1-2-3/G®: The Complete Reference

Mary Campbell

Osborne **McGraw-Hill**

Berkeley New York St. Louis San Francisco
Auckland Bogotá Hamburg London Madrid
Mexico City Milan Montreal New Delhi Panama City
Paris São Paulo Singapore Sydney
Tokyo Toronto

Osborne **McGraw-Hill**
2600 Tenth Street
Berkeley, California 94710
U.S.A.

Osborne **McGraw-Hill** offers software for sale. For information on software, translations, or book distributors outside of the U.S.A., please write to Osborne **McGraw-Hill** at the above address.

This book is printed on recycled paper.

1-2-3/G®: The Complete Reference

1234567890 DOC 99876543210

ISBN 0-07-881651-3

Acquisitions editor: Elizabeth Fisher
Technical reviewer: Lauren Wendell
Project editor: Janis Paris
Text design: Stefany Otis and Peter Hancik
Cover art: Bay Graphics Design, Inc.
Color separation: Phoenix Color Corporation
Screen production: InSet Systems, Inc.
Printer: R.R. Donnelley & Sons Company

TABLE OF CONTENTS

ACKNOWLEDGMENTS

I would like to thank the following individuals who contributed so much to this revision:

Gabrielle Lawrence, who worked along with me to explore all the new features of 1-2-3/G, and Jody Fordham, who created the 1-2-3/G screens needed for this book.

Liz Fisher, Acquisitions Editor, Osborne/McGraw-Hill, who coordinated all the resources necessary to produce a finished product. Wendy Goss, who coordinated the many pages of manuscript as they flowed between the people needed to create and review the manuscript. Judy Wohlfrom, who handled all the production tasks for the book. Janis Paris and Kathy Krause, who juggled all the right pieces and managed to meet our print date. Louise Sellers, who did a fine job of proofing.

To the many, many individuals at Lotus who offered help in different ways.

Lauren Wendell, who took time from her busy schedule to review the manuscript. Lauren's knowledge of the product and timely review of the many pages of manuscript were an immense help. Also special thanks to Scott Richardson, Mary Beth Rettger, and Alexandra Trevelyan. Many individuals on the 1-2-3/G team were an enormous help, including Kathy Rolan, John Allyn, Gina Blaber, Scott Brumit, Jim Buccigross, Matthew Christian, Jim Coluprisco, Joe Gaulesky, Sandy Gibson, Chris Hyland, Jim King, Tim Lawson, Paul Nolan, Claudia Rawal, Lois Rosenbaum, Martha Stammers, Tammy Tenney, and Martha Warkentin. Other Lotus 1-2-3/G experts who lent assistance were Caron Keenhold, Meg McAdams, Michael Morizio, and Marsha Telesetsky.

1-2-3/G provides an easy-to-use interface between 1-2-3 features and the OS/2 operating system environment and marks Lotus' entry into the growing OS/2 market.

About This Book

1-2-3/G: The Complete Reference is designed to serve the needs of both new and experienced users.

If you are a novice user, you should start at the beginning of the book and work up through Chapter 11 (where you will print your first documents). A good second step is then to work through the remaining "Getting Started" chapters at the beginning of each section.

If you are a user already familiar with 1-2-3 basics, you will also want to read Part One on the graphical user interface as a starting point. You may then skip to the "Getting Started" chapters at the beginning of each new section or review the table of contents and focus on topics with which you want to gain familiarity, such as data management features, keyboard alternative macros, or command macros. Throughout the book, boxes in the text summarize important information, and a detailed index will help you find the precise topic you are looking for.

How This Book Is Organized

This book is divided into seven sections, or parts. Part One covers the graphical user interface. Part Two focuses on 1-2-3/G's worksheets and the many commands that make 1-2-3 the leading spreadsheet product on the market today. Part Three covers the new Solver and Backsolver technology. Part Four covers how to create and print graphs. Part Five introduces the data management features, including external database access. Part Six focuses on keyboard and command language macros.

Part Seven consists of several appendixes on varied topics such as OS/2 essentials, installation, release differences, the Lotus character set, and a command map to all the 1-2-3/G commands.

Conventions Used in This Book

Understanding the conventions used in this book should make your task of learning about 1-2-3/G easier:

- Command sequences are shown with initial letters in uppercase (as in Worksheet Erase)
- User input is indicated in boldface (for instance, type: **John Doe**)
- Small capitals have been used for the names of function keys (such as in press ALT-F4)
- @Function keywords (such as @INFO) are shown in capital letters, although you may use either upper- or lowercase letters when making entries
- Filenames are shown in uppercase (as in FILENAME.DOC)
- Macros are shown in uppercase with braces (for instance, the {READ} command)

Additionally, the index provides special sections for @functions and macros for ease of reference.

WHY THIS BOOK IS FOR YOU

1-2-3 has been available for many years, but 1-2-3/G is the first spreadsheet package to operate under the OS/2 environment—opening up a whole new world of graphical user interface. Features like the new Solver and Backsolver utilities make problem solving easier, while a new note and preview utility give you the productivity aids you need to utilize spreadsheet applications more effectively.

This book first introduces you to certain features of the OS/2 operating system and then takes you step-by-step through the basic and advanced applications of your 1-2-3/G program. Numerous examples have been included to illustrate these steps, along with discussions of the differences in the new 1-2-3/G for users who already have some familiarity with 1-2-3.

1-2-3/G: The Complete Reference has been written to serve the needs of both new and experienced users. New users will appreciate the tutorial-style chapters that introduce each major section, while experienced users will find the chapters on advanced techniques especially helpful. Experienced users will also find this volume to be a valuable reference tool. Included are complete reference sections on @functions (see Chapter 9) and command language macros (see Chapter 23).

All users will appreciate the detailed reference materials in the appendixes, the boxes used to highlight important information in the text, the "tips" designed to save you time, and the supplemental command map—which shows the menu structure of all of 1-2-3/G's commands.

Introduction to the Graphical User Interface

Getting Started with the New Graphical User Interface
Using Windows and the Desktop
Working with 1-2-3/G Tools and Utilities

PART ONE

Getting Started with the New Graphical User Interface

ONE

Starting 1-2-3/G
The Mouse Versus the Keyboard
Working with a Window
Working with the Desktop
Using Other Graphic Elements

Because 1-2-3/G runs under the OS/2 Presentation Manager, the product has a new look and feel. There are many options for interfacing with the product that were not possible in the character-based releases of 1-2-3. If you have used the character-based releases, you will be pleased to learn that 1-2-3/G still supports previous ways of accomplishing tasks. Moreover, you can mix and match 1-2-3/G and Presentation Manager commands.

This book offers you several different approaches for learning to use 1-2-3/G. The best approach will depend on your experience with prior releases of 1-2-3 and the skill level you are attempting to build.

If you want a quick overview of some of the differences between 1-2-3/G and other 1-2-3 releases, you can spend a few hours working through each of the "Getting Started" chapters. You will begin with this chapter and continue with Chapters 4, 13, 15, 18, and 21. When you finish, you will have not only an overview, but some hands-on practice, and can decide which features to explore in more detail. If you don't yet have 1-2-3/G installed on your machine, start with Chapter 2 and proceed through the book, skipping the "Getting Started" chapters just listed, since you will not be able to complete the hands-on exercises. If you don't want to read all the details of a specific section, you can skip some of the material, using it later as a reference when needed.

You can proceed from start to finish if you want to experience every aspect of the product, including the hands-on exercises in Chapter 1. This approach will transform you into an expert user.

Although OS/2 version 1.2 is the preferred operating system for 1-2-3/G, you can run the program under OS/2 version 1.1. 1-2-3/G does not run with the DOS operating system. Your choice of OS/2 versions affects some of the features available to you. For example, some of the print drivers available for OS/2 1.2 do not work in OS/2 1.1. Your choice of OS/2 version also determines the appearance of some of the graphical elements on screen; for instance, some warning screens in 1.2 display a stop sign whereas in 1.1 they display a hand. The version, however, does not affect the way you use 1-2-3/G.

1-2-3/G lets you use several spreadsheets and files simultaneously. It also lets you organize views of multiple files on screen. OS/2 also allows you to view different applications on-screen simultaneously. 1-2-3/G uses OS/2's capabilities to offer you a 1-2-3/G *desktop,* the surface in which 1-2-3/G is displayed, and which can include a variety of other windows in which to manipulate your data. If you have worked with OS/2, you have already mastered some of the techniques of working efficiently with 1-2-3/G's desktop and windows. If you have never used OS/2, learning about 1-2-3/G will provide you with some of the basic skills you need to work with OS/2's desktop and windows.

Starting 1-2-3/G

You will use the same procedure to start 1-2-3/G, regardless of which release of OS/2 you are using. Since the screen from which you will be selecting 1-2-3/G looks very different under the two releases, separate instructions for loading 1-2-3/G are provided for each version.

If you are running OS/2 1.1, follow these steps:

1. Start your system with the A drive empty. The Start Programs window should appear on screen. If you followed the 1-2-3/G installation instructions in Appendix A, "System Requirements and Installation," 1-2-3/G should be an option in this window, as shown in Figure 1-1.

2. If you want to work with the keyboard, use the DOWN ARROW key to highlight 1-2-3/G and press ENTER. To start 1-2-3/G with the mouse,

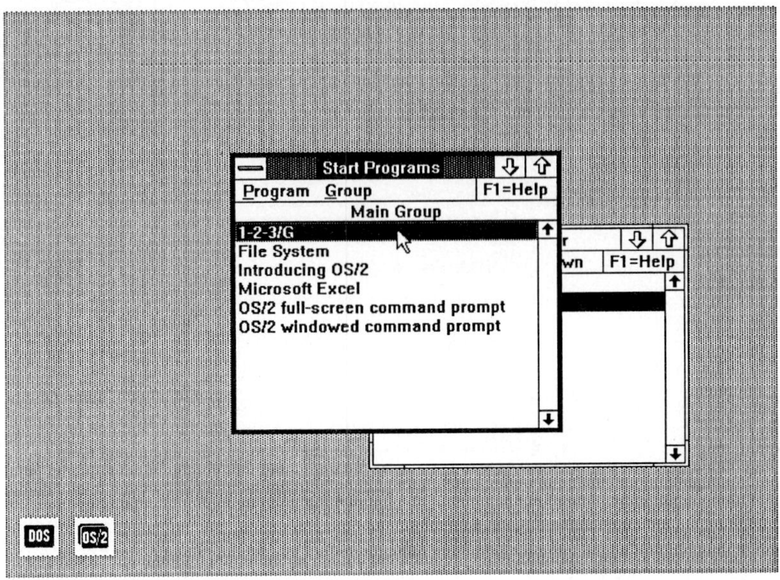

Figure 1-1. Start Programs window for OS/2 1.1

move the mouse pointer (the arrow) to 1-2-3/G and press the left mouse button twice in rapid succession.

If you are running OS/2 1.2, follow these steps:

1. Start your system with the A drive empty. The Group-Main window (for the Main programs) should appear on your screen, as shown in Figure 1-2. If you followed the 1-2-3/G installation instructions in Appendix A, 1-2-3/G should be displayed as an option in this window, although you will need to scroll down the screen to see it (press the DOWN ARROW key or click the bottom arrow box in the bar on the right side of the window).

2. If you want to work with the keyboard, use the DOWN ARROW key to highlight 1-2-3/G and press ENTER. To make the same selection with the mouse, move the mouse pointer (the arrow) to 1-2-3/G and press the left mouse button twice in rapid succession to start 1-2-3/G.

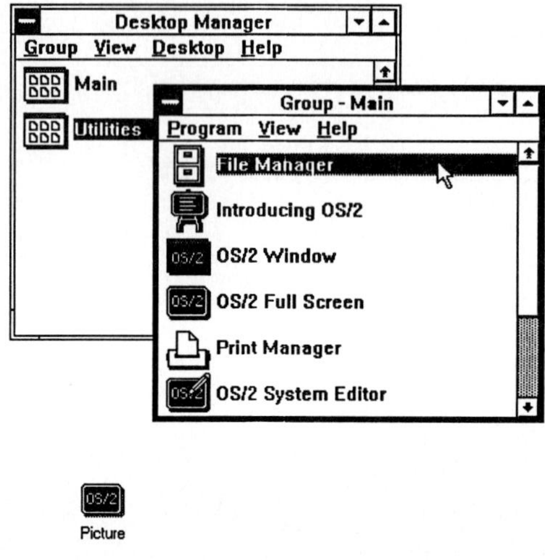

Figure 1-2. Group-Main window for OS/2 1.2

Regardless of which operating system you are using, your initial 1-2-3/G screen will look like Figure 1-3.

The Mouse Versus the Keyboard

You can choose between the keyboard and mouse for any 1-2-3/G task. If you already know how to perform some tasks in 1-2-3, you may want to use the keyboard for these tasks in 1-2-3/G. Working with windows and the desktop is new to 1-2-3/G, so you should plan to use the mouse for these features. Although keyboard instructions are also included, try to ignore these if you have a mouse, and instead force yourself to learn the mouse procedures. This section focuses on mouse techniques.

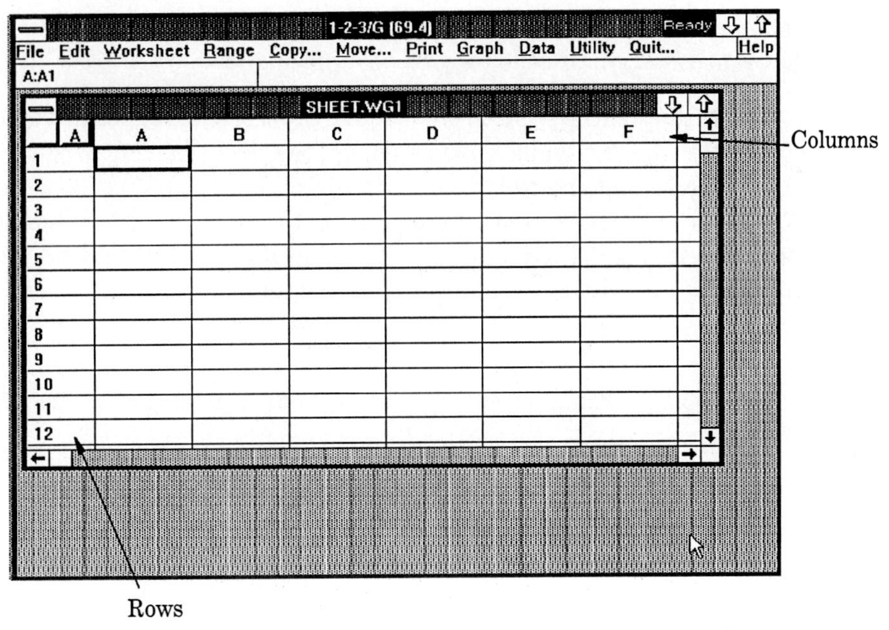

Figure 1-3. Initial 1-2-3/G desktop and worksheet window

The window that appears when you start 1-2-3/G is the worksheet window, with which you will begin to work in Chapter 4, "Getting Started with Worksheets." The window has a grid pattern that marks it off in rows and columns. Each row and column forms a cell, referred to by column letter and row number. Follow these steps to try some of the new mouse techniques in the window that appears after you start 1-2-3/G:

1. Move the mouse by rolling it across your desk until the mouse pointer (the arrow) is located in column C and row 4.

2. Press the left mouse button.

   The process of pressing the left mouse button is known as *clicking,* and it selects the cell where the mouse pointer is located.

3. Move the mouse pointer to D2 and press the right mouse button.

This procedure is also called clicking, but pressing the right mouse button rather than the left mouse button adds the cell to the current selection of cells instead of replacing it.

4. With the mouse pointer still in D2, press the left mouse button and hold it down while moving the mouse. Stop moving when you have selected all the cells from D2 to F15.

This procedure is called *dragging* the mouse. The difference between this and clicking is that you hold the left button down and move the mouse while making your selection.

The only other technique that you can use with a mouse is a *double-click:* two clicks in rapid succession. You can try this option in the next section.

Working with a Window

You do everything in 1-2-3/G within a window. What you can do in the window depends on whether it is a *tool* window or a *utility* window that offers specialized features. The two 1-2-3/G tools, *graph* and *worksheet,* provide windows that differ significantly, but the same basic techniques to operate window commands work in all windows. You will create worksheets in worksheet tool windows. You will create graphs in graph tool windows. There are also utility windows that allow you to use the Solver utility to find problem solutions, the Note utility to attach notes to cells, and the Help utility to access context-sensitive on-screen help. You will try out the features in a worksheet window and then take a look at some other window types.

Working with the Window Control Menu

You can pull down the window control menu from the upper-left corner of a window using either the keyboard or the mouse.

If you are using a mouse, try this now:

1. Move the mouse to the upper-left corner of the window. The mouse pointer should be in the window control box that looks like this:

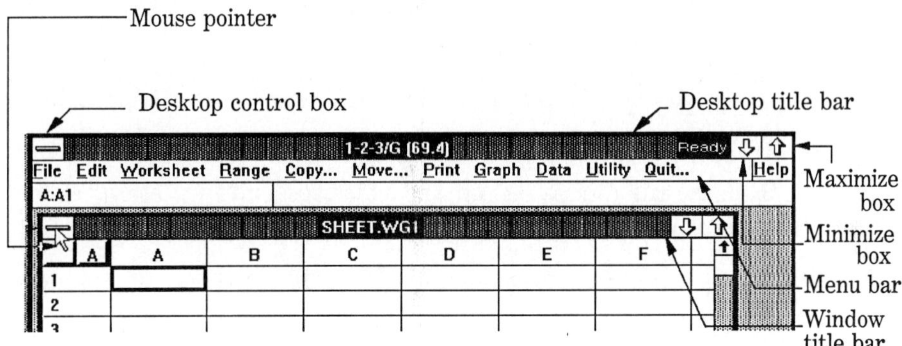

2. Press the left mouse button once with the mouse pointer on the window control box. The window control menu appears like this:

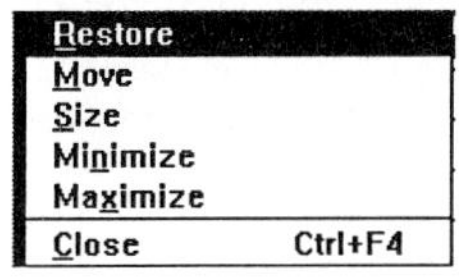

3. Move the mouse pointer to an area of the window outside the pull-down menu and click the left button. The pull-down menu disappears.

If you are using the keyboard, try this now:

1. Press ALT-MINUS to activate the window control menu.

2. Press ESCAPE and the pull-down menu disappears.

Changing the Window Size

You can change the size of a window in two ways with a mouse. You can use the minimize and maximize boxes in the upper-right corner of the screen. Also, you can drag the borders of the window to change its size if you use a mouse. To make the same change with the keyboard, you need to use the window control menu and the arrow keys.

Try these options if you are using a mouse:

1. Move the mouse pointer to the right edge of the current window. The mouse pointer changes to a double-sided arrow.

2. Press the left mouse button and drag the window edge a little to the right.

3. Release the mouse button and you will see the window widen as it is redrawn.

4. Again, place the mouse at the right edge of the window until the mouse pointer changes to the double-sided arrow.

5. Press the left mouse button and push the right edge in toward the left a little, and then release the mouse button.

6. Move the mouse pointer to the lower-right corner. Notice that the mouse pointer becomes a double-sided diagonal arrow. You can drag here to change both width and height.

7. Move the mouse pointer to the maximize box in the upper-right corner of the window and click it. The window becomes full-screen size and the maximize box becomes the *restore box.* Clicking it would restore the original size.

8. Click the minimize box. The window is reduced to an *icon,* a small symbol—in this case representing a worksheet, like this:

9. Double-click the icon to restore the size.

Try this if you are using the keyboard:

1. Press ALT-MINUS to activate the window control menu.
2. Type **S** to select Size.
3. Press the RIGHT ARROW key several times to stretch the right side.
4. Press ENTER to finalize the change.
5. Repeat step 1, and then type **N** to select Minimize.
6. Repeat step 1, and then type **R** to select Restore.

Changing the Window Location

You can relocate windows on the screen. This allows you to see data in other active worksheets or tools located beneath the current window. You can use the menu to move a window or drag it by the control bar.

With the mouse, try this:

1. Move the mouse pointer to the window title bar where the name of the window is displayed.
2. Press the left mouse button and drag this bar to a new location.

When you release the mouse button, the window is relocated.

With the keyboard, try this:

1. Press ALT-MINUS to activate the window control menu.
2. Type **M** to select Move.
3. Press the DOWN ARROW key to move the window down a little.
4. Press ENTER to finalize the change.

Opening and Closing Different Window Types

1-2-3/G has a number of different kinds of windows. You open the windows in different ways using commands specific to each window. Once opened, all of the window types can be closed with the same set of closing options.

1-2-3/G provides both a worksheet tool and a graph tool. Each of these tools has different types of windows. In addition, there are a number of utility windows, including a Note utility, a Help utility, and a Solver utility. The windows for each of these have unique functions even though the same techniques work for all three utilities. As you open new windows, notice the change in options in the menu bar, as shown in Figure 1-4.

You can close the current window in several ways. Double-clicking the window control box in the upper-left corner of the window closes it.

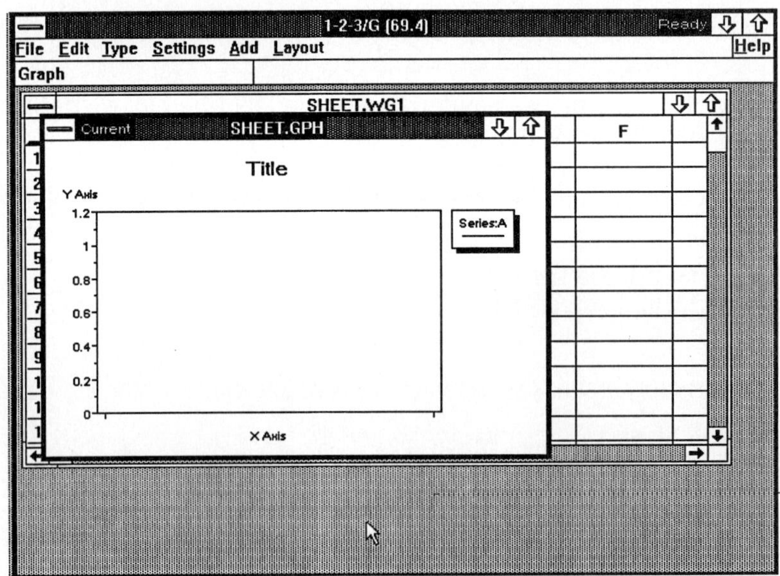

Figure 1-4. Graph window

Pressing CTRL-F4 also closes the current window. You can also press ALT-MINUS to activate the window and select Close from the menu. You can select menu commands by clicking the mouse or typing the underlined letter in the command word. Each instruction specifies the command to be selected, but you can determine the selection technique that fits your needs. Try these mouse and keyboard options for opening and closing windows:

1. Select Graph View by clicking Graph and then View, or by pressing F10 (Menu) and typing **GV**.

   A graph window like the one in Figure 1-4 appears. From now on, you will be told which menu commands to select. Although you will not always be reminded to click each menu option or type the underlined letter in the desired selection, this selection procedure works for all menus.

2. Press CTRL-F4 to close the window. A prompt asks if you want to save the window.

3. Select No.

4. Select Utility Solver to display the Solver window:

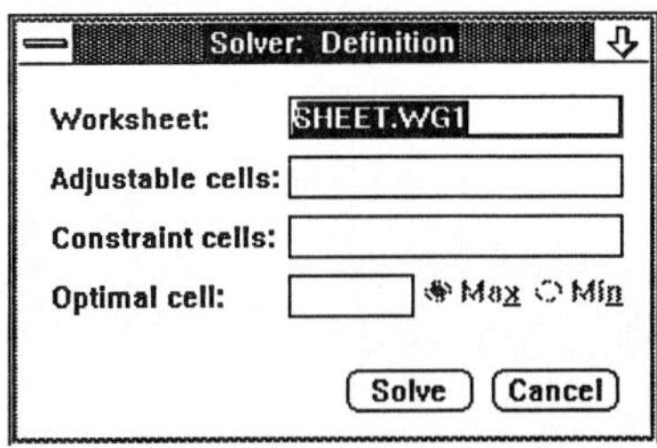

5. Press ALT-MINUS and then type **C** to close the Solver window.

6. Press F1 (Help) to display a Help window.

7. Double-click the Help window control box to close the window.

8. Select Utility Note to display a Note window.

9. Press ALT-MINUS, and then type **C** to close this window.

Working with the Desktop

The desktop control menu allows you to tailor the size and location of the desktop and to manipulate the windows that display on the desktop. The commands are separate from the menu items in the menu bar and pull down from the desktop control box in the upper-left corner of the screen. You can click this box with the mouse to pull down the menu, or you can press ALT-SPACEBAR.

You can use the menu to make changes to the desktop, or you can use the mouse directly for certain tasks. For changing the size or location, it's quickest to use the mouse.

Changing the Desktop Size

You can change the desktop size by dragging its borders with the mouse. You can also use the Size option from the desktop control menu.

Follow these steps to change the desktop size from the desktop control menu with the keyboard:

1. Press ALT-SPACEBAR to activate the desktop control menu.
2. Select Size.
3. Press the DOWN ARROW twice to make the desktop a little larger.
4. Press ENTER to finalize your selection.
5. Repeat step 1, and then select Minimize.
6. Press ALT-ESCAPE repeatedly to move to the next Presentation Manager task until the icon for 1-2-3/G is highlighted.
7. Select Restore.

Follow these steps to change the desktop size with a mouse:

1. Move the mouse pointer to the right edge of the desktop.
2. Press the left mouse button and move toward the left to shrink the desktop.

3. Click the maximize box in the upper-right corner of the desktop.

4. Click the restore box for the desktop.

Changing the Desktop Location

You can move the desktop around on the screen just as you can move windows. If you use a mouse, the technique is the same as for windows—just drag the desktop control bar. With the keyboard, use the desktop control menu. Try this now:

1. Move the mouse to the desktop control bar, press the left mouse button, and drag the bar down to a new location.

2. With the keyboard, press ALT-SPACEBAR, type **M** to select Move, and press the DOWN ARROW key to move the desktop down a little.

3. Depending on whether you are using a mouse or the keyboard, repeat step 1 or 2 to place the desktop in its original location. You will need to drag it up a little or use the UP ARROW to relocate it.

Changing Windows

The desktop control menu allows you to work with the different windows on the desktop. You can use options in the desktop control menu to rearrange the placement of windows on your screen. This menu also allows you to activate any of the open windows on the desktop.

Your first task will be to add a few windows to the desktop to provide additional windows to work with. Follow these steps to add the windows and try the desktop control menu options affecting windows:

1. Select File.

   Remember, you can click File in the menu or press F10 (Menu) to activate the menu bar and type **F** to select File.

2. Select New.

3. Click OK or press ENTER to open a new worksheet file.

1-2-3/G will use the name SHEET with the next sequential number appended to the end as the name for the new worksheet file added to the screen.

4. Select Graph View to open a graph window.

   The window that appears is a graph window, although it does not display a graph since there is no data selected to display on the graph. Assuming that you have not changed the default settings, the new windows are stacked on top of the existing windows with the most recent window on top and active.

5. Move the mouse to the desktop control menu box and click the box with the left mouse button or press ALT-SPACEBAR to activate the desktop control menu.

6. Select Window.

7. Select Tile.

   You can click with the left mouse button or type **T** to select Tile. The three open windows are arranged on the desktop like floor tiles. You can identify the active window by the highlighting in the window title bar.

8. Repeat steps 5 and 6, and then select Stack.

   You can click Stack with the left mouse button or type **S** to select Stack. The active window is at the top of the stack.

9. Repeat steps 5 and 6, but click the name of a window other than the active window (the active window has a check next to the name) or use the DOWN ARROW key to highlight the name of the window and press ENTER. The window selected becomes the active window.

Closing the Desktop

Closing the desktop is the same as ending your current 1-2-3/G session. The 1-2-3/G desktop is removed from the screen, and the Start Programs (OS/2 1.1) or Group-Main (OS/2 1.2) windows return for your next selection. If there are open windows in 1-2-3/G, you may need to respond to a prompt to indicate whether you wish to save the files before exiting. Follow these steps to end a 1-2-3/G session in different ways:

1. Double click the desktop control box to close the desktop.

   If you have made entries on the worksheet, you will need to decide whether to save the windows. If you are prompted by 1-2-3/G about saving a file for a window, click No in the box that appears on the screen. This action indicates that you do not want to save the worksheet.

2. Double click the 1-2-3/G icon in the Start Programs or Group-Main window to start a new 1-2-3/G session.

3. Press ALT-F4 to close the desktop.

4. Repeat step 2 to start a new session.

5. Click Quit in the menu, and then click Yes to close the desktop and end the session.

6. Repeat step 2 to start a new session.

7. Press ALT-SPACEBAR, move the highlight to Close, and then press ENTER.

8. Repeat step 2 to start a new session.

Using Other Graphic Elements

Other on-screen graphic elements make things easier—if you have a mouse. Although you can accomplish these tasks using the keyboard, this section focuses on mouse shortcuts. You will learn how to change the row height and the column width. You will also see how easy it is to make a menu selection with a quick click. Follow these steps to try all three tasks:

1. Move the mouse pointer to the border between column A and column B in the column heading area. Notice how the mouse pointer changes into a double-sided arrow.

2. Press the left mouse button and drag to the right. When you release the button, the column is widened.

3. Move the mouse pointer to the border between row 2 and row 3 in the row heading area that contains the row numbers. Again, the mouse pointer changes to a double-sided arrow, this time with the arrow heads pointing up and down rather than right and left.

4. Press the left mouse button and drag down to increase the height of row 2. When you release the mouse button, the height of row 2 is finalized.

5. Move the mouse pointer to Range in the menu bar near the top of the screen.

6. Click the left mouse button. A pull-down menu appears.

7. Move the mouse pointer to Format in the pull-down menu.

8. Click the left mouse button.

A *dialog box* appears on the screen, presenting options to be defined by the user to complete the worksheet command.

9. Move the mouse pointer to the Cancel box within the dialog box and click the left mouse button. The box disappears from the screen.

You will learn more about the different graphical objects as you work with all of the 1-2-3/G windows in subsequent chapters.

Using Windows and the Desktop

TWO

Although 1-2-3/G maintains much of its compatibility with earlier character-based releases, its screen displays are much more versatile. It uses OS/2 features to provide a desktop work surface with one or more windows in which to work with your information. In this chapter you will learn a few OS/2 essentials to allow you to start a new 1-2-3/G session. You will also learn all the basics of desktop windows with a special emphasis on worksheet windows. In Chapter 3, you will learn more about the windows for other 1-2-3/G tools and utilities.

OS/2 and 1-2-3/G

1-2-3/G is the latest 1-2-3 product designed to take advantage of the OS/2 operating system. Like other operating systems such as DOS or UNIX, OS/2 is a controlling program that coordinates the resources of the computer and lets you run other programs. The operating system provides support for tasks like printing, copying, and deleting files. Since the operating system supports running multiple programs, you can create an accounting system, manage a database to keep track of your clients, and produce reports to measure how well you are doing in the same session.

The OS/2 operating system offers several advantages over its predecessor, DOS. DOS is limited to 640K of RAM. RAM (random access memory) is the area in which the computer stores programs and data. As your programs and applications grow and develop, this storage maximum limits both program features and the amount of data the program can handle. Some programs and hardware have found solutions to the problem from within DOS. For example, 1-2-3 Release 3 included DOS extenders to provide access to memory beyond the DOS 640K limit. Hardware, such as extended memory cards, lets you add RAM to the basic memory in your machine. The additional memory is referred to as extended or expanded memory. Extended and expanded memory are different types of hardware that provide the same feature of making more RAM available to the operating system. This additional RAM is only useful when the program you are using can use extended memory. In OS/2, you can add up to 48 megabytes of RAM. This lets application developers provide additional features that a DOS-based application could not support with its RAM limitations. 1-2-3/G uses the additional RAM to provide features such as graphical preview display, which lets you see exactly how your worksheet or graph will appear when printed.

Another advantage of the OS/2 operating system is *multitasking.* Multitasking means that the computer is doing more than one thing at a time. DOS can handle only one task at a time. For example, you may start running a program that processes end-of-the-month data. With DOS, you must wait until the program finishes to start another program. With OS/2, you can start running the program and then tell the operating system that you want to work with another application. While the computer is processing the end-of-the-month data, you can be composing a letter or drafting next year's budget. OS/2 doesn't make you wait; it can run simultaneously with other applications.

A third feature of OS/2, introduced with OS/2 version 1.1, is the Presentation Manager. The Presentation Manager (PM) provides a graphical user interface. This means that any Presentation Manager application is not limited to placing characters on the screen like earlier character-based releases of 1-2-3. You can use any size, shape, or color to represent data shown on the screen. This lets Presentation Manager applications use symbols to represent application features. For example, you can reduce the size of Presentation Manager applications to icons (small symbols that represent a larger object). By looking at the icons, you can quickly see which applications are running. 1-2-3/G uses the graphical user interface to draw your worksheet and graphs using colors, fonts, and attributes.

OS/2 keeps track of each application separately and allows you to switch to whichever application you want quickly and consistently. With OS/2, programs are available to you with a minimum of keystrokes. OS/2 manages the job of storing the program and data in RAM, and it remembers exactly where you are in each application and keeps track of the steps it must perform. OS/2 also keeps track of how each application appears. When you switch to an application, OS/2 draws the screen just as if you are running the application by itself. The other activities continue in the background.

What Is the Desktop?

In a Presentation Manager application, every application is placed in a Presentation Manager window. 1-2-3/G calls its Presentation Manager window a desktop. The *desktop* is the surface where 1-2-3/G or a Presentation Manager application displays data and information needed to run the program. When you start running OS/2, you already have one or more OS/2 windows open, with names like Start Programs, DOS Command Prompt, and Print Spooler, depending on the version and your computer setup.

You might use either OS/2 1.1 or OS/2 1.2. The two versions of OS/2 are similar but differ somewhat in the names of the OS/2 window selections and the appearance of desktop graphical objects. For example, OS/2 1.1 uses the Start Programs window whereas OS/2 1.2 refers to the same window as Group-Main. Also the arrows in the upper-right corner of the initial OS/2 1.1 screen have shafts, while those in OS/2 1.2 have only arrowheads.

Using a Presentation Manager Window

OS/2 provides several Presentation Manager windows as well as the ones that you open for applications like 1-2-3/G. To move between applications, you need to learn how to select the window you want. Once you know how to select a Presentation Manager window, you can start opening new ones and changing how they appear.

OS/2 initially provides several Presentation Manager windows depending on which OS/2 release you're using. If you are using OS/2 version 1.1, you have a Start Programs window, and you can have DOS Command Prompt and Spooler Queue Manager windows. If you disable the spooler, the spooler window will not appear. Figure 2-1 shows how the initial screen may appear if you are using OS/2 version 1.1. You can select a Presentation Manager window by pressing CTRL-ESCAPE. This activates the Task Manager window, which lists all available Presentation Manager windows.

If you are using OS/2 version 1.2, your screen displays the Group-Main and Desktop Manager windows. Your screen may also display DOS and Print Manager icons. Figure 2-2 shows how the initial screen

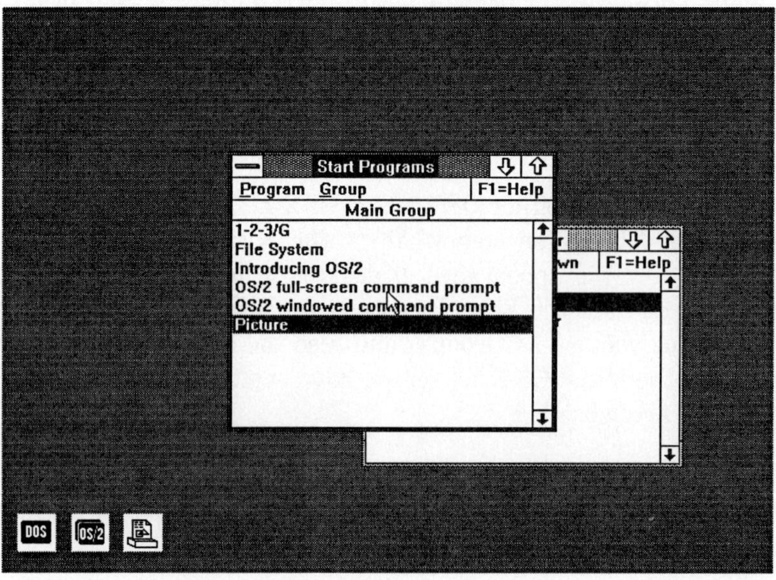

Figure 2-1. Opening screen for OS/2 version 1.1

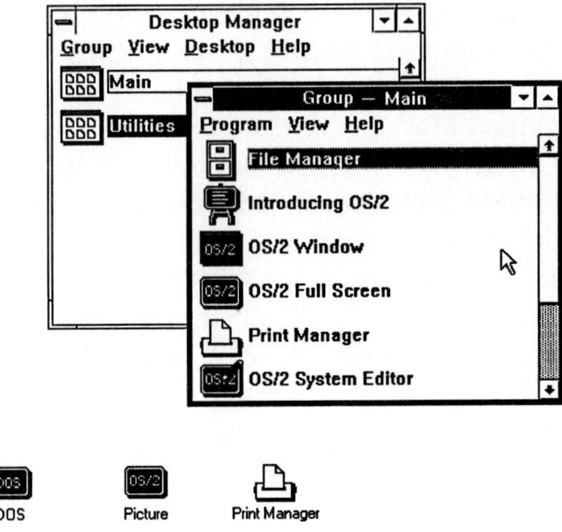

Figure 2-2. Opening screen for OS/2 version 1.2

may appear if you are using version 1.2. You can select a Presentation Manager window by pressing CTRL-ESCAPE. This activates the Task List window, which lists all of the Presentation Manager windows available.

To select a Presentation Manager window from the Task Manager or Task List window, use the UP ARROW and DOWN ARROW to highlight the window name you want and press ENTER. You can move to the window name quickly by typing the first letter of the window name. Each time you type a letter, OS/2 moves the highlight to the next item in the list that starts with the selected letter. With a mouse, you can select the Presentation Manager window by pointing with the mouse to the window name and double-clicking the left mouse button. (Remember, double-clicking means pressing the mouse button twice quickly.)

OS/2 has other methods for choosing a Presentation Manager window. All of the windows can be represented as icons. As you learned, icons are symbols that represent a larger object—in this case, a Presentation Manager window. Table 2-1 lists several Presentation Manager windows that appear in OS/2. You can select a Presentation Manager window by double-clicking the icon that represents the desired Presentation Manager window. The icons appear at the bottom of the screen. They will not appear when another Presentation Manager window uses the display area. You can also switch between windows until you are at the Presentation Manager window you want. When you press ALT-ESCAPE, OS/2 makes the next Presentation Manager window listed in the Task Manager or Task List the current window.

Using a mouse, you can also click a Presentation Manager window that appears behind the active window. As an example, suppose you want to make the Desktop Manager window active in Figure 2-2. You can point to any visible part of the Desktop Manager window and click the mouse. Since you are selecting the object in the window you are clicking, be sure not to click an object in the Presentation Manager window you don't want. A good practice is to click the title bar (the top line, which contains the window name). Clicking the title bar selects a window without making any choices in the Presentation Manager window.

OS/2 Program Groups

OS/2 works with groups of programs. Instead of listing all the programs together, OS/2 provides multiple groups. This makes it easier to find a program because the list in each group is shorter. OS/2 initially provides two groups: Main and Utilities. Main includes programs like OS/2 command windows, the File System or File Manager, and 1-2-3/G. The Utilities group contains applications like the Control Panel, OS/2 System Editor, and commands that format a disk.

With OS/2 version 1.1, if the group containing the application you want to start is not listed in the Start Programs window, you may need to change the group. To change the group, click Group with the mouse. Group and Program are both listed in the menu bar. With a keyboard, you can activate the menu bar by pressing F10 or holding down ALT until Program is highlighted. Menus have underlined letters. You can type the underlined letter in the menu choice to select the menu item. To select Group, type G. You can also change the highlight's position with the arrow keys and press ENTER when the highlight is on the menu item you want. Using a mouse, you can select a menu item by pointing to it and clicking the left mouse button.

Presentation Manager Window	Version 1.1 Icon	Version 1.2 Icon
1-2-3/G		1-2-3/G
Control Panel		Control Panel
Desktop Manager (1.2 only)		Desktop Manager
File System (1.1) or File Manager (1.2)		File Manager
OS/2 full-screen command prompt (1.1) or OS/2 Full screen (1.2)	OS/2	OS/2 Full Screen
OS/2 System Editor	OS/2	OS/2 System Editor - Untitled
OS/2 windowed command prompt (1.1) or OS/2 Window (1.2)		OS/2 Window
Spool Queue Manager (1.1) or Print Manager (1.2)		Print Manager
Start Programs (1.1) or Group - Main (1.2)		Group - Main
Task Manager (1.1 only)		
DOS command prompt	DOS	DOS

Table 2-1. Icons That Represent Desktops

With OS/2 version 1.2, each group has a program group window. Initially, the Group-Main window is open. If you want to start a program or application from another group, you must open the group's program window by selecting Desktop Manager from the Task List. The Desktop Manager desktop lists all program groups. Use the arrow keys to highlight the group you want and press ENTER. With a mouse, point to the group you want and double-click the mouse. Clicking the mouse moves the highlight to the group but does not select it. Once a group is selected, OS/2 opens a program group window for the selected group.

Differences Between OS/2 Versions 1.1 and 1.2

Most of the differences between versions 1.1 and 1.2 are the icons and the window names. The two versions of OS/2 also use other icons, which vary. In the upper-right corner of Presentation Manager windows are minimize and maximize boxes that you can use to change the size of the window. In OS/2 version 1.1, the boxes are shown in the upper-right corner of the Start Programs and Task Manager windows, as shown in Figure 2-1. Figure 2-2 shows the same boxes with a different style of arrows in the Group-Main and Desktop Manager windows. Versions 1.1 and 1.2 also use different icons. For example, version 1.1 will display a hand where version 1.2 will display a stop sign. The icon differences only affect 1-2-3/G when it displays certain message boxes that contain symbols on the left side. However, the steps you perform when you see either message box are the same.

The other noticeable differences between releases are the Presentation Manager window names. While some are the same, a few are different. For example, the Task Manager in version 1.1 is called Task List in version 1.2. However, the choices you make in the two Presentation Manager windows are the same.

Starting 1-2-3/G

The 1-2-3/G installation process adds 1-2-3/G to the Start Programs or Group-Main Presentation Manager window. You can start 1-2-3/G from the Presentation Manager or directly from an OS/2 command prompt. Once you start 1-2-3/G, the screen looks like Figure 2-3. The 1-2-3/G desktop shown in the figure may differ from your desktop in two respects. The letters and numbers that appear along the top and left of the worksheet in this figure and the figures in the rest of the book do not use the gray default background color. In addition, the character size is changed to use the larger System Proportional font that 1-2-3/G initially provides. 1-2-3/G uses this font if you have not installed fonts for OS/2. Both of these changes make the figures in this book easier to read.

If you are using OS/2 version 1.1, you will see the Start Programs window as soon as you turn on your computer and OS/2 is running. If you added 1-2-3/G to the Main Group when you installed 1-2-3/G, you can start 1-2-3/G by highlighting 1-2-3/G in the list and pressing ENTER. If you have a mouse, you can start 1-2-3/G by pointing to 1-2-3/G and

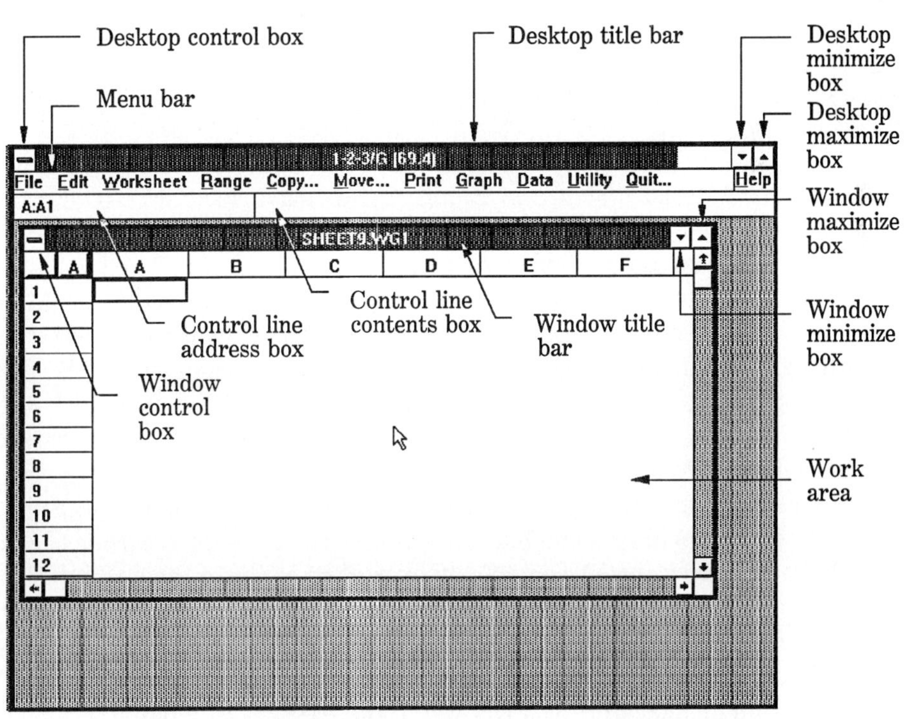

Figure 2-3. 1-2-3/G's initial desktop

double-clicking. If you have 1-2-3/G included in a different group, you need to change the group listed in the Start Programs window before you can start 1-2-3/G.

If you are using OS/2 version 1.2, you will see the Group-Main window as soon as you turn on your computer and OS/2 is running. If you added 1-2-3/G to your Main group when you installed 1-2-3/G, you can start 1-2-3/G by highlighting 1-2-3/G in the list and pressing ENTER. If you have a mouse, you can start 1-2-3/G by pointing to 1-2-3/G and double-clicking. If 1-2-3/G is in a different group, you need to change to that group of applications before starting 1-2-3/G.

You can also start 1-2-3/G by using an OS/2 command prompt. Both the Main Group in the Start Programs window and the Group-Main window include selections for a full-screen or window OS/2 command prompt. If you select an OS/2 command prompt (either full screen or window), you can start 1-2-3/G by changing the directory to \123G, typing **cd \123G**, and pressing ENTER. If you installed 1-2-3/G on a different directory, substitute the directory name for 123G. After changing the directory, type 123G and press ENTER to load 1-2-3/G on the desktop.

1-2-3/G's Desktop

The 1-2-3/G desktop shown in Figure 2-3 displays several features you will use in a 1-2-3/G session. These features remain consistent as 1-2-3/G adjusts the desktop to display your data.

1-2-3/G's desktop has four parts. The first line in a 1-2-3/G desktop is the *desktop title bar.* Like other Presentation Manager windows, the title bar contains the name of the application or program. In 1-2-3/G, the desktop title can also be a desktop file. Initially, 1-2-3/G displays 1-2-3/G in this location. In the left corner of the title bar is the *desktop control box.* This icon lets you set the appearance of the application or program. OS/2 calls this box the System Menu icon in other Presentation Manager windows. The minimize and maximize icons are in the right corner of the title bar. These icons let you quickly expand or contract the desktop size with a mouse. 1-2-3/G also uses the desktop title bar to display mode indicators such as Ready and Menu. You can use the *mode indicator* to check the type of information that 1-2-3/G expects from you. Table 2-2 lists the mode indicators you will see in the desktop title bar.

The next line of the desktop is the *menu bar.* This is where 1-2-3/G displays the first selections available with a menu. 1-2-3/G has different

Indicator	Meaning
CMD	Appears during the execution of a macro.
Edit	An entry is being edited. Edit is generated when your entry contains an error that 1-2-3/G wants you to edit. You can also generate it by pressing the F2 (Edit) key to change a cell entry. 1-2-3/G commands enter Edit mode when you are entering text in a text box.
Error	1-2-3/G has encountered an error. 1-2-3/G displays a message box describing the problem. Select a command button from the message box to proceed.
Help	The Help window is active.
Label	1-2-3/G has determined that you are entering a label.
Link	An external database link needs updating.
Mem	Memory is low. You will want to relinquish memory before continuing so 1-2-3/G has enough memory to perform the desired tasks.
Menu	1-2-3/G is waiting for you to make a menu selection.
Msg	1-2-3/G is displaying a message.
Point	1-2-3/G is waiting for you to point to a cell or range. As soon as you begin to type, Point mode changes to Edit mode.
Ready	1-2-3/G is idle and waiting for you to make a new request.
SST	This macro indicator appears during single-step execution for a macro instead of CMD.
Step	Step mode is selected for macros.
Value	1-2-3/G has decided that you are entering a value.
Waitnj	1-2-3/G is processing your last task and cannot begin a new task until the Wait indicator disappears.

Table 2.2. Desktop Mode Indicators

menus for the various tools and utility windows. Like most Presentation Manager applications, the menu bar includes Help so you can quickly display help for the current topic you are working with.

The third line of the desktop is the *control line.* The control line describes the data you are using. The control line contains data that you are entering and editing as well as selecting cells that 1-2-3/G commands use. The control line is divided in half. The left half, the address box, shows the location of the data you are using. The right half, the contents box, shows the data or text you are using.

The remaining area on the 1-2-3/G desktop is called the *work area.* The work area might contain spreadsheet data, a graph, utility data, or a combination of these. The work area display changes as the data you are working with changes. In 1-2-3/G, the work area contains one or more windows. Each window has a window title bar with the name of the displayed utility, graph, or worksheet file.

What Are Windows?

Windows are 1-2-3/G's way of looking at worksheet or graph data. Another type of window is a utility window, which offers a special feature like notes or keystroke recording. Each window contains the name of the utility or filename stored in the window. 1-2-3/G lets you use 16 windows at a time. These windows can be all worksheet tool windows or a combination of window types. Utility windows like Solver and Help only allow one window open at one time; tool windows can have several open at the same time.

Although the menu in each window type is different, there are some common elements between windows. The menus are activated in the same way and some windows share common menu choices. The various window types also share other elements like title bars at the top of windows and scroll bars at the side.

Types of Windows

1-2-3/G has two types of windows. Tool windows contain data commands used to manipulate data on worksheets and graphs. Utility windows contain windows for utilities like Note, Solver, Help, and Keystroke Editor.

You can size worksheet and graph windows to your liking. You can both move and size some utility windows like the Help window. You can only move others, such as the Note window.

Why Use Multiple Worksheet Windows?

Multiple windows offer several advantages over the single window offered in the earlier character-based releases of 1-2-3. First, with several windows, you can work with more than one file at once by storing each file in a window. 1-2-3/G lets you use up to 16 windows simultaneously. You can put each of the files you want to work with on your 1-2-3/G desktop. Second, you can work with several types of information at once. You can continue to view worksheet data while you use a Help or Note utility window.

Working with the 1-2-3/G Desktop

1-2-3/G's desktop provides many features that you can use as you work with 1-2-3/G. Many of the changes you can make to the 1-2-3/G desktop you can also make to other Presentation Manager windows. With the 1-2-3/G desktop, you can change the desktop's size and position as well as use other options to change how windows on the desktop appear. Most of these features are available through the desktop control menu.

Activating the Desktop Control Menu

The desktop control menu lets you change the size and position of the desktop and close the desktop. In later chapters, you will learn about additional tasks that you can perform with commands in this menu. To activate the desktop control menu, you can use the keyboard or mouse. The desktop control menu is connected to the desktop control box shown in the upper-left corner of Figure 2-3. With the keyboard, you can activate this menu by pressing ALT-SPACEBAR. With a mouse, you can activate the desktop control menu by pointing to and clicking the desktop control box. A desktop control menu like this will appear:

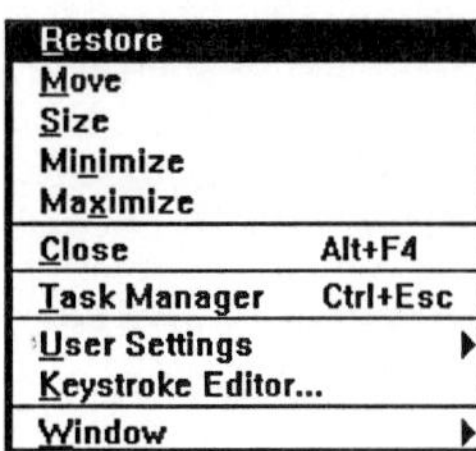

The first six menu items in this box are also found in other Presentation Manager windows. In the desktop control menu, these commands control the size and location of the desktop. You will also find these commands in the window control menu. As you learn how to change the size and position of 1-2-3/G using the desktop control menu (or its equivalents using a mouse), you can also apply the same commands to change the size and position of other Presentation Manager windows from the window control menu.

When you activate a menu, you will notice *accelerator keys* next to some of the menu choices. Accelerator keys are keys you can press instead of activating the menu and selecting the menu item. For example, next to Task Manager (OS/2 1.1) or Switch to (OS/2 1.2), you will see CTRL-ESCAPE. This means that instead of activating the desktop control menu and selecting Task Manager (OS/2 version 1.1) or Switch to (OS/2 version 1.2), you can press CTRL-ESCAPE. These accelerator keys provide a quicker way to perform commands.

To select one of the items in the desktop control menu, you can use the same steps you used to select a menu item in an OS/2 Task Manager or Task List window. You can use the UP ARROW and DOWN ARROW to highlight the desired menu item and press ENTER to select it. You can also type the underlined letter in each menu item to select that menu item. With a mouse, you can point to the menu item you want and click the left mouse button.

Changing the Desktop Size and Location

Once you know how to activate the desktop control menu, you can change the desktop size and position. You can also make these changes without the desktop control menu if you use the mouse. You can make a quick change to the size using the maximize and minimize boxes.

Changing the Size of the Desktop

You can change the size of the desktop with the desktop control menu or the mouse. To change the size of the desktop with the mouse, follow these steps:

1. Move the mouse pointer to the edge of the desktop until it becomes a white double-sided arrow.

2. Drag the mouse to move to the new position for the desktop edge. (Remember, dragging means holding down the mouse button while you move the mouse to a new position.) As you drag the mouse, 1-2-3/G draws a shaded outline to indicate the new desktop edge.

3. Release the mouse button when the outline represents the desired desktop location. 1-2-3/G will redraw the desktop to use the new size.

You can also change the size of the desktop with the keyboard with these selections from the desktop control menu:

1. Press ALT-SPACEBAR to activate the desktop control menu.

2. Select Size. 1-2-3/G presents a shaded outline on the desktop edge to indicate that the desktop size will change.

3. Press an arrow key to move the mouse pointer to a desktop edge you want to change. For example, if you press the UP ARROW, the mouse pointer moves to the top desktop edge.

4. Press the UP ARROW and DOWN ARROW keys to alter the top edge of the desktop.

With a mouse, the change is even easier:

1. Move the mouse pointer to the left edge of the desktop.

2. Press the left mouse button and push or pull on the edge of the desktop to change the size.

As you move the mouse, 1-2-3/G draws a shaded outline to indicate the new desktop edge. When the desktop is the size you want, release the left mouse button and 1-2-3/G will redraw the desktop using the new size. You can also change the size from the lower-right corner and push or pull the mouse diagonally to change both height and width at once.

As you change the size of the desktop, 1-2-3/G may make some changes to reflect the desktop's new size. As the desktop size decreases, 1-2-3/G may use multiple lines for the menu bar. Also, 1-2-3/G adjusts the size of the windows in the desktop so the window is the same size relative to the desktop. The worksheet window also shrinks to reflect the new desktop size.

Quickly Changing the Desktop Size

You can change the size of the desktop with the Size option in the desktop control menu; however, you can change the size more quickly using the Maximize, Minimize, and Restore choices in the desktop control menu. These options also use the two icons on the right side of the title bar. Minimizing a 1-2-3/G desktop or Presentation Manager window reduces the desktop or window to an icon. Maximizing a 1-2-3/G desktop or Presentation Manager window expands the desktop or window to fill the entire screen. Restoring the desktop or Presentation Manager window returns the desktop or window to the size it had before you maximized or minimized it.

To shrink the desktop size with a mouse, use the icons. Of the two icons, clicking the left one (the downward-pointing arrow) on the right side of the title bar minimizes the desktop. Using the keyboard, activate the desktop control menu and select Minimize. Once the desktop is minimized, the screen displays the desktop as the 1-2-3/G icon. Minimizing the 1-2-3/G desktop also activates the Task Manager or Task List. When you click the 1-2-3/G icon in the lower portion of the screen, the screen displays the same desktop control menu. You can even select Move if you want to move the icon. Double-clicking the icon or selecting 1-2-3/G from the Task Manager or Task List by pressing ENTER performs the same action as selecting Restore after clicking the 1-2-3/G icon. Selecting Restore returns the desktop to the size it had before you selected Minimize.

From the worksheet window, you can also click the right icon on the title bar. This maximizes the desktop to use your entire screen. You can maximize the desktop using the keyboard by activating the desktop control menu and selecting Maximize. Once the desktop is maximized, the maximize icon in the desktop title bar changes to the restore icon, which contains an up and a down arrow combined. At this point, selecting Restore from the desktop control menu or clicking the restore icon returns the desktop to the size it had before you maximized it.

Moving the Desktop

You can relocate the desktop on your screen. You can move the desktop with the desktop control menu or by using the mouse. To move the desktop with the mouse:

1. Move the mouse pointer to the title bar of the desktop.
2. Drag the mouse by pressing the left mouse button and moving the mouse while holding down the button.
   As you drag the mouse, 1-2-3/G draws a shaded outline to indicate where you are moving the desktop.
3. When the outline is where you want the desktop, release the mouse button and 1-2-3/G will move the desktop to the new position.

You can also move the desktop with the keyboard using the desktop control menu. Follow these steps if you are using the keyboard:

1. Activate the desktop control menu.
2. Select Move. 1-2-3/G adds a shaded outline above the desktop edge to indicate the desktop's position.
3. Press the arrow keys to relocate the shaded outline to indicate the new desktop's position.
4. When the desktop is where you want it, press ENTER and 1-2-3/G will redraw the desktop using the new position. OS/2 lets you move the desktop so part of the desktop display is beyond the edge of the screen.

Selecting the Active Window

As you add multiple windows to the 1-2-3/G desktop, you must tell 1-2-3/G the window you want to use. To select a window with the keyboard, follow these steps:

1. Activate the desktop control menu.

2. Select Window.

   This presents an additional menu listing Tile, Stack, and the names of all the available 1-2-3/G windows. The name of a window is the filename stored in a graph or worksheet window or the name of the utility for a utility window. Next to each window is a number between 1 and 0 or a letter between A and F.

3. Type the letter or number next to the window name or highlight the window name and press ENTER.

With a mouse, if a portion of the window you want is on the desktop, you can click a part of the window that you want. If the window is not visible, you can make your selection from the menu.

Tiling and Stacking Windows

While you can position and size every open window, if you have several windows open at once, positioning and sizing each window can be time-consuming. 1-2-3/G has two options for positioning and sizing all open windows. The option you use depends on the number of windows open and how you want to see the open windows that are not the current window.

One option is to divide the work area between all open windows. This is called *tiling.* To tile windows, select Window and Tile from the desktop control menu. Figure 2-4 shows several tiled windows. Utility windows such as the Note and Solver windows shown in Figure 2-4 cannot be resized. The size of the graph and worksheet windows is changed to share the remaining room equally. Since the space allocated to each window decreases as the number of windows increases, you will not want to tile windows with many windows. Also, tiling windows uses all windows; you cannot choose which windows are tiled.

Another option is stacking windows. To stack windows, select Window and Stack from the desktop control menu. Stacking windows makes all graph and worksheet windows the same size. (Utility windows are not affected by this.) The windows are then stacked on top of each other

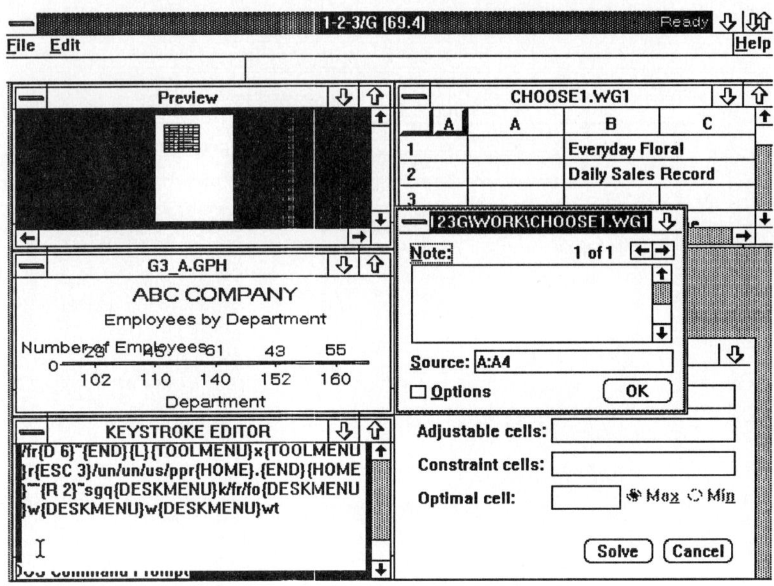

Figure 2-4. Tiled windows

so the title bar of each open window is visible. Figure 2-5 shows several stacked windows. Stacking windows makes it easy to choose a window with a mouse, since you can quickly click the title bar of the window you want.

Working with a Window

Working with a 1-2-3/G window is like working with the desktop. You can change the size and position of a window. Most of the keystrokes or mouse selections are the same. Instead of using the desktop control menu, you use the window control menu. The icon for the window

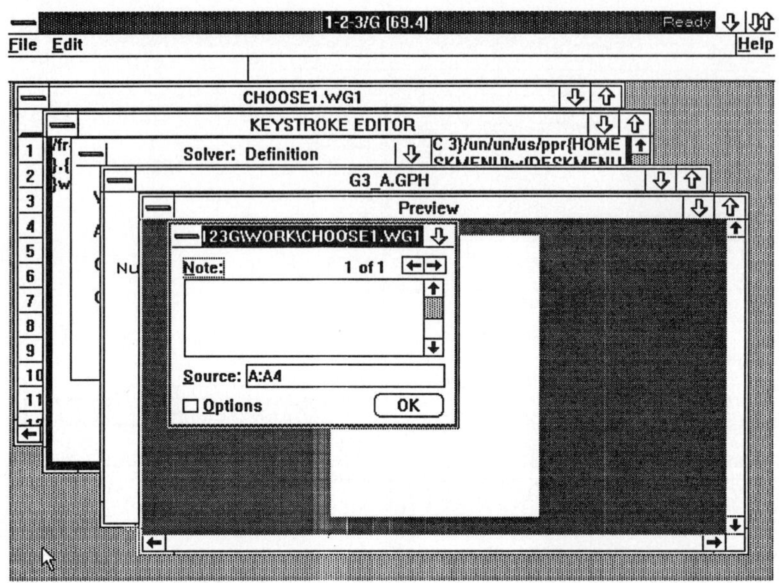

Figure 2-5. Stacked windows

control menu appears in the upper-left corner of the window and looks like the icon for the desktop control menu.

To activate the window control menu, you have several options. With the keyboard, you can activate this menu by pressing ALT-MINUS. With a mouse, you can activate the window control menu by pointing to and clicking the window control box. Figure 2-6 shows the window

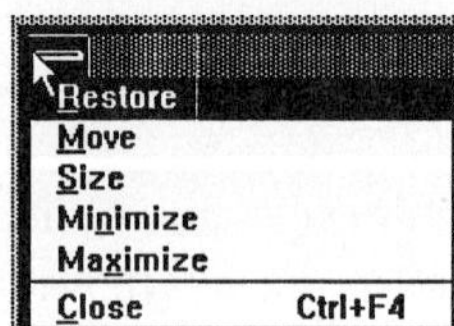

Figure 2-6. Window Control menu for a worksheet window

control menu. These six menu items perform the same tasks as those in the desktop control menu except that they are performed in the window attached to the window control menu. The window control menus for some utilities do not include all six options. You can select items in the window control menu using the same steps as for the desktop control menu.

Changing the Window Size and Location

Once you know how to activate the window control menu, you can change the window size and position. Options in the menu include selecting a custom size, minimizing or maximizing the size, restoring the size, moving the window, or closing it. You can access these menu options with the keyboard or the mouse. You can use the mouse to change the window size quickly with the minimize, maximize, and restore icons.

Changing the Size of the Window

You can change a window's size with the window control menu or the mouse. To change the size of the window with a mouse, follow these steps:

1. Move the mouse pointer to the edge of the window until it becomes a white double-sided arrow.

2. Press the mouse button and drag the mouse to move to the new position for the window edge. As you drag the mouse, 1-2-3/G draws a shaded outline to indicate the window's size.

3. When the outline is the size you want the window to be, release the mouse button.

   1-2-3/G will redraw the window using the new size. You can only resize active windows with a solid yellow border. You cannot change the size of windows that have a wavy blue line in the border. (Monochrome monitors will present these as slightly different shades.) When you move the mouse pointer to a window's edge in this case, the mouse pointer will not change to a double-sided arrow.

You can also change the size of the window with the keyboard using the window control menu. To change the window's size using the keyboard:

1. Activate the window control menu.
2. Select Size.
   Some utility windows do not have this option since you cannot adjust some utility window sizes. 1-2-3/G draws a shaded outline to indicate the window's position and size.
3. Press an arrow key to determine which window edge to change.
   For example, if you press the DOWN ARROW first, 1-2-3/G assumes that you want to change the bottom window edge. Subsequently pressing the UP ARROW and DOWN ARROW keys further alters the bottom edge of the window. In the same way, pressing the RIGHT ARROW moves the mouse pointer to the right edge of the window. As you press the LEFT ARROW and RIGHT ARROW keys, you will alter the right edge of the window. As you press the arrow keys, 1-2-3/G changes the window's outline to indicate the new window's size.
4. When the window outline is the size you want, press ENTER.
   1-2-3/G redraws the window to use the outlined size.

Quickly Changing the Size of a Window

Besides changing the size of the window with the Size option in the window control menu, you can change the size quickly using the Maximize, Minimize and Restore choices in the window control menu or their icons on the right side of the window title bar. Minimizing a 1-2-3/G window reduces it to an icon. Following are the different icons a 1-2-3/G window can use:

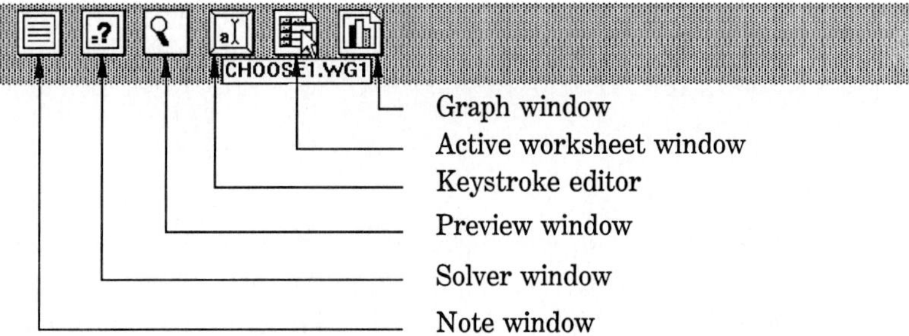

Maximizing a 1-2-3/G window expands it to fill the entire desktop. Restoring the window returns to the size it had before you maximized or minimized it. Some utility windows do not have Minimize, Maximize, and Restore options for their window control menu.

To shrink the window size with a mouse, click the minimize icon in the right side of the title bar. Using the keyboard, activate the window control menu and select Minimize. Once the window is minimized, the screen displays it as one of the icons shown previously. Minimizing a window activates the window shown below the window before it was minimized. When you click a 1-2-3/G window icon, 1-2-3/G displays the window control menu for the selected window. When you minimize a window, 1-2-3/G does not include it in the windows that are tiled or stacked by selecting the appropriate choices in the desktop control menu. Double-clicking the icon performs the same action as selecting Restore after clicking the window's icon. Selecting Restore returns the window to the size it had before you selected Minimize.

You can also click the maximize icon on the window title bar. This maximizes the window. You can maximize the window with the keyboard by activating the window control menu and selecting Maximize. Once the window is maximized, the maximize icon in the window title bar changes to the restore icon, which is an up and a down arrow combined. At this point, selecting Restore from the window control menu or clicking the restore icon returns the window to the size it had before you maximized it.

Moving the Window

You can also move the window, either with the window control menu or with the mouse. To move the window with a mouse, move the mouse pointer to the window title bar. Then drag the mouse to move the window. As you drag the mouse, 1-2-3/G draws a shaded outline to indicate where you are moving the window. When the outline is where you want the window, release the mouse button and 1-2-3/G will move the window display to the new position.

You can also move the window with the keyboard using the window control menu. To move the window, activate the window control menu and select Move. 1-2-3/G adds a shaded outline above the window edge to indicate the window's position. As you press the arrow keys, 1-2-3/G moves the shaded outline to indicate the new window's position. When the window outline is where you want it, press ENTER and 1-2-3/G will redraw the window to use the outlined position. OS/2 will let you move the window so part of the window is beyond the edge of the desktop.

You can also move icons using the same mouse actions or keystrokes you use to move a window. When you move an icon, 1-2-3/G has some limitations that affect where the icons can appear. Icons cannot overlap. If you try moving an icon on top of another one, 1-2-3/G moves the original icon to the right of the lower icon. Also, you cannot move an icon off the desktop.

Closing Windows

When you are finished using a window, you have several choices for removing the window from the screen, depending on the type of window. One option available for all windows is selecting Close from the window control menu. This option also has an accelerator key, CTRL-F4 (Close Tool), as displayed next to it in the window control menu. You can close the Help, Solver, and Note utility windows by pressing ESCAPE repeatedly. In addition, 1-2-3/G closes all windows when you close the 1-2-3/G desktop. For graph and worksheet windows, you don't have to close a window when you are finished. When you retrieve a file into a graph or worksheet window, the retrieved file will replace the graph or worksheet file in the window.

Closing the 1-2-3/G Desktop

When you are finished using 1-2-3/G, you will want to close the desktop, which is synonymous with ending your 1-2-3/G session. Closing the desktop frees the RAM the computer uses to store 1-2-3/G data, enabling you to use the memory for other applications. Also, closing the 1-2-3/G desktop ensures that you can save any open data files that you want. To close the desktop, you can activate the desktop control menu and select Close. You can also activate this command with the accelerator key ALT-F4 (Close Desktop). If any graph or worksheet window contains unsaved data, 1-2-3/G will ask if you want to save the graph or worksheet data. From a worksheet, you can also close the 1-2-3/G desktop by selecting Quit from the menu bar and then selecting Yes when 1-2-3/G presents the confirmation box. This uses the same keystrokes as earlier releases of 1-2-3. 1-2-3/G's keystroke compatibility lets people who have used prior releases of 1-2-3 quickly adapt to 1-2-3/G and thus focus their attention on new features.

Working with 1-2-3/G Tools and Utilities

THREE

All of the work you do with 1-2-3/G will be displayed in different windows on 1-2-3/G's desktop. Although the 1-2-3/G windows share some basic features, each window type also has some unique options. The window type (tool or utility) is determined by whether you are working with a 1-2-3/G tool or utility, which are the two types of windows 1-2-3/G uses. This chapter explains the types of tasks you can perform in each window and the unique features offered by the special window types.

1-2-3/G Tool Windows

1-2-3/G provides two types of tool windows. The worksheet tool window displays a worksheet and any data you have stored on it. A graph tool window displays a graph. The data displayed in the windows is stored in files. Worksheet windows display files with an extension of .WG1 and graph windows display files with the .GPH extension. The appearance of each window is different, since 1-2-3/G tailors the window to each specific type of information or task.

Worksheet Windows

Worksheet windows contain most of the data that you use with 1-2-3/G. You can use a worksheet window to build spreadsheet models and construct databases. The other 1-2-3/G windows are designed to handle more specialized needs, such as graphs and cell notes.

A worksheet contains text, numbers, and formulas, storing these different types of data in cells. A *cell* is located at the intersection of each column, row, and sheet. 1-2-3/G uses columns, rows, and sheets to divide the worksheet area.

Initially, you only see part of the first sheet in the worksheet file although there are 256 sheets with the identical row and column construction. A cell can contain any type of data and has a specific cell address. A *cell address* consists of a sheet letter between A and IV for the 256 sheets a worksheet file can contain. Then comes a colon and a column letter—a letter between A and IV for the 256 columns in each sheet. Following the column letter is the row number. This is a number between 1 and 8192 for the 8192 rows each sheet in the worksheet file contains. Figure 3-1 illustrates how a worksheet is structured.

The Worksheet Window Display

The worksheet window is divided into two areas: a title bar at the top of the window and a worksheet area below the title bar. As shown in Figure 3-2, the title bar includes the window control box, the filename, and the minimize and maximize icons (which you saw in Figure 2-3 in the last chapter). 1-2-3/G also uses this area for mode indicators like Ready, which tells you that 1-2-3/G is ready for you to make an entry. Below the title bar is the worksheet area. A worksheet window can display up to five worksheet file sheets at once if you use the Worksheet Window Perspective command. Each sheet in the worksheet area has a border containing the column letters, row numbers, and sheet letters. In the upper-left corner are two boxes. On the right is the sheet letter box, which lets you select an entire sheet for some 1-2-3/G commands. On the left is the worksheet file box, which lets you select the entire worksheet file for some 1-2-3/G commands. The lines that define the columns and rows create the worksheet *grid.*

When you are in a worksheet, you can select a cell or cells. The cell you are using (where an entry is positioned, or that a selected command

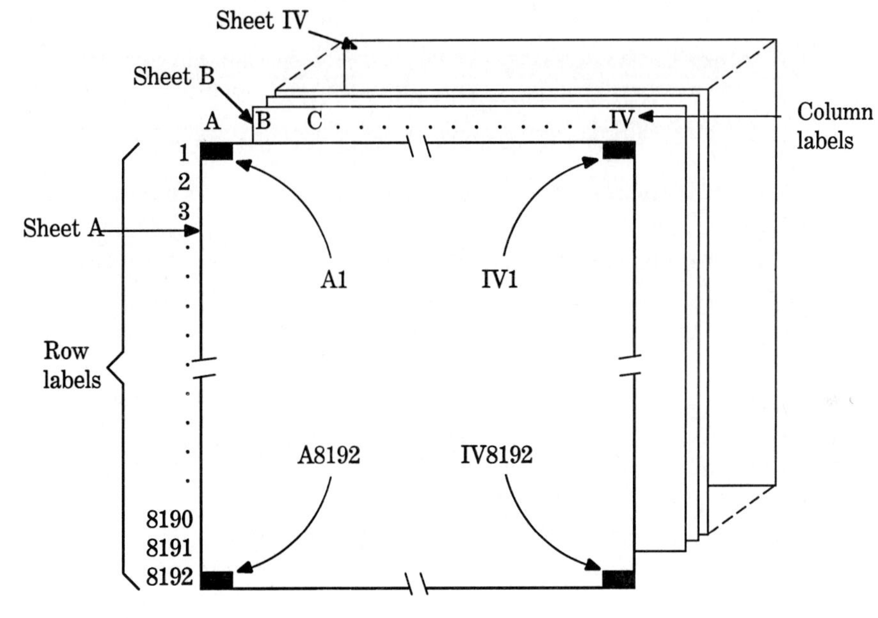

Figure 3-1. Worksheet structure

will be using) is called the *current cell.* When a worksheet window is the active window, 1-2-3/G displays the cell address of the current cell in the address box, which is the left side of the control line. The right side of the control line, the contents box, displays the cell entry as 1-2-3/G stores it.

Worksheet Window Indicators

1-2-3/G has three types of indicators for telling you about the current 1-2-3/G session. In Chapter 2, "Using Windows and the Desktop," you learned about the mode indicators 1-2-3/G uses to let you know the type of entry 1-2-3/G expects you to make.

A worksheet uses cell indicators to describe attributes for the cell address displayed in the address box. Cell indicators describe the cell's format, protection status, and show whether the cell has a note added with the Note utility. These indicators appear to the left of the worksheet filename in the title bar, and are provided with the commands or

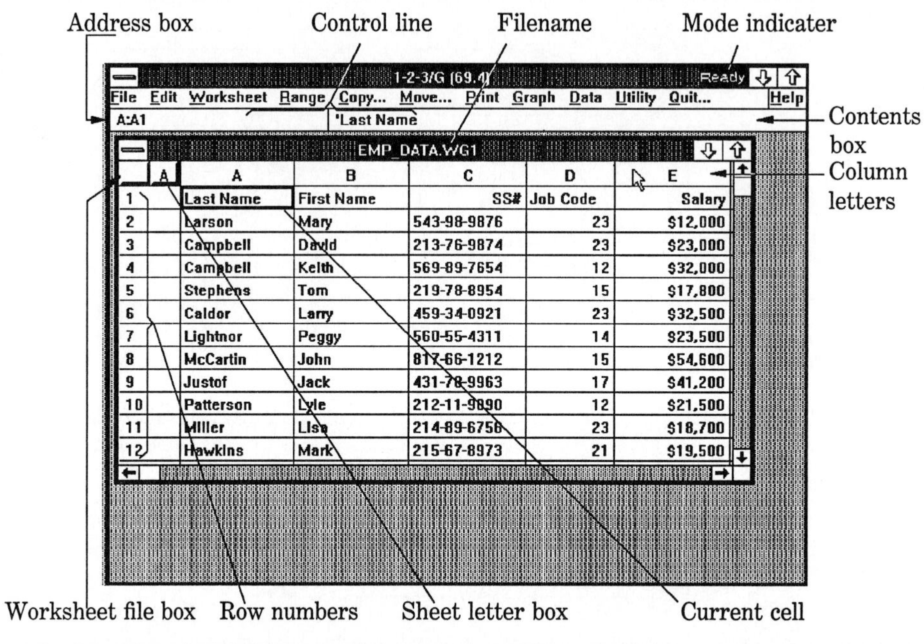

Figure 3-2. Worksheet window

features that create them. A worksheet window also uses status indicators to display information about the worksheet in the window. These indicators appear to the right of the filename in the window title bar, and are listed in Table 3-1.

Graph Windows

Graph windows contain graphs that you create using data from worksheet files. Figure 3-3 shows a sample graph window. It includes the window control box, the filename, and the minimize and maximize icons in its title bar. In addition, indicators like Preview and Manual sometimes appears in the title bar. Below the title bar is the graph. A graph window allows you to select the different parts of a graph, which are called *objects*. An object can be part of the data in the graph or can be a title. The menu for a graph tool window provides features for determining how the graph appears.

Indicator	Meaning
Bound	The cell pointer is restricted to cells selected before the Bound mode is enabled.
Calc	The worksheet needs to be recalculated. A changed cell may affect formula results. This indicator appears when recalculation is set to manual. You must press F9 to recalculate the worksheet file. This indicator also appears when 1-2-3/G is performing background recalculation and is automatically recalculating worksheet formulas.
Circ	The worksheet contains a circular reference—that is, a cell that refers to itself. You can find an address of one of the circular reference cells with the Worksheet Status command.
End	The END key has been pressed. Cell pointer movement is affected by the next key or key combination pressed.
Find	The Data Query Find command is limiting which database records you can move to with the cell pointer.
Group	The worksheet file contains two or more sheets in Group mode, causing some commands to affect all the sheets that are part of the group.
Input	The Range Input command is limiting the cell pointer's movement to only unprotected cells in the selected range.
RO	The status of the current file is read only. This means that you cannot save any of your changes to the file with this filename.

Table 3-1. Worksheet Status Indicators

When a graph tool window is the active window, 1-2-3/G displays the name of the selected object in the graph file with the graph object name in the address box. The contents box displays the object's contents. For example, if the selected object is the graph's first title, the control line would display First_Title in the address box and the title text in the contents box.

1-2-3/G Utility Windows

The other windows you will use in 1-2-3/G are utility windows. Unlike worksheet and graph windows, utility windows don't store data in a file

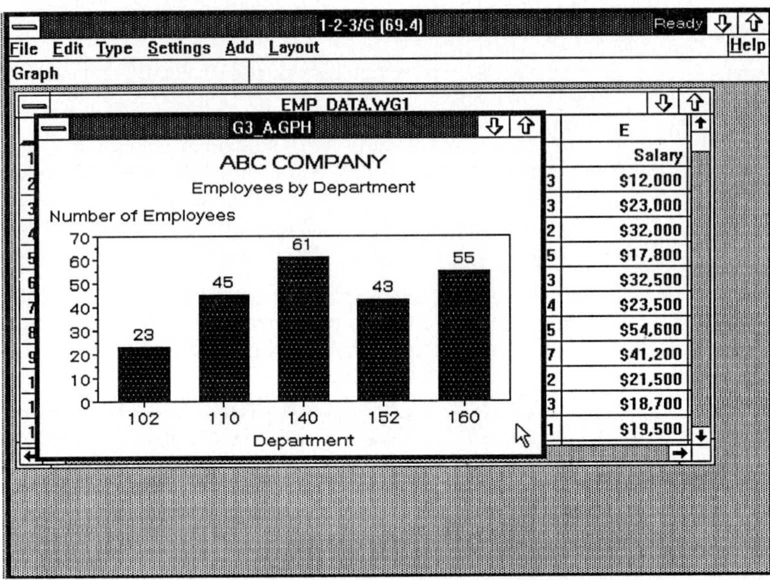

Figure 3-3. Graph window

that they create. Also, utility windows provide specialized features. For example, you can see the keystrokes you have entered or see how a graph or worksheet will appear when printed. Some utility windows have their own menu. You can open only one of each type of utility window at a time.

The Help Window

You can open a window to an online reference source at will. Just press the F1 (Help) key or point to Help in the menu bar and click the left mouse button. If you are performing a 1-2-3/G task, 1-2-3/G supplies information related to your current task. If you want additional help or help with a different subject, select Main Index on the Help window to change the help topic.

Figure 3-4 displays the help window that 1-2-3/G provides when you seek help while editing a cell. 1-2-3/G recognized that you pressed the F2 (Edit) key and then displayed this help information in case you needed additional information on editing your entry. Several words or phrases at the bottom of this Help window let you display different text in the Help window. These are *command buttons.* You can select one by typing the underlined letter or by pointing to the text and clicking the left mouse button. These buttons are

Main Index	Displays the main index that lets you select the window type for which you want assistance
How do I . . .	Displays a list of tasks you may want to perform in the window type described by the first word below the Help window title bar

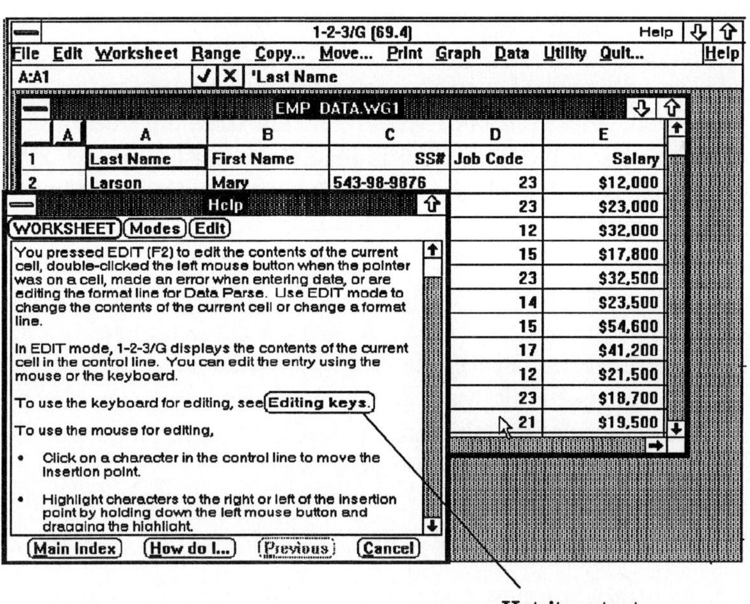

Figure 3-4. Help window

Previous	Displays the Help topic you saw last, turning gray when you are using the first Help screen
Cancel	Closes the Help window and makes the window you used last the active window

You can also close the Help window by pressing ESCAPE, selecting Close from the window control menu, or selecting the Cancel button in the Help window.

The Help window also has a window control menu, which you can use to move, change the size of, or maximize the Help window. You can also make these changes with a mouse. The solid yellow border indicates that you can make the Help window any size. When a Help window contains more text than 1-2-3/G can fit in the Help window, a vertical scroll bar appears.

1-2-3/G has a hierarchical help structure. This means that when the help topic is Worksheet, only topics that you would use in a worksheet window are listed. The line below the title bar is called the *context line,* and it lists the help topics that are above the displayed help topic in the help system's hierarchy.

There are several ways to select a help topic. One is to select a hot-item text. *Hot-item* text appears within the help description as red or boldface (more boldface than is displayed in Figure 3-4). Pointing to the hot-item text and clicking the left mouse button displays the help topic information for the selected hot-item text. For example, in Figure 3-4, "Editing keys" is hot-item text. With a keyboard, you can highlight hot-item text by pressing the LEFT ARROW and RIGHT ARROW keys. As you press the LEFT ARROW and RIGHT ARROW keys, 1-2-3/G highlights the context window buttons, the hot-item text, and the command buttons. When the item you want is highlighted, press ENTER. You can also choose a help topic belonging to one of the buttons in the context window by highlighting the desired button and pressing ENTER.

The Note Window

The Note utility is a new addition to 1-2-3/G. This utility lets you add to a worksheet cell documentation that you can use to explain an entered value or text. You can also use the Note utility to document a worksheet formula. You can add up to four notes to a cell, and each note can contain up to 511 characters.

To open a Note window, select Utility Note from the worksheet tool menu. A Note utility window might look like this:

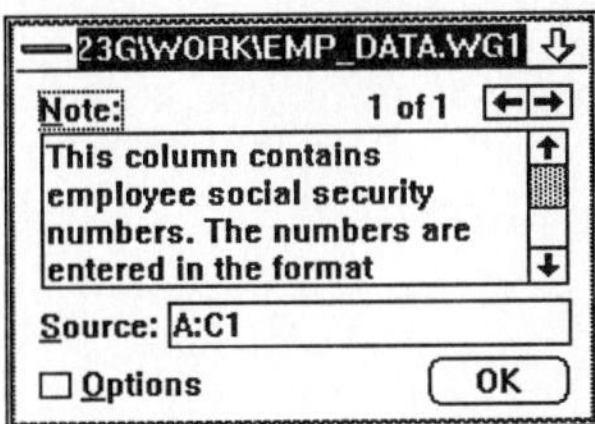

The OK command button closes the Note window and stores the notes for a cell with the worksheet containing the cell. You can also close the Note window by pressing CTRL-BREAK once or ESCAPE several times (BREAK being coupled with PAUSE on the enhanced keyboard and SCROLL LOCK on the PC keyboard). Alternately you can close the Note utility by selecting Close from the window control menu. Each Note window can be moved, minimized, and restored using its window control menu. A Note utility window has the same filename in its title bar as the worksheet file that contains the cell with the attached note.

The Solver Window

The Solver utility is a unique problem-solving utility offered with 1-2-3/G. The Solver utility finds a combination of numbers for a problem that fits a given set of constraints. You can use this feature to find numeric solutions to a problem. The Solver utility has several windows, which let you define the problem, monitor its progress, select an answer, display information about cells the Solver uses, and make a guess.

To open a Solver window, select Utility Solver from the worksheet tool menu to see a window like this:

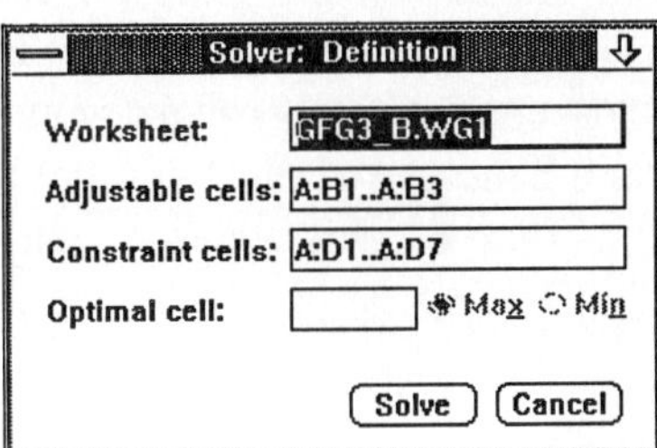

The Cancel command button closes the window without saving the addresses selected for the problem. You can also close the Solver utility by pressing CTRL-BREAK once or ESCAPE several times. Alternately, you can close the Solver utility by selecting Close from the utility's window control menu. You can also use this menu to move, minimize, and restore a Solver window.

The Keystroke Editor Window

1-2-3/G provides a keystroke recording utility that facilitates macro creation. 1-2-3/G automatically records every keystroke you make in its recorder, up to a limit of 16,384 bytes. The keystroke history is useful when you need it but doesn't occupy desktop space when you don't.

Using the Keystroke Editor to create macros prevents errors, since you can inadvertently omit a keystroke from a macro if you enter the macro keystrokes manually. The Keystroke Editor is also useful to record and play back a set of keystrokes that you have already performed. You can use this feature to query a database, change some data, and requery.

To open the Keystroke Editor, select Keystroke Editor from the desktop control menu to show a window like this:

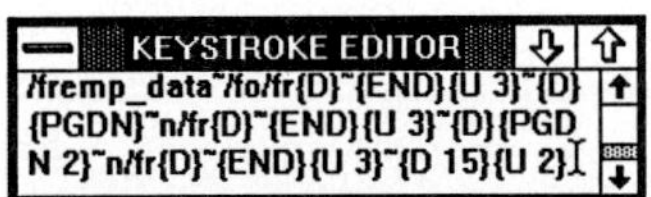

You can also open this window by selecting Utility Macros Keystroke Editor from the worksheet tool menu. You can close the Keystroke Editor window by selecting Close from the Keystroke Editor's window control menu or by pressing CTRL-F4 (Close). When the Keystroke Editor is closed from the desktop view, 1-2-3/G continues to record your keystrokes. Using a mouse or the Keystroke Editor's window control menu, you can also change the size and position of this window with the techniques you learned in Chapter 2, "Getting Started with the New Graphical User Interface."

The Preview Window

1-2-3/G's Preview window lets you see how graphs and worksheets will look before you print them. If the preview is what you want, you can go ahead and print. If not, you can close the Preview window, make changes, and preview the graphs or worksheets again. With the Preview utility, you don't waste time printing graphs and worksheets that aren't correct.

1-2-3/G opens a Preview utility window when you select Screen preview as part of the printing process. Your screen will look like this:

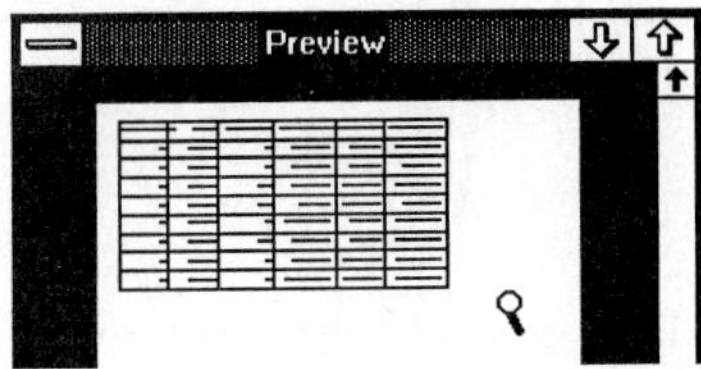

In a Preview window, you can use the utility's commands to enlarge or reduce the previewed output. To close the window, select Close from the window control menu or press CTRL-F4 (Close Tool). You can also change the size and position of the Print Preview window using a mouse or the window control menu.

The Keyboard

You use the keyboard to make cell entries and to make menu selections, since 1-2-3/G provides compatibility with the keystrokes used in earlier releases of 1-2-3. Figure 3-5 shows the standard enhanced IBM keyboard used with most computers that run 1-2-3/G. The location of a few keys differs between keyboards; this should not change how you use 1-2-3/G. This chapter covers all keys and provides a single reference source for all keyboard functions. Later chapters point out individual features as needed.

The enhanced keyboard has three basic sections, as shown in Figure 3-5. The main section keys are in most cases identical to the key assignments on a regular typewriter. Table 3-2 lists special key combinations and additional uses for the regular typewriter keys.

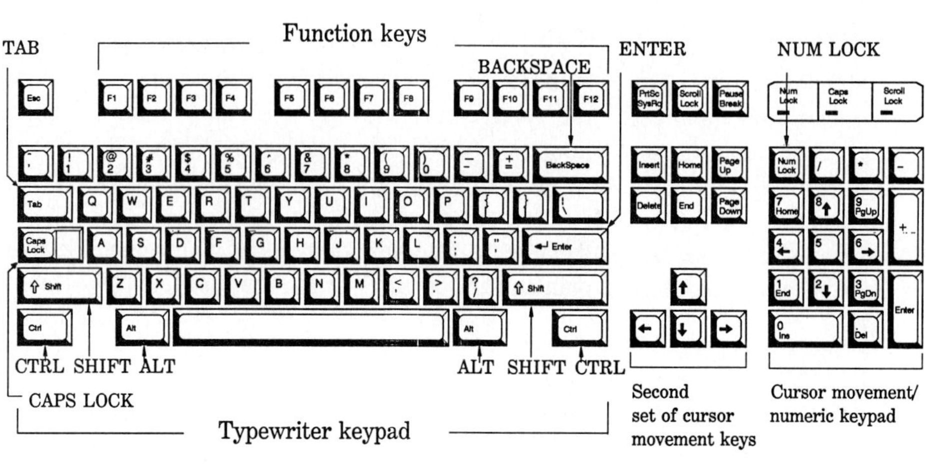

Figure 3-5. IBM enhanced keyboard

Keys	**Action**
ALT	Used in combination with other keys.
ALT-BACKSPACE (Undo)	Undoes the effect of the last action if Undo is enabled.
ALT-ESCAPE (Next Application)	Activates the next Presentation Manager application according to the application names in the Task Manager or Task List.
ALT-SPACEBAR (Desktop Control)	Activates the desktop control menu.
ALT-MINUS (Window Control)	Activates the window control menu.
BACKSPACE	Deletes the character to the left (destructive backspace) when in Edit mode.
CAPS LOCK	Produces capital letters. Toggles on and off each time it is pressed. Does not affect the number keys at the top of the keyboard or the special symbols at the tops of keys. (Use SHIFT to access these.)
CTRL	Used in combination with other keys.
CTRL-BREAK	Returns you to Ready mode, canceling one or more selections. Equivalent to pressing ESC enough times to return to Ready mode.

Table 3-2. Special Key Combinations (*continued on next page*)

Keys	Action
CTRL-ESCAPE (Task List)	Activates the Task Manager or Task List window to choose a Presentation Manager application to activate.
ENTER	Finalizes the last entry made. In a dialog box with Enhanced setting (the default), ENTER selects the item with the dotted outline and moves to next level, or if at the last level, finalizes the dialog box and performs its command. In a dialog box with Standard setting, ENTER finalizes the dialog box and performs its command.
ESCAPE	Cancels the last request. In a dialog box with Enhanced setting (the default), ESCAPE moves the dotted outline to the previous level or, if the dotted outline is on the highest level in the dialog box, leaves the dialog box without performing its command. With Standard setting, ESCAPE leaves the dialog box without performing its command.
NUM LOCK	Toggles numeric keypad between cell pointer movement (off) and numeric entries (on).
SCROLL LOCK	Toggles scroll display between scrolling a line of the display every time an arrow key is pressed, and moving the display screen around a fixed pointer.
SHIFT	Causes letter keys to produce capitals. Allows you to access the special symbols at the top of the number and letter keys. Also combines with some function keys.
SHIFT-ENTER (Confirm)	Finalizes a dialog box and performs its command.
SHIFT-ESCAPE (Cancel)	Quits a dialog box without executing its command.
SHIFT-TAB	Shifts the worksheet in the window to show the next set of columns to the left; equivalent to CTRL-LEFT ARROW.
TAB	Equivalent to CTRL-RIGHT ARROW; shifts the display to show the next set of columns to the right.

Table 3-2. Special Key Combinations

Along the top of the keyboard are the ESCAPE key, used to back out of an entry or dialog box, and the function keys, labeled F1 through F12. Each program uses function keys for tasks or commands specific to the program. Presentation Manager programs use F1 for Help and ALT-F4 to close the program. 1-2-3/G assigns these keys the special functions shown in Table 3-3. Pressing a function key causes 1-2-3/G to take the

Function Key	Assignment
F1 (Help)	Opens a Help window to provide context-sensitive help.
F2 (Edit)	Allows you to alter the contents of the current cell without reentering all the information. You can add or delete just a few characters if you wish.
F3 (Name)	Displays a list of range names, function names, macro commands, or template filenames. The information listed is based on the entry you made before pressing F3.
F4 (Abs)	Allows you to toggle from a relative address to an absolute or mixed address.
F5 (Goto)	Moves your cell pointer to the range or address you enter after pressing the key, or select from a list of ranges.
F6 (Window)	Functions as a toggle, moving you into the other pane when the worksheet window has two panes. (See Chapter 5.)
F7 (Query)	Repeats the last Data Query operation.
F8 (Table)	Repeats the last Data Table command.
F9 (Calc)	Recalculates all worksheet formulas. Useful when worksheet recalculation is set to manual. In a graph window, redraws the most recent graph.
F10 (Menu)	Activates the menu.
F11 (Help Index)	Displays the index of help topics when a Help window is active.
ALT-F1 (Compose)	Creates characters that are not on the keyboard.
ALT-F2 (Step)	Switches Step mode on and off. Step mode executes macros one step at a time.
ALT-F3 (Run)	Runs a selected macro.
ALT-F4 (Close Desktop)	Closes the desktop.
CTRL-F6 (Next Tool)	Activates the next window in the list that is displayed by selecting Window from the desktop control menu. Useful for switching between graph and worksheet tools.
SHIFT-F2 (Trace)	Opens a Trace dialog box that displays macro instructions as 1-2-3/G performs them.
SHIFT-F3 (Options)	Displays a dialog box to select options for the Copy, Edit Paste Special, and Range Erase commands.
SHIFT-F4 (Bound)	Turns Bound on and off, which lets only the cell pointer move to unprotected cells in the selected range.
SHIFT-F6 (Hide)	Displays or rehides hidden columns, rows, or sheets.
SHIFT-F7 (Group)	Turns Group mode on or off. Group mode applies formatting changes made in one sheet to every sheet in the group.
SHIFT-F8 (Detach)	Attaches or detaches the cell pointer to the selected range.

Table 3-3. Function Key Assignments

requested action when it is in Ready mode. The exceptions are F1 (Help), F3 (Name), F4 (Abs), and ALT-F4 (Close), which function in Ready as well as other modes. As you can see from the table, several of the function keys combine with ALT, CTRL, and SHIFT keys to perform additional tasks.

The keys to the far right serve a dual purpose, providing both the numeric keypad and the movement keys. These keys have both numbers and direction arrows or other writing on them. When NUM LOCK is enabled (the keyboard light below NUM LOCK is on), pressing these keys produces a number. When NUM LOCK is disabled (the light is off), pressing these keys moves the cell pointer in the direction described in Table 3-4. As you can see from the table, sometimes these keys are combined with CTRL to provide additional movement features.

Each time you press the NUM LOCK key, it toggles between enabled and disabled. Fortunately, the enhanced keyboard has a second set of navigational keys that allows you to enable NUM LOCK and use the numeric keypad exclusively for numbers while you use the second set of navigational keys to move the cell pointer. The gray keys, *, /, –, +, and ENTER on this keypad, are included a second time merely to be handy when you are entering numbers with the numeric keypad.

Here's a brief example of how to use the movement keys. Take a look at the multisheet worksheet window in Figure 3-6. The commands for displaying multiple worksheets in one worksheet window are covered in Chapter 5, "Building Blocks for Worksheets." The cell pointer is in B:B3, as shown by cell address in the address box in the control line. Using either the keypad or the gray cursor keys will move the cell pointer to new locations. Table 3-5 shows the new location of the cell pointer if you press the listed keys when the cell pointer is in location B:B3.

The function of these keys will become clearer as you develop your worksheet models. There are also keys for accessing other sheets within the current worksheet file, as well as additional files open in memory. Commands for adding worksheet windows and retrieving files into the worksheet windows are covered in more detail in Chapter 6, "Managing Worksheet Data and Other File Options." Commands for changing the number of sheets that appear in a worksheet window are covered in Chapter 5, "Building Blocks for Worksheets."

Tip: Focus first on the basic keys for cell pointer movement. Trying to learn too many keys may confuse you. Five basic entries are all you need to get started. Press the HOME key to move to A1, and use the four arrow keys to move in other directions. If you hold down the arrow keys, they will repeat and move you around very quickly.

Keys	Action
HOME	Moves the cell pointer to the home position or upper-left corner of the worksheet. When in Edit mode, moves the cell pointer to the beginning of the entry.
UP ARROW	Moves the cell pointer up one cell on the worksheet.
DOWN ARROW	Moves the cell pointer down one cell on the worksheet.
RIGHT ARROW	Moves the cell pointer one cell to the right.
LEFT ARROW	Moves the cell pointer one cell to the left.
PGUP	Moves the cell pointer up the number of rows displayed in the window.
PGDN	Moves the cell pointer down the number of rows displayed in the window.
END followed by an arrow key	Moves the cell pointer to the end of your entries in the direction indicated by the arrow key when the cell pointer is on a cell containing an entry. When the cell pointer is on a blank cell, takes the cell pointer to the next cell in the direction that has an entry.
CTRL-RIGHT ARROW	Moves your window into the worksheet to show the next set of columns to the right.
CTRL-LEFT ARROW	Moves your window into the worksheet to show the next set of columns to the left.
CTRL-HOME	Moves the cell pointer to A:A1 in the current worksheet.
END, CTRL-HOME	Moves the cell pointer to the cell with the address that has the sheet letter of the last sheet used, the column letter of the right-most column used in any sheet, and the row number of the last row used in any sheet for the current worksheet file.
CTRL-PGUP	Moves the cell pointer to the next worksheet.
CTRL-PGDN	Moves the cell pointer to the previous worksheet.
END, CTRL-PGUP	Functions much like the END key, but moves across sheets from the current sheet toward the last sheet. The cell pointer remains in the same location as in the present worksheet, except the current worksheet becomes the worksheet with a nonblank entry at an intersection of blank and nonblank cells. If your cell pointer is in A:B3, pressing END, places the cell pointer in IV:B3 if all the sheets are blank.
END, CTRL-PGDN	Functions much like the END key, but moves across sheets toward the first sheet. The cell pointer remains in the same location as in the present worksheet, except the current worksheet becomes the worksheet with a nonblank entry at an intersection of blank and nonblank cells.

Table 3-4. Movement Key Functions

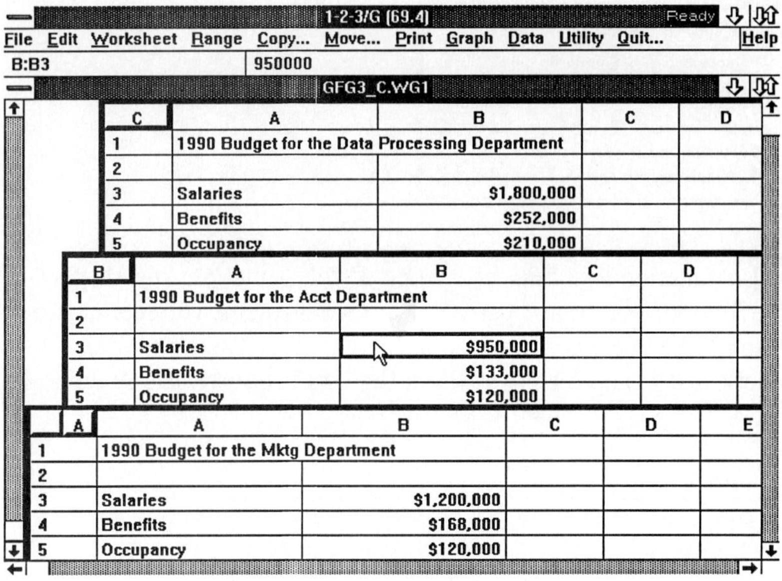

Figure 3-6. Multisheet worksheet file

Adding a Function-Key Map

Since each window uses different function-key assignments, you may want a constant reminder of the tasks the function keys perform. As you press the ALT, SHIFT, or CTRL keys, 1-2-3/G updates the function-key map for the task 1-2-3/G will perform when you combine ALT, SHIFT, or CTRL with a function key. Another advantage of displaying the map is that you can click these keys with the mouse to make a selection.

To add a function-key map, select Utility from the main menu by typing / or pressing F10 (Menu) then type **U**. Next select User Settings and Preferences by typing **U** and **P**. Finally, using this dialog box:

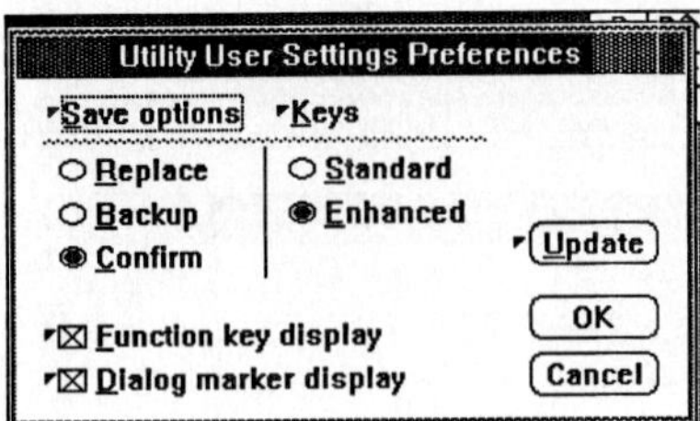

add a function-key map by typing **F** for Function key display. To hide the function-key map, perform the same menu command and type **F**. When the check box next to Function key display contains an X, the function-key map displays; when the box is empty, the function-key map

Key Sequence	New Cursor Location
LEFT ARROW	B:A3
RIGHT ARROW	B:C3
UP ARROW	B:B2
DOWN ARROW	B:B4
END, DOWN ARROW	B:B5
END, UP ARROW	B:B1
END, RIGHT ARROW	B:IV3
END, LEFT ARROW	B:A3
PGUP	B:B1 (cannot move up one full screen)
PGDN	B:B7 (number of rows down will be same as number of rows displayed on screen)
HOME	B:A1
CTRL-RIGHT ARROW	B:G3
CTRL-LEFT ARROW	B:A3
CTRL-PGDN	A:B3
CTRL-PGUP	C:B3
END, CTRL-PGDN	A:B3
END, CTRL-PGUP	C:B3

Table 3-5. Key Sequence Cursor Locations

disappears. Making this kind of menu selection is discussed in more detail later in the chapter.

Once you add a function map, 1-2-3/G also adds the indicators Caps, Num, and Scroll above the function-key map. They appear in a superimposed indicator box when the function map is displayed and indicate whether the CAPS LOCK, NUM LOCK, and SCROLL LOCK keys are toggled on or off.

Selecting Keyboard Compatibility

The keyboard in 1-2-3/G can be compatible with other Presentation Manager applications or with prior releases of 1-2-3. Keyboard compatibility affects how 1-2-3/G interprets ENTER and ESCAPE in dialog boxes that display options for 1-2-3's commands. Dialog boxes are described later in this chapter. If your keyboard is set to be compatible with other Presentation Manager applications, pressing ENTER in a dialog box finalizes your dialog box selections and performs the associated command. Pressing ESCAPE takes you out of the dialog box and returns you to Ready mode. This is the Standard keyboard setting. If your keyboard is set to be compatible with other 1-2-3 releases, pressing ENTER selects the dialog box component with the dotted outline and pressing ESCAPE backs you out of the current menu level. This is the Enhanced keyboard setting. Unlike the Standard setting, Enhanced does not finalize the dialog box. Enhanced keyboard compatibility is more convenient if you are accustomed to using other 1-2-3 releases and if you make selections by pressing ENTER. The 1-2-3/G default is set to Enhanced to support character-based releases of 1-2-3/G. You may want to change the keyboard compatibility to Standard if you are using many Presentation Manager applications and you want ENTER and ESCAPE to behave as they do in other Presentation Manager applications.

To change the keyboard compatibility, follow these steps:

1. Select Utility.

2. Select User Settings and Preferences.

3. From the dialog box just presented, change the keyboard compatibility by selecting Keys and Standard.

To return the keyboard compatibility to Enhanced, perform the same steps, replacing Standard with Enhanced.

Using a Mouse

1-2-3/G takes full advantage of the Presentation Manager's graphical user interface. One of the advantages of a graphical user interface is that it lets you use a mouse. Rather than typing and pressing keys to select commands, you can simply point to a command and click the mouse. For some tasks, such as moving between cells or changing the size and position of a window or desktop, a mouse is easier. For other tasks, such as data entry, you must use a keyboard. Using a mouse makes working with 1-2-3/G more flexible.

A mouse is easy to use. Once the mouse is connected and installed and the operating system has loaded the necessary software (part of booting up), you can start using the mouse. Place your hand over the mouse with your fingers touching the mouse buttons. With 1-2-3/G, you will use the left mouse button most of the time and the right button only for special tasks. If you prefer, you can switch the buttons through the Presentation Manager Control Panel program, although the book uses the default settings for the mouse. Some mouse devices have three buttons, but 1-2-3/G does not use the middle button.

As you move the mouse, 1-2-3/G indicates the mouse location on screen with a graphical pointer. Since you want to be able to move the mouse around quickly, place it on a flat area. Some mice require special pads; others will accept any flat surface. If your work surface is cluttered and you run into something as you move the mouse, simply pick the mouse up, move it to another area, and continue.

On screen, the mouse pointer looks different, depending on what you're pointing to. 1-2-3/G adjusts the mouse pointer's appearance to reflect your current task. Table 3-6 shows the different mouse pointer shapes. Next to each symbol and description is the task 1-2-3/G will perform while the mouse pointer has the shape shown. The mouse pointer's appearance reminds you what you can do from your current position. 1-2-3/G constantly updates the mouse pointer's appearance as you move across the screen. For example, as you move the pointer from

Symbol	Description	Task you can perform
	White arrow	Selects object below white arrow.
	White double-sided arrow	Resizes desktop, window, column, or row depending on the pointer's position.
I	I-beam	Selects position to enter and edit data.
	Hourglass	None. 1-2-3/G is busy performing a task and wants you to wait until 1-2-3/G is finished.
	Gray arrow	None. You are pointing at something 1-2-3/G will not let you select.
	Black double-sided arrow	Creates or changes the size of a worksheet pane. A pane splits a window in two so you can look at two parts of a worksheet file at the same time.
?	Question mark	Selects a Help window hot-item text.
	Magnifying glass	Magnifies or reduces the display of the printed output in a Preview window.

Table 3-6. Mouse Pointer Appearance

the bottom to the top of Figure 3-7, the mouse pointer starts as a white arrow, changes to a white double-sided arrow as it crosses the desktop border, returns to a white arrow in the desktop background, returns to a white double-sided arrow as it crosses the window border, returns to a white arrow in the worksheet window, changes to an I-beam in the contents box of the control line, and finally returns to a white arrow in the menu bar and desktop title bar.

Using a mouse is very different from using a keyboard. To select something with a mouse, you usually click the mouse. As you know, clicking the mouse means pointing to the item you want and pressing the left mouse button; double-clicking means pointing to the item you want and pressing the left mouse button twice quickly; and dragging means pointing to the object you want and then holding down the left

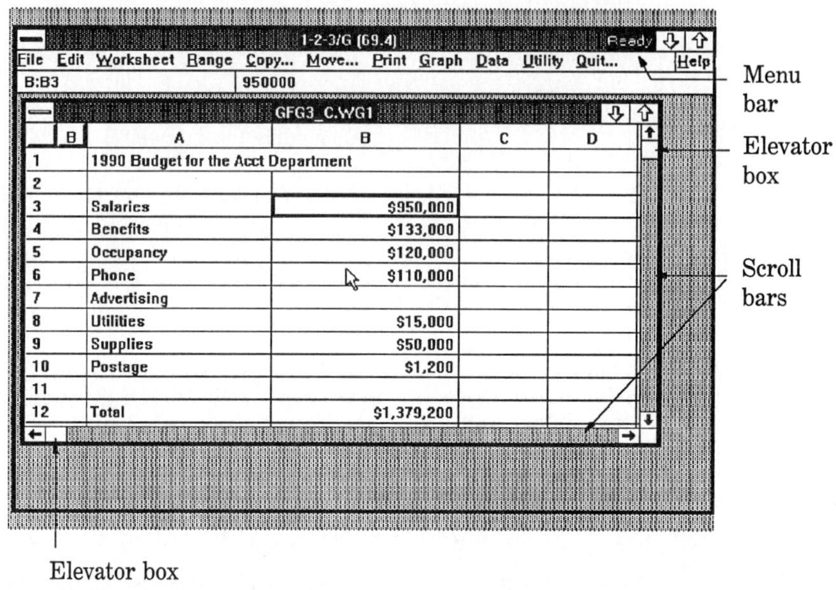

Figure 3-7. Worksheet window showing worksheet tool menu

mouse button as you drag the mouse to the new location. When you resize a window with a mouse you are dragging a mouse. If you run out of space on your work surface while dragging the mouse, simply lift the mouse while holding the left mouse button down, and move the mouse to a new location. This takes practice but works well when you have a small work area.

Tip: Make sure that your work area is clean. A dirty mouse is not only hard to move but its movement does not properly record on the screen.

Tip: Clear the area on which you move the mouse. Also, make sure you have a large enough area so you don't waste time moving the mouse from one side of the mouse work area to the other.

Scroll Bars

The two bars along the right and bottom of every worksheet are *scroll bars.* Scroll bars also appear in other windows to indicate that the window contains more information than can be seen. For example, Help windows include scroll bars when the help topic display is more than can fit in the Help window. Some 1-2-3/G dialog boxes use scroll bars when a list is longer than the space reserved for the list elements. You can use scroll bars to change your position in a window or dialog box. You access scroll bars via the mouse; just click the scroll bar's position and 1-2-3/G moves you to the appropriate location in the window or dialog box list. Your current position in the window or dialog box list is marked on the scroll bar with an elevator box (refer to Figure 3-7), which you can use to scroll through a window or list quickly. You can also scroll a worksheet to change the area of the display that appears in the window. Scrolling in a worksheet does not change the worksheet's cell pointer position. The cell pointer remains at the address shown in the address box on the control line.

To move to another location with the scroll bar, point the mouse above or below the elevator box in a vertical scroll bar or to the left or right of the elevator box in a horizontal scroll bar. When you click the mouse, the display in the window or dialog text box scrolls in the direction selected, one window at a time. You can choose a location close to the elevator box or far away—the result will be the same.

You can also drag the elevator box, that is, point to an elevator box in the scroll box and drag the elevator box to a new position. Dragging the elevator box scrolls the display so that the elevator's position indicates your location within the window. This scrolls the worksheet display more than one screen length at a time, which occurs when you click the mouse on a scroll bar.

Scroll bars also include arrows at the ends. Click on these arrows to scroll the display one line at a time in the direction of the arrow. It's more efficient to use these arrows than to switch your hand from the mouse to the keyboard.

Menus

The menu bar in the second line of the desktop is available whenever you need it. Menus are the backbone of the 1-2-3/G program and allow you to access all of its features. You can activate the menu by typing **/** (slash), as used in other releases of 1-2-3 or by pressing F10 (Menu). With a mouse, simply click the desired menu item.

Once you activate the menu, 1-2-3/G displays the menu choices. The desktop title bar describes the highlighted menu option. You can point to different menu items with the navigational keys. As you move from item to item, the description changes accordingly. For instance, when you move the highlight to Worksheet in the menu bar, the description displays a "Change global settings; modify worksheet file; change window display"—providing an overview of your choices under Worksheet.

Making and Canceling Selections

To select a menu item, you can either type the underlined letter of the menu item (for example, **W** for Worksheet), move to the item with your cell pointer, and press ENTER, or you can click the menu item. These methods invoke the selected command or present a menu for further selections. Each subsequent menu level is selected in the same manner as the previous selection, with each level refining your initial choice further. Each menu item has a unique underlined letter.

If you make a mistake, you have several choices. Pressing ESCAPE removes the last selection you made. Each time you press ESCAPE, you go back to the previous menu level until you are eventually returned to Ready mode. You can press ESCAPE repeatedly to back out of a menu completely. You can also press CTRL-BREAK which takes you out of the menu system and to Ready mode. Some commands provide a Cancel command button that you can press to abandon your menu selections and return to Ready mode. If a dialog box is not on screen, you can cancel the menu selections by clicking a cell or another menu.

Tip: Highlighting alone does not select a menu option. Remember to press ENTER after highlighting your selection.

The Main Menu

The first menu in 1-2-3/G is the main menu. It appears constantly in the menu bar and changes to match the active tool or utility window. The second line in Figure 3-7 shows the worksheet tool menu. The other tool menu bars are the

Graph tool:

File Edit Type Settings Add Layout Help

Note utility:

File Edit Help

Keystroke editor utility:

File Edit Options Run Help

Preview utility:

File Edit Zoom Goto Print Help

Solver utility:

File Solve Answer Report Options Help

While the rest of this chapter focuses on the worksheet tool menu, the procedure for making menu selections is the same for the other menus. From here on, the text refers to selecting menu items, whether you use the keyboard or a mouse.

Pull-Down Menus

Once you select a menu item from the main menu, 1-2-3/G presents a pull-down menu. A *pull-down* menu looks like this Worksheet pull-down menu:

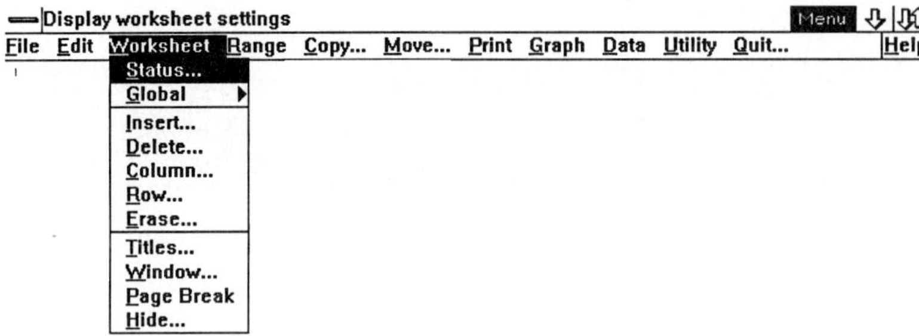

All of the menu items in the main menu except Copy, Move, and Quit have pull-down menus. You can select an item from a pull-down menu by typing the underlined letter, clicking the desired menu item, or using the UP ARROW, DOWN ARROW, HOME, and END keys to highlight a choice before pressing ENTER to select it. If you press LEFT ARROW or RIGHT ARROW, 1-2-3/G displays the pull-down menu of the next menu item in the menu bar. For example, after you select File, pressing the RIGHT ARROW displays the Edit pull-down menu. A pull-down menu appears below the menu item to which it belongs.

Pull-down menus use two symbols to indicate what you will see when you select a particular menu item. An ellipsis (...) indicates a dialog box. (As described later, a dialog box lets you provide different types of information 1-2-3/G uses to perform the command.) A right arrow indicates that selecting the highlighted item displays a cascading menu. A pull-down menu also uses grayed text to indicate selections that are not available. Some commands display accelerator key options. As described earlier, accelerator keys are keys you can press instead of selecting the menu commands. A pull-down menu may be divided into sections with lines that mark related commands.

Cascade Menus

A *cascade menu* connects to a pull-down menu or another cascade menu. Cascade menus cascade across the worksheet as shown in Figure 3-8. 1-2-3/G displays a right arrow after a menu item if selecting it will display a cascade menu. When you select Worksheet, 1-2-3/G displays a right arrow next to Global (as illustrated in the pull-down menu just shown). If you select Global, you'll see a right arrow next to Attributes. When you select Attributes the cascade menu displays. If you look at

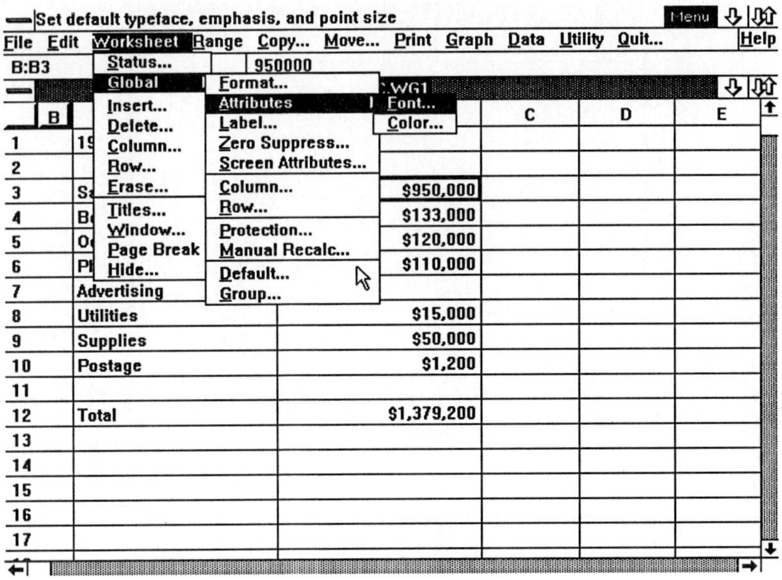

Figure 3-8. Cascading menus

Figure 3-8 you will see the cascade menu options Font and Color. With all cascade menus, selecting one of the choices performs the command, displays another cascade menu, or displays a dialog box.

Dialog Boxes

Dialog boxes let you enter command information. Figure 3-9 shows the dialog box for the Print Printer command, discussed in Chapter 11, "Printing." Dialog boxes have several features in common. The title bar displays the command name. You can use the title bar to move the dialog box on the 1-2-3/G desktop using the mouse just as you use the window title bar to move a window. Some dialog boxes, like the one in Figure 3-10, include minimize icons. Chapter 7, "Changing the Worksheet Appearance," discusses how you can use the Range Format

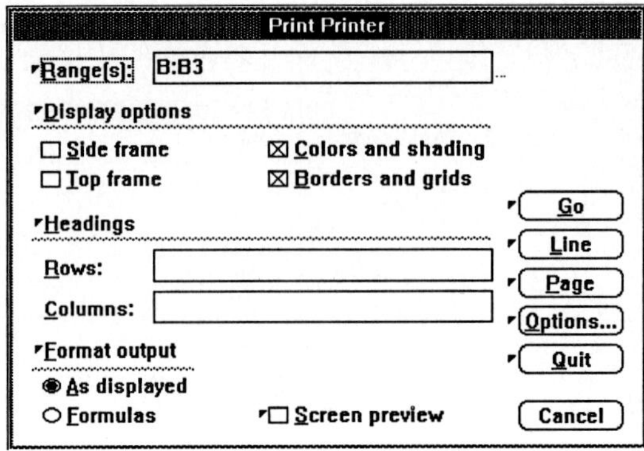

Figure 3-9. Print Printer dialog box

command to improve the appearance of worksheet entries. When you begin to select a range, the dialog box looks like this:

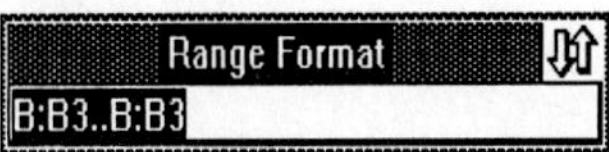

It's easier to select cells in a minimized dialog box. Most dialog boxes reduce to this size when you begin to select cells in the worksheet

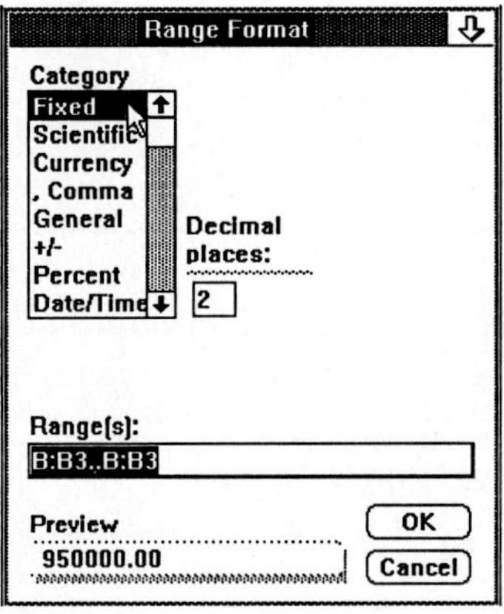

Figure 3-10. Range Format dialog box

window. A dialog box also contains different types of prompts and displays, or *components*, including dialog markers, text boxes, list boxes, information boxes, option buttons, check boxes, and command buttons, all of which will be discussed shortly. The components that appear in a dialog box depend on the information the command needs and the options you can choose for the command. You can move from one component to another by pressing TAB and SHIFT-TAB. 1-2-3/G marks the current position with a dotted box like the one around Range in Figure 3-9. You can select the outlined item by pressing ENTER. You can also change an item outlined within a group by pressing the arrow keys. For example, pressing the RIGHT ARROW or DOWN ARROW in Figure 3-9 moves the dotted box from Range to Display options, which is the next dialog box item marked with a dialog marker.

Dialog Markers

When a dialog box contains many types of information, you need to know where the keystrokes will affect it. Dialog markers mark the dialog box components that you can select by typing the underlined letter. Dialog markers are important when you are selecting dialog box components with the keyboard. The small triangle dialog markers are shown in Figure 3-9. As shown in the Print Printer dialog box, you can type **R** to select Range, **D** to select Display options, **H** to select Headings, **F** to select Format output, **S** to select Screen preview, **G** to select Go, **L** to select Line, **P** to select Page, **O** to select Options, or **Q** to select Quit.

If you are using the mouse, dialog markers are not as important; usually you can just select the dialog component you want without first selecting the component that is hierarchically above. For example, to select Side frame from Figure 3-9 with a mouse, simply click Side frame instead of first selecting Display options and then selecting Side frame. If you are using a mouse to select dialog box components, you may want to hide the dialog markers by selecting Utility User Settings Preferences and the Dialog marker display check box. Select OK to finalize your selections in the dialog box.

Text Boxes

For some commands, you must type in text. This can be the text you want to appear at the top of every printed page, the range a command uses, or the file you want the command to use. You enter this information in a text box, such as the Range(s), Rows, and Columns boxes in Figure 3-9. The type of information you enter depends on the command. The text above or in front of the text box describes the information that 1-2-3/G wants to know. If 1-2-3/G wants a cell or range (multiple cells), you can select cells with the arrow keys or the mouse. When you begin the selection process, 1-2-3/G minimizes the entire dialog box to let you select the range more easily. For a text entry, pressing the arrow keys in these boxes moves the I-beam that marks where 1-2-3/G will insert your characters.

Some text boxes have an attached list box that appears directly below them. When you select an item from a list box, 1-2-3/G places that item in the text box. Pressing DOWN ARROW moves the outline that marks the current position from the text box to the list box.

List Boxes

A *list box,* then, displays a list of possible selections. The highlighted selection is the one 1-2-3/G will use. You can change the highlighted item with the arrow keys. HOME highlights the first item in the list; END highlights the last. List boxes include a scroll bar that you can use to change the highlighted item. Figure 3-10 shows a list for selecting cell format. The items in the list box depend on the command and are described with the text above the list box. The list box can include filenames, fonts, and names of cells in the worksheet file. Another list box is presented when you select File Retrieve. You can use the list box to select the name of the file you want to retrieve. As mentioned, a list box can be attached to a text box so that selecting an item in the list box enters the item in the attached text box. Conversely, typing an entry in a text box highlights the item in the list box.

Information Boxes

A dialog box can also contain a box that displays information about a highlighted list box item. As the highlighted item in the list box changes, the text in the information box changes. The information box text depends on the type of items shown in the list box. The text may include the size, date, and time a file was saved last or the source of a link that brings data from other Presentation Manager applications into 1-2-3/G. In Figure 3-10, the Preview information box displays how the selected format will appear using the current cell's entry. The number in the current cell will appear when you highlight one of the formats shown above. The formats let you change how a number appears. You cannot alter the items displayed in the information box.

Option Buttons

The choices in some dialog boxes are limited to option buttons. You can select only one of these. If you are working with files, for example, you only have a limited number of drives that can contain the files. When you save a file, you must select which drive you want to use.

Option buttons are represented as small circles next to the descriptive text for the option. You can use option buttons to select disk drives, set label alignment in cells, set column width, and hide or display a column. When you select one of these buttons, you are replacing any previous selection for that option. To select an option button with a mouse, click either the option button or the text that appears next to it.

Check Boxes

Other dialog box options also have a limited number of choices but let you select more than one (for example, you can display both a function-key map and the dialog markers). These dialog box options use check boxes. Check boxes contain an X when the option is selected and are blank when the option is not. To select a check box with a mouse, click either the check box or the text that appears next to it.

Sometimes check boxes appear as gray. This occurs when a range is selected before selecting a command that alters the appearance of the cells. For example, you can boldface, italicize, strikeout, and underline the text in a cell. If you select more than one cell before you enter the Range Attribute Font command, the check boxes under Attributes are grayed, indicating that all cells selected before you selected the Range

Attribute Font command will use the original font attributes. When the check boxes are initially gray, selecting the check box once removes the check box for all cells selected, and selecting the check box again selects the check box for all cells.

Command Buttons

The last dialog box component is a command button. Figure 3-10 shows two command buttons labeled OK and Cancel. Selecting the command button performs the described action. Most dialog boxes have an OK and a Cancel button. The Cancel button, equivalent to pressing CTRL-BREAK, cancels both the command and the dialog box and returns you to Ready mode. The OK command button finalizes the selections in the dialog box and performs the command using the selections made in the dialog box. The OK command button is also selected when you choose an entry from the last level of the dialog box. For example, when you use Range Format to select how 1-2-3/G will display numbers in one or more cells, after you select the format you want, you select the cells to which this format will be applied. When you press ENTER to finalize the cell selection, you are also selecting the OK command button since this is the last entry that this dialog box needs to complete the Range Format command. Some commands have more or different command buttons.

1-2-3/G Worksheets

Getting Started with Worksheets
Building Blocks for Worksheets
Managing Worksheet Data and Other File Options
Changing the Worksheet Appearance
Copying and Moving Worksheet Data
@Functions in Worksheets
Using Multiple Windows and Links
Printing
Building Advanced Worksheet Applications

PART TWO

Getting Started with Worksheets

FOUR

The worksheet tool allows you to create financial models that can help you analyze budgets, sales projections, and staffing needs, or project costs. The worksheet tool is an accurate and efficient way to make calculations that require modification or are needed repeatedly.

You will make entries in worksheet cells (the intersection of a row and a column) to create your models; these entries can be placed in the first sheet (sheet A) or in any of the 255 sheets in the worksheet file.

You can choose various numeric formats and other display attributes for your data. You can change the size of rows and columns. And you can print your data when finished. In this chapter you will use many of the worksheet features to create a budget model. First you'll create a budget for the Cleveland Division of Allied Piano Company, and then you'll create budgets for the other divisions.

Making the Entries for the Cleveland Division

You will use sheet A in the empty worksheet displayed when you first start 1-2-3/G to make budget entries for the Cleveland Division of Allied Piano as shown in Figure 4-1. First, move to each of the cell addresses below and enter the text as shown:

A5: Salaries
A6: Benefits
A7: Material Cost
A8: Advertising
A9: Interest Expense
A10: Utilities
A11: Taxes
A12: TOTAL EXPENSES
B1: Allied Piano Company
B2: 1990 Budget
B3: Cleveland Division

Each of these entries is a label, one of the two types of entries 1-2-3/G permits in a worksheet cell. Some of these labels are longer than the current width of the cell where they are entered and will be temporarily truncated when you make an entry in the cell to the right. Later you will learn how to adjust for this by widening the cell columns.

1-2-3/G (69.4) Ready
File Edit Worksheet Range Copy... Move... Print Graph Data Utility Quit... Help
A:A1

SHEET6.WG1

A	A	B	C	D	E	F
1		Allied Piano Company				
2		1990 Budget				
3		Cleveland Division				
4						
5	Salaries	567500				
6	Benefits	79450				
7	Material Cost	245000				
8	Advertising	45000				
9	Interest Expense	21000				
10	Utilities	1800				
11	Taxes	27900				
12	TOTAL EXPENSES	987650				

Figure 4-1. Model budget entries

The other type of entry in a worksheet cell is a value. Values can consist of numbers, formulas, or @functions. Formulas and @functions perform calculations, make comparisons, or manipulate text entries. Complete the following value entries by typing the exact set of keystrokes shown:

B5: 567500
B6: +B5*.14

Entry B6 is a formula that uses the figure in entry B5 to compute benefits, as benefits are normally a percentage of salaries.

B7: 245000
B8: 45000
B9: 21000
B10: 1800
B11: 27900
B12: @SUM(B5. .B11)

This last entry is an @function. It sums the contents of each row in the range B5..B11. The results of this are identical to entering the formula +B5+B6+B7+B8+B9+B10+B11. Although the exact appearance of the worksheet will depend on the font in use, it will look something like Figure 4-2.

Changing the Appearance of the Entries

Although the worksheet entries just completed represent correct budget projections, they are difficult to read. The long labels in column A are truncated, and the value entries lack comma separators for the thousands position. In addition, the heading would be better presented in larger characters. 1-2-3/G can make all of these changes with ease.

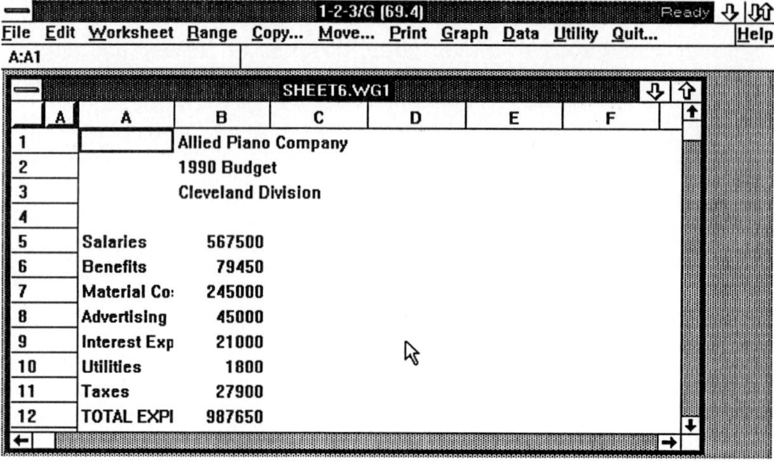

Figure 4-2. Model after completing basic entries in columns A and B

Changing the Column Width

You can change the width of any worksheet column to accommodate your data. You can either pick a set width or have 1-2-3/G adjust the width to meet the need of the largest entry within the column. Try changing the width of column A with these steps:

1. Move the cell pointer to column A, using the arrow keys or click the mouse on any cell in column A.
2. Select Worksheet Column. A dialog box like this appears:

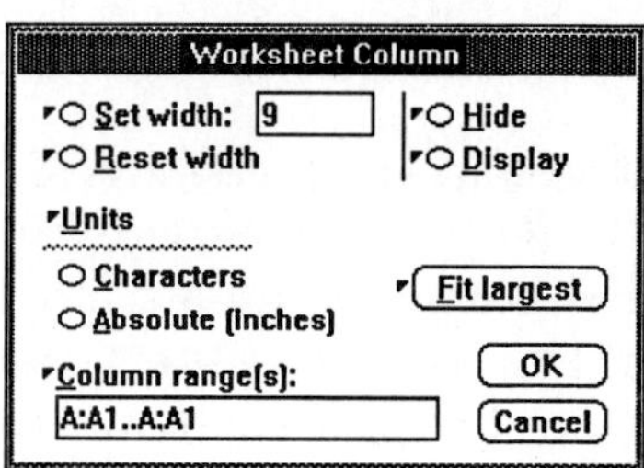

3. Click Fit largest or type **F** to have 1-2-3/G widen column A for the largest entry.

Changing the Format for Value Entries

1-2-3/G's formats for numbers include currency, percentages, and dates. If none of the standard options meet your needs, you can even create custom formats. The numbers on the current sheet will be easier to read if you add a comma as a thousands separator. Follow these steps to make the change:

1. If you are using a mouse, preselect the cells to be formatted by moving the mouse pointer to B5, pressing the left mouse button, dragging down to B12, and then releasing the left mouse button. If you are using the keyboard, simply move the cell pointer to B5.

2. Select Range Format to display a dialog box of format optons.

3. Click the mouse on the option **, Comma** or type **,**.

4. Type **0**, for 0 decimal places, and press ENTER.

5. If you are using a mouse, click OK to accept the range. If you are using the keyboard, expand the range to B12 by using the DOWN ARROW key, and then press ENTER. Don't be alarmed when the dialog box shrinks to aid in your selection of a range.

Each of the numbers on the sheet will display with a comma separator.

Font Changes

A Font choice dictates both character style and size for text entries. 1-2-3/G allows you to specify both screen and print fonts. Helvetica 8 point is 1-2-3/G's default font for screen display. Helvetica indicates the character style and 8 point indicates the size. Larger point sizes produce larger characters, which could be used, for example, to set off the entries in B1..B3 from the others. Follow these steps to change these entries to Courier 12 point:

1. Move the cell pointer to B1. Use the arrow keys if you're working from the keyboard; click the mouse after positioning the pointer if you're using the mouse.

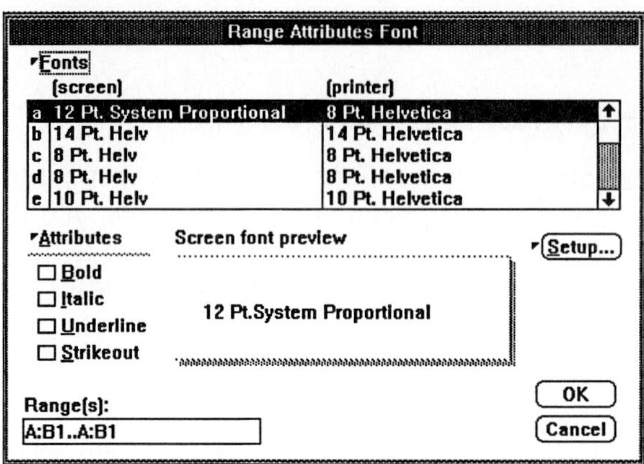

Figure 4-3. Range Attributes Font dialog box

2. Select Range Attributes Font and the dialog box in Figure 4-3 appears.

3. If you are using a mouse, click the scroll bar at the right of the font options until 12 Pt. Courier appears and then click the 12 Pt. Courier option. Click the Range text box and select cells B1..B2 by clicking B1 and dragging to B2. The dialog box temporarily disappears while you make the selection. Click OK to complete the change or press ENTER.

With the keyboard the same task can be accomplished by pressing TAB to activate the font options. Next type **R** to select 12 Pt. Courier. Press TAB to move through the other dialog box options until the Range box is active and then type **B1.B3** and press ENTER.

Figure 4-4 shows the change in entries B1..B3 after the new font is selected.

Copying Data to Other Sheets

To create budgets for other divisions of the Allied Piano Company, you will copy categories from the Cleveland budget to other sheets in the

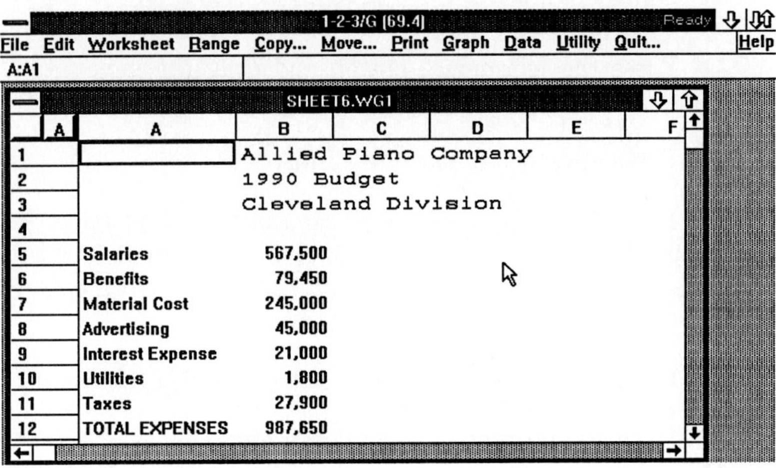

Figure 4-4. New font selected

file. 1-2-3/G also supports adding new worksheets to the desktop and adding the information to these sheets. You will learn about linking multiple sheets in later chapters in this section.

First copy the budget categories, then copy part of the heading. The division name and the figures for each department will be entered for each new sheet. Follow these steps:

1. Move the cell pointer to the first budget category, Salaries, in A5 of the current sheet, sheet A, or click the mouse pointer on A:A5.

2. Select Copy.

3. Move the cell pointer down to A:A12, which contains the last budget category on the current sheet, to include the range of labels.

4. Press ENTER to accept the From range that tells 1-2-3/G the data you want to copy.

5. Press CTRL-PGUP and move to B:A5.

Cell A5 is the first cell you want to copy to on the new sheet, sheet B.

6. Press the left mouse button and drag the mouse to B:A12 or type . and move the cell pointer to B:A12.

7. Press CTRL-PGUP to move to C:A5.

8. Press ENTER to accept the To range and place copies of the budget categories in B:A5..B:A12 and C:A5..C:A12. The copies were placed on both sheets since the To range spanned the beginning To locations on sheets B and C.

9. Press ALT-MINUS then type an **X** to maximize the window size.

10. Select Worksheet Window Perspective to view sheets A through C overlapping and then move the cell pointer to A:A5 as shown in Figure 4-5.

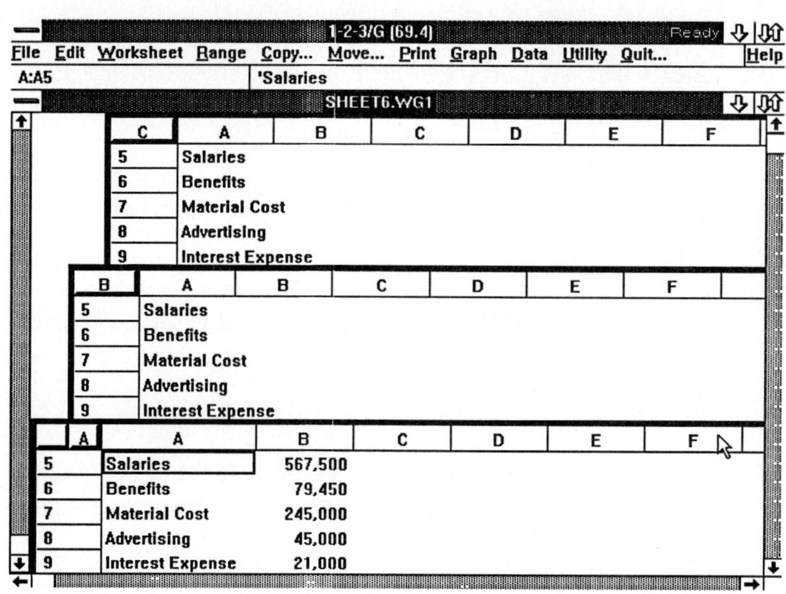

Figure 4-5. Perspective view showing three sheets

You can move between sheets A, B, and C by using with CTRL-PGUP and CTRL-PGDN or by clicking the mouse on the desired sheet.

11. Move the cell pointer to A:B12 or click the mouse pointer on A:B12. This is the cell that contains the total of the budget expenses on sheet A.

12. Select Copy.

13. Press ENTER to accept the From range that consists of a single cell.

14. Press CTRL-PGUP.
    Cell B12 is the first cell in the range you want to copy to. This will provide a total for the expenses on sheet B.

15. Type a period to lock the beginning of the To range or click the first cell and drag to the last cell.

16. Press CTRL-PGUP to move to C:B12.
    This is the last cell in the range you want to copy to.

17. Press ENTER to accept the To range.
    This will copy the total expense formula in A:B12 to B:B12 and C:B12 since the To range includes both sheets. When the copy is completed, the new copies of the formula used to calculate the total display zero.

18. Move the cell pointer to A:B1 or click the mouse pointer on A:B1.

19. Select Copy.

20. Move the cell pointer to A:B2. This selects the cells A:B1..A:B2.

21. Press ENTER to accept the From range that tells 1-2-3/G the data you want to copy.

22. Press CTRL-PGUP and move to B:B1. This is the first cell you want to copy to on the new sheets.

23. Type a period to lock in the beginning of the To range.

24. Press CTRL-PGUP to move to C:B1.

If you prefer, you can complete the selection process for the To range with the mouse by clicking the cell in each sheet with the right mouse pointer then using CTRL-PGUP to move to the next sheet.

25. Press ENTER to accept the To range.

26. Move the cell pointer to A:B6, since this is the benefits formula that you want to copy to sheets B and C.

27. Select Copy and press ENTER or click the To range.

28. Type **B:B6.C:B6** or drag the mouse pointer to select the correct cells.

29. Press ENTER or click the check box to complete the copy process.

30. Select Worksheet Window Clear to return to a single sheet perspective.

Using the Group Mode

The entries in sheet A have already been formatted to display with commas. In addition, column A has been widened to accommodate the label entries. Although you can make these changes separately on each of the other sheets there is an easier way. You can use the Worksheet Global Group command to apply the changes to as many other sheets as you want. Once the Group mode is enabled, any additional changes to formats and other sheet attributes will be applied to all the sheets in the group. To invoke the Group mode option for sheets A through D, follow these steps:

1. Move the cell pointer to sheet A.

   Sheet A must be the current sheet as you will use the Copy option in the Group command to make an entire group of sheets use the same format, font, and width settings as sheet A.

2. Select Worksheet Global Group. A dialog box like the one in Figure 4-6 will appear.

3. Select Enable by clicking on it or typing **E**.

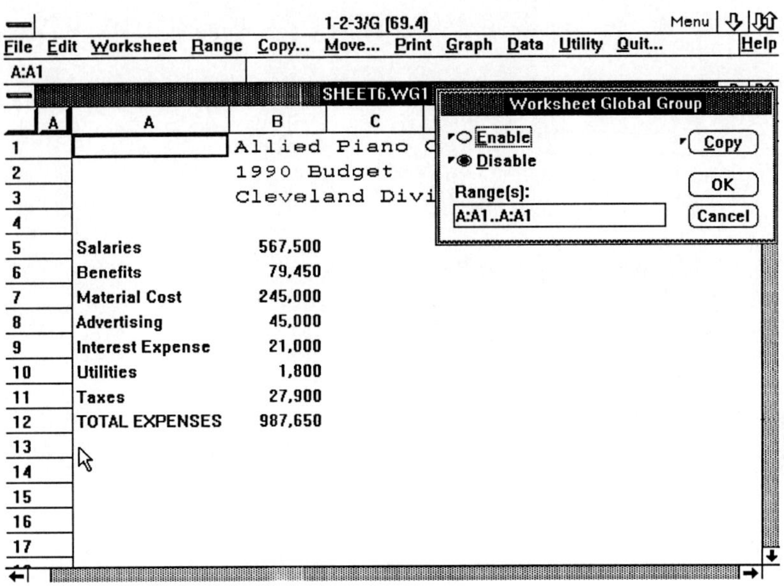

Figure 4-6. Worksheet Global Group dialog box

4. If you are using a mouse, click the range box. Typing **E** on the keyboard places you in the box.

5. Type **A:.C:** as the range.

6. Click Copy or press TAB four times and then press ENTER to select Copy.

7. Click the OK button or press ENTER to finalize.

8. Add the following entries to sheets B and C.

   B3: Portland Division
   C3: Grand Rapids Division

Notice in Figure 4-7 that the entry in B:B3 uses the same font as A:B3, since you copied the settings from sheet A to the entire group using the Group mode. If you had not been in sheet A, 1-2-3/G would have applied

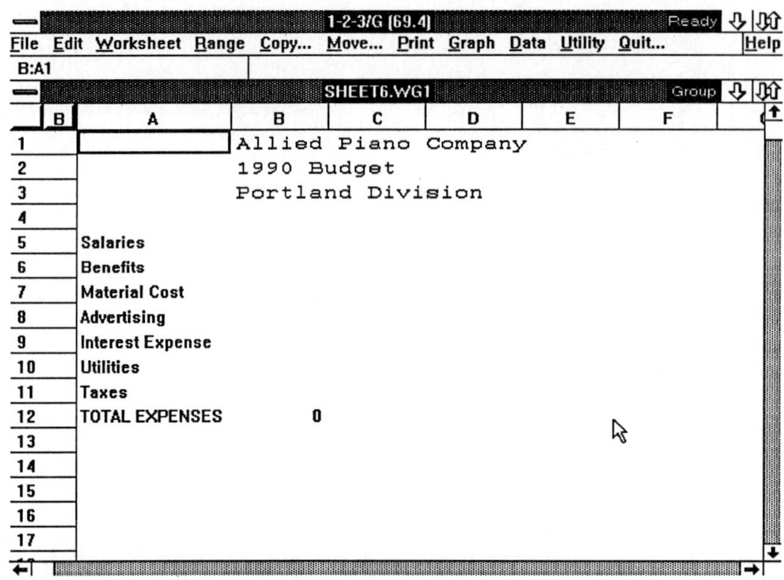

Figure 4-7. Entries selected with the Group mode

the settings from whichever sheet had been current. If this happens accidentally, use Undo to restore the proper settings.

Adding Data for the Other Divisions

As you enter data for the other divisions, the entries in B5..B11 will be formatted with commas automatically since you applied format with the Group mode. Complete these data entries for the Portland and Grand Rapids Divisions, respectively:

B:B5: 689456
B:B7: 177243
B:B8: 35679
B:B9: 18456

B:B10: 2311
B:B11: 3857
C:B5: 352344
C:B7: 334436
C:B8: 34234
C:B9: 163583
C:B10: 1541
C:B11: 44556

Figure 4-8 shows some of the entries arranged via the Perspective option.

Select Worksheet Window Perspective to look at the entries on your sheets. You will notice that the benefit calculation originally recorded in sheet A supplies the numbers in B6 in sheets B and C. All of the numbers are also formatted with commas. When you are ready to return to a single sheet you can select Worksheet Window Clear to eliminate the Perspective option.

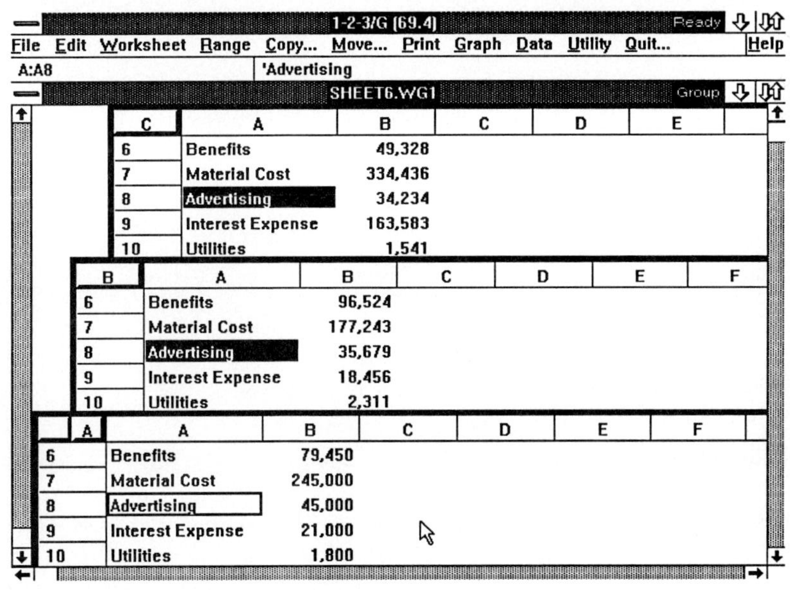

Figure 4-8. Additional entries in Perspective view

Building Blocks for Worksheets

FIVE

Everything you do with 1-2-3/G depends on the entries you make in worksheet cells. These entries are the basis for financial models and projections, files used in the data management environment, and even for the graphs you create. In 1-2-3/G, you can make many types of entries, tailoring them to the task you are performing.

This chapter discusses the various entry types that 1-2-3/G supports. You will learn how to make entries and how to control their placement on the worksheet. You will also learn how to have 1-2-3/G make some automatic entries for you. In addition, you will discover how to select and name ranges on the worksheet. Finally, you will find out how 1-2-3/G stores the worksheet information that will affect how you make entries.

The Worksheet

The worksheet window displayed when you start 1-2-3/G shows only the upper-left corner of the first sheet in the worksheet file. This is a very small corner of a very large worksheet—remember, the 1-2-3/G worksheet consists of 256 columns and 8192 rows. The columns are identified by letters beginning with column A on the far left and continuing to column IV on the far right. The rows are identified by numbers, starting with row 1 at the top of the sheet. The entire worksheet is organized just like the small section visible in the worksheet window.

1-2-3/G also provides multiple sheets in one worksheet file, with each sheet arranged like the first one. The only difference between the first sheet and any others is the sheet level indicator at the intersection of the row and column labels. The letters assigned to sheets always start with the initial A level. Subsequent sheets are assigned the letters B through Z, followed by AA through AZ, BA through BZ, and so on, until the 256th level (IV) is assigned.

1-2-3/G provides multiple sheets automatically. If you want to save a multiple-sheet 1-2-3/G worksheet to a .WK1 file, you must copy data on sheets other than the first sheet to other 1-2-3/G worksheet files and save each as a separate .WK1 file. If you only have entries on sheet A of the 1-2-3/G file, just save the worksheet to a file with a .WK1 extension to use it in Release 2.

Tip: In similar applications, use sheets consistently. If you create multiple-sheet worksheets, try to establish a pattern for your entries. Don't use sheet A for the consolidated information one time and sheet D the next time. The same is true for the location of macros, data criterion entries, and an extract range.

Since the worksheet is a replacement for green-bar columnar pads, it's worth making a size comparison. The space for one entry on a green-bar sheet is about 1 1/8 by 1/4 inches. If you multiply this area by the number of cells in the first sheet in your 1-2-3/G worksheet, the equivalent of your electronic sheet would require a piece of green-bar paper over 23 feet wide and 170 feet long! And 1-2-3/G provides 256 of these sheets.

The electronic worksheet window can be used to view any part of a worksheet. You can use special key combinations to move to any of these sheets. All the sheets are "stacked" in memory, as illustrated in Figure 5-1.

You can also use the mouse or the desktop control menu to move between windows, as discussed in Chapter 2. As you learned, these

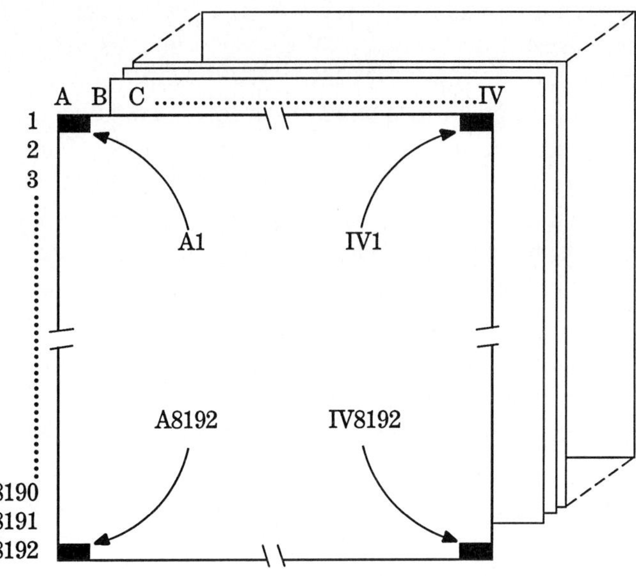

Figure 5-1. Multiple sheets available in each file

windows can be stacked or tiled in memory. Unlike moving from sheet to sheet in one file, as you move from one worksheet file to another, you are changing the active window.

You can make entries in any of the cells on any sheet, within the memory limitations of your system. Each cell can only contain one entry at a time, however. If you make a second entry in a cell that already contains information, the existing information is replaced by the new information.

Types of Entries

1-2-3/G supports label entries and value entries. These two entry types serve as the building blocks for both simple and sophisticated worksheet models. *Label entries* contain at least one text character. Examples include Accounting, Sales, John Smith, 111 Simmons Lane, and 456T78. Even the last example, which contains mostly numbers, has one letter character and is therefore categorized as a label entry. You cannot use label entries in arithmetic operations. *Value entries,* on the other hand, are either numbers or formulas. Most value entries are used in arithmetic operations.

1-2-3/G determines the type of entry for a particular cell by reading the first character you type in the cell. Once 1-2-3/G determines the entry type, you can only change it by pressing ESCAPE and starting a new entry in the cell, or by editing the cell to remove or add a label indicator. A *label indicator* is a single character that appears at the front of each label entry and tells 1-2-3/G how to display the entry in the cell.

Tip: Learn to check the mode indicator as you perform data entry—this will save you considerable time and energy. One quick look tells you whether 1-2-3/G is treating your entry as a number or a label.

As you make an entry into a cell, 1-2-3/G displays the location of the entry in the address box on the left side of the control line. The characters in your entry are displayed in the contents box on the right side of the control line. An insertion point marks where characters are added as you type. A sample entry looks like this:

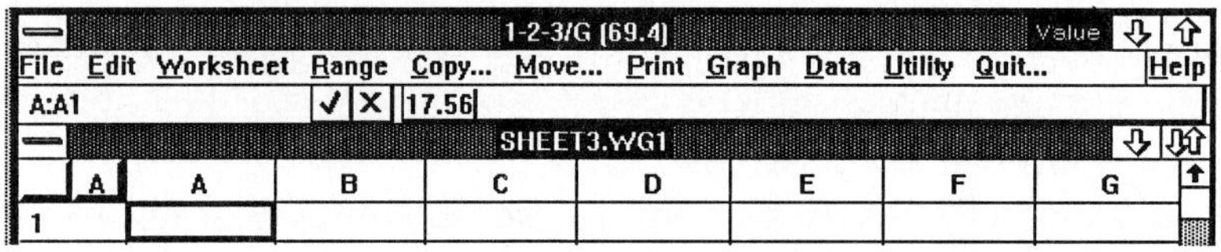

1-2-3/G [69.4] Value
File Edit Worksheet Range Copy... Move... Print Graph Data Utility Quit... Help
A:A1 ✓ X 17.56
SHEET3.WG1
A A B C D E F G
1

As soon as your entry fills the first line of the contents box, the box expands, allowing you to enter as many as 512 characters, and to view and edit your complete entry. When you click the mouse in the contents box, 1-2-3/G moves the insertion point to the mouse I-beam. The I-beam is so named because it resembles the letter I and appears like this:

File Edit Worksheet Range Copy... Move... Print Graph Data Utility Quit... Help
A:A1 ✓ X 'To test the Range Justify command, we will type a series of long labels in Column A.

An icon box to the left of the contents box displays both confirm (✓) and cancel (X). You can finalize an entry by clicking the confirm icon. If you prefer, you can click the cell to finalize it. With the keyboard, you can press one of the navigational keys or ENTER to finalize the entry, which causes it to appear in the worksheet cell, as shown in Figure 5-2.

If you attempt to finalize an entry that contains an error, 1-2-3/G beeps and moves the insertion point to the location of the error.

Tip: Use the mouse or cell pointer movement keys to finalize your entry. You can save a keystroke on most entries if you finalize by moving the cell pointer rather than pressing ENTER and then moving to a new cell.

When the entry is a formula, the results appear on the worksheet. For example, if cell A1 contains 10 and A2 contains 5, entering the formula **+A1/A2** in cell A3 causes a 2 to appear in A3 on the worksheet. Otherwise, the entry appears as typed, except that the current format option is applied. For example, if you enter **.4** and the format is Percent, your entry displays as 40% in the cell. In the contents box, however, the entry appears exactly as you typed it.

Tip: Use the special keys introduced in Chapter 3 to position the cell pointer for an entry. Although the arrow keys move you to any location on the worksheet, there are some shortcuts. You can press the F5 (Goto) key, type an address like **D3** or **C:F2**, and 1-2-3/G immediately positions the cell pointer in the new address.

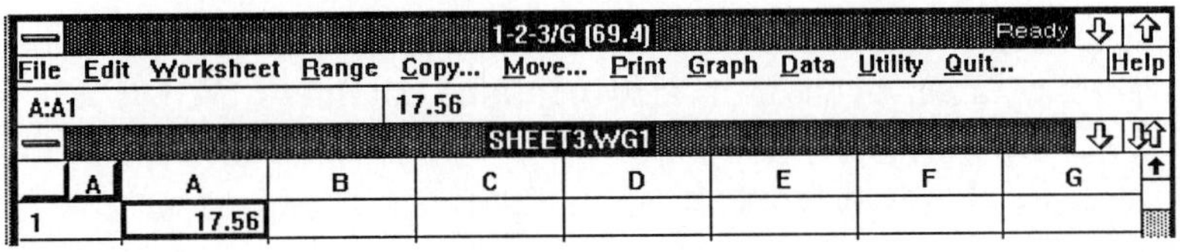

1-2-3/G [69.4] Ready
File Edit Worksheet Range Copy... Move... Print Graph Data Utility Quit... Help
A:A1 17.56
SHEET3.WG1

A	A	B	C	D	E	F	G
1	17.56						

Figure 5-2. Finalized cell entry

Label Entries

You can use label entries whenever you want to enter text or character data into a worksheet cell. Labels can contain descriptive information, as well as character data. There are no restrictions on the characters that you can enter within a label.

1-2-3/G supports the full IBM Multilingual Character Set (code page 850), including numbers and symbols. These codes provide access to international symbols and many special characters not directly accessible from the keyboard. All of these symbols are listed in Appendix E.

You can enter the desired character with the @CHAR function described in Chapter 9, "@Functions in Worksheets," or through the Compose key sequence. To use Compose, press ALT-F1, and then the key combination representing the desired character. For example, to generate an uppercase "E" with a circumflex (or caret), you can use the @CHAR function with the entry 210, as in **@CHAR(210)**. Alternately, you can press ALT-F1 and type an **E** and a caret ^.

Some of the key label entry rules are summarized in the "Rules for Labels" box. Labels can be up to 512 characters long. The space re-

Rules for Labels

- Labels cannot be longer than 512 characters.
- An entry is automatically recognized as a label if the first character is an alphabetic character, any character other than 0 through 9, or any of the following:

  . + − $ or (@ = < > or any currency symbol

- Any entry that contains letters or editing characters is considered a label, even if it also contains numbers. When a label begins with a numeric digit or symbol, you must type a label indicator before the label.
- Labels longer than the cell width will borrow display space cells to the right if those cells are empty.

quired for label entries with the same number of characters may vary since 1-2-3/G uses a proportional font by default. If you don't have the default 8-point Helvetica font installed under OS/2, 1-2-3/G displays the screen information in Courier, which is not a proportional font, and your screens will look quite different than the examples in this book. The examples in this book use a System Proportional 12-point font. This font, like the default, is proportional, but is larger so you can see the examples more clearly.

1-2-3/G displays as much of the label as possible in the cell you use for the entry. If the label is longer than your cell width and the cells to the right are empty, 1-2-3/G borrows space from them so the label can be displayed completely. You can change the Worksheet Global Label Cell Display option to prevent long labels from borrowing space from empty cells. This command is covered in Chapter 7, "Changing the Worksheet Appearance." If the adjacent cell is not empty, 1-2-3/G truncates the display. The extra characters are stored internally and are displayed if the cell is widened or the contents of cells to the right are erased.

As descriptive information, a label might be a report heading containing the company name placed in a cell near the top of the worksheet. Labels can also be column headings indicating the months of the year, row headings indicating account names, or descriptive text placed anywhere on the worksheet. Label entries can also record text data anywhere on the worksheet. Part numbers, employee names, sales territories, and warehouse locations are all examples of data containing text characters.

When you type a letter as the first entry in a cell, 1-2-3/G generates a default label indicator that establishes the entry as a label and controls the display of the entry within the cell. If a label begins with a number, you must type a label indicator before you enter the label, since 1-2-3/G determines the type of an entry by the first character entered in a cell. However it is generated, the label indicator appears in the contents box but does not appear in the worksheet cell.

Tip: Spaces and special characters that are not numeric characters are treated as labels. If you start an entry with a space or a nonnumeric character, you can save a keystroke by not typing the label indicator.

You can use label indicators to control the placement of an entry in a cell. 1-2-3/G provides five label indicators for this purpose, explained in the "Label Indicators" box. The apostrophe is the default label indicator—that is, the one 1-2-3/G generates for you when you type character data. It left justifies an entry within the cell. You must type the apostrophe yourself if your entry begins with a number—for example, '134 Tenth Street or '213-78-6751. (The hyphens in the second entry count as text.)

If you don't type the label indicator, you can't finalize the first example (the address) in a cell. You can finalize the second example (the social security number) without a label indicator, but it does not appear as a social security number. 1-2-3/G interprets the hyphens as minus signs and performs two subtractions, resulting in an entry of −6616. If you press F2 (Edit) and move to the front of the entry, you can type a label indicator, instructing 1-2-3/G to treat the minus signs as hyphens and display the entry as a social security number.

The other two label indicators that you can use for entry placement are the double quotation mark (") and the caret (^). The double quotation mark right justifies label entries, while the caret centers entries within the cell.

In Chapter 7, you will learn how to alter the default label indicator with Worksheet Global Label. For now, if you want something other than left justification, type the appropriate label indicator before you start typing your entry.

Label Indicators

1-2-3/G provides a default label indicator of ', which left justifies a label. You can change this default with a menu command (see Chapter 7) or by typing a different indicator at the beginning of the label entry. The label indicators and their effects are as follows:

'	Left aligned (the default setting)
"	Right aligned
^	Center aligned
\	Repeat the character that follows until the cell is filled
¦	Displays but does not print the label. This label prefix is also used to indicate where a page break should occur

1
2
3
G

Two additional label indicators perform special functions. The backslash (\) causes the characters that follow it to be repeated until the entire cell is filled with this pattern. For example, entering **\–** fills the cell with dashes. You might use * to fill all the cells in one row of the worksheet to divide the worksheet assumptions and the sales projections section. (You can use any character to create dividing lines.) You can also use \ to make multiple characters repeat: \+ – results in a pattern of alternating + and – symbols repeated for the width of the cell. The other type of label indicator is a vertical bar (¦). A label that uses the vertical bar indicator appears in the worksheet but does not print. You can use this label indicator to create explanations within a report that do not appear when the report is printed.

Labels make a worksheet easier to read and allow you to enter text data. Since a worksheet is primarily involved in projections and calculations, however, you also need a way to handle numeric entries.

Value Entries

1-2-3/G treats value entries as numeric entries. They must follow much more rigid rules than label entries. There are two basic types of value entries: *numbers* and *formulas.* Like labels, numbers are constants; they don't change as the result of arithmetic operations. Formulas are not constants, since the results they produce depend on the current number values of the variables they reference. Numbers and constants are covered separately, because 1-2-3/G handles them differently. Dates and times are special types of numbers, and are discussed in their own section.

Numbers

The box "Rules for Numbers" summarizes the rules for entering numeric constants. Numeric entries don't have a special beginning indicator like labels, but they can contain only certain characters.

- You cannot add spaces and other characters to a numeric entry—except the letter "E" when it is used to denote a scientific notation entry. When you are using the Automatic format, any valid format for the supported value entries is acceptable.
- You can't substitute alphabetic characters for numeric digits, as you can on a typewriter. Using the lowercase "l" for a numeric 1, or

an uppercase "O" for a numeric 0 (zero) causes an invalid entry for a value.

- For date and time entries, the automatic format allows additional characters in numeric entries. Any characters in one of 1-2-3/G's valid date or time entries are accepted and stored as a date or time serial number. These special date and time characters are discussed in further detail later in this chapter.

Tip: Entries you think of as numbers may be labels to 1-2-3/G. It is common to refer to social security numbers, phone numbers, part numbers, and purchase order numbers. Although these entries are called numbers, they may not be considered number values to 1-2-3/G because

Rules for Numbers

- Numbers cannot exceed 512 characters; however, the limitation for decimal accuracy and significant digits is 18.
- If the first key you press is a numeric digit or one of these symbols

    + − . ($

  the entry is treated as a number.
- Only the following symbols can appear in a number entry:

    0 1 2 3 4 5 6 7 8 9 . + − $ ( ) E @ ^ %

- The last five of these cannot begin a numeric entry.
- You can only use one decimal.
- You can only enter spaces and commas as part of a numeric entry with automatic formats, or when you have changed the international punctuation settings.

of alphabetic characters or special symbols. You must enter these numbers as labels in 1-2-3/G.

Size Numbers can be as large as 10^99 or as small as 10^−99, where the caret symbol (^) represents exponentiation (that is, 10^{99} or 10^{-99}). You can use up to 512 characters to represent the numbers, although you must still adhere to the numeric size limits of the package.

If you wish, you can use the scientific notation to enter large numbers. Scientific notation is a method of entering a number along with the power of ten that it will be multiplied by. In this format, the letter "E" (or "e") separates the number from the positive or negative power of 10 that will be used. This kind of notation represents very large or very small numbers in a minimum of space. The following examples should help clarify scientific notation:

9.76E+4 = 97,600
3.86e−05 = .0000386

The number that follows E must be between −99 and 99 to conform with the entry size that 1-2-3/G allows. Although you cannot exceed this limitation for entries, 1-2-3/G can store calculated numbers that are much larger and smaller. The storage limitations are numbers between 10^−4093 and 10^4093 when the number is the result of calculations.

Entry In one sense, entering numbers is easier than entering labels, since you just make your entry using the allowable characters and then press either ENTER or an arrow key, or use the mouse to select the confirm icon or another cell. You don't need a special character at the beginning of a numeric entry.

As soon as you type any of the allowable characters, the mode indicator changes from Ready to Value. Once 1-2-3/G determines that you are entering a value, you must continue typing only characters that are allowable as values. If you attempt to finalize an entry that contains unacceptable characters, 1-2-3/G places you in Edit mode so you can make necessary corrections.

Looking at a few numeric entries may clarify the entry process and the 1-2-3/G displays such entries in a cell, as shown in Figure 5-3.

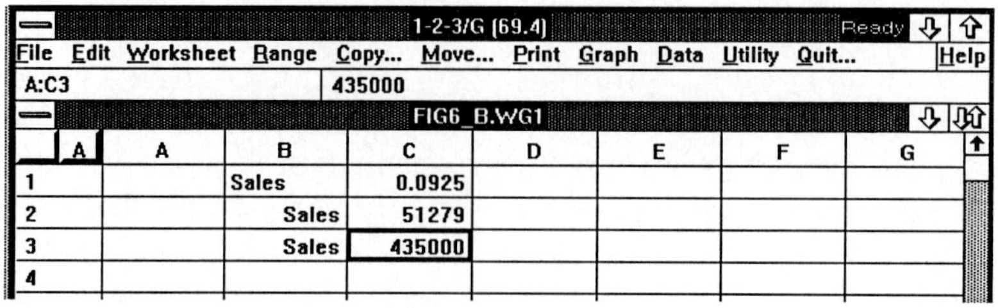

1-2-3/G (69.4) Ready

File Edit Worksheet Range Copy... Move... Print Graph Data Utility Quit... Help

A:C3 435000

FIG6_B.WG1

A	A	B	C	D	E	F	G
1		Sales	0.0925				
2		Sales	51279				
3		Sales	435000				
4							

Figure 5-3. Numeric entries

1-2-3/G will convert an entry of 4.35E+05, since the number is not too large for decimal display. If you enter .0925, a zero is added in front of the decimal.

The numbers you enter initially are right aligned in the cell. In Chapter 7, you will learn techniques for changing the alignment of numbers within cells.

Display The numbers you enter are shown both in the contents box and the worksheet. They are also stored internally. The form of the numbers may be slightly different in each case. 1-2-3/G can store and display numbers of up to 18 significant digits. If you enter a number with more than 18 significant digits, it is rounded to fit within the 18-digit display limitation. The number displayed on the worksheet depends on the format for the cell and the length of the number in relation to the cell width.

When 1-2-3/G displays a number in a cell, it displays as many digits as the cell width. Minus signs and formatting characters also occupy one space in the display. Numeric entries longer than this limit are not handled by borrowing space from cells to the right, as with labels. The entries are either shown in scientific notation, a rounded form, or as asterisks representing an overflow situation. The cell format and the composition of the number determines the display.

If the General format is in effect, 1-2-3/G displays the number as you have entered it if possible. If the integer portion of the number is too large, 1-2-3/G converts the display to scientific notation. If the integer portion of the number fits, but some or all of the decimal digits do not, the cell value is rounded to fit within the display. However, when the General format is not in effect, 1-2-3/G displays these numbers as a series of asterisks (*********). The default cell width is nine positions, so long numbers don't fit unless you expand the width of the column, which you will learn how to do in Chapter 7.

The following example shows how 1-2-3/G responds to long numeric entries.

1. If **.000000000134** is entered, the worksheet display changes this to scientific notation and displays the number as 1.340E−10.

2. If **9578000000** is entered, 1-2-3/G shows the entry as 9.578E+09 in the cell. The entry appears in its original form in the contents box.

You have no control over the format of the data in the contents box or the internal storage of a number. In both cases, 1-2-3/G retains as much accuracy as possible (18 decimal digits maximum for the menu bar and internal storage). You can control the accuracy of the number that appears on the worksheet by selecting a format. (You will learn how to do this in Chapter 7, where you will also learn how to format date and time serial numbers.)

Date and Time Serial Numbers

1-2-3/G uses date and time serial numbers to represent the date and time. 1-2-3/G can record in a worksheet cell any date between December 31, 1899 and November 21, 9999. 1-2-3/G can record any time.

Rather than remembering dates as labels, such as 20-Aug-1990, 1-2-3/G assigns each date a unique serial number. This way, you can enter dates and times in a worksheet file and use the date and time serial numbers in calculations. Thus, by assigning the date 20-Aug-1990 the serial number 33105, 1-2-3/G can calculate the difference between your entry and another date entry or generate a new date that is a specified number of days away.

1-2-3/G records times as the time's proportion to an entire day. For example, at 6:00 P.M., three-fourths of the day has elapsed so the time serial number is .75. Time numbers range between 0 for midnight to 1 for midnight of the next day. You can combine date and time serial numbers, as in 33105.75, which represents 6:00 P.M. on 20-Aug-1990. These are regular numbers that 1-2-3/G uses to represent times and dates.

To prevent confusion, 1-2-3/G lets you enter dates and times in one of the formats shown in Table 5-1. When you enter an acceptable date in a cell using one of the formats, 1-2-3/G converts your entry to a date or time serial number. The following example shows how 1-2-3/G responds to date and time entries.

1. If **12-Dec-1990** is entered, the worksheet display changes this to 33219 in the cell and in the contents box.
2. If **12:53:49** is entered, 1-2-3/G shows the entry as .5373727 in the cell and .537372685185185 in the contents box.
3. If **3:62 PM** is entered, since this is not an acceptable value or time, 1-2-3/G switches to Edit mode so you can change the entry to a valid time by changing the 6 to a 1.

As this last example shows, 1-2-3/G can recognize a valid date and time. For example, you can only enter February 29 for a leap year. Chapter 7 explains how you can display these date and time serial numbers as the dates and times they represent. For now, you can enter your dates and format them later.

Formulas

Formulas are the second type of value entry. Unlike number and label entries, they produce variable results depending on the numbers that

Format	Example	Result
DD-Mon-YY	15-Mar-91	33312
DD-Mon	15-Mar	33312
Mon-YY	Mar-91	33298
MM/DD/YY	03/15/91	33312
HH:MM:SS AMPM	1:59:02 PM	.582662
HH:MM AMPM	1:59 PM	.582639
HH:MM:SS	13:59:02	.582662
HH:MM	13.59	.582639

Table 5-1. Date and Time Formats for Entering Dates and Times

they reference. This ability makes formulas the backbone of worksheet features. They allow you to make what-if projections and to look at the impact of changing variable values. To produce an updated result with a formula, you don't need to change the formula. Simply change one of the values that the formula references, and the entire formula will be recalculated for you. Formulas follow the same basic rules as numbers in terms of allowable characters. In addition, formulas support the use of cell references, range names assigned to a group of cells, and operators that define specific operations to 1-2-3/G.

1-2-3/G has three types of formulas: arithmetic, logical, and string formulas, summarized in the "Formula Types" box.

Formula Types

- Arithmetic formulas involve constants, cell references, and the arithmetic operators (+, −, *, /, and ^). Arithmetic formulas calculate the formula entered and return its result. Examples are A2*A3, or Sales − Cogs (where Sales and Cogs are names of cells that contain numerical data).
- Logical formulas involve cell references, constants, and comparison operators (< >, =, < =, > =, <, and >). These formulas evaluate the condition listed to determine whether it is true or false. If the condition is false, the formula returns a 0; if the condition is true, the formula returns a 1. An example of a logical formula is +C2< =500.
- String formulas permit you to join two or more character strings. You can use the concatenation character (&) to join string variables or constants—for example, +"Sales for the "&"Midwest "&"Region".
- Functions provide predefined formulas for a variety of calculations, including mathematical formulas, financial calculations, logical evaluations, statistical computations, and string manipulation. Functions begin with the @ symbol and contain a list of specific operations for arguments within parentheses.

A few rules pertain to all formulas:

- Formulas cannot contain spaces, except for the spaces in range names or string variables.
- The first character of a formula must be one of the following:

  + – (@ # $. 0 1 2 3 4 5 6 7 8 9

- Formulas contain special operators to define the operation you want to perform. Operators are assigned priorities in 1-2-3/G, as shown in the "Operation Priorities" box. (1-2-3/G's documentation refers to this as "Operation Precedence.")
- Formulas can also contain numeric constants or string constants (such as 77 or "sales total"), cell references (such as F4 or Z3), special built-in functions (such as @MIN), or range names (such as TOTAL).

Arithmetic Formulas Arithmetic formulas calculate numeric values. These formulas are built with *arithmetic operators* and references to values in other cells in the current worksheet file, or to values in other worksheet files. The value references are to either the cell address in the current sheet (such as A1 or Z10), cells in other sheets within the current file (such as B:A1 or D:F10), cells in other files on disk, or a name assigned to a cell or cells (such as Cash or Interest). For now, you can concentrate on references to cells in the current file, using both the current worksheet and other sheet references. Linkages to external files are covered in the section "External Link Formulas" later in the chapter. You will also learn how to assign range names in the section "Naming Cell Ranges" later in the chapter.

The arithmetic operators used in 1-2-3/G are + for addition, – for subtraction, / for division, * for multiplication, and ^ for exponentiation. For example, an instruction to multiply 3 times 4 would be written as 3*4. These operators are listed in the "Operation Priorities" box.

Tip: Ignoring 1-2-3's operator priorities will yield incorrect formula results. You must use parentheses to group references if you want to change the priority order that 1-2-3/G uses to calculate formulas.

There are some things to keep in mind when entering cell references. Cell references without sheet letters preceding them are assumed to reference cells on the sheet where the formula is entered.

Operation Priorities

1-2-3/G has a variety of operators for arithmetic, logical, and string formulas. Often, more than one operator is used in a formula. In this situation, it is important to know which operation 1-2-3/G evaluates first. This table provides the priority order for each operation within 1-2-3, with the highest number corresponding to the highest priority. If several operators in a formula have the same priority, they are evaluated from left to right.

Priority	Operator	Operation Performed
8	(	Parenthesis for grouping
7	^	Exponentiation
6	+ −	Positive and negative indicators
5	/ *	Division and multiplication
4	+ −	Addition and subtraction
3	= <> < > <= >=	Logical operators
2	#NOT#	Complex not indicator
1	#AND# #OR# &	Complex and, complex or, and string operator

In the sample formulas, you may have wondered why there is a plus sign at the beginning of the formula. To multiply the current contents of C1 by the contents of C2, you might want to enter C1*C2—however, this won't work. As soon as you type the initial C, 1-2-3/G flags the cell as a label entry, and shows the entry as a label on the worksheet rather than giving the result of the formula calculation.

You need a formula indicator, and the + is the logical choice, since it requires only one additional keystroke and does not alter the formula. (Actually, any numeric character that does not affect the formula result is acceptable.) Therefore, place a + at the front of all formulas that begin with a cell address. You can enter the formula just discussed as +C1*C2, for example. This formula is entered in cell E1 on the work-

1-2-3/G (69.4) Ready

File Edit Worksheet Range Copy... Move... Print Graph Data Utility Quit... Help

A:E1 +C1*C2

FIG6_C.WG1

A	A	B	C	D	E	F	G
1		Sales	0.0925	33219	4743.3075		
2		Sales	51279	0.5373727			
3		Sales	435000	0.6333333			
4			1.340E-10				
5			9.578E+09				
6							

Figure 5-4. Formula in E1

sheet shown in Figure 5-4. The result of the formula appears on the worksheet, while the formula itself is displayed in the contents box when the cell pointer is selecting the cell. Formula results are displayed on the worksheet automatically unless you change the worksheet format to Text, an option covered in Chapter 7.

To enter a formula like the one used in the previous example, but with references to cells on different sheets, you need to make a minor modification. The sheet letter precedes both of the cell addresses. In Figure 5-5, to compute the total sales of widgets, you need the number of units stored in cell B2 on sheet B, and the cost of a widget stored in B2 on sheet C. So, you enter the formula in A:B2 as **+B:B2*C:B2.**

1-2-3/G (69.4) Ready

File Edit Worksheet Range Copy... Move... Print Graph Data Utility Quit... Help

A:B2 +B:B2*C:B2

FIG6_E.WG1

A	A	B	C	D	E	F	G
1	Total Sales for January						
2	Widgets	94650					
3	Stoves						
4	Pipes						

Figure 5-5. Formula with a reference to other sheets

Parentheses are the only way to change the order of operations. Otherwise, operators in formulas are evaluated according to the priority list, and operators with the same precedence are evaluated from left to right. For example, 3+4*5 equals 23, but (3+4)*5 equals 35. In the first expression, multiplication has a higher priority than addition, so it is carried out first.

1-2-3/G allows a maximum of 32 sets of parentheses in one expression, so you can use them liberally to override the natural priority order. With nested parentheses, the priority sequence applies within each set of parentheses. Here is an example of priority order within nested parentheses:

```
4*((1+2)*2)/2+3
↑  ↑  ↑ ↑  ↑
3rd | 2nd| 5th
   1st  4th
```

You have learned how to build a formula by typing cell addresses and arithmetic operators. This method works well if you are good at remembering the cell addresses you want to use and don't make typing mistakes. However, a second method of formula construction can alleviate both of these potential problems. This new method lets you point to the cell references you wish to include in the formula and then type only the arithmetic operators. You can use either the mouse or the cell pointer to point to the desired cell references. After you type an operator, simply move your mouse pointer or cell pointer to the cell whose value you want to include in the formula. Watch the mode indicator change from Value to Point as you move your cell pointer. To select a cell with a mouse, point to the cell and click the left mouse button. To finalize the cell selected, either type the next operator or, if you have reached the end of the formula, press ENTER or click the confirm icon. If you type another operator, the cell pointer returns to the formula's entry cell, and 1-2-3/G waits for you to select another value to add to the formula.

Tip: Blank cells have a zero value. Referencing a blank cell in a formula is the same as referencing a cell that contains a zero. Thus, +A1*A2 equals zero if either A1 or A2 contain a zero. The only exception to this rule is @COUNT, which is covered in Chapter 9.

Here is a sample worksheet that is developed using the pointing method:

1-2-3/G [69.4] Ready

File Edit Worksheet Range Copy... Move... Print Graph Data Utility Quit... Help

A:E1 +C1*C2

FIG6_C.WG1

A	A	B	C	D	E	F	G
1		Sales	0.0925	33219	4743.3075		
2		Sales	51279	0.5373727			
3		Sales	435000	0.6333333			

To produce this example, enter **.0925** in C1 and **51279** in C2. The mouse pointer is then moved to E1 and the left mouse button is clicked. A + is typed, and then the mouse pointer is moved to C1 and the left mouse button is clicked, putting 1-2-3/G in Point mode. An asterisk for multiplication is then typed, returning the cell pointer to E1. With 1-2-3/G still in Point mode, the mouse pointer is moved to C2 and the left mouse button is clicked. Finally, the confirm icon is clicked and the formula appears in cell E1, as shown in this example.

To complete the same example using only the keyboard for pointing, you would start with the same entries in C1 and C2. Next, move the cell pointer to E1. Type a + and then press the LEFT ARROW key twice to change to Point mode and move to cell C1. Type a * for multiplication, which also finalizes the C1 in the formula. Press LEFT ARROW twice and DOWN ARROW once to switch to Point mode and select the cell C2. Finally, press ENTER to display 4743.3075 in E1 and +C1*C2 in the contents box.

You can use the pointing method when there are multiple sheets in a file and you want to access cell values from more than one sheet. Use the special key combinations introduced in Chapter 3 to move to another sheet and then move around within the sheet to select the correct cell.

This may seem like more work than typing in cell references. However, the pointing method speeds up the testing and verification process for your model, because it forces you to verify cell references visually and therefore eliminates many formula errors that result from incorrect cell or sheet references.

Tip: Always use the pointing method when creating formulas that reference other sheets. Otherwise, you can easily type in an incorrect reference.

Logical Formulas Logical formulas use the *logical operators* to compare two or more values. Such formulas can evaluate a series of complex decisions or influence results in other areas of the worksheet. As noted in the "Operation Priorities" box, the logical operators are = for equal, < > for not equal, < for less than, > for greater than, < = for less than or equal to, and > = for greater than or equal to. The logical operators all have the same priority and are evaluated from left to right in an expression. All the logical operators are lower in formula calculation priority than the arithmetic operators.

Unlike arithmetic formulas, logical formulas don't calculate numeric results. They produce a result of either zero or one, depending on whether the evaluated condition is true or false. If the condition is true, 1 is returned; if the condition is false, 0 is returned. For example, if C1 contains .0925, the logical expression +C1> =500 returns 0, since the condition is false.

1-2-3/G also has a few *compound operators.* These operators are used either to negate a logical expression or to join two logical expressions. The negation operator #NOT# has priority over the other two compound operators, #AND# and #OR#. #AND# and #OR# can join two expressions, as in

```
C1> =500#AND#C2=50
```

In this example, the expression returns a 1 for true only if both conditions are true.

#NOT# negates an expression. For instance, the formula

```
#NOT#(A1=2#AND#D2=1)
```

returns a 1 for true only if the value of cell A1 is not equal to 2, and the value of cell D2 is not equal to 1. (If #OR# replaced #AND# in this formula, the formula would be true if cell A1 were not equal to 2, or cell D2 were not equal to 1.) For practical purposes, you are more likely to use the not equal logical operator, < >, than the more cumbersome #NOT# operator. The formula

```
A1< >2#AND#D2< >1
```

is easier to read than

#NOT(A1=2#AND#D2=1)

and its meaning is identical.

One application of logical operators in a worksheet is the calculation of a commission bonus. Figure 5-6 shows a calculation to determine the quarterly commission check for salesperson John Smith. The calculation has two components: the regular commission, and a bonus for meeting sales quotas.

The regular commission is 10 percent of total sales. The bonus is calculated by product. Each salesperson has a $50,000 quota for each of three products. A bonus of $1,000 is given for each product for which the sales quota is met. A salesperson could thus gain $3,000 by meeting the quota for all three products.

To build the model shown in the figure, first a number of labels are entered in cells B2 through A7. Next, **John Smith** is entered in C4, and **56000, 45000,** and **3000** are entered in C5 through C7. These numbers

1-2-3/G [69.4] Ready

File Edit Worksheet Range Copy... Move... Print Graph Data Utility Quit... Help

A:D14 +C10+C11

FIG6_G.WG1

A	A	B	C	D	E	F	G
1							
2		Commission Calculation					
3							
4	Employee:		John Smith		Quotas Met		
5	Sales Product A:		56000		1		
6	Sales Product B:		45000		0		
7	Sales Product C:		3000		0		
8			104000		1		
9							
10	Commission:		10400				
11	Bonus:		1000				
12							
13							
14	Total Commission Plus Bonus			11400			
15							
16							
17							

Figure 5-6. Total commission calculation

are totaled in C8 by entering the formula **+C5+C6+C7** in that cell. The label **Quotas Met** is entered in E4.

The logical formula **+C5>50000** is now entered in E5. When the formula is finalized, a 1 is returned if sales of product A are greater than 50,000, but a 0 is returned if they are equal to or less than this number. Similarly, **+C6>50000** is entered in E6, and **+C7>50000** is entered in E7. Finalizing the formula produces the result of the logical formula in both cases. The total formula, **+E5+E6+E7**, is placed in E8 to determine the number of bonus categories.

Additional labels **Commission:** and **Bonus:** are entered in A10 and A11. **+C8*.1** is then entered in C10, and **+E8*1000** is entered in C11. A label for total commission is placed in A14, and the final formula is entered in D14 as **+C10+C11**.

String Formulas String or text formulas allow you to join or concatenate two or more groups of characters. This enables you to access and manipulate character data to build headings, correct errors, and convert text formats to a satisfactory format for reporting. There is only one operator for string formulas, the ampersand (&). If you want to join the string John with the string Smith, you could type the string formula **+ "John"&"Smith"** to produce JohnSmith, or **+ "John"&" "&"Smith"** to produce John Smith.

String formulas let you alter data previously entered in a worksheet, so you can use it to correct errors or change formats. For example, if names are entered in a worksheet with the last name first, you can combine string functions such as @RIGHT, @LEFT, and @MID if you want to reverse the sequence. (String functions are explained in Chapter 9.)

Tip: Since blank cells are equivalent to zero, referencing a blank cell in a string formula returns ERR, indicating an error in the formula. If you make an entry in the cell, ERR disappears. You can type a label indicator if you want the cell to represent an empty string, often known as the *null string.*

@Functions 1-2-3/G's built-in *@functions* are a special category of mulas. You can use them alone or as part of a formula you create. The entire algorithm or formula for the calculations represented in a function have been worked out, tested, and incorporated into the package features. You just need to supply the values that the operators work with. There are functions for performing arithmetic operations, string manipulation, logical evaluation, statistical calculations, and date and time arithmetic. They all have the same general format and must abide by the same entry and calculation rules. All functions use the Value mode when the formula is entered.

Functions all start with an @ sign. This is followed by a function keyword, which is a character sequence representing the calculation being performed. The keyword is followed by arguments enclosed in parentheses. These arguments define the function's specific use in a given situation. A few of 1-2-3/G's functions are

@SUM	Calculates a sum or total
@ROUND	Rounds a number to a certain number of decimal places
@NPV	Calculates the net present value

1-2-3/G has over 100 of these built-in @functions, spanning calculations in financial, mathematical, logical, statistical, string, and other applications. @functions are covered thoroughly in Chapter 9.

Figure 5-7 illustrates the use of the @SUM function to produce a total. After you enter appropriate numbers and labels, enter the sum function in E6 by typing @, pressing F3, and selecting the keyword

1-2-3/G (69.4) Ready

File Edit Worksheet Range Copy... Move... Print Graph Data Utility Quit... Help

A:E6 @SUM(C6..D6)

FIG6_1.WG1

A	A	B	C	D	E	F	G
1							
2			Boston Fireworks, Inc.				
3			June Sales (000 omitted)				
4							
5			1986	1987	TOTAL		
6	Sparklers		500	540	1040		
7	Rockets		700	756			
8	Fountains		1200	1296			

Figure 5-7. Using @SUM

SUM. You can also type **SUM(** but using F3 makes 1-2-3/G do all the work for you. Then move the mouse pointer to C6 (the beginning of the range to be summed), and drag the mouse to D6 to select cells C6..D6. Lock this reference in place as the beginning of the range by typing a period. Next, move the cell pointer to the value in D6 and type another period. As a last step, enter the closing parenthesis), and press ENTER to finalize the entry and produce the sum shown in the figure. The remaining two @SUM formulas are entered in the same way.

You can also use the @SUM function across sheets in 1-2-3/G. You might have the data for three of a company's subsidiary operations in sheets B through D. To produce a consolidated travel expenses total in sheet A, you might use a formula like this in sheet A:

@SUM(B:B4..D:M4)

External Link Formulas Like functions, *external link formulas* are a special type of formula. With an external link formula, the cell reference the formula uses is in another worksheet file. 1-2-3/G indicates that the data comes from another file by including the filename in double angle brackets (≪ ≫) before the range or cell address the formula uses.

It's easy to create external link formulas. As with other formulas, you can type the filename and the address the formula uses from the other file. For example, you can type

+ ≪BUDGET.WG1≫A:C20

This formula returns the value of A:C20 from the BUDGET.WG1 worksheet file. You can also point with the mouse if your worksheet file is in an open worksheet window and you can see the other worksheet file on the screen. As an example suppose you want to multiply the value in C1 in the EXTERN1 worksheet file by the value in B6 in the EXTERN2 worksheet file, and store the result in C3 in the EXTERN1 worksheet file. First, you must type + to start the formula. Then you can include C1 by clicking the cell. Finalize the C1 entry by typing *. For the value from the other file, point to B6 in the EXTERN2 file; 1-2-3/G will include both the ≪EXTERN2.WG1≫ and the A:B6 in the formula.

To finalize the formula +C1*<<EXTERN2.WG1>>A:B6, select the confirm icon. You can combine external links in formulas with references to cells in the current sheet, as in this example. You can use an external link in most formulas.

Tip: If you type an external link in a formula, include the sheet letter. 1-2-3/G assumes that you want sheet A if you don't include a sheet letter. However, you supply the sheet letter so the formula uses the correct value when you want to use a value from a different sheet.

How 1-2-3/G Treats Formulas 1-2-3/G offers a number of recalculation options that affect the frequency of recalculation and the order of formula evaluation. You will probably begin using 1-2-3/G with the default settings, but you should be aware of the alternatives when you begin to build more sophisticated models.

By default, 1-2-3/G uses minimal intelligent background recalculation—that is, 1-2-3/G deals with recalculation much more efficiently than did past releases. 1-2-3/G can now determine which cells require recalculation, recalculating only this minimum number of cells rather than the entire worksheet every time you change a variable on a sheet. This efficient recalculation method is performed in the system background, thereby allowing you to continue with additional worksheet entries. Instead of the Wait mode indicator that you saw during recalculation for past releases, you will see the Calc indicator at the bottom of the screen until the background recalculation is completed. Unless your worksheet is very large, you will hardly notice the amount of time required to perform these calculations—1-2-3/G is one of the fastest spreadsheet packages marketed.

1-2-3/G offers further processing efficiency for users who have 80287 or 80387 math coprocessor chips installed in their systems, because it can automatically recognize and use these chips. With natural recalculation, 1-2-3/G's default setting, 1-2-3/G calculates the values referenced in the formula before evaluating the formula. 1-2-3/G bears the burden of determining the appropriate order for evaluating formulas, and backward references do not occur.

Reference Types The cell address references in 1-2-3/G's formulas can be relative, absolute, or mixed. These three reference types are covered in detail in Chapter 8 in connection with the Copy command.

They are mentioned here as well, however, because you must enter references in one of the three formats when you type in your original formulas, even though the reference type doesn't affect the original calculation. The "Reference Types" box illustrates the three reference type formats.

Notice that the mixed type addresses have several different options, since mixed is a combination of relative and absolute. Only portions of the address are absolute; the other part of the address may vary depending on where it is copied. The way that you enter cell references in your original formula can have long-term and widespread consequences if the formula is copied.

Adding Notes

1-2-3/G has a Note utility that you can use to annotate formulas or other entries with text to describe your entry. This feature allows you to describe the logic behind a formula or the source for a value. With a separate Note utility, you can work with all of the notes in the file at once. In Release 3, you had to work with each cell's note individually.

1
2
3
G

Reference Types

1-2-3/G has three different reference types. These types do not affect the original formula, but do affect Copy operation. You can type the absolute indicators ($) where required or add them with the F4 (Abs) key when you are in Point mode. The mixed reference type actually has a number of forms, depending on which parts of the address are held constant and which are allowed to change.

Relative references: A:A2, A:B10, A:Z43
Absolute references: $A:$A$2, $A:$B$10, $A:$Z$43
Mixed references: $A:A$2, $A:$A2, A:B$10, A:$B10, A:$A$3, $A:A2

To enter a note for a cell, select Utility Note. This presents the dialog box shown below.

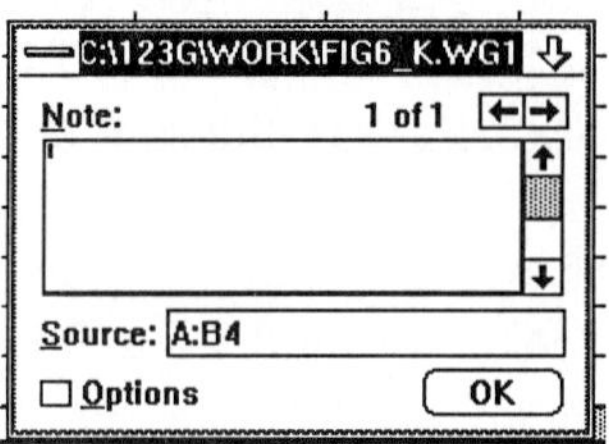

You don't need to be positioned on the cell where you want to add a note. To add a note to a specific cell, edit the address listed under Source. This address is initially the cellpointer's address when you select Utility Note. When Source contains the desired cell, you can type a note of up to 512 characters. Each cell can have up to four notes. To switch between notes for a cell, use PGUP and PGDN. After you select the OK command button, 1-2-3/G displays an N on the left side of the window title bar when the cell pointer is on a cell that has a note.

The Note utility has other options. When you select the Options check box, the Note utility window is expanded. From the list box under List, you can select the note that appears in the left half of the Utility window. For each note, the list box includes the cell and the first few characters of the note. You can use the arrow keys, mouse, or scroll bar to change the highlighted note. Besides displaying the highlighted note in the left half of the Utility window, you can also delete the highlighted note by selecting the Delete command button. If you select the Reset command button, you are erasing all of the notes in the worksheet file. You can also create a list of the note addresses and contents by selecting Table. When you select Table, to display the table contents, you must select a cell with space adjacent to it in any open worksheet. This is the first cell of the table. The table lists the cells with notes, as well as the notes.

The notes you enter in a Note utility window are stored with the worksheet named in the utility's title bar. Changes that you make in a Note utility window for one worksheet do not affect the notes stored with other worksheets. The worksheet that you affect with the Note utility is the last worksheet window that is active before you activate the

Note utility window. For example, if the worksheet SHEET is current and SHEET1 and SHEET2 are in open worksheet windows, the worksheet name that appears in the Note utility window is SHEET. If you switch to SHEET1 and then to the Note utility window, the Note utility operates with the SHEET1 worksheet file. 1-2-3/G keeps the notes for each worksheet file separate.

Correcting Errors in Entries

1-2-3/G offers a variety of error correction techniques, which are summarized in the "Error Correction Methods" box. The method you use depends mostly on whether you have finalized the entry to be corrected (by pressing ENTER or one of the arrow keys, or selecting the confirm icon or another cell with the mouse).

When an entry is short and has been finalized, retyping is a good correction method. This replaces the incorrect contents of the cell with your new entry.

If the Undo feature is active, you can press ALT-BACKSPACE or select Edit Undo to remove the effect of an entry. The Undo feature removes the effect of previous commands, entries, or actions you performed. The advantage of the Edit Undo command is that 1-2-3/G displays the abbreviated command or action it will undo if you select Undo from the Edit pull-down menu. In addition to reversing the effect of commands and actions, you can also undo the effect of edit changes. 1-2-3/G can undo up to 20 actions.

Table 5-2 lists the commands and actions that 1-2-3/G cannot undo. If Undo is currently disabled, you can activate it by selecting the Enable option button under Undo in the dialog box that appears when you select Worksheet Global Default. This only enables Undo for subsequent entries. Enabling Undo does not let you undo the effect of commands and entries you made before Undo was enabled. In addition, Undo uses part of your computer's resources that you may want to dedicate to your worksheets. If your worksheets are too large, your hard disk becomes full, or you are running many Presentation Manager applications, you may want to disable Undo so that you can use the computer's memory for other applications.

Error Correction Methods

If data is in the menu bar but not yet entered in the cell:

- Use the ESCAPE key to erase the entire entry.
- Use the BACKSPACE key to delete one character at a time until the erroneous character has been eliminated.
- Press F2 (Edit); then use HOME, END, RIGHT ARROW, and LEFT ARROW to move within the entry. Use BACKSPACE to delete the character in front of the cursor, and DELETE to erase the character above the cursor.
- Press ALT-BACKSPACE to remove the current entry.

If data has already been entered in the cell:

- Retype the entry; the new entry will replace the old.
- Press F2 (Edit), then use HOME, END, RIGHT ARROW, and LEFT ARROW to move within the entry. Use BACKSPACE to delete the character in front of the cursor, and DELETE to erase the character above the cursor.
- If the UNDO feature is enabled, press ALT-BACKSPACE. This eliminates the tasks and commands that you have performed, one task or command for every time you press ALT-BACKSPACE or select Edit Undo.

A quick-fix option for an unfinalized entry is pressing ESCAPE or clicking the cancel icon, which makes your entire entry disappear. However, if you have not finalized an entry, the most common error correction technique is to use the BACKSPACE key, which functions as a destructive backspace. This approach is ideal when the last character you typed is incorrect.

Placing yourself in Edit mode by pressing the F2 (Edit) key is a good way to correct errors in entries that have been finalized. Move to

Command or Action	
Data External Create command	File Utility Restore Desktop
Data External Delete command	Graph Menu commands
Data External Use command	Move the cell pointer
Data Query Modify command	Print menu commands
Desktop control menu commands	Quit command
Edit Link commands	Range Goto command or the F5 (Goto) key
File Admin Links-Refresh	Recalculating the worksheet
File Erase command	Scroll the worksheet in the window
File New Command for a graph file	Select cells, ranges, collections or worksheet
File Open command for a graph file	Utility Macros commands
File Print commands	Utility User Settings Commands
File Utility Archive Desktop	Window control menu commands
File Utility Copy Desktop	Worksheet Global Default

Table 5-2. Commands and Actions that You Cannot Undo

the cell entry you wish to edit and press F2. The mode indicator in the desktop title bar will change to Edit, and an insertion point will appear at the end of the entry in the contents box. This insertion point marks your place in the entry as you move within it and make changes. It also marks where the characters that you type are added to the entry. Edit mode is also a handy solution when you are working with long, incomplete entries where the error is near the beginning of the entry.

The cell pointer movement keys take on new functions in Edit mode, as follows:

Key	Action
HOME	Moves the cursor to the first character in your entry—not to A1 as it does outside of Edit mode.
END	Moves the cursor immediately to the last character in your entry. You don't have to press an arrow key to have END take an action, as you do in Ready mode.

RIGHT ARROW and LEFT ARROW	Move the cursor one character at a time in your entry.
CTRL-RIGHT ARROW and CTRL-LEFT ARROW	Move the cursor five characters at a time in your entry.
UP ARROW and DOWN ARROW	Move the cursor one line above or below in your entry when the entry contains more than one line. If the entry contains only one line, these arrow keys finalize the entry.
BACKSPACE	Deletes the previous character in the entry.
DELETE	Removes the character in front of the insertion point.

You can also use the mouse to select your position by moving the mouse pointer in the contents box so it appears as an I-beam. When you click the mouse, the insertion point moves to the mouse pointer's position.

Tip: Using the Point mode to modify an existing formula is more difficult than using Edit. Since Edit changes the operation of many of the special keys, it is often easier to type a formula change than to point to it. If you want to use Point, press F2 to change from Edit to Point mode. If you want to add additional formula references to the end of a formula, just press F2 once more to switch from Point to Value mode. Once you are in Value mode, you can point in any direction.

If you have left out a character in an entry, move the cell pointer to the character that follows the desired location, and type the character you wish to add. You can also delete multiple characters. By dragging a mouse or using the SHIFT key with the arrow keys, you can highlight multiple characters in the entry. You can also highlight all characters from the insertion point to the beginning or the end of the entry with SHIFT-HOME or SHIFT-END. To delete the highlighted characters, press DELETE. (DELETE normally deletes only one character, but when multiple characters are highlighted, it deletes all highlighted characters.)

You can also use the error correction techniques to change the justification of a label entry by altering the label indicator that appears at the beginning of the entry. Simply press F2 and then HOME to move to the front of the entry. Press DELETE to remove the label indicator, and then type a caret (^) or double quote ("). When you finalize the entry by clicking the confirm box or pressing ENTER, this entry uses the new label justification character. This same editing approach works with long label entries and complicated formulas.

Ranges

Most of the formulas discussed in this chapter have operated on individual cells—for example, C1*C2 or B:C2+D:F2, where the value in one cell was multiplied by the value in another cell, or the values in two cells were added. The one exception was the @SUM function example which used of a *range* of cells. When using 1-2-3's built-in functions and other commands, you will often work with more than one cell at a time. This is not difficult as long as the range of cells forms a contiguous rectangle. Ranges can be large rectangles of cells, or they can be as small as a single cell.

A range specification always includes two cell addresses separated by periods. If you type a range address, you only need to type one period; 1-2-3/G will supply the second one. If you specify a range address by pointing, and if the address already appears in a range format with two addresses separated by a period, you can use the arrow keys or mouse to enlarge or contract the range.

The entries B1..B10, F2..F2, and A3..C25 are all examples of range specifications. You can change any single cell address to a range reference within a formula by typing a period after the address as you are specifying the range. With a mouse, you drag the mouse from one cell to another while holding down the left mouse button. With the mouse, you can also select the first corner of the range and then point to the opposite corner. Instead of clicking the opposite corner, hold down the SHIFT key while clicking the range's opposite corner. 1-2-3/G will highlight the range that is defined with the two selected cells.

As an example, an entry of B1 will appear as B1..B1 if you type a period after B1 while 1-2-3/G is expecting a range specification. With @SUM, type **@SUM(**, point to B1 and type a period, and then type).

The entry appears as @SUM(B1..B1). To expand the range, move the cell pointer down or to the right before typing the closing parenthesis.

You can type in cell ranges just like a single address, or highlight them with your cell pointer or a mouse, or specify them with a range name. To specify the cells of a range, use the cell names of two diagonally opposite corners of the rectangle, separated by one or two periods. For example, you can specify the range shown in Figure 5-8 as B4.C8, B4..C8, B8..C4, B8.C4, C8..B4, C8.B4, C4..B8, or C4.B8. However, the most common way to represent a range is by specifying the upper-left cell first and the lower-right cell last. Also, since 1-2-3/G will supply the second period, you can save a keystroke by typing **B4.C8**.

Tip: When 1-2-3/G references the selected range to use with a command, you can type a decimal point to change the orientation of a range. If you need to expand or shrink a highlighted range from the beginning rather than the end, you can press ESC and start over. A better approach is to press the period, which activates a different corner of the current range and allows you to use the arrow keys to push and pull on the range area from this corner. For example, the range A1..D10 initially has D10 as the active corner. The first time you press the period, A10 is active, the second time A1, and the third time D1.

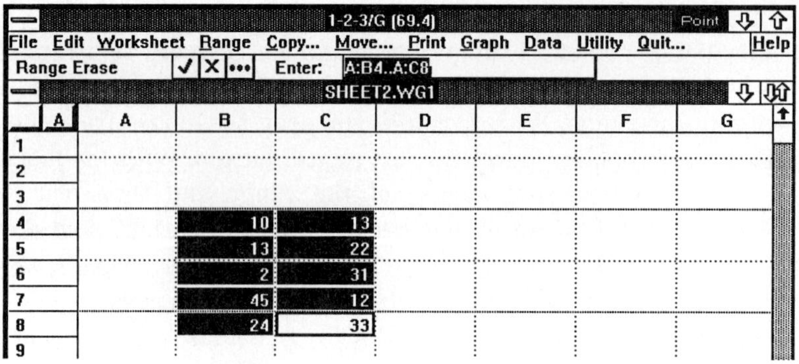

Figure 5-8. Highlighted range

Ranges in 1-2-3/G can also span sheets in a file. You saw one example of this with the @SUM function used to consolidate travel expenses. When specifying ranges across multiple sheets, you must choose diagonally opposite corners for the range on the first and last sheet in the range. The size of the range in each sheet is always the same.

In this case, the period option allows you also to change the orientation of the beginning and ending sheets for the range by switching the diagonally opposite corners that specify the range. Typing a period changes the corners used to indicate the range, allowing you to change the anchor point for the range, and enabling you to expand or contract the range from different sides of the range. 1-2-3/G marks the anchored cell in the range address by displaying the anchored corner in a different color.

When specifying a range encompassing multiple cells on each sheet, you can specify all the cells in the range on the first sheet (as in B:D2..B:E4) and then use CTRL-PGUP to extend this range to other sheets like C, D, and E, with a final range specification of B:D2..E:E4. To specify this same range, you can also start with the cell pointer in D2 of sheet B, and extend the range to the remaining sheets so that it reads B:D2..E:D2; then you can extend the range on the last sheet. Both methods produce the same range.

Collections

Collections are a new feature of 1-2-3/G that let you work with a selection of cells and ranges. Unlike ranges, collections don't have to be a contiguous group of cells. The collection can include many ranges and cells. You can use collections with many 1-2-3/G commands. This lets you format and copy a group of cells that are not in a contiguous range. An example of a collection is A3..B3,A4..C4,B6,A2..B2,A12,B13,C14. As you can see, a collection is a combination of cell and range addresses joined by commas. The exact collection delimiter is the punctuation chosen with Utility User Settings International Number format Argument (as discussed in Chapter 6). The only limitation is that the entire collection address cannot exceed 512 characters.

There are three ways to specify a collection in 1-2-3/G. You can type the collection address. As with typing a cell address for a formula, this method is prone to errors, since you cannot visually check each cell that you are including. You can also select and then name the collection and use its name with the 1-2-3/G command that will use the collection. Finally, you can highlight the collection.

Highlighting a collection is a simple method of selecting the cells and ranges you want to use, whether you are using the mouse or the keyboard. With a mouse, you must select the first cell or range that is part of the collection. When you are ready to select the next range or cell, you must detach the cell pointer from the current range so you can move it to a new range. Move the cell pointer to the first cell of the next range or cell you want to select. Hold down the right mouse button while you drag the mouse across the range to include in the collection. Using the right mouse button tells 1-2-3/G that you want to use the newly selected range or cell in addition to the previously selected cells. You can continue selecting new cells and ranges to add to the collection by using the right mouse button.

With a keyboard, when you highlight a collection, you select its first cell or range. When you are ready to select the next range or cell, you must detach the cell pointer from the current range so you can move it to a new range. To detach the cell pointer, press SHIFT-F8 (Detach). Once the cell pointer is detached, you can select the next cell or range, by moving the cell pointer to the next cell you want to use in the collection. Hold down the SHIFT key while you move the cell pointer to the opposite corner of the range or cell address you are adding to the collection. When the range or cell is selected, release the SHIFT key and move to the corner of the next cell or range you want to add to the collection. You can continue moving the cell pointer to a new corner and using the SHIFT key to select the cells and ranges that are part of the collection until you are finished selecting the collection.

Regardless of how you select a collection, for commands such as Range Input, you will want to consider the order in which you make your selections. Since commands like Range Input are used to control input, you need to make your entries within a collection specified for this command in the order in which the individual components of the collection are specified. Using A1..A3, C2..C4 allows a different entry order than using C2..C4, A1..A3. Once the collection is selected, you can use the collection in 1-2-3/G formulas and commands.

Working with Ranges and Collections

Ranges offer several features that make it easier to use 1-2-3/G. You can name cells, ranges, and collections. A range name is easier to remember than the cell, range, or collection address that the range name describes. Also, using a range name lets you document the formulas, since you can assign meaningful names to the ranges in a formula. You can also use ranges and collections to limit input into cells in a range or collection. With the Range Input command and Bound mode, you can limit cell pointer movement to the cells in a selected range.

Methods of Specifying Cell Ranges and Collections

There are a variety of ways to specify the range or collection you want to work with. The easiest method is pointing using the arrow keys or the mouse. Pointing lets you visually verify the range or collection as you define it, since it highlights the cells as you expand or contract the range or collection. The way you select a range or collection depends on whether you use the keyboard or the mouse.

For many Commands 1-2-3/G suggests a range beginning at a location of the cell pointer E3. If your cell pointer is positioned at the beginning of the desired range before you invoke the menu, you just need to move with the arrow keys to complete the range. 1-2-3/G will highlight the range when you use this method.

When 1-2-3/G is in Ready mode, you can select a range by anchoring one corner of the range and selecting the range's opposite corner. To anchor a range to the cell pointer's position, press CTRL-. (CTRL-period). As you move the cell pointer to the opposite corner for the range, the first cell becomes the range's anchor point and 1-2-3/G highlights all cells between the two corners of the range.

It is preferable to have 1-2-3/G generate the cell addresses in a range whenever possible. However, you can always type a cell reference in response to one of the range prompts. For example, you can type **1..3** to select the range consisting of rows 1 through 3. To select columns in a range, type the column letters. To select sheets in a range, type the sheet letters followed by colons, as in **A:..D:**. When you use the pointing method, 1-2-3/G always adds the sheet letters, even if the references are both on the same sheet. If you are typing the range yourself, you only need to type the cell addresses, unless the data is in another sheet or file.

Naming Cell Ranges

In some respects, all worksheet cells automatically have names, since they have unique cell addresses by which you can reference them. You are already familiar with column/row addresses such as A2, U7, or AX89 from a single-sheet perspective, and D:A2, D:F10, G:A2 from a multiple-sheet perspective. It is clear exactly what cell you mean when you use these addresses. If you leave out the sheet level indicator, 1-2-3/G assumes that you want the cell address on the current sheet. Although it is never incorrect to add a sheet level, it is only required when the referenced cells are on another sheet. Likewise, a file reference is only required when you are referencing a range in another file.

Although the location of the cell is evident, it is not clear what is contained in cells named A2, U7, or A:X89. Is it the interest rate, the number of employees, or the Los Angeles Dodgers' batting average? It can take time to move the cell pointer to the cell every time you need to remember a particular cell's contents.

The Range Name commands provide a solution for this dilemma. You can use these commands to assign names to ranges of any size—names that provide meaningful information about the contents of the groups of cells they reference. If cell A10 contains sales for 1989, for example, you might assign it the name SALES_89. If cells B3..B25 contain all the expenses for a certain department, you might assign a range name like TOTAL_EXPENSES.

Tip: Some commands remember the last range they used. Commands like Data Fill (described in Chapter 5) and Print (in Chapter 11) remember the last range used, and suggest it for the next use of the command. To change these suggested ranges, you can use ESCAPE to eliminate the range, or BACKSPACE to set the beginning of the range to the location of the cell pointer when you invoked the command.

Range names assume added importance with multiple worksheets. When you can access multiple worksheets in one file, it is more convenient to access data in other sheets by using a name like Sales rather than remembering that it is stored in <<BUDGET>> A:D13..A:D42.

This feature also makes it easier to link data across several files. You can only assign range names within open worksheet files (that is, files in memory), although you must use sheet or file indicators to assign names to sheets other than the current sheet or file.

1-2-3/G allows you to assign any name to any range of cells, provided that the name does not exceed 15 characters. Once you assign a range name, you can use it in exactly the same way that you use a cell address, range, or collection. For example, you could create a formula for a profit calculation using these assigned range names: +SALES_89–TOTAL_EXPENSES. 1-2-3/G keeps the range name in the formula, even when you edit it. See the Creating Range Names box, which provides some additional tips on range names.

Creating Range Names

1-2-3/G has few restrictions in range names, but it is helpful to add a few for the sake of clarity:

- 1-2-3/G doesn't prevent you from using spaces in range names; however, you should avoid them. The name TOTAL SALES could be mistaken for two range names, but TOTAL_SALES is clearly one name.
- You can use arithmetic operators in range names, but they, too, can cause problems. TOTAL*SALES could be confusing as a range name. It might be interpreted as a request for an arithmetic operation that would multiply TOTAL by SALES.
- Again, although they are permitted, avoid names that could be confused with a cell address, such as A3 or D4.
- Don't give ranges the same name as functions, macro commands, or 1-2-3 key names.
- Don't start range names with numbers because they cannot be included in a formula. For example, SALES_86 is acceptable, but 56 is not acceptable as a range name.

1-2-3/G has many new range name options, including support for undefined range names. You can finalize a formula even if it includes range name references that have not been created. If you delete an assigned range name used in a formula, 1-2-3/G converts the range name reference to the corresponding range address. 1-2-3/G has a Range Name Undefine command that retains an existing range name but disassociates it from any specific range reference.

Assigning Range Names

There are two basic methods for assigning range names. Usually, you will invoke the Range Name Create command to enter your range names. You can use the Range Name Labels command in special cases where you want to name a single cell using a name in an adjacent worksheet cell.

Creating New Names The easiest way to name a cell, range, or collection is to select it. After positioning the cell pointer, select Range Name Create, type your range name, and select the OK command button. If you don't select the cell, range, or collection before you select Range Name Create, you will want to select the cell, range, or collection after providing the range name. Once the cell, range, or collection is selected, choose the OK button from the dialog box. You can select the cell, range, or collection by typing the addresses or by pointing with the mouse or keyboard.

For example, consider the commands Range Name Create SALES D:A1 and Range Name Create EXPENSES B2..B6. In the first example, the named range is on another sheet in the active file. In the second example, the range name refers to B2..B6 in the sheet that is current when you select the Range Name Create command.

1-2-3/G allows you to assign more than one name to a range. For example, suppose that you have data in cells F4..F25 that represents expenses for 1989, and you name this range EXPENSES_89. Now suppose that you want to use these expenses to project next year's budget. You might want to assign this same range of cells the name PREVIOUS_YR_EXP for use in your budget calculations.

1-2-3/G has a special feature for accessing names once they have been assigned: the F3 (Name) key. When you are using a command that expects a range, you can press F3 to access the list of names you have assigned. You can then select a name from the list for use with the command you entered.

To create the formula, move to B5 and type + to start the formula. To use the first range name, press F3 (Name). This lists all of the cells, ranges, and collections named in the current worksheet file. This list also includes the names of other open worksheet files. If you select a worksheet name, you can select from the range names in the selected worksheet file.

Creating Range Names with Existing Worksheet Labels The Range Name Labels command can save you data entry time when assigning range names, if conditions are right. First, the name you plan to use must already exist on the worksheet as a label entry. It must also be in a cell adjacent to the cell you plan to name. You can only assign a range name to a single cell with this command, so if you are naming more than one cell in a range, you must use the Range Name Create command. You can use Range Name Labels to assign several range names at once.

The cells in B3..B10 in Figure 5-9 can all have range names assigned with one execution of the Range Name Labels command. To do

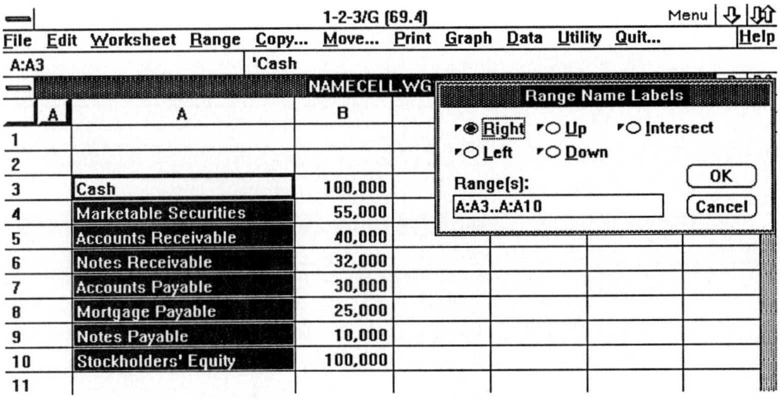

Figure 5-9. Selecting the range and direction

this, select the range A3..A10 and select Range Name Labels. Since the range of cells to which you are assigning names is to the right of the labels, choose Right next as shown in the figure. Finally, select the OK command button to name the cells. 1-2-3/G only uses the first 15 characters as a limit on range names.

You can also give unique names to the cells in a range. Figure 5-10 shows a worksheet that can use the Range Name Labels Intersect command. When you select a range like A1..D4 and Range Name Labels Intersect, 1-2-3/G does not name any cells in the first row and column of the range, instead using this column and row to name the other cells in the range. The range names of each cell after the first row and column are a combination of the label in the first column and the label in the first row. When you type + and press F3 (Name), you can see the list of field names 1-2-3/G creates. Using the worksheet shown in Figure 5-10, some of the range names are COGS_1990, PROFIT_1990, and SALES_1990. While you cannot use this option for every occasion, it's a great time saver when available.

Deleting Range Names

Assigned range names use a small amount of 1-2-3/G's internal memory. If you are not using some of your old range names, consider deleting them to free up the space that they use. It is best to delete a range name as soon as you know it is no longer required, since later on you may forget whether or not you need it.

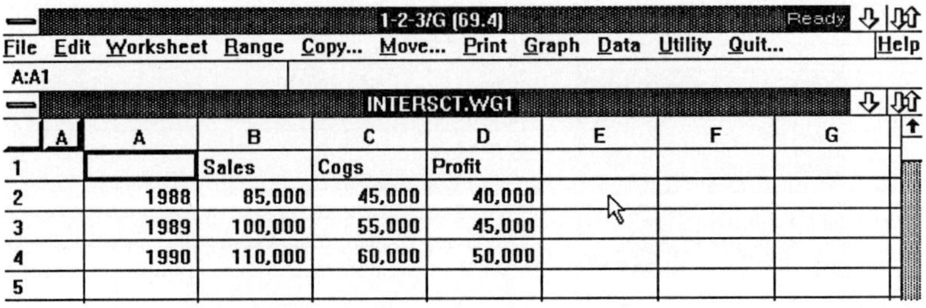

1-2-3/G [69.4] Ready

File Edit Worksheet Range Copy... Move... Print Graph Data Utility Quit... Help

A:A1

INTERSCT.WG1

A	A	B	C	D	E	F	G
1		Sales	Cogs	Profit			
2	1988	85,000	45,000	40,000			
3	1989	100,000	55,000	45,000			
4	1990	110,000	60,000	50,000			
5							

Figure 5-10. Worksheet set up to use intersecting range names

To delete a range name, select Range Name Delete. 1-2-3/G will present a list of all the assigned range names, including other worksheet files, so you can select a range name from another open worksheet window. When you delete a range name, 1-2-3/G replaces all instances of the range name in the worksheet file with the last cell, range, or collection address that the range name represented.

Resetting Range Names

If you have many names to delete, the Range Name Reset command can speed up the process when you are deleting most or all of your range names. Range Name Reset deletes all range names, so it is perfect when you want to create all new names. When you have a large number of names and want to delete all but a few, it may be quicker to delete them all and then use Range Name Create to reenter the names you want to keep. When you select Reset, you don't have to make any additional choices.

Range Name Undefine also removes range names from the active list of range names. Unlike Range Name Delete, Range Name Undefine does not eliminate notes that may be attached to range names. It also does not remove the range name reference in formulas, although the formulas containing undefined ranges evaluate to ERR. If you use Range Name Create later to reinstate undefined range names, the notes will still be there. If you use the Delete or Reset commands to remove a range name, the note is also deleted and must be reentered when you reinstate the range name.

Tip: Remember to check the file you are in before using Range Name Reset to delete all ranges and range notes. If Undo is not enabled, there is no way to restore notes you have Reset, unless you have a copy of the worksheet on disk. To safeguard your notes, check the active file to ensure that you are in the right file before invoking the Reset option.

Creating a Table of Range Names

When you have many range names, you may want to look over the cell addresses that each range name represents. You can check the address to which a range name is assigned by using the Range Name Create command to display the list of names. When a range name in the list is highlighted, 1-2-3/G displays the cell, range, or address list in the Ranges text box. Selecting the Cancel command button ensures that the assignment is not changed. This works well for a single range name; however, it is not a good alternative when you want to check a number of ranges, since repeating the sequence for each range takes too much time.

A better solution is to use the Range Name Table command to build a table of range names and the cell addresses they identify. This table, displayed in any empty area of a worksheet, can document all the range names your worksheet uses.

Before executing the required command sequence, choose a good table location, with enough free space so you won't overwrite data or important formulas if the table is longer than you expect. You might even want to move to a new sheet so that the table will have no impact on existing model entries. When you are ready to create the table, select Range Name Table and respond to 1-2-3/G's prompt by typing or pointing to the desired table location in any open worksheet window. 1-2-3/G permits you to supply just the upper-left corner of the table range, and then uses as much space as it needs for the table. When you create a table with the Range Name Table command, the range names are listed in alphabetical order. With 1-2-3/G, the entries in column E of the table list the type of range that the range name represents. This includes Range for one cell or a range, Coll for a collection, and Ref for a range reference that represents data in another worksheet file.

Using Filenames and Wildcard References with Range Names

Although range names like SALES or BUDGET are the most common form of reference used, you can also use a filename as part of the range name reference when you want to access a range in a file other than the current file. The standard double angle bracket notation is used around the filename, as in <<C:\123R3\BUDGET.WK3>>SALES.

You can also use a question mark within the angle brackets as a wildcard, and 1-2-3/G will search all active files. Use the wildcard notation only when the range name is unique among the active files. If you enter this notation in a command or formula, 1-2-3/G displays an error message if it does not find a match, or if it finds multiple matches. To look for the range name SALES in this manner, you would type **<<?>> SALES** in a formula or a command that expects a range.

Tip: 1-2-3/G does not convert wildcard references to range addresses when you delete the range name. Normally, if you delete a range name, 1-2-3/G converts formula entries that reference the deleted name to the appropriate cell addresses. This does not occur with wildcard references.

Practical Applications for Range Names

Assigning range names may seem like much unnecessary extra work. For very small models, they may not be worthwhile. For larger ones, however—especially multiple-sheet models—range names offer a significant payback. They make formulas much more readable. They also help prevent incorrect formula references, since you see a descriptive name rather than a cryptic cell address. As data becomes further removed from the formula location, the payback becomes greater—you cannot see the data on the screen at the same time as the formula, and thus cannot verify the accuracy of the cell addresses used.

When you use range names, you can insert rows, columns, and sheets in the middle of a range, and the range reference will be adjusted automatically. The references are also updated if you delete rows, columns, or sheets from a range. If you want to see the updated references in a table, however, you must execute the Range Name Table command again, since the table is not automatically updated when changes are made.

Limiting Cell Movement in a Range

When you are developing models for someone else, you will probably only want them to be able to change some of the cells. Also, when you are making data entries, you may only want to make entries in selected cells, leaving other cells unchanged. You can tell 1-2-3/G to limit cell pointer movement to a range of cells with the Range Input command or the Bound mode. With the Range Input command, you can move the cell pointer to any unprotected cell in a range. With the Bound mode, you can move the cell pointer to all cells in the range selected before the Bound mode is enabled.

Using the Range Input Command

The Range Input command is combined with 1-2-3/G's protection features to limit the cells to which a cell pointer will move. The protection features of 1-2-3/G let you select the cells that you can change with Range Input. Once the cells that you want to change are unprotected, the Range Input command allows you to restrict cell pointer movement to unprotected cells within the input range. Range Input is useful for controlling the location of the cells available for entry during data input. The steps for using this command are as follows:

1. Set up the worksheet with all needed labels and formulas. In other words, design your worksheet before restricting the cell pointer.

2. Select Range Unprotect to remove protection from the cells requiring data entry. Unprotecting cells also changes their appearance, by default, to green text with a white background.

3. Select the cell, range, or collection of cells that you want to be able to change while the Range Input command is in effect. Then select the OK command button.

4. Select Range Input and select the range or collection of cells in which you want to allow input. You can use F3 (Name) to select a named range or collection. The range or collection can include both protected and unprotected cells, since 1-2-3/G only lets you edit the unprotected cells in the range or collection.

Your screen will display Input in the window title bar. While the Range Input command is in effect, 1-2-3/G will not let you perform any commands. You can edit or enter new data in cells in the specified range. You can also use ESCAPE, HOME, END, ENTER, F1 (Help), F2 (Edit), F4 (Abs), BACKSPACE, or any of the arrow keys to complete your entries. The cell pointer always remains within the input range, since that is the only area where you can make entries. While Range Input is in effect, the END and HOME keys move you to the first or last unprotected cell in the input range. When you use the mouse to point to a cell that you cannot change, the mouse pointer becomes gray. If you select a collection for this command, pressing the arrow keys moves the cell pointer to the next cell according to the order of the cells and ranges listed in the collection address. If the selected range or collection includes multiple sheets, you must use the arrow keys, rather than CTRL-PGUP and CTRL-PGDN, to switch between the sheets. Pressing either ESCAPE or ENTER without making an entry cancels the Range Input command. The Range Input command is also used in the macro environment to assist with automating applications.

Using the Bound Mode

The Bound mode lets you select the cells to edit. Once the Bound mode is enabled, you can only move to the selected cells. Unlike the Range Input command, you do not have to unprotect the cells you want to change. To use the Bound mode, first select the range or collection to which to limit cell pointer movement, and then press SHIFT-F4 (Bound).

When the Bound mode is in effect, Bound appears in the window title bar. 1-2-3/G moves the cell pointer to the top visible cell in the selected range or collection. If the selected range or collection is not visible in the worksheet window, 1-2-3/G moves the worksheet in the window to display the first cell in the selected range or collection in the worksheet file. This can only happen when the cell pointer is detached. Unlike the Range Input command, the Bound mode leaves the selected cells highlighted.

In the Bound mode, you can edit or add new data to cells in the specified range. You can use the arrow and directional keys or the mouse to select the desired cell. Table 5-3 lists how the different keys affect cell pointer movement in the Bound mode. In certain situations, the keys may behave differently. When you are at the first cell of a range and try to move to a prior cell, or at the last cell of a range and try to move to the next cell, you move to the previous or next range within the collection you select for the Bound mode. If you only select a single range for the Bound mode, moving beyond one corner of the range moves you to the opposite range corner. The same is true when you move from opposite ends of a collection—moving to the prior cell in the first cell of a collection or moving to the next cell in the last cell of a collection moves the cell pointer to the collection's opposite corner.

Key	Action
RIGHT ARROW	Moves to the next cell to the right or, if on the last selected cell in the row, moves to the first cell in the following row.
LEFT ARROW	Moves to the previous cell to the left or, if on the first selected cell in the row, moves to the last cell in the previous row.
ENTER	Moves to the next cell to the right or, if on the last selected cell in the row, moves to the first cell in the following row.
SHIFT-ENTER	Moves to the previous cell to the left or, if on the first selected cell in the row, moves to the last cell in the previous row.
UP ARROW	Moves to the cell above or, if on the first selected cell in the column, moves to the last cell in the previous column.
DOWN ARROW	Moves to the cell below or, if on the last selected cell in the column, moves to the first cell in the previous column.
TAB	Moves the cell pointer to the next corner in the current range, moving in a clockwise direction.
SHIFT-TAB	Moves the cell pointer to the previous corner in the current range, moving in a counterclockwise direction.
HOME	Moves the cell pointer to the first cell in the current range column.
CTRL-HOME	Moves to the first cell in the first range selected for the Bound mode collection.
PGUP	Moves the cell pointer to the lower-right corner of the next range in the collection.
PGDN	Moves the cell pointer to the upper-left corner of the previous range in the collection.
CTRL-PGUP	Moves the cell pointer to the same cell in the previous sheet of a multiple-sheet range.
CTRL-PGDN	Moves the cell pointer to the same cell in the next sheet of a multiple-sheet range.

Table 5-3. Keys Available in the Bound Mode

Unlike the Range Input command, you cannot use the SHIFT-F8 (Detach) key while in Bound mode. This affects how you enter a collection that a formula uses. Also, unlike Range Input, Bound will let you perform menu commands. The Bound mode is temporarily turned off during the Point mode of editing a cell, the Find mode of the Data Query Find (covered in Chapter 19), when you press F5 (Goto) or use the Range Goto command, hide columns and rows (covered in Chapter 7), add titles (covered in Chapter 7), or divide the worksheet window into panes (covered in Chapter 7). If the Bound mode is temporarily turned off, it returns when you have finished with the mode or command that disabled it. When you are finished with the Bound mode, press SHIFT-F4 (Bound) again to toggle it off. With a mouse, you can also disable the Bound mode by selecting a cell that is not part of the range or collection selected for the Bound mode.

Generating a Series of Values

The Data Fill command can save you considerable time when you are preparing a worksheet model. Use it to generate a series of dates, invoice numbers, purchase order numbers, new account numbers, or identification numbers for new employees, among other things. Whenever you need to enter a series of data with evenly spaced values in either ascending or descending sequence, Data Fill can handle the task.

To use Data Fill, place your cell pointer in the first cell of the row or column in which you want the series generated, and select Data Fill. To produce a dialog box select the range or collection to use for a series. As with other 1-2-3/G commands that use ranges, you can select the range before or after you select Data Fill. If you select the range before you select the command, the range will continue to be highlighted after 1-2-3/G generates the values; if you select the range after you select Data Fill, the selected range is not highlighted when the command is finished. To switch between parts of this dialog box, use TAB or press ENTER. If you press ENTER (as opposed to TAB) after accepting or altering the stop value, you will also select OK and 1-2-3/G will perform the command. 1-2-3/G then prompts you for the first number in the series (the start value) and suggests the default value of 0. You can accept this value or type another number. The prompt for the increment value, or step, is next. You can accept the default of 1, or type any positive or negative number for the increment before pressing ENTER. A positive step creates a series of ascending numbers and a negative step creates a series of descending numbers. The fourth necessary part of the dialog box is a stop value. As long as the default stop value of 8192 is greater than or equal to your planned stop value, you can just select OK and allow 1-2-3/G to determine a stop value, based on the size of the range and other values you have supplied. If 8192 is not large enough, type a new stop value before selecting OK or another option in the dialog box.

For example, suppose you need to enter the data for a group of consecutively numbered invoices. Rather than entering the invoice numbers, you can use the Data Fill command to create them for you. To enter invoice numbers in cells A2..A20 of a worksheet, select the range A2..A20 and select Data Fill. Press TAB or click the Start text or text box. For the start value, type **1004**, representing the first invoice number that you want. For the increment, type **1**. Since you want to use the default settings for Series and Order, select the OK command button.

Remember, there are two situations that stop generation of entries in a fill series. Make sure that the range is large enough and the stop value is high enough. 1-2-3/G stops generating values as soon as either condition is exceeded. Consider what happens if you accept the default stop value of 8192. This number exceeds the start value, and it also far exceeds the range, so the range area specified is what stops the generation of fill values. If you typed **1009** as the stop value, your results would be quite different, since the stop value would have been reached before the end of the range. In that case, the Data Fill command would only fill A2..A7.

Tip: If you want Data Fill to fill every cell in the range, make the stop value larger than what you expect the last value in the fill range to be.

Using the Data Fill Options

1-2-3/G does not limit generating values to simple increments. You can use the Data Fill command to work with dates and times. The Data Fill dialog box also includes Series and Order options that make the Data Fill command applicable in situations where you need a series with nonsequential entries such as exponential growth. Many of the Series options work with date increments such as quarterly or monthly. The Series options include how 1-2-3/G interprets the step value and how this command fills in a range containing multiple rows and columns.

When you are using Data Fill with dates or times, you can type the start, step, and stop values as dates or times. This lets you generate a series of dates or times. The dates and times must be in a date and time format that 1-2-3/G will accept for directly entering dates and times into a cell.

If the range selected for Data Fill uses the Automatic format, as described in Chapter 7, 1-2-3/G automatically formats the cells as dates and times using the format of the start, step, and stop values. If the range selected for Data Fill does not use an Automatic format, 1-2-3/G displays the time or date serial numbers using the format of the range.

The options for Data Fill Series are described in the "Data Fill Series Options" box. To use one of the Data Fill Series options, select the appropriate option button under Series. If you are using the keyboard, use the TAB key to move to these options.

The third special option of the Data Fill command determines how 1-2-3/G fills a range containing multiple columns and rows. 1-2-3/G has two options. You can fill each column in the range or collection selected before preceding with the next column. This is the default setting of Column under Order in the Data Fill text box. Alternatively, you can fill each row in the range or collection selected before preceding with the next row. You can select this option by choosing the Row option under Order. When the selected range includes only a single column or row, the order selected does not affect the results.

For example, suppose you need to enter a series of dates for Monday through Friday for two weeks, entering the first week's dates in B2..F2 and the second week's dates in B8..F8. First, select the collection to contain the date by selecting B2..F2,B8..F8. When you select Data Fill, you can press TAB or click the start value to bypass the fill range that you have already selected. If the first date you need is January 7, 1991, you can enter **7-Jan-91** and get a serial date number of 33245. Type **1** for the increment and **99999** for the stop value. Since dates have high serial numbers, you usually have to provide a stop value much higher than 1-2-3/G's default. Press TAB to switch to the Series option buttons and select the Weekday option button with the SPACEBAR on the keyboard or click the Weekday option button with the mouse. Select OK. 1-2-3/G first fills the range B2..F2 and then fills the range B8..F8 with date serial number. After the formatting options covered in Chapter 7 have been used and additional entries have been made, the worksheet will display the entries like dates. You will learn how to improve the appearance of your worksheets in Chapter 7.

Data Fill Series Options

The Data Fill command has the following series options, which control the increment between the generated values:

Linear	Makes the increment between each generated value the same as the increment specified with Step. This is the default series option.
Growth	Increases or decreases the values the Data Fill command generates by the last value multiplied by the value entered in the Step text box.
Power	Makes the increment between each generated value the prior value raised to the power specified in the Step text box.
Year	Increases or decreases the generated values by the number of years entered in the Step text box. This option adds 365 days for most years and 366 days for leap years.
Quarter	Increases or decreases the generated values by the number of quarters entered in the Step text box.
Month	Increases or decreases the generated values by the number of months entered in the Step text box. This option keeps track of the number of days in each month.
Week	Increases or decreases the generated values by the number of weeks entered in the Step text box.
Weekday	Increases or decreases the generated values by the number of days entered in the Step text box, so the date number is for a day between Monday and Friday. This option skips over Saturday and Sunday. A date for Saturday or Sunday only appears if the date serial number entered in the Start text box is for a Saturday or Sunday.
Day	Increases or decreases the generated values by the number of days entered in the Step text box.

Data Fill Series Options (Continued)

- Hour — Increases or decreases the generated values by the number of hours entered in the Step text box.
- Minute — Increases or decreases the generated values by the number of minutes entered in the Step text box.
- Second — Increases or decreases the generated values by the number of seconds entered in the Step text box.

How 1-2-3/G Stores Your Worksheets

1-2-3/G has greater data storage capabilities than previous releases. These differences may change how you organize large worksheets. Since 1-2-3/G operates under OS/2, it can contain over 536,870,912 cells of data (256 columns * 8192 rows * 256 sheets). The 1-2-3/G desktop can have as many as 16 windows open at once, and uses a different record to file information on your system.

How OS/2 Uses Memory

1-2-3/G can use up to 16Mb of RAM and virtual memory. (RAM are computer chips in your computer that provide temporary storage for any application that you are using.) When RAM is full, OS/2 uses *virtual memory*—free space on your system hard disk that OS/2 reserves to store additional information used during a work session. Since OS/2 allocates part of the hard disk for virtual memory, the amount of disk space you have to use with your other applications decreases when you run OS/2 rather than DOS. Since the disk is used for virtual memory, the free space you have on your OS/2 disk drive increases the amount of virtual memory you have. If the OS/2 disk space is less than 6Mb, 1-2-3/G cannot load parts of the 1-2-3/G program. When this happens, you should delete files that you no longer use from the system drive on which OS/2 is installed.

Using RAM is faster than using virtual memory. Since virtual memory is stored on a disk, the operating system must access the disk each time it uses information stored in the virtual memory. This takes longer than retrieving the information from RAM. This means that you can enhance the computer's performance for a specific task by closing the Presentation Manager applications and 1-2-3/G windows that you are not using. Since it doesn't need to keep the information for the unused windows in memory, OS/2 can put more of 1-2-3/G processing in RAM. OS/2 is responsible for moving information between RAM and virtual memory.

Tip: Periodically review the contents of your OS/2 disk drive, searching for and deleting files that you no longer need. Also find the files you no longer use but do not want to delete. You can copy these files to a floppy disk, store them in a safe location, and delete them from the hard disk.

How 1-2-3/G Uses Memory

Earlier releases of 1-2-3 kept track of the cells that had entries, their contents, and their formatting information. With 1-2-3/G, most of this information is stored in blocks. 1-2-3/G divides the cells in each worksheet column into 256 blocks, each containing 32 cells. When you enter information in any one of the 32 cells in a block, 1-2-3/G allocates memory for each cell in the block. This means that entering data in A1 and B1 uses more memory than entering data in A1 and A2, because you have entered data in two blocks. 1-2-3/G allocates the blocks of memory in the larger area where OS/2 has placed your worksheet file in memory.

1-2-3/G also allocates memory based on the sheets used. Each time you make an entry on a new sheet, 1-2-3/G allocates information for the sheet as well as for the block containing the entry.

When you work in 1-2-3/G, memory blocks are allocated for performing operations. As these blocks are allocated, they become fragmented. The remaining blocks may become too small for 1-2-3/G to use. When 1-2-3/G is low on memory, it displays Mem in the desktop title bar, indicating that it didn't have enough memory to perform the last command or accept the last entry. You should save the file, close the window or erase the worksheet, and then retrieve the worksheet file into the blank worksheet window or open a new worksheet window. When you retrieve a file, 1-2-3/G allocates a larger area of memory and removes any unused areas of memory.

Review the suggestions in the box "Steps for Increasing Memory." In addition, if low memory is a persistent problem and you frequently use large worksheets, you may want to consider purchasing more RAM chips to boost the total amount of RAM and virtual memory that 1-2-3/G and OS/2 can use. Memory allocation is primarily an issue as you develop complex worksheet models. You shouldn't lack memory when you create simple worksheets.

Leaving 1-2-3/G

When you have finished using 1-2-3/G, you will want to save your work with File Save, and then exit 1-2-3/G. Exiting 1-2-3/G means closing all

Steps for Increasing Memory

When you are low on memory, you should remedy this problem via some of the following methods before you continue using 1-2-3/G:

- Disable the Undo feature by selecting Worksheet Global Default Set Undo Disable.
- Press END and CTRL-HOME to find the last worksheet that has an entry. This alerts you that you have a worksheet with entries that you don't need. Delete unneeded worksheets with the Worksheet Delete Sheet command.

Steps for Increasing Memory (Continued)

- Display the worksheet in Map mode by selecting Worksheet Window Map Mode Enable. This highlights the cells in the worksheet that contain entries.
- Use Worksheet Delete (Column, Row, or Sheet) to eliminate unneeded items or use File Extract with specific ranges to make a smaller worksheet.
- Close unnecessary 1-2-3/G windows and Presentation Manager windows that you are not using. Pressing CTRL-F4 (Close Tool) closes 1-2-3/G windows and pressing ALT-F4 closes Presentation Manager windows. You can also close the window by selecting Close from the window control menu. Reducing windows to icons does not save memory.
- Convert formulas you no longer need to their values with the Range Value command (see Chapter 8). Formulas use more memory than their values.
- Move your data closer together using the Move command (discussed in Chapter 8). A worksheet with entries closer together uses less memory than a worksheet with entries spread further apart.
- Remove formatting information from blank cells using the Range Erase command with the Settings check box selected in the Range Erase Options dialog box (described in Chapter 7). 1-2-3/G uses some memory to store the formatting information even if the cells are blank. Since 1-2-3/G uses memory for each attribute, you will want to eliminate all unnecessary attributes on your worksheet.
- Save the file, close the worksheet window, and open the file again. This combines the smaller pieces of unused memory into a larger piece that 1-2-3/G can use.
- Limit the use of Group mode. Assigning format settings to all sheets requires a significant amount of virtual memory space.

windows on the desktop and returning to another OS/2 window. To quit 1-2-3/G, select Quit from the menu bar. You can also press ALT-F4 (Close Tool) or select Close from the desktop control menu for the same effect. When 1-2-3/G closes a window that has changed, it asks if you want to save the file in the window. You can choose Yes to update the file, No to abandon any unsaved changes, or Cancel to stop 1-2-3/G from closing its OS/2 window.

You can also close 1-2-3/G from the OS/2 Task Manager or Task List box. With OS/2 version 1.1, highlight 1-2-3/G in the Task Manager window, select Task from the menu bar, and select Close. With OS/2 version 1.2, highlight 1-2-3/G in the Task List window, and then select End Task command button. Unfortunately, when closing 1-2-3/G in this way, you don't have the opportunity to save changes made in the windows.

Once you quit 1-2-3/G, you cannot return to the same session. When you end a 1-2-3/G session, OS/2 erases the memory it used for 1-2-3/G and the data files.

You can also end a 1-2-3/G session by turning off your computer. While this works, it is a bad solution. Turning off the computer ends all OS/2 applications. You may have other OS/2 applications in which you want to save data. It's good to develop the habit of closing each OS/2 application before turning off the computer.

Managing Worksheet Data and Other File Options

SIX

Naming and Using Files
Filenames and File Types
The File Menu Options
Creating and Using Templates
Working with Multiple Files
External File Links
Using Desktops
Other Ways to Work with Files
Worksheet Customization Options
Displaying Current Status of Worksheet Options

The worksheets discussed so far have all been stored as part of your computer's random access memory (RAM). Information stored in RAM is instantly accessible—you can change, add to, and delete such information very quickly. However, continued storage of information in RAM depends on the power to your system being maintained without interruption. If you lose power to your computer even briefly everything stored in RAM will be permanently lost.

Clearly, you need a more permanent means of storage, and normally disk files are used for this. The 1-2-3/G program itself is a file. That is why it is permanently available on your disk. If the program is lost from memory, you can restore it by reloading it from your disk.

This chapter focuses on the data files that contain information on the applications you have created on 1-2-3/G. You will learn how to save, retrieve, and delete files. You will also learn to combine files, and to perform other file-management operations. While the focus is on worksheet files, many of the same commands are also used in graphs. After you learn how to manipulate files with the File menu within the worksheet tool menu, you will be able to perform the same operations with the File menu within the graph tool menu. You will also learn how to customize your worksheet files and how to store this information for use in subsequent sessions.

Naming and Using Files

1-2-3/G uses disk files for the permanent storage of all worksheet information. You can maintain these files on either hard or floppy disks. You can transfer them from one disk to another by saving the worksheets to several disks with the File Save command or by using operating system copy commands. Because 1-2-3/G runs under OS/2, you must follow the OS/2 file naming conventions.

Tip: If you are using OS/2's new High Performance File System (HPFS), you may want to limit your filenames to no more than 12 characters even though the new file system permits more. When you attempt to access these files with 1-2-3/G, you will only be able to see 12 characters of the filename on your screen.

Filenames and File Types

The 1-2-3/G program creates three types of data files: worksheet files, graph files, and print files. 1-2-3/G automatically appends an extension to each filename that allows you to distinguish one file type from another. In addition, 1-2-3/G has many files of its own that are part of the program and its various features.

OS/2 supports two different file allocation systems. With OS/2 1.1, your only choice is the File Allocation System (FAT) that is identical to the DOS file allocation system. With OS/2 1.2, you can use FAT or the HPFS. Your choice affects the way the disk is formatted and your options for filenames.

The FAT system imposes an 8-character limit on filenames, and a three-character limit on filename extensions. A period (.) separates the filename from the extension. The High Performance File System (HPFS) imposes a 254-character limit on filenames. With the HPFS, you can have several parts to a filename simply by separating each part with a period. This lets you have multiple extensions with a varying number of characters in each extension.

Some filenames that are acceptable to the operating system could be confusing. You can use KBD$, PRN, NUL, COM1, COM2, COM3, CLOCK$, LPT1, LPT2, LPT3, CON, SCREEN$, POINTER$, and MOUSE$ when followed by an extension, but you should avoid these names since they represent device names used by OS/2.

A filename and extension can contain any characters that you can generate with the keyboard except

```
" / \ [ ] : | < > + = ; & ,
```

1-2-3/G automatically changes lowercase characters in your filename entries to uppercase. Although you can include spaces in the filename, many operating system commands such as COPY and PRINT use spaces to separate parts of the operating system command. An underscore (_) is a better way to separate filenames into words. Examples of valid filenames are SALES, REGION_1, EMPLOYEE, and SALES_85.

If your operating system only accepts up to eight characters for a filename but you enter one longer than that, 1-2-3/G truncates the filename after the eighth character. SALES_REGION_1 thus becomes SALES_RE, which is indistinguishable from other filenames with the same first eight characters.

1-2-3/G distinguishes file types by the file extension. The file types in Table 6-1 list all of the extensions for data files and special file types used by 1-2-3/G.

You can also supply your own extension for any file type. If you supply the extension when you create a file, you must supply it every time you access that file. If you use 1-2-3/G's default extensions, the package supplies them for you when you retrieve or open a file. The only exception is the use of external file links in 1-2-3/G. In this situation, you must supply the filename extension and the special << >> symbols that enclose the filename.

File Type	Extension
Worksheet	.WG1 (Release 1-2-3/G)
	.WK3 (Release 3)
	.WK1 (Release 2)
	.WKS (Release 1A)
	.WR1 (Symphony Release 1.1)
Print	.PRN (Unencoded)
	.ENC (Encoded)
Graph	.GPH
Fonts	.LVF
Temporary	.TMP
Default Settings	.SET
Programs	.EXE
Program messages	.MSG
	.RI (Database driver only)
Help Window data	.HLP
Miscellaneous files	.DLL (Dynamic link libraries)
	.BCF (Identifies database drivers)
	.DBL (Drivers for different countries)
	.BMP (Bitmap picture file)
	.PML, .TML (Translation files)

Table 6-1. 1-2-3/G File Types

Subdirectories

On a hard disk system, you can create subdirectories for storing files. Subdirectories create logical rather than physical divisions on the hard disk, and make it easy to find related files within a particular directory. Setting up subdirectories is much like setting up a filing system to manage the large amount of paper information you probably receive. Just as you would not throw all this paper in one desk drawer and expect to find something easily, you don't want to place all your files on the hard disk randomly, but in organized subdirectories.

When you install 1-2-3/G, directories will be created for you automatically. Unless you override the default names, a directory named 123G will be added to your root or main directory; a subdirectory 123G\WORK will be added for storing worksheet files and graphs; and 123G\TEMPLATE will be added for storing worksheet templates or patterns used as the basis for new worksheets. 123G\BACKUP will be created for backup copies of worksheet files, and 123G\TEMP will be created to store temporary files.

Within a directory, each filename and extension combination must be unique. You can have two files named BUDGET in the same directory, as long as they have different extensions. You can use the same filename and extension more than once as long as the files are in different subdirectories. For example, you can have the filename BUDGET.WG1 in the subdirectory ACCT and in the subdirectory FIN. The contents of these files may be the same or different. Even if the files originally contain the same data, they are two separate physical files, and an update to one does not affect the other.

If you are using subdirectories, 1-2-3/G must know the drive and the path name in order to find a file. The drive designation is the drive letter followed by a colon; for example, A:, B:, or C:. The path name tells 1-2-3/G what directory the file is in. Higher level directories are always listed first. \SALES indicates that the file is in the higher level directory SALES, whereas \SALES\REGION\ONE indicates that the file is several levels down from the top directory, in a subdirectory called ONE. If you are not familiar with the ins and outs of subdirectories, review your operating system manual for more information on this subject.

The File Menu Options

You access commands that create and retrieve files through the File menu options. The pull-down menu shown here appears when you activate the File command from the worksheet tool:

Although this is 1-2-3/G's most comprehensive set of file options, other tools and utilities offer many of these same file selections. You will want to refer to the next sections when working with other tools as well as the worksheet. These sections cover the worksheet menu options in detail.

Saving a File to Disk

You must save to a disk file any worksheet model in RAM if you want it to be available in later 1-2-3/G sessions. Use the File Save command to place a copy of the current worksheet on your disk. You can use this command to save a new worksheet, and to save an updated, existing worksheet.

Unlike earlier character-based releases, 1-2-3/G assigns a name to your file from the time you first see it on the screen. Since multiple files can be shown on a 1-2-3/G desktop, this name is used to identify the file uniquely and allow you to move easily from one window to another. You can provide the name for a new file, or you can allow 1-2-3/G to name it. If 1-2-3/G provides the name, the filename is SHEET followed by the lowest unused number starting with SHEET.WG1 for 0. Initially, these files are empty and 1-2-3/G deletes them when you close the worksheet window or replace the window's contents with another file.

If only one tool (worksheet or graph) window is on the 1-2-3/G desktop when you invoke File Save, 1-2-3/G displays the filename that also appears in the window's title bar. You can accept the displayed filename, or enter a new name in response to 1-2-3/G's prompt, and press ENTER. You can also press F3 (Name) to list the existing files in the current directory. From the list box, highlight your choice and press ENTER or click your choice from the list.

If the file has been saved before, 1-2-3/G displays the following message box:

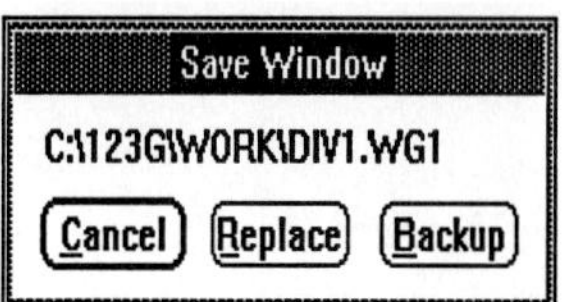

The command buttons in the box allow you to replace or back up the existing file, or cancel the File Save command. Select Replace if you want the current worksheet to replace the existing file. If you want to create a backup copy of the worksheet, select the Backup command button. When you back up a file, 1-2-3/G copies the existing version of the file to the backup directory before replacing it with the new file. If you decide not to save the file, select Cancel to return to Ready mode.

Tip: Backing up your worksheets prevents you from losing your work, since you can always return to the backup copy.

1-2-3/G automatically appends .WG1 to the filename. You can choose any file extension, but then you have to reenter this extension every time you access the file. For example, you can add a .WK3 extension if you want the file translated to a Release 3 format. You can directly save a 1-2-3/G worksheet file to a Release 2 format if the worksheet file has data in only one worksheet. If the worksheet file uses more than one worksheet, you must copy each sheet's data to a new worksheet or use the File Xtract command discussed later. 1-2-3/G cannot save files in a Release 1A (.WKS) or Symphony format (.WR1). When you save data to a Release 3 (.WK3) or Release 2 format (.WK1), 1-2-3/G warns you that you will lose data. Since many 1-2-3/G features are unavailable in Releases 2 and 3, the information for 1-2-3/G specific features is lost. 1-2-3/G temporarily stores the 1-2-3/G specific worksheet information in Release 3 files that you save, so if you use the Release 3 file during the current session, the 1-2-3/G specific information is still available. Entries longer than 240 characters are truncated in Release 2 files. The box "Transferring Files Between 1-2-3 Releases" presents more information on creating files for character-based releases.

You can save a file to a different drive or directory by specifying the drive and directory designation along with the filename—for example, C:\SALES\REGION\FILE1. If you need to add or delete characters in the current filename and path specification, use the LEFT ARROW and RIGHT ARROW keys to navigate. You can remove the filename and extension by pressing ESCAPE once. Pressing ESCAPE a second time removes the drive and path information as well. The filename and extension also disappear when you type a new entry.

Transferring Files Between 1-2-3 Releases

Although you can work with files from other 1-2-3 releases 1-2-3/G, there are a number of subtle points that affect your ability to read and write these files. Here are some considerations:

- If you retrieve a .WK3 or .WK1 file, save it as a .WG1 file if you no longer need it in earlier releases. This will improve performance.
- Range names in prior releases will display as cell addresses if they referenced a single cell.
- Functions that were created by add-in's display as @? in the 1-2-3/G sheet.
- Translate prior release macros if you plan to use them in 1-2-3/G. You will learn more about the translate procedure in Chapter 23.
- When you save a 1-2-3/G file to a Release 3 file, some of the attributes will not appear in Release 3 since they are not Release 3 options. However, these attributes will still be available in 1-2-3/G if you later retrieve the Release 3 file, since they are stored in an extended format record. If you save to a file type for another release, these extended settings are permanently lost.
- If you save a .WG1 file as a Release 3 file, you'll lose named print settings but not named graph settings.
- When you save a .WG1 file to a Release 3 file, only sheets for worksheets containing data are created.
- You cannot save a sealed or multiple-sheet .WG1 file as a .WK1 file.
- Labels longer than 240 characters are truncated when you save a 1-2-3/G file to a .WK1 file. Formulas longer than 240 characters are saved and continue to function unless you edit them—if you edit them they will be truncated after 240 characters.
- External file references are converted to labels in a .WK1 file.
- Functions that are part of 1-2-3/G but not prior releases are converted to the label @ISEMPTY(DJS).

Transferring Files Between 1-2-3 Releases (Continued)

- Undefined ranges are converted to ERR in .WK1 files.
- Characters than are not part of the LICS character set are lost when you write a 1-2-3/G worksheet as a .WK1 file.
- You may need to change the setting for Worksheet Global Default Release 2 if you see strange characters on the screen. 1-2-3/G supports both ASCII and LICS translation.

Saving Multiple Files

When you have more than one tool window open, the File Save command presents different options because you can save several files.

Whenever multiple tool (worksheet or graph) windows are on the 1-2-3/G desktop, 1-2-3/G displays [All Modified] in the File name text box when you invoke File Save. If you only want to save the active tool window using a different name, type the new filename. You can press TAB to choose different options for saving multiple tool window files. When you select Current file only, the File Save command saves only the current file using the same filename. When you select All files, 1-2-3/G saves all files in the desktop using the same names. When you select the File by file option button, 1-2-3/G displays the dialog box where you can enter the filename used to save the file as well as a description and password, as described in the section "Using Passwords and Descriptions with Files" later in this chapter. For each file that has already been saved, 1-2-3/G displays the Backup, Cancel, and Replace Command buttons. You can choose whether to replace or back up the existing file, or cancel the File Save command.

Translating Files to Other Formats

If you need to translate 1-2-3/G data into a format like dBASE, DIF, or Multiplan, save the file as in a prior release of 1-2-3. Then use the Translate utility in the previous release of 1-2-3 to translate the data into the necessary format.

Retrieving a File from Disk

The File Retrieve command lets you retrieve a file from your disk. When 1-2-3/G loads a worksheet file into a worksheet window, the information currently in worksheet window is erased. If you have not saved that information on disk, 1-2-3/G asks you whether to save the existing file first.

When you enter the File Retrieve command, 1-2-3/G displays the dialog box shown in Figure 6-1. This dialog box allows you to select the worksheet file that you want to retrieve. With a keyboard, use the TAB key to switch between the different parts of the dialog box. With a mouse, point to the dialog box item you want and then click. From the File name text box, you can enter the filename of the desired worksheet. You can also change the drive and directory information. The list box under the File name text box lists the worksheet files in the current directory by .. to indicate the parent directory and any subdirectory names in the current directory. If you highlight a filename in the list box, the Selected file information box displays the date and time the file was saved and its size. You can choose a file by pressing ENTER, or

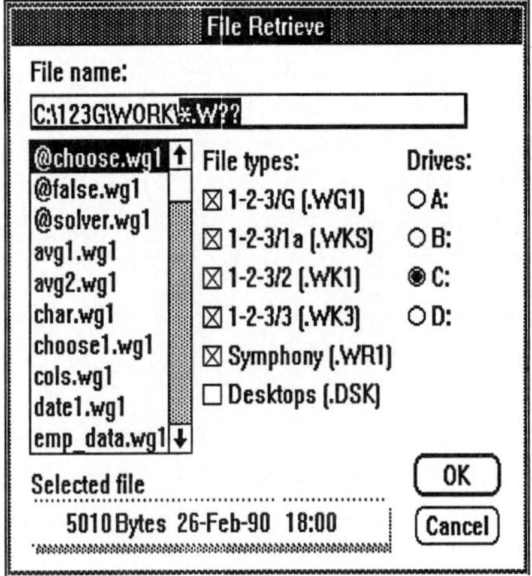

Figure 6-1. Dialog box for retrieving files

double-clicking the desired filename. You can select the types of files that appear in the desktop by choosing the appropriate check box under File types. When you pick a check box, the file list includes files of that type. You can quickly change the drive of the files that the file list box displays by selecting or clicking a valid drive option button. Once you select the drive, you can change the directory by choosing the subdirectory at the bottom of the files list. Once the filename and path are entered in the File name text box or highlighted in the file list box, select OK. With a mouse, you can double-click the file in the file list box to select the file and the OK command button.

If you select a worksheet file with an extension other than .WG1, 1-2-3/G translates the file to use with 1-2-3/G. This lets you use your worksheet files from other 1-2-3 releases and Symphony without using a conversion program. When 1-2-3/G retrieves a Release 2 file, it follows the setting of the Worksheet Global Default Release 2. This command has two options. The LICS option uses Lotus International Character Set to translate the characters in the worksheet file. The ASCII option is for Release 2 files created with the ASCII NO-LICS driver available with Release 2.01. You must select the ASCII option if you load a Release 2 file and special characters in the file don't appear correctly. When Release 3 retrieves a Release 1A or Symphony file, it loads the data into memory and names the worksheet file with the same name and a .WG1 file extension. You cannot save .WG1 files in a Release 1A or Symphony format.

Using Passwords and Descriptions with Files

When you save a file, you can add a password of up to 15 characters so that only people who can supply the password can access the file. Passwords offer a measure of protection for the worksheet. You can also add a file description of up to 80 characters when you save a file.

If you want to specify a password when saving a file, enter the filename, press the SPACEBAR, type a **p**, and then press ENTER.

1-2-3/G displays the same dialog box that you see when you select File by file as an option for the File Save command. 1-2-3/G prompts for the password, which can be up to 15 characters. The password is not displayed when you type it; instead, each character is represented by an asterisk in the menu bar.

Passwords are case-sensitive—you must correctly duplicate your use of upper- and lowercase when you access the file later. When you press ENTER, the New indicator changes to Verify and you are prompted to enter the password again for verification. If the passwords entered on both occasions are not an exact match, 1-2-3/G will display an error message.

The second prompt for the password also offers a way to stop the addition of the password: simply press ESCAPE. Once you have pressed ENTER for the final time after verification, the password is added to the disk, and you must use it every time you retrieve the file.

To access a file with a password, select the command you wish to use in working with the file, such as File Retrieve. 1-2-3/G then generates a password prompt.

1-2-3/G waits for you to enter the password, and lets you enter it twice, if needed. If in two tries you cannot reproduce the password *exactly* as it was originally entered, 1-2-3/G does not retrieve the file and displays an error message.

To change the password of a password-protected file, save the file again. When 1-2-3/G displays the filename followed by [pp], press END to move to the end of the filename or click the filename to remove the [pp], press SPACEBAR and then type **p.** 1-2-3/G prompts you once to verify the old password, and then to add and verify a new password.

To remove the password of a password-protected file, save the file again. When 1-2-3/G displays the filename followed by [pp], press END or click the filename to remove the [pp] and press ENTER. You must enter the password again before you can save the file without the password protection.

You follow similar steps to add a description to a file, but you don't need to enter it a second time for verification. If you want to specify a description, after entering the filename press SPACEBAR and type **d** before pressing ENTER. 1-2-3/G prompts for a description, which can be up to 80 characters. When you press ENTER, 1-2-3/G saves the file with the description.

Adding Existing Files to the Desktop

When you use one file at a time, you open the file with the File Retrieve command. When you execute another File Retrieve command or the Worksheet Erase command, the current file is erased from memory. To use multiple files in memory, you can use the File Open command to open a file without affecting the other files in memory.

When you use File Open, a dialog box appears to let you select the file you want to open. This dialog box is almost identical to the File Retrieve dialog box. Unlike the File Retrieve dialog box, the File Open dialog box includes a Tool names list box. This list box lets you select whether the opened window is a worksheet tool window containing worksheet data or a graph tool window containing a graph, as discussed in Part Four. When you change the highlighted tool, 1-2-3/G changes the file types in the list box from worksheet to graph files or vice versa. Once you enter the filename and path in the File name text box or highlight them in the file list box, select OK. With a mouse, you can double-click the file in the file list box to select the file and the OK command button.

When you open a worksheet file, 1-2-3/G adds another worksheet window to the desktop and retrieves the selected file into that worksheet window. When you are finished with the worksheet window, you can close it by pressing CTRL-F4 (Close Tool) or selecting Close from the Window Control menu. If the file has not been saved when you close the window, 1-2-3/G asks if you want to save the file.

Adding New Files to the Desktop

Besides adding existing files to the 1-2-3/G desktop, you can add new files to the desktop. This lets you create a new worksheet model while maintaining other windows on the desktop. The File New command opens a new window with a new file in the desktop.

After you select File New, 1-2-3/G displays a dialog box. The first text box is the name of the new file this command creates. You can accept 1-2-3/G's default name of SHEET plus the next unused sheet number or you can provide your own filename. If you provide the name yourself, you can give the file a meaningful name that will be easier to remember. The File New dialog box has a Tool names list box that lets you select whether the opened window is a worksheet tool window containing worksheet data or a graph tool window containing a graph. When you change the highlighted tool, 1-2-3/G changes the default filename from SHEET to GRAPH or vice versa. The Template name text box lets you select the name of the template that the new file uses. Template files are described later in this chapter, under "Creating and Using Templates." Once the dialog box is completed, select OK.

When you open a new worksheet file, 1-2-3/G adds another worksheet window to the desktop, in which it places a blank worksheet file with the name provided in the File New dialog box. You can switch between windows, save the contents of the window, or close the window, as you can when using other tool windows.

Changing the Current Directory

The File Directory command permits you to change the disk drive or directory for your current 1-2-3/G session. This is an easier way to use a different directory than providing the path for the File Open, File Retrieve, and File Save commands. When you select File Directory, 1-2-3/G displays the existing directory. You can press ENTER to accept it, or type a new directory or path name.

Erasing Files from the Disk

You should remove files that you no longer need from your hard disk. This will free up additional space that OS/2 can use for virtual memory. You can remove the files with OS/2's DEL command or you can use 1-2-3/G's File Erase command. The advantage of File Erase is that you remain in 1-2-3/G. You can use the menu to perform the task and you can retrieve a file and look at it to make sure that you want to delete it. The File Erase command lets you delete a worksheet or a desktop file.

Once you select the file, 1-2-3/G asks you to confirm your choice by selecting the OK command button. If you elect not to proceed, select the Cancel command button. If the worksheet file that you select is password protected, 1-2-3/G asks you for the password. You must correctly enter the password before this command can delete the file.

Determining What Files Are on Your Disk

As your list of worksheet models and other 1-2-3/G files grows longer, you may have trouble remembering all the files that you have on a disk. You can always use the OS/2 DIR command or the File Manager program to see a list of your files, but you can also use the File Admin Table command to list the files on a disk.

1-2-3/G's File Admin Table command creates a table in the worksheet containing a list of files and related information. When you select File Admin Table, you are presented with the dialog box shown in Figure 6-2. Underneath File type, you can select the types of files for which information will be listed. The first column of file types lists options that pertain to files. The second column of file types provides information about specific types of files.

If you select Active, the table includes all open worksheet files. If you select Links, the table includes all worksheet files linked by formulas to the current worksheet file. If you select Edit links, the table includes all worksheet files linked by the Edit Link command to the current worksheet file. If you select Connected drives, the table lists the connected hard- and floppy-disk drives installed in the computer. If you select Desktop windows, the table includes all open 1-2-3/G and Presentation Manager windows. You can also select the type of file to display by choosing Worksheet, Graph, Print, or Other.

If you choose Worksheet, the table includes worksheet files from all releases of 1-2-3/G and Symphony. If you want to limit the table to a specific release, edit the extension in the File name text box. If you select Graph, the table includes files with a .GPH extension. If you select Print, the table includes files with a .PRN extension. Other includes all the filenames in the current disk and directory selected.

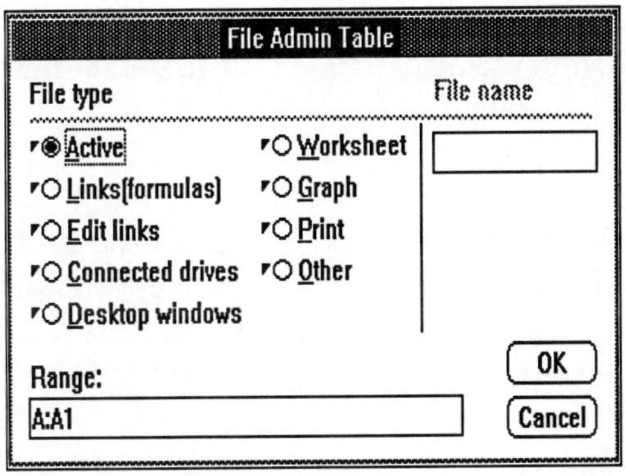

File Admin Table
File type
File name
Active
Links(formulas)
Edit links
Connected drives
Desktop windows
Worksheet
Graph
Print
Other
Range:
A:A1
OK
Cancel

Figure 6-2. File Admin Table dialog box

If you select Worksheet, Print, Graph, or Other, you can alter the File name text box. By editing the path name, directory, and filename indicator in this text box, you can determine which files 1-2-3/G includes in the table. The selected directory can include the ? and * wildcard characters that work just as they do in OS/2. The question mark represents any single character in the filename and the asterisk specifies that any characters are accepted from that point to the end of the filename.

Once you select the type of files you want to list, 1-2-3/G prompts for the location of the table. Either select the cell with the mouse or arrow pointer keys, or type the cell address or range in which you want to place the upper-left corner of the table. The table will use as many rows as necessary to list the files, and two to nine columns, depending upon the file type selected. The table writes over the worksheet's current contents, so be sure to select an area where the worksheet has plenty of available space. The information in the table depends on the file type selected. Figure 6-3 shows tables created with the File Admin Table command. You can select the column headings and date and time formats before or after performing the Table command.

Tip: When you create a table with File Admin Table, use an empty sheet for the table to ensure that the table won't overwrite any other data.

Combining Information from Two Files

The File Combine options allow you to bring information from other worksheet files into your current worksheet. With this capability you can produce budget consolidations, or build a new worksheet using components of several existing worksheet files.

The five Combine options are Copy, Add, Subtract, Multiply, and Divide. All five options depend on the location of the cell pointer in the current worksheet since the cell pointer is the first cell the command uses for combining files. The Combine Copy option was essential in earlier releases that did not support multiple-sheet files, or sheets referenced with external links. Although you can still use the File Combine Copy command for many applications, you will probably want to employ links and multiple-sheet files as you work with applications that use several types of data. The Add, Subtract, Multiply, and Divide options automatically perform arithmetic operations between the contents of the

1-2-3/G [69.4] Ready

File Edit Worksheet Range Copy... Move... Print Graph Data Utility Quit... Help

A:H16 +<<AVG1>>A:D15

TBL_LIST.WG1

A	A	B	C	D	E	F	G	H	I
1	Graph (*.GPH)	Date	Time	Size					
2	CHOOSE.GPH	01-Mar	10:29:06	0					
3	G3_A.GPH	26-Feb	16:47:14	4,972					
4	WORK\	08-Feb	16:38:42	<DIR>					
5									
6	Desktop	Horiz	Vertical			Min	Max	Window	Reservation
7	Windows	Posit	Position	Width	Height	Stat	Stat	Type	Status
8	SHEET.WG1	-0.06	-0.059	9.53	6.31	0	1	Worksheet	Reservation
9	SOLVER	0.044	0	4.44	3.02	0	0	Solver	N/A
10	G3_A.GPH	0.294	1.529	6.24	4.32	0	0	Graph	Reservation
11	1-2-3/G	-0.06	-0.059	9.53	7.18	0	1	Desktop	N/A
12	Screen	0	0	9.41	7.06	0	1	Screen	N/A
13									
14	Links								Formula in
15	(formulas)	Date	Time	Size					Column H
16	AVG1.WG1	11-Feb	20:03:16	2,763				249.75	+<<AVG1>>A:D15
17	AVG2.WG1	11-Feb	20:07:18	3,426				410.7188	+<<AVG2>>A:D15

Figure 6-3. Tables created with the File Admin Table command

current file and the external file being combined; you don't have to enter formulas. The file combinations are performed with the File Combine command, which displays the dialog box shown in Figure 6-4. From here, you can choose how the two files are combined, whether all or only a part of the incoming file is used, and the name of the incoming file.

Using the Copy Option to Copy to the Current Worksheet

The Copy option for the File Combine command allows you to replace the contents of current worksheet cells with the contents of cells in a file on disk. The replacement begins at the cell pointer's location in the current file, and the extent of the replacement depends on how many cells are copied from the worksheet file on disk. The Copy option lets you copy values, labels, and formulas from the file on disk.

You have two options for determining the extent of the replacement. First, you can bring in an entire file. This operation takes each nonblank cell in the incoming disk file, and replaces an appropriate number of

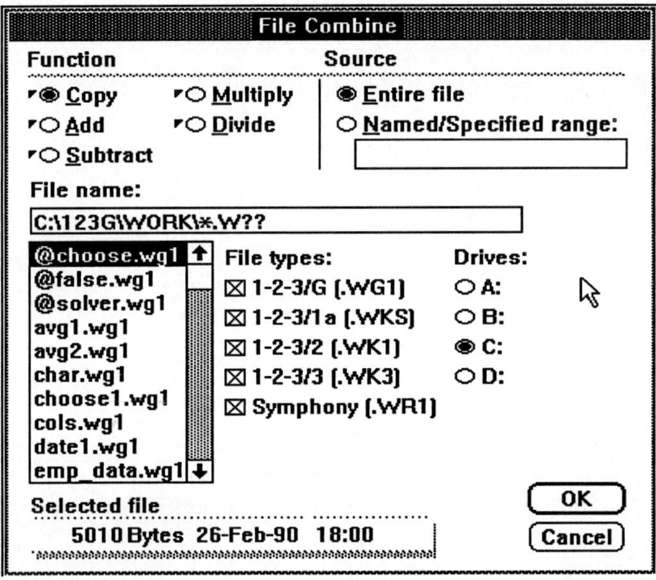

Figure 6-4. File Combine dialog box

cells in the current worksheet. The location of the replaced cells is determined by the location of the cell pointer at the time of the File Combine command, and by the contents of the incoming file. Displacement of cells in the current file matches the dimensions of the replacement data, with the base point being the cell pointer location.

Suppose you have a worksheet file named HEADING that contains 12 Month Projection in E1 and Jan through Dec in A3..L3. The months and title are named Months. Your current worksheet file is blank in B1..M3. Position your cell pointer in B1 and select File Combine. Select the Entire file option button under source. Under the File name text box and list box, type the filename **HEADINGS** or select HEADINGS.WG1 from the list. You can use the File types check boxes and the Drives option buttons to change the files that appear in the file list. The results look like Figure 6-5. The File Combine command overwrites the existing contents of cells starting at B1.

1-2-3/G (69.4) Ready

File Edit Worksheet Range Copy... Move... Print Graph Data Utility Quit... Help

A:B1

SALEPROD.WG1

A	A	B	C	D	E	F	G
1						12 Month Projection	
2							
3		JAN	FEB	MAR	APR	MAY	JUNE
4	Sales - Product A	1,300	1,442	1,599	1,773	1,966	1,995
5	Sales - Product B	500	700	980	1,372	1,921	1,950
6	Sales - Product C	850	859	867	876	885	898
7	Sales - Product D	1,120	1,159	1,200	1,242	1,285	1,304
8	Sales - Product E	3,500	3,833	4,197	4,595	5,032	5,107
9	Sales - Product F	1,200	1,500	1,875	2,344	2,930	2,974
10	Sales - Product G	2,550	3,137	3,858	4,745	5,837	5,925
11	**Total**	11,020	12,630	14,576	16,947	19,856	20,154
12							

Figure 6-5. Heading entries added with the File Combine command

Tip: Use the File Combine or Copy command if you only need to copy data once and will not need to update the values copied. If you want to data to be updated constantly, use a formula that contains external references.

Tip: If you are only combining part of the incoming file, name the ranges in the incoming file you are combining. Range names are easier to remember than the range addresses they represent.

Using the Mathematical Functions to Combine Worksheets

The other options for the File Combine command perform a mathematical function using the values in the current and the incoming worksheet files. The mathematical calculations begin at the cell pointer's location, and the extent of the mathematical file combination depends on how many cells are in the selected range or the entire worksheet file. Only numeric values are involved in the mathematical computation. Labels and formulas are ignored, and the label and formula entries in the current worksheet are retained for those cells. For formulas in the incoming worksheet, 1-2-3/G only uses the values of the formulas in the mathematical computation.

The four additional options let you add, subtract, multiply or divide. The Add option adds the values and numerical formula results of the incoming worksheet to the current worksheet. The Subtract option subtracts the values and numerical formula results of the incoming worksheet from the values in the current worksheet. The Multiply option multiplies the values and numerical formula results of the incoming worksheet by the values in the current worksheet. The Divide option divides the values and numerical formula results of the incoming worksheet by the values in the current worksheet.

Tip: If you have worksheet files for various divisions, you can perform a quick consolidation with File Combine Add.

Once you combine data in the worksheets, you should save it using a different name to protect your original data. As you look at the results in the combined sheet, notice that the resulting entries after the file combination are values, not formulas.

Saving Part of a Worksheet

The File Xtract command enables you to save part of a current worksheet to a new or existing file. A specified section of the worksheet is saved as a worksheet file, using the extension you provide to select the file format. Using this command you can construct new models from sections of an existing worksheet. You can also split large worksheet files into smaller worksheet files. The new file includes the selected worksheet data as well as the worksheet settings.

Worksheet sections are saved either as formulas or values. If you choose Formulas, 1-2-3/G saves formulas as they are entered, adjusting the cell addresses for the new position in the extracted file. When using the Formulas option, remember that 1-2-3/G adjusts all cell formulas as if they are all relative. Absolute and mixed cell references are adjusted in the new file location, although they remain absolute or mixed in the new worksheet file. When labels and values are extracted, the result is the same whether you select Formulas or Values, since labels and values do not reference other cells.

Extracting formulas that reference cells outside the extract range can lead to error. For instance, if you extract E1..H12, and E2 has a formula that refers to A1, the entry in A2 in the extracted file that represents the entry in E2 of the original file will refer to cell IS1 since the reference is adjusted for copying the formula from E2 to A2 as 1-2-3/G creates the extracted file. This cell therefore does not contain what you expect. Similar problems occur when you combine the extracted formulas with an existing worksheet using the Copy command: Some of the formulas will reference inappropriate cells in the current worksheet and thereby cause errors.

If you choose Values, the extracted worksheet contains values and labels of the current values of the selected cells. When you use the Values option, only calculated results and labels are retained in the new file. All formulas are replaced by the results of the formula calculations.

The procedure for using either option is to select File Xtract and choose either Formulas or Values. You can type a filename to use for the extracted worksheet cells. You can also press F3 (Name) to list the existing files in the current directory. Once the filename is entered, you can enter a file description and, if you select the Set password check box, you can enter a password. Once you have selected the filename, you must select the range or collection of cells to extract to the new worksheet. If you select the range before you enter the File Xtract command, 1-2-3/G includes the selected range in the Range(s) text box. When you select OK, 1-2-3/G creates a worksheet file containing the data you have selected. If you choose an existing filename for the extracted file, you must confirm your choice with Cancel, Replace, or Backup.

Adding Text Files to the Worksheet

The File Import command allows you to transfer to your worksheet the data from a word processing program or other package that generates standard ASCII text input. You must be sure that the word processor does not include special characters in the file. (Most word processors have an option for eliminating special characters from the text file.) 1-2-3/G creates a standard ASCII text file every time you use the Print File command.

1-2-3/G has two basic options for importing text data into a worksheet: Text and Numbers. These options determine how the data is placed in the worksheet. Use the Text option when you want to import the entire file as a range of labels. Use the Numbers option to import the ASCII file in a delimited format with each piece of data separated by commas.

When you import data as text, each line of the imported file becomes one long, left-justified label. You end up with a column of long labels. Once the data is imported, you can use Data Parse to split the labels into individual pieces.

The Numbers option is for importing delimited data files. If you use this option, characters enclosed in double quotation marks, as well as all numbers, are imported. Blanks and characters not in quotation marks are eliminated in the import process. The bottom of the OS/2 window in Figure 6-6 shows a delimited ASCII file. Each number in a line of the text file generates a numeric cell entry, and each quote-enclosed label creates a left-justified label cell. Entries from the same line of a text file produce entries in the same row of the worksheet, proceeding from left to right of the row with each new entry.

1-2-3/G imposes a size limit of 8192 lines on the imported file. The maximum number of characters in a line is 512. Since a label at the beginning requires one character, the real potential for import is 511 characters. When you use the Text import option, the entire entry is placed in one cell. With the Numbers option, every comma-delimited and quote-enclosed entry is placed in a separate cell.

Figure 6-6 shows two ASCII text files, although only the bottom file has its data delimited. You would need to use a different importing option for these two files. To import the first file, move the cell pointer to A1 and select File Import Text. Choose the ASCII.PRN file from the file list and select OK. Figure 6-7 shows the results in the bottom worksheet. You will notice from the address box that each entry is a long label with the entire line in the one label. For the second ASCII file, select File Import Numbers with the cell pointer on A1. The resulting worksheet is shown in the top of Figure 6-7 (sheet B). In this

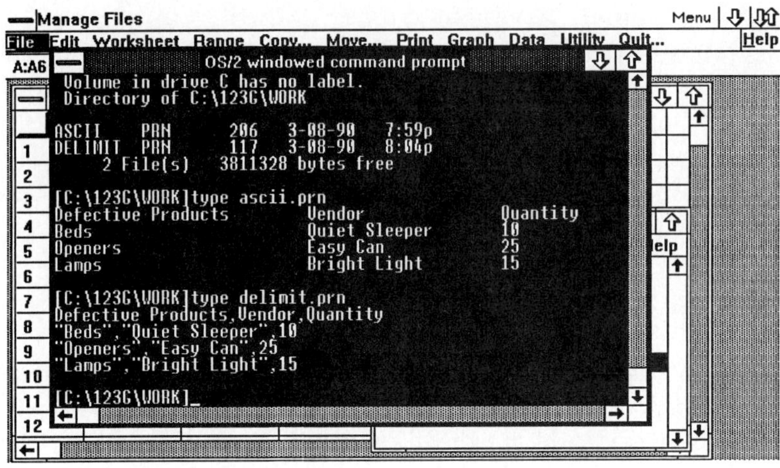

Figure 6-6. ASCII files

1-2-3/G (69.4) Ready

File Edit Worksheet Range Copy... Move... Print Graph Data Utility Quit... Help

A:A1 'Defective Products Vendor Quantity

SHEET.WG1

B	A	B	C	D	E	F
1						
2	Beds	Quiet Sleep	10			
3	Openers	Easy Can	25			
4	Lamps	Bright Light	15			
5						

A	A	B	C	D	E	F	G
1	Defective Products Vendor Quantity						
2	Beds Quiet Sleeper 10						
3	Openers Easy Can 25						
4	Lamps Bright Light 15						
5							

Figure 6-7. File Import with Text and with Numbers

instance, the text enclosed in quotes is imported while the text without quotes is omitted.

When you import text, 1-2-3/G uses the full IBM Multilingual Character Set (international code page 850) to decipher the characters. If the imported file uses special characters that don't translate properly, select the Country option button under File translation in the File Import Text or File Import Numbers dialog box to obtain the closest character match.

Sharing 1-2-3/G Files

When you use a network, more than one user may want to use a file concurrently. With OS/2, this situation may arise even without a network since you might use the file in one OS/2 window then try using it in another OS/2 window. A network and the OS/2 operating system handle file-sharing by assigning file reservations. A *file reservation* is a privilege that restricts file modifications to the one user holding the file reservation. Before someone else can modify the file, the first user must release the reservation. Then the next user can obtain the reservation and modify the file. Most of the time, by default, 1-2-3/G obtains the reservation automatically when you retrieve a file, and releases the reservation when you erase the worksheet or close the window containing the worksheet. If 1-2-3/G cannot get the reservation (because another user has it), 1-2-3/G asks if you want the file read-only. Selecting Yes retrieves the file and displays RO in the desktop title bar, indicating that you cannot save the file using the same filename. However, 1-2-3/G provides the File Admin Reservation command so that you can control obtaining and releasing a reservation.

When you select File Admin Reservation, the dialog box offers three choices. Get obtains a reservation for the active file if you do not have it. Release releases the file reservation so another network user or another OS/2 application can obtain it. Setting determines when 1-2-3/G gets a reservation. (Once you've chosen Setting, you must choose either Automatic or Manual.) The default setting of Automatic means that 1-2-3/G gets the file reservation when you load the file. The Manual option means that you only get the file reservation by selecting File Admin Reservation Get.

You will only notice file reservations when you cannot obtain one. If you try retrieving a file being used by a network user or another OS/2 application, 1-2-3/G will ask if you want to retrieve the file without the reservation. If you select No, the command to retrieve the file will be canceled. If you select Yes, 1-2-3/G loads the file with an RO (read-only) indicator in the window title bar. This means that you cannot modify the file and save it with the same name; however, 1-2-3/G will let you save the file with a different name. If you select File Admin Reservation Get and 1-2-3/G cannot obtain the file reservation, you'll see an error message. When you try using the file with a command like File Import or Print File, 1-2-3/G tells you that the file reservation is already taken.

Protecting Worksheets

A password limits access to a file by preventing unauthorized access. You may want to provide access yet prevent inadvertent damage to important model formulas and format settings. For example, if you spend several hours building an attractive model for another user, you may want to prevent the user from undoing your formatting changes. A file password does not offer this protection, since once users have access to a file they can make any changes to it. When a file is sealed however, the user cannot perform any command listed in the following list:

File Admin Reservation Setting
Graph Name Create
Graph Name Delete
Range Attributes Border
Range Attributes Color
Range Attributes Font
Range Attributes Precision
Range Format
Range Label
Range Name Create
Range Name Delete
Range Name Labels
Range Name Reset
Range Name Undefine
Range Protect
Range Unprotect
Range Zero Suppress
Worksheet Column
Worksheet Row
Worksheet Hide
Worksheet Global Attributes
Worksheet Global Format
Worksheet Global Column
Worksheet Global Row
Worksheet Global Zero Suppress
Worksheet Global Label
Worksheet Global Screen Attributes
Worksheet Global Protection
Worksheet Global Manual Recalc
Worksheet Global Group

Another type of seal lets you prevent the user from changing the file reservation setting, but lets the user make formatting changes to a worksheet.

To seal a worksheet, select File Admin Seal. Select File seal to disable the commands in this list. Select Reservation setting to prevent the user from changing the file reservation setting. After selecting File seal or Reservation seal, you must enter the password twice, just as you enter a file password twice. The password must follow the same rules as file protection passwords. The file is not sealed permanently until you save the worksheet file. When a file has the file or reservation sealed, the worksheet doesn't change but the commands that cannot be used are grayed. If you later need to make formatting changes, you must remove the seal with the File Admin Seal Disable seal command.

Creating and Using Templates

Templates are files that 1-2-3/G uses as a pattern for new worksheet files. You can use templates to change the default fonts your worksheet will use. When you create a new worksheet, 1-2-3/G retrieves the template file and uses it as the basis for the new worksheet. Any entries in the template file appear in all files that use the template file. You can use templates to select the default formatting that you want for each worksheet. You can also use a template as the basis for a group of worksheets that use the same entries. For example, you can create a template that has the months in A:B3..A:M3 so that every file that uses that template automatically has the months in the worksheet.

To create a template file, create the worksheet file that you want to use as a template. When you are planning a template, consider the formatting changes that you make most frequently and decide if you want to include them in every worksheet automatically. When you are ready to use the worksheet file as a template, save it to the template directory, which is C:\123G\TEMPLATE unless you change it. The filename of the template can be any name, but 1-2-3/G will choose it as the default template if you name it DEFAULT.

Once you have saved the template file, you are ready to use it. When you enter File New, you can select the template to be used in the template box. By default, 1-2-3/G uses the DEFAULT.WG1 template file, but you can select another template file by typing the filename or by pressing F3 (Name) and choosing one from the list. When you use the Worksheet Erase command, the new empty worksheet does not use the template. Initially the default WG1 template file that 1-2-3/G provides is set to create the same worksheet file you get when you select Worksheet Erase.

Working with Multiple Files

1-2-3/G lets you work with multiple files in memory at the same time. Chapter 2 described how you can move between the files rapidly by choosing the window that you want to use. You can use multiple worksheets in several 1-2-3/G commands such as Copy and Move. 1-2-3/G allows you to open up to 16 tool and utility windows at once. With multiple files, an *active* window is a window that 1-2-3/G has in its memory; the *current* window is the one that you are currently using.

Using Multiple Files in Commands

Most 1-2-3/G commands can use ranges from different files. Most commands can only use open files. For example, you must select an open file for the From or To ranges for the Copy, Range Transpose, and Range Values commands. For instance, assume that you want to copy to the current worksheet the values in the TOTAL range in a YEARLY worksheet file. When you select Range Values, 1-2-3/G initially chooses the current cell or selected range for the From range. You can type a new range such as **<<C:\123G\YEARLY.WG1>>TOTAL.** With a mouse, you can point to the worksheet you want to use and 1-2-3/G automatically supplies the <<C:\123G\YEARLY.WG1>>as part of the From range address. You can also use a range in another worksheet when defining the To range.

External File Links

You can establish links between the current worksheet and data stored in cells or ranges in open worksheet files or files on disk. You can use this feature to reference data in another file, and 1-2-3/G will update the link as the reference data changes. In earlier releases of 1-2-3, you needed to enter data in each worksheet that used the data. This meant that you had to check constantly that the data in each worksheet contained the most up-to-date values. With external file links, you can create links to external files, and 1-2-3/G updates their values every time you load a file or use the File Admin Links-Refresh command.

To refer to a value in another worksheet file, precede the cell address, range address, or range name by the filename surrounded by the file delimiter of double angle brackets (<< >>). If the file is a .WG1 file, you can omit the filename extension. If the file is in another directory, you should include the path information such as <<C:\123G\BUDGET>>.

1-2-3/G does not adjust filenames in external file links as you rename files. For example, if you enter **+<<SHEET>>A:A4** and then rename the SHEET worksheet file to NAMES, the external file link remains +<<SHEET>>A:A4 and returns a value of ERR since the file is no longer available.

1-2-3/G also supports a wildcard feature that allows you to access a specified range name in any open file. If you use ? as the file reference for a range name's source, 1-2-3/G searches for the range name in all open worksheet files and uses the range values it finds. You cannot include the ? wildcard with a cell address since 1-2-3/G does not accept a formula with this type of external file link.

A formula that computes the yearly total for a company with several divisions might look like this: +<<DIV1>>SALES + <<DIV2>>SALES+ <<DIV3>>SALES. Each division has its own worksheet file. The first worksheet of each file contains the summary information for the entire year. The summary worksheet for the entire company adds the different ranges for each of the division's summary worksheets. The formula uses range names rather than cell addresses so that 1-2-3/G can adjust the range names if the cells in the ranges are moved.

Refreshing File Links

To recalculate values from other files, use the File Admin Links-Refresh command. When you use this command, 1-2-3/G rechecks all formulas in your current worksheet that refer to values in other files, and automatically checks values from other files when the other worksheet files are open.

Moving External File Links

When you rename a file, 1-2-3/G doesn't adjust external file links to use the new filename. Instead, you must use the File Admin Move Links command to alter the filename in all external file links. When you enter this command, 1-2-3/G presents a dialog box like the one shown in Figure 6-8. Under Current source is a list of every worksheet file to which the active worksheet file has an external file link. You can select the file you want to change by typing the filename in the text box or selecting the filename from the list box. Under New source are all of the potential worksheet files to which you can move the link. 1-2-3/G lists all of the worksheet files in the current directory. As with the Current source, you can select a new file by typing the filename or selecting a name from the list. When you select OK, 1-2-3/G replaces the filename in every external file link formula that has the filename selected under Current source with the filename selected under New source. This does not change the cells or ranges the external file link uses— it only changes the filename.

Tip: If a file is linked to other files, include the path name. This way, the worksheet can find the values it needs even when another directory is current. If 1-2-3/G cannot find the file in the current directory, the formula containing the link to an external file returns ERR.

Tip: Use range names rather than cell addresses for external file links. 1-2-3/G does not adjust cell references if you move them, but if you use range names 1-2-3/G will automatically register if you move the linked cells in the external file.

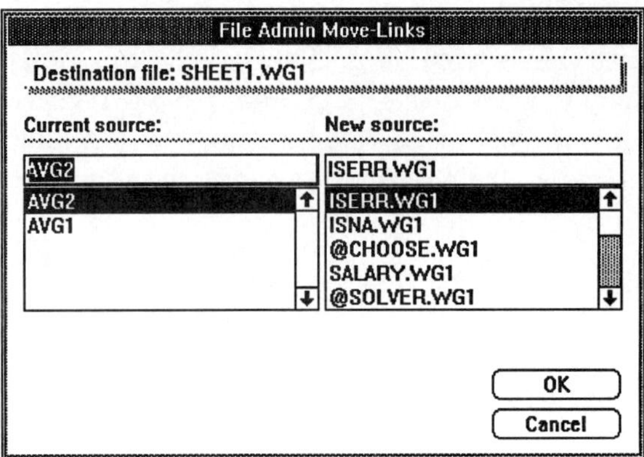

Figure 6-8. File Admin Move-Links dialog box

Using Desktops

Besides graph and worksheet data files, 1-2-3/G supports desktop files. A desktop file stores the position and size of every window on 1-2-3/G's desktop. With a desktop, instead of telling 1-2-3/G every worksheet file that you want to use, you can specify the desktop to use and 1-2-3/G will load all the desktop files onto the desktop and position every window in the same place.

When you have more than one file on the desktop, 1-2-3/G assumes that you want to save the desktop as well as the files. When you select File Save, 1-2-3/G has a check in the Save desktop check box to indicate that you will save the desktop as well as the worksheet files. The text box below contains the filename of the desktop. You can accept 1-2-3/G's default of DESK followed by the next unused number, or you can provide a more meaningful name. If you don't want to save the desktop, unselect the Save desktop check box. Once the desktop is saved, the desktop name appears next to 1-2-3/G in the title bar.

To retrieve a desktop, select the desktop filename in the File Retrieve or File Open dialog box. 1-2-3/G loads every file in the desktop and returns the window to its last location and size on the desktop. If the desktop is not empty when you retrieve or open a desktop, the desktop retrieved is merged with the current desktop's contents.

You can also use a worksheet file in more than one desktop. For example, if you use a worksheet in several desktops, each desktop remembers the worksheet position and the size of the window. Each desktop probably has different size and placement information for the same worksheet file. The desktop records the window size, placement and file in the window, but not the file contents, which are only saved with the file itself. In this way, you can use the same worksheet in several desktops and be certain that the files in every desktop window are using the most current information.

When you are finished with a desktop, the File Erase command lets you delete a desktop file. If you just want to remove the desktop file and all windows from the 1-2-3/G desktop, select File Utility New desktop. This command closes all open windows and any desktop files.

Tip: If you rename the directory containing desktops, the desktop files will no longer work since they continue to refer to files with the previous directory name.

Other Ways to Work with Files

1-2-3/G provides several commands and features besides those on the File menu that are useful for working with files. These other 1-2-3/G commands let you change how 1-2-3/G saves your files when you select File Save, select the windows 1-2-3-/G adds to the desktop when you load 1-2-3/G and permanently change the directory 1-2-3/G uses (rather than changing it temporarily with the File Directory command). You can also create a special worksheet file that 1-2-3/G loads every time you use 1-2-3/G. Once you have your models developed, you can protect your investment by protecting worksheet cells and by sealing the file. You can also change the default settings the worksheet files use for such features as recalculation and date and time formats. This offers additional worksheet protection beyond adding a password with the File Save command.

You make many of these changes by first selecting Utility User Settings from a worksheet tool menu or selecting User Settings from the desktop control menu. These changes are only in effect during the current 1-2-3/G session unless you select the Update command button.

The Update command button tells 1-2-3/G to store all of the default settings changes to the 123G.SET file. Since this affects all default settings, the changes you make in one default settings dialog box are saved when you select Update, regardless of which dialog box you select Update from. This also applies to the Update command button that is part of the Worksheet Global Default dialog box.

Changing How 1-2-3/G Saves Your Files

When you save a file with an existing name, you are accustomed to choosing between Cancel, Replace, and Backup. However, you can set 1-2-3/G to take a specific action instead of prompting you. This allows you to replace or back up files automatically. To change how 1-2-3/G saves your files, select Utility User Settings Preferences. Under Save options, select the appropriate option button. If you choose Backup, all files that you save are automatically backed up to the backup directory, which is C:\123G\BACKUP by default. If you choose Replace, all files that you save automatically replace the existing version on disk. If you choose Confirm, 1-2-3/G prompts you to select between Cancel, Replace, and Backup whenever you save a file.

Creating a Worksheet File that Loads Automatically

1-2-3/G can automatically load a specific worksheet file every time you boot. All you have to do is name the worksheet file AUTO123.WG1 and place it in the default working directory.

This feature enables you to create a worksheet that contains help information for your application, and that documents the names of files to retrieve for different applications.

Changing the Initial Startup Window

When you start 1-2-3/G, you see a worksheet window containing a new file. These are other options for starting with an existing file or restoring the desktop as is was when you last left 1-2-3/G. To select how 1-2-3/G sets up the desktop when you boot, select Utility User Settings

Startup from the worksheet tool menu or User Settings Startup from the desktop control menu. From the dialog box select the type of files you want to see when you start a 1-2-3/G session. Selecting New file, the default, starts 1-2-3/G with a new worksheet file in a worksheet window. Under Tool name, you can select whether the new window is a graph or worksheet tool window. Selecting Old file starts 1-2-3/G with a worksheet window containing the file that you select using the text box, list box, and Drives option buttons. Use this option if you usually use the same worksheet file when you first load 1-2-3/G. The Tool option lets you select whether the file that is opened is a graph file or a worksheet file. The third option, Restore, tells 1-2-3/G to save all of the windows and their contents to the desktop each time you leave 1-2-3/G. When you next load 1-2-3/G, it reads this information and opens the same windows with the same worksheet files. Finally, select the Update command button to have 1-2-3/G add your selection for the default startup window to its 123G.SET file.

Temporarily and Permanently Changing the Directories 1-2-3/G Uses

To change the disk drive or directory for file saving and retrieval for the current 1-2-3/G session, you can use the File Directory command. You can also change the directory 1-2-3/G uses for backups, templates, and temporary files. From the dialog box, which you access by selecting Utility User Settings Directory, you can change the directories 1-2-3/G uses. The working directory is the directory 1-2-3/G initially uses for File commands. The backup directory is where 1-2-3/G copies your files when you select Backup. The file template directory is the directory containing files that you can use for templates. The temporary directory is the directory where 1-2-3/G stores temporary files during a work session—such as the files 1-2-3/G creates to store your actions so you can use the Undo feature.

To change the directories 1-2-3/G uses, select Utility User Settings Directories, or select User Settings Directories from the desktop control menu. To change a directory, select the type of directory and type the new directory information. To make these changes part of every 1-2-3/G session, select the Update command button to have 1-2-3/G store these changes to 123G.SET, which stores your default settings.

Using Operating System Commands

Unlike prior DOS releases of 1-2-3, 1-2-3/G does not have a System command since OS/2 allows you to open additional windows and access the OS/2 system commands. Since each window or desktop is maintained separately, you can continue using 1-2-3/G as you open additional OS/2 windows. You will want to perform system commands to copy files, print files, and format disks.

To open an OS/2 window, select Start Programs from the OS/2 version 1.1 Task Manager window, or Group-Main from the OS/2 version 1.2 Task List window. From this list, you can open an OS/2 command prompt window that fills the screen or a smaller window. This presents an OS/2 command prompt that looks just like a DOS command prompt.

Worksheet Customization Options

1-2-3/G has several customization options that alter how you work with worksheets. These options include the international settings 1-2-3/G uses for dates, times and numbers, protecting worksheet cells, choosing how the worksheet is recalculated, and disabling Undo. You can alter these customization options to match how you are using the worksheet.

Protecting Worksheet Cells

A completed worksheet often represents hours or days of work in planning, formula entry, and testing. Once you have created a well-planned and tested worksheet application, you will want to protect it from accidental keystrokes or option selections that could overwrite formulas or other vital data. 1-2-3/G provides features that prevent this damage to important cells.

Tip: Watch your screen for information about the current protection status. Use Worksheet Status to see the global protection status for the current file. Look in the window title bar for PR to identify individual entries with a protected status.

1-2-3/G's protection features let you determine which cells are protected and which ones accept entries. You can also temporarily disable the protection mechanism without changing a cell's basic definition as a protected or unprotected cell. Finally, 1-2-3 provides a command that you can use with cell protection to restrict the cell pointer to a single input range on the worksheet.

Tip: You should group input entries on an input form on one sheet where possible. This approach saves the operator entry time, and also makes it easy for you to protect the cells in all the other sheets and leave the entry cells on the input sheet unprotected.

1-2-3/G's protection process requires that you first decide which worksheet cells you want to protect. All cells are protected by default. If you want to allow entries in certain cells, you can unprotect them with Range Unprotect. You can then turn on the worksheet's protection features, and these unprotected cells will still permit entries. You turn on protection with a Global option under the Worksheet menu.

Tip: The effect of Group mode applies to Range Protect and Range Unprotect. If Group mode is on, changes to the protection status of the current worksheet apply to all the sheets in the group.

Deciding What Cells to Protect

1-2-3/G establishes a default status of protected for every worksheet cell. However, you can make an entry anywhere on a new worksheet because the protection features of the package are initially turned off. If you turn on the worksheet protection, each cell is protected, and 1-2-3/G rejects any additional entries. For this reason, it's important to decide what cells should accept entries before turning on worksheet protection.

You can think of the worksheet protection feature as a fence placed around every cell. The fences don't protect the contents of cells in a new worksheet, since none of the fence gates are closed. The Worksheet Global Protection Enable command closes all the gates, thereby protecting the contents of the cells. Use Range Unprotect to tear down fences around cells that you don't want to protect. When the gates are closed with Worksheet Global Protection Enable, you will still be able to change these cells.

The Range Unprotect command strips cell protection from a range of one or many cells. To unprotect a range, select Range Unprotect and either point to the limiting cells or type the range or collection address. You can also select the cells to unprotect before you select Range Unprotect. If you change your mind, you can use the Range Protect command to restore protection for the cell. Unprotecting a cell highlights it on a monochrome display, or makes it green on a color display. You can use the Worksheet Global Screen Attributes command to change the color of the unprotected cells. Removing protection has no other effect on a cell unless the worksheet protection features (discussed in the next section) are turned on; a U appears in the window title bar when the cell pointer is on the unprotected cell.

Enabling Worksheet Protection

As noted, the Worksheet Global Protection Enable command "closes the gate" on every protected worksheet cell, ensuring that protected cells cannot be altered. It also places PR in the window title bar when the cell pointer is on a protected cell.

Unless you alter the default cell protection with Range Unprotect, you cannot make entries in any worksheet cell once protection is enabled. You can enter characters from the keyboard while pointing to one of these cells, but you'll see the error message indicating that the cell is protected when you attempt to finalize the entry. If you use the Range Unprotect command to remove protection from some of the cells, you can make entries in these cells.

You may need to turn Protection off after enabling it; if so, you can select Worksheet Global Protection Disable, allowing you to suspend worksheet file protection temporarily so you can change a formula, for example.

Tip: If you need more protection, use File Admin Seal. Anyone who knows how to enable worksheet protection also knows how to disable it. Use File Admin Seal to lock the current worksheet settings; a password is then required to unlock it.

Recalculating the Worksheet

In 1-2-3/G a new improved calculation method offers minimal, intelligent, background recalculation. In other words, 1-2-3/G no longer recalculates the entire worksheet every time you make a new entry in a worksheet cell—it only recalculates the formulas affected by the new entry and knows which cells are affected. Recalculation now takes place as a background activity, so that you can continue with your other worksheet tasks while 1-2-3/G is updating the worksheet formula results.

You should only perform some tasks—like printing, changing formulas to values with Range Values, or altering the layout of entries with Range Transpose—when the recalculation has completed. You can wait for the Calc indicator to disappear from the window title bar, or you can press F9 to have the calculations done in the foreground. The latter approach is better, since you won't be able to proceed until 1-2-3/G finishes, and all of your machine's resources will be dedicated to the recalculation effort. You access all of the recalculation options via the Worksheet Global Recalc command.

1-2-3/G's recalculation features have three different setting categories, all of which you select from the dialog box for the command. The left half of the dialog box determines the order in which the worksheet formulas are reevaluated, and the right half determines when the worksheet is recalculated. The Iterations option specifies how many times each formula that is part of a circular reference is reevaluated.

Timing of Recalculation

The default setting for a worksheet file is Automatic recalculation. This means that with any new number, changed number, or new formula, 1-2-3/G recalculates all worksheet formulas affected by your change. The time needed for this recalculation depends on the number and complexity of the worksheet formulas and the number of formulas affected by your change. Since 1-2-3/G recalculates in the background, you can continue with other tasks, although part of your computer's resources are dedicated to the recalculation. If you have a series of entries to make, and don't need instant recalculation of results for each individual entry, you can use Manual recalculation, so that 1-2-3/G doesn't do any recalculations until you request them. The Manual option is also desirable when you are running OS/2 applications and you don't want to slow the other OS/2 applications by having 1-2-3/G use part of the computer's processing power to recalculate your worksheet files.

To change when 1-2-3/G recalculates formulas, select Worksheet Global Manual Recalc and the Manual option button. When the Manual option is in force, 1-2-3/G doesn't recalculate the worksheet unless you turn Automatic back on, or press the F9 (Calc) key. The Manual option can speed up your data entry, since you can enter everything before using system resources to recalculate.

Order of Recalculation

The default setting for recalculation order is Natural. This means that 1-2-3/G examines each worksheet formula for dependencies on other formulas, and determines which formulas must be calculated first to provide the results needed by the formulas to be reevaluated next. Before the Natural recalculation order was introduced, the only options were Rowwise or Columnwise recalculation.

Rowwise recalculation evaluates all the formulas in row 1, then all the formulas in row 2, and so on. Unfortunately, if a formula in row 1 references a value in a row further down the worksheet, the earlier formula will reference a value from a prior recalculation. The same type of problem occurs with Columnwise recalculation, when early columns reference values further to the right that have not yet been recalculated so that your worksheet does not have the correct formula results. Natural recalculation order averts these problems.

If you want recalculation done in Rowwise or Columnwise order, rather than Natural order, you can enter Worksheet Global Manual Recalc Rowwise or Worksheet Global Manual Recalc Columnwise. You might want to use the other recalculation orders when you import data from another worksheet package. Changing the recalculation order is primarily done in macros that process large worksheets.

Iterations of Recalculation

One is the default setting for the number of iterations for a recalculation. This means that when 1-2-3/G finds a set of circular reference formulas, it evaluates the formulas in the circular reference once. 1-2-3/G also uses this number for Rowwise and Columnwise recalculation methods to tell 1-2-3/G how many times to recalculate each formula.

In calculations that involve a circular calculation pattern, one iteration is not sufficient. This is because each calculation depends on the result of some other calculation, with the final result referring back to one of the earlier calculations. In situations like this, 1-2-3/G cannot identify a clear recalculation sequence for the formulas. Multiple calculations are required so that each calculation approximates the correct answer a little more closely.

Increasing 1-2-3/G's iterative count can solve the problem with circular references. This increase means that 1-2-3/G recalculates these formulas more than once each time the worksheet is automatically calculated or the F9 (Calc) key is pressed.

The formulas in Figure 6-9 illustrate a circular reference requiring iteration for resolution. When the formulas are first entered, C3 displays as 0 and C2 displays as 200. Since these two formulas are dependent on each other, each recalculation refines the accuracy of the result. The results after several recalculations with the F9 (Calc) key indicate that slight changes continue to occur over the next several recalculations, until a final approximation is reached. 1-2-3/G can calculate this value the first time if the iteration count is set higher. You can change the number in the Iteration text box, but it must be between 1 and 50.

Displaying Current Status of Worksheet Options

When you go back to a worksheet you used earlier, you may not remember all the options you chose for it. Luckily, 1-2-3/G lets you

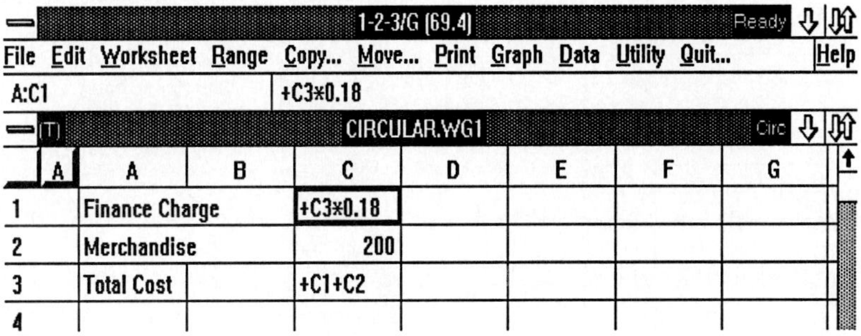

1-2-3/G [69.4] Ready

File Edit Worksheet Range Copy... Move... Print Graph Data Utility Quit... Help

A:C1 +C3*0.18

(T) CIRCULAR.WG1 Circ

A	A	B	C	D	E	F	G
1	Finance Charge		+C3*0.18				
2	Merchandise		200				
3	Total Cost		+C1+C2				
4							

Figure 6-9. Worksheet containing a circular cell reference

display the settings for all the worksheet options. Many of these settings are for the current worksheet, displaying the settings on one worksheet in a file may produce different results than looking at the worksheet settings in a different sheet in the same file.

Select Worksheet Status to display a Worksheet Status dialog box like the one shown in Figure 6-10. With this command, you can monitor the settings for the sheet format, display options, recalculation settings, colors, and other information. When you select the OK command button, 1-2-3/G returns you to the Ready mode.

Under Format, the Worksheet Status dialog box displays the defaults for the numeric format, font, label alignment, value alignment, and zero display. You select the default numeric format with Worksheet Global Format. You select the default font with Worksheet Global Attributes Font. You select the default label and value alignment with Worksheet Global Label. You pick the default zero display with Worksheet Global Zero Suppress.

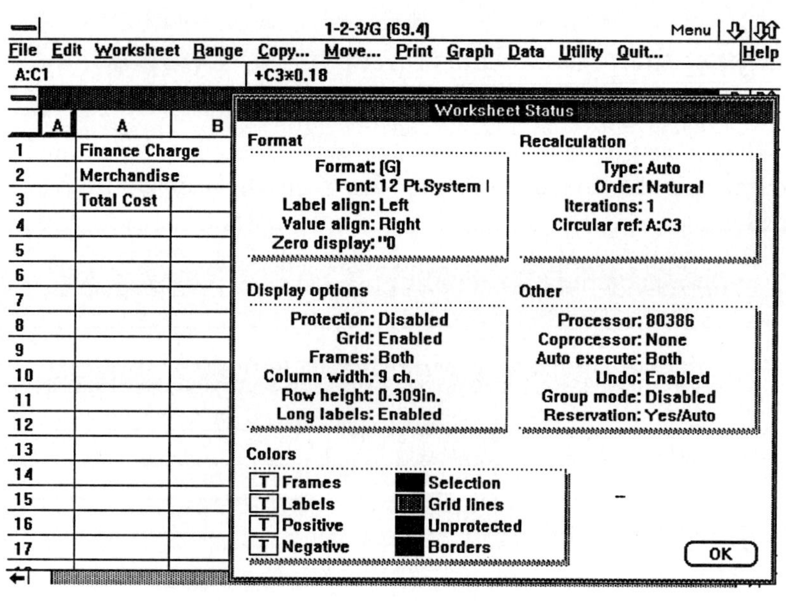

Figure 6-10. Worksheet Status dialog box

Under Recalculation, 1-2-3/G lists the settings of the Worksheet Global Manual Recalc command and the first cell in any circular reference. You can use the Worksheet Global Manual Recalc command to change the settings. The circular reference information just helps you find an unintentional circular reference.

Under Display options, 1-2-3/G displays whether the worksheet protection is enabled, grid lines are displayed, row and column borders are displayed, default column width, default row height, and whether long labels will borrow display space from adjacent cells. You change the worksheet protection status with the Worksheet Global Protection command.

Under Other, 1-2-3/G lists information that doesn't belong in the other boxes in the Worksheet Status dialog box, including the system processor (such as an 80386), the math coprocessor (which the computer uses to perform computations faster), whether 1-2-3/G will execute auto-execute macros from .WG1 files or other format files, whether Undo is enabled or disabled, whether Group mode is enabled or disabled, and when 1-2-3/G gets the reservation for a file.

The final section of the Worksheet Status dialog box lists the colors 1-2-3/G uses for different parts of the screens. You set all of these colors with the Worksheet Global Screen Attributes command.

International Format Options

The remaining customization options are in the dialog box shown when you select Utility User Settings International from the worksheet tool menu or User Settings International from the desktop control menu. This command allows you to customize the display for numeric punctuation, currency, date, and time. You can also select how 1-2-3/G measures distances, sorts labels, and the character page 1-2-3/G uses for File Import and Print File. The dialog box you use to make these customization options is shown in Figure 6-11.

Changing How 1-2-3/G Sorts Labels

1-2-3/G has three different methods of sorting labels. The different methods determine how 1-2-3/G handles labels containing numbers and the differences between lower- and uppercase. To use a different sorting

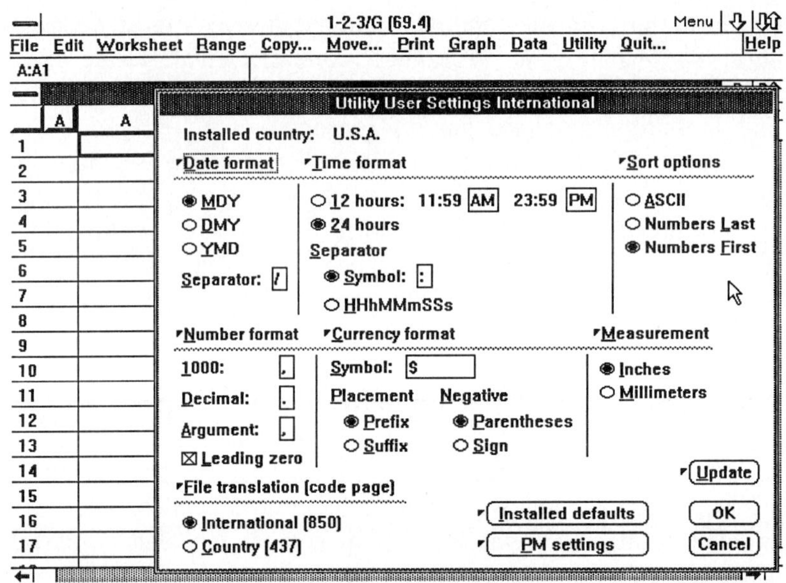

Figure 6-11. Utility User Settings International

method select ASCII, Numbers Last, or Numbers First under Sort options.

If you select ASCII, the labels in the sort range are sorted according to their ASCII values. For example, the label Smith has an ASCII values of 83, 109, 105, 116, and 104. With ASCII values, spaces and symbols have the lowest numbers, then the digits 0 through 9, then uppercase letters, and finally lowercase letters. This sort order means that the case of the entry can determine its position in the sorted list.

The two other options sort upper- and lowercase entries the same way. If you select Numbers Last, the labels are sorted in alphabetical order (regardless of case) and with numbers sorted after letters. If you select Numbers First, the labels are sorted in alphabetical order (regardless of case) and with numbers sorted before letters. The sort order also depends on the country selected, since countries alphabetize their letters in different ways.

Selecting Punctuation Characters

The numeric format indicators you can control are the decimal point, the thousands separator for numbers, and the argument separator in functions and macros. The default decimal point separator is a period, but you can change it to a comma as long as the thousands separator is not a comma. The default thousands separator is a comma, and you can change it to a period, apostrophe, or a space. The argument separator is initially set as a comma; you can change it to a period or a semicolon. The argument separator cannot be the same character as the decimal point separator. Like all options in the dialog box, the number formats are easy to change. Select Number format and either 1000, Decimal, or Argument, and type the character that you want to use. You can also click 1000, Decimal, or Argument with a mouse to select the option. You can also select or deselect the Leading zero check box to choose whether 1-2-3/G displays a zero in front of the decimal point—as in 0.5—or omits this leading zero—as in .5.

Tip: If you plan to use 1-2-3/G with different country settings, use the semicolon as the separator since a semicolon works as a separator regardless of the argument separator chosen.

Selecting Currency Display

Currency format in the dialog box allows you to choose the currency symbol, where the symbol is placed, and how negative values appear. By selecting Currency format and Symbol, you can type a currency symbol of up to five characters that you want 1-2-3/G to use. You can use any Lotus Character Set (see Appendix E) character for a currency symbol. Some of these require that you use the ALT-F1 (Compose) key followed by the character's compose sequence. Some of the most common currency symbols are £ for Pounds (L=,) and ¥ for Yen (Y=.).

You can change the position of the currency symbol by selecting the Prefix or Suffix option button below Placement. As you would expect, Prefix places the currency symbol before the value and Suffix places the currency symbol after the value.

You can also determine how negative numbers appear when formatted with the Currency or Comma format. 1-2-3/G has two options. You can display negative numbers enclosed in parentheses by selecting the Parentheses option button under Negative (the default). You can display negative numbers with a preceding minus sign by selecting the Sign option button under Negative.

Setting How 1-2-3/G Measures Distances

For some commands like column width, row height, or print margins, you can tell 1-2-3/G the absolute distance you want to use. This distance is measured in the English or metric system. By default, 1-2-3/G uses inches, the English system, to measure distances. If you are more accustomed to using the metric system, select the Millimeters option button under Measurements. 1-2-3/G will change all measurements to the current selected measurement unit. Also, prompts that expect a distance such as column widths and row heights will include inches or millimeters to let you know the measurement system being used.

Selecting the Character Set

When you import text and print to a text file, 1-2-3/G uses the IBM Multilingual Character Set (international code page 850) to convert the characters from the import file or to the text file. A code page tells 1-2-3/G (or any other program that uses multiple code pages) the character that each ASCII code represents. If you want to use code page 437 instead, select the Country option button under File translation. You should only make this change if you are importing or exporting files and the characters look incorrect.

Selecting a Group of Settings

Besides selecting a group of settings when you select a country in 1-2-3/G's install program, you can select a group of settings with the Presentation Manager. To do so, activate the OS/2 Control Panel program. With OS/2 version 1.1, select Preferences from the menu bar and then select Country. With OS/2 version 1.2, select Options from the menu bar and then select Country. You should see an OS/2 dialog box that you can use to select a country from the list of settings.

When in 1-2-3/G, you can tell 1-2-3/G to use the settings made with the OS/2 Control Panel program by selecting the PM settings option button. This changes the date, time, number, and currency format options. Using the country selected with the Presentation Manager does not change the sort options, measurement, and File translation code page. You can return to the settings assigned to the country chosen with the 1-2-3/G Install program by choosing the Installed defaults command button. This returns the settings in the Utility User Settings International dialog box to the settings that belong to the chosen country listed at the top of the dialog box.

Update

Any changes you make with the Utility User Settings or Worksheet Global Default commands are in effect only for the current session. The next time you load 1-2-3/G, the original worksheet global default settings will be in effect. To make your changes permanent, select the Update command button from any Utility User Settings or Worksheet Global Default dialog box. This will make your changes the new global default values, and they will be in effect the next time you load 1-2-3/G into memory.

Changing the Worksheet Appearance

SEVEN

This chapter describes the features that 1-2-3/G provides for altering the appearance of the worksheet. You will learn how to make changes to the whole worksheet or to a range of cells. You will learn how to work with a group of sheets from a file to apply changes to one sheet and have it affect the other sheets in the group. You will explore the various menu options for making changes to a worksheet. Next, you will learn how to limit changes to a smaller area as you apply the change to a range. The last section of the chapter discusses the specific format options that 1-2-3/G provides in greater detail.

Global, Range, and Group Changes

There are numerous commands that affect the appearance of the worksheet. Most can be applied either globally or to a specific range or collection of cells. If you combine Group mode with Worksheet or Range commands, your options expand further. Although you must make some global changes through the Utility User Settings command, you can make most with Worksheet Global. Normally, you can find the same options on a more limited basis in the pull-down menu for the Range command.

As an example, contrast the various ways to change the format of cells. The Worksheet Global Format command changes the appearance of an entire sheet from the global setting of General to another display format. If Group mode is on, every sheet in the group has its global format altered. Figures 7-1 and 7-2 show the impact of a global format change with and without Group mode on for sheets A through C.

The Range Format command changes the appearance of just the cells within a specified range. Again, the range affected is in the current sheet, or, with Group mode on, the same range in all sheets included in the Group range. If you make the changes in Figure 7-1 and 7-2 with a Range command rather than a global format change, the results are identical. Without Group mode on, formatting the range in sheet A leaves sheets B and C unaffected. The same change with Group mode on for sheets A through C also applies to sheets B and C.

A range format option has priority over a Worksheet Format option. This enables you to select a Worksheet option that matches your needs for most of the worksheet cells, and still change the appearance of individual cells. In Figure 7-3, the Worksheet Global Format command has set the overall format to Currency, and then Range Format has changed C3..C5 to Percent format. Changing the global format again would change every numeric worksheet cell except C3..C5, because a range format instruction was applied to them.

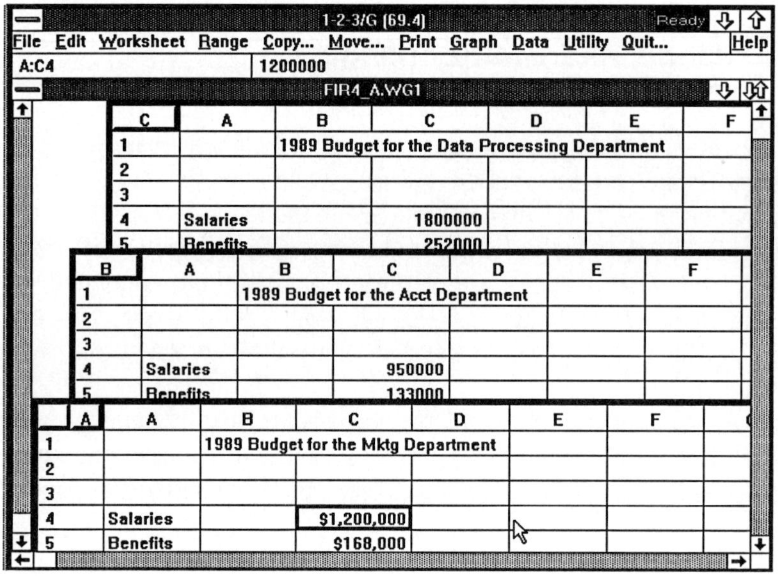

1-2-3/G [69.4] Ready
File Edit Worksheet Range Copy... Move... Print Graph Data Utility Quit... Help
A:C4 1200000
FIR4_A.WG1

C	A	B	C	D	E	F
1		1989 Budget for the Data Processing Department				
2						
3						
4	Salaries		1800000			
5	Benefits		252000			

B	A	B	C	D	E	F
1		1989 Budget for the Acct Department				
2						
3						
4	Salaries		950000			
5	Benefits		133000			

A	A	B	C	D	E	F
1		1989 Budget for the Mktg Department				
2						
3						
4	Salaries		$1,200,000			
5	Benefits		$168,000			

Figure 7-1. Global format change with Group mode off

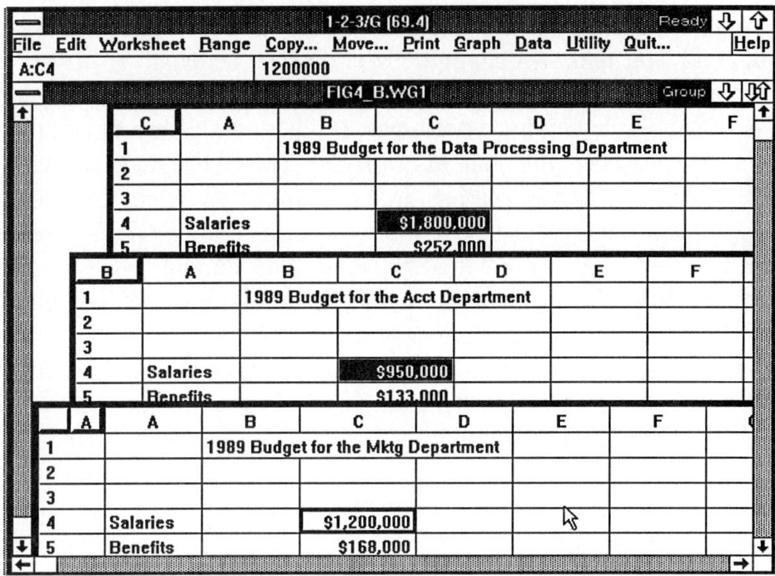

Figure 7-2. Global format change with Group mode on

1-2-3/G (69.4) Ready

File Edit Worksheet Range Copy... Move... Print Graph Data Utility Quit... Help

A:C3 0.1

(P1) FIG4_C.WG1

A	A	B	C	D	E	F	G
1							
2							
3	Growth Product A		10.0%				
4	Growth Product B		15.0%				
5	Growth Product C		12.0%				
6							
7			1989	1990	1991	1992	1993
8	Sales Product A		$123,560	$135,916	$135,916	$135,916	$135,916
9	Sales Product B		$56,700	$65,205	$65,205	$65,205	$65,205
10	Sales Product C		$95,600	$107,072	$107,072	$107,072	$107,072

Figure 7-3. Combining global and range formats

Before changing your worksheet, you should always determine the portion of your file that will be affected by the change. Then select the command that makes a change of the desired scope.

You can enable the Group mode by selecting Worksheet Global Group Enable. If you have not already selected a range to be affected by Group commands, you can also display the Worksheet Global Group dialog box by pressing SHIFT-F7 (Group). Once you select Enable, 1-2-3/G prompts you for the range containing at least one cell in each worksheet that you want to include in the group. You cannot select a collection address. Once Group mode is enabled, a Group mode indicator appears in the window title bar. When you make a formatting change to any of the worksheets in the group, the change applies to all worksheets in the group. All worksheets in the group are affected if you use any of the Range or Worksheet commands. Most other 1-2-3/G commands that use a range, such as Copy and Move, also use every sheet in the group when you select one sheet within the group.

You can also retroactively apply formatting changes from one sheet to the other sheets in the group. When you select Worksheet Global Group or press SHIFT-F7 (Group) and select Copy, 1-2-3/G applies the selected formats in the current sheet to every sheet in the group. When you are finished with the Group mode, you can select Worksheet Global Group Disable or press SHIFT-F7 (Group). After Group mode is disabled, 1-2-3/G remembers the sheets that are in the group. When you later select Worksheet Global Group Enable, 1-2-3/G displays the last group you selected. If you press SHIFT-F7 (Group), 1-2-3/G automatically reenables Group mode using the same range you selected last time. Every time you press SHIFT-F7 (Group), 1-2-3/G alternates between enabling and disabling Group mode. If you want to change the range of sheets used in the Group mode, you must use the Worksheet Global Group command.

In addition, Group mode moves you from sheet to sheet, keeping the cell pointer on the same column and row. In other words, if you press CTRL-PGUP from cell A3 on sheet A, you will be in cell A3 on sheet B. Without Group mode, CTRL-PGUP would have placed you in the cell that was active the last time you used sheet B.

If you have several sheets in the window at once, notice that the current cell appears with the usual cell pointer highlight. In the other sheets in the group, the cells with the same row and column address are highlighted, as in Figure 7-2. When you select a command that affects the same range in every sheet in the group, as you select the range in

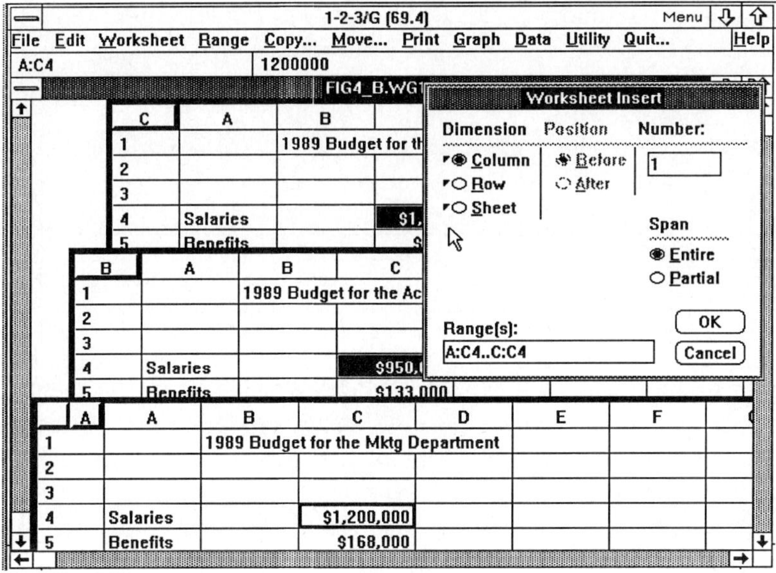

Figure 7-4. Worksheet Insert dialog box

the current worksheet, 1-2-3/G automatically selects the same range in every sheet in the group, as in Figure 7-4. The exception to this is made if you exclude sheets in the range as you select the range.

Worksheet Changes

1-2-3/G has several commands that you can use to change the appearance of the worksheet. You can add and delete columns, rows, and worksheets. You can even lock the titles or descriptive labels at the side or top of your screen—this enables to look at data in remote parts of the worksheet and still have these labels in view. You can split the worksheet window vertically or horizontally and use each section as a window to view a different part of the worksheet. In addition, you can display multiple sheets of the same worksheet file in one window. You can create a map of the worksheet to identify cells that contain formulas, values, and labels. You access all the Worksheet commands through this Worksheet pull-down menu:

You can activate this menu by clicking Worksheet in the menu bar or activating the menu with / or F10 (Menu) and pressing ENTER while the Worksheet command is highlighted. You can also simply type **W**.

This chapter discusses the Worksheet menu options that are found under Insert, Delete, Column, Row, Window, Titles, Hide, and Global on the Worksheet pull-down menu.

If you've made many mistakes and wish to eliminate all of the entries on your worksheet, or if you have saved the worksheet file and are ready to work on a new application, you can use the Worksheet Erase command to remove the worksheet file from the worksheet window. The empty worksheet file that is put in its place does not use the file template described in Chapter 6. When you select Worksheet Erase 1-2-3/G presents the following screen:

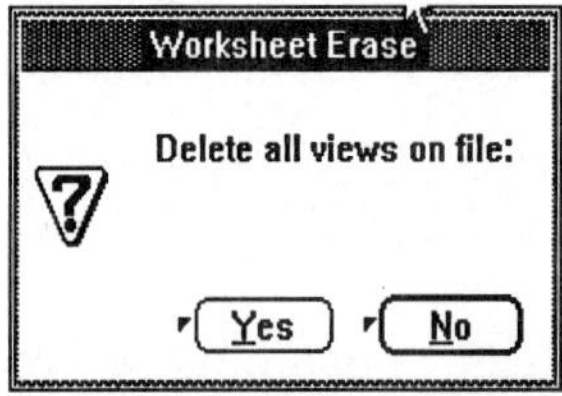

Notice that the cell pointer is initially positioned over the No option on the confirmation screen. This prevents you from losing your worksheet files if you accidentally press ENTER. You must confirm your selection or abandon the operation. You can also remove a worksheet from the 1-2-3/G desktop by closing the worksheet window. When you close a worksheet window, 1-2-3/G asks if you want to save the file if it contains unsaved changes. The Worksheet Erase command does not have this option. A similar command, Range Erase, clears a range on one or more worksheets; it is covered later in the chapter with the other Range commands.

Tip: ALT-BACKSPACE (Undo) is your only hope for reversing the effect of Worksheet Erase. This will only work if your Undo feature is enabled at the time of the erase operation. In other words, once you have erased a worksheet, there is no way to bring the contents of memory back without Undo, unless you have saved a copy of the worksheets on disk.

Undoing Worksheet Changes

1-2-3/G provides a powerful Undo feature that can return a worksheet to its former status. When Undo is enabled, each time you select Edit Undo or press ALT-BACKSPACE (Undo), 1-2-3/G will reverse (undo) the last entry or command taken. Repeatedly pressing ALT-BACKSPACE can undo the effects of up to 20 commands or entries. Although many spreadsheet packages now provide an undo feature to disable single commands, the ability to back out of a series of actions makes 1-2-3/G's undo feature the most sophisticated undo feature offered in any package. Pressing ALT-BACKSPACE (Undo) when Undo is disabled has no effect (Undo will be grayed in the Edit menu).

You can use Undo to eliminate format changes, worksheet insertions and deletions, sorting, the effects of macros, and most other changes to the worksheet. You can't undo external activities like printing or saving a file with Undo.

To enable Undo, use Worksheet Global Default Set Undo Enable. To disable Undo, use Worksheet Global Default Set Undo Disable. Undo was covered in Chapter 5.

Enabling Undo increases the amount of memory required for 1-2-3/G. The exact memory requirements are determined by the amount of memory 1-2-3/G must use to store the effect of the commands. For example, undoing a cell format requires a small amount of additional memory, whereas undoing a sort of a large database can require extensive storage space.

Insert Commands to Add Rows, Columns, or Sheets

You can use the Worksheet Insert command to add blank rows, columns, or sheets to a worksheet. The maximum columns and sheets are 256 and the maximum rows are 8192.

Adding rows and columns is different than adding sheets. You add new rows above the current row, and you add new columns to the left of the current column. You can add new sheets before or after the current sheet.

Inserting is a little like cutting rows, columns, and sheets from the end of the worksheet and pasting them back at another location. Since the full complement of rows, columns, and sheets are in a worksheet from the beginning, the insertions cannot enlarge the size of the worksheet.

With 1-2-3/G, you can insert a partial row, column, or sheet. If you select the Partial check box under Span in the Worksheet Insert dialog box, you can supply a range that affects the amount of the insertion. If you select Entire, an entire row, column, or sheet is inserted.

You can insert rows and columns to add a heading for a report, or to include new or unexpected information. Adding blank rows and columns can also make your worksheet more readable. You can add sheets to restructure your entire worksheet. For example, you might choose to use a sheet for another product line or department. You can also store tables and macros on separate sheets. Since you can add a sheet at any time, your additions do not disrupt an existing model design.

When you use the Worksheet Insert command, 1-2-3/G assumes that you want to add rows and columns at the cell pointer location. However, you can change where the insertion occurs. You can add new sheets before or after the current sheet.

Inserting Columns and Rows

When you insert entire columns and rows, you needn't make a second menu choice to indicate the position of the new row or column. Position your cell pointer in the *column to the right* of or in the *row below* the insertion. 1-2-3/G always inserts columns to the left of the selected range, and rows above the selected range. After you select Worksheet Insert, 1-2-3/G displays the dialog box shown in Figure 7-4. You can insert columns, rows, or sheets by clicking the appropriate option or typing the underlined letter.

Once you select Column or Row, 1-2-3/G prompts for number of columns or rows to add. There are two ways to select the number of columns or rows. One method is to select a range containing the number of columns or rows you want to add. As with other commands that use a range, you can select a range before entering the Worksheet Insert command and 1-2-3/G will supply the range in the Range(s) text box. If you don't select a range before entering the Worksheet Insert command, the range initially consists of the cell pointer's location. Selecting the OK command button at this point adds one column or row. You can change the first cell of this range by pressing ESCAPE or BACKSPACE with the keyboard or clicking the starting cell. Once the starting position is selected, type a period and drag the cell pointer to the range's opposite corner with the arrow keys or the mouse. You can expand the range across columns or down rows, covering the number of rows or columns you wish to insert. The number of columns or rows 1-2-3/G adds is determined by the number of columns or rows in the selected range.

The other way to select the number of columns or rows to add involves pressing TAB or clicking the text box under Number, and typing the number of columns or rows to be added. This text box initially lists the number of columns, rows, or sheets (depending on the option button selected under Dimension) in the selected range. You can supply a different number to change the number of columns, rows, or sheets 1-2-3/G will add with this command.

When you insert columns, rows and sheets, 1-2-3/G adjusts the cell formulas to refer to the moved cells. For example, if C1 contains the formula +A1+B1 and you insert a column between columns A and B, the formula in D1 becomes +A1+C1. When you insert rows, columns, or sheets in the middle of a range, the range is automatically expanded. This applies to range names that have been assigned as well as to ranges used in formulas. For example, Figure 7-5 shows an @SUM formula for departmental expenses. When two additional rows are inserted in the range, the formula is automatically adjusted to include two extra cells, as shown in Figure 7-6. If entries are made in these rows, a new total will display, as shown in Figure 7-7.

Inserting Sheets

Each new worksheet file automatically provides sheets A through IV. Although you cannot expand beyond these 256 sheets, you can move blank sheets from the end of the stack to a location in the middle of the stack. This capability is useful if you are creating new sheets in a specific order and realize that you forgot to enter one. Rather than adding the new sheet at the end of the existing stack, you can add it at a desired location with the Worksheet Insert command.

1-2-3/G (69.4) Ready

File Edit Worksheet Range Copy... Move... Print Graph Data Utility Quit... Help

A:D15 @SUM(D5..D14)

(C0) FIG_AA.WG1

A	A	B	C	D	E	F	G
1							
2							
3		Expenses - Jan 89					
4				JAN			
5	Salaries			$8,000			
6	Building Operations			1,100			
7	Travel			850			
8	Supplies			500			
9	Depreciation			1,200			
10	Equipment Maintenance			750			
11	Shipping Expense			400			
12	Data Processing Costs			2,100			
13	Printing & Duplicating			640			
14	Other			1,030			
15	Total Expenses			$16,570			
16							
17							

Figure 7-5. Worksheet computing department expense

1-2-3/G (69.4) Ready

File Edit Worksheet Range Copy... Move... Print Graph Data Utility Quit... Help

A:D17 @SUM(D5..D16)

(C0) FIG_AA.WG1

A	A	B	C	D	E	F	G
1							
2							
3		Expenses - Jan 91					
4				JAN			
5	Salaries			$8,000			
6	Building Operations			1,100			
7	Travel			850			
8	Supplies			500			
9							
10							
11	Depreciation			1,200			
12	Equipment Maintenance			750			
13	Shipping Expense			400			
14	Data Processing Costs			2,100			
15	Printing & Duplicating			640			
16	Other			1,030			
17	Total Expenses			$16,570			

Figure 7-6. Worksheet after adding two rows

A	A	B	C	D	E	F	G
1							
2							
3		Expenses - Jan 91					
4				JAN			
5	Salaries			$8,000			
6	Building Operations			1,100			
7	Travel			850			
8	Supplies			500			
9	Postage			200			
10	Cleaning Supplies			300			
11	Depreciation			1,200			
12	Equipment Maintenance			750			
13	Shipping Expense			400			
14	Data Processing Costs			2,100			
15	Printing & Duplicating			640			
16	Other			1,030			
17	Total Expenses			$17,070			

Figure 7-7. Worksheet with two rows inserted and filled

Unlike 1-2-3 Release 3, where only the first sheet is available in a new worksheet file, 1-2-3/G automatically provides 256 sheets in all worksheet files. If you use the Worksheet Window Perspective command (described in the section "Window Perspective Command" later in this chapter), you will see a perspective view of two to five of the sheets, as in Figure 7-8. To record data on sheets beyond the first, just change the current sheet with CTRL-PGUP.

To insert sheets before or after the current sheet, use Worksheet Insert and then select Sheet. Next, decide whether the new sheets should be inserted before or after the current sheet. If Group mode is enabled and the current worksheet is part of the defined group, the inserted sheets are inserted after the first sheet in the group. After selecting either Before or After, you can type the number of sheets to insert if you want to add more than 1, or you can select a range that contains the number of sheets to be inserted.

In addition, you can insert a partial sheet. When you insert a partial sheet, the selected range has one or more sheets inserted in its location while the remainder of the worksheet is not affected. You can use a partial sheet insertion to move entries from one sheet to another. In

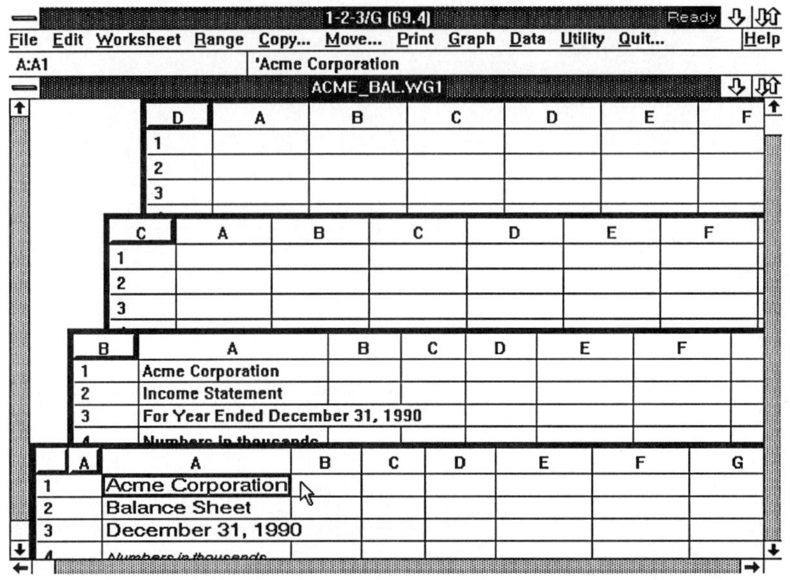

Figure 7-8. A perspective window of four worksheets

Figure 7-9, the worksheet on the left shows the worksheet before any changes are made. For this worksheet file, the range B:A2..C:A3 is the range you want to select to insert a partial sheet. This range tells 1-2-3/G to insert two sheets for the range A2..A3, starting in the current sheet. To add the partial sheet, select Worksheet Insert Sheet Before. You can select Partial by pressing TAB and typing a **P**, or by clicking the Partial option button. After you select Partial, you can click the OK button or press ENTER to insert the partial sheet. Once the partial sheet is added, the worksheet on the right in Figure 7-9 is produced. As you can see, the range B:A2..B:A3 has two sheets inserted in front of it so the data in these cells is now in D:A2..D:A3. The remainder of sheet B is unchanged.

Deleting Rows, Columns, or Sheets

1-2-3/G also lets you delete complete and partial rows, columns, or sheets that are no longer required. As with the Worksheet Insert command, it is easiest to use the Worksheet Delete command when you

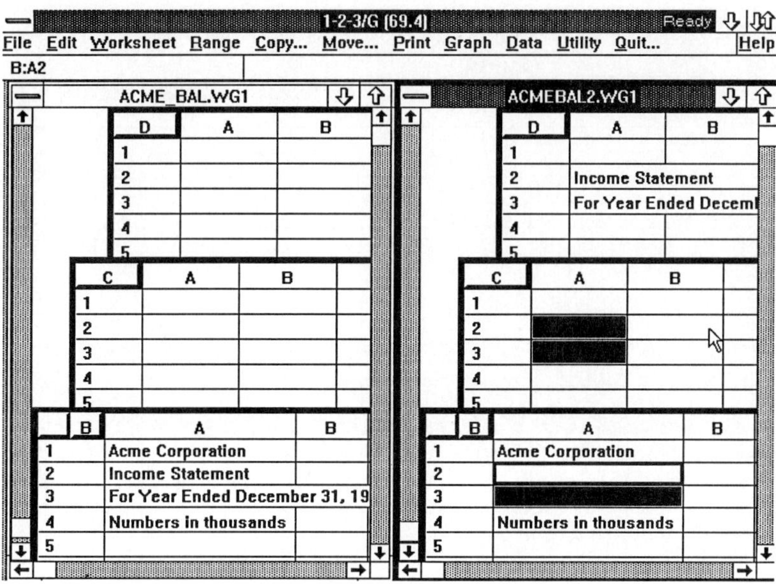

Figure 7-9. Adding a partial sheet to a worksheet

position your cell pointer to the desired location prior to execution. If you are deleting rows, place the cell pointer in the uppermost row to be deleted. If you are deleting columns, position the cell pointer in the leftmost column to be deleted. If you are deleting sheets, locate the pointer in the first sheet to be deleted. You can also select the range that contains the columns, rows, or sheets that you want to delete before you select Worksheet Delete. Note that you cannot delete protected cells when worksheet protection is enabled, nor can you delete columns, rows, or sheets in a sealed worksheet file.

The rows, columns, or sheets that you delete can be blank, or they can contain worksheet data, including formulas. When deleting rows or columns, be sure that the formulas and data in them are not referenced by other worksheet cells. If such references exist, these cell and range references are replaced by ERR in formulas. If you delete columns, rows, or sheets that are part of a range address or name, 1-2-3/G contracts the range address used in formulas and referenced by range names. This occurs whether the deleted columns, rows or sheets are at the beginning, end, or middle of a range. Figure 7-10 shows the formula

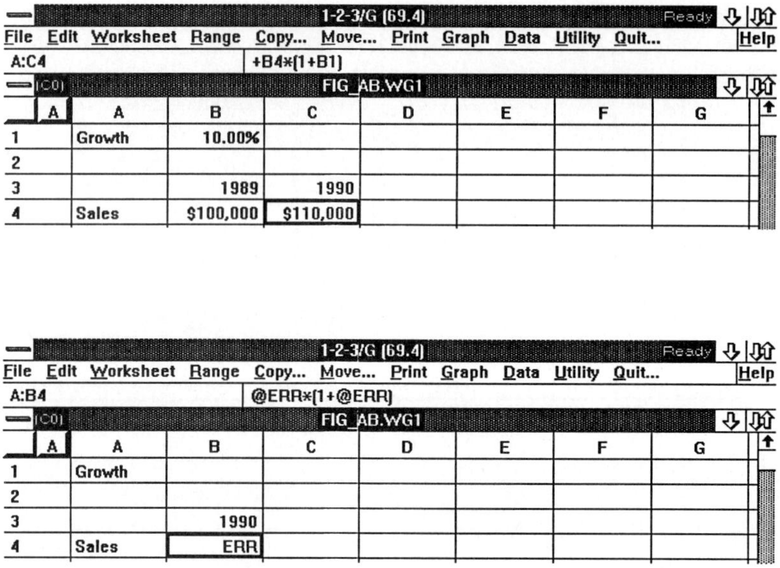

1-2-3/G (69.4) Ready

File Edit Worksheet Range Copy... Move... Print Graph Data Utility Quit... Help

A:C4 +B4*(1+B1)

(C0) FIG_AB.WG1

A	A	B	C	D	E	F	G
1	Growth	10.00%					
2							
3		1989	1990				
4	Sales	$100,000	$110,000				

1-2-3/G (69.4) Ready

File Edit Worksheet Range Copy... Move... Print Graph Data Utility Quit... Help

A:B4 @ERR*(1+@ERR)

(C0) FIG_AB.WG1

A	A	B	C	D	E	F	G
1	Growth						
2							
3		1990					
4	Sales	ERR					

Figure 7-10. Worksheet before and after deleting critical cells

result that displays after column B is accidentally deleted. Before making large-scale deletions, you should save your worksheet to disk or make sure that the Undo command is enabled. (To enable Undo, enter Worksheet Global Default Set Undo Enable.)

You can delete entire sheets full of entries with the Worksheet Delete Sheet command. Be cautious, however; 1-2-3/G does not first verify the deletion, and file backups or the Undo feature are the only available means of recovery. After entering the command, specify the range of sheets to be removed. For example, to delete sheet C from the sheets shown in either side of Figure 7-9, select Worksheet Delete Sheet and select a range containing one or more cells from sheet C. When you click OK or press ENTER, the data in sheet D is moved and renamed as sheet C.

Tip: Save the file before deleting entire sheets. Otherwise, deleting the wrong sheets can quickly destroy an afternoon's work. You should save your work frequently in case you select the Worksheet Delete Sheet command by accident.

Deleting Partial Rows, Columns, or Sheets

Just as you can insert partial columns, rows, and sheets, you can delete them. When you delete partial columns, rows, and sheets, the remaining contents of the worksheet shifts to fill the gaps left in the worksheet. To delete partial columns, rows, or sheets, select the Partial option button under Span before selecting the OK command button. The range that you select determines the number of columns, rows, or sheets to be removed and also determines the columns, rows, and sheets that are affected by the partial deletion.

Note that when you delete partial sheets, the selected range has one or more sheets deleted in its location while the remainder of the worksheet file is not affected. You can use a partial sheet deletion to move entries from one sheet to another.

Freezing Titles

When you have a large worksheet, you will want to lock the descriptive information in place on the screen. This allows you to look at data anywhere on the worksheet and still see your data heading labels.

With the Worksheet Titles command, you can freeze titles at the top of your screen, the side of your screen, or both. The command freezes titles that are currently above and to the left of the cell pointer location.

Once titles are frozen on the screen, you cannot move into these cells. If you try moving to a title with the arrow keys, 1-2-3/G beeps. If you try moving to a title with the mouse, the mouse pointer changes from white to gray, indicating that the title is unavailable for selection. If you need to make spelling corrections or other changes in these locked cells, you can use the F5 (Goto) key or the Range Goto command.

Tip: Group mode causes title changes to apply to all sheets in the active file. If Group mode is on, titles are frozen at the same time in all worksheets that are part of the group.

Freezing Horizontal Titles

When worksheet data extends below the bottom of a worksheet, you can freeze titles horizontally. This allows you to move below the edge of the worksheet into rows far below the normal display, and still have identifying labels visible at the top of the screen. To freeze titles horizontally, simply move your cell pointer below the title columns you want to freeze, and select Worksheet Titles Horizontal. Figure 7-11 shows a worksheet with titles frozen horizontally. Notice that the figure starts with row 1, which displays the horizontal titles, but the data displayed is from row 18 to 22.

Freezing Vertical Titles

If your worksheet data extends beyond the screen display, you can freeze titles vertically. This allows you to move across the screen into columns far to the right of the normal display, and still have identifying labels visible on the left side of the screen. To freeze titles vertically, simply move your cell pointer to the right of the title columns you want to freeze and select Worksheet Titles Vertical.

Freezing Titles in Both Directions

You may want to freeze titles in both directions when the data in your worksheet is both longer and wider than the screen, and has descriptive titles both at the top and the left side. To freeze titles in both directions, move the cell pointer below and to the right of the title columns you want to freeze, and then select Worksheet Titles Both.

1-2-3/G [69.4] Ready

File Edit Worksheet Range Copy... Move... Print Graph Data Utility Quit... Help

A:A22 1133

PART_NO.WG1

A	A	B	C	D	E	F	G
1	Part No.	Cost	Warehouse				
18	8876	$0.79	1				
19	9931	$2.00	1				
20	4452	$1.50	4				
21	3311	$1.75	5				
22	1133	$1.00	2				

Figure 7-11. Titles remain on the screen after freezing

Clearing Titles

Worksheet Titles Clear unfreezes any titles that you have frozen. This command removes the worksheet titles that are set, regardless of your cell pointer location.

Splitting a Window

You can split the window into two vertical or horizontal sections and then move your cell pointer within either pane to bring into view whichever cells you choose. Having two panes in your window allows you to look at information in two completely different areas of the current worksheet file at the same time.

If you decide to divide the window into horizontal or vertical panes, the size of each pane depends on the cell pointer location at the time you request the split. The split is placed to the left of or above the cell pointer location, based on whether you choose a vertical or horizontal split.

The command for splitting the worksheet is Worksheet Window, which produces the following dialog box:

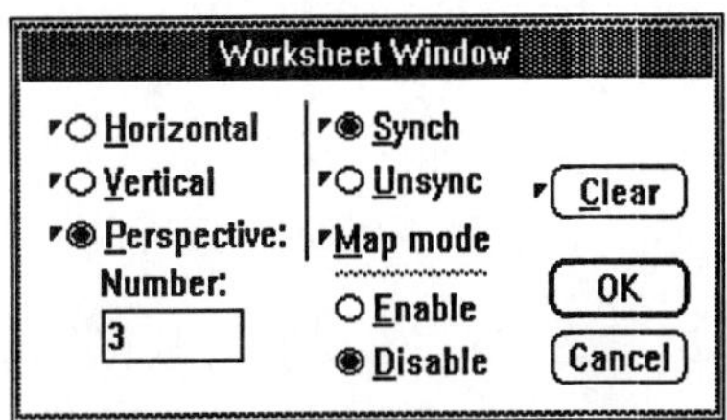

Notice there is no option for splitting the window in both directions at once: 1-2-3/G has a two-pane limitation.

The Worksheet Window dialog box also contains the Synch and Unsynch options, which determine whether movement in one pane will cause a corresponding shift of information in the second pane. The remaining choices provide special displays within the worksheet window that are described in the sections "Using the Map Option to View Worksheet Information" and "Window Perspective Command." You can also split the window by using the mouse, as described in the next section.

Splitting the Window Horizontally

A horizontal pane split is appropriate when you need the entire window width to show two different sections of a worksheet file. To split the window horizontally, move the cell pointer to the row immediately below the desired split location, and select Worksheet Window Horizontal. The window splits into two different panes, whose the height is dictated by the cell pointer's location at the time of the request. Figure 7-12 shows an example of a worksheet split into two panes. You can press F6 (Window) to move the cell pointer into the second pane, and the cell pointer is moved to show different rows in the worksheet.

To split the window into two panes with a mouse, position the mouse pointer so it is a vertical double-sided arrow.

Next, drag the mouse to where you want to split the window. When you release the mouse, 1-2-3/G splits the window into two panes at the mouse's location. Using a mouse lets you split a window somewhere other than exactly between rows. Also, you can adjust the split between panes by moving the mouse pointer to the border where the window is split. When the mouse pointer is a double-sided black arrow, drag the

1-2-3/G (69.4) Ready

File Edit Worksheet Range Copy... Move... Print Graph Data Utility Quit... Help

A:C26 @SUM(C4..C23)

EMP_DEPT.WG1

A	A	B	C	D	E	F	G
1			New Employees By Department				
2							
3	DEPT.	1975	1976	1977	1978	1979	1980
4	100	51	66	83	82	73	53
5	120	33	93	31	38	29	12
6	130	20	28	95	25	39	78
7	140	88	59	0	33	53	73
8	145	23	31	32	7	22	39
9	150	84	18	72	59	47	76

A	A	B	C	D	E	F	G
21	235	21	99	70	73	82	4
22	240	42	66	9	7	88	34
23	245	26	55	5	28	1	9
24							
25							
26	TOTAL	805	1120	845	937	910	775
27							

Figure 7-12. Horizontally split screen

mouse to the new location to split the window. With a mouse, you can also quickly switch between panes by clicking a cell in the pane you want to use. Each pane has its own scroll bars, which you can use to scroll the part of the worksheet that appears in the pane.

Once the window is split, you can use the arrow keys to move the cell pointer around in either pane. In Figure 7-12, the cell pointer is in the TOTAL line. You can also move the second pane to a different sheet while the first pane remains on the original sheet.

Splitting the Screen Vertically

A vertical pane split is appropriate when you want the full length of the window but don't require the full width. Cell pointer position at the time of the request again determines the size of the two panes: The split occurs to the left of the column in which the cell pointer is located.

You could also split the worksheet in Figure 7-12 vertically. To do so, position the cell pointer in column D and select Worksheet Window Vertical. If you then press the F6 (Window) key and move the cell pointer to column P, you should see the display shown in Figure 7-13. As

1-2-3/G [69.4] Ready

File Edit Worksheet Range Copy... Move... Print Graph Data Utility Quit... Help

A:P9 55

EMP_DEPT.WG1

A	A	B	C	A	N	O	P
1			New Employ	1			
2				2			
3	DEPT.	1975	1976	3	1987	1988	1989
4	100	51	66	4	29	75	61
5	120	33	93	5	86	81	6
6	130	20	28	6	5	46	4
7	140	88	59	7	91	84	41
8	145	23	31	8	66	80	92
9	150	84	18	9	37	24	55
10	160	64	89	10	46	78	46
11	175	85	22	11	36	57	100
12	180	5	92	12	45	68	58
13	190	21	36	13	58	9	33
14	195	5	65	14	76	51	33
15	200	0	85	15	29	89	46
16	210	62	45	16	67	35	8
17	220	31	23	17	42	58	42

Figure 7-13. Vertically split screen

with the Horizontal option, you move the cell pointer into the second pane with F6 (Window). Each time you press F6 (Window), the cell pointer moves into the opposite pane.

To split the window into two vertical panes with a mouse, position the mouse pointer so that it is a horizontal double-sided arrow. Then drag the mouse to where you want to split the window. When you release the mouse, 1-2-3/G splits the window into two panes at the mouse's location. Using a mouse lets you split a window somewhere other than exactly between columns. Also, you can adjust the split between panes by moving the mouse pointer to where the window is split. When the mouse pointer is a double-sided black arrow, drag the mouse to the new location to split the window. With a mouse, you can also quickly switch between panes by clicking a cell in the pane you want to use. Each pane has its own scroll bars, which you can use to scroll the part of the worksheet that appears in the pane.

Moving in Both Windows at Once

By default, 1-2-3/G has the two panes synchronized. In other words, if you move in one pane, the other pane automatically scrolls the same distance to match it. With horizontal panes, moving the cell pointer from column A to column Z in one pane makes the other pane scroll automatically to match. With vertical panes, moving from row 1 to row 120 in one pane automatically makes the other pane also move to row 120. With horizontal panes, each pane has its own vertical scroll bar but the window has only one horizontal scroll bar, since scrolling to the left or right scrolls both panes. With vertical panes, each pane has its own horizontal scroll bar but the window has only one vertical scroll bar, since scrolling up or down scrolls both panes.

Moving in One Window at a Time

Sometimes you will want information, such as a table, to remain stationary while you move in the other pane. You can make this change from either pane by selecting Worksheet Window Unsync. When you use Unsync, the two displays are totally independent. Each pane has its own vertical and horizontal bar to control scrolling. If you like, you can show the same worksheet area in both panes. To return to a synchronized mode, invoke Worksheet Window Sync. The Sync and Unsync options also affect pane movement when you use a perspective view showing multiple sheets.

Clearing the Second Window

When you decide to return to a single window display, select Worksheet Window Clear. If the screen is split horizontally, the single window obtains its default settings from the top pane. If the screen is split vertically, the settings for the left pane are used. Selecting Worksheet Window Clear also disables the Map mode display and sets a perspective view to display a single worksheet in the window.

Using the Map Option to View Worksheet Information

As your worksheet grows, it can be difficult to monitor all of its entries. The Map mode allows you to audit the entries in the worksheet to determine if they contain numbers, labels, or formulas, and to find out where they are placed on the sheet. The type of entry within a cell can pinpoint an important change in the structure of a model.

When you display a worksheet in Map mode, 1-2-3/G narrows the display of the columns and rows, allowing many columns and rows to display on the screen at once. Label entries display as backslash (\), numbers display as number signs (#), and formulas display as plus signs (+). To invoke this view, select Worksheet Window Map mode Enable; to clear it again, select Worksheet Window Map mode Disable or Worksheet Window Clear. Different colors are used to display the data types for \, #, and + located in the cells.

Figure 7-14 shows a model with 1991 budget entries. These entries extend to column N, and are totaled in column O and at the bottom of each column. If one of the @SUM functions is accidentally entered as a number, the Map mode will reveal the error. After selecting Worksheet Window Map mode Enable, the display in Figure 7-15 is the result. You can see from this display that column O and row 13 do contain formulas in the required location, based on the "+" entries. If you encountered a "#" in any of these locations, you would need to explore the model further and make the required changes.

1-2-3/G [69.4] Ready
File Edit Worksheet Range Copy... Move... Print Graph Data Utility Quit... Help
A:A1
BUDGET91.WG1

A	A	B	C	D	E	F	G	H
1				1991 Budget for the Marketing Department				
2								
3			Jan	Feb	Mar	Apr	May	Jun
4	Salaries		$1,200,000	$1,218,000	$1,236,270	$1,254,814	$1,273,636	$1,29
5	Benefits		168,000	170,520	173,078	175,674	178,309	18
6	Occupancy		120,000	121,800	123,627	125,481	127,364	12
7	Phone		259,500	263,393	267,343	271,354	275,424	27
8	Advertising		1,050,000	1,065,750	1,081,736	1,097,962	1,114,432	1,13
9	Utilities		19,000	19,285	19,574	19,868	20,166	2
10	Supplies		67,000	68,005	69,025	70,060	71,111	7
11	Postage		3,500	3,553	3,606	3,660	3,715	
12								
13	Total		$2,887,000	$2,930,305	$2,974,260	$3,018,873	$3,064,157	$3,11

Figure 7-14. Model with budget entries for an entire year

Window Perspective Command

To view the worksheet with a perspective view of multiple sheets, shown in some of the earlier examples in this chapter, select Worksheet Window Perspective. 1-2-3/G uses the current sheet as the first sheet, and

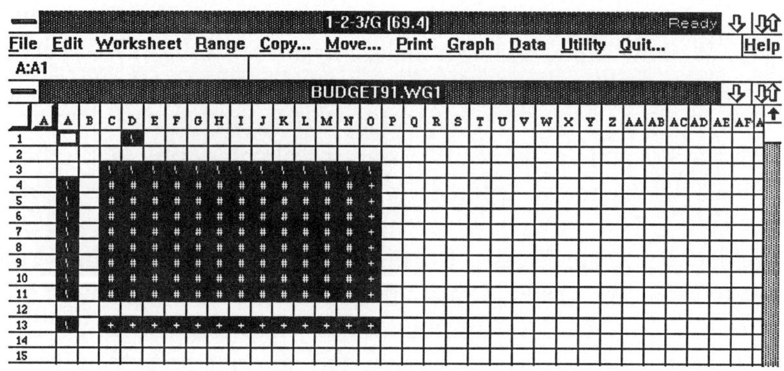

Figure 7-15. Map view of the worksheet

shows you as many as four more sheets. By default, 1-2-3/G shows three sheets at once. By changing the value in the Number text box under Perspective to a number between 2 and 5, you can change the number of sheets that appear in a perspective view. A worksheet window in a perspective view has a second vertical scroll bar on the left side of the worksheet window. This scroll bar indicates the sheet position in the file. By moving the elevator box in the scroll bar, you can change the sheets that appear in the worksheet window.

Column Commands

Unless you change the default width, every column on a new worksheet is nine characters wide. The actual number of characters that can fit in a cell depends on the width of each character. Formatting characters such as decimal points, commas, and currency symbols also require additional display space.

When you enter labels that are too long for the column width, they are truncated for display if the cells to their right are not empty. If the adjacent cells are empty, 1-2-3/G borrows space from them to show the complete label entry—that is, unless you have restricted the display of long labels with the Range Label or Worksheet Global Label command. Numbers that are too long are either rounded to fit the cell width or displayed as asterisks, depending on the format in effect for the cell. In earlier releases of 1-2-3, the General format truncated numbers without rounding. 1-2-3/G follows these rules governing the General default display of numbers:

- 1-2-3/G attempts to display your entry as you enter it.
- If the integer portion of the entry exceeds the cell width, 1-2-3/G switches to scientific notation.
- If the integer portion fits within the cell width but the decimal portion does not, 1-2-3/G rounds the value.

The Worksheet Column command lets you change column widths and select columns that are hidden in the worksheet display. As with other Worksheet commands, if the Group mode is enabled, the changes that you make to columns of one sheet in the group are repeated in every sheet in the group.

Set Width

The Worksheet Column dialog box looks like this:

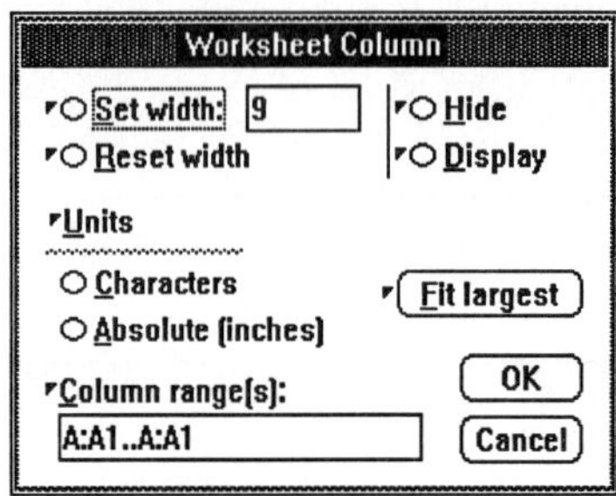

The options Set width, Reset width, and Fit largest change the width of the selected column or columns chosen for the command. Make sure to position your cell pointer in a cell of the first column to be changed before requesting the command. The Column range(s) option selects the columns affected by the other options in the dialog box. As with other 1-2-3/G commands that use a range or collection, you can select a range or collection containing one cell from each column, that you want to change with the Worksheet Column command, and 1-2-3/G automatically supplies the range or collection address in the Column range(s) text box.

To change the width of a column, select Worksheet Column Set width. Next, either enter the desired number of characters and press ENTER, or move with the RIGHT ARROW and LEFT ARROW keys until the column is the desired width, and press ENTER. The second method is best, since if you guess wrong about the desired number of characters, you have to start over with Worksheet Column Set width.

You can also select a column's width by using average character width or an absolute distance measured in inches or millimeters. By default, 1-2-3/G uses the average character width as the measurement for column width. This also means that as you change the global font and character size (as described later), 1-2-3/G adjusts the column width accordingly. If you select Absolute, 1-2-3/G changes the measurement in the Set width text box from number of characters to inches or millimeters, and displays inches or millimeters after Absolute to indicate whether inches or millimeters were chosen with the Utility User Settings International Measurement command.

You can use Set width to change the width of multiple columns. If you select a range or collection containing multiple columns before you select this command, the column width change applies to every column in the selected range or collection. You can also use the Worksheet Column dialog box to select the range or collection containing the columns this command affects. From the dialog box, you can select Column range(s) and enter a range or collection containing a cell from each column to change. If you have selected the column's width first, press TAB to switch to the Column range(s) text box or click the text box with the mouse. If you select Column range(s) before choosing Set width, press TAB or click the restore icon to return to the Worksheet Column dialog box and select an option. As an example, the display width for columns D through G in Figure 7-16 is reduced to 3 by selecting the range D7..G7, selecting the command Worksheet Column Set width, and typing 3 before selecting OK by clicking the command button or pressing ENTER.

With a mouse, you can change the column width more quickly by moving the mouse pointer to the right side of the column border to be changed. When the mouse pointer changes to the shape of a horizontal white double-sided arrow, drag the mouse to the new position for the end of the column. As you drag the mouse, 1-2-3/G draws a dotted line

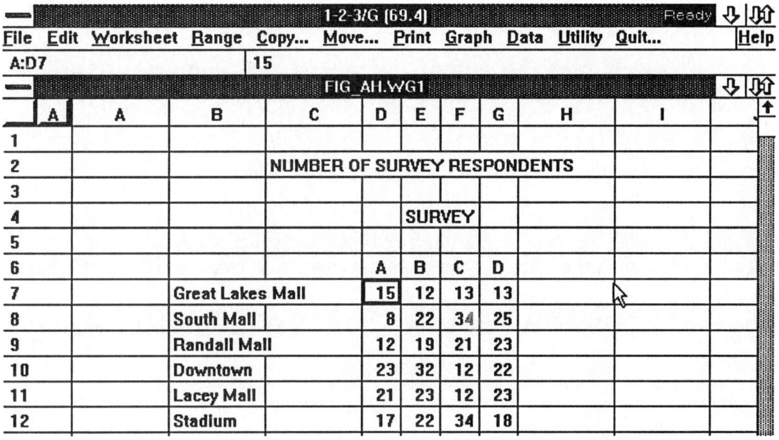

1-2-3/G [69.4] Ready

File Edit Worksheet Range Copy... Move... Print Graph Data Utility Quit... Help

A:D7 15

FIG_AH.WG1

A	A	B	C	D	E	F	G	H	I
1									
2			NUMBER OF SURVEY RESPONDENTS						
3									
4					SURVEY				
5									
6				A	B	C	D		
7		Great Lakes Mall		15	12	13	13		
8		South Mall		8	22	34	25		
9		Randall Mall		12	19	21	23		
10		Downtown		23	32	12	22		
11		Lacey Mall		21	23	12	23		
12		Stadium		17	22	34	18		

Figure 7-16. Worksheet with columns D, E, F, and G using a width of 3

indicating where it will place the end of the column. When you release the mouse, the column is widened or narrowed to the dotted line's position. As you drag the mouse, the control line displays the column width in characters. If multiple columns are selected (the entire columns are highlighted), changing the width of one of the highlighted columns changes the width of every highlighted column.

Fit Largest

While you can use Set Width to change the column width, 1-2-3/G provides a simpler entry when you want to adjust the column width to fit the entries in the column. The Fit Largest option takes the guesswork out of setting column widths. When you select Worksheet Column Fit Largest, 1-2-3/G makes each column in the selected range or collection as wide as the longest entry in each column. The following worksheet is an example:

1-2-3/G (69.4) Ready

File Edit Worksheet Range Copy... Move... Print Graph Data Utility Quit... Help

A:A1 'Last Name

EMP_DATA.WG1

A	A	B	C	D	E	F	G
1	Last Name	First Name	SS#	Job Code	Salary	Location	
2	Larson	Mary	543-98-987	23	$12,000	2	
3	Campbell	David	213-76-987	23	$23,000	10	
4	Campbell	Keith	569-89-765	12	$32,000	2	

In this worksheet, some of the entries are wide and some are narrow. If the remaining entries in this column are going to be the same width, you may want to change the column width of the columns A through F so there is enough display space where it is needed. To adjust all of these columns, select A1..F1 and select Worksheet Column Fit Largest. The beginning of your worksheet will now look like this:

1-2-3/G (69.4) Ready

File Edit Worksheet Range Copy... Move... Print Graph Data Utility Quit... Help

A:A1 'Last Name

EMP_DATA.WG1

A	A	B	C	D	E	F	G
1	Last Name	First Name	SS#	Job Code	Salary	Location	
2	Larson	Mary	543-98-9876	23	$12,000	2	
3	Campbell	David	213-76-9874	23	$23,000	10	
4	Campbell	Keith	569-89-7654	12	$32,000	2	

Tip: When using Worksheet Column Fit Largest, check for any lengthy columns that you don't want 1-2-3/G to use to determine the column's width. For example, reports often contain long heading that borrow display space from adjacent empty cells. If your worksheet contains these long labels, don't use the Worksheet Column Fit Largest command on that column.

Reset Width

Once you have used Worksheet Column Set Width or Fit largest to change the width of a column, its width is different from the width of its neighbors. If that width ceases to be useful, you can return the column to the global column width with the Reset width command. If you select a range or collection containing multiple columns before selecting this command, each column in the selected range or collection is reset. You can also reset multiple columns with this command by first selecting Worksheet Column Column Range(s) and a range collection containing one or more cells from the columns you want to reset. When you finish selecting the range or collection, click the restore icon in the upper-right corner of the minimized dialog box or press TAB and select Reset Width.

If you are uncertain of the current global width, you can select Worksheet Status. Under Display options, 1-2-3/G lists various display default settings, including the default column width. When you select OK by clicking the command button or pressing ENTER, 1-2-3/G returns you to Ready mode.

Hidden Columns

Worksheet Column Hide allows you to hide or temporarily eliminate individual columns from the display. In effect, it cuts a section of the worksheet temporarily. You can use this option to eliminate confidential or proprietary information from the display. You can restore hidden columns to the display at any time, since the data is not erased. When you select Worksheet Column Hide, 1-2-3/G prompts for a range or collection containing at least one cell from each column you want to hide. You can use the mouse or the arrow keys to select this range or collection before clicking the OK command button or pressing ENTER. You can also select the range or collection of columns to be hidden before selecting Worksheet Column Hide.

Besides using this command to hide columns, you can also hide columns by giving them a column width of zero via the Worksheet Column Set width command.

Tip: Use Range Format Hidden to eliminate any range from display, and thus display a group of cells as blank. This allows you to hide the information in a row or rectangle on the worksheet without hiding the entire column.

The Worksheet Column Display command redisplays hidden columns. It displays the column letters of the formerly hidden columns with asterisks next to them. After selecting the command, you can choose a range or collection containing one or more cells from columns you want to display. You can include columns that already display in the range or collection. With the range selected, press ENTER or click the OK command button to display the previously hidden columns.

Tip: Column Hide and Delete Column produce very different results. When you hide a column, it is removed from the display only temporarily. When you delete a column, the column and its contents are permanently removed from the worksheet—its entries are lost unless you have a retrievable copy of the model on disk.

Row Commands

1-2-3/G also has settings for rows. By default, every row on a new worksheet is the same height. As you change the fonts, 1-2-3/G adjusts the height of the row to match the tallest font selected for any cell in the row. You can change the height of a row and can also hide and display rows. If you change a row's height or change whether a row appears in a worksheet that is part of a group when Group mode is enabled, these changes are repeated in every sheet in the group. The command for changing row settings, Worksheet Row, produces the following dialog box:

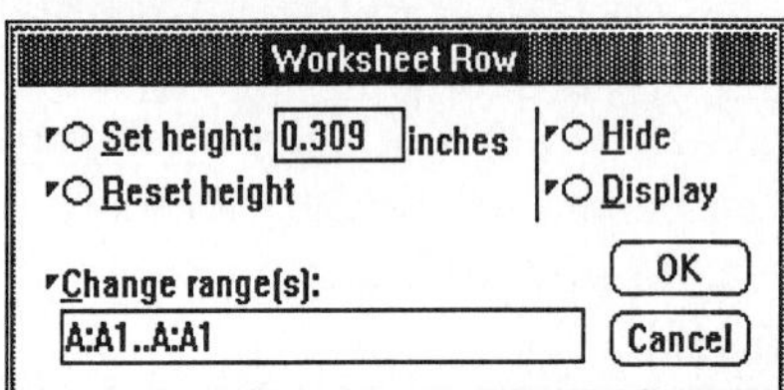

Set Row Height

You can adjust the height of individual rows in the worksheet. The Set height option changes the height of the selected row or rows. The Change range(s) option selects the rows that will be affected by the other options in the Worksheet Row dialog box. As with other 1-2-3/G commands that use a range or collection, you can use the Worksheet row command to select a range or collection containing one cell from each row to be changed, and 1-2-3/G automatically supplies the range or collection address in the Change range(s) text box.

To change the height of a row select Worksheet Row Set height. Row height is measured either inches or millimeters, depending on the measurement chosen with Utility User Settings International. Next, you can either enter the desired number of inches or millimeters, or you can press the UP ARROW and DOWN ARROW keys until the row is the desired height. Each time you press the UP ARROW or DOWN ARROW, the row height is increased by 0.25 inches or millimeters. The second method is best, since it lets you select the row height visually. When you have selected the new row height, click OK or press ENTER to select the OK command button and change the row height.

You can also use the Worksheet Row Set height command to change the height of multiple rows. If you select a range or collection containing multiple rows before you select this command, the row height change applies to all rows in the selected range or collection. You can also use the Worksheet Row dialog box to choose the range or collection containing the row this command affects. From the dialog box, select Change range(s) and a range or collection containing a cell from each row to change. If you have selected the row's height first, press TAB to switch to the Change range(s) text box or click the text box with the mouse. If you select Change range(s) before choosing Set height, press TAB or click the restore icon to return to the Worksheet Row dialog box and select another option.

You can set the height of worksheet rows more quickly by using the mouse. To change the height of a row, move the mouse pointer to the line below the row number that you want to change. When the mouse pointer is the vertical white double-sided arrow, drag the mouse to the new position for the bottom of the row. As you drag the mouse, 1-2-3/G draws a dotted line indicating where it will place the bottom of the row. When you release the mouse, the row height becomes taller or shorter depending on the dotted line's position. As you drag the mouse, the control line displays the height of the row. If you select multiple rows by selecting the row numbers in the row border, changing the height of one of the selected rows changes the height of every selected row.

Reset Row Height

Once you have used Worksheet Row Set height to change the height of a row, its height is different from the height of its neighbors. If that row height ceases to be useful, you can return the height to the global row height with the Reset height command. To use this command, place the cell pointer in a cell in the row to be changed and select Worksheet Row Reset height to return the row's height to 0.309 inches or 7.845 millimeters. If you select a range or collection containing several rows before selecting this command, each row in the selected range or collection is reset. You can also reset multiple rows by first selecting Worksheet Row Change range(s) and then selecting a range collection that contains one or more cells from the rows you want to reset. When you finish selecting the range or collection, click the restore icon in the upper-right corner of the minimized dialog box or press TAB and select Reset height.

You can quickly check the default row height by selecting Worksheet Status. Under Display options, 1-2-3/G lists the default row height among other things. When you select OK by clicking the command button or pressing ENTER, 1-2-3/G returns you to Ready mode.

Hidden Rows

Worksheet Row Hide allows you to hide individual rows from the display. In effect, it masks a section of the worksheet temporarily. You can use this option to hide confidential or proprietary information from the display. You can restore hidden rows to the display at any time, since the data is not erased. When you select Worksheet Row Hide, 1-2-3/G prompts for a range or collection containing at least one cell from each row you want to hide. You can use the mouse or the arrow keys to select this range or collection before clicking the OK command button or pressing ENTER. You can also select the range or collection of rows to be hidden before selecting Worksheet Row Hide.

You can continue to use the hidden rows in your formulas. You can also hide rows by setting their height to zero with the Set height option in the Worksheet Row dialog box. As with hidden columns, you can display hidden rows and hide them again by pressing SHIFT-F6 (Hide), which is a toggle.

The Worksheet Row Display command redisplays hidden rows. It displays the row numbers of the hidden rows marked with asterisks. After selecting Worksheet Row Display, you can choose a range or collection containing cells from the rows you want to display. You can include rows that already display in the range or collection. With the range selected, press ENTER or click the OK command button to display the previously hidden rows.

Tip: Worksheet Row Hide and Worksheet Delete Row are not the same commands. When you hide a row, the row is removed from the display only temporarily. When you delete a row, the row and its contents are permanently removed from the worksheet—the deleted rows entries are lost unless you have a copy of them on disk.

Hiding Sheets

1-2-3/G's Worksheet Hide command allows you to remove sheets from display and then redisplay them. You can use this command for one or more consecutive sheets at once. Figure 7-17 shows three of the sheets in the current worksheet file. There are many additional sheets, representing other departments in the company. To work with sheets A, D, and E, moving between them frequently, you will want to hide sheets B and C. You cannot move the cell pointer to hidden sheets, even with the F5 (Goto) key. As with hidden columns and rows, you can temporarily display hidden sheets by pressing SHIFT-F6 (Hide).

Figure 7-17 shows a perspective view of the file with sheets B and C in the display. Move to sheet B and select Worksheet Hide Enable, as in Figure 7-18. Expand the range to include sheet C by pressing CTRL-PGUP and ENTER. Your screen will now display sheets A, D, and E, as shown in Figure 7-19.

The Worksheet Hide command is also a good option when you want to eliminate confidential or proprietary data from view or want to print a range that does not include the hidden data. You can also use Worksheet Global Format Hidden to hide all the data on a worksheet.

Global Commands

Global commands affect the entire worksheet. All rows, and columns, and all cells in all rows and columns are affected by the changes you make with the Worksheet Global command options. However, these

1-2-3/G: DESK5.DSK [69.4] Ready

File Edit Worksheet Range Copy... Move... Print Graph Data Utility Quit... Help

A:C3 1200000

FIG_AI.WG1

C	A	B	C	D	E	F
1		1991 Budget for the Data Processing Department				
2						
3	Salaries		$950,850			
4	Benefits		$153,450			
5	Occupancy		$198,700			

B	A	B	C	D	E	F
1		1991 Budget for the Acct Department				
2						
3	Salaries		$950,000			
4	Benefits		$133,000			
5	Occupancy		$120,000			

A	A	B	C	D	E	F	G
1		1991 Budget for the Mktg Department					
2							
3	Salaries		$1,200,000				
4	Benefits		$168,000				
5	Occupancy		$120,000				

Figure 7-17. Worksheet file with multiple sheets

1-2-3/G: DESK5.DSK [69.4] Edit

File Edit Worksheet Range Copy... Move... Print Graph Data Utility Quit... Help

C:A1

FIG_AI.WG1

D	A	B	C
1		1991 Budget for the	
2			
3	Salaries		$1,75
4	Benefits		$25
5	Occupancy		$210,000

Worksheet Hide

◉ Enable

○ Disable

Range(s): b:a1..c:a1

OK

Cancel

C	A	B	C	D	E	F
1		1991 Budget for the Data Processing Department				
2						
3	Salaries		$950,850			
4	Benefits		$153,450			
5	Occupancy		$198,700			

B	A	B	C	D	E	F	G
1		1991 Budget for the Acct Department					
2							
3	Salaries		$950,000				
4	Benefits		$133,000				
5	Occupancy		$120,000				

Figure 7-18. Hiding the B and C sheets

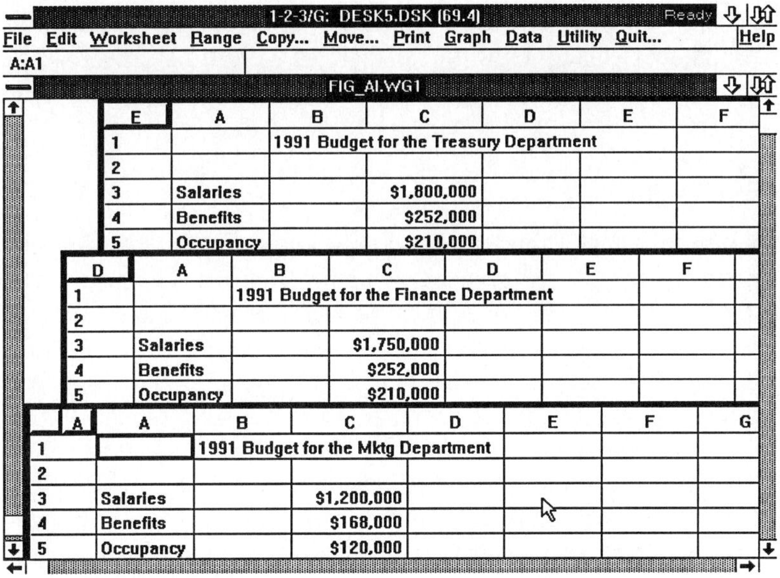

Figure 7-19. Worksheet file after hiding sheets

commands only change the current sheet. If Group mode is enabled, the global changes affect every sheet within the group. The options available under the Global menu are shown in Figure 7-20.

In this chapter, you will use Global Column, Row, Format, Attributes, Zero Suppress, Label, and Screen Attributes. In addition, you

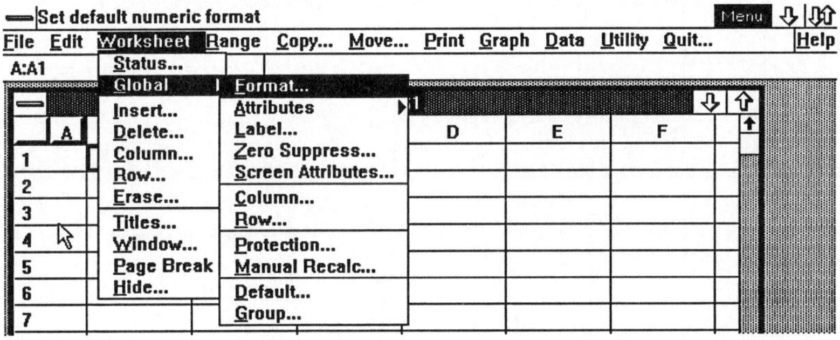

Figure 7-20. Worksheet Global cascade menu

have already benefitted from the Group mode setting, which can also affect a global change if the range includes all sheets. In Chapter 6, you learned how to make a few global changes with the Utility User Settings options and Worksheet Global Default. These changes affect not only the current session but all subsequent sessions.

Column Width

It would take much too long to change the column width for the entire worksheet with the Worksheet Column command. If you want to affect every column, it is more efficient to use a global change. Also, it uses less of the computer's memory to change the global column width than to change the column width of many columns to the same width. In addition, a global change is documented on the Worksheet Status dialog box, so it is easy to see the currently selected width. You can change the width of every column on the worksheet with Worksheet Global Column, with which you can make all worksheet columns any width from 1 to 240 characters or an equivalent width using an absolute inch or millimeter scale. The default setting is nine characters using the default font.

Since Worksheet Global Column affects the entire worksheet, you needn't position your cell pointer before invoking it. The example in Figure 7-21 shows columns of numbers, all of which contain fewer than the default setting of 9 positions. Shrinking the size of the columns would allow you to display more information on the sheet. By selecting

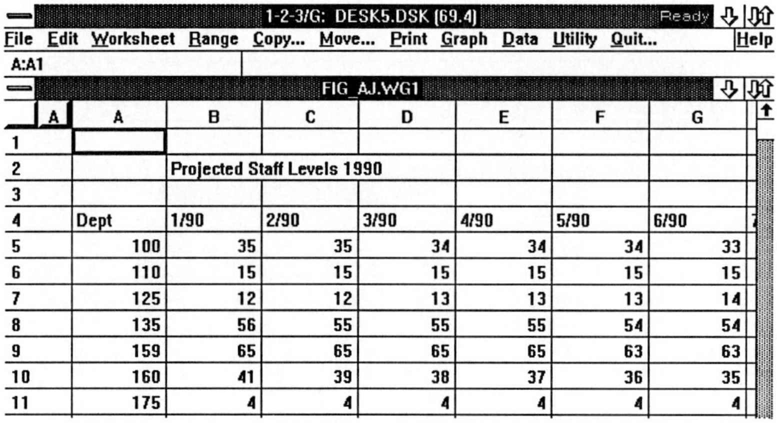

1-2-3/G: DESK5.DSK [69.4] Ready

File Edit Worksheet Range Copy... Move... Print Graph Data Utility Quit... Help

A:A1

FIG_AJ.WG1

A	A	B	C	D	E	F	G
1							
2		Projected Staff Levels 1990					
3							
4	Dept	1/90	2/90	3/90	4/90	5/90	6/90
5	100	35	35	34	34	34	33
6	110	15	15	15	15	15	15
7	125	12	12	13	13	13	14
8	135	56	55	55	55	54	54
9	159	65	65	65	65	63	63
10	160	41	39	38	37	36	35
11	175	4	4	4	4	4	4

Figure 7-21. Worksheet using a default column width of 9

Worksheet Global Column, typing 5, and selecting the OK command button, you can change the display to match the one shown in Figure 7-22. As with the Worksheet Column Set width command, you can also use the LEFT ARROW and RIGHT ARROW keys to change the column width.

The Worksheet Column command takes precedence over the Global Column command. You can use both commands if you have a worksheet where all but one column is narrow. Worksheet Global Column can set the narrow width for the entire worksheet. You can then move your cell pointer to the column that must be wider, select Worksheet Column Set width, and specify the necessary width for that column only.

Row Height

It would take too much time and memory to change the row height for the entire worksheet with the Worksheet Row command. A better alternative is to alter the global row height with the Worksheet Global Row command. The Worksheet Status dialog box lists the global row height, which provides better documentation than altering individual row heights with the Worksheet Row command. With the Worksheet Global Row command, you can make all the rows on your worksheet any height up to ten inches or 254 millimeters. The default setting is determined by the default font.

Since the Worksheet Row command affects the entire worksheet, the cell pointer can be in any cell on the sheet to be changed. The

1-2-3/G: DESK5.DSK (69.4) Ready

File Edit Worksheet Range Copy... Move... Print Graph Data Utility Quit... Help

A:I4

FIG_AJ.WG1

A	A	B	C	D	E	F	G	H	I	J	K	L
1												
2		Projected Staff Levels 1990										
3												
4	Dept	1/90	2/90	3/90	4/90	5/90	6/90	7/90				
5	100	35	35	34	34	34	33	33				
6	110	15	15	15	15	15	15	15				
7	125	12	12	13	13	13	14	14				
8	135	56	55	55	55	54	54	54				
9	159	65	65	65	65	63	63	63				
10	160	41	39	38	37	36	35	35				
11	175	4	4	4	4	4	4	4				

Figure 7-22. Worksheet using a default column width of 5

example in Figure 7-23 shows two worksheets. The worksheet on the left has the global row height changed to fit more lines on the screen. This change is made by selecting Worksheet Global Row, typing .27, and selecting the OK command button. While this is not much of a difference in each row, it is enough to squeeze a few more rows into the worksheet window. If you decide to return the global row height to the appropriate height for the default font, you can select the Reset check box, which returns the value in the text box to the appropriate row height for the default font.

The Worksheet Row command takes precedence over the Worksheet Global Row command. You can use both commands in a worksheet where you want to change the height of all but a few rows. Worksheet Global Row can set the row height for the entire worksheet. You can then select the rows requiring a different height, select Worksheet Row Set height, and specify the row height needed for the selected rows.

Tip: Don't reduce the global row height so much that it makes the characters hard to read. If you want to change the number of rows that fit on the screen, change the font used to display the entries.

1-2-3/G (69.4) Ready

File Edit Worksheet Range Copy... Move... Print Graph Data Utility Quit... Help

C:A1 'SS#

EMP_DATA.WG1

A	A	B	C
1	Last Name	First Name	SS#
2	Larson	Mary	543-98-9876
3	Campbell	David	213-76-9874
4	Campbell	Keith	569-89-7654
5	Stephens	Tom	219-78-8954
6	Caldor	Larry	459-34-0921
7	Lightnor	Peggy	560-55-4311
8	McCartin	John	817-66-1212
9	Justof	Jack	431-78-9963
10	Patterson	Lyle	212-11-9090
11	Miller	Lisa	214-89-6756
12	Hawkins	Mark	215-67-8973
13	Hartwick	Eileen	313-78-9090
14	Smythe	George	560-90-8645
15	Wilkes	Caitlin	124-67-7432
16	Deaver	Ken	198-98-6750
17	Kaylor	Sally	312-45-9862
18	Parker	Dee	659-11-3452
19	Preverson	Gary	670-90-1121
20	Samuelson	Paul	219-89-7080

C	A	B
1	SS#	Last Name
2	569-89-7654	Campbell
3	459-34-0921	Caldor
4	817-66-1212	McCartin
5	431-78-9963	Justof
6	313-78-9090	Hartwick
7	560-90-8645	Smythe
8	312-45-9862	Kaylor
9		
10		
11		
12		
13		
14		
15		
16		
17		

Figure 7-23. Changing the global row height to display more rows

Number Format

You can also change numeric format on a global basis. The numeric format determines how 1-2-3/G displays the numbers. Selecting a format does not affect how 1-2-3/G stores the numbers or uses them in calculations. The default setting is General format, but if you want all of your entries to be in Currency, Percent, Scientific, or any of the other available formats, you can reformat every worksheet cell with the Worksheet Global Format command and the format specification of your choice. The "Format Options" box lists the standard formats that you can select. Figure 7-24 displays a worksheet created with the General format setting. You can greatly improve the appearance of this worksheet with Worksheet Global Format Currency. After the initial command sequence, type **0** to indicate zero decimal places, and press ENTER. The newly formatted worksheet looks like Figure 7-25.

You can use any of the options in the "Format Options" box. Some formats require more worksheet space than others, however. If the display changes to asterisks when you change your format, you must widen your columns to accommodate the new format or select a different format. A Range Format command always takes precedence over a Worksheet Global Format change. The options available with Worksheet Global Format are covered under the Format Options section later in the chapter.

Using the Group mode while making a formatting change causes the change to affect all sheets in the group. If you choose Currency in

1-2-3/G: DESK5.DSK (69.4) Ready

File Edit Worksheet Range Copy... Move... Print Graph Data Utility Quit... Help

A:A1

FIG_AK.WG1

A	A	B	C	D	E	F	G
1							
2							
3		Budget	Actual	Diff.			
4	Salaries	120678	125690	-5012			
5	Supplies	34578.5	34250	328.5			
6	Rent	6789	6955.5	-166.5			
7	Postage	325	400.2	-75.2			
8	Ins.	1235	1350	-115			
9	Legal	4500	5000	-500			

Figure 7-24. Worksheet using the General format

Format Options

This table is a quick reference to 1-2-3/G's formatting features.

Format	Entry	Display
Fixed 2 decimal places	5678	5678.00
	−123.45	−123.45
Scientific 2 decimal places	5678	5.68E+03
	−123.45	−1.23E+02
Currency 2 decimal places	5678	$5,678.00
	−123.45	($123.45)
, (comma) 2 decimal places	5678	5,678.00
	−123.45	(123.45)
General	5678	5678
	−123.45	−123.45
+/ −	4	++++
	−3	−−−
	0	.
Percent	5	500%
0 decimal places	.1	10%
Date (D1)	24-Sep-91	24-Sep-91
Time (T1)	12:00	12:00:00 PM
Text	+A2*A3	+A2*A3
Automatic	$5	$5
Automatic	15-Aug-92	15-Aug-92
Parentheses with Currency	−5	(−$5)
Label	(305)349-1235	'(305)349-1235

the active sheet, all of the sheets in the group will have a format of Currency. If Group mode is not enabled, changing the format on one sheet has no effect on another sheet in the group.

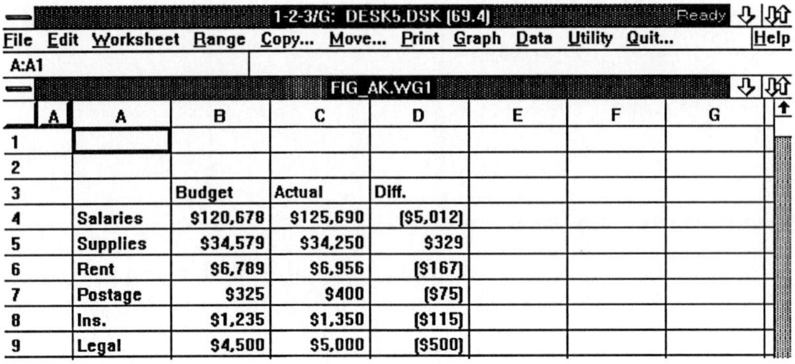

1-2-3/G: DESK5.DSK [69.4] Ready

File Edit Worksheet Range Copy... Move... Print Graph Data Utility Quit... Help

A:A1

FIG_AK.WG1

A	A	B	C	D	E	F	G
1							
2							
3		Budget	Actual	Diff.			
4	Salaries	$120,678	$125,690	($5,012)			
5	Supplies	$34,579	$34,250	$329			
6	Rent	$6,789	$6,956	($167)			
7	Postage	$325	$400	($75)			
8	Ins.	$1,235	$1,350	($115)			
9	Legal	$4,500	$5,000	($500)			

Figure 7-25. Worksheet using the Currency format

Changing the Worksheet's Default Justification

The default worksheet setting for labels provides left justification for every label entry and right justification for every value entry. This means that an apostrophe is generated as the first character of every label entry. As you learned in Chapter 5, you can always center a label entry by typing the center justification character yourself. For example, entering **^Sales** centers the label Sales in its cell. You can also right justify a single entry by beginning your label entry with a double quotation mark ("). 1-2-3/G does not have a manual method for changing the default justification of values or for telling 1-2-3/G to not use adjacent cells to display long labels.

1-2-3/G's Range Label command lets you change the justification of a range of entries. However, if you want to change the justification of all or most of your entries, neither the single entry method nor the Range Label command is an adequate solution. For such circumstances, 1-2-3/G provides the Worksheet Global Label command to change the default alignment for worksheet entries. This command also changes the global setting for whether long labels borrow display space from adjacent cells. To make the change, select Worksheet Global Label and select the justification you want from the menu, as shown here.

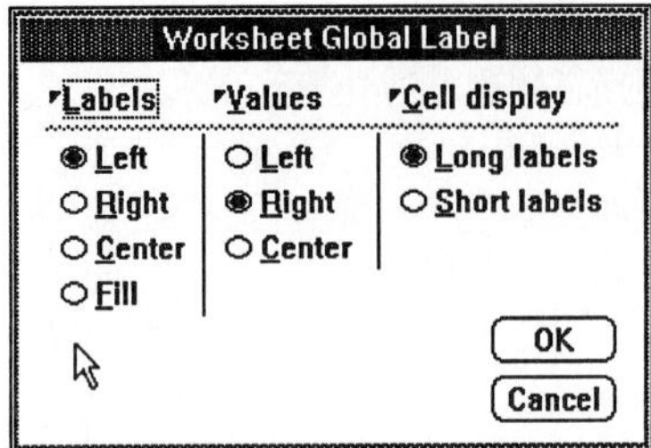

When you use the Worksheet Global Label command, all entries that don't have their justification set manually or with the Range Label command are affected. Under Labels, you can select Left, Right, Center, or Fill to automatically supply an apostrophe, double quote, caret, or backslash label prefix, respectively. Under Values, you can select Left, Right, or Center to change the alignment of values. The formula results use the alignment based on the results of the formula. If the formula is a string formula, the formula uses the label prefix for labels. If the formula is a number or logical formula, the display of the formula's result uses the alignment selected for values.

You can also determine whether long labels borrow display cells from the adjacent empty cells. When you initially make entries that extend beyond the length of the cell, the long labels overlap the neighboring cells if they are blank. This is because the Long Labels option button under Cell display is selected in the Worksheet Global Label dialog box. If you select Short labels, long labels don't borrow the display space.

Changing the global worksheet setting affects all cells in the current worksheet. You can override this setting with the Range Label command described later.

Selecting the Worksheet Font

Fonts define the appearance of characters on your screen and on your printer, affecting both character size and typeface. Since 1-2-3/G uses Presentation Manager's graphical interface, it has access to all fonts installed in the Presentation Manager, as well as a few special font attribute options whose definitions are supplied with 1-2-3/G. These options let you use different fonts for your worksheet cells.

Besides the typeface style, you can select the size of the font, and font attributes such as boldface and italics. The typeface is the general style of the characters. Some fonts are relatively plain, while others are

1-2-3/G [69.4] Ready

File Edit Worksheet Range Copy... Move... Print Graph Data Utility Quit... Help

B:A1 'Acme Corporation

ACME_BAL.WG1

A	A	B	C	D
1	Acme Corporation			
2	Balance Sheet			
3	December 31, 1990			
4	*Numbers in thousands*			
5				
6	ASSETS			
7	Curent Assets			
8	Cash			$250
9	Notes Receivable			$320
10	Amounts Receivable			$590
11	Total Current Assets			$1,160
12	Plant Assets	Cost	Dep	Book
13	Land	$500	—	$500
14	Buildings	$980	$400	$580
15	Factory Equipment	$575	$50	$525
16	Total Plant Assets			$1,605
17	Intangible Assets	Cost	Amort	Book
18	Copyrights	$1,100	$400	$700
19	Patents	$1,200	—	$1,200

B	A	B
1	Acme Corporation	
2	Income Statement	
3	For Year Ended December 3	
4	Numbers in thousands	
5		
6	Sales	
7	Gross Sales	10000
8	Returns on Sales	4
9	Net Sales	9996
10		
11	Cost of Goods Sold:	
12	Initial Inventory	60
13	Purchases	350
14	Inventory For Sale	410
15	Ending Inventory	75
16	Cost of Goods Sold	335
17		
18	Expenses:	
19		

Figure 7-26. Worksheet file using different fonts

much fancier with many embellishments. Notice the contrast in the Helvetica font on the left and the System Proportional font on the right in Figure 7-26. The size of a font is measured in points, where each point equals 1/72 of an inch.

To choose the font that 1-2-3/G uses as the global font for the worksheet, select Worksheet Global Attributes Font. You can choose the global font, any attributes, and Setup to choose the fonts that appear in the list box under Font, as shown in this dialogue box:

1-2-3/G [69.4] Menu

File Edit Worksheet Range Copy... Move... Print Graph Data Utility Quit... Help

A:A1

Worksheet Global Attributes Font

Fonts

	(screen)	(printer)
a	12 Pt. System Proportional	8 Pt. Helvetica
b	14 Pt. Helv	14 Pt. Helvetica
c	8 Pt. Helv	8 Pt. Helvetica
d	8 Pt. Helv	8 Pt. Helvetica
e	10 Pt. Helv	10 Pt. Helvetica

Attributes: ☐ Bold ☐ Italic ☐ Underline ☐ Strikeout

Screen font preview: 12 Pt.System Proportional

Setup... OK Cancel

The list box under Font lists the typeface and size combinations from which you can choose. On the left are the fonts that 1-2-3/G uses to display the worksheet on your computer screen; on the right are the fonts that 1-2-3/G uses when it prints your worksheet. Your Worksheet Global Attributes Font dialog box probably lists Helvetica 8 point first, since it's the default global font. The examples in this book use a larger font, System Proportional 12 point, to make the figures easier to read. To select a font from the list, click the desired font or select Fonts and type the letter of the desired font. As you change the selected font, 1-2-3/G changes the font in the Preview box so you can see whether you have chosen the correct font. Under Attributes, which you can select by clicking the desired check box or pressing TAB, you can choose whether the global font uses boldface, italic, underline, or strikeout. Select OK by clicking the command button or pressing ENTER. All worksheet cells in the current sheet (or all sheets within a group, if Group is enabled) that do not have their font selected with the Range Attributes Font command use the font and attributes you have chosen. If Group is enabled the impact extends from the current sheet to all sheets in the group.

All of the font commands assume that you have installed the font with OS/2. If the font is not installed with OS/2, the uninstalled font appears as Courier. 1-2-3/G includes a Courier and System Proportional font that you can use for display, but you cannot use these fonts to print worksheets. (The Courier font that 1-2-3/G provides is different than the Courier font that you can install with OS/2.) If you have not installed fonts yet, see Appendix A for detailed instructions.

Tip: If you want to change the global font for one worksheet, change the font from the Worksheet Global Attributes Font dialog box. If you want to change the global font for all worksheets in the file, use Setup to change font A in the font list.

Zero Display

You can choose how zero values are displayed on the worksheet. Initially, a zero value results in a cell containing and displaying 0. The zero value options in 1-2-3/G can hide zero values, display zero values, or display a label in every zero location on the worksheet. The zero values remain the same, and they can be referenced for calculations; but any cell with a zero value can appear, be hidden, or appear as a label.

To suppress the display of zeros on the worksheet, use Worksheet Global Zero Suppress Yes. To restore the display, use Worksheet Global Zero Suppress No. To display the zero values as labels, use Worksheet Global Zero Suppress Label and enter a label to display in place of zero values. The label uses the value alignment selected for the cell. You can override the alignment by supplying a label prefix character as part of the label.

The one problem with zero suppression is that 1-2-3/G will write over a zero-suppressed cell if you type a new entry there, because the cell appears blank. For a solution to this problem, see "Protecting Workshop Cells" in Chapter 6.

You can also change how zeros display within a range by using the Range Zero Suppress command, which overrides the Worksheet Global Zero Suppress for the range chosen with the command.

When you select Range Zero Suppress, you can choose between Yes (hide zeros), No (display zeros), and Default (use the setting made with the Worksheet Global Zero Suppress command). You cannot use the Range Zero Suppress command to display a different label than the label chosen with the Worksheet Global Zero Suppress command. Once you select the zero display option, you can select the range that the command uses. After you select a range and choose OK, 1-2-3/G applies the zero display selection to the chosen range and uses the global zero display option for the other cells in the worksheet.

Tip: 1-2-3/G only lets you supply one label for zero suppression. If you want to use more than one label for zero values in a worksheet, use the Worksheet Global Zero Suppress command for the first label and create user-defined formats to represent other zero values.

Tip: Zeros may still appear in a worksheet, even when Global Zero is suppressing zeros or displaying them as labels. The worksheet will display zeros if it contains cells that appear as zero due to the cell's format. To convert these values to actual zeros, use the @ROUND function covered in Chapter 9.

Screen Colors

You can customize the screen's appearance in two ways. You can use the Control panel program described in Appendix A. You can also use the

Worksheet Global Screen Attributes command. You can use this command to change the screen colors, or, if you are using a monochrome monitor, you can use varying shades. You can also select whether 1-2-3/G shows the grid lines, column frames, and row frames.

When you select Worksheet Global Screen Attributes, 1-2-3/G displays a dialog box that lets you select the sheet object or settings to change. By selecting Sheet object, you can select whether you are changing the color of the grid lines, the background of the row and column frames, the text of the row and column frames, the current selection, default background of all cells, color of the characters in unprotected cells, and the color of the range lines added with the Range Attributes Border command (discussed later). Once you select the color to change, you can choose a color that you want for the selected object. The boxes below Palette show how each color appears. If you are using a mouse, you can quickly change many screen attributes by clicking the sheet object to change and the color you want. If you want to select colors for multiple objects with the keyboard, select the object to change by typing the letter or using the arrow keys to move the dotted outline to the object you want to change and pressing ENTER. Then move the dotted outline under Palette to the color you want and press the Spacebar to select the color. If you type the letter or press ENTER, you will also select the OK command button. You can return the dotted outline to the Sheet object section by pressing SHIFT-TAB to continue selecting colors for other sheet objects.

You can also use the Worksheet Global Screen Attributes command to determine whether 1-2-3/G displays grid lines, the column frame, and the row frame. You can include them by selecting the appropriate check box and remove them by unselecting the appropriate check box. The column frame is the row at the top of a worksheet that identifies each column below it. The row frame is the column at the right of a worksheet that identifies each row to the right. The sheet letter and file selector appear only when the worksheet uses both a column frame and a row frame. When a column frame and row frame are displayed, you can use the mouse to change the column width and row height without using the Worksheet Column Set width or Worksheet Row Set height commands. If these frames are hidden, you must use the menu commands to change the column width or row height. When you are done selecting the screen settings, you can select the OK command button with the keyboard by pressing ENTER or clicking the OK command button.

Changing Worksheet Cell Colors

You can supplement your font selections with color selections. You can affect both the text in a cell and its background color.

To change the color of the cells, select Worksheet Global Attributes Color. For all cells, or cells with labels, positive values or negative values, you can change the color of the text and the color of the background. 1-2-3/G displays the current selections next to each option. As you change the colors, 1-2-3/G changes the colors of the boxes to match your selections.

To change the color with a mouse, click the type of cell you want to change under Text or Background, and then click the color you want for the selected cell's text or background color. You can alternate between choosing one of the option buttons in the top of the dialog box and the color for the selected text or background in the bottom of the dialog box. When you have finished choosing colors, click the OK command button.

To change the color with the keyboard, type a **T** for Text or a **B** for Background and then type one of the underlined letters to select the type of cell you want to change. After choosing the cell type, select the color to change by moving the dotted outline to the color you want and press SPACEBAR. Don't press ENTER if you are selecting multiple colors, since pressing ENTER also selects the OK command button. To select another type of cell for which to set the color, press TAB or SHIFT-TAB to move the markers to object you want to select. You can alternate between choosing the cell type and the color by repeating these steps. After choosing the last color to change, press ENTER instead of SPACEBAR to select the OK command button as you choose the color.

Choosing All under Text or Background changes the color for all of the cell types, unless you have chosen a different color for one of the other cell types. When you have finished choosing colors, click the OK command button. The changes that you make with this command only affect the current worksheet unless the current worksheet is part of a group and Group mode is enabled. When Group mode is enabled, this command affects all sheets in the group.

Range Changes

1-2-3/G has several range commands that you can use to change the appearance of a selected group of cells in the worksheet file. For the range or collection selected, your choices will override changes made to the worksheet with global commands. Many of these commands determine how your entries look. These commands let you select the colors, font, and formatting characters 1-2-3/G uses to display your entries. You can access all the range commands through the Range pull-down menu, which is shown in Figure 7-27.

This section discusses the Range menu options found under Erase, Format, Attributes, Label, Justify, and Zero Suppress. There are many similar commands in the Worksheet menu. However, the commands in the Worksheet menu apply to the entire worksheet, while the range commands only apply to the cells selected in a range. In addition, many of the settings in the Worksheet menu are listed in the Worksheet Status dialog box since they apply to all worksheet cells. The range settings are not listed and only apply to the cells that they are used with. 1-2-3/G displays the range settings by displaying range indicators in the window title bar when the cell pointer is on a cell that has one of the range command settings listed in Table 7-1.

The range commands only apply to the range that you select for the command. With the range commands, you can select the range the command uses by using the mouse, pressing the arrow keys, typing the range address, or pressing F3 (Name) and selecting the range name from

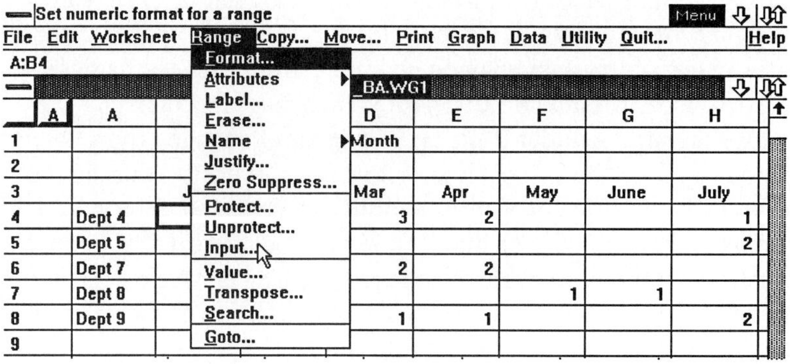

Figure 7-27. Range pull-down menu

Cell Indicator	Command that Adds Indicator	Meaning of Indicator
~	Range Attributes Precision	The precision of calculations made in the cell is set
( )	Range Format (Parens)	Values in the cell are enclosed in parentheses
(,*n*)	Range Format Comma (,)	Cell is formatted with Comma format, with the number of decimal digits set by *n*
(+)/(−)	Range Format +/−	Cell is formatted with +/− format
(A)	Range Format Automatic	Cell is formatted with Automatic format
(C*n*)	Range Format Currency	Cell is formatted with Currency format, with the number of decimal digits set by *n*
(D*n*)	Range Format Date/Time	Cell is formatted with Date/Time format, with the date/time format number indicated by *n*
(F*n*)	Range Format Fixed	Cell is formatted with Fixed format, with the number of decimal digits set by *n*
(G)	Range Format General	Cell is formatted with General format
(H)	Range Format Hidden	Cell is formatted with Hidden format
L	Edit Link Create	Cell is linked to another worksheet or Presentation Manager application
(L)	Range Format Label	Cell is formatted with the Label format
N	Utility User Settings Note	Cell has one or more notes
(P*n*)	Range Format Percent	Cell is formatted with Percent format with the number of decimal digits set by *n*
PR	Range Protect	Cell is protected and worksheet protection is enabled
(S*n*)	Range Format Scientific	Cell is formatted with Scientific format with the number of decimal digits set by *n*
(T)	Range Format Text	Cell is formatted with Text format
U	Range Unprotect	Cell is unprotected
(U)	Range Format User	Cell is formatted with a user-defined format

Table 7-1. Cell Indicators

the list. If Group mode is enabled and you use a range command for one sheet in the group, the command applies to all sheets in the group. When you select the range that command uses, 1-2-3/G automatically supplies the sheet letters so that entire group is included in the command. You can make the command affect only a single sheet in the group by typing the range address to use and including the sheet letters in the range address.

Erasing Cell Ranges

The Range Erase command eliminates the entries in a range of cells, whether they are numbers, labels, or formulas. You can select whether 1-2-3/G erases the cells' contents and/or settings.

Figure 7-28 shows a worksheet containing miscellaneous entries in E1..G13 that are no longer required. To remove these entries, select the collection of ranges, and select Range Erase. The results are shown Figure 7-29. Range Erase just needs to know the cell, range, or collection to erase. You can select the options icon (the box with the three dots) to produce this dialog box:

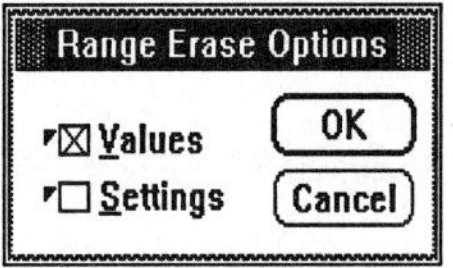

You can also display the Range Erase Options dialog box by pressing SHIFT-F3 (Options). When you select the Values check box the Range Erase command removes the selected cells' contents. When you select the Settings check box, the Range Erase command removes the selected cells' properties. You can select one or both check boxes. When you select the OK command button, 1-2-3/G returns to the prompt for the cells to delete. When you select the confirm icon or press ENTER, 1-2-3/G deletes the contents and/or properties of the selected cells. You can display the Range Erase Options dialog box at any point before you select the confirm icon or press ENTER. Note that if worksheet protection is enabled, the Range Erase command does not work.

1-2-3/G [69.4] Ready

File Edit Worksheet Range Copy... Move... Print Graph Data Utility Quit... Help

B:F12 'and lines to create

ASSUME.WG1

B	A	B	C	D	E	F	G
1					134	346	
2		ASSUMPTIONS			143	13478	
3		Sales Growth					
4		Product A	10.0%				
5		Product B	12.0%		Box is created with		
6		Product C	9.0%		Range Attributes Border command		
7							
8	Sales		1989	1990	1991	1992	1993
9	Product A		100000				
10	Product B		50000				
11	Product C		45000		You can use underlining		
12	Cost of Goods Sold					and lines to create	
13	Profit					dividing lines	

Figure 7-28. Extraneous worksheet entries

Range Format Commands

Range format commands change the format for a specified range of cells on the worksheet. Any valid range or collection described in Chapter 5

1-2-3/G [69.4] Ready

File Edit Worksheet Range Copy... Move... Print Graph Data Utility Quit... Help

B:F13

ASSUME.WG1

B	A	B	C	D	E	F	G
1							
2		ASSUMPTIONS					
3		Sales Growth					
4		Product A	10.0%				
5		Product B	12.0%				
6		Product C	9.0%				
7							
8	Sales		1989	1990	1991	1992	1993
9	Product A		100000				
10	Product B		50000				
11	Product C		45000				
12	Cost of Goods Sold						
13	Profit						

Figure 7-29. Results of Range Erase

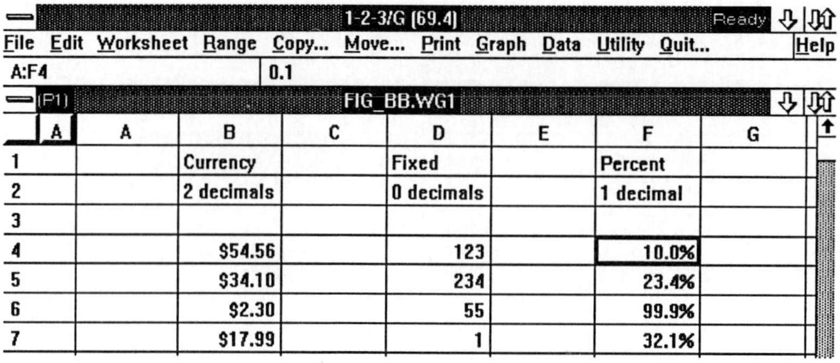

1-2-3/G [69.4] Ready

File Edit Worksheet Range Copy... Move... Print Graph Data Utility Quit... Help

A:F4 0.1

(P1) FIG_BB.WG1

A	A	B	C	D	E	F	G
1		Currency		Fixed		Percent	
2		2 decimals		0 decimals		1 decimal	
3							
4		$54.56		123		10.0%	
5		$34.10		234		23.4%	
6		$2.30		55		99.9%	
7		$17.99		1		32.1%	

Figure 7-30. Formatted Percent numbers

can be affected. The range can be as small as one cell, or it can be a row, column, or rectangle of cells on one or many sheets.

Tip: Plan your format layout as carefully as you plan your worksheet design. You cannot create well-designed models without adequate planning. As you lay out a worksheet design on paper, add color highlighting or some other indication of the formats and attributes you want to use. You can make the format changes as a first step in the model creation process, or you can wait until you have entered your data.

Figure 7-30 shows an example of the use of the Range Format command. In the worksheet shown, the range from B4..B7 has been set to currency format, the range from D4..D7 to fixed format, and the range F4..F7 to percent format.

To use the Range Format command to change the format of a group of cells, follow these steps:

1. Preselect the range you want to format or move your cell pointer to the upper-left cell to be formatted. This allows you to specify the range using only the arrow keys.

2. Select Range Format.

3. Select the Percent format from the menu, either by typing **P**, clicking Percent from the list, or moving to Percent and pressing ENTER.

4. If the format requires a certain number of decimal places, type the desired number of decimal places or accept the default of two decimal places. If you have not already selected a range, click the Range(s) text box to select a range, or press ENTER or TAB to select the range. If you selected a range before selecting Range Format, click the OK command button or press ENTER twice.

5. 1-2-3/G requests the range to format. Specify the range by using the RIGHT ARROW and DOWN ARROW keys to move to the lower-right cell to be formatted. If you are formatting just one cell, don't move the cell pointer. With a mouse you can click the first cell in the range then drag the mouse to the range's opposite corner. To supply a collection address, add the next range by typing a comma or selecting the next range with the right mouse button. After all the cells to format are highlighted, click the OK command button or press ENTER; the cells will display using the new format.

As with Worksheet Global Format changes, changes in format for a range of cells don't affect the internal storage accuracy of your numbers and calculated results. Suppose you decide to display an entry with no decimal places, but internally six or more places are stored. When that cell is used in a calculation, the full internal accuracy is applied, because 1-2-3/G maintains entries with an accuracy of approximately 18 decimal digits. In the "Changing the Precision of Calculations" section, later in this chapter, you will learn how to set the internal accuracy of the numbers that 1-2-3/G uses in calculations.

Range Format commands always take priority over Worksheet Global Format commands. When constructing new worksheets, determine which format will be used more than any other, and use Worksheet Global Format to establish this format. Then, where necessary, use Range Format commands to alter the format of individual cells or ranges.

The Range Format command has a feature not found in the Worksheet Global Format command. Once a cell is formatted with a range command, the window title bar displays a format indicator for the cell. (F2) means Fixed with two decimal places, (C0) means Currency with zero decimal places, and so on. Table 7-1 shows these cell indicators.

You can use the Range Format commands with multiple sheets in two ways. First, with the Group mode option, you can make a format change on the current sheet and have it apply to every sheet in the group. Second, you can supply a range that spans sheets for the Range Format command. In this case, you could format cells F2..H25 as Currency on sheets B, C, and D by selecting the range B:F2..D:H25 in response to the prompt. The format options are covered in their own section later in the chapter.

Changing the Justification of Entries

By default, 1-2-3/G places labels at the left side of cells and values on the right side of cells. You already know how to change the default alignment of an individual label by preceding it with a caret (^) for center justification or a double quotation mark (") for right justification. You also know how to change the global alignment of labels and values with the Worksheet Global Label command. You can use the Range Label command to make the same change on a smaller area. The Range Label command presents options identical to the Worksheet Global Label command, but each column has a Global option button to return the range to the setting made with Worksheet Global Label command, and you must supply the range that the Range Label command uses. You can supply the range or collection the Range Label command uses before selecting the command or after selecting the option buttons for the alignment and display space selections. The Range Label command affects cells containing entries as well as blank cells in the range. If you make an entry in one of these blank cells at a later time, its alignment will be established by the selection made for Range Labels. In earlier releases of 1-2-3, this command only changed labels that already contained entries, and never affected values. The Cell display column is also different from earlier releases of 1-2-3 since you can select for a range whether cells borrow display space from adjacent cells (Long labels), are truncated to display only in the cell's display space (Short labels), or use the global setting in effect for the worksheet (Global).

You can use the Range Label command to select left, right, or center justification for an existing range of entries. Labels originally entered using the default label prefix of an apostrophe (') are left justified and values are right justified, as shown in this worksheet:

1-2-3/G [69.4] Ready
File Edit Worksheet Range Copy... Move... Print Graph Data Utility Quit... Help
A:G2 19567
DAYS.WG1

A	A	B	C	D	E	F	G
1	Day 1	Day 2	Day 3	Day 4	Day 5	Day 6	Day 7
2	8347	13408	12039	32940	35901	29051	19567

If you enter Range Label and select Label and Right to change the orientation of the labels to the right side of each cell, the results look like this:

1-2-3/G [69.4] Ready
File Edit Worksheet Range Copy... Move... Print Graph Data Utility Quit... Help
A:A1 "Day 1
DAYS.WG1

A	A	B	C	D	E	F	G
1	Day 1	Day 2	Day 3	Day 4	Day 5	Day 6	Day 7
2	8347	13408	12039	32940	35901	29051	19567

When you change the alignment of values, 1-2-3/G does not add anything to the cell's contents or any cell indicator to the window title bar to indicate that the value has its alignment altered. Entering the command again and choosing Center under both Labels and Values displays each label in the center of the cell, as shown here:

1-2-3/G [69.4] Ready
File Edit Worksheet Range Copy... Move... Print Graph Data Utility Quit... Help
A:A1 ^Day 1
DAYS.WG1

A	A	B	C	D	E	F	G
1	Day 1	Day 2	Day 3	Day 4	Day 5	Day 6	Day 7
2	8347	13408	12039	32940	35901	29051	19567

You can use the Left option to change either of these results back to the original display format. You can also choose Fill under Labels to fill each cell with repeated cell contents. In addition, you can left align values, as in:

1-2-3/G [69.4] Ready
File Edit Worksheet Range Copy... Move... Print Graph Data Utility Quit... Help
A:A1 \Day 1
DAYS.WG1

A	A	B	C	D	E	F	G
1	Day 1Day 1	Day 2Day 2	Day 3Day 3	Day 4Day 4	Day 5Day 5	Day 6Day 6	Day 7Day 7
2	8347	13408	12039	32940	35901	29051	19567

The last option for Labels and Values is Global, which selects the global setting made with the Worksheet Global Label command.

Selecting the Font for a Range

Earlier, you learned how to use the Worksheet Global Attributes Font command to choose the font 1-2-3/G uses for your worksheet. 1-2-3/G also has a Range Attributes Font command that you can use to apply font selections to a smaller area of a worksheet. When you select Range Attributes Font, you see a dialog box similar to the Worksheet Global Attributes Font dialog box. However, you can also select the range or collection the command uses with the addresses entered in the Range(s) text box. The Range Attributes Font command overrides the global font chosen with Worksheet Global Attributes Font.

To change the font for a range, select Range Attributes Font. From the dialog box, select Font and the desired font. There are many combinations of typefaces and sizes. Under Attributes, which you can select by clicking the check box you want or pressing TAB, you can choose whether the font selected uses boldface, italics, underline, or strikeout. If a range or collection is selected when you select Range Attributes Font, these check boxes are gray, indicating that the selected cells will not have their font attributes changed unless you explicitly select one of the check boxes. When the check boxes are gray, you must select a check box once to remove the attribute from all cells or twice to add the attribute to all cells. You select these check boxes by clicking them or the accompanying text, typing the underlined letter of the attribute, or moving the dotted outline to the attribute and pressing the spacebar. As you make changes in the dialog box, 1-2-3/G displays how the selections will appear in the Preview box. After you select the font and/or attributes, select or accept the range or collection the command uses. When you select OK by clicking the command button or pressing ENTER, all cells listed in the Range(s) text box use the selected font and attributes.

The Range Attributes Font dialog box includes a Setup command button that you can use to change the fonts that appear in the list for both the Worksheet Global Attributes Font and the Range Attributes Font dialog box. Changing the font list in one setup screen affects the font list in both option lists.

Adding Lines to a Worksheet

You can enhance your worksheet by adding lines to it. You can use lines to separate one section of a worksheet from another, or to separate column headings from the data below. Lines are added to a worksheet along grid lines. When you add lines to a worksheet, you may want to hide the grid lines to emphasize the lines that you add. To add lines to a worksheet, select Range Attributes Border. Under Frame, you select whether 1-2-3/G draws a border around all sides of each selected range, or whether it only draws the line on the right, left, top, or bottom side of each range. Under Inside, you select whether 1-2-3/G adds lines between each row in each range (Horiz), between each column in each range (Vert), or between each row and each column in each range (All). Once you select the location for the lines, you can select the line style. Style A adds a solid line, styles B and C add dotted lines, and style D removes any line created with the other three styles. When you select a line position and style, 1-2-3/G draws the line style in the box next to the selected position option. When you select the ranges that this command uses, each range is treated separately. You can use TAB or click the mouse to switch to other line positions and line styles if you want to add several positions and styles at once. When you select OK by pressing ENTER after selecting the range or by clicking the command button, 1-2-3/G draws the selected line types in the selected range. If you want to remove some lines later, select the options for Frame and Inside and select line style D.

Tip: If you are adding lines to your worksheet with Range Attributes Border, you will probably want to remove the grid lines to make the lines stand out. You can remove the grid lines by selecting Worksheet Global Screen Attributes Settings Grid lines.

Changing a Range of Cell Colors

You can select the cell colors of a range with the Range Attributes Color command. These settings can override the global worksheet setting that you made with Worksheet Global Attributes Color.

Selecting Range Attributes Color, displays a dialog box that is identical to the worksheet dialog box with three exceptions. First, the dialog box only displays the selected colors for the cell type colors that you change from the default. Second, the Range Attributes Color dialog box includes a Reset command button that you can select to change all of the colors for the cell types to the colors set with the Worksheet Global Attributes Color command. Third, the Range Attributes Color dialog box includes a Range(s) text box that selects the cells that the Range Attributes Color command changes. You can choose this range or collection before you select the Range Attributes Color command. You can also choose the range or collection after selecting the last color if you press ENTER or click the Range(s) text box.

Range Justify

The Range Justify command is as close as 1-2-3/G comes to providing word processing features. It adjusts the length of a line of text to fit within margin limitations.

With the Range Justify command, you can enter one or more long labels in a column and, after the entry is complete, you can decide how wide the display should be by selecting a justify range. If that range is two cells wide, for example, the long labels will be redistributed so that they take up more rows but display only in two columns.

Range Justify doesn't provide full word processing support, but it does allow you to write readable documentation on the screen, or write a short memo that references worksheet data. This feature frees you from having to concentrate on the length of your entry as you type. When you have entered all of your data, 1-2-3/G adjusts the line length according to your specifications.

Figure 7-31 shows some long labels entered into A1..A6 of the worksheet. The labels are all of different lengths. Suppose you decide to confine the display to columns A through C. (The labels are entered in column A and will remain in that location; what you are changing is the space they borrow for display purposes.) To make the change, take the following steps:

1. Move your cell pointer to the beginning of the range you will use for display—A1 in the example.

2. Select Range Justify.

	A	B	C	D	E	F	G
1	To test the Range Justify command, we will type a series of long labels in Column A.						
2	Then we will attempt to confine the display of these long labels to the first three						
3	columns. To do this we will use Range Justify and specify our justify range as A1..C1.						
4	The labels will be shortened to use only the allotted spaces and will require						
5	additional spreadsheet rows for the display.						

Figure 7-31. Worksheet containing long labels

3. Select the range A1..C1 by pressing the RIGHT ARROW key or by dragging the mouse from A1 to C1.

4. Click the confirm icon or press ENTER. Your justified data should look like Figure 7-32.

To widen the display again, move your cell pointer to A1 and start the process over. For example, you might want to specify A1..F1 as the justify range to use the first six columns for the display.

If there is information in column A or in cells after the end of the justify range, the Range Justify command will displace that information

	A	B	C	D	E	F	G
1	To test the Range Justify command,						
2	we will type a series of long labels						
3	in Column A. Then we will attempt						
4	to confine the display of these long						
5	labels to the first three columns.						
6	To do this we will use Range Justify						
7	and specify our justify range as						
8	A1..C1. The labels will be shortened						
9	to use only the allotted spaces and						
10	will require additional spreadsheet						
11	rows for the display.						

Figure 7-32. Worksheet with long labels justified

as it expands the long label down the worksheet. Since the label was originally entered in column A, *only* the cell entries in column A are displaced. Even if the justify range includes columns A through C, and there is information in the cells to the right of column A, that information is not displaced. For instance, a table in cells B10..C14 would be unaffected by the paragraph rearrangement shown in Figure 7-32. Instead, the label display in column A would be truncated in rows 10 through 14, just as it is when an entry to the right of any long label truncates the label display.

You can also select multiple rows in the justification range. When the selected range contains more than one row, 1-2-3/G justifies the range only if the current range is large enough to fit the reformatted text. If the range is not large enough, 1-2-3/G displays a message instead of rearranging the text. Selecting multiple rows also prevents 1-2-3/G from shifting the remaining contents in the first column of the range. When the range contains multiple rows, the data outside of the range in any column does not change.

In addition, you can justify a multiple-sheet range, either by selecting a range that spans multiple sheets, or by selecting a range from a sheet that is part of a group when 1-2-3/G is in Group mode. When you justify a multiple-sheet range, the ranges on each sheet are justified separately. For example, suppose you select the range A:A1..A:F1 when sheet A is part of a group containing sheets A through D. Assuming that Group mode is enabled, when you select the range, 1-2-3/G justifies sheet A using the range A:A1..A:F1, then sheet B using B:A1..B:F1, sheet C using C:A1..C:F1, and sheet D using D:A1..D:F1.

Changing the Precision of Calculations

When 1-2-3/G calculates numbers, it uses their full precision. That is, if you multiply 5.3*6.8985315, 1-2-3/G returns 36.56221695. If these represent two measurements and each measuring device measure the amount to different precision, you don't gain a more accurate measurement by using all digits after the decimal point. Since the first measurement is made to the nearest tenth, the area you calculate is only accurate to the nearest hundredth (a tenth times a tenth is a hundredth). You can select different levels of precision for the numbers that 1-2-3/G uses in calculations by selecting Range Attributes Precision and the Limited precision option button. In the text box, type the number of decimal digits

1-2-3/G will use in calculations. For the two measurement example, you can enter **1** so that 1-2-3/G rounds the numbers after the first digit after the decimal point. After you make a selection, you must select the range to be changed. The range you select chooses the values that use the limited precision rather than the formula that uses the values. For example, consider this worksheet:

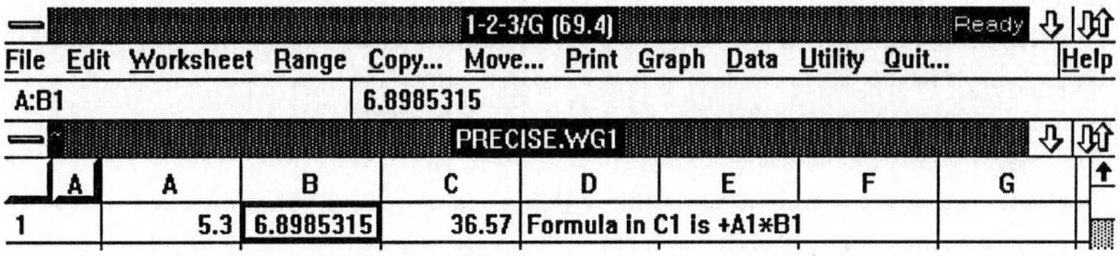

1-2-3/G (69.4) Ready

File Edit Worksheet Range Copy... Move... Print Graph Data Utility Quit... Help

A:B1 6.8985315

PRECISE.WG1

A	A	B	C	D	E	F	G
1	5.3	6.8985315	36.57	Formula in C1 is +A1*B1			

You would select the range A1..B1. As with other commands that use a range, you can pick the range before you select the command or after choosing a precision option. When you change the precision of a range, the window title bar displays ~ when the cell pointer is on a cell with a limited precision. When you use a limited precision with the two values, the formula returns 36.57. When you want to return to full precision, select Range Attributes Precision Full Precision and the desired range to return to the default setting.

Format Options

Except for Reset, you can select format options either through the Worksheet Global Format or the Range Format command. Since Reset reverses Range Format commands by changing the range back to the global setting, you don't need this option on the Worksheet Global Format menu. The following format options are summarized for you in the "Format Options" box shown earlier in the chapter.

With both the Worksheet Global Format and the Range Format command, 1-2-3/G displays how the selected format will appear. The value that appears in the Preview box is the cell pointer's value. If the cell pointer is pointing to a blank cell or a label, 1-2-3/G uses a sample value or date such as 123.12 or the current date. You can use the Preview box to confirm that you are selecting the desired format.

Fixed Format

The Fixed format lets you choose the number of places to the right of the decimal point to display. Like the General format, it does not display dollar signs or commas.

If you use the Fixed format option and the numbers you enter or calculate with formulas don't contain enough decimal places, zeros are added. For example, if you enter **5.67** in a cell that you formatted as Fixed with four decimal places, your entry displays as 5.6700. With Fixed format, you can select from 0 to 15 decimal places. If the column is not wide enough to display all decimal places, asterisks appears in the cell. Leading zero integers are added for decimal fraction numbers if you select the Leading zero check box in the Utility User Settings International dialog box.

Scientific Format

The Scientific format displays numbers in exponential notation. You can choose from 0 to 15 decimal places in the first, or multiplier, portion of the expression, which distinguishes the Scientific format option from the scientific notation display generated by the General format option. With General, if scientific notation is required for a very large or very small number, 1-2-3/G determines the number of decimals in the multiplier. With Scientific format, you make this decision when you establish the format.

Scientific notation is useful when you need to display very large or very small numbers in a limited cell width. This notation is primarily used in scientific and engineering applications and is not acceptable on most business reports.

Currency Format

The Currency format places a currency symbol next to each entry. It also adds a separator between thousands and hundreds and between millions and thousands. This format shows negative numbers in parentheses or with the minus sign. With the U.S. default country setting, 1-2-3/G uses $ before the number for a currency symbol, a comma for the thousands separator, and parentheses around negative numbers. You can change these settings with the Utility User Settings International command described in Chapter 6.

You can specify from 0 to 15 decimal places for this format, although the most common settings are 0 for whole dollars, and 2 to show both dollars and cents. The default setting is 2. To show dollars and cents, you just have to press ENTER after selecting Currency from either the Worksheet Format or Range Format dialog box option list. Using the Range command, you also need to specify the size of the range to format.

Comma Format

The Comma format is just like the Currency format, but it does not use the currency symbol. As with the Currency format, negative numbers are usually shown in parentheses and commas are added as separators.

You can display from 0 to 15 decimal places with this format. Enter the number of decimal places when prompted with the default. If you wish to accept the default (2), just press ENTER.

General Format

General is the default format. Unlike the other formats, this format does not provide consistent displays, since it depends on the size of the number you enter. Very large and very small numbers display in scientific notation when the General format is in effect. Some numbers appear as they are entered, while others receive a leading zero, or are rounded to a number of decimal digits that fits in the selected column width. The General format also suppresses trailing zeros after the decimal point.

General format does not let you choose the number of zeros for the display, and it often produces a display with varying numbers of decimal places in the entries. There is also no way to establish the number of digits for the multiplier when you use the Scientific format option for very small and very large numbers. When you display a number in scientific notation with the General format, 1-2-3/G displays as many digits as fit within the column.

Here are some sample entries in General format:

Entry	General Display
10000000000	1.000E+10
2345678	2345678
234.76895432	234.76895

General format uses a (G) indicator. A numeric digit is not present, since the command doesn't expect you to decide the number of decimal digits to show.

+/− Format

The +/− format is one of the most unusual 1-2-3/G formats. It creates a series of plus (+) or minus (−) signs to represent the size of the number in the cell, producing a sort of bar graph. These signs change to asterisks if the size of the bar exceeds the column width. When the value of the cell is zero, a period (.) displays on the left side of the cell. This format is also the only numeric format that is initially left aligned within the cell.

The +/− format creates the following horizontal displays from the entries shown:

Entry	+/− Display
0	.
5	+++++
−4	−−−−
−3.85	−−−

The indicator (+)/(−) will appear in the command line when the cell pointer is on any cell that has been formatted with the +/− format using the Range Format command.

Tip: Use a monospace font (such as Courier) with cells that use the +/− format. The − sign in proportional fonts such as System Proportional, Helvetica, and Times Roman is much narrower than the +, so a large negative number will seem shorter than the same number multiplied by −1 (made into a positive number).

Percent

You can use the Percent format to display percentages attractively, appending the % symbol to each cell. You can choose any number of decimal places between 0 and 15.

Entries to be formatted as percentages are stored as decimal fractions. For example, ten percent is entered as .1 or 10%. 1-2-3/G stores this number as .1. When you apply the Percent format, the number you have entered is multiplied by 100 before the % symbol is added. Thus, an entry of .1 becomes 10%, and an entry of 10 becomes 1000%.

Date/Time Format

You use the Date/Time format for date and time entries. As described in Chapter 5, 1-2-3/G provides a single serial number that represents both the date and the time. The whole number portion of the entry represents the date, and the fractional portion of the entry represents the time.

Tip: Format the cells into which you will enter dates and times before you make your entries. It is easier to check that you are entering the correct dates and times if the date and time serial numbers to which 1-2-3/G converts your entries appear as the dates and times they represent.

With 1-2-3/G, you can enter dates and times by typing the date or time in one of the date and time formats that the Range Format dialog box provides. You can also access date and time serial numbers with some of the @ functions described in Chapter 9. @TODAY returns the date serial number for the current date. @NOW returns the combined date and time serial number for the current date and time. Neither @NOW nor @TODAY requires function arguments; you just enter them into worksheet cells as either @NOW or @TODAY. If these functions return the incorrect date or time, your computer does not have the correct date and time entered into its system. You can use the Control Panel program to change the computer's date and time.

1-2-3/G shows dates as serial numbers representing the number of days from December 30, 1899 to the current day. For example, the serial number for September 24, 1986, is 31679. Before you format that number as a date, it appears as 31679 on your worksheet. Fortunately, Date formats provide a number of other options. You can display the date as 24-Sep-86, 24-Sep, Sep-86, 09/24/86, or 09/86. All of these formats are much easier to understand than a serial date.

For each cell that contains both a time and date serial number portion, you must decide whether to apply a Date or a Time format, since you cannot apply both formats to the same cell. That is, although the @NOW function places both a time and a date in a cell, you can only display one at a time—the one you see depends on the format you choose.

As with dates, you will probably want to use the special Time formats to make the time easier to read. The Time format options are just as varied as the Date formats. You can display a time of 10:00 P.M. as 10:00:00 PM, 10:00 PM, 22:00:00, or 22:00.

There are four Time formats. Two use the AM and PM designation, and the other two are international formats that use the settings made under Time format in the Utility User Settings International dialog box. For more information, see Chapter 6 under "International Format Options." By default, the two international time formats use a 24-hour day.

You can use date and time entries in a variety of applications, such as to represent shipment receipts or line processing time. You can also use them to represent loan due dates, appointment dates, or order dates.

Automatic Format

The Automatic format is 1-2-3/G's most powerful formatting choice. It converts your entry to one of the other format types as you make a value entry in the cell. You must enter the value in a valid Range Format sequence. For example, you must enter a date in one of the acceptable date formats, except month/day, which 1-2-3/G interprets as a division formula. Automatic can supply the correct format for a variety of different data types. It allows you to make entries as you wish to see them, and uses the edit characters within your first entry in a cell to determine how the data will display. 1-2-3/G then stores the data from your entry in its numeric form.

A cell with an Automatic format can successfully handle Currency, Comma, Fixed, Percent, Scientific, and Date/Time formats. If you change a cell with an existing entry to Automatic, 1-2-3/G uses the General format. Cells with an Automatic format display (A) in the window title bar. If you enter a formula or label in a cell containing a label, the cell retains the Automatic format. Any formula displays its results in General format.

Figure 7-33 shows the effects of Automatic format in column B, assuming that the entries in column A were entered exactly as shown. Column C shows how these entries are stored, and column D shows the cell indicator that appears when the cell pointer is on the entry in column B. After you type your entry and press ENTER, the (A) for Automatic format is replaced by one of 1-2-3/G's other format entries.

If you want the cell entry formatted as Currency, precede your entry with a dollar sign. The entry $5 in a cell formatted as Automatic

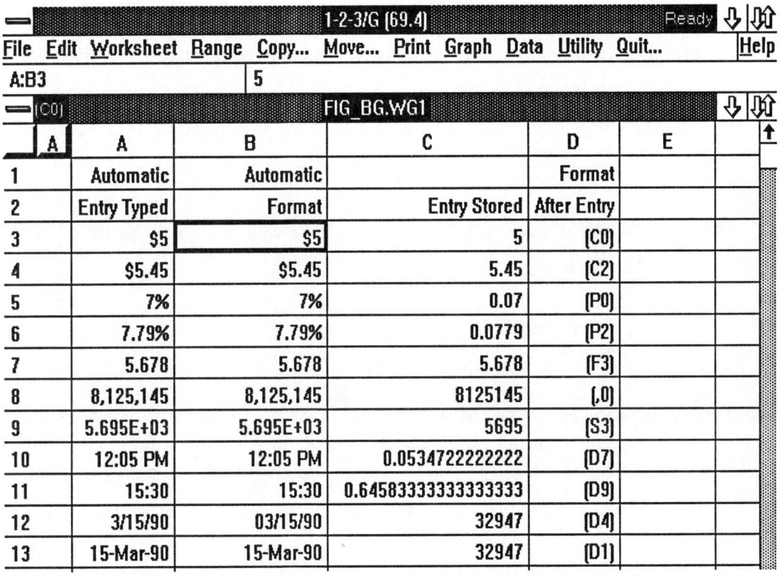

1-2-3/G [69.4] Ready

File Edit Worksheet Range Copy... Move... Print Graph Data Utility Quit... Help

A:B3 5

(C0) FIG_BG.WG1

A	A	B	C	D	E
1	Automatic	Automatic		Format	
2	Entry Typed	Format	Entry Stored	After Entry	
3	$5	$5	5	(C0)	
4	$5.45	$5.45	5.45	(C2)	
5	7%	7%	0.07	(P0)	
6	7.79%	7.79%	0.0779	(P2)	
7	5.678	5.678	5.678	(F3)	
8	8,125,145	8,125,145	8125145	(,0)	
9	5.695E+03	5.695E+03	5695	(S3)	
10	12:05 PM	12:05 PM	0.0534722222222	(D7)	
11	15:30	15:30	0.6458333333333333	(D9)	
12	3/15/90	03/15/90	32947	(D4)	
13	15-Mar-90	15-Mar-90	32947	(D1)	

Figure 7-33. Effects of Automatic format

displays as $5 and the (A) cell indicator changes to (C0). An entry of 7.79% is stored as .0779, with a format of Percent with two decimal place (P2), so it displays as you entered it. The entry 5.678 displays as 5.678, with a format of Fixed with three decimal places (F3). An entry of 8,125,145 is stored as 8125145 in the cell, with a display format of Comma with zero decimal places (C0). The entry 5.695E+03 is stored as 5695 in the cell, and displays as entered. A time entry of 12:05 or 12:05 PM is stored as .5208333333, and formats the cell with either (D9) or (D7), depending on which entry you used. The entry 3/15/90 or 15-Mar-90 is stored as 32947, the date serial number for 3/15/90, and formats the cell as dictated by the style of your entry. Thus, if you use 3/15/90, the format for the cell is (D4); if you use 15-Mar-90, the format is (D1).

Tip: Automatic format occurs only once for a cell. Once you make an entry into an Automatic format cell, 1-2-3/G changes the cell's format to match the format of the entry. If you make a new entry in the cell, it retains the cell format of the first entry. To change the format, you must use the Range Format command.

Text Format

Text format allows you to display actual formulas, rather than the results of formula calculations. Using Text format causes a cell to display exactly what you enter. If your entry was a formula, 1-2-3/G also stores the result of the formula, and you can access the results with a reference to the cell.

The following table shows how different entries appear when you format a cell as text:

Entry	Text Display
+A1+A2	+A1+A2
+A3*A4/A5	+A3*A4/A5
Sales	Sales
23.56	23.56

When the cell pointer is on a cell formatted as text with a Range command, the indicator (T) appears in the window title bar.

Label Format

The Label format adds a label indicator at the front of values entered after the format is applied. Existing value entries are not changed to labels. Cells formatted with the Label format display an (L) indicator in the window title bar. This type of format is ideal for numbers that you don't want treated as values, such as social security numbers, ZIP codes, and phone numbers.

This format only affects entries that you type. When 1-2-3/G generates a series of entries with Data Fill, the label prefix is not added, and the values display in General format.

Hidden Format

Hidden format displays a cell as a blank; that is, 1-2-3/G suppresses the display of the cell. Even though they don't appear on the worksheet the cell's contents are still stored internally and are accessed when you reference the cell in a formula. In fact, the contents of the cell will display in the contents box when you move your cell pointer to the cell. You can hide the contents further by enabling worksheet protection, as discussed in Chapter 6. When a worksheet is protected, 1-2-3/G displays PR in the window title bar and does not display the contents of hidden cells in the contents box.

With the Hidden format, all entries appear as blanks, regardless of type. The cell indicator for a hidden cell, when the format is applied with a Range command, is (H). Figure 7-34, shows the cell pointer in a hidden cell, and the contents displayed in the contents box.

The main use of hidden cells is in macro applications. If a worksheet is kept completely under macro control, the Hidden format can provide a measure of security. For more about macros, see Part Six, "1-2-3/G's Macro Features."

Parentheses Format

The Parentheses format causes 1-2-3/G to enclose all numeric values in parentheses. Unlike the other formats, this format is supplemental to any existing format. A cell formatted as Currency remains formatted as

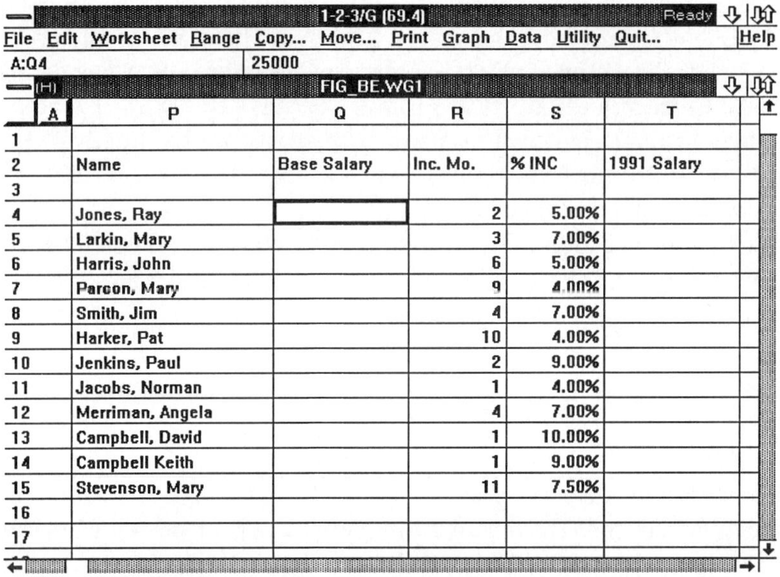

1-2-3/G (69.4) Ready

File Edit Worksheet Range Copy... Move... Print Graph Data Utility Quit... Help

A:Q4 25000

(H) FIG_BE.WG1

A	P	Q	R	S	T
1					
2	Name	Base Salary	Inc. Mo.	% INC	1991 Salary
3					
4	Jones, Ray		2	5.00%	
5	Larkin, Mary		3	7.00%	
6	Harris, John		6	5.00%	
7	Parcon, Mary		9	4.00%	
8	Smith, Jim		4	7.00%	
9	Harker, Pat		10	4.00%	
10	Jenkins, Paul		2	9.00%	
11	Jacobs, Norman		1	4.00%	
12	Merriman, Angela		4	7.00%	
13	Campbell, David		1	10.00%	
14	Campbell Keith		1	9.00%	
15	Stevenson, Mary		11	7.50%	
16					
17					

Figure 7-34. Numbers hidden with the Hidden format

Currency while it is enclosed in parentheses, as in ($5). Likewise, cells in the Percent, Date, Time, or Scientific formats all retain their existing format. Even the format indicator in the title bar shows both formats, with Currency and Parentheses represented as (C0( )).

User-Defined Formats

In addition to all of 1-2-3/G's predefined formats, you can create your own formats to display numbers, date serial numbers, time serial numbers, and formula results. You create user-defined formats by using the Format Description Language characters listed on the following pages. When you select User as the format, you must choose which of the 64 potential user-defined formats to use. The list of user-defined formats lists the format definition for each choice or the phrase Undefined if the selected user format doesn't have a definition. Once you select the user-defined format from the list, you can create or alter the format definition. Then, once you enter the format definition, you can select the

OK command button or select the range that applies for a Range Format command. User-defined formats display a (U) cell indicator in the window title bar. While user-defined formats are easy to use once the format definition is established, the hardest part is creating the definition. The definition you enter depends on the type of data you want to use with the user-defined format. As you enter the format definition, 1-2-3/G displays how the format will appear in a cell.

User-defined formats are good for the additional display options you have with dates and times. To tell 1-2-3/G that the format definition is for a date or time, start the format definition with a T. If it is a date, use the following characters to build a format description.

Format Entry	Results
D	Display 1-31 representing the day of the month
DD	Display 01-31 representing the day of the month
WDAY	Display the three-letter abbreviation for the day's name
WEEKDAY	Display the day's name spelled in full
M or MO	Display 1-12 representing the month's number
MM or MMO	Display 01-12 representing the month's number
MON	Display the three-letter abbreviation for the month
MONTH	Display the month spelled in full
YY	Display 00-99 as the last two digits of the year
YYYY	Display 1899-9999 as the digits of the year

With the format entries that display letters (WDAY, WEEKDAY, MON, and MONTH), the case of the entry in the format definition determines the case of the entry in the cells formatted with the format definition. For example, with a date of 15-APR-91, the format of TWEEKDAY, MON D returns MONDAY, APR 15; a format of TWeekday, Mon D returns Monday, Apr 15; and a format of Tweekday, mon d returns monday, apr 15. The formatting entries that return digits can be in upper- or lowercase. The format definition can also include spaces, commas, and other punctuation marks where you want them to appear. These features let you create date formats that are not available by selecting Date/Time for a formatting selection.

You can enter the following formatting entries for user-defined time formats:

Format Entry	Results
h or hh	Display 1-12 representing the hour of the day using a 12-hour clock (when AMPM is used) or 0-23 representing the hour of the day using a 24-hour clock (when AMPM is omitted)
H or HH	Display 01-12 representing the hour of the day using a 12-hour clock (when AMPM is used) or 00-23 representing the hour of the day using a 24-hour clock (when AMPM is omitted)
M or MI	Display 1-59 representing the minute of the hour
MM or MMI	Display 01-59 representing the minute of the hour
S	Display 1-59 representing the second of the minute
SS	Display 01-59 representing the second of the minute
AMPM	Display AM or PM to indicate before or after noon

In user-defined time formats, the format entry for minutes must be included directly after the hour so 1-2-3/G does not display the month instead. The other formatting entries can be upper- or lowercase. The AMPM format actually displays the before noon and after noon indicators selected with the Utility User Settings International Time format command. By default, these indicators are AM for before noon and PM for after noon. You can combine date and times into a single format, such as Weekday, Mon d H:MM AMPM, which displays Monday, Apr 15 6:00 PM for 6 PM on Monday, April 15.

You can also employ user-defined formats for numbers. The number format entries can contain two- or three-parts format definitions. Each part defines a format for a range of values and is separated from the other parts by a semicolon. If the format definition has two parts, the first part applies to zero and positive numbers and the second part applies to negative numbers. If the format definition has three parts, the first part applies to positive numbers, the second part applies to zeros, and the third part applies to negative numbers. Each part of a numeric user-defined format starts with an N or n. Numeric format definitions can contain the following format entries:

Format Entry	Results
9	Indicates that a digit should occupy the position or be left blank if the value does not have a digit for the position
0	Indicates that a digit should occupy the position, even if the digit is a zero
%	Displays the value as a percentage by multiplying the value by 100 and appending a %
,	Displays a thousands separator at the indicated position
.	Displays a decimal separator at the indicated position
E−	Displays the value in scientific notation, with the value after the − selecting the power of 10 by which the number is multiplied. Positive exponents do not include the + after the E
E+	Displays the value in scientific notation, with the value after the + selecting the power of 10 by which the number is multiplied. Positive exponents include the + after the E

You select the thousands and decimal separators in the Utility User Settings International dialog box under Number format. The case of the E determines the case of the E in the scientific formatted number. The 9's and 0's represent the digits in the values. For example, using 9999999 to represent 4560 displays 4560, while using 0000000 displays 0004560. The 9's and 0's are often combined, primarily using 9's in front of the decimal point and 0's after the decimal point. Using 0's after the decimal point lets you align the values, just as selecting the number of decimal digits for Fixed, Currency, Comma, Scientific and Percent lets you align the decimal points. When you combine these formats into a single format definition, sample format definitions include N999999.00;N0;N(999999.00). When you apply this format to 8934.1, 0, and −14893.1023, they appear as 8934.10, 0, (14893.10). You can use the formats with numbers to customize display formats and provide more formats than those listed in the Range Format or Worksheet Global Format dialog boxes.

Both date and time and the numeric user-defined formats can include other entries. One type of entry is text. If 1-2-3/G doesn't understand part of your entries as an established formatting entry, it displays the characters recorded in the formatted entries. For example, the format N99999;Nzero;N –99999 displays zeros as the label zero. If the text you want to add could be interpreted as a valid formatting entry, enclose it in quotes. You can also precede the potentially confusing character with a backslash. Examples of this are

T"Date : "Mon d. or T\Date : Mon d.

1-2-3/G will confuse the initial D as the formatting entry d for day of the month without the quotes or backslash. Using text also has an advantage with logical formulas. The format of N"True";N"False";N"Error in formula" displays logical formulas that return a value of 1 or true as True, and logical formulas that return a value of 0 or false as False. You can also use the asterisk at the end of a format definition. The asterisk fills the width of the column with the character that follows the asterisk.

Copying and Moving Worksheet Data

Moving Information
Copying Information
Converting Formulas to Values
Transposing Data
Using the Clipboard to Copy and Move Information
Using 1-2-3/G's Search and Replace Features

EIGHT

This chapter focuses on menu commands that duplicate and reposition your entries and extend your productivity in using the worksheet. You will learn additional commands on the worksheet tool menus.

You will learn how to cut and paste worksheet entries to make 1-2-3/G do much of the work of model creation. You can use these techniques to build new worksheets with a minimum of effort, and can apply them again to restructure existing models to meet your current needs. You will learn to use the Copy and Move commands to handle these tasks for you. You will also learn how to use the Presentation Manager's Clipboard to share data between Presentation Manager applications. Range commands will also boost your productivity by locating required entries quickly. If you prefer, you can also have 1-2-3/G replace the entries with something else once it locates them.

Moving Information

Creating a worksheet is sometimes a trial-and-error process, during which you attempt to obtain the most effective placement of data. 1-2-3/G's Move command permits you to move a range of cells to another location on one of the sheets in the active file. You must specify both a From and a To range. The From range marks the original location of the data to be moved, and the To range is the new location you have selected. 1-2-3/G will prompt you for these ranges. You can use any of the normal methods for specifying a range location, including range names, typing cell addresses, and pointing with arrow keys or a mouse.

It is easiest to specify the From range by selecting the cell, range, or collection before invoking the command. You can preselect the range by pointing and dragging the worksheet area with the mouse or by using CTRL and a period to select the range with the keyboard. Alternately, you can place your cell pointer on the upper-left cell in the range to move before selecting Move from the menu bar. When you select Move, 1-2-3/G assumes that the current cell or selected range or collection is the one to be moved. To expand this range, move the cell pointer in the direction you want; the beginning cell remains anchored in place. You can move a single sheet or a multiple-sheet range or collection.

If you want to change the beginning of the range 1-2-3/G suggests, press ESCAPE or BACKSPACE to unlock the range beginning. Move your cell pointer to the first cell in the range or collection you wish to move, type a period, and move to the end of the range or select a new range with a mouse. Or, you can just type a new range when presented with 1-2-3/G's prompt. When you select a new range with a mouse, the selected range automatically replaces any range displayed in the control line. When the range is selected, click the To range prompt (any part of the To range address), or press ENTER or TAB.

Unless you are typing the range reference, you must move your cell pointer to the area on the worksheet designated as the To range. If you position your cell pointer before invoking the Move command, the From and To range will display the selected cell as their selected addresses. Since the suggestion for To is a single cell, you don't need to press ESCAPE to unlock the beginning of the range. Just move to or click the desired beginning cell for the To range, or type the beginning cell from the keyboard. You just need to specify the beginning cell for To, even if you are moving many cells. When you select a single cell, 1-2-3 assumes that the selected cell is the starting point where the From range is moved.

1-2-3/G will move data even when you specify a To range that is not large enough to contain all of the entries. It simply starts at the beginning of the specified range and continues to use whatever additional space it needs.

When both the To and From ranges are selected, click the confirm icon or press ENTER after selecting the To range. If you press TAB, 1-2-3/G switches to the From range. 1-2-3/G moves the cells as long as the To and From range don't contain protected cells (worksheet protection is enabled). The moved cells contain all of the cell entries and format information of the original cells.

The Move command can move one or many worksheet cells. The example in Figure 8-1 shows a long label that is not in the center of the worksheet. It's time consuming to reenter the label in a more central location; you can move it more quickly with Move. Place the cell pointer in A1 and select Move. Since the From range is the cell pointer location, click the To range prompt to accept the current From entry and edit the To range selection. You can also press ENTER or TAB to accept the current cell address for the From range. To select a To range, click C1 or move the cell pointer to C1, and click the confirm icon or press ENTER to accept C1 as the To range. Figure 8-2 shows the worksheet after the move is complete. Although the label displays in multiple cells, you can move it by specifying only one cell each for the From and To ranges.

As another example, suppose that you want to move the entries in cells A2..C15 to the right in the worksheet shown in Figure 8-3. These cells contain numbers, labels, and formulas. (The formulas are shown in Figure 8-4.) To move all these entries at once, select Move and the From range A2..C15. When the To range is requested, select B2. You only need one cell to tell 1-2-3/G where to begin the To range; it

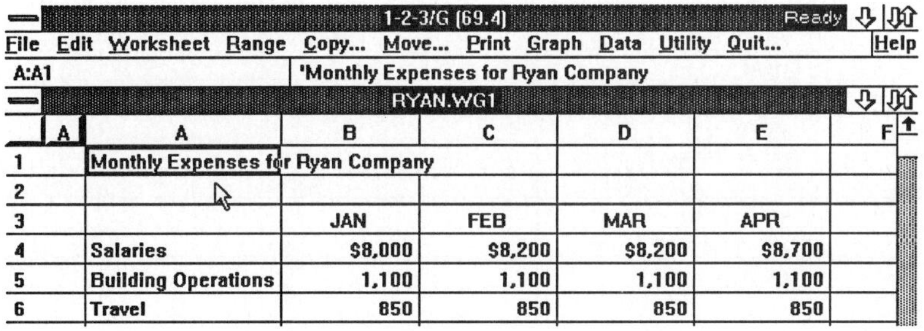

1-2-3/G [69.4] Ready

File Edit Worksheet Range Copy... Move... Print Graph Data Utility Quit... Help

A:A1 'Monthly Expenses for Ryan Company

RYAN.WG1

A	A	B	C	D	E	F
1	Monthly Expenses for Ryan Company					
2						
3		JAN	FEB	MAR	APR	
4	Salaries	$8,000	$8,200	$8,200	$8,700	
5	Building Operations	1,100	1,100	1,100	1,100	
6	Travel	850	850	850	850	

Figure 8-1. Long label to be moved

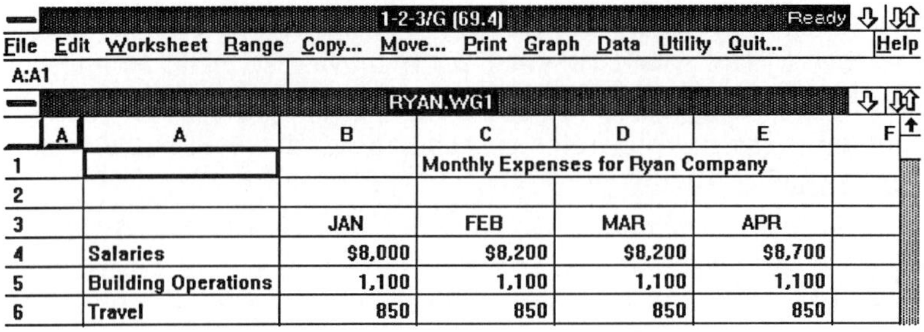

1-2-3/G (69.4) Ready

File Edit Worksheet Range Copy... Move... Print Graph Data Utility Quit... Help

A:A1

RYAN.WG1

A	A	B	C	D	E	F
1			Monthly Expenses for Ryan Company			
2						
3		JAN	FEB	MAR	APR	
4	Salaries	$8,000	$8,200	$8,200	$8,700	
5	Building Operations	1,100	1,100	1,100	1,100	
6	Travel	850	850	850	850	

Figure 8-2. Result of moving label

automatically uses B2..D15 as the complete To range. Figure 8-5 shows the worksheet after the move; notice how the formulas are adjusted to reflect their new locations. Note also that the From and To ranges overlap. 1-2-3/G can handle this. While 1-2-3/G can move all sizes of ranges, you cannot use the Move command to move collections.

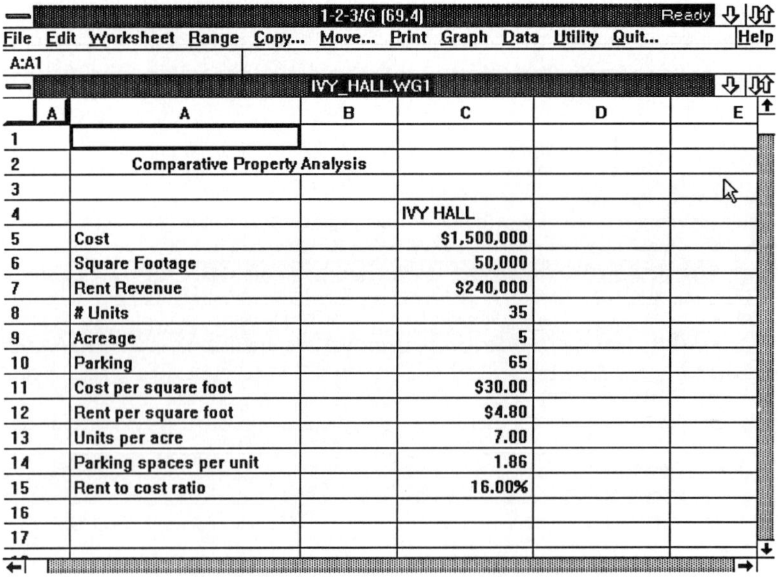

1-2-3/G (69.4) Ready

File Edit Worksheet Range Copy... Move... Print Graph Data Utility Quit... Help

A:A1

IVY_HALL.WG1

A	A	B	C	D	E
1					
2	Comparative Property Analysis				
3					
4			IVY HALL		
5	Cost		$1,500,000		
6	Square Footage		50,000		
7	Rent Revenue		$240,000		
8	# Units		35		
9	Acreage		5		
10	Parking		65		
11	Cost per square foot		$30.00		
12	Rent per square foot		$4.80		
13	Units per acre		7.00		
14	Parking spaces per unit		1.86		
15	Rent to cost ratio		16.00%		
16					
17					

Figure 8-3. Entries in A2..C15 to be moved

1-2-3/G (69.4) Ready

File Edit Worksheet Range Copy... Move... Print Graph Data Utility Quit... Help

A:C11 +C5/C6

(T) IVY_HALL.WG1

A	A	B	C	D	E
1					
2	Comparative Property Analysis				
3					
4			IVY HALL		
5	Cost		$1,500,000		
6	Square Footage		50,000		
7	Rent Revenue		$240,000		
8	# Units		35		
9	Acreage		5		
10	Parking		65		
11	Cost per square foot		+C5/C6		
12	Rent per square foot		+C7/C6		
13	Units per acre		+C8/C9		
14	Parking spaces per unit		+C10/C8		
15	Rent to cost ratio		+C7/C5		
16					
17					

Figure 8-4. Display of formulas

1-2-3/G (69.4) Ready

File Edit Worksheet Range Copy... Move... Print Graph Data Utility Quit... Help

A:B2 ' Comparative Property Analysis

IVY_HALL.WG1

A	A	B	C	D	E
1					
2		Comparative Property Analysis			
3					
4				IVY HALL	
5		Cost		$1,500,000	
6		Square Footage		50,000	
7		Rent Revenue		$240,000	
8		# Units		35	
9		Acreage		5	
10		Parking		65	
11		Cost per square foot		+D5/D6	
12		Rent per square foot		+D7/D6	
13		Units per acre		+D8/D9	
14		Parking spaces per unit		+D10/D8	
15		Rent to cost ratio		+D7/D5	
16					
17					

Figure 8-5. Result of Move in Figure 8-3

When you move a named range, 1-2-3/G adjusts the range address that the range name refers to. If you move the upper-left or lower-right corner of an existing range, the range address expands or contracts to reflect the new corner location of the range. This assumes that you are moving to another location in the same worksheet file. Otherwise, formulas that use the range evaluate to ERR. Moving other cells in the range does not affect the range's address. If you move a named range to another sheet, the range name remains in the file and refers to the range in the worksheet file selected for the To range. If you move a range of cells to another file and replace that file, the To file reflects the originating file and cell reference. The range in the new worksheet has no name. If you move data in a cell to the upper-left or lower-right corner of a range, a range name becomes undefined, and the range addresses in formulas are replaced with ERR. This problem also occurs when you move an entry to another cell that is used by a formula.

Tip: If you want to move an entry to a cell or a corner of a range that is used in a formula, use the Copy command to copy the entry to the new location then erase the contents of the cell from the original location.

Moving Rows, Columns, and Sheets

A new 1-2-3/G feature allows you to move entire columns, rows, sheets, and files. To move a column, row, sheet, or worksheet file with a mouse, click the column letter, row number, sheet letter, or file selection box. To select a column, row, sheet, or worksheet file with the keyboard, type the column letter, row number, or sheet letter followed by a colon or filename in double angle brackets. Examples of a range of columns, rows, or sheet selections are A:A..A:C, A:1..A:5, and C:..G:. To select the entire worksheet, you might enter **≪SHEET.WG1≫**. As these examples show, you can select a range of columns, rows, and sheets. The only difference between moving columns, rows, sheets, and worksheet files is that the To and From range must refer to a column, row, sheet, or file to match the size of the From range. For example, if the From range is C:..G:, R: or ≪SHEET2.WG1≫A: are valid From ranges, but R:A1 is not, since it is a cell address while the From range is a column address.

Moving Data Between Files

1-2-3/G allows you to move data between files. This allows you to use information entered in one file in another if you decide to restructure an application.

Figure 8-6 shows two worksheet files that you can use to move data between sheets. In these two worksheets, the data in A4..C7 in the DUE_60 worksheet needs to be moved to A4..C7 in the DUE_90 worksheet. To move these cells, select Move and the range A4..C7. When you click the To range or press ENTER or TAB to select the To range, type **<<DUE_90>>A:A4** or click A:A4 in the DUE_90 worksheet file. After moving the cells, the two worksheets look like Figure 8-7.

Copying Information

1-2-3/G's copying features extend your productivity more than any other single feature. Copy permits you to enter a label, formula, or number in

1-2-3/G (69.4) Ready

File Edit Worksheet Range Copy... Move... Print Graph Data Utility Quit... Help

A:A3 'Name

DUE_60.WG1

A	A	B	C	D	E	F
1	Customer Accounts With Overdue Accounts As Of 9/30/91					
2	60 Days Overdue					
3	Name	Account Number	Amount			
4	Jones, Amy	398843	1452.42			
5	Madigan, Samuel	434394	2048.68			
6	Smith, Michael	573742	129.44			
7	Williams, Carol	792277	1398.81			

DUE_90.WG1

A	A	B	C	D	E	F
1	Customer Accounts With Overdue Accounts As Of 12/31/91					
2	90 Days Overdue					
3	Name	Account Number	Amount			
4						
5						
6						
7						
8						

Figure 8-6. Data to move between worksheets

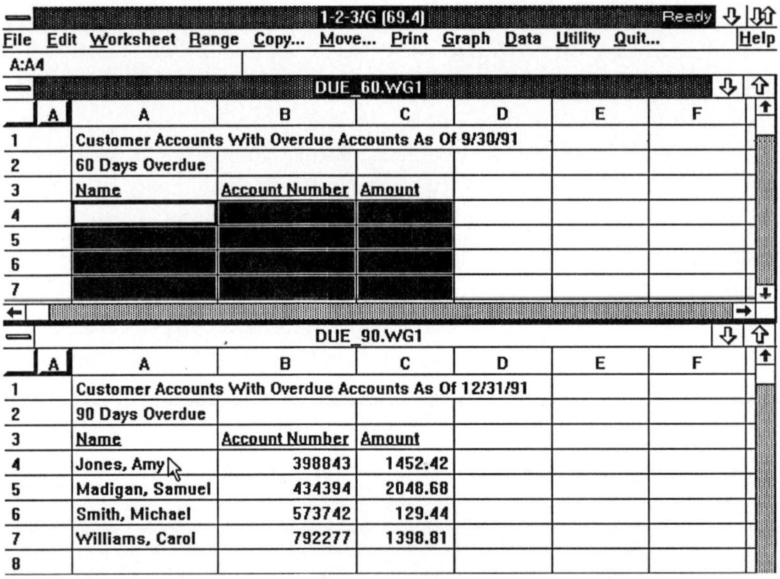

1-2-3/G (69.4) Ready

File Edit Worksheet Range Copy... Move... Print Graph Data Utility Quit... Help

A:A4

DUE_60.WG1

A	A	B	C	D	E	F
1	Customer Accounts With Overdue Accounts As Of 9/30/91					
2	60 Days Overdue					
3	Name	Account Number	Amount			
4						
5						
6						
7						

DUE_90.WG1

A	A	B	C	D	E	F
1	Customer Accounts With Overdue Accounts As Of 12/31/91					
2	90 Days Overdue					
3	Name	Account Number	Amount			
4	Jones, Amy	398843	1452.42			
5	Madigan, Samuel	434394	2048.68			
6	Smith, Michael	573742	129.44			
7	Williams, Carol	792277	1398.81			
8						

Figure 8-7. Data after moving to another worksheet

one cell and copy it to many new locations. This feature is especially valuable for formulas, since 1-2-3/G adjusts the formulas to conform to their new locations. With a worksheet file containing 256 sheets, you can set up calculations for a business entity on one sheet and copy it to 5, 10, or more additional sheets. Using this approach, you can enter data for other business entities immediately, without entering any formulas.

Although there is only one Copy command in the main menu, 1-2-3/G has two other commands that copy worksheet entries. Although you will use Copy more than the other two, both Range Value and Range Transpose are useful in many situations. The Range Value command copies the current formula result instead of the formula. The Range Transpose command changes the orientation of the range as it copies the range. Entries in a column can be copied to a row or vice versa, and entries that span sheets can be copied to a single row or column. Since Range Value and Range Transpose affect the composition of a range on the worksheet, they are located under Range in the main menu and will be covered separately in the sections "Converting Formulas to Values" and "Transposing Data" later in this chapter.

The Copy command performs its task in a variety of situations. You can Copy the contents of one cell to another cell, or to a range of many cells. You can speed up the copying process by copying a range of cells to a second range of the same size. You can copy a range of cells to a second range whose size is a multiple of the original range. In addition, you can copy data to other sheets or other files. The Copy command also has an options icon, which you can use to select the data to be copied. The data you are copying can be in any worksheet file, either in an active worksheet or on disk. The area to which you copy must be in an active file. What follows are examples for each of these uses.

Suppose a label entry is placed in cell A1, like this:

1-2-3/G (69.4) Ready
File Edit Worksheet Range Copy... Move... Print Graph Data Utility Quit... Help
A:A1 'Cash
SHEET.WG1

A	A	B	C	D	E	F	G
1	Cash						
2							

To copy this label to another cell, it's easiest to first place your cell pointer on A1. When you select Copy, 1-2-3/G asks what you want to copy from. Since your cell pointer is already positioned on A1, just press ENTER or TAB, or click the box to finalize the From range and activate the To prompt. (If the cell pointer is not positioned at the beginning of the From range, press ESCAPE before moving it to the correct From location.) ENTER moves you to the next part of the command and finalizes the command at the last part, while pressing TAB cycles through the choices a command uses. After you specify the From location, 1-2-3/G's next prompt requests the To range. Using the preceding illustration, to copy label entry to B3, move the cell pointer to B3 with arrow keys or the mouse in response to this prompt. Press ENTER or click the confirm icon. The completed copy operation generates a second label in B3, like this:

1-2-3/G (69.4) Ready
File Edit Worksheet Range Copy... Move... Print Graph Data Utility Quit... Help
A:A1 'Cash
SHEET.WG1

A	A	B	C	D	E	F	G
1	Cash						
2							
3		Cash					

The next example again starts with the Cash entry in A1, but this time you will copy the entry to many cells. The beginning of the operation is the same: Place the cell pointer on A1 and select Copy. Press ENTER or TAB or click the box following the To prompt in response to the From range prompt, since you only want to copy the one cell. To copy this label to D1..D51, move the cell pointer to D1. Type a period to lock the beginning of the To range in place, and move the cell pointer down to D51. With a mouse, click D1 and drag the mouse to D51. Press ENTER or click the confirm icon. As a result, the label will be copied into every specified cell from D1 down, like this:

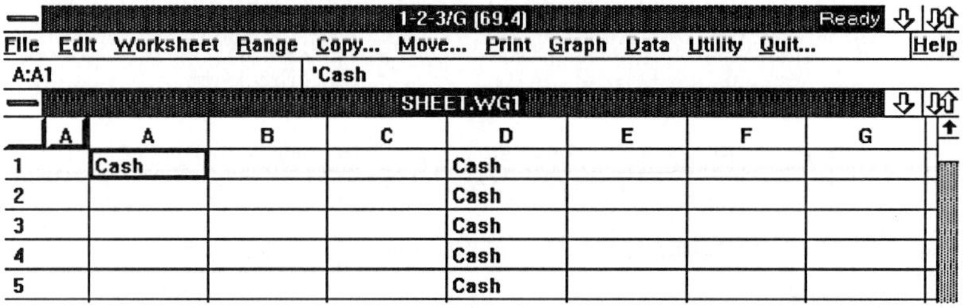

1-2-3/G (69.4) Ready

File Edit Worksheet Range Copy... Move... Print Graph Data Utility Quit... Help

A:A1 'Cash

SHEET.WG1

A	A	B	C	D	E	F	G
1	Cash			Cash			
2				Cash			
3				Cash			
4				Cash			
5				Cash			

Figure 8-8 shows a worksheet with labels in A3..A15. The Copy command can copy these labels to a second range of the same size as the

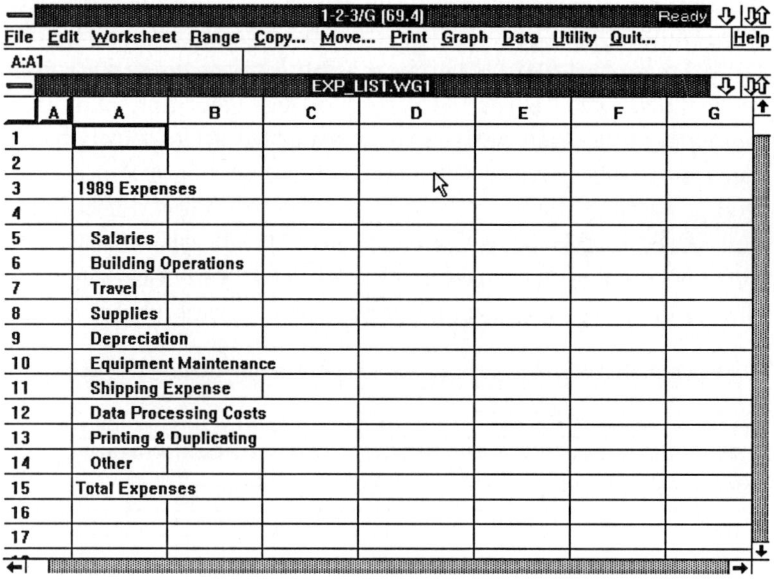

1-2-3/G (69.4) Ready

File Edit Worksheet Range Copy... Move... Print Graph Data Utility Quit... Help

A:A1

EXP_LIST.WG1

A	A	B	C	D	E	F	G
1							
2							
3	1989 Expenses						
4							
5	Salaries						
6	Building Operations						
7	Travel						
8	Supplies						
9	Depreciation						
10	Equipment Maintenance						
11	Shipping Expense						
12	Data Processing Costs						
13	Printing & Duplicating						
14	Other						
15	Total Expenses						
16							
17							

Figure 8-8. Label entries to be copied

original. The best way to begin is to select the range before you select the command or to place the cell pointer in the upper-left cell in the range, A3 in this example. Select Copy. Then, if you have not yet chosen the range to copy, move the cell pointer to select the column entries to the bottom of the From range, as shown in Figure 8-9 (the entries are all long labels within column A) or use the mouse to select the range A3..A15. Press ENTER or click the To prompt, and 1-2-3/G prompts for the To range. At this point, move the cell pointer to the first cell in the To range; in Figure 8-9, this is E3. Since 1-2-3/G knows that the To range must match the From range in size and shape, you only need to specify the upper-left corner of the To range. Then press ENTER or click the confirm icon, producing the results shown in Figure 8-10. With just a few keystrokes, you have duplicated an entire range of label entries much faster than anyone could type them.

The next use of Copy copies one row or column of entries to many rows or columns in one operation. The following example uses the labels in Figure 8-11. To copy these labels, select the range A1..A12 and select Copy. This time, you want to copy the labels to B1..B12, C1..C12,

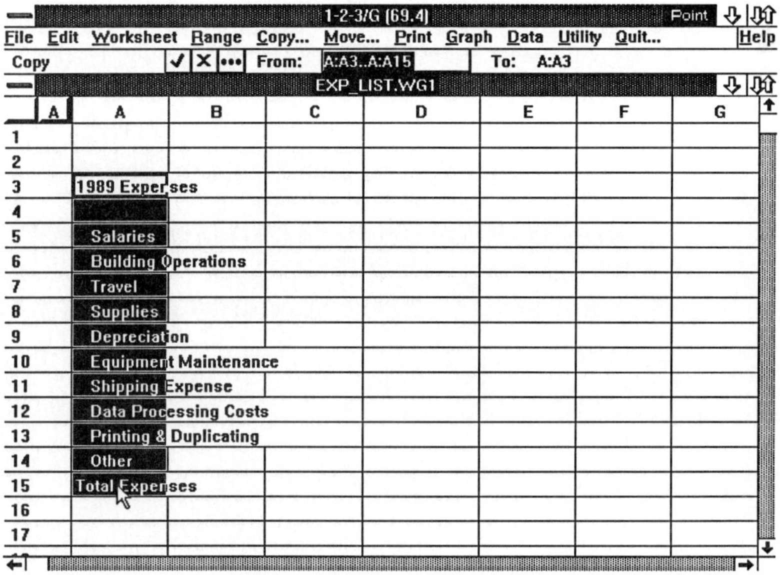

Figure 8-9. From range for labels

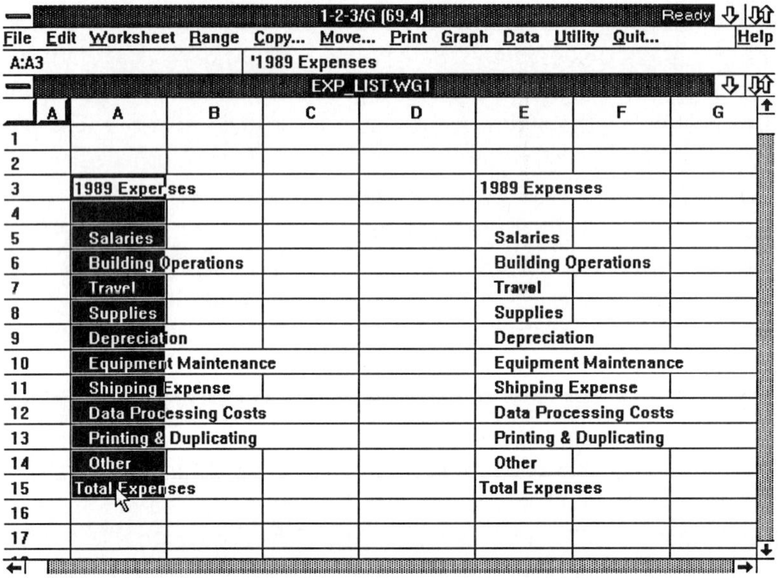

Figure 8-10. Result of copying labels

D1..D12, and E1..E12. When 1-2-3/G requests the To range, therefore, move the cell pointer to the top of the first column where the labels are to be copied, B1, and type a period to lock the beginning of the range in place.

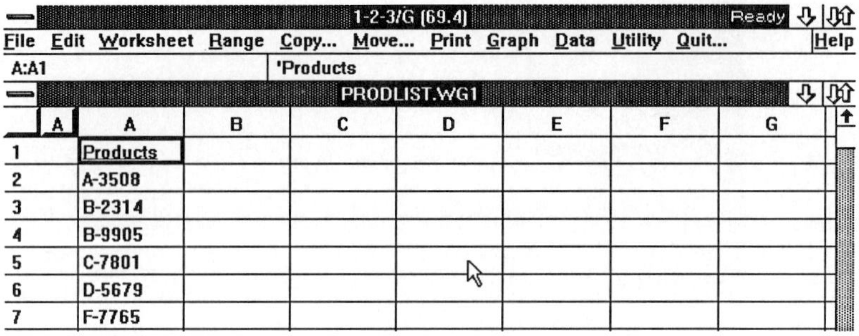

Figure 8-11. Column of label entries

Since 1-2-3/G knows it is copying a partial column of labels that extends down to row 12, you only need to indicate how far across the worksheet this partial column should be copied. To do this, move the cell pointer to E1. With a mouse, you can select the range by clicking B1 and dragging the mouse to E1. When the range is selected, click the confirm icon or press ENTER to produce the display in Figure 8-12.

You can also copy to other sheets entries in a rectangular range on one sheet. Although the information in the From range is on the same sheet in this example, you can just as easily obtain it from another sheet. First, highlight the rectangle of cells to copy. In Figure 8-13, this is A:A1..A:G6. There are cells without entries in this range because they are part of the defined range that includes the entries across the top and down the sides. Including the empty cells in this copy operation can offer another advantage if you have used range formats on the empty cells: The copy operation copies the range formats as well as the data. Specify the To range as B:A1..D:A1—or the first cell in each worksheet where you want this rectangle copied. Figure 8-14 shows part of the data copied to three new sheets.

Using Collections with the Copy Command

With 1-2-3/G, you can use collections with the Copy command. As an example, using the data in Figure 8-15, when you copy the collection

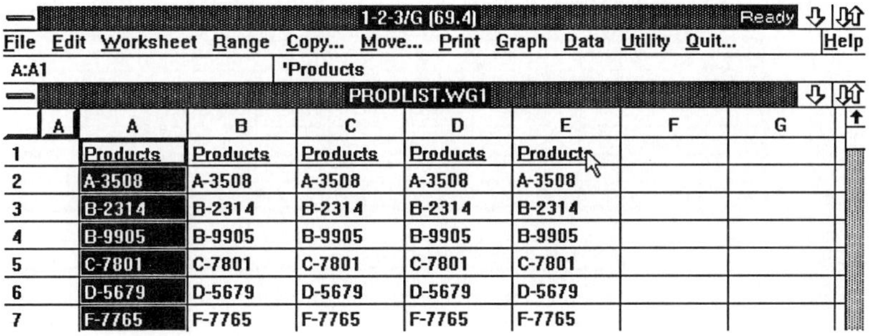

1-2-3/G [69.4] Ready

File Edit Worksheet Range Copy... Move... Print Graph Data Utility Quit... Help

A:A1 'Products

PRODLIST.WG1

A	A	B	C	D	E	F	G
1	Products	Products	Products	Products	Products		
2	A-3508	A-3508	A-3508	A-3508	A-3508		
3	B-2314	B-2314	B-2314	B-2314	B-2314		
4	B-9905	B-9905	B-9905	B-9905	B-9905		
5	C-7801	C-7801	C-7801	C-7801	C-7801		
6	D-5679	D-5679	D-5679	D-5679	D-5679		
7	F-7765	F-7765	F-7765	F-7765	F-7765		

Figure 8-12. Result of copying to many locations

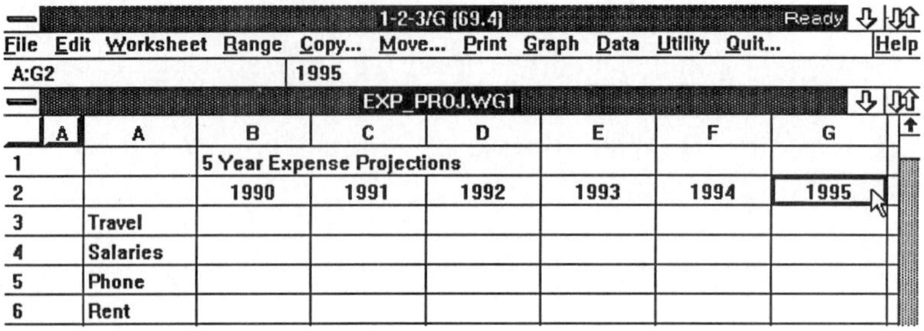

1-2-3/G (69.4) Ready

File Edit Worksheet Range Copy... Move... Print Graph Data Utility Quit... Help

A:G2 1995

EXP_PROJ.WG1

A	A	B	C	D	E	F	G
1		5 Year Expense Projections					
2		1990	1991	1992	1993	1994	1995
3	Travel						
4	Salaries						
5	Phone						
6	Rent						

Figure 8-13. Range to be copied

A:B2..A:F2,A:A3..A:B5,A:A7..A:F8 to B:B2, the results are shown in Figure 8-16. When you copy a collection, the first cell in the To range corresponds to the first cell in the From range. For example, in Figure 8-16, the first cell copied is placed in B:B2 which corresponds to A:B2.

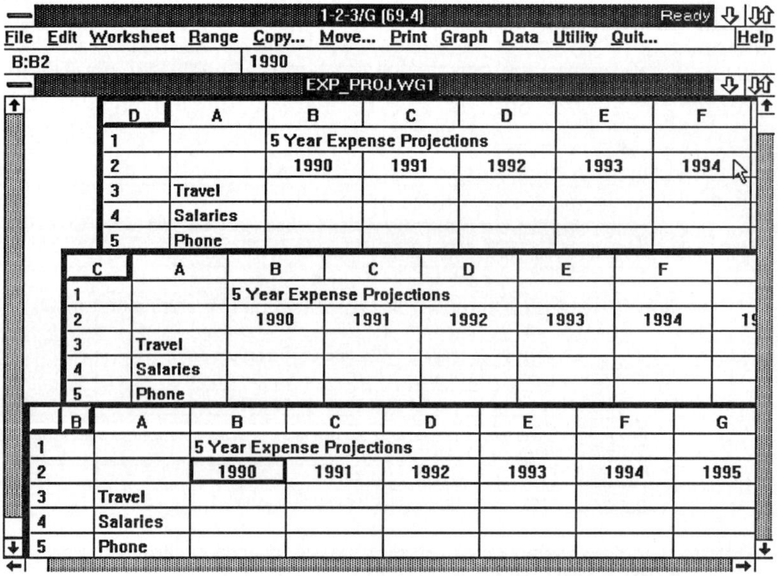

1-2-3/G (69.4) Ready

File Edit Worksheet Range Copy... Move... Print Graph Data Utility Quit... Help

B:B2 1990

EXP_PROJ.WG1

D	A	B	C	D	E	F
1		5 Year Expense Projections				
2		1990	1991	1992	1993	1994
3	Travel					
4	Salaries					
5	Phone					

C	A	B	C	D	E	F
1		5 Year Expense Projections				
2		1990	1991	1992	1993	1994
3	Travel					
4	Salaries					
5	Phone					

B	A	B	C	D	E	F	G
1		5 Year Expense Projections					
2		1990	1991	1992	1993	1994	1995
3	Travel						
4	Salaries						
5	Phone						

Figure 8-14. Multiple-sheet range to which the range is copied

1-2-3/G Ready

File Edit Worksheet Range Copy... Move... Print Graph Data Utility Quit... Help

A:A7 'Sales Growth

GROWTH2.WG1

B	A	B	C	D	E	F
1	Second Set of Assumptions					
2						
3						
4						
5						
6						
7						
8						

A	A	B	C	D	E	F	G
1	First Set of Assumptions						
2		1989	1990	1991	1992	1993	
3	Sales	100,000	110,000	123,200	141,680	157,265	
4	Cogs	45,000	49,500	55,440	63,756	70,769	
5	Profit	55,000	60,500	67,760	77,924	86,496	
6							
7	Sales Growth		10%	12%	15%	11%	
8	Cogs %		45%				

Figure 8-15. Selected collection to copy

1-2-3/G (69.4) Ready

File Edit Worksheet Range Copy... Move... Print Graph Data Utility Quit... Help

A:A7 'Sales Growth

GROWTH2.WG1

B	A	B	C	D	E	F
1	Second Set of Assumptions					
2		1989	1990	1991	1992	1993
3	Sales	100000				
4	Cogs	45000				
5	Profit	55000				
6						
7	Sales Growth					
8	Cogs %					

A	A	B	C	D	E	F	G
1	First Set of Assumptions						
2		1989	1990	1991	1992	1993	
3	Sales	100,000	110,000	123,200	141,680	157,265	
4	Cogs	45,000	49,500	55,440	63,756	70,769	
5	Profit	55,000	60,500	67,760	77,924	86,496	
6							
7	Sales Growth		10%	12%	15%	11%	
8	Cogs %		45%				

Figure 8-16. Result of copying a collection

The copies of the other cells in the collection are the same relative number of cells away from the first cell in the collection. If the From range is too close to the worksheet border to fit all of the cells in the collection, 1-2-3/G displays an error message. You can also use a collection for the From range to make new copies in noncontiguous cells. As an example, in Figure 8-17 the repeated copies of the words "No flights" are made by copying B4 to the collection B5..B13,C15..D17,D6,D8, D11..D13,E10..E14,E16..E17,F7,F11..F17.

Copying to Larger Areas than a Range or a Collection

The Copy command accepts other types of To and From ranges besides range and collection addresses. You can use the Copy command to copy entire columns, rows, sheets, and worksheet files. To select a column, row, sheet, or worksheet file with a mouse, click the column letter, row

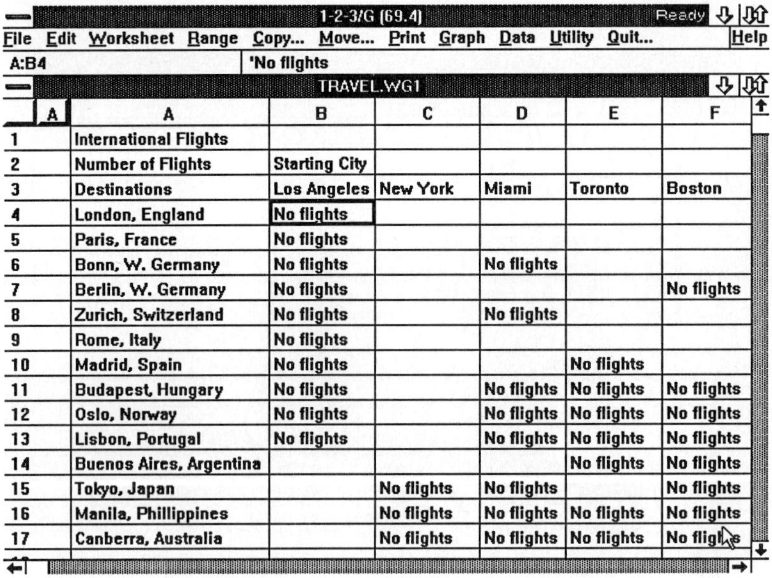

1-2-3/G (69.4) Ready

File Edit Worksheet Range Copy... Move... Print Graph Data Utility Quit... Help

A:B4 'No flights

TRAVEL.WG1

A	A	B	C	D	E	F
1	International Flights					
2	Number of Flights	Starting City				
3	Destinations	Los Angeles	New York	Miami	Toronto	Boston
4	London, England	No flights				
5	Paris, France	No flights				
6	Bonn, W. Germany	No flights		No flights		
7	Berlin, W. Germany	No flights				No flights
8	Zurich, Switzerland	No flights		No flights		
9	Rome, Italy	No flights				
10	Madrid, Spain	No flights			No flights	
11	Budapest, Hungary	No flights		No flights	No flights	No flights
12	Oslo, Norway	No flights		No flights	No flights	No flights
13	Lisbon, Portugal	No flights		No flights	No flights	No flights
14	Buenos Aires, Argentina				No flights	No flights
15	Tokyo, Japan		No flights	No flights		No flights
16	Manila, Phillippines		No flights	No flights	No flights	No flights
17	Canberra, Australia		No flights	No flights	No flights	No flights

Figure 8-17. Copying a cell to a collection

number, sheet letter, or file selection box. To select a column, row, sheet, or worksheet file with the keyboard, type the column letter, row number, or sheet letter followed by a colon or filename in double angle brackets. Examples are A..C, 1..5, C:..G:, and <<SHEET.WG1>>. As these examples show, you can select a range or collection of columns, rows, and sheets. You can also combine them, as in A..C,1..5 to copy columns A through C and rows 1 through 5. The only difference between copying columns, rows, sheets, and worksheet files is that the To and From range must refer to the same type of column, row, sheet, or file. For example, if the From range is C:..G:, then R: or <<SHEET2.WG1>>A: are valid From ranges, but R:A1 is not, since it is a cell address while the From range is a sheet address.

Copying Between Files

1-2-3/G will duplicate entries from one worksheet file in another file. This allows you to enter data once and use it in as many files as necessary without any additional typing. This both saves time and ensures consistency between application models.

Figure 8-18 shows two worksheet files. The data in A2..B8 in the SELLPLAN worksheet is copied to A2 in the SELL_RPT worksheet file. To copy these cells, select Copy and the range A2..B8. When you

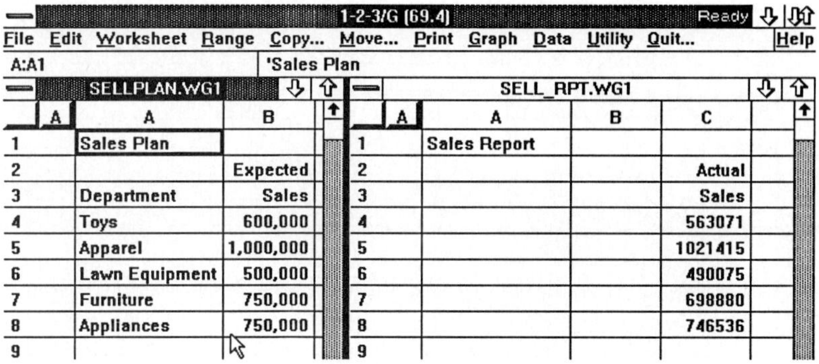

1-2-3/G (69.4) Ready

File Edit Worksheet Range Copy... Move... Print Graph Data Utility Quit... Help

A:A1 'Sales Plan

SELLPLAN.WG1

A	A	B
1	Sales Plan	
2		Expected
3	Department	Sales
4	Toys	600,000
5	Apparel	1,000,000
6	Lawn Equipment	500,000
7	Furniture	750,000
8	Appliances	750,000
9		

SELL_RPT.WG1

A	A	B	C
1	Sales Report		
2			Actual
3			Sales
4			563071
5			1021415
6			490075
7			698880
8			746536
9			

Figure 8-18. Two worksheet files containing data

press ENTER or TAB or click the To range to provide the To range, type **≪SELL_RPT≫A:A2** or click A:A2 in the SELL_RPT worksheet file. When you point to the file to use in a 1-2-3/G command, 1-2-3/G supplies the filename for you. After copying the cells, the two worksheets look like Figure 8-19.

If you want to copy to more than one file, use a collection such as ≪SHEET.WG1≫A:A1,≪SHEET1.WG1≫B:A1, which copies to the destination, you select the From range starting in A:A1 of the SHEET.WG1 worksheet file and in B:A1 of the SHEET1.WG1 worksheet file.

Copying Formulas

Copying numbers works the same way as copying labels. Copying formulas is even more valuable. It is important to understand exactly how 1-2-3/G treats cell references when copying formulas.

Since copying formulas requires adjusting cell references to calculate based on the new location, you should have a complete understanding of cell addressing. This topic was introduced in Chapter 5, "Building Blocks for Worksheets," but is expanded in this section to cover the three addressing options completely.

Certain types of cell and range addresses are not adjusted at their new location as you copy them in formulas, regardless of the address

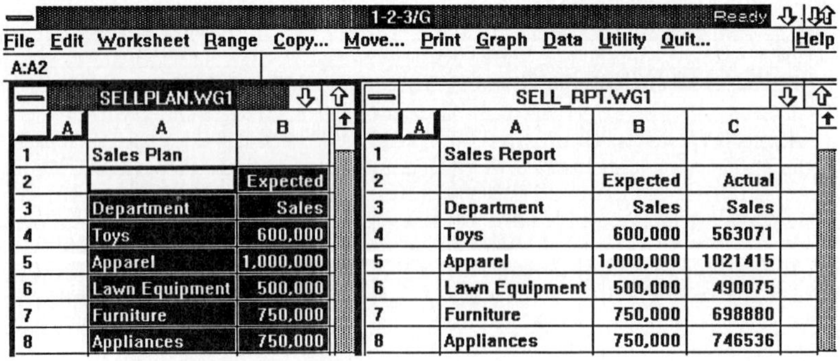

1-2-3/G Ready

File Edit Worksheet Range Copy... Move... Print Graph Data Utility Quit... Help

A:A2

SELLPLAN.WG1

A	A	B
1	Sales Plan	
2		Expected
3	Department	Sales
4	Toys	600,000
5	Apparel	1,000,000
6	Lawn Equipment	500,000
7	Furniture	750,000
8	Appliances	750,000

SELL_RPT.WG1

A	A	B	C
1	Sales Report		
2		Expected	Actual
3	Department	Sales	Sales
4	Toys	600,000	563071
5	Apparel	1,000,000	1021415
6	Lawn Equipment	500,000	490075
7	Furniture	750,000	698880
8	Appliances	750,000	746536

Figure 8-19. Copying data between worksheet files

type the formula addresses use. Undefined ranges, unnamed ranges, and named collections are not adjusted. On the other hand, when you copy data to another worksheet file, 1-2-3/G adjusts the formula references to refer to data in the new file. The exception is external link formulas, since they continue referring to the original file before and after they are copied. The cell address used in the external link formula, however, is adjusted. Copying the formula + <<LINKSHT>>A1 down a cell, for example, will cause the copy of the formula to read + <<LINKSHT>>A2.

Relative References

Relative references are the addresses generated when you enter regular cell addresses into formulas. A19, D2, and X15 are all relative references, as are D:H5, A:Z2, and SALES. This is the normal reference style used with formulas in 1-2-3/G. When a formula is created using cell addresses with this reference style, 1-2-3/G not only records the cell addresses for the formula, but also records their relative distance and direction from the cell containing the formula.

For example, when you enter the formula **+A1+A2** in A3, 1-2-3/G remembers facts that are not shown in the worksheet. Specifically, 1-2-3/G remembers the distance and direction that it must travel to obtain each of the references in the formula. You can see the effect of this in the following worksheet:

1-2-3/G (69.4) Ready
File Edit Worksheet Range Copy... Move... Print Graph Data Utility Quit... Help
A:A3 +A1+A2
ADD.WG1

A	A	B	C	D	E	F	G
1	12	18	2	78	22	67	66
2	15	22	3	4	13	25	22
3	27						

For A1, 1-2-3/G knows that this reference is in the same column as the formula result, but two rows above it. A2 is in the same column, one row above the result. This concept adds great power to the Copy command. Suppose you want the same type of formula in B3, and you want it to add the values in B1 and B2. The Copy command performs this operation quickly, since it remembers the directions for the formula's relative references.

To make this transfer, place the cell pointer on A3, select Copy, and press ENTER or click the box following the To range prompt. Then move the cell pointer to B3 as the To location and press ENTER again or click the confirm icon. The formula is replicated into B3 and, in addition, adjustments are made that make the formula appropriate for B3, as shown here:

1-2-3/G (69.4) Ready

File Edit Worksheet Range Copy... Move... Print Graph Data Utility Quit... Help

A:B3 +B1+B2

ADD.WG1

A	A	B	C	D	E	F	G
1	12	18	2	78	22	67	66
2	15	22	3	4	13	25	22
3	27	40					

Try this again, but this time copy from B3 across the remainder of the row. Select Copy with the cell pointer on B3, and press ENTER or click the box following the To range prompt. With the keyboard, move the cell pointer to C3 as the beginning of the To range, type a period, move the cell pointer to G3, and press ENTER again. With a mouse, click C3 and then drag the mouse from C3 to G3 before clicking the confirm icon. Figure 8-20 shows that the appropriate formulas are copied across the row.

You should use relative references in formulas any time you want the formula adjusted during the copying process. Figure 8-21 shows another worksheet with a column of formulas. To copy the formulas, select the range C3..C5 with the arrow keys or with the mouse, and

1-2-3/G (69.4) Ready

File Edit Worksheet Range Copy... Move... Print Graph Data Utility Quit... Help

A:C3 +C1+C2

ADD.WG1

A	A	B	C	D	E	F	G
1	12	18	2	78	22	67	66
2	15	22	3	4	13	25	22
3	27	40	5	82	35	92	88
4							
5							
6							

+C1+C2 +D1+D2 +E1+E2 +F1+F2 +G1+G2

Figure 8-20. Result of copying formulas across a row

1-2-3/G (69.4) Ready

File Edit Worksheet Range Copy... Move... Print Graph Data Utility Quit... Help

A:C3 +B3*(1+C7)

GROWTH.WG1

A	A	B	C	D	E	F	G
1							
2		1989	1990	1991	1992	1993	
3	Sales	100,000	110,000				
4	Cogs	45,000	49,500				
5	Profit	55,000	60,500				
6							
7	Sales Growth		10%	12%	15%	11%	
8	Cogs %		45%	43%	50%	44%	

Figure 8-21. A column of formulas

select Copy. Since 1-2-3/G displays the range to copy, press ENTER or TAB, or click the To range prompt. With the keyboard, move the cell pointer to D3, type a period, and move the cell pointer to F3, before pressing ENTER to finalize the To range. With a mouse, click D3 and drag the mouse to F3 before selecting the confirm icon. Figure 8-22, which contains the results of the copying process, is changed to a text format so that you can review 1-2-3/G's work in copying the formulas.

Figure 8-23 shows some formula entries in an earlier model, where labels are copied across sheets. Now that the formulas are added, you can copy them across sheets as well, saving data entry time. The absolute reference (see the next section) to Expense Growth percentage

1-2-3/G (69.4) Ready

File Edit Worksheet Range Copy... Move... Print Graph Data Utility Quit... Help

A:F3 +E3*(1+F7)

(T) GROWTH.WG1

A	A	B	C	D	E	F
1						
2		1989	1990	1991	1992	1993
3	Sales	100,000	+B3*(1+C7)	+C3*(1+D7)	+D3*(1+E7)	+E3*(1+F7)
4	Cogs	45,000	+C3*C8	+D3*D8	+E3*E8	+F3*F8
5	Profit	55,000	+C3-C4	+D3-D4	+E3-E4	+F3-F4
6						
7	Sales Growth		10%	12%	15%	11%
8	Cogs %		45%	43%	50%	44%

Figure 8-22. Result of copying formulas, displayed as text

1-2-3/G [69.4] Ready

File Edit Worksheet Range Copy... Move... Print Graph Data Utility Quit... Help

A:C3 +B3*(1+$C$8)

(C0) EXP_PROJ.WG1

A	A	B	C	D	E	F	G
1		5 Year Expense Projections - Eastern Region					
2		1990	1991	1992	1993	1994	1995
3	Travel	$50,000	$51,250	$52,531	$53,845	$55,191	$56,570
4	Salaries	$80,000	$82,000	$84,050	$86,151	$88,305	$90,513
5	Phone	$10,000	$10,250	$10,506	$10,769	$11,038	$11,314
6	Rent	$12,000	$12,300	$12,608	$12,923	$13,246	$13,577
7							
8	Expense Growth		2.50%				

Figure 8-23. Data from the multiple-sheet model used earlier

on sheet A ensures that the entries for all four regions use the same growth rate projection. First, move the cell pointer to A:C3 and select Copy. Expand the range to A:G6 with the arrow keys or the mouse. Press ENTER or TAB, or click the To prompt. Next, use CTRL-PGUP and move the highlighting to the same cell as the beginning of the range, but in the next sheet. Type a decimal point, press CTRL-PGUP two more times to select B, and then press ENTER or click the confirm icon to produce the results shown in Figure 8-24.

When you copy a formula using relative range names, 1-2-3/G adjusts the formula to use the adjusted cell, range, or collection address that the original range name represents. After you copy a formula using a range name, the original copy continues using the range name while the range name in the copied formula is replaced with an adjusted cell, range, or collection address.

Absolute References

Absolute references are cell addresses that you want held constant—in other words, you don't want them adjusted when they are copied to a different location. You want this kind of reference for, say, a single interest rate, a specific value in an assumption block, or a table in a fixed location. Even when you copy this formula to other sheets, the sheet, column, or row portions of an absolute address are not adjusted.

Entering absolute cell references in formulas requires a little extra work, because absolute references must have a $ in front of the sheet,

1-2-3/G (69.4) Ready

File Edit Worksheet Range Copy... Move... Print Graph Data Utility Quit... Help

B:C3 +B3*(1+$A:$C$8)

(C0) EXP_PROJ.WG1

D	A	B	C	D	E	F
1		5 Year Expense Projections - Northern Region				
2		1990	1990	1991	1992	1993
3	Travel	$65,000	$66,625	$68,291	$69,998	$71,748
4	Salaries	$78,000	$79,950	$81,949	$83,997	$86,097
5	Phone	$12,000	$12,300	$12,608	$12,923	$13,246

C	A	B	C	D	E	F	
1		5 Year Expense Projections - Southern Region					
2		1990	1990	1991	1992	1993	1
3	Travel	$76,000	$77,900	$79,848	$81,844	$83,890	$8
4	Salaries	$45,000	$46,125	$47,278	$48,460	$49,672	$5
5	Phone	$3,400	$3,485	$3,572	$3,661	$3,753	

B	A	B	C	D	E	F	G
1		5 Year Expense Projections - Western Region					
2		1990	1990	1991	1992	1993	1994
3	Travel	$15,600	$15,990	$16,390	$16,799	$17,219	$17,65
4	Salaries	$90,800	$93,070	$95,397	$97,782	$100,226	$102,73
5	Phone	$7,650	$7,841	$8,037	$8,238	$8,444	$8,65

Figure 8-24. Result of copying formulas across sheets

column, and the row portion of the address. $A$4, $F$87, $A:$X$1, and $SALES are all absolute references. 1-2-3/G doesn't work with the relative direction and distance that must be traveled to obtain these values when they are used in a formula. Instead, it remembers the absolute cell address.

There are two ways to enter the $'s during formula entry. You can type them wherever they are required, or you can have 1-2-3/G enter them for you. For example, the worksheet in Figure 8-25 requires formulas that use both relative and absolute references, since there are varying Sales Growth rates but one fixed Cogs (cost of goods sold) percentage that applies to all years. The formulas already entered for the 1990 sales used only relative references. The formula for cost of goods sold (row 4) requires both a relative reference to sales for the current year, and an absolute reference to the Cogs% (cell C8). An absolute reference is required because the same Cogs% is used for all years. The formula is +C3*$C$8 for 1990, +D3*$C$8 for 1991, and so forth.

1-2-3/G (69.4) Ready

File Edit Worksheet Range Copy... Move... Print Graph Data Utility Quit... Help

A:C3 +B3*(1+C7)

GROWTH.WG1

A	A	B	C	D	E	F	G
1							
2		1989	1990	1991	1992	1993	
3	Sales	100,000	110,000				
4	Cogs	45,000	49,500				
5	Profit	55,000	60,500				
6							
7	Sales Growth		10%	12%	15%	11%	
8	Cogs %		45%				

Figure 8-25. Model requiring relative and absolute references

To enter this formula in cell C4 (it will later be copied to other cells in row 4), place the cell pointer in C4 and type +. The first cell reference needed in the formula is the 1990 Sales figure in C3, so use the UP ARROW to point to C3 or click the cell with the mouse. Since you want to multiply this figure by the Cogs%, next type *, which represents multiplication.

Now, move the cell pointer to C8 to reference the Cogs%. If you needed a relative reference, you would press ENTER now or click the confirm icon. However, since you want an absolute reference to this cell, $'s are needed first. 1-2-3/G will enter them for you if you press F4 (Abs). The first time you press F4, the reference becomes $C$8. You can continue to press F4 to cycle through all the possibilities:

Absolute reference	A:$C$8—first time
Mixed address	$A:C$8—second time
Mixed address	$A:$C8—third time
Mixed address	$A:C8—fourth time
Mixed address	A:$C$8—fifth time
Mixed address	A:C$8—sixth time
Mixed address	A:$C8—seventh time
Relative reference	C8—eighth time

The F4 (Abs) key cycles through the possibilities again if you continue to press it. If the address is a range address, 1-2-3/G changes both parts of the address so both corners of the range use the same absolute, mixed, or relative address. If the address is a range name, pressing F4, (Abs) alternates between relative and absolute references.

Once the cell reference has the dollar signs added in both positions, press ENTER or click the confirm icon to accept it. If another arithmetic operation is required in the formula, typing the arithmetic operator would also have accepted the $ placement. (For instance, typing + to continue the formula would accept the $A:$C$8 reference.) You can also use the F4 (Abs) key when you are typing a formula. For the example in C4, you could type **+A:C3*A:C8**. With the insertion point at the A:C8 address, you can convert the relative address to an absolute address by pressing F4 (Abs). Using the F4 (Abs) key in the Edit and Value mode lets you convert to absolute addresses in existing formulas.

The formula +A:C3*$A:$C$8 is now entered, containing both an absolute and a relative reference. The result of the calculation as recorded in cell C4 is the same as if both relative references are used. Only when the formula is copied to new locations does the difference become apparent.

Figure 8-25 shows a formula recorded in cell C5 needed to calculate the profit for 1990. This formula is simply +C3−C4, with both references relative. Now you can copy three years' formulas at once. To do this, select the range C3..C5 and select Copy. Press ENTER or TAB or click the To prompt to accept the From range. Next, move to D3 as the first location in the To range and type a period. Then move across to F3, and press ENTER. With a mouse, click D3 and drag the mouse to F3 before selecting the confirm icon. Figure 8-26 shows the results of the copying process.

The formulas in the different cells are shown in Figure 8-27. If the formula in C4 did not use an absolute reference for the Cogs%, 1-2-3/G would attempt to increment the cell reference for each new formula, and the copied formulas in D3..F3 would reference blank cells.

As you can see, you can combine relative and absolute references to create formulas that meet your specific needs.

Mixed Addresses

1-2-3/G has one more reference type: a *mixed address*, which combines relative and absolute features in one cell reference. Cell and range addresses can use mixed addressing, but range names cannot.

1-2-3/G [69.4] Ready

File Edit Worksheet Range Copy... Move... Print Graph Data Utility Quit... Help

A:C4 +C3*A:$C$8

GROWTH.WG1

A	A	B	C	D	E	F	G
1							
2		1989	1990	1991	1992	1993	
3	Sales	100,000	110,000	123,200	141,680	157,265	
4	Cogs	45,000	49,500	55,440	63,756	70,769	
5	Profit	55,000	60,500	67,760	77,924	86,496	
6							
7	Sales Growth		10%	12%	15%	11%	
8	Cogs %		45%				

Figure 8-26. Result of copying relative and absolute references

Since a cell address is composed of a row and a column reference, you can make one component absolute while leaving the other relative. This gives you the flexibility, for example, to have the column portion of an address updated when a formula is copied across the page, while keeping the row portion of the same address constant when the formula is copied down the worksheet.

Figure 8-28 presents an application where the mixed addressing feature is useful. In this worksheet, the 1989 figures are historic numbers, and all of the projections for subsequent years use these figures as base numbers. Sales projections for each product use the appropriate growth factor from C4..C6. For Product A, for example, the sales figure from 1989 is multiplied by 110 percent. You could write this formula in

1-2-3/G [69.4] Ready

File Edit Worksheet Range Copy... Move... Print Graph Data Utility Quit... Help

A:F5 +F3-F4

(T) GROWTH.WG1

A	A	B	C	D	E	F	G
1							
2		1989	1990	1991	1992	1993	
3	Sales	100,000	+B3*(1+C7)	+C3*(1+D7)	+D3*(1+E7)	+E3*(1+F7)	
4	Cogs	45,000	+C3*A:$C$8	+D3*A:$C$8	+E3*A:$C$8	+F3*A:$C$8	
5	Profit	55,000	+C3-C4	+D3-D4	+E3-E4	+F3-F4	
6							
7	Sales Growth		10%	12%	15%	11%	
8	Cogs %		45%				

Figure 8-27. Formulas from Figure 8-26 displayed

1-2-3/G [69.4] Ready

File Edit Worksheet Range Copy... Move... Print Graph Data Utility Quit... Help

A:D9 +C9*(1+$C4)

ASSUME.WG1

A	A	B	C	D	E	F	G
1							
2		ASSUMPTIONS					
3		Sales Growth					
4		Product A	10.0%				
5		Product B	12.0%				
6		Product C	9.0%				
7							
8	Sales		1989	1990	1991	1992	1993
9	Product A		100,000	110,000	121,000	133,100	146,410
10	Product B		50,000	56,000	62,720	70,246	78,676
11	Product C		45,000	49,050	53,465	58,276	63,521
12	Cost of Goods Sold		87,750	96,773	106,733	117,730	129,873
13	Profit		107,250	118,278	130,451	143,892	158,734
14							
15							
16							
17							

Figure 8-28. An application of mixed addressing

cell D11 as **+C9*(1+C4)**. This would work for this one year, but it would cause a problem when copied across to subsequent years, since C4 would be updated to D4, E4, and so on.

Using $C$4 in this formula would present another problem, since the Product A formulas could not be copied down for Product B and Product C. If you use an absolute reference for C4, the copied formulas could not reference C5 and C6. The ideal situation would be to freeze the column portion of the address, but allow the row portion to vary. Mixed addressing enables you to do this. If you write the formula reference as **$C4**, only the column portion of the address is absolute; the row portion can vary during the copying process.

It will take some thought and planning to decide how to construct the address type you need. You might elect just to use a different formula for each of the product types. However, for 25 products rather than 3, the mixed addressing feature saves a great deal of time, since it allows you to devise one formula for all situations.

The formula devised for D9 is +C9*(1+$C4). Because of mixed addressing, you can use this formula for all of the sales projections.

Copy D9 to the range D9..G11. The formulas automatically created in E11..G13 are as follows:

D10: +C10*(1+$C5)
D11: +C11*(1+$C6)
E9: +D9*(1+$C4)
F9: +E9*(1+$C4)
G9: +F9*(1+$C4)
E10: +D10*(1+$C5)
F10: +E10*(1+$C5)
G10: +F10*(1+$C5)
E11: +D11*(1+$C6)
F11: +E11*(1+$C6)
G11: +F11*(1+$C6)

Using mixed addressing, you can enter one formula in D9 and have 1-2-3/G generate the other 11 formulas for you in D10..D11, E9..G11. Although mixed addressing is not useful in all situations, it produces a significant payback under appropriate circumstances.

Copy Command Options

The Copy command has several options in addition to the From and To ranges. The Copy command options let you select the type of information that 1-2-3/G copies. To select the Copy command options, press SHIFT-F3 (Options) or click the options icon any time after you select Copy from the menu bar and before you finalize the command. The options icon is the three-dot icon after the cancel icon. When you press SHIFT-F3 (Options) or click the options icon, 1-2-3/G displays the Copy Options dialog box shown in Figure 8-29.

The Copy Options dialog box contains three parts. You use the first part to select the types of entries that the Copy command copies. The check boxes for Label, Number, and Formula determine the entry types 1-2-3/G copies. By default, these three check boxes are selected to indicate that 1-2-3/G will copy all types of entries. You can unselect a check box to tell 1-2-3/G to ignore certain types of entries during the copy process. For example, suppose you want to copy the numbers and

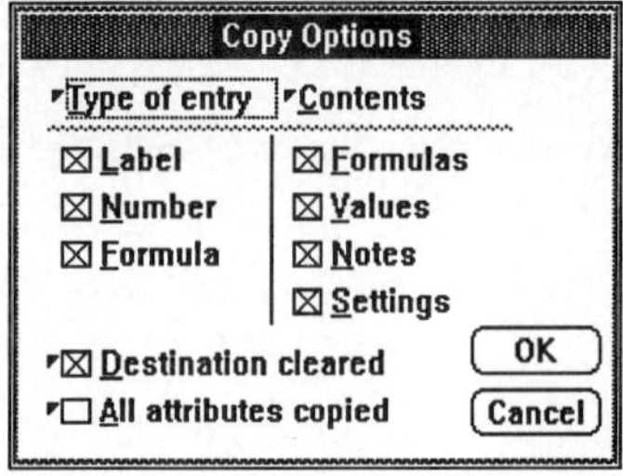

Figure 8-29. Copy Options dialog box

labels from Figure 8-28 without copying the formulas to sheet B. One method would be to select the collection A:A1..A:G8,A:A9..A:C13 as the From range. Another option is to select sheet A as the From range by clicking the A in the intersection of the column and row border or by typing **A:** as the From range. Next, click the options icon or press SHIFT-F3 (Options) and unselect Formula under Type of entry. When you select OK to leave the Copy Options dialog box, you can proceed with the command and select sheet B as the To range. If the B sheet is visible, you can select sheet B by clicking the B in the intersection of the column and row border or by typing **B:**. When you select the confirm icon or press ENTER, 1-2-3/G copies the labels and value entries to sheet B, as shown in Figure 8-30.

You use the second part of the Copy Options dialog box to select the attributes of the copied cells that the Copy command copies. You can use the options to select whether the Copy command copies a cell's formula or its values, the notes, or the formatting settings that are assigned to the cell. By default, 1-2-3/G copies all parts of the cells to the From range. By unselecting some of the check boxes, you can change the information of the cells that the Copy command copies. With the Formulas check box selected, 1-2-3/G copies the formulas of the cells in the From range. This assumes that the Formula check box is selected under Type of entry; otherwise, the Formulas check box has no effect. If the Values check box is selected, 1-2-3/G copies the values of the cells in the From range. This means that the labels and numbers in the From range are copied. If Values is selected but Formulas is not, the Copy command copies the values of the formulas to the To range as values instead of formulas. With Notes selected, 1-2-3/G copies the notes of the

1-2-3/G (69.4) Ready

File Edit Worksheet Range Copy... Move... Print Graph Data Utility Quit... Help

B:A1

ASSUME.WG1

B	A	B	C	D	E	F	G
1							
2		ASSUMPTIONS					
3		Sales Growth					
4		Product A	10.0%				
5		Product B	12.0%				
6		Product C	9.0%				
7							
8	Sales		1989	1990	1991	1992	1993
9	Product A		100000				
10	Product B		50000				
11	Product C		45000				
12	Cost of Goods Sold						
13	Profit						

Figure 8-30. Copying just labels and numbers

cells in the From range. If you unselect the Notes check box, the notes are not copied to the To range. If the Settings check box is selected, 1-2-3/G copies the format attributes of the From range to the To range. If you unselect the Settings and Destination cleared check boxes, the copied cells take on the formats of the original cells in the To range. You can also use the Settings check box to copy formatting to cells without copying cell data by unselecting the Formulas, Values, Notes, and Destination cleared check boxes. For example, if you use the Copy command with A: as the From range and B: as the To range from the worksheet in Figure 8-31, you can use the Copy Command Options to copy only the settings. After selecting the Copy command but before clicking the confirm icon or pressing ENTER, press SHIFT-F3 and unselect Formulas, Values, Notes, and Destination cleared. When you select the OK command button and the To and From range before finalizing the Copy command, the worksheet looks like Figure 8-32.

The third part of the Copy Options dialog box determines whether 1-2-3/G clears the destination before it copies the cells, and how 1-2-3/G copies column, row, sheet, and worksheet file attributes. When selected, the Destination cleared check box erases all cell contents of the To range before copying the cells. For example, if you copy the cell's contents without also unselecting the Destination cleared check box, existing data in the To range may remain after the copy is completed

1-2-3/G [69.4] Ready

File Edit Worksheet Range Copy... Move... Print Graph Data Utility Quit... Help

B:A1 'Acme Corporation

ACME_BAL.WG1

A	A	B	C	D
1	Acme Corporation			
2	Balance Sheet			
3	December 31, 1990			
4	*Numbers in thousands*			
5				
6	ASSETS			
7	Curent Assets			
8	Cash			$250
9	Notes Receivable			$320
10	Amounts Receivable			$590
11	Total Current Assets			$1,160
12	Plant Assets	Cost	Dep	Book
13	Land	$500	—	$500
14	Buildings	$980	$400	$580
15	Factory Equipment	$575	$50	$525
16	Total Plant Assets			$1,605
17	Intangible Assets	Cost	Amort	Book
18	Copyrights	$1,100	$400	$700
19	Patents	$1,200	—	$1,200

B	A	B
1	Acme Corporation	
2	Income Statement	
3	For Year Ended December 3	
4	Numbers in thousands	
5		
6	Sales	
7	Gross Sales	10000
8	Returns on Sales	4
9	Net Sales	9996
10		
11	Cost of Goods Sold:	
12	Initial Inventory	60
13	Purchases	350
14	Inventory For Sale	410
15	Ending Inventory	75
16	Cost of Goods Sold	335
17		
18	Expenses:	
19		

Figure 8-31. Worksheet with formats to copy

1-2-3/G [69.4] Ready

File Edit Worksheet Range Copy... Move... Print Graph Data Utility Quit... Help

B:A1 'Acme Corporation

ACME_BAL.WG1

A	A	B	C	D
1	Acme Corporation			
2	Balance Sheet			
3	December 31, 1990			
4	*Numbers in thousands*			
5				
6	ASSETS			
7	Curent Assets			
8	Cash			$250
9	Notes Receivable			$320
10	Amounts Receivable			$590
11	Total Current Assets			$1,160
12	Plant Assets	Cost	Dep	Book
13	Land	$500	—	$500
14	Buildings	$980	$400	$580
15	Factory Equipment	$575	$50	$525
16	Total Plant Assets			$1,605
17	Intangible Assets	Cost	Amort	Book
18	Copyrights	$1,100	$400	$700
19	Patents	$1,200	—	$1,200

B	A	B
1	Acme Corporation	
2	Income Statement	
3	For Year Ended Dece	
4	*Numbers in thousands*	
5		
6	Sales	
7	Gross Sales	10000
8	Returns on Sales	4
9	Net Sales	9996
10		
11	Cost of Goods Sold:	
12	Initial Inventory	60
13	Purchases	$350
14	Inventory For Sale	$410
15	Ending Inventory	$75
16	Cost of Goods So	335
17		
18	Expenses:	
19		

Figure 8-32. Copying formats using Copy command options

because it was not replaced by incoming data. The Destination cleared check box also has an affect when the From range includes blank cells. For example, consider this worksheet:

1-2-3/G [69.4] Ready

File Edit Worksheet Range Copy... Move... Print Graph Data Utility Quit... Help

A:A1 'Acme Company

REPORT1.WG1

A	A	B	C	D	E	F
1	Acme Company	Date:	02-Feb-91			
2				Income Statement		
3	For the Year Ended December 31, 1990			Yearly Report		

Suppose you want to copy A1..C3 to D1. This range includes blank cells in A2 and B2..C3. If you want to copy this range to D1, the results are different depending on whether the Destination cleared check box is selected. When the Destination cleared check box is selected, the copy looks like this:

1-2-3/G [69.4] Ready

File Edit Worksheet Range Copy... Move... Print Graph Data Utility Quit... Help

A:A1 'Acme Company

REPORT1.WG1

A	A	B	C	D	E	F
1	Acme Company	Date:	02-Feb-91	Acme Company	Date:	02-Feb-91
2						
3	For the Year Ended December 31, 1990			For the Year Ended December 31, 1990		

1-2-3/G erases the range D1..F3, which corresponds to the From range of A1..C3. The empty cells in A2 and B2..C3 replace the entries in D2 and E2..F3. If the Destination check box is not selected, after copying the worksheet looks like this:

1-2-3/G [69.4] Ready

File Edit Worksheet Range Copy... Move... Print Graph Data Utility Quit... Help

A:A1 'Acme Company

REPORT1.WG1

A	A	B	C	D	E	F
1	Acme Company	Date:	02-Feb-91	Acme Company	Date:	02-Feb-91
2				Income Statement		
3	For the Year Ended December 31, 1990			For the Year Ended December 31, 1990		

The empty cells in A2 and B2..C3 don't replace the entries in D2 and E2..F3. The copy of the range leaves intact any cell contents in the To range that correspond to empty cells in the From range.

The last option for the Copy command is the All attributes copied check box. When this check box is selected and the To and From ranges include columns, rows, sheets, or worksheet files, 1-2-3/G copies all of the cell format information, as well as all of the column, row, sheet, or worksheet file attributes. For example, copying column F to column H with the All attributes copied check box selected copies both the cell contents of column F and the attributes of column F such as column width. If the All attributes copied check box is not selected, 1-2-3/G only copies the cell contents of column F to column H, since the column settings are not copied.

Converting Formulas to Values

You will want formulas in most models since they update the model as you revise assumptions. Sometimes you don't want the model values to vary because certain values may have been accepted as goals or target numbers. This would be true of the budgeted dollar amounts in various categories, for example. You need the model to use your projections in this situation, and monitor actual performance against the budgeted amounts. 1-2-3/G provides the perfect way to do this via the Range Value command, which freezes a cell's value as the current formula result and eliminates the formula.

The Range Value command copies to a new location the values produced by formulas. It copies only the values displayed in worksheet cells, not the formulas that produce these values. Thus, the original worksheet can still change as new values are entered for assumptions, but the copy is not affected by changes in the assumptions. To freeze formula values in their current location with the Range Valve command, use the same range for From and To. Thus, the original formula values are replaced with fixed values.

Tip: Be sure all your formula values are up to date before converting formulas to fixed values. If the Calc indicator appears in the window title bar, wait until it disappears. If you are referencing linked cells in other worksheet files, use File Admin Links-Refresh to ensure that you have the most recent values.

As an example of fixing values, the entry in B3 in the following worksheet displays as a number in the worksheet cell but as a formula in the contents box:

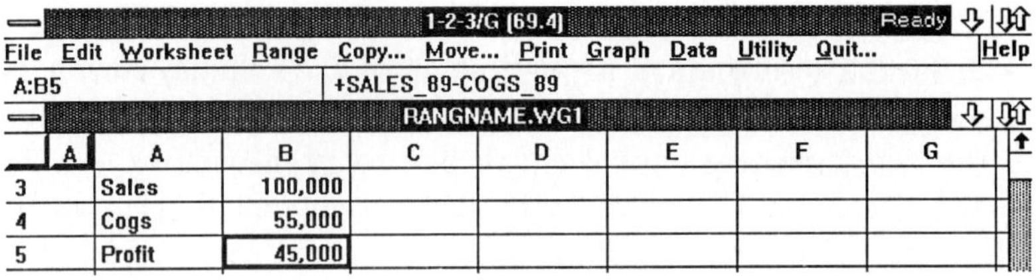

1-2-3/G [69.4] Ready

File Edit Worksheet Range Copy... Move... Print Graph Data Utility Quit... Help

A:B5 +SALES_89-COGS_89

RANGNAME.WG1

A	A	B	C	D	E	F	G
3	Sales	100,000					
4	Cogs	55,000					
5	Profit	45,000					

The same cell after using Range Value, with B3 as a From and a To range, is now a value in both places:

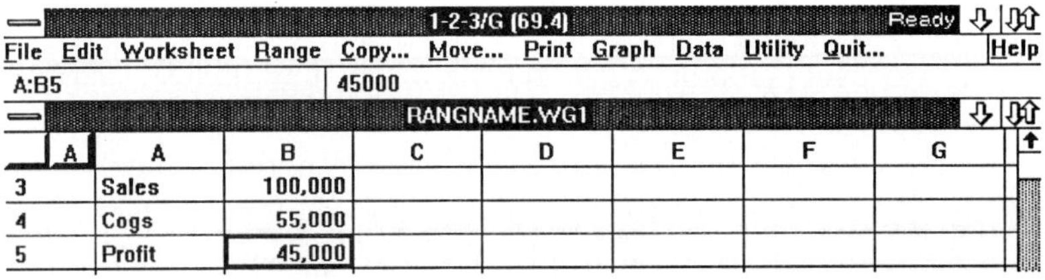

1-2-3/G [69.4] Ready

File Edit Worksheet Range Copy... Move... Print Graph Data Utility Quit... Help

A:B5 45000

RANGNAME.WG1

A	A	B	C	D	E	F	G
3	Sales	100,000					
4	Cogs	55,000					
5	Profit	45,000					

Notice that the worksheet display is the same, but the contents box now shows the cell as containing a value rather than a formula. The new copy of range values also has the original cell's properties. The Range Value command does not have the options the Copy command has.

You can also use Range Value on ranges that span worksheets, if you have a multiple-sheet range you wish to convert. If you want to convert a single cell's formula to a value quickly, you can press F2 (Edit) and F9 (Calc). The difference between using Range Value versus F2 and F9 is the function keys recalculate the cell's formulas an additional time.

You can also use the Range Value command with a collection. This means only the values of selected cells are copied to the new location. The resulting copy ignores cells in the To range that do not have a corresponding cell copied from the From range. Figure 8-33 shows a worksheet with a highlighted collection of F3..F4,F6 copied to H3.

Transposing Data

Sometimes you want to rearrange a range of entries that you have made in a worksheet. You may have changed your mind about the best

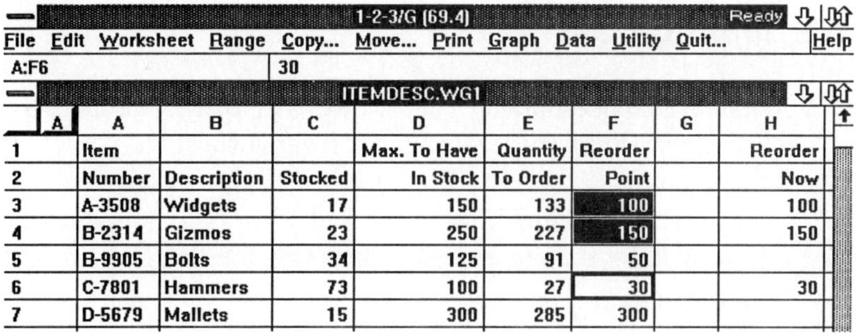

A	A	B	C	D	E	F	G	H
1	Item			Max. To Have	Quantity	Reorder		Reorder
2	Number	Description	Stocked	In Stock	To Order	Point		Now
3	A-3508	Widgets	17	150	133	100		100
4	B-2314	Gizmos	23	250	227	150		150
5	B-9905	Bolts	34	125	91	50		
6	C-7801	Hammers	73	100	27	30		30
7	D-5679	Mallets	15	300	285	300		

Figure 8-33. Copying the values of a collection

presentation method, or you may want to use an existing worksheet model as the basis for a new, reorganized worksheet model.

1-2-3/G provides the Range Transpose command for changing the orientation of data entered horizontally across a row, vertically across a column, or perpendicularly in multiple worksheets. You can reorganize the data to rotate its orientation. For example, you can reorganize a row of data so it goes down a column or so it has one entry in several worksheets. As With Range Value, when you transpose data, 1-2-3/G copies the values of the original data rather than the formulas and entries that created the values. The steps for transposing data are summarized in the "Transposing Data" box.

Since the Range Transpose command operates on single or multiple rows or columns in single or multiple sheets, it offers a wide variety of options. Before using any of these options, the formulas in any cells that you are transposing should have up-to-date values. If Calc is displayed in the window title bar, wait until 1-2-3/G finishes the background recalculation. Also, if the cells that you are transposing contain links to other files, you might want to use File Admin Links-Refresh to refresh these links before starting.

To begin the transpose operation, select Range Transpose. Next, select a From range (the original location of your data) in response to 1-2-3/G's prompt by using the arrow keys, the mouse, or by typing a range name—you can also use F3 (Name). This range cannot be a collection. As with other range commands, you can select this range before beginning and 1-2-3/G will display the selected range in the From

Transposing Data

You can transpose data in your worksheet to reorganize an entire application without reentering data. Follow these steps:

1. Use File Admin Links-Refresh if you need to update calculations or links to external files, and wait for any Calc indicator to disappear.

2. Select Range Transpose.

3. Select the entire range containing entries that you want to transpose. Press ENTER or TAB or click the To text box.

4. Select the first cell in the To range. If both of your ranges are single-sheet ranges and you want a Rows/Columns transposition, press ENTER or click the OK command button. The transposition will occur now. 1-2-3/G automatically performs a Range Value command with the Range Transpose command, since it copies the values instead of the formulas to the To range.

5. If either range contains multiple sheets, or you want to select the Transposition type, select the option button for the desired transposition type. The selections are

Rows	Columns to change the orientation of data within each sheet
Columns	Worksheets to change columns of data in a worksheet to columns on other worksheets
Worksheets	Rows to change rows of data in a worksheet to rows on other worksheets

If you want to transpose a single-sheet range to a multiple-sheet range, press TAB instead of ENTER to select a transposition type option button.

text box. Press ENTER or TAB to move to the To text box or click the text box. For the To range, you can use the arrow keys, the mouse, or supply a range name to select the cells that the copied data will use. 1-2-3/G uses the first cell that you select as the starting point for transposing data. You may want to include cells from multiple sheets if you are transposing data to multiple sheets or you want to select the type of transposition 1-2-3/G performs. If the From and To range are single-sheet ranges, when you press ENTER or select the OK command button 1-2-3/G automatically transposes column data into a row, and row entries into a column, using a special copy process. If the From and To range span multiple worksheets, 1-2-3/G does not perform the transposition until you select the transposition type. You can also select the transposition type by pressing TAB or selecting a transposition type option button with the mouse.

If 1-2-3/G prompts you for a transposition type, you have three options. The Rows/Columns option performs the same transpose operation as the single-sheet operation. Within each sheet, the orientation of data in the From range is reversed in the To range: Rows are changed to columns and columns to rows. With the Worksheets/Rows selection, the data in the first row of each worksheet's From range is copied to the first worksheet. Data from the second row in each worksheet is copied to the second worksheet, and so on until all the rows in the From range are transposed. With a Columns/Worksheets transposition, the first column in the From range on each worksheet is copied to the first worksheet in the To range, the data from the second column of each worksheet is copied to the second worksheet, and so on until all the columns in the From range are transposed.

If some of the cells in the To range already contains data, their contents are replaced as a result of the transposition operation. As formulas in a From range are copied to a To range, the resulting entries in the To range are always the converted value of the formula.

Single-Sheet Transposition

In Figure 8-34, the original worksheet entries for a single-sheet transposition are shown in cells A3..B5. To complete the operation, select

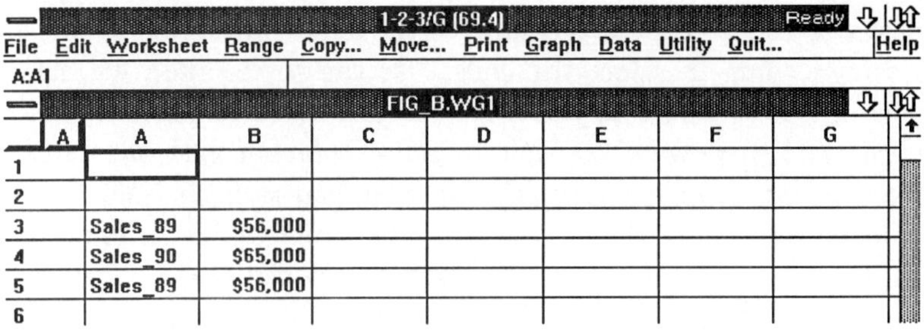

1-2-3/G [69.4] Ready

File Edit Worksheet Range Copy... Move... Print Graph Data Utility Quit... Help

A:A1

FIG_B.WG1

A	A	B	C	D	E	F	G
1							
2							
3	Sales_89	$56,000					
4	Sales_90	$65,000					
5	Sales_89	$56,000					
6							

Figure 8-34. Entries for a transposition operation

Range Transpose and select the range A3..B5. Select D1 as the beginning of the To range and select the OK command button (pressing ENTER selects the OK command button) to complete the transposition. The results are shown horizontally in D1..F2 in Figure 8-35.

Multiple-Sheet Transposition

Multiple-sheet transpositions can either transpose several sheets, as if you had performed several single-sheet transpositions, or can slice through a series of sheets and bring into one sheet the data from a row or column of these sheets.

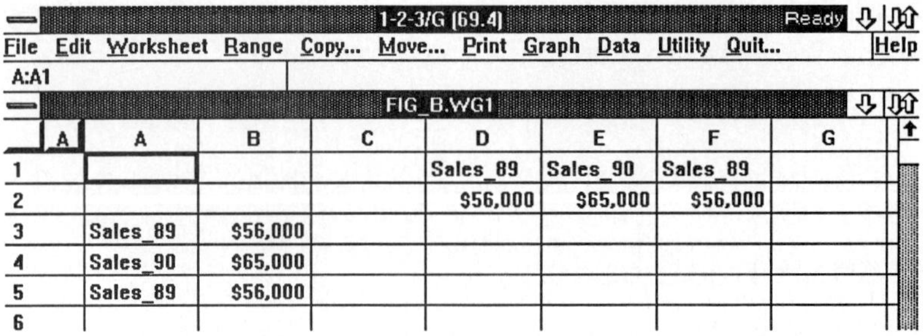

1-2-3/G [69.4] Ready

File Edit Worksheet Range Copy... Move... Print Graph Data Utility Quit... Help

A:A1

FIG_B.WG1

A	A	B	C	D	E	F	G
1				Sales_89	Sales_90	Sales_89	
2				$56,000	$65,000	$56,000	
3	Sales_89	$56,000					
4	Sales_90	$65,000					
5	Sales_89	$56,000					
6							

Figure 8-35. Results of the transposition operation shown in D1..F2

First you will learn a way to complete several row-to-column transpositions without making separate requests. The data in Figure 8-36 shows a section from three different worksheets that display discount percentages by customer type and amount purchased for three different regions. To place Customer Type/Amount data across the top row rather than down the left-hand column, you can use the Rows/Columns option.

First, select Range Transpose. Specify the From range as A:A3..C:E6. Next, specify the To range as A:A10 on the sheet you are copying to. Although you may want the new orientation to replace the old data, you don't want to use overlapping From and To ranges. First transpose the data; then move it to replace the old entries, to ensure an error-free operation. Select the Rows/Columns option button under Transposition and select the OK command button. The worksheet now shows the transposed data, as shown in Figure 8-37.

Figure 8-38 in the next example contains a series of worksheets showing sales contest winners from three regions. If you want all the first-place winners in one list, second-place winners in another, and

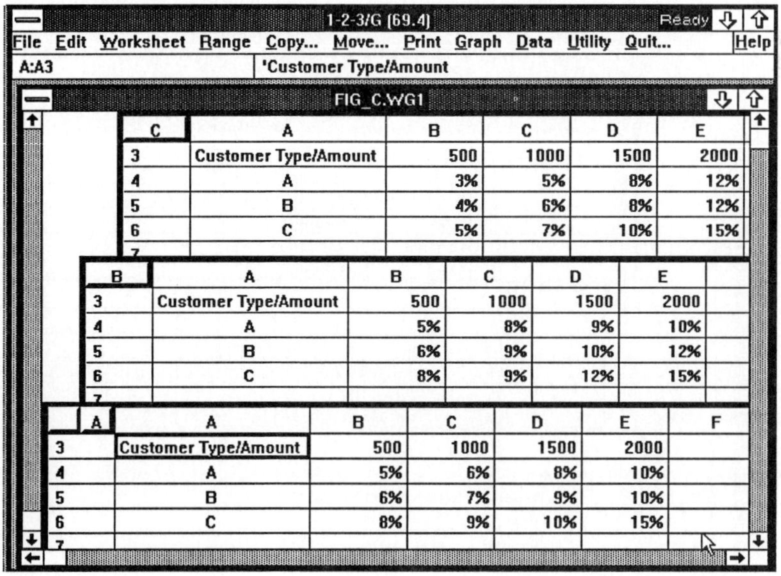

1-2-3/G [69.4] Ready

File Edit Worksheet Range Copy... Move... Print Graph Data Utility Quit... Help

A:A3 'Customer Type/Amount

FIG_C.WG1

C	A	B	C	D	E
3	Customer Type/Amount	500	1000	1500	2000
4	A	3%	5%	8%	12%
5	B	4%	6%	8%	12%
6	C	5%	7%	10%	15%

B	A	B	C	D	E
3	Customer Type/Amount	500	1000	1500	2000
4	A	5%	8%	9%	10%
5	B	6%	9%	10%	12%
6	C	8%	9%	12%	15%

A	A	B	C	D	E	F
3	Customer Type/Amount	500	1000	1500	2000	
4	A	5%	6%	8%	10%	
5	B	6%	7%	9%	10%	
6	C	8%	9%	10%	15%	

Figure 8-36. Entries from three different range name tables

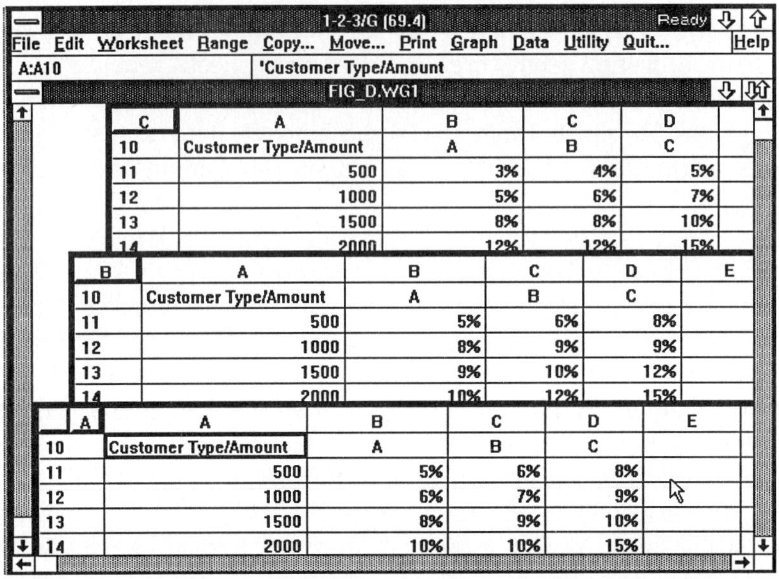

1-2-3/G (69.4) Ready

File Edit Worksheet Range Copy... Move... Print Graph Data Utility Quit... Help

A:A10 'Customer Type/Amount

FIG_D.WG1

C	A	B	C	D
10	Customer Type/Amount	A	B	C
11	500	3%	4%	5%
12	1000	5%	6%	7%
13	1500	8%	8%	10%
14	2000	12%	12%	15%

B	A	B	C	D	E
10	Customer Type/Amount	A	B	C	
11	500	5%	6%	8%	
12	1000	8%	9%	9%	
13	1500	9%	10%	12%	
14	2000	10%	12%	15%	

A	A	B	C	D	E
10	Customer Type/Amount	A	B	C	
11	500	5%	6%	8%	
12	1000	6%	7%	9%	
13	1500	8%	9%	10%	
14	2000	10%	10%	15%	

Figure 8-37. Entries from the three sheets in Figure 8-36 transposed in a new location

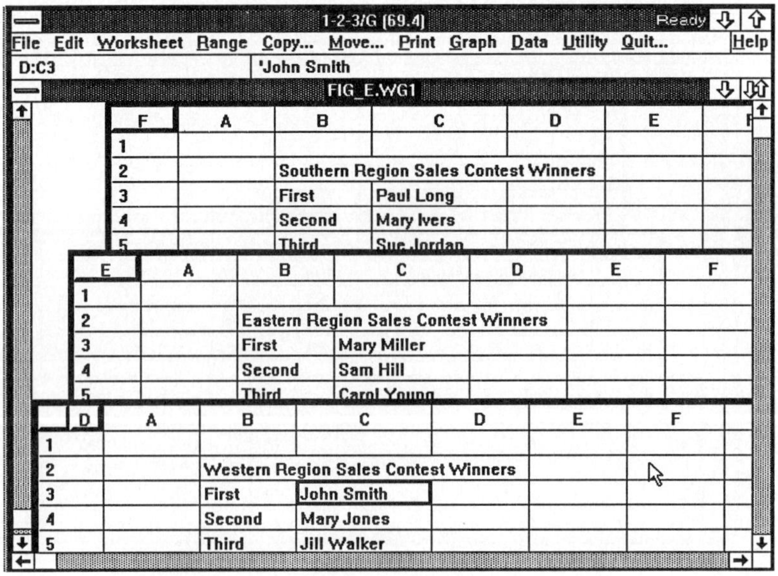

1-2-3/G (69.4) Ready

File Edit Worksheet Range Copy... Move... Print Graph Data Utility Quit... Help

D:C3 'John Smith

FIG_E.WG1

F	A	B	C	D	E
1					
2		Southern Region Sales Contest Winners			
3		First	Paul Long		
4		Second	Mary Ivers		
5		Third	Sue Jordan		

E	A	B	C	D	E	F
1						
2		Eastern Region Sales Contest Winners				
3		First	Mary Miller			
4		Second	Sam Hill			
5		Third	Carol Young			

D	A	B	C	D	E	F
1						
2		Western Region Sales Contest Winners				
3		First	John Smith			
4		Second	Mary Jones			
5		Third	Jill Walker			

Figure 8-38. Sales contest winners from three regions

third-place winners in another, you can employ the Columns/Worksheets option. First, check that the worksheet file has an empty area to receive the data. Since sheets D, E, and F contain the data to be transposed, sheets A, B, and C can contain the new entries. Sheets A, B, and C are set up with headings in B2, and the words "Western Region," "Eastern Region," and "Southern Region" in C3..C5 of each sheet. After the preliminary setup, select the range D:C3..F:C5 and select Range Transpose. The range D:C3..F:C5 automatically appears as the From range. Specify the To range as A:D3 and select the Columns/Worksheet option button. 1-2-3/G will transpose the data so that it displays on the sheets as shown in Figure 8-39.

The third type of multiple-sheet transposition involves moving data from several worksheets and placing it into the first row on one sheet. In Figure 8-40, the worksheet file has three sheets that display the total sales information by year for three regions. In a set of consolidated reports by year, you might want to show all of the 1989 data for all three regions on one sheet. Select Range Transpose and A:B3..C:D5 as

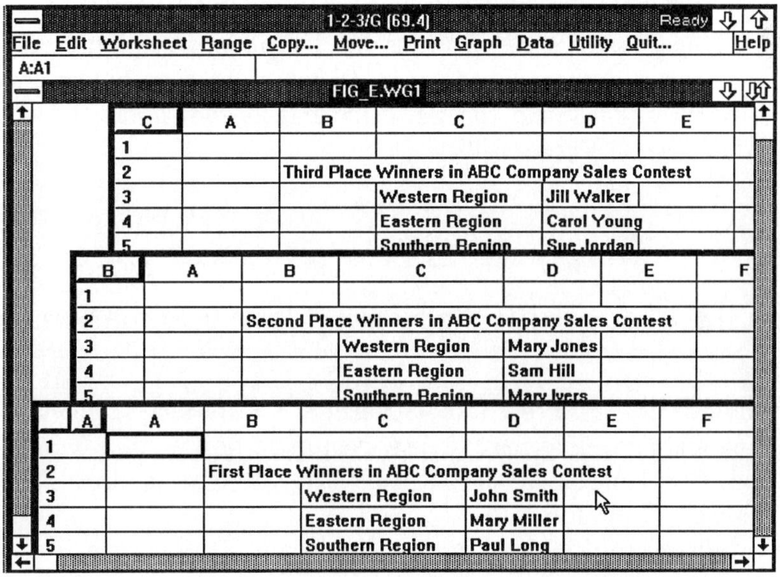

Figure 8-39. Data from Figure 8-38 after transposition

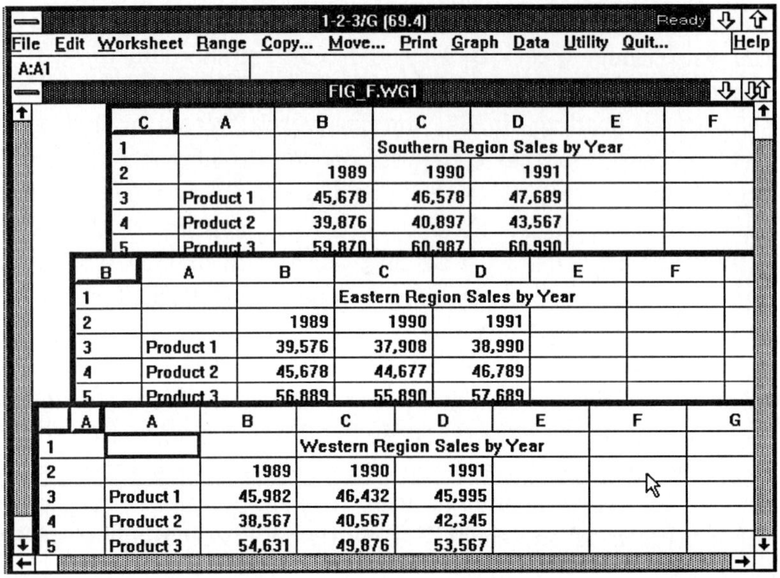

1-2-3/G [69.4] Ready

File Edit Worksheet Range Copy... Move... Print Graph Data Utility Quit... Help

A:A1

FIG_F.WG1

C	A	B	C	D	E	F
1			Southern Region Sales by Year			
2		1989	1990	1991		
3	Product 1	45,678	46,578	47,689		
4	Product 2	39,876	40,897	43,567		
5	Product 3	59,870	60,987	60,990		

B	A	B	C	D	E	F
1			Eastern Region Sales by Year			
2		1989	1990	1991		
3	Product 1	39,576	37,908	38,990		
4	Product 2	45,678	44,677	46,789		
5	Product 3	56,889	55,890	57,689		

A	A	B	C	D	E	F	G
1			Western Region Sales by Year				
2		1989	1990	1991			
3	Product 1	45,982	46,432	45,995			
4	Product 2	38,567	40,567	42,345			
5	Product 3	54,631	49,876	53,567			

Figure 8-40. Total sales information

the From range. Select D:B3 as the To range, assuming that you want to use the prepared sheets in Figure 8-41 for the results. Select Worksheet/Rows and the OK command button to see the transposed data shown in Figure 8-42.

Using the Clipboard to Copy and Move Information

You can use the Presentation Manager's Clipboard as another way to copy and move information. It's even more flexible than 1-2-3/G's Copy and Move commands, since it can work with data in other Presentation Manager applications.

Since the Clipboard is provided by the Presentation Manager, any application that is designed to use the Clipboard can access the information that is in it. These applications support what is called the dynamic

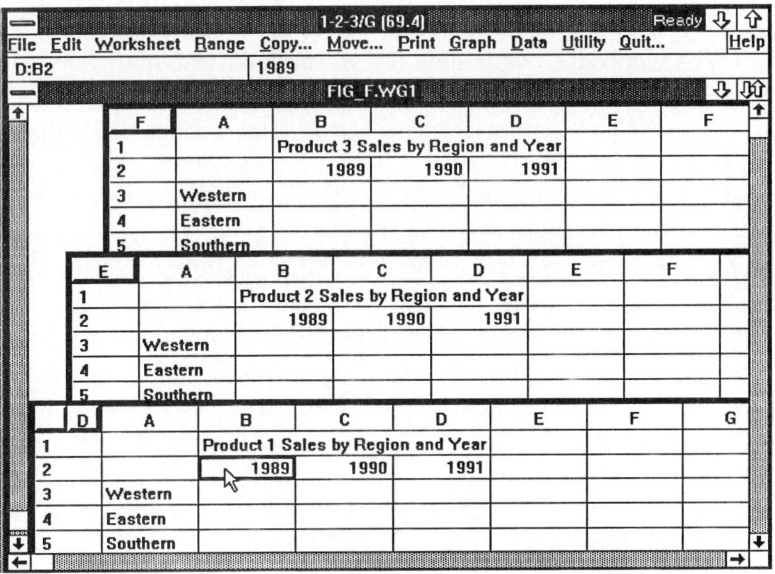

Figure 8-41. Sheets prepared for the transposed data

1-2-3/G (69.4) Ready

File Edit Worksheet Range Copy... Move... Print Graph Data Utility Quit... Help

D:A1

FIG_F.WG1

F	A	B	C	D	E	F
1		Product 3 Sales by Region and Year				
2		1989	1990	1991		
3	Western	54,631	49,876	53,567		
4	Eastern	56,889	55,890	57,689		
5	Southern	59,870	60,987	60,990		

E	A	B	C	D	E	F
1		Product 2 Sales by Region and Year				
2		1989	1990	1991		
3	Western	38,567	40,567	42,345		
4	Eastern	45,678	44,677	46,789		
5	Southern	39,876	40,897	43,567		

D	A	B	C	D	E	F	G
1		Product 1 Sales by Region and Year					
2		1989	1990	1991			
3	Western	45,982	46,432	45,995			
4	Eastern	39,576	37,908	38,990			
5	Southern	45,678	46,578	47,689			

Figure 8-42. Results of the transposition of Figure 8-40

data exchange (DDE). Besides 1-2-3/G, other applications that can use the Clipboard include Borland's SideKick and Microsoft's Excel.

The Clipboard commands are in the Edit pull-down menu shown in Figure 8-43. 1-2-3/G displays the available selections in black, graying the unavailable menu selections. For example, since you cannot place a collection on the Clipboard, 1-2-3/G grays the Cut and Copy commands, which place data on the Clipboard if a collection is selected when you select Edit. Likewise, Paste and Paste Special are gray when the Clipboard is empty, since they transfer Clipboard information to the worksheet.

Using the Clipboard to copy and move data is similar to using the Copy command, but the To range, From range, and Copy Options dialog box are separated. Since you copy data to the Clipboard and paste information from the Clipboard with separate commands, you can perform these operations at different times. This lets you copy data from 1-2-3/G or another Presentation Manager application. In addition, the data in the Clipboard remains there until it is replaced with new data. This lets you paste data repeatedly in different 1-2-3/G worksheets or different Presentation Manager applications.

When moving and copying data with the Clipboard, you must first copy the data to the Clipboard. You can copy up to 64K. 1-2-3/G has two commands that copy data to the Clipboard, depending on whether you want to remove the original data from the worksheet. First you select the cell or range to place in the Clipboard. Remember, you cannot store a collection in the Clipboard. Also, you cannot copy an entire column, row, sheet, or worksheet file to the Clipboard. Unlike the Copy and Move command, the Clipboard doesn't let you select the cell or range after you select the 1-2-3/G command. To copy data to the Clipboard and

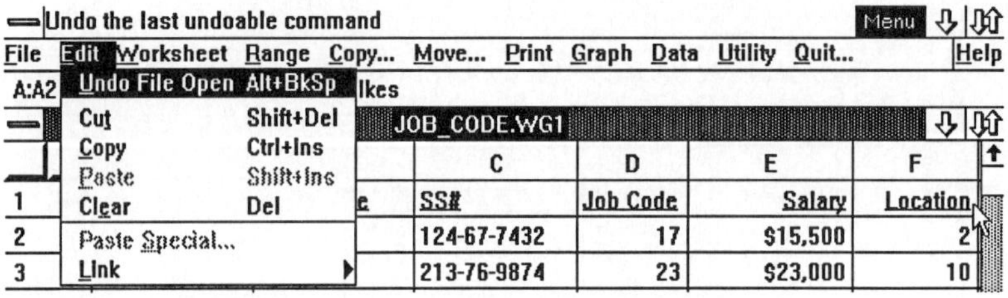

Figure 8-43. Edit pull-down menu

leave the original intact, select Edit Copy or press the accelerator key CTRL-INSERT. To copy data to the Clipboard and remove the original data, select Edit Cut or press the accelerator key SHIFT-DELETE. When you add data to the Clipboard, you are also erasing any data stored in the Clipboard up to that point. As with the Copy command, copying data to the Clipboard also copies the cells' addresses, entries, formats, and notes.

Other Presentation Manager applications have similar commands for copying their data to the Clipboard. In Borland's SideKick Notepad, the Edit menu includes Copy, Cut, and Paste commands that you can use to transfer data to and from the text files that the Notepad uses. In Microsoft's Excel, the Edit menu has the same Copy, Cut, Paste, and Paste Special commands that 1-2-3/G uses. Once data is in the Clipboard, you can only view the Clipboard's contents by pasting it.

When the data is in the Clipboard, you are ready to paste it to a 1-2-3/G worksheet or another Presentation Manager application. 1-2-3/G has two commands for pasting Clipboard data to a worksheet. Using the Edit Paste command is like using the Copy command without changing the initial settings of the Copy Options dialog box. Before you select Edit Paste, move the cell pointer to the first cell where the data from the Clipboard will be pasted. Select Edit Paste or press the accelerator key SHIFT-INSERT. 1-2-3/G will copy the Clipboard data to the worksheet starting at the current cell. If the Clipboard data contains 1-2-3/G formulas, 1-2-3/G adjusts the formulas as if you are copying with the Copy command. If the Clipboard data is from another Presentation Manager application, 1-2-3/G stores the data in different cells, depending on the format of the data in the Presentation Manager application.

You can also use the SHIFT-INSERT accelerator key to copy data from the Clipboard to the current cell. If you press SHIFT-INSERT while in Edit mode, 1-2-3/G adds the Clipboard's contents starting at the insertion point. If the Clipboard contains worksheet data, the copied information will include unneeded characters that you can delete. If the Clipboard data contains text, such as text from a note created in Borland's SideKick Notepad, the copied data only contains unusual characters where the Clipboard text is broken into lines.

The second 1-2-3/G command for copying the Clipboard data to the worksheet is the Edit Paste Special command. Using this command is like using the Copy command and changing the settings with the Copy Options dialog box. Before you select Edit Paste Special, move the cell pointer to the first cell where the data from the Clipboard will be pasted. Select Edit Paste Special (this command does not have an accelerator key). 1-2-3/G displays the Edit Paste Special dialog box, which contains the settings that appear in the Copy Options dialog box. These settings let you alter the type of information that is copied from the Clipboard. When you select the OK command button, 1-2-3/G copies the Clipboard data to the worksheet, starting at the current cell and using the settings selected in the dialog box. Any formulas copied to the worksheet are copied as if you are using the Copy command (assuming that the Formula and Formulas check boxes are selected). If the Clipboard data is from another Presentation Manager application, the appearance of the copied data depends on how the other Presentation Manager copied the data to the Clipboard.

The graph tool window also uses the Clipboard to transfer data. Chapter 17, "Advanced Graph Techniques," discusses how you can use the Clipboard with graphs. Although most of the techniques are the same as using the Clipboard in a worksheet tool window, the graph tool window uses the data stored in the Clipboard in a different way than a worksheet tool window.

Using 1-2-3/G's Search and Replace Features

With 1-2-3/G's Range Search command, you can search for character strings within formulas and labels. This feature is especially useful in a large worksheet where you need to locate a particular entry but you have no knowledge of its cell address. The area that you search can span sheets if you are uncertain which sheet you want to search. With the Find option you can find the first occurrence of your entry, or continue to search through a specified range of the worksheet file. You can use Range Search to search either formulas, labels, or both. You can also select whether the case of the entry you are finding must match the case of the entry in the worksheet.

The Range Search command offers a Replace option. With this option, you supply a replacement string, which 1-2-3/G uses as a substitute for the character string you find within matching entries. This feature is useful if you need to replace cell references or range names in a large range of formula entries. You can replace the first occurrence or all occurrences. If you prefer, you can proceed through the selected range, finding one occurrence at a time.

Tip: You may want to replace matching entries one at a time until you are certain that the search string you entered is matching correctly. This isn't necessary if you need to change all occurrences of A:$D$9 to D:$A$9, because you will probably only find correct matches. But, if you want to change the A in A:$D$9 to D, replacing all A's with D could be a disaster: Entries like AB10 would be changed to DB10, and all A's in range names would be changed to D's. As a rule, be as specific as possible when performing a replace.

Using Search

The Range Search command lets you locate a string of characters in a range of formulas or labels. 1-2-3/G can scan a large range much more quickly than you can. You might want to scan a large range of data for a vendor name, or for a range name that you are considering deleting. When looking for a range name, use the Formulas option for the Range Search command to scan only the cells with formula entries. When looking for text stored in a label cell, you can restrict your search to cells that contain labels.

To find the name Campbell in the data in Figure 8-44, select Range Search and highlight the cells that contain name entries, as shown in the dialog box in Figure 8-44. This range can include the visible cells, can extend beyond the area visible in the worksheet window, or can include entire columns, rows, sheets or worksheet files. As with other Range commands, you can select the range to search before you select Range Search. After selecting the appropriate range, click the Search for text box or press ENTER or TAB. Type **Campbell.** Select the Labels and the Find option buttons. Unselect the Any case check box. This prevents Campbell from matching with campbell or CAMPBELL. After entering the text to find, select the Next command button. The first occurrence of the cell containing the first occurrence of the string is highlighted. The address and part of the cell's contents are shown in the Selected cell information box. Select either Next to look for additional occurrences, or Quit to end the Find operation. When 1-2-3/G has found the last occurrence of the search string, it displays a message indicating that all

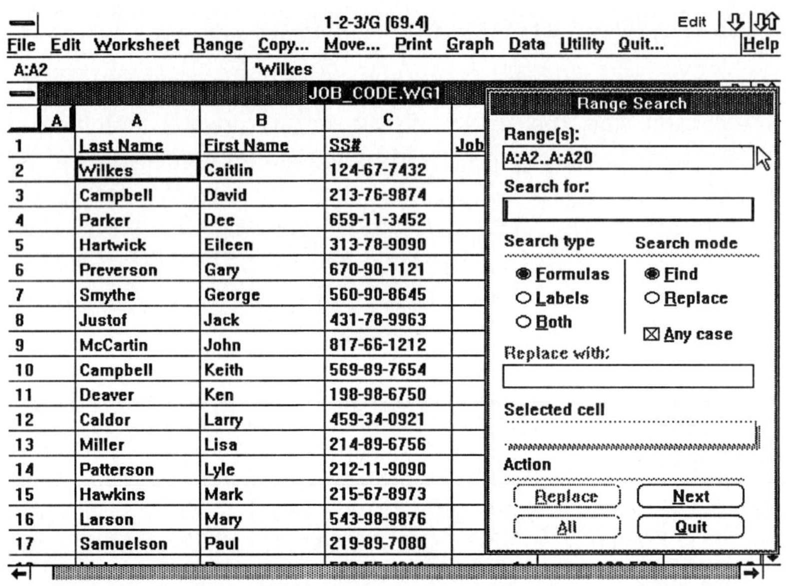

Figure 8-44. Section of large worksheet

occurrences of the search string are found. When you see this message, click the OK command button or press ENTER to return to Ready mode.

Using Replace

The Replace option not only locates strings but allows you to replace them with other entries. This example uses the data in Figure 8-44. Assume that you want to change to Camper the second occurrence of the last name Campbell. You could find the entry, quit, and then change it; or you can use Replace. Begin a Replace operation by selecting Range Search, selecting column A by clicking the column letter or typing **A:**. After selecting the range to search, click the Search for text box or press ENTER or TAB to switch from the Range(s) text box to the Search for text box. Next, type **Campbell**. Select the Labels and the Replace option buttons. The Replaced with box becomes black as 1-2-3/G prompts you for the replacement entry. Type **Camper** and press ENTER

1-2-3/G [69.4] Ready

File Edit Worksheet Range Copy... Move... Print Graph Data Utility Quit... Help

A:A10 'Camper

JOB_CODE.WG1

A	A	B	C	D	E	F
1	Last Name	First Name	SS#	Job Code	Salary	Location
2	Wilkes	Caitlin	124-67-7432	17	$15,500	2
3	Campbell	David	213-76-9874	23	$23,000	10
4	Parker	Dee	659-11-3452	14	$19,800	4
5	Hartwick	Eileen	313-78-9090	15	$31,450	4
6	Preverson	Gary	670-90-1121	21	$27,600	4
7	Smythe	George	560-90-8645	15	$65,000	4
8	Justof	Jack	431-78-9963	17	$41,200	4
9	McCartin	John	817-66-1212	15	$54,600	2
10	Camper	Keith	569-89-7654	12	$32,000	2
11	Deaver	Ken	198-98-6750	23	$24,600	10
12	Caldor	Larry	459-34-0921	23	$32,500	4
13	Miller	Lisa	214-89-6756	23	$18,700	2
14	Patterson	Lyle	212-11-9090	12	$21,500	10
15	Hawkins	Mark	215-67-8973	21	$19,500	2
16	Larson	Mary	543-98-9876	23	$12,000	2
17	Samuelson	Paul	219-89-7080	23	$28,900	2

Figure 8-45. Data altered with the Replace option

or click the Next command button. Since you don't want to replace the first occurrence of Campbell, select Next to move to the next occurrence without changing the current entry. Now select Replace to complete the change. Since there are no additional entries, you are finished. 1-2-3/G displays a message indicating that it can find no more matching entries. You can press ENTER or click the OK command button to return to Ready mode.

Other menu options for Replace are All to change all the records at once, and Quit to return to Ready mode when you don't wish to make further changes. Figure 8-45 shows the altered data.

@Functions in Worksheets

Chapter 5 introduced 1-2-3's @functions and included @function examples providing prerecorded formulas that could save you time. Other @functions provide features that cannot be expressed in a formula. For example, you can use the database statistical @functions both to locate needed data and perform a computation. Other @functions manipulate strings, locate table entries, or perform a condition test.

1-2-3/G provides 106 documented @functions as well as a few undocumented ones. These include all of the @functions in previous releases as well as some new @functions only found in 1-2-3/G.

Following the Rules for Function Entries

1-2-3-/G treats @functions as value entries. Functions are easy to use as long as you follow a few simple rules. You must type an @ symbol, a function keyword, and, for most @functions, arguments enclosed in parentheses. Never include spaces in an @function entry. The one exception is the use of spaces within character strings used as @function arguments, as in "Jim Smith" where a space separates the two words in the string.

Copying @Function Keywords

Since you must spell @function keywords correctly, you may want 1-2-3/G to insert them for you. Just press F3 (Names) after typing the @ symbol to see a list of @function names.

The @function names are presented in alphabetical order. You can move quickly through this list by typing the first letter in the @function keyword, or by using the DOWN ARROW and UP ARROW keys. You can also use the scroll bar at the left side of the box. With the mouse, either drag the elevator box or click the scroll arrows to move to a new area in the list. Once you highlight the keyword you need, press ENTER or click OK with the mouse to add the keyword to your entry. 1-2-3/G also adds the open parenthesis for @functions that require arguments. You can complete the entry of arguments by typing or pointing to each argument with the mouse or arrow keys.

@Functions Without Arguments

Arguments allow you to customize the use of an @function in a specific situation. A few @functions perform only one specific task or computation, leaving no room for customization. When you use these @functions, you just need to enter the @ symbol and a keyword.

@Functions that require no arguments include @ERR, @FALSE, @NA, @NOW, @PI, @TODAY, and @TRUE.

@Functions Requiring Arguments

Most @functions need arguments. Your arguments tell 1-2-3/G what data you want to use with an @function and control its features. There are no defaults that substitute for missing arguments. For example, the @TIME function has a syntax that looks like this:

@TIME(*hour,minutes,seconds*)

If you specify a time of 9:30 as @TIME(9,30), omitting the seconds, 1-2-3/G beeps and places you in Edit mode. You must use a 0 for the seconds argument and record the @function as @TIME(9,30,0). If the syntax for an @function shows arguments, you must always include them. The only exception is an optional argument, which is shown in brackets,

@VDB(*cost,salvage,life,start_period,end_period*
[,*depreciation*][,*switch*])

In this example, you must provide *cost, salvage, life, start_period,* and *end_period* function arguments, even if the function's argument equals zero. In addition, you have the option of providing a depreciation and/or a switch function argument. When a function includes optional arguments, you must include the commas that indicate which argument the function uses.

You can categorize @function arguments in several ways. Some arguments are position dependent and others are not. In addition, different arguments expect different types of data. Lastly, there are different ways of defining the argument data to 1-2-3/G. You will find these details covered with each @function.

Entering Arguments Where the Sequence Is Important

You must enter position-dependent arguments in the exact order in which they are shown in syntax. For example, the syntax for @PMT is

@PMT(*principal,rate,term*)

You must provide the three arguments in this exact sequence. For @functions that aren't position dependent, you just need to supply a list of arguments, in any order. The @functions that aren't position dependent are primarily statistical @functions that average, count, or sum a range of entries. For example, @SUM(A4,B5..B10,D2) and @SUM(D2,A4,B5..B10) both produce the same result.

Whenever you enter an @function with multiple arguments, you must use an argument separator between each pair of arguments. You can use either a comma or a semicolon as a separator.

Argument Data Types

You can also categorize arguments by the type of data needed for the argument. You can enter values for some arguments, but only labels or cell addresses for others. If you enter the wrong data type for an @function, the @function returns ERR. For example, the @TRIM function removes leading, trailing, and consecutive spaces from a string.

If you provide a value rather than a label for the argument, the function equals ERR. The "@Function Reference" in this chapter describes the correct data type for each argument used by an @function.

String Arguments Arguments that require string entries must be enclosed in quotes if you place the string within the @function. One example is this argument:

@TRIM(" This string contains extra spaces ")

If the string is stored in a cell, the cell entry doesn't need the quotes. You can reference the cell entry with either a cell address or range name. You might enter @TRIM(A7) or @TRIM(Text). If the cell is in another worksheet file, you can use an external file reference using double angle brackets to refer to it, as in

@TRIM(<<BUDGET.WG1>>Text)

Note that quotes are never used with a cell address or range name even though they contain a string. You only need to use quotes when entering the string directly in the @function.

You can also provide a string as an argument by using a string formula. In the previous example, you could have created the string in a formula that looked like this:

@TRIM(+" This string "&"contains extra spaces ")

You can also use a string formula that refers to cell addresses or range names, as in @TRIM(+A7&C2). In addition, you can use another @function that will return a string as the @function's result, as in @STRING(@RIGHT(A25,10)). You will learn more about using @functions as arguments for other @functions in various examples.

Value Arguments You can place a value directly in an @function without using quotes. You might enter @ROUND(854.67,1), using both decimal fractions and integers where appropriate.

A value representing a percent can be expressed as either a decimal fraction or a percent. To record the @PMT function using 9 percent interest, you might enter

@PMT(Principal,.09,Term)

or

@PMT(Principal,9%,Term)

As with strings, you can use a cell address or range name. You can use an external file reference to access the value you want to use in an @function if the value is in another worksheet file. You can also use another @function that returns a value or an arithmetic formula, as in

@ROUND(@PI,2)

or

@ROUND(A7/C2,2)

Range Arguments Some @functions expect a range for an argument. You can supply the range as a range address. For example, you could enter

@NPV(.09,A7..A20)

where A7..A20 is a range that supplies the series of cash flows used by the @function.

To specify a range, you can use any two of its opposite corners. For example, you can also enter the range A3..B10 as A10..B3, B3..A10, or B10..A3.

You can use a range name or external file reference to access a range of entries. You cannot use a single cell address when the @function expects a range. Since 1-2-3/G doesn't convert the single address into a range address, the value you expect is not returned.

In most cases, you can use range arguments that span worksheets. (See the section "Arguments That Span Sheets" later in the chapter.)

List Arguments A list argument can be a collection. This means that 1-2-3/G accepts one-cell references and ranges. You have additional options when the @function accepts a list. @SUM(A1..A5,B1..B25), for example, totals the values in two ranges, while @SUM(A2,F4,G3..H6) totals the values in two individual cells and a range. You can only use a list for @functions that accept them. Supplying a list when an @function expects a range will probably produce an error. 1-2-3/G will assume that the second list component is actually the next argument rather than a part of the range argument.

Arguments that Span Sheets

Most @functions that support ranges can use ranges that span worksheets. To specify a range that spans sheets, you must include the worksheet letters in the reference or use a range name. As when you specify a single-sheet range, you must supply diagonally opposite corners of the range. This means that the beginning and end of the range refers to cells on different sheets. If you want to sum cells A3..B10 on sheets C, D, and E, you could enter the @function as @SUM(C:A3..E:B10). You could access the same group of cells with @SUM(C:A10..E:B3), @SUM(E:B10..C:A3), or @SUM(E:B3..C:A10). All of these are equivalent to @SUM(C:A3..C:B10,D:A3..D:B10,E:A3..E:B10), but as you can see, it's easier to enter a multiple-sheet range.

Some @functions don't accept a range that spans worksheets. @HLOOKUP and @VLOOKUP are in this category. You must use one worksheet for the table range in these @functions.

Typing Argument References

You can type the entries required for an @function and its arguments. You needn't worry about the case you use for the @function keyword or sheet and column references within an address. You need only to enter a range with the correct case when you use a field in an external database table with a database statistical @function. There are even some external database packages for which case does not matter. Check the documentation for your package to find out if case matters. To be safe, just use the capitalization used for the names entered for the database fields.

You type the @function exactly as you type any other value entry. No special indicator is needed at the front of the entry. For instance, to enter a formula to sum the contents of B7..E25, you could type @SUM(B7..D25). Remember @sum(b7..d25) is also acceptable. For consistency, @function cell words and cell addresses are shown in uppercase throughout this book.

Pointing to Argument References

If you are an experienced mouse user, the pointing method is a quicker way to enter an @function. Even if you use the keyboard, the pointing method reduces errors through incorrectly specified references.

To enter the @SUM formula that adds the contents of B7..D25 with a minimum of typing, follow these steps:

1. Type the @ symbol.

2. Press F3 and then select SUM from the list of @function names. You can use the arrow keys to highlight the correct @function name or click it with the mouse.

3. Move the cell pointer to B7 either with the arrow keys or the mouse.

4. Select cells B7..D25. With the mouse, drag the mouse from B7 to D25 with the left button depressed. With the keyboard, type a decimal point and then move the cell pointer to D25. Either method highlights all the cells from B7..D25.

5. Type the closing) and either press ENTER or click the check box with the mouse to finalize your entry. The pointing approach may seem longer than typing since each step is described in detail. Actually, this approach saves time once you have mastered it.

@Functions with Optional Argument Entries

Most @functions require argument entries, although you've seen a few @functions that never use arguments. Some @functions have optional arguments in addition to required arguments. This means that you can use the @function with only the required arguments, or you can add the optional arguments for a specialized application. Within the @function descriptions, optional arguments are shown in brackets.

Nesting @Functions

Since cell entries can be up to 512 characters, you have ample space to enter even the most complicated @function. This includes an @function that uses one or more other @functions for arguments.

You can use any @function for an argument within another @function if the first @function results in the type of data needed by the second. Suppose that you want to compute the amount of a loan payment. If you need to borrow for three different expenses, the principal is the sum of these three entries. Since you need a value entry for the principal you will have no problem using @SUM to provide the argument representing the principal. The formula entry for the @PMT function might look something like this:

```
@PMT(@SUM(B3..B5),INTEREST,TERM)
```

You must fulfill all the requirements for each @function entry. Keep in mind that:

- Each @function must start with an @ symbol.
- You must use parentheses for each @function that requires an argument.
- A comma must follow an @function used as an argument within another @function that has other arguments following the @function argument.

Tip: If you enter an @function that returns ERR, check that the parentheses match properly. Also check for missing commas or extra spaces.

Tip: When you cannot locate the problem in a nested @function, temporarily place a label indicator at the front of the entry. Copy the @function to as many additional cells as there are nesting levels. Edit each copy to remove the label indicator. Also make each of the copies contain only one @function to help locate the problem.

Categories of @Functions

1-2-3/G provides eight categories of @functions. Each @function category provides a group of related capabilities. If you use one @function in a category, you will want to take a quick look at the entire set of @functions within the category. You might have related needs that the other @functions can meet.

The @function categories are:

- Database statistical functions
- Date and Time functions
- Financial functions
- Logical functions
- Mathematical functions
- Special functions
- Statistical functions
- String functions

The best way to increase your use of @functions is to read the descriptive information for each of the @function categories. Then you can take a closer look at specific @functions in the "@Function Reference" section later in this chapter.

Database Statistical @Functions

Database statistical @functions perform calculations on selected records in a 1-2-3/G database table.

You can use database statistical @functions with any worksheet database table. To use database statistical @functions with an external database, you must have a DataLens driver for the database product that you used to create the external database. Also, using external database tables causes 1-2-3/G to recalculate the @function when any value on the worksheet changes. Database statistical @functions that refer to internal tables are only recalculated when one of the @function arguments changes.

Syntax of Database Statistical Functions

Most of the database statistical @functions have the same three arguments, which must follow the same pattern. You can use the arguments in the "@Function Reference" section for @DQUERY, the only exception, and follow this pattern for all of the other database statistical @functions:

@DFUNC(*input,field,criteria*)

The first argument is the location of the database that the @function uses. You can use one or more input ranges when defining a database statistical @function. If you use more than one database table as input, separate each with an argument separator such as a comma. 1-2-3/G can distinguish a second input range from the field argument by examining arguments from the back to the front of the entry.

After defining the input, you must tell 1-2-3/G which field you want to use when performing computations. You can define the field argument as the offset column in the input table. 1-2-3/G counts beginning with zero. You can also use the field name to specify the field that you want to work with. In fact, when the input argument includes more than one table range, you must use a field name rather than an offset number. When you use a field name, you must enclose it in quotation marks. The field name must be unique in the database or 1-2-3/G returns ERR. Case is not important in your entry unless you are working with an external database table, in which case it is safest to use the same case you used in the database field name unless you are certain that your database product is not case sensitive.

The criteria argument refers to the records you want to select from the database. You use the same process to enter these criteria that you use to find or extract records in a database table. That is, you can enter a field name on the worksheet and in the cell below the field name, and then enter the value or label entry you wish to match. If you want all records where the STATE field contains NY, you would type STATE in a cell and NY in the cell in the row directly beneath STATE. You can name these entries and use either the name or the range address to reference them in the @function argument. If you have never worked with a 1-2-3/G database, refer to Chapter 19 for more about criteria.

Database Statistical Function Options

Table 9-1 lists all the database statistical @functions. Notice that the arguments for each @function except @DQUERY follow the same pattern. This consistency allows you to perform many different calculations with database statistical @functions using the same input and criteria areas. If you enter the references to each of the arguments as an absolute reference or a range name, you can copy one database statistical @function to many different cells, editing only the @function keyword to produce a variety of calculations on the selected records.

Date and Time Functions

Date and time @functions allow you to perform calculations involving date and time entries. You can use these @functions to enter a date or time serial number into a worksheet cell. You can also use them to work with an existing entry as a date, time, or a component of a date or time such as months or hours.

1-2-3/G assigns a unique date serial number to every date between December 31, 1899 and December 31, 2099. December 1, 1899 is assigned the date serial number 1. December 31, 2099 is assigned the date serial number 73050 because it is 73,049 days after December 31, 1899.

Times are also assigned serial numbers, which are decimals. Midnight is represented by .000000. 11:59:59 P.M. is represented as .999999. The decimal .25 is 6 A.M., .5 is noon, and .75 is 6 P.M.

These date and time serial numbers are only used for internal storage. These numbers allow you to subtract any two dates to determine how many days separate them, or to add a fixed number of days to a date like a loan origination date to determine a loan due date.

Function	Use
@DAVG(*input, field,criteria*)	Computes the average for a field in selected records
@DCOUNT(*input, field,criteria*)	Counts nonblank entries in selected database records
@DGET(*input, field,criteria*)	Retrieves a value or label from a database table
@DMAX(*input, field,criteria*)	Returns the maximum value from a field in selected database records
@DMIN(*input, field,criteria*)	Returns the minimum value from a field in selected database records
@DQUERY(*function*[,*ext-arguments*])	Performs a function in an external database
@DSUM(*input, field,criteria*)	Computes the total for a field in selected records
@DSTD(*input, field,criteria*)	Calculates a standard deviation for a database field representing entries for a population
@DSTDS(*input, field,criteria*)	Calculates a standard deviation for a database field representing entries for a population sample
@DVAR(*input, field,criteria*)	Calculates a variance for a database field representing entries for a population
@DVARS(*input, field,criteria*)	Calculates a variance for a database field representing entries for a population sample

Table 9-1. Database Statistical @Functions

Storing dates and times as serial numbers allows you to sort your data in date sequence or to determine whether a specific date or time has been reached.

When you assign one of the date formats to these numbers, you can present them in an understandable fashion. You can use either Range format or Worksheet Global format, depending on the number of cells you wish to display as a date or time. Besides the standard format options, you can use 1-2-3/G's custom formats to create your own format for a date or time entry.

Date Functions

Date @functions record a specific date in a cell, perform a date computation, or extract part of a date entry. You can also use a date @function to calculate the difference between two dates. Table 9-2 lists all the date @functions.

The arguments for date @functions vary by @function. @DAY, @MONTH, and @YEAR expect a date serial number for an argument since they extract the portion of the date specified by their keyword. The undocumented @WEEKDAY function also expects a date serial number. @WEEKDAY returns the number of the day of the week represented by the date serial number. When you use these @functions with a combined date/time serial number, 1-2-3/G uses only the date portion of the number.

The @DATE function creates a date serial number. You must enter the three components of a date as arguments. The specific order of the three arguments must always be *year, month,* and *day.*

Time Functions

Time @functions allow you to extract a component of time from a time serial number or record a time serial number in a cell. Time serial

Function	Use
@D360(*start-date,end-date*)	Determines the number of days between two dates, assuming a 360-day year
@DATE(*year,month,day*)	Returns a date serial number
@DATEVALUE(*string*)	Returns a date serial number
@DAY(*date-number*)	Returns a day number
@MONTH(*date-number*)	Returns a month number
@NOW	Returns a combined date/time number corresponding to the current system date
@TODAY	Returns a date number corresponding to the current system date
@YEAR(*date-number*)	Returns a year number

Table 9-2. Date @Functions

@functions are similar to date @functions, except they work with times. Table 9-3 lists the time @functions.

Like date @functions, the time @function arguments vary by function. The @HOUR, @MINUTE, and @SECOND functions expect a time serial number for an argument and return the time component specified by the @function.

The @TIME function records a time serial number in a cell if you provide the hour, minutes, and seconds for arguments. You must provide each of the arguments in the order shown.

Financial Functions

The financial @functions perform computations for depreciation and cash flow. They allow you to analyze investment options and perform computations involving the time value of money. As you can see in Table 9-4, each @function has unique and position-dependent arguments, which means you must follow the order of presentation given in this text.

Financial Function Rules

Many financial @functions require the use of interest rates and terms (time periods) for arguments. Interest rates must always be expressed as decimals or percentages. If you want to indicate an interest rate of 9 percent you can enter either .09 or 9%. An entry of 9 is treated as 900%.

Function	Use
@HOUR(*time-number*)	Returns an hour number
@MINUTE(*time-number*)	Returns a minute number
@NOW	Returns a combined date/time number corresponding to the current system date
@SECOND(*time-number*)	Returns a second number
@TIME(*hour,minutes,seconds*)	Returns a time number
@TIMEVALUE(*string*)	Returns a time number

Table 9-3. Time @Functions

Function	Use
@CTERM(*interest, future-value, present-value*)	Calculates compounding periods for an investment
@DDB(*cost,salvage,life,period*)	Calculates double-declining balance depreciation
@FV(*payments,interest,term*)	Calculates the future value for an investment
@IRR(*guess,range*)	Computes the internal rate of return
@NPV(*interest,range*)	Calculates net present value
@PMT(*principal,interest,term*)	Computes a payment
@PV(*payments,interest,term*)	Computes the present value
@RATE(*future-value,present-value,term*)	Computes a periodic interest rate
@SLN(*cost,salvage,life*)	Calculates straight-line depreciation
@SYD(*cost,salvage,life,period*)	Calculates sum-of-years-digits depreciation
@TERM(*payments,interest, future-value*)	Calculates the number of payments required to reach a future value
@VDB(*cost,salvage,life,start-period,end-period*[,*depreciation*][,*switch*])	Calculates variable-declining balance depreciation

Table 9-4. Financial @Functions

When an @function uses a term and an interest rate, they must both reference the same unit of time. An interest rate of 1.5 percent a month and a term of five years don't make sense. When you use an annual rate, use an annual term such as five years. When you use a term of 12 months, use a monthly interest rate like 1.5 percent.

Types of Financial Functions

You can use four different @functions to compute depreciation. Your selection depends on whether you want straight line (@SLN), double-declining balance (@DDB), variable-declining balance (@VDB), or sum of the year's digits.

Several financial @functions are useful for investment and loan computations. Each of these @function focuses on the time value of money. The idea is that a dollar today is worth more than a dollar received on some future date.

Logical Functions

Logical @functions are designed to work with conditions that can be either true or false. These conditions are known as Boolean conditions. A Boolean condition test returns either a 0 for false or a 1 for true. Later you will learn how a simple 0 or 1 can add power and flexibility to your models.

Logical @functions provide a way around the limitation of spreadsheets to place a single entry in a cell. By returning one of two values, they allow you to choose a course of action in two situations. The @IF function is the most powerful @function in this group and is often combined with other logical @functions that check for errors or other conditions to let you perform two different calculations depending on the result of a condition test.

You can use the logical @functions in many different ways, including the following:

- Testing for the values ERR or NA to determine if an error condition or unavailable data conditions exist
- Checking for information about ranges or range names
- Checking to see if a cell is empty
- Testing to see if a cell contains the type of data you need

Arguments for the logical @functions can be values, addresses or range names referencing values, or special values like NA and ERR. Single cell ranges are required for @functions like @ISERR and @ISNA. Except for @IF and @ISNAME, the logical @functions return either a 0 representing false or a 1 representing true.

Table 9-5 shows a complete list of the logical @functions. Keep these @functions in mind when you want to create macros that perform condition tests. Simple and logical operators used in condition tests are summarized in the boxes "The Simple Logical Operators" and "The Compound Logical Operators."

Mathematical Functions

Mathematical @functions perform both simple and complex tasks. You can use a mathematical @function for a simple computation like rounding or obtaining the absolute value of a number. You can also use

Function	Use
@FALSE	Returns a logical 0
@IF(*condition,x,y*)	Evaluates a condition and returns one of two values
@ISEMPTY(*x*)	Tests for a blank
@ISERR(*x*)	Tests for ERR
@ISNA(*x*)	Tests for NA
@ISNAME(*x*)	Checks to see if a range name exists
@ISNUMBER(*x*)	Checks for a value entry
@ISRANGE(*x*)	Checks for a range
@ISSTRING(*x*)	Checks for a label
@TRUE	Returns a logical 1

Table 9-5. Logical @Functions

mathematical @functions for more complex operations like square root and the trigonometric @functions that work with angles.

Although most business models use the @ROUND function, many of the other mathematical @functions are primarily used in engineering,

The Simple Logical Operators

1 2 3 G

Simple logical operators compare two or more values. The basic conditions you can check for with these operators are equal to, greater than, and less than. You can also use the last two conditions in combination with the first condition. The simple logical operators and their meanings are

=	Equal to
>	Greater than
<	Less than
> =	Greater than or equal to
< =	Less than or equal to
< >	Not equal to

The Compound Logical Operators

You can use compound logical operators to join two logical expressions or to negate an expression. The compound logical operators and a sample use for each one are

#AND#	C1=2#AND#D1=7	Both conditions C1=2 and D1=7 must be true for this expression to evaluate as true
#OR#	C1=2#OR#D1=7	If either condition is true, the statement evaluates as true
#NOT#	#NOT#C1=3	This statement negates C1=3. The #NOT# operator has priority over #AND# and #OR#.

manufacturing, and scientific applications. Table 9-6 lists all the mathematical @functions.

The trigonometric @functions all work with angles. These angles are expressed in radians, a unit of measure that equates the radius and the arc length. If the @function returns an angle size in radians, you can convert the radians to degrees if you multiply the radians by 180/@PI. Trigonometric @functions that expect angles for arguments, like @SIN, @COS, and @TAN, require that you express angle sizes as radians. If you only know degrees in the angle, multiply the degrees by @PI/180 to convert them to radians.

Special Functions

You can think of special @functions as a group of miscellaneous @functions. These @functions provide advanced features that do not fit into other @function categories.

Function	Use
@ABS(x)	Calculates an absolute value
@ACOS(x)	Calculates the inverse cosine
@ASIN(x)	Calculates the inverse sine
@ATAN(x)	Calculates the inverse tangent
@ATAN2(x,y)	Calculates the inverse tangent using y/x
@COS(x)	Calculates the cosine of an angle
@EXP(x)	Calculates the value of e raised to a power
@INT(x)	Returns the integer portion of a number
@LN(x)	Calculates the natural log
@LOG(x)	Calculates the common log
@MOD(x,y)	Calculates the remainder for x/y
@PI	Returns the value 3.1415926536
@RAND	Returns a random number
@ROUND(x,n)	Rounds a number to a requested number of decimal places
@SIN	Calculates the sine
@SQRT(x)	Returns the square root
@TAN(x)	Calculates the tangent

Table 9-6. Mathematical @Functions

Not all special @functions provide related features. There are special @functions like @@, @CELL, and @CELLPOINTER that provide information about a cell. Other @functions within the group—like @INFO, @SHEETS, and @SOLVER—provide information about the current worksheet, window, or session.

Some of these @functions work with a tabular range. You can use @HLOOKUP, @VLOOKUP, and @INDEX to return an appropriate entry from a table.

@ERR and @NA are also part of this category. These functions indicate an error, or that the value required for a calculation is not a value.

Table 9-7 is a complete list of all special @functions. Refer to this list when you are working with macros; often one of these functions can help you complete a macro task with ease.

Statistical Functions

Statistical @functions perform simple statistical computations on the list of entries. The list can consist of individual cell addresses and ranges,

Function	Use
@? and @??	Indicate an unknown function
@@	Provides indirect addressing
@CELL(*attribute,location*)	Returns information about a cell
@CELLPOINTER(*attribute*)	Returns information about the current cell
@CHOOSE(*x,list*)	Returns an entry from a list
@COLS(*range*)	Returns the number of columns in a range
@COORD(*worksheet,column,row,absolute*)	Creates a cell address
@ERR	Returns the value ERR
@HLOOKUP(*x,range,row-offset*)	Returns a table entry
@INDEX(*range,column,row*[*,worksheet*])	Returns a table entry
@INFO(*attribute*)	Returns system information
@NA	Returns the value NA
@ROWS(*range*)	Returns the number of rows in a range
@SHEETS(*range*)	Returns the number of sheets in a range
@SOLVER(*query-string*)	Provides information about the Solver utility
@VLOOKUP(*x,range,col-offset*)	Returns a table entry

Table 9-7. Special @Functions

or collections. You can use either names or addresses to refer to any of the entries in a list.

The cells within a list normally contain values for all the statistical @functions except @COUNT. The @COUNT function can tabulate the number of entries whether or not they contain values or labels.

Blank cells within a list are ignored as long as they are part of a range. Blank cells identified specifically are treated as if they contain a zero, which has a significant effect on the @AVG computation. Entering @AVG(B3..B5) returns 7.5 if B3 is blank, B4 contains 10, and B5 contains 5. If you compute the average with the entry @AVG(B3,B4,B5), the result is 5, since B3 is specifically included in the computation.

Label entries are treated as zero when referenced with one of the statistical @functions. Labels can have the same effect on an @AVG entry as a blank cell.

All of the statistical @functions except @SUMPRODUCT have corollary database statistical @functions. Use the database statistical @functions whenever you want to perform a calculation on a selected group of records.

Table 9-8 lists all of the statistical @functions. The function @SUMPRODUCT displays *list* as an argument with the other @functions in this category. When you use @SUMPRODUCT, the list must consist of a series of ranges that are identical in size. The @SUMPRODUCT function multiplies elements of each range and then adds the products of all the separate multiplications.

String @Functions

String @functions work with characters. You can also refer to character entries as text entries. These are entries that you place in cells as label entries or include within @functions by enclosing them in quotes.

Function	Use
@AVG(*list*)	Calculates an average
@COUNT(*list*)	Counts nonblank entries
@MAX(*list*)	Returns the maximum value
@MIN(*list*)	Returns the minimum value
@STD(*list*)	Computes the standard deviation for a population
@STDS(*list*)	Computes the standard deviation for a population sample
@SUM(*list*)	Totals values in list
@SUMPRODUCT(*list*)	Computes the sum of a series of products
@VAR(*list*)	Computes the variance for values in a population
@VARS(*list*)	Computes the variance for values in a population sample

Table 9-8. Statistical @Functions

You can use the string @functions to extract part of a string from a cell entry. String @functions can change the case of a text entry to upper-, lower-, or proper case. String @functions locate or change text in entries. String @functions can compare two entries or duplicate a string until a cell is filled. Most string @functions perform a straightforward conversion or extraction from a string. However, several string @functions display a character when a code is specified or locate the position of an entry within a string. Table 9-9 lists all of the string @functions.

You can supply string arguments as a cell address, a range address or name, or by placing the entry directly within the @function. If you

Function	Use
@CHAR(*x*)	Returns a character from the IBM Multilingual Character Set
@CODE(*string*)	Returns the IBM Multilingual Character Set code
@EXACT(*string1*,*string2*)	Compares two strings
@FIND(*search-string*, *string*,*start-number*)	Returns the location of a search-string within another string
@LEFT(*string*,*n*)	Extracts characters from a string
@LENGTH(*string*)	Returns the length of a string
@LOWER(*string*)	Converts a string to lowercase
@MID(*string*,*start-number*,*n*)	Extracts characters from the middle of a string
@N	Returns an entry as a value
@PROPER(*string*)	Converts a string to proper case
@REPEAT(*string*,*n*)	Repeats a string
@REPLACE(*original-string*,*start-number*,*n*, *new-string*)	Replaces part of a string
@RIGHT(*string*,*n*)	Extracts characters from the right side of a string
@S(*range*)	Returns an entry as a label
@STRING(*x*,*n*)	Converts an entry to a label
@TRIM(*string*)	Removes spaces from a string
@UPPER(*string*)	Converts a string to uppercase
@VALUE(*string*)	Converts to a value a string that looks like a value

Table 9-9. String @Functions

place the entry in the @function, you must enclose it in quotes, as in @REPEAT("ABC",3). If ABC is stored in a cell, no quotes are needed in either the cell or the @function.

Many of the string @functions work with part of a string. 1-2-3/G uses position numbers to reference each character in a string, making it easy to identify the needed components. You must always express string position numbers as positive integers. If you use a negative integer, 1-2-3/G returns ERR. If you use a number with a decimal, 1-2-3/G drops it and uses only the integer portion of the number. No rounding occurs; for example, 1-2-3/G truncates a value of 5.7 to 5 when you use it as a position number for a string.

Position numbers always start with 0 rather than 1. In the string ABC, A is position 0, B is position 1, and C is position 2. Any spaces within the string are assigned position numbers, although the label indicator at the beginning of a string is not.

An empty string is a string that contains nothing but a label indicator. It has a length of 0. It is not, however, equivalent to a blank cell without a label indicator.

@Function Reference

Each of the following sections describes an @function. The sections include a brief description, a syntax section, and at least one example.

The @@ Function

@@ is a special function that provides an indirect addressing capability. Rather than place an address in a formula, @@ lets you supply an address containing the address of another cell, the contents of which are used in the formula.

Syntax

@@(*cell*)

The *cell* argument is the address of a cell. The contents of the cell direct you to another address. It is this second level of addresses that makes this @function a little difficult to understand at first.

The cell referenced by @@ contains a string that looks like a cell address. The contents of the cell supplied by the argument can look like a regular cell address such as Z10, A4; a range name such as SALES or BUDGET; or a string formula that creates a string that looks like an address, such as +"A"&"1", which creates the string A1.

Example

The worksheet in Figure 9-1 uses @@ to determine which of the key variable values to use. The model shows the annual sales and commissions for a sales staff. You can set up the model to accept a quick change to the commission percent with @@.

In this example, the base rate for the company is set at 7 percent, but this percentage can be as high as 12 percent if the period is profitable. The @@ function is used to make a quick adjustment to a higher commission. The formula in C2 of the model is @@($A$10)*B2. A10 in turn contains a reference to one of the commission percentages in E1..E5. The referenced entry must be a string variable that displays a cell address. It is currently e4, so the commission is calculated using an 11 percent rate. Note that either an upper- or lowercase "e" in the

1-2-3/G (69.4) Ready

File Edit Worksheet Range Copy... Move... Print Graph Data Utility Quit... Help

A:C2 @@($A$10)*B2

SHEET_50.WG1

A	A	B	C	D	E	F
1	Salesman	Total Sales	Commission		7.00%	
2	RKL	$1,500,890.00	$165,097.90		8.50%	
3	HYT	$2,306,789.00	$253,746.79		9.00%	
4	REW	$1,000,950.00	$110,104.50		11.00%	
5	MAC	$957,850.00	$105,363.50		12.00%	
6	DIL	$998,750.00	$109,862.50			
7	SAM	$1,234,750.00	$135,822.50			
8			$879,997.69			
9						
10	e4					

Figure 9-1. Using @@ to select a commission rate

cell address produces the same results. To change the commission to another rate, just change A10. If you change the entry in A10 to E2, all the commissions are recalculated, and the total commissions in C8 will drop to $679,998.22.

Tip: You may need to use F9 (Calc) with @@. If you use the @function to refer to a cell that contains a formula, a 0 is returned. Pressing F9 eliminates the problem by forcing 1-2-3/G to recalculate the worksheet.

@ABS

@ABS is a mathematical @function that calculates the absolute value of a number.

Syntax

@ABS(x)

The argument x can be any value entry.

Example

You can use @ABS when you are interested in the magnitude of a difference. For example, suppose you want to monitor cash overages and shortages in the cash registers of a retail establishment. Consistent cash overages and shortages indicate a cash control problem that should be corrected. If you monitor both overages and shortages, adding their + and – signs, they might cancel each other out. However, looking at the absolute value of the overages and shortages provides a look at the total amount of the differences.

If you add a restaurant's cash overages and shortages by adding absolute values for each day, the positive and negative numbers reported will not cancel each other partially.

You might combine the @ABS function with @IF and @STRING. The two @functions compute the total at the bottom of a customer's bill. If the amount of the charges exceeds the credit payments, the total amount is positive and equals the absolute value of the sum. If they are not equal, there have been more payments than charges and the customer has a credit balance. One way of performing the test for a positive value is:

@ABS(@SUM(E5..E10))=@SUM(E5..E10)

The complete entry is

```
@IF(@ABS(@SUM(E5..E10))=@SUM(E5..E10),"You owe $ "
&@STRING(@SUM(E5..E10),2),"Credit balance of $ "
&@STRING(@ABS(@SUM(E5..E10)),2))
```

The entry is a little long, but it provides correct results for all customer bills. Formulas like this take time, but their flexibility makes the effort worthwhile.

Tip: If you use @ABS to reference a cell containing a string, the result is zero.

@ACOS

@ACOS is a mathematical @function that performs a trigonometric calculation. It returns the inverse cosine of an angle. The arc cosine represents an angle from 0 to 180 degrees, but the result is expressed in radians. This angle is located between the hypotenuse (side opposite the right angle) and the side adjacent to the right angle. If you prefer to work with the result in degrees, you can convert it by multiplying the result by 180/@PI.

Syntax

@ACOS(x)

The argument x is the cosine of an angle. A cosine can be any value from -1 to 1.

Example

Suppose that you are at the top of a cliff in a lighthouse 100 feet above the water and want to know the angle required to make a projectile reach a boat approximately 200 feet away. You can use the @ACOS function to calculate the answer. You could find the number of degrees with these calculations:

cos of angle = 100/200
cos of angle = .5
@ACOS(.5)*180/@PI = 60 degrees

@ASIN

@ASIN is a mathematical @function that determines the arcsine or inverse sine of a number.

Syntax

@ASIN(x)

x is the sine of an angle, which can range from −1 to 1.

Example

Suppose that you need to roll a barrel into a truck. The truckbed is three feet off the ground at point A and the board used to roll the barrel is six feet long touching the ground at point B. If you want to position a support where the board meets the ground, you need to know the size of angle ABC where point C is the ground directly beneath point A. The sine of this angle is equal to 3/6 or 0.5. Using the @ASIN function @ASIN(.5)*180/@PI shows that the angle equals 30 degrees.

@ATAN

@ATAN is a mathematical @function that calculates the arctangent or inverse tangent of an angle.

Syntax

@ATAN(x)

x is the tangent of an angle, which can range from −1 to 1.

Example

Suppose that you are playing a game of championship pool and need to pass the ball from point A to point B in the diagram in Figure 9-2. The tangent between the pocket and the bumper is equal to 4/3 or 1.3333333. @ATAN(1.3333333) is 0.927295 radians. When this result is multiplied by 180/@PI, you have 53.1301 degrees.

@ATAN2

@ATAN2 is a mathematical @function that returns the 4 quadrant arctangent, or the angle in radians whose tangent is *y/x*

Syntax

@ATAN2(*x*,*y*)

x is the x coordinate of the angle and *y* is the y coordinate of the angle.

Example

An angle with an X-axis coordinate of 1 and a Y-axis coordinate of 0.5 has an arctangent of @ATAN2(1,.5) or 0.463647 radians.

@AVG

@AVG is a statistical @function that computes the average or mean for a range of values.

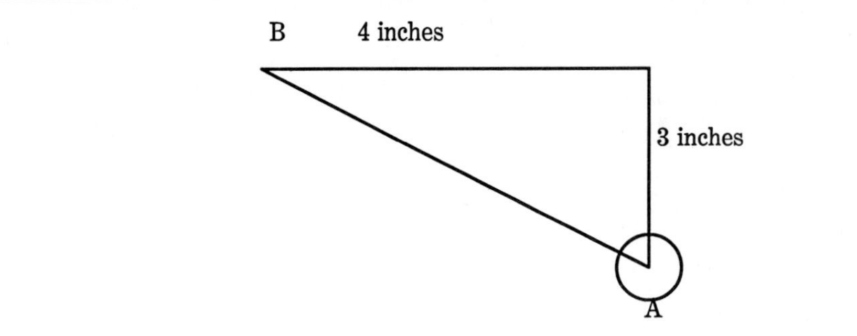

Figure 9-2. Making the pool shot

Syntax

@AVG(*list*)

List can consist of one or more cell addresses, range addresses, or range names referring to individual cells, ranges, or collections. A list can contain a range that spans sheets in a worksheet file.

Example

You can use @AVG to obtain the average for values in a range. For example, you might have a simple listing of bid amounts in B4..B11. If you want to determine the average bid amount, you can just enter @AVG(B4..B11).

Tip: Be careful with label entries in a range referenced by @AVG. Although the label is treated as 0, it adds one to the divisor used in the average computation. Individual references to blank cells create the same problem, causing your average computation to be incorrect

@CELL

@CELL is a special @function that obtains information about a cell. There are 58 different pieces of information you can request about a cell with this @function.

Syntax

@CELL(*"attribute",location*)

Attribute can be any one of the 58 attributes shown in Table 9-10. Attributes that begin with "s" check the global setting. You can supply the attribute within the @function, but it must be enclosed within quotes.

Example

You can use the @CELL function to check a cell's status for zero suppression. If the user inadvertently changed the setting, this

Attribute String	Results
address	The address of the current cell; for example, $K$3
bborder/sbborder	The bottom border pattern returned as letter A, B, C, or D
blcolor/sblcolor	Background palette color A through P
bvcolorneg/sbvcolorneg	Background palette color for negative values, A through P
bvcolorpos/sbvcolorpos	Background palette color for positive values, A through P
calcprecision/ scalcprecision	Calculating precision, NA for full precision or 0 through 15 if limited by Range Attributes
col	A number between 1 and 256, representing the column number
color	Color setting for negative values, 1 for color, 0 if not color
contents	The contents of the cell
coord	The cell address that includes the worksheet letter; for example, $A:$K$3
filename	The current path and filename
flcolor/sflcolor	Foreground palette color for labels A through P
fontattrib/sfontattrib	The font attribute represented as a string of four digits. From left to right the digits represent bold, italic, underline, and strikeout
fontid/sfontid	The font ID A through T
fontnamep/sfontnamep	The name of the printer font
fontnames/sfontnames	The screen font
fontpointp/sfontpointp	Printer font point size
fontpoints/sfontpoints	Screen font point size
fvcolorpos/sfvcolorpos	Foreground palette color for positive values
fvcolorneg/sfvcolorneg	Foreground palette color for negative values
format/sformat	The current format of the cell. Choose from:
	A for Automatic
	C0-C15 for Currency with 0 to 15 decimal places
	D1 for *DD-MMM-YY*
	D2 for *DD-MMM*
	D3 for *MMM-YY*
	D4 for *MM/DD/YY*, *DD/MM/YY*, *DD.MM.YY*, or *YY-MM-DD*
	D5 for *MM/DD*, *DD/MM*, *DD.MM*, or *MM-DD*
	D6 for *HH:MM:SS AM/PM*

Table 9-10. Attribute Strings for @CELL (*continued on next page*)

Attribute String	Results
	D7 for *HH:MM AM/PM*
	D8 for *HH:MM:SS, HH.MM.SS, HH,MM,SS,* or *HHhMMmSSs* (all 24-hour)
	D9 for *HH:MM, HH.MM, HH,MM,* or *HHhMMm* (all 24-hour)
	F0-F15 for Fixed with 0 to 15 decimal places
	G for General, labels or blank cells
	H for Hidden
	L for Label format
	P0-P15 for Percent with 0 to 15 decimal places
	T for Text
	S0-S15 for Scientific with 0 to 15 decimal places
	,0-,15 for Comma with 0 to 15 decimal places
	+ for +/− format
	U for User format
lborder/slborder	Left border pattern A through D
longlabel/slonglabel	Long label setting; 0 if short, 1 if long
parentheses/sparentheses	Parentheses format; 0 if not (Parens), 1 if (Parens)
prefix/sprefix	Label prefix for the cell. The label prefix ^ will appear for centered entries, ' for left-justified entries, " for right-justified entries, \ for repeating labels, | for non-printing label, and blank for an empty or numeric cell
protect/sprotect	Protection status of the cell; with 1 representing protected and 0 representing unprotected
rborder/srborder	Right border pattern, A through D
row	A number between 1 and 8192 representing the row number
sheet	A number between 1 and 256 representing the worksheet letter
tborder/stborder	Top border pattern, A through D
type	The type of data in the cell. The value types are b for blank, v for numeric, and l for label
vprefix/svprefix	Value alignment, ' if left-aligned, " if right aligned, ^ if centered
width	A number between 1 and 240 representing the current cell width
zerosuppress/ szerosuppress	Zero suppression status; 0 if not suppressed, 1 if suppressed

Table 9-10. Attribute Strings for @CELL

@function reminds him or her to change the setting back before printing a report. The entry in A17 is

```
@IF(@CELL("zerosuppress",A1)=1,"","You accidentally changed
the status of zero suppression, please set it to Yes")
```

If you are checking the status, you must recalculate the worksheet before relying on the results of this @function, since it is not automatically recalculated when you make changes with range commands.

@CELLPOINTER

@CELLPOINTER is a special @function that provides information about the cell in which the cell pointer is located. This @function is almost identical to @CELL. However, it looks at the cell containing the cell pointer rather than at a location that you specify. If you move the cell pointer and recalculate the worksheet, another result would appear for a cell containing @CELLPOINTER.

Syntax

@CELLPOINTER("*attribute*")

Attribute is one of 58 different options shown in Table 9-10.

Example

Figure 9-3 shows the @CELLPOINTER function entered in columns C and E. The cell pointer is in A1. Column C is formatted as General to display the return values, and column E is formatted as the text to display @CELLPOINTER formulas.

Figure 9-4 shows a more sophisticated @CELLPOINTER application that combines @CELLPOINTER and @VLOOKUP. The table in A9..B11 shows a few entries for fonts. This could be expanded to include all font options. The letters in column A are matched against the letters returned with @CELLPOINTER("fontid") and return a string that is more readable. B2 contains the entry

@VLOOKUP(@CELLPOINTER("fontid"),A9..B11,1)

1-2-3/G (69.4) Ready

File Edit Worksheet Range Copy... Move... Print Graph Data Utility Quit... Help

A:A1 1234.678

(,2) SHEET_53.WG1

A	A	B	C	D	E	F
1	1,234.68		$A$1		@CELLPOINTER("address")	
2			1		@CELLPOINTER("col")	
3			1		@CELLPOINTER("row")	
4			1234.678		@CELLPOINTER("contents")	
5			1		@CELLPOINTER("protect")	
6			,2		@CELLPOINTER("format")	
7			v		@CELLPOINTER("type")	
8			15		@CELLPOINTER("width")	
9			$A:$A$1		@CELLPOINTER("coord")	
10			1	Sheet	@CELLPOINTER(F10)	
11			C:\123G\F2\FIG7_53.WK3		@CELLPOINTER("filename")	

Figure 9-3. Examining the current cell with @CELLPOINTER

With the cell pointer on B6, it returns the entry from B11 to B2 where the @function combination is entered. If you change the settings with the Range command, you must recalculate the worksheet with F9 (Recalc) to see the updated setting.

For more information on @CELLPOINTER, refer to @CELL, since the two @functions have identical applications.

1-2-3/G (69.4) Ready

File Edit Worksheet Range Copy... Move... Print Graph Data Utility Quit... Help

A:B6 'This is 12 point Helvetica

FONTS.WG1

A	A	B	C	D	E	F	G
1							
2		Font used for the current cell is 12 point Helvetica					
3							
4		This is 8 point Helvetica					
5		This is 14 point Helvetica					
6		This is 12 point Helvetica					
7							
8	Lookup Table for font						
9	A	Font used for the current cell is 8 point Helvetica					
10	B	Font used for the current cell is 14 point Helvetica					
11	F	Font used for the current cell is 12 point Helvetica					

Figure 9-4. Combining @CELLPOINTER with @VLOOKUP

@CHAR

@CHAR is a string @function. It allows you to specify a code from the IBM Multilingual Character Set and returns the character.

Syntax

@CHAR(*x*)

x is an integer from 1 to 6143.

Tip: For a quick look at many options, enter @CHAR with a cell address for an argument. Substitute various values in the cell to see a range of options.

Example

You can add a trademark symbol with the formula

+"Market Analysis Model "&@CHAR(169)

Dividing lines can be added with

@REPEAT(@CHAR(190),80) in A3 and A5

@CHOOSE

The @CHOOSE function returns a value from a list of value options that are part of the @function arguments. @CHOOSE is one of the Special @functions.

Syntax

@CHOOSE(*x*,*list*)

x is the number of the list entry that you want the @function to return. It is an offset from the beginning of the list, with 0 representing the first entry in the list; *list* is a set or group of labels or values.

Example

The worksheet in Figure 9-5 shows the @CHOOSE function determining a shipping cost from a warehouse location. In the list for @CHOOSE, warehouse 1 adds $5.00 shipping charges, warehouse 2 adds $10.00, warehouse 3 adds $15.00, warehouse 4 adds $3.00, and warehouse 5 adds $20.00.

The Warehouse codes are in column A. The Item numbers are in column B. The Quantity and Unit Prices are in columns C and D respectively. The calculation for shipping cost requires the @CHOOSE formula. A dummy value is used for warehouse 0, since all @CHOOSE lists start with 0. A $0 shipping charge is therefore included in the list. The function is recorded in E2 as @CHOOSE(A2,0,5,10,15,3,20). The cell is formatted as Currency, and the formula is copied down the column E. Total Cost in the model, shown in column F, is simply the entry in column C times the entry in column D plus the Shipping cost from column E.

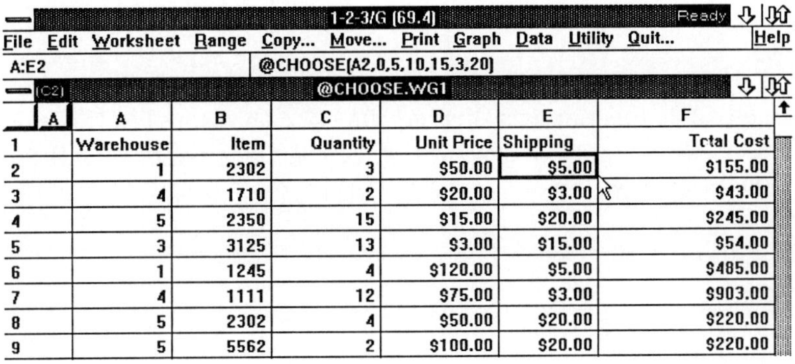

1-2-3/G (69.4) Ready

File Edit Worksheet Range Copy... Move... Print Graph Data Utility Quit... Help

A:E2 @CHOOSE(A2,0,5,10,15,3,20)

(C2) @CHOOSE.WG1

A	A	B	C	D	E	F
1	Warehouse	Item	Quantity	Unit Price	Shipping	Total Cost
2	1	2302	3	$50.00	$5.00	$155.00
3	4	1710	2	$20.00	$3.00	$43.00
4	5	2350	15	$15.00	$20.00	$245.00
5	3	3125	13	$3.00	$15.00	$54.00
6	1	1245	4	$120.00	$5.00	$485.00
7	4	1111	12	$75.00	$3.00	$903.00
8	5	2302	4	$50.00	$20.00	$220.00
9	5	5562	2	$100.00	$20.00	$220.00

Figure 9-5. Choosing the correct value

@CLEAN

The @CLEAN function is an undocumented @function that removes from a string characters that have Lotus Character Set values of less than 32. These include some special characters that you can import into 1-2-3/G.

Syntax

@CLEAN(*string*)

String is a string in quotes, or a cell or range address, or a name that contains a string.

Example

The following example shows the original strings and the strings this function returns:

```
@CLEAN("☺☻ This is ¶text")
```

equals

```
This is text
```

@CODE

The @CODE function is a String @function that supplies the code from the IBM Multilingual Character Set (called "code page 850") that corresponds to a character.

Syntax

@CODE(*string*)

String can be a string or a cell containing a string or a string formula.

Tip: Codes between 65 and 90 correspond to uppercase letters. For example, a lowercase "a" is 97 and an uppercase "A" is 65.

Example

The following examples show the values returned by @CODE:

Function	Equals
@CODE("$")	36
@CODE("V")	86
@CODE("@")	64

@COLS

@COLS is a special @function that determines the number of columns in a specified range.

Syntax

@COLS(*range*)

Range is a range address or a range name.

Example

You might have a worksheet that projects sales for a varying number of months. You can determine the number of months forecast by the model with @COLS(SALES_STATS) if the range name SALES_STATS is assigned to the data.

@COORD

The @COORD function is a special @function that lets you create a cell address. You must supply an entry corresponding to each component of the cell address.

Syntax

@COORD(*worksheet,column,row,absolute*)

Worksheet is a value from 1 to 256 representing the sheet number. The number 1 is sheet A and the number 256 is sheet IV.
Column is a value from 1 to 256 representing the column number (1 stands for column A and 256 stands for column IV).
Row is a value between 1 and 8192, corresponding directly to the row number you want to use.
Absolute is a value from 1 to 8. The numbers correspond to the entries in Table 9-11.

Example

Figure 9-6 shows detail expense entries for expense codes 1001 and 1002. Other sheets contain the remaining expense codes, which are assigned sequentially.

Sheet A allows you to enter the month, year, and expense code type for which you need information. The formula in A:B5 uses these entries in the @COORD function. The sheet number is computed by subtracting 999 from the expense account number. To access 1001, the formula would subtract 999 from 1001, resulting in 2 or sheet B. The column number is supplied as the month+1, since the month data starts in column B (column 2). Since 1985 data is in row 2, the year location is the year entered less 1983. The data for 1987 is in row 4. When @COORD is combined with the @@ function, the resulting value for expense account 1001 for May 1987 is returned.

Value	Example	Worksheet	Row	Column
1	$A:$B$4	Absolute	Absolute	Absolute
2	$A:B$4	Absolute	Relative	Absolute
3	$A:$B4	Absolute	Absolute	Relative
4	$A:B4	Absolute	Relative	Relative
5	A:$B$4	Relative	Absolute	Absolute
6	A:B$4	Relative	Relative	Absolute
7	A:$B4	Relative	Absolute	Relative
8	A:B4	Relative	Relative	Relative

Table 9-11. Values for the Absolute Argument in @COORD

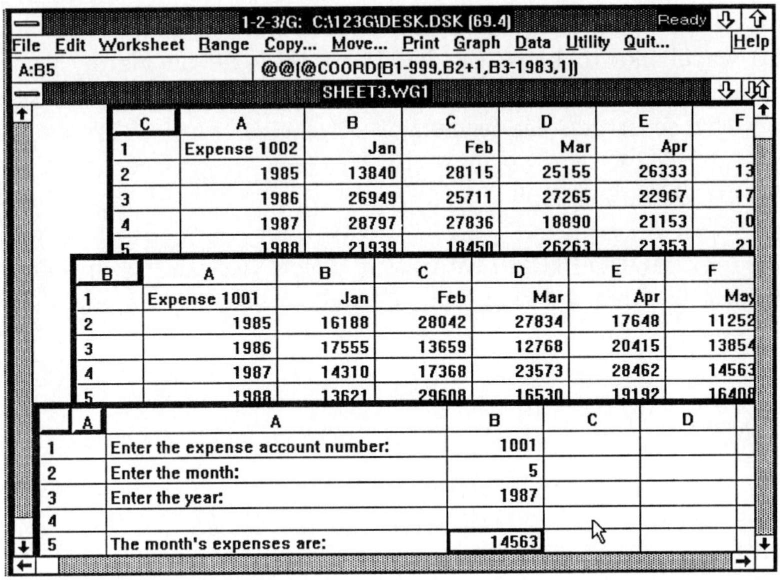

1-2-3/G: C:\123G\DESK.DSK [69.4] Ready

File Edit Worksheet Range Copy... Move... Print Graph Data Utility Quit... Help

A:B5 @@(@COORD(B1-999,B2+1,B3-1983,1))

SHEET3.WG1

C	A	B	C	D	E	F
1	Expense 1002	Jan	Feb	Mar	Apr	
2	1985	13840	28115	25155	26333	13
3	1986	26949	25711	27265	22967	17
4	1987	28797	27836	18890	21153	10
5	1988	21939	18450	26263	21353	21

B	A	B	C	D	E	F
1	Expense 1001	Jan	Feb	Mar	Apr	May
2	1985	16188	28042	27834	17648	11252
3	1986	17555	13659	12768	20415	13854
4	1987	14310	17368	23573	28462	14563
5	1988	13621	29608	16530	19192	16408

A	A	B	C	D
1	Enter the expense account number:	1001		
2	Enter the month:	5		
3	Enter the year:	1987		
4				
5	The month's expenses are:	14563		

Figure 9-6. Using @COORD to generate a cell address

@COS

@COS is a mathematical @function that computes the cosine of an angle.

Syntax

@COS(*x*)

x is a number representing the radians in an angle.

Example

Given some information about a plot in the shape of a right triangle, a surveyor can determine the length of a side of the triangle.

The longest side of the plot of land is 50 feet, as shown in Figure 9-7. There is a 60-degree angle where the surveyor is standing. He or she would like to know the length of the side on his or her left. In mathematical terminology, this side is called the adjacent side. The surveyor constructs the formula

@COS(60°) = x/50

The @COS(60*@PI/180) returns .5, which you can use in the equation to solve for an x value of 250. @PI/180 translated the angle size from degrees into radians.

@COUNT

The @COUNT function determines the number of cells containing entries within a list of cell addresses or ranges. It is a statistical @function.

Syntax

@COUNT(*list*)

List is a series of cell addresses, ranges, or collections.

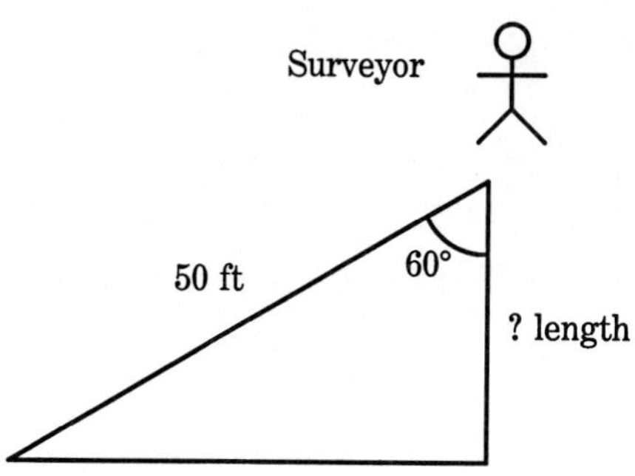

Figure 9-7. Determining the length of the side of a plot of land

Example

You might use @COUNT to determine the number of travel reports processed this month where column D contains the initials of the person who processed the travel report. Records without an entry in column D are still open. The formula @COUNT (D5..D100) will count the number of initials entered in column D, assuming rows 1 through 4 are used to contain column headings and other types of information. The result of the formula is the number of travel reports processed.

Tip: To count records in a database selectively use @DCOUNT. This function allows you to use criteria to specify what records you want included in the count.

@CTERM

The @CTERM function returns the number of compounding periods needed to attain a future value for an investment. 1-2-3/G uses the formula for this financial @function.

natural log(future-value/present-value)
natural log(1 + *periodic interest rate*)

Syntax

@CTERM(*interest,future-value,present-value*)

Interest is the fixed interest rate per compounding period.
Future-value is the value of the investment at some point in the future.
Present-value is the current value of the investment.

Example

Suppose that you have $5,000 to invest today. You think that you can get an 11 percent return on your investment and want to know how long it will take to triple your initial investment. Assuming that the compounding occurs monthly,

```
@CTERM(11%/12,15000,5000)
```

provides the answer, 120.39708 months. If you divide this result by 12, 10.03 years will display as the result.

@D360

@D360 is a date @function that calculates the number of days between two dates, assuming a 360-day calendar year.

Syntax

@D360(*start-date*,*end-date*)

Start-date is a date serial number for the starting date of a period. *End-date* is the date serial number for the ending date for the period.

Example

If you deposit $100,000 in a bank from April 1 to August 16, you might want to know how much interest you will earn, assuming that the bank pays 9 percent using a 360-day year. The entry

```
+100000*@D360(@DATE(90,4,1),@DATE(90,8,15))/360*.09
```

returns 3350, which is the interest earned. The same calculation based on a 365-day year is

```
+100000*(@DATE(90,8,15)−@DATE(90,4,1))/365*.09
```

which returns 3353 as the interest.

@DATE

The @DATE function allows you to create a date number when you supply each of the date components. Date numbers allow you to perform date arithmetic.

Syntax

@DATE(*year,month,day*)

Year is a number between 0 and 199. 1900 is represented by 0 and 2099 is represented by 199.
Month is a number between 1 and 12.
Day is a number between 1 and 31 that is valid for the month number specified. Since month 9 (September) only has 30 days, 31 would not be an appropriate day entry for September. Likewise, 28 is the highest number you can use for month 2 (February) unless the year number specified is a leap year, when 29 is acceptable.

Example

Suppose you obtain a 30-day loan on July 15, 1990. You can have 1-2-3/G determine the loan due date for you so you don't have to worry about which months have 30 days and which ones have 31. The loan origination date might be entered as @DATE(90,7,15). The due date is computed by adding 30 days to this date as in @DATE(90,7,15). A data format would need to be applied to the results.

Tip: You can also enter a date in the *DD-MMM-YY, DD-MMM,* or Long International Date format. 1-2-3/G automatically converts such entries to date serial numbers. This approach is quicker than the @DATE function.

@DATEVALUE

The @DATEVALUE function converts a label entry that looks like a date into a date number.

Syntax

@DATEVALUE(*string*)

String is a label entry in any of 1-2-3/G's valid date formats.

Example

If you have dates entered as labels to record the date a video tape was checked out and the date it was returned, you can use @DATEVALUE in your computation of the rental charges. The formulas to subtract the two dates are located in column E and follow the format of

(@DATEVALUE(D5)−@DATEVALUE(C5))*2.25

assuming that column D contains labels for the return dates, column C contains labels for the checkout dates, and $2.25 is the daily rental charge.

@DAVG

The @DAVG function computes an average from selected database records. You control record selections by entering criteria on the worksheet. @DAVG is a database statistical @function.

Syntax

@DAVG(*input,field,criteria*)

Input refers to the entire database, including the field names in the first row. It can be a range or ranges referring to one or more database tables.

Field is the offset of a field in the database table or the name of an actual database field.

Criteria are your specifications of the records you want selected.

For more information on these arguments see the section "Syntax of Database Statistical Functions" earlier in this chapter and Chapter 19 on data management.

Example

You might use the @DAVG function and the database in Figure 9-8 to calculate an average salary for employees in job code 23. Note that the database is defined as being located in A1..F12. The function uses the Salary field, and the criteria used in the selection are located in A15..A16 with an entry of

@DAVG(A1..F12,4,A15..A16)

returning $21,550.

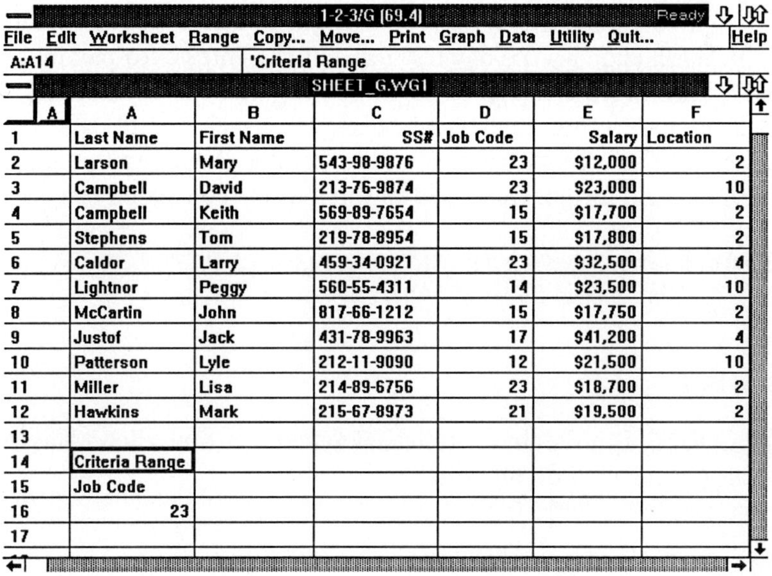

1-2-3/G [69.4] Ready

File Edit Worksheet Range Copy... Move... Print Graph Data Utility Quit... Help

A:A14 'Criteria Range

SHEET_G.WG1

A	A	B	C	D	E	F
1	Last Name	First Name	SS#	Job Code	Salary	Location
2	Larson	Mary	543-98-9876	23	$12,000	2
3	Campbell	David	213-76-9874	23	$23,000	10
4	Campbell	Keith	569-89-7654	15	$17,700	2
5	Stephens	Tom	219-78-8954	15	$17,800	2
6	Caldor	Larry	459-34-0921	23	$32,500	4
7	Lightnor	Peggy	560-55-4311	14	$23,500	10
8	McCartin	John	817-66-1212	15	$17,750	2
9	Justof	Jack	431-78-9963	17	$41,200	4
10	Patterson	Lyle	212-11-9090	12	$21,500	10
11	Miller	Lisa	214-89-6756	23	$18,700	2
12	Hawkins	Mark	215-67-8973	21	$19,500	2
13						
14	Criteria Range					
15	Job Code					
16	23					
17						

Figure 9-8. Database for use with the database statistical functions

@DAY

The @DAY function computes the day of the month when you supply a valid date number.

Syntax

@DAY(*date-number*)

Date-number is a value between 1 and 73050. The number 1 represents December 31, 1899 and the number 73050 represents December 31, 2099.

Example

You can build a schedule of dates that are exactly one month apart. As an example, suppose that you want to extract the day from a loan origination date so you can use it to generate payment due dates. The @DAY function supplies the day in each entry using the day from the origination date.

You can also use @DAY as part of a more complex date entry. @DAY still supplies the day number, but the entries for month and year are a little more complex since you must allow for a different entry in each of these other components once you reach month 12. You might create date entries with the following formula assuming the first date is in A4 and the formula is copied to the rest of the column or row:

```
@IF(@MONTH(A4)=12,@DATE(@YEAR(A4)+1,1,@DAY(A4)),
@DATE(@YEAR(A4),@MONTH(A4)+1,@DAY(A4)))
```

@DCOUNT

@DCOUNT is a database statistical @function that allows you to count entries in selected database table records.

Syntax

@DCOUNT(*input,field,criteria*)

Input refers to the entire database, including the field names in the first row. It can be a range or ranges referring to one or more database tables.

Field is the offset of a field in the database table or the name of an actual database field. If you use an offset, remember that the first database field has an offset of zero.

Criteria are the specifications of the records you want selected. They include at least one field name with an entry beneath it to indicate acceptable entries for the field. For more on these argument entries, refer to the section "Syntax of Database Statistical Functions" earlier in this chapter and Chapter 19 on Data Management.

Example

You might use the @DCOUNT function and the database in Figure 9-8 to count the salary entries for records with a job code of 23. Note that the input is defined as A1..F12. The field number to refer to the salary is 4 and the criteria used in the selection are in A15..A16. Since @DCOUNT counts only records with a nonblank entry in the specified field, choose the field that you count carefully. For example, some records need not have a location assignment, but all records should have a salary. Your formula entry would be @DCOUNT(A1..F12,2,A15..A16) and return 4.

@DDB

@DDB is a financial @function that calculates depreciation with the double-declining balance method.

Syntax

@DDB(*cost,salvage,life,period*)

Cost is a value entry representing the amount you paid for the asset.

Salvage is a value entry representing the value of the asset at the end of its useful life.

Life is the expected useful life of the asset—that is, the number of years needed to depreciate the asset from its cost to its salvage value.

Period is the specific time period for which you are attempting to determine the depreciation expense. Normally the year for which you are calculating depreciation expense, *period* must be a value or a reference to one.

Example

Figure 9-9 uses @DDB to determine the proper depreciation expense for each year in an asset's five-year life. The cost of the asset was $11,000, and its salvage value is $1,000.

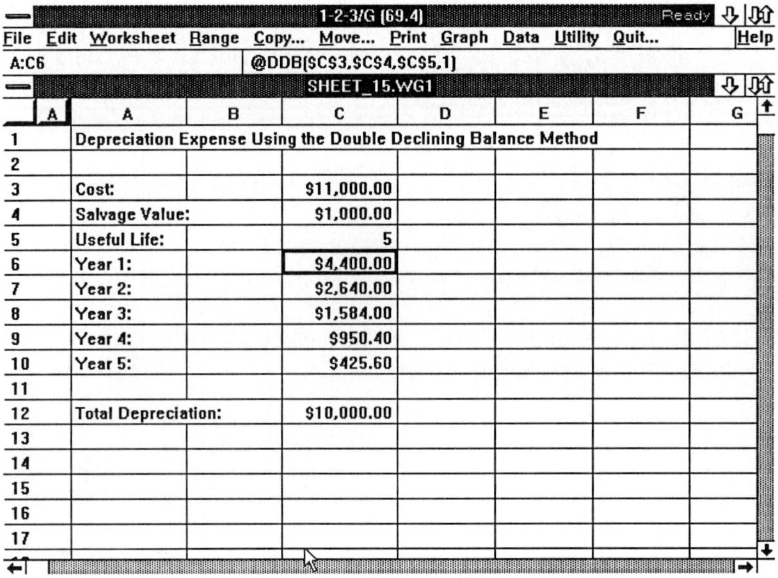

1-2-3/G (69.4) Ready

File Edit Worksheet Range Copy... Move... Print Graph Data Utility Quit... Help

A:C6 @DDB($C$3,$C$4,$C$5,1)

SHEET_15.WG1

A	A	B	C	D	E	F	G
1	Depreciation Expense Using the Double Declining Balance Method						
2							
3	Cost:		$11,000.00				
4	Salvage Value:		$1,000.00				
5	Useful Life:		5				
6	Year 1:		$4,400.00				
7	Year 2:		$2,640.00				
8	Year 3:		$1,584.00				
9	Year 4:		$950.40				
10	Year 5:		$425.60				
11							
12	Total Depreciation:		$10,000.00				
13							
14							
15							
16							
17							

Figure 9-9. Double-declining balance depreciation

@DGET

@DGET is a database statistical @function that returns a value for a record that meets a set of criteria. If more than one record in the database table matches the criteria, @DGET returns ERR.

Syntax

@DGET(*input,field,criteria*)

Input refers to the entire database, including the field names in the first row.
Field is the offset of a field in the database table or the name of an actual database field. If you use an offset, remember that the first database field has an offset of zero.
Criteria are the specifications of the records you want selected. They include at least one field name with an entry beneath it to indicate acceptable entries for the field. For more on the arguments see the section "Syntax of Database Statistical Functions" earlier in this chapter or Chapter 19.

Example

The @DGET function in Figure 9-10 uses the database (sheet C) and criteria (B:C1..B:C2) to return the social security number of the employee with the last name of Canfield. Note that the database is defined as being located in C:A1..C:E12, the SSN field is searched, and the criteria used in the selection are located in B:C1..B:C2.

@DMAX

@DMAX is a database statistical @function that allows you to locate the maximum value in a field within a selected group of records.

Syntax

@DMAX(*input,field,criteria*)

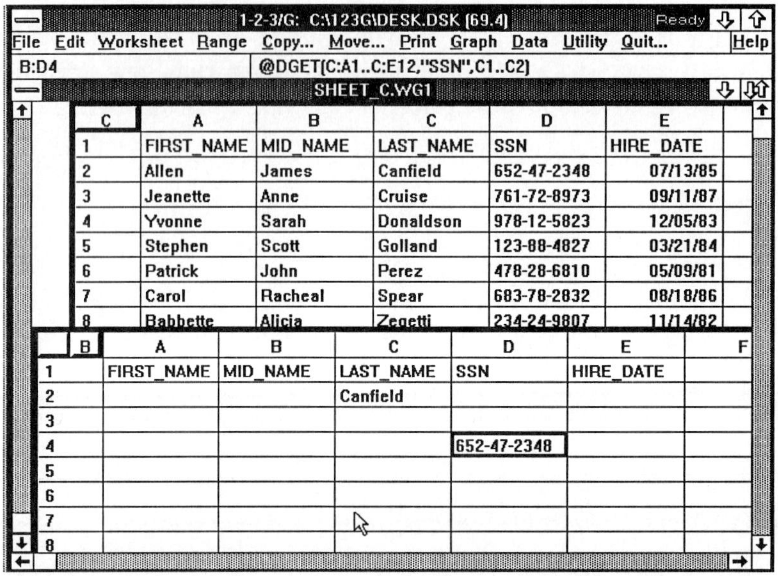

1-2-3/G: C:\123G\DESK.DSK (69.4) Ready

File Edit Worksheet Range Copy... Move... Print Graph Data Utility Quit... Help

B:D4 @DGET(C:A1..C:E12,"SSN",C1..C2)

SHEET_C.WG1

C	A	B	C	D	E
1	FIRST_NAME	MID_NAME	LAST_NAME	SSN	HIRE_DATE
2	Allen	James	Canfield	652-47-2348	07/13/85
3	Jeanette	Anne	Cruise	761-72-8973	09/11/87
4	Yvonne	Sarah	Donaldson	978-12-5823	12/05/83
5	Stephen	Scott	Golland	123-88-4827	03/21/84
6	Patrick	John	Perez	478-28-6810	05/09/81
7	Carol	Racheal	Spear	683-78-2832	08/18/86
8	Babbette	Alicia	Zegetti	234-24-9807	11/14/82

B	A	B	C	D	E	F
1	FIRST_NAME	MID_NAME	LAST_NAME	SSN	HIRE_DATE	
2			Canfield			
3						
4				652-47-2348		
5						
6						
7						
8						

Figure 9-10. Using @DGET to find a social security number

Input is a range or ranges that refer to the entire database, including the field names in the first row.

Field is the offset of a field in the database table or the name of an actual database field. If you use an offset, remember that the first database field has an offset of zero.

Criteria is a range containing the specifications of the records you want selected.

Example

You can use the @DMAX function and the database in Figure 9-8 to determine the maximum salary for employees with a job code of 23. Note that the database is defined as being located in A1..F12. The

Salary field is used, and the criteria used in the selection are located in A15..A16. The entry is:

@DMAX(A1..F12,4,A15..A16)

and returns 32500.

@DMIN

@DMIN is a database statistical @function that you can use to obtain the minimum value in a field within a selected group of database records.

Syntax

@DMIN(*input,field,criteria*)

Input refers to the entire database, including the field names in the first row. It can be a range or ranges referring to one or more database tables.
Field is the offset of a field in the database table or the name of an actual database field.
Criteria are the specifications of the records you want selected.

For more on arguments, see the "Syntax of Database Statistical Functions" section earlier in this chapter or Chapter 19.

Example

You can use the @DMIN function and the database in Figure 9-8 to determine the minimum salary for employees with a job code of 23. Note that the database is defined as being located in A1..F12, the Salary field is used, and the criteria used in the selection are located in A15..A16. The formula entry is @DMIN(A1..F12,4,A15..A16) and returns 12000.

@DQUERY

@DQUERY is a database statistical @function that sends a command to an external database management program. This @function allows you to perform a command in the external database program without leaving 1-2-3/G.

Syntax

@DQUERY(*function*[,*ext-arguments*])

Function is a command in another database-management program. This argument is a string, cell reference, or formula that evaluates to a string. The string this function uses is the external database command the function performs.
Ext-arguments are the arguments the external command uses. These must match the order and type that the external database command expects.

Example

The database and criteria in Figure 9-11 are used with the @DQUERY function to locate the employees in the EMP_BENE external database that participate in the company's medical, dental, and long-term disability plans. The Data Query commands use range name EMP_BENE

1-2-3/G (69.4) Ready

File Edit Worksheet Range Copy... Move... Print Graph Data Utility Quit... Help

A:E10 @DQUERY("SIGN",E3)

(G) SHEET_F.WG1

A	A	B	C	D	E	F	G	H
1	Type 1 for Medical or 0 for not participating:				1			
2	Type 1 for Life or 0 for not participating:				0			
3	Type 1 for Dental or 0 for not participating:				1			
4	Type 1 for LTD or 0 for not participating:				1			
5	Type 1 for Pensions or 0 for not participating:				0			
6	Then press F7.							
7								
8	Criteria area:							
9	SSN	NAME	MEDICAL	LIFE	DENTAL	LTD	PENSION	YEARS
10			SIGN	SIGN	SIGN	SIGN	SIGN	
11								
12	Output Area:							
13	SSN	NAME	MEDICAL	LIFE	DENTAL	LTD	PENSION	YEARS
14	652-47-2348	Allen Canfield	1		1	1		4
15	358-95-2594	Andrew Jeck	1		1	1		6
16								
17								

Figure 9-11. Using @DQUERY in a database query

assigned to the external database as the input range, A9..H10 as the criteria, and A13..H13 as the output range. "SIGN" is a function that returns a 1 if the field contains a positive number, a −1 if the field contains a negative number, or a 0 if the field contains a 0.

@DSTD

@DSTD is a database statistical @function that determines the standard deviation of a set of values, or how much variation there is from the average of the values. The values used in this calculation are from selected records in the database. The standard deviation is the square root of the variance and uses the calculations shown for the @STD function.

Syntax

@DSTD(*input,field,criteria*)

Input refers to the entire database, including the field names in the first row.
Field is the offset of a field in the database table or the name of an actual database field.
Criteria are the specifications of the records you want selected.

Example

This function performs the following:

$$\sqrt{\frac{\sum(x_i - \text{AVG})^2}{n}}$$

You can use the @DSTD function and the database in Figure 9-8 to determine the standard deviation of salaries for employees in job code 23. The criteria are located in A15..A16. The formula of @DSTD(A1..F12,4,A15..A16) returns the standard deviation of 7438.5818541.

@DSTDS

@DSTDS is a database statistical @function that determines the standard deviation of a set of values, or how much variation there is from the average of the values for a sample of the population. The values used in this calculation are from selected records in the database. The standard deviation is the square root of the variance.

Syntax

@DSTDS(*input,field,criteria*)

Input refers to the entire database, including the field names in the first row.
Field is the offset of a field in the database table or the name of an actual database field.
Criteria are the specifications of the records you want selected. For more on the arguments, see "Syntax of Database Statistical Functions" earlier in this chapter or Chapter 19.

Example

Using the @DSTD function and the database in Figure 9-8, you can determine the standard deviation of salaries for employees in job code 23 when this group is treated as a sample of the population. The criteria are located in A15..A16. The formula of @DSTDS is @DSTDS(A1..F12, 4,A15..A16) to return the result of 8589.3344717.

@DSUM

@DSUM is a database statistical @function that allows you to determine the total of values in a field within a selected group of database records.

Syntax

@DSUM(*input,field,criteria*)

Input refers to the entire database, including the field names in the first row.
Field is the offset of a field in the database table or the name of an actual database field.
Criteria are the specifications of the records you want selected. For more on the arguments, see "Syntax of Database Statistical Functions" earlier in this chapter or Chapter 19.

Example

You can use the @DSUM function and the database in Figure 9-8 to determine the total of salaries for employees with a job code of 23. Note that the database is defined as being located in A1..F12, the Salary field is selected to total, and the criteria used in the selection are located in A15..A16. The entry would be @DSUM(A1..F12,4,A15..A16) and return a result of 86200.

@DVAR

@DVAR is a database statistical @function that you can use to compute the variance of the records in a population. It assumes that the entire population is selected by the criteria you specify.

Syntax

@DVAR(*input,field,criteria*)

Input refers to the entire database, including the field names in the first row.
Field is the offset of a field in the database table or the name of an actual database field. If you use an offset, remember that the first database field has an offset of zero.
Criteria are the specifications of the records you want selected. For more on arguments, see "Syntax of Database Statistical Functions" or Chapter 19.

This function uses the following formula:

$$\frac{\sum(X_i - \text{AVG})^2}{n}$$

where X_i is the ith item in the list, and n is the number of items in the list.

Example

You might use the @DVAR function and the database in Figure 9-8 to calculate the variance in salary for employees with a job code of 23. Assuming a database in A15..A16, and salaries in column E. Your entry might be @DVAR(A1..F12,4, A15..A16) and return 55332500.

Tip: Use the @DVARS function when you are not working with an entire population. Using @DVAR in this situation would provide less accurate results.

@DVARS

@DVARS is a database statistical @function that computes the variance for a selected group of records when they represent a population sample.

Syntax

@DVARS(*input,field,criteria*)

Input refers to the entire database, including the field names in the first row.
Field is the offset of a field in the database table or the name of an actual database field.

Criteria are the specifications of the records you want selected.

For more on these arguments, see "Syntax of Database Statistical Functions" or Chapter 19.

Example

You can use the @DVARS function and the database in Figure 9-8 with criteria located in A15..A16 to determine the variance for salaries of employees with a job code of 23. If the database is in A1..F12, and salaries are in column E, your entry would be @DVARS(A1..F12,4, A15..A16) and return the result of 73776666.66

@ERR

@ERR is a special @function that returns the value ERR in the cell where it is entered and any cell that references it.

Syntax

@ERR

The @ERR function has no arguments.

Tip: 1-2-3/G generates ERR on its own when errors are made in the entry of a formula, or in one of the arithmetic operations in a formula. The effect of both ERR conditions is the same, even though they are generated in different ways. The ERR will ripple through all formulas in the worksheet.

Example

To prevent incorrect entries in a field, you can combine @ERR with @IF. Suppose that the only valid values for a field are 0 through 3. To flag errors in a column where your entries are made, you might enter formulas like this in an adjacent column:

@IF(A4> =0#AND#A4< =3,"",@ERR)

@EXACT

@EXACT is a string @function that allows you to determine if two strings are exactly equal. When @EXACT compares the two strings, they must match in capitalization to be considered equal.

Syntax

@EXACT(*string1*,*string2*)

String1 can consist of any text entry or a cell that contains text. A formula that returns text is also acceptable.
String2 accepts the same entries as *string1*.

Example

Several examples of @EXACT follow:

Function	Returns
@EXACT("Mary Brown", "MARY BROWN")	0
@EXACT("2144","2144")	1
@EXACT(2144,"2144")	ERR since *string1* is a numeric, not a text entry

@EXP

@EXP is a mathematical @function that raises the base e (2.718282) to a specific power. @EXP is the inverse of @LN.

Syntax

@EXP(*x*)

x is the power to which you want to raise e. This argument must be a numeric value or a reference to one, and cannot exceed 230 if you wish to display the function's result. *x* can be as high as 11,356 and still fit 1-2-3/G's internal storage requirements.

Examples

Function	Returns
@EXP(1)	2.718282
@EXP(10)	22026.46
@EXP(@LN(5))	5

@FALSE

@FALSE is a logical @function that always returns a logical 0 representing false.

Syntax

@FALSE

This function has no arguments.

Example

@FALSE and its counterpart @TRUE can be used to determine if the number of items ordered equals the number of items billed. If the items ordered are in column B and the number billed are in column C, you might enter @IF(B3=C3,@TRUE,@FALSE). You can use the @SUM function to add these 0's and 1's after copying this formula down in column D to determine the number of discrepancies in the orders.

@FIND

@FIND is a string @function that searches for a string within another string and returns the position of the search string.

Syntax

@FIND(*search-string,string,start-number*)

Search-string is a character sequence or a reference to a cell containing one.
String is a sequence of characters or a reference to a cell containing one.
Start-number is the position in the string where you wish to begin your search. Remember that the leftmost character in the string is character 0. The maximum starting location can be one less than the number of characters in the string.

Example

You can use @FIND to locate a space or unique character within an entry. In a name in A3, you might have a first name followed by a space and the last name. You can locate the space with the entry @FIND(" ",A3,0).

If the name entry is entered as last name followed by a comma, a space, and the first name, you can use @FIND to help extract the first name. To extract the first name from the entry, you can use this formula:

@RIGHT(A3,@LENGTH(A3)−@FIND(" ",A3,0)−1)

This formula works regardless of the length of the first or last name entry.

@FV

@FV is a financial @function that computes the future value of an investment based on the assumption that equal payments are generated at a specific rate over a period of time.

Syntax

@FV(*payment,interest,term*)

Payment is a value representing the amount of the equal payments for the investment over the length of the term.
Interest is a value representing the periodic interest rate earned by the investment.
Term is a value representing the number of periods for the investment.

Example

Suppose that you plan to deposit $500 a month for each of the next 36 months, and will continue to earn interest on this money at the rate of 12 percent compounded monthly. You can use the @FV function to calculate the future value for this ordinary annuity. The formula entry is @FV(C1,C2/12,C3), which is the same as @FV(500,1%,36) given 500 in C1, .12 in C2, and 36 in C3. This example assumes that interest is paid at the end of the year and that your next contribution is always made on the last day of the year. This function returns 21538.

You can adapt this formula to work with an annuity due. Make these changes:

@FV(*payment,interest,term*)*(1+*periodic-interest-rate*)

This is appropriate when you must make contributions on the first day of the year. Assuming that you make annual payments of $5000 at the beginning of each year, and that this money will earn interest at a rate of 10 percent, the value at the end of ten years is represented by this formula:

@FV(5000,10%,10)*(1+10%)

This formula would return $87,655.83, the value of your annuity after ten years.

@HLOOKUP

@HLOOKUP is a special @function that you can use to search a table for an appropriate value to use in your worksheet. Unlike @VLOOKUP, which uses a vertical orientation for its search operation, @HLOOKUP performs its search across the worksheet in a horizontal orientation.

Syntax

@HLOOKUP(*x*,*range*,*row-offset*)

x is the entry in your worksheet that is compared against the table entry. When you use numeric values, 1-2-3/G looks for the largest value in the table that is not greater than the code. An entry for *x* that is greater than the last table value is considered to match with the last value in the table. When you use string values, the search is for an exact match.

Range is a range containing one or more rows on a worksheet.

Row-offset is a number that determines which row should be consulted for the return value when a matching *x* value is located. The first row beneath the row of *x* values has a row offset of 1.

Example

Figure 9-12 shows a table located in cells C3..F7. The following codes return the values shown from the table, assuming that you provided the listed offsets:

Code	Offset	Return Value
4.5	1	22
11	2	2
15	3	77
0	1	11
99	1	44
4.5	0	4.5
11	1	22
15	2	3
102	1	44
−1	1	ERR

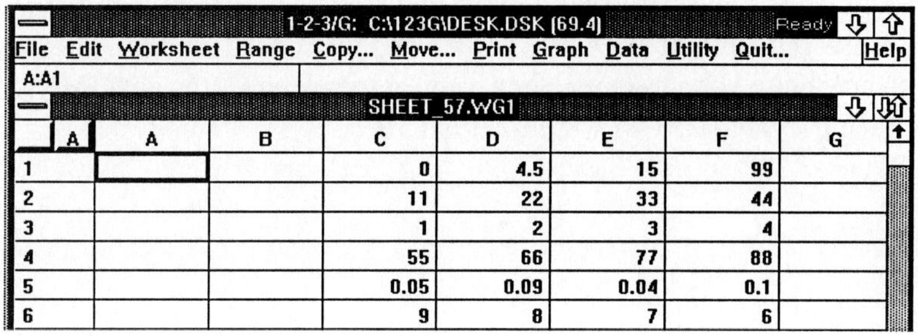

1-2-3/G: C:\123G\DESK.DSK (69.4) Ready

File Edit Worksheet Range Copy... Move... Print Graph Data Utility Quit... Help

A:A1

SHEET_57.WG1

A	A	B	C	D	E	F	G
1			0	4.5	15	99	
2			11	22	33	44	
3			1	2	3	4	
4			55	66	77	88	
5			0.05	0.09	0.04	0.1	
6			9	8	7	6	

Figure 9-12. Sample horizontal table

Tip: Compare the code against the 0 column of the table when you need an exact match. Remember that 1-2-3/G returns a matching value for numeric codes even if there is not an exact match. So, if you only want to use the value returned by @HLOOKUP or @VLOOKUP when the match is exact, compare it against the values with an offset of 0. Your formula might look something like this:

```
@IF(B7=@HLOOKUP(B7,$TABLE,0),@HLOOKUP(B7,$TABLE,1),
    "No exact match")
```

@HOUR

@HOUR is a date/time function that allows you to extract a number representing the hour from a time number.

Syntax

@HOUR(*time-number*)

Time-number is a value between .000000 and .999988. Midnight is represented by .000000 and 11:59:59 P.M. is represented by .999988.

Example

If you want to record the delivery hour for packages received, you might capture the time at receipt and use the @HOUR function to access the specific hour. If a receipt time was entered in C3 as @TIME(10,30,0), entering @HOUR(C3) would return 10.

@IF

@IF is a logical @function that allows you to determine a result based on a condition test.

Syntax

@IF(*condition*,*x*,*y*)

Condition is a logical formula testing for equality, inequality, less than, or greater than. The formula can be recorded in the @function or stored in a cell and referenced.
x is a value or label returned if the condition tests true.
y is a value or label returned if the condition tests false.

Example

You can use the logical @IF function to determine allowances for FICA and FUTA taxes. To calculate FICA, the formula must compare the projected salary to a $48,000 FICA cap (that is, the highest amount of salary on which an employer would pay FICA tax). If the projected salary is less than $48,000, FICA tax is calculated as the salary multiplied by 7.65 percent. If, however, the salary is equal to or greater than the cap amount, FICA tax is paid on $48,000 at the rate of 7.65 percent. The formula entry would be @IF(A4<48000,A4*.0765,48000*.0765) where A4 contains the salary.

The FUTA calculation, for unemployment tax, follows a similar pattern. The formula to calculate FUTA is

@IF(A4<7000,A4*.06,7000*.06)

This states that the FUTA tax is 6 percent of salary if the salary is less than $7,000, but 6 percent of $7,000 if the salary exceeds that amount.

@INDEX

@INDEX is a special @function that returns a value from a table. You must specify the exact location of the entry you want returned.

Syntax

@INDEX(*range*,*column*,*row*[,*worksheet*])

Range is the location of the table where you will locate the return value.
Column is the offset of the column you want to use for a return value.
Row is the offset of the row you want to use for a return value. The offset is applied from the beginning of the table. The first row in the table has an offset of 0.
Worksheet is an optional argument that allows you to specify the sheet offset for a table that spans sheets. The first worksheet in the table range has an offset of zero. If you don't supply the *worksheet* argument, 1-2-3/G assumes that you want to use the first worksheet in the range.

Example

Figure 9-13 illustrates a commission application that uses Total Sales and Region values to index the proper commission percentage. The table is located in A1..G3. The return value is selected from the row sales region minus 1, since tables begin with row 0, not row 1. The return value is selected from the column calculated as

(Total Sales amount divided by $10,000) minus 1

The percent obtained from this function is multiplied by the sales figure to determine commissions.

1-2-3/G: C:\123G\DESK.DSK (69.4) Ready

File Edit Worksheet Range Copy... Move... Print Graph Data Utility Quit... Help

A:D7 @INDEX($A$1..$G$3,(B7/10000)-1,C7-1)*B7

(C2) SHEET_59.WG1

A	A	B	C	D	E	F	G
1	5.00%	6.00%	7.50%	9.00%	12.00%	15.00%	20.00%
2	6.00%	7.00%	8.00%	9.00%	13.00%	18.00%	25.00%
3	8.00%	9.00%	12.00%	15.00%	18.00%	23.00%	30.00%
4							
5							
6	Salesman	Total Sales	Region	Commission			
7	White	$50,000.00	2	$6,500.00			
8	Savage	$30,500.00	3	$3,660.00			
9	Greene	$41,000.00	1	$3,690.00			
10	Parsel	$65,000.00	3	$14,950.00			
11	Murray	$54,500.00	2	$7,085.00			

Figure 9-13. Finding the appropriate value with @INDEX

Tip: If the @INDEX @function returns ERR, check for an argument that exceeds the size of the range or a negative argument value.

@INFO

@INFO is a special function that provides access to system information that would not otherwise be available.

Syntax

@INFO(*attribute*)

Attribute is one of 11 strings, as shown in Table 9-12.

Attribute	Returns
directory	Path
memavail	Amount of memory available
memused	Memory used
mode	0 Wait
	1 Ready
	2 Label
	3 Menu
	4 Value
	5 Point
	6 Edit
	10 Help
	99 All other modes
numfile	Number open files
origin	Address of cell pointer
osreturncode	Value returned by system command
osversion	Operating system version
recalc	Recalculation mode
release	1-2-3/G release
system	Operating system
totmem	Total memory

Table 9-12. Attribute Strings for @INFO

Example

Figure 9-14 shows a worksheet with a status area established. The area is assigned a range name of STATUS. This allows you to go to this area quickly. Because OS/2 performs disk swapping (see Appendix B), the results the "*totmem*" and "*memavail*" attributes return are not as reliable as under DOS.

@INT

@INT is a mathematical function that extracts the integer portion of a number. Any entry after the decimal point in the number is dropped.

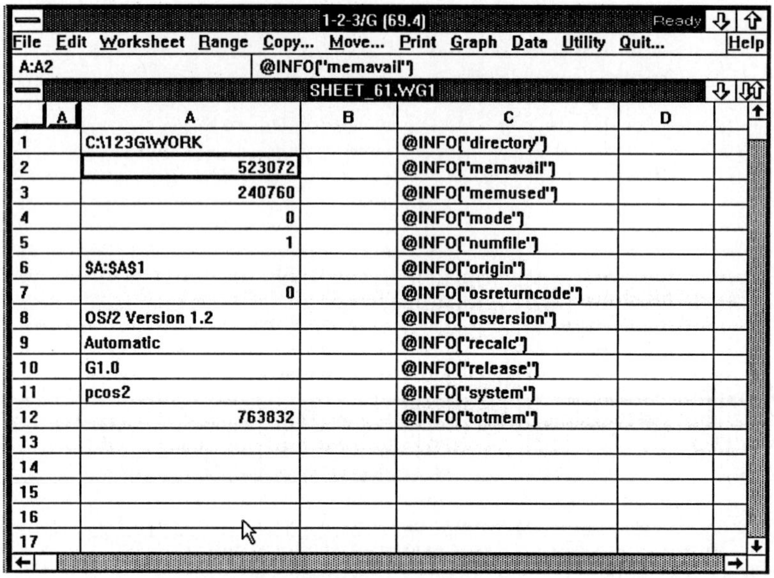

1-2-3/G [69.4] Ready

File Edit Worksheet Range Copy... Move... Print Graph Data Utility Quit... Help

A:A2 @INFO("memavail")

SHEET_61.WG1

A	A	B	C	D
1	C:\123G\WORK		@INFO("directory")	
2	523072		@INFO("memavail")	
3	240760		@INFO("memused")	
4	0		@INFO("mode")	
5	1		@INFO("numfile")	
6	$A:$A$1		@INFO("origin")	
7	0		@INFO("osreturncode")	
8	OS/2 Version 1.2		@INFO("osversion")	
9	Automatic		@INFO("recalc")	
10	G1.0		@INFO("release")	
11	pcos2		@INFO("system")	
12	763832		@INFO("totmem")	
13				
14				
15				
16				
17				

Figure 9-14. @INFO providing information about the current 1-2-3/G session

Syntax

@INT(x)

x is a value entry.

Example

You can use @INT to calculate the number of wallets that can be created from different sized pieces of cowhide—the production of partial wallets is not of interest. If you store .6789 in E1 as the amount of leather needed for a single wallet and store the cowhide sizes beginning in A4, the first formula would be @INT(A4/$E$1).

@IRR

@IRR is a financial @function that calculates the rate of return for an investment. The internal rate of return is the rate at which your initial investment is equal to the present value of cash flows that you expect to be generated in the future.

Syntax

@IRR(*guess*,*range*)

Guess is an estimate of the internal rate of return, expressed as a percentage or a decimal. 1-2-3/G uses your initial guess to approximate the internal rate of return. It continues to refine the initial guess until it can approximate the final result to within .0000001. If it is not this close after 30 tries, ERR is returned.
Range is a range name or address of the location where the expected future cash flows are located.

Tip: Check that the result you obtain is reasonable. If you question the result, try another guess to see if it has an impact on the solution.

Example

You can use the @IRR function to analyze the stream of projected cash flows shown in A2..A7. As required to represent the initial investment, the first number in the range is negative. A guess of 12 percent is placed in D2. The formula for the internal rate of return is placed in E2, as @IRR(D2,A2..A7). In this example, the function returns 19.58 percent given entries of –42500, 14500, 4500, 18500, 21000, and 15000 in A2..A7.

@ISAAF

@ISAAF is an undocumented logical @function that checks if a named add-in function is attached. This function is used when add-ins are combined with 1-2-3/G. The @function returns a 1 if the named function is attached, or a 0 if 1-2-3/G does not recognize the name as an attached add-in function.

Syntax

@ISAAF(*name*)

Name is the name of an add-in function that you want to check.

Example

You can store the result of @ISAAF in a cell and test it. For example, to check for a function @TAILOR, you would enter @ISAAF("tailor").

@ISAPP

@ISAPP is an undocumented logical @function that checks whether a named add-in is attached. You can use this function when you use add-ins with 1-2-3/G. The @function returns 1 if the named add-in is attached, or 0 if 1-2-3/G does not recognize the name as an attached add-in.

Syntax

@ISAPP(*name*)

Name is a string representing the name of an add-in that you want to check.

Example

You can store the result of @ISAPP in a cell and test it. For example, to check for an add-in called Linear, you would enter @ISAPP("linear").

@ISEMPTY

@ISEMPTY is a logical @function that checks for a blank cell. The @function returns a 1 if the cell is blank and a 0 if there is anything in the cell. A cell that contains nothing but a label indicator is not a blank cell.

Syntax

@ISEMPTY(*x*)

x is a cell address or a range name.

Example

You can store the result of @ISEMPTY in a cell and test it. You might use this test to control a macro or display a message. Referring to a range named SSNO, you might enter this in B4:

@ISEMPTY(SSNO)

In another cell, you might enter

@IF(B4=1,"","You must supply a Social Security Number")

@ISERR

@ISERR is a logical function that checks a cell to see if it contains or equals an ERR value. The @function returns a 1 if the cell contains ERR, and a 0 if it does not.

Syntax

@ISERR(*x*)

x can be a formula, text, cell address, or range name.

Example

You enter ERR on a worksheet for a price that is about to change. This ERR entry could be generated by placing @ERR in the cell, or it could be the result of an incorrect formula. When this cell is referenced to supply the unit cost for multiplication, it causes ERR to appear in other locations in the worksheet.

If you don't want ERR to ripple through the worksheet like this, use the @ISERR function in conjunction with @IF as in @IF(@ISERR(A1),0,A1*B1). This allows you to confine ERR to one location.

@ISNA

@ISNA is a logical @function that tests a cell for the value @NA.

Syntax

@NA(*x*)

x can be a formula, text, cell address, or range name.

Application

Like ERR, NA can ripple through a worksheet. Every cell referencing a cell containing NA also displays as NA. Using @ISNA with @IF allows you to stop the display of NA at the first cell where data is missing.

@ISNA only recognizes the value NA, not the label of NA.

Example

Figure 9-15 shows the @ISNA function combined with @IF. The @IF function checks the condition @ISNA(D3). If D3 is equal to NA, the condition is considered true because @ISNA evaluates as 1. On a true condition, the error message "Missing Unit Price" displays. If D3 is not equal to NA, column E contains the result of column C times column D.

@ISNAME

@ISNAME is a logical function that allows you to check 1-2-3/G's internal table for a range or collection name.

Syntax

@ISNAME(*string*)

String is a text entry that you want to check against 1-2-3/G's internal table of range and collection names.

1-2-3/G [69.4] Ready

File Edit Worksheet Range Copy... Move... Print Graph Data Utility Quit... Help

A:E3 @IF(@ISNA(D3),"MISSING UNIT PRICE",C3*D3)

(C2) ISNA.WG1

A	A	B	C	D	E	F	G
1							
2	Order Number	Date	Quantity	Price	Total		
3	12760	30-Sep	3	$3.50	$10.50		
4	12781	01-Oct	4	NA	MISSING UNIT PRICE		
5	12976	01-Oct	12	$12.20	$146.40		
6	13076	02-Oct	32	$13.75	$440.00		
7	13079	02-Oct	14	$5.25	$73.50		
8	13099	02-Oct	5	$9.84	$49.20		
9	13123	02-Oct	3	NA	MISSING UNIT PRICE		

Figure 9-15. Checking for missing data

Table 9-13 shows the various return values you can expect, along with their meanings.

Example

You might combine @ISNAME with @IF to display an error message. This formula displays an error message when a range name needed in calculations has not been defined:

```
@IF(@ISNAME("TOTAL_BUDG")=0,"You must define TOTAL_BUDG","")
```

@ISNUMBER

@ISNUMBER is a logical function that checks an entry to see if it is a value.

Syntax

@ISNUMBER(*x*)

x is the data you wish to check.

Example

If you want to check C6 to ensure that the ZIP code was entered as a numeric value, use the formula

@IF(@ISNUMBER(C6)," ","ERROR - Entry must be numeric")

Value	Meaning
1	String is not a name
2	String is an undefined name
3	String is a range name
4	String is a collection name
5	String is an external range name
6	String is an external database table

Table 9-13. Return Values for @ISNAME

That is, if the entry in C6 is numeric, a blank label is placed in E6, where the formula is located. If the cell contains a nonnumeric value, an error message appears. This type of error check allows the operator to glance at column E quickly for error flags, rather than having to study entries individually.

@ISRANGE

@ISRANGE is a logical @function that checks whether a range name is defined to 1-2-3/G.

Syntax

@ISRANGE(*x*)

x is a label reference to a cell that you want checked against 1-2-3/G's internal list of range names.

Example

Figure 9-16 shows the first worksheet in a file used to summarize data. If the range the formula will add does not exist, the @IF function displays a message to let you know.

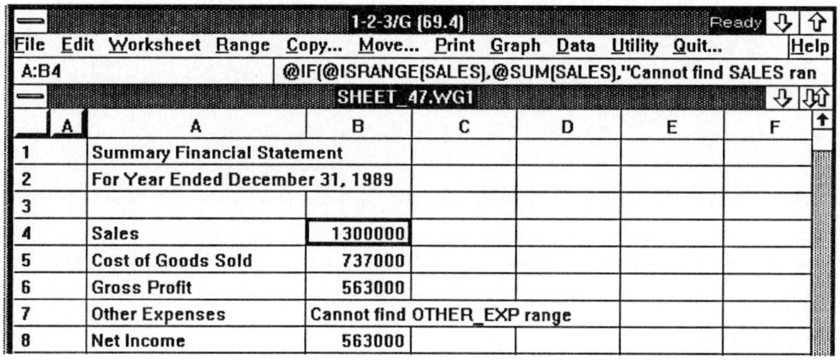

1-2-3/G (69.4) Ready

File Edit Worksheet Range Copy... Move... Print Graph Data Utility Quit... Help

A:B4 @IF(@ISRANGE(SALES),@SUM(SALES),"Cannot find SALES ran

SHEET_47.WG1

A	A	B	C	D	E	F
1	Summary Financial Statement					
2	For Year Ended December 31, 1989					
3						
4	Sales	1300000				
5	Cost of Goods Sold	737000				
6	Gross Profit	563000				
7	Other Expenses	Cannot find OTHER_EXP range				
8	Net Income	563000				

Figure 9-16. Using @ISRANGE to check that a range is defined

@ISSTRING

@ISSTRING is a logical @function that checks whether an entry is a string.

Syntax

@ISSTRING(x)

x can be any type of entry, including a number, formula, or label.

Example

The worksheet in Figure 9-17 shows name and address information entered in column C. If you want to check C2..C5 to ensure that the data was entered as strings, use a formula like the one in E2:

@IF(@ISSTRING(C2)," ","Entry is invalid - it is numeric")

This formula states that if the entry in C2 is a string, a blank is placed in E2, where the formula is located. If the cell contains something other than a string value, as shown in the worksheet, an error message

1-2-3/G (69.4) Ready

File Edit Worksheet Range Copy... Move... Print Graph Data Utility Quit... Help

A:E2 @IF(@ISSTRING(C2)," ","Entry is invalid - it is numeric")

SHEET_48.WG1

A	A	B	C	D	E	F	G
1							
2		Name:	3		Entry is invalid - it is numeric		
3		Address:	4102 Caroline St.				
4		City:	Gates Mills				
5		State:	Ohio				
6		Zip:	44040				

Figure 9-17. Using @ISSTRING tc validate data

appears. This type of error check can allow the operator to glance at column E quickly for error flags, rather than having to study entries individually.

@LEFT

@LEFT is a string @function that extracts a specified number of characters from the beginning of a character string.

Syntax

@LEFT(*string*,*n*)

String is a label containing a series of text characters.
n is a value representing the number of characters you wish to extract from the left side of the string.

Example

You might use @LEFT in a worksheet where the state code is the first two characters in a lengthy part number. The entry is extracted with @LEFT(A3,2) if the first part number is in A3. This formula is copied down the column of the worksheet to complete the extract for all part numbers.

You can extract data even when the length of the desired element varies. You will need to use other @functions to locate and extract the correct number of characters.

@LENGTH

@LENGTH is a string @function that allows you to determine the number of characters in a string.

Syntax

@LENGTH(*string*)

String is a series of text characters.

Example

You can use the @LENGTH function to determine the number of characters in names. The formula @LENGTH(A1) might be copied down the column C to return the length of all the entries in column A.

@LN

@LN is a mathematical @function that returns the natural log of a number. A natural log uses a base of 2.718282, which is known as the base e.

Syntax

@LN(x)

x is a value or a cell address or range name that refers to a value.

Example

Here are a few examples:

Function	**Returns**
@LN(9)	2.197224
@LN(1.5)	0.405465

@LOG

@LOG is a mathematical @function that calculates the log of a number.

Syntax

@LOG(x)

x is a value or an address or range name that refers to a value.

Example

Here are the results returned by 1-2-3/G from a few examples of @LOG:

Function	Returns
@LOG(10)	1
@LOG(100)	2
@LOG(190)	2.278753

@LOWER

@LOWER is a string @function that converts the case of a label entry to lowercase.

Syntax

@LOWER(*string*)

String is a label or a reference to a label or text formula that you want to convert to lowercase.

Example

As an example, entering @LOWER("THESE ARE CAPITALS") returns "these are capitals". Entering @LOWER("This Is Proper Case") returns "this is proper case".

Tip: To use @LOWER to change text entered with incorrect capitalization, first enter the function in an empty area of the worksheet, referencing the data to be corrected. You will need to restructure the data in a different location before copying it back, and you want to be sure you do not overlay important data in the process of doing so. After the formulas are entered, you can freeze the function results in the cells with F2 (Edit) followed by F9 (Calc). Then transfer them with Move. Alternatively, you can use Range Value to freeze the formulas as values and copy them all in one step. After verifying the accuracy of the data, you can erase the work area that originally contained the formula.

@MAX

The @MAX function is a statistical function that determines the maximum value within a list of cell addresses or ranges.

Syntax

@MAX(*list*)

List is a series of cell addresses, ranges, or collections.

Example

The @MAX function can be used to obtain the highest bid in a group of vendor bids. The bids are entered in B4..B11, with the corresponding vendor names in column A. The @MAX function is placed in B13 as @MAX(B4..B11); it returns a maximum bid of $8,700.00 from the range of bids that include 5498, 6500, 8700, 4100, 3900, 8100, 5600, and 4300.

If you enter additional vendor bids, they are included in the calculation automatically, as long as you insert them somewhere in the middle of the range. If you add your entries at the beginning or end of the range, 1-2-3/G doesn't automatically expand the defined range to include them.

@MID

@MID is a string @function that extracts a series of characters from anywhere in a string.

Syntax

@MID(*string,start-number,n*)

String is the string you want to extract from.
Start-number is an integer that specifies the starting character within the string using 0 as the first character.
n is an integer representing the number of characters to be extracted.

Example

Examples are of @MID are

Function	**Returns**
@MID("abcdefghi",3,3)	def
@MID("123"&"456",1,512)	23456

Tip: The @RIGHT and @LEFT functions are actually special versions of @MID that extract from the right or left edge of a string. When 0 is the start number, @MID is functionally equivalent to @LEFT, since it begins extracting with the leftmost character in the string.

@MIN

The @MIN function is a statistical @function that determines the minimum value within a list of cell addresses or ranges.

Syntax

@MIN(*list*)

List is a series of cell addresses, ranges, or collections.

Example

You can use the @MIN function to find the lowest bid in a group of vendor bids. The bids are located in B4..B11, and the minimum is found with the function @MIN(B4..B11). If you enter additional vendor bids, they are included in the calculation automatically, as long as you inserted them somewhere in the middle of the range. If you add your entries at the beginning or end of the range, 1-2-3/G doesn't automatically expand the range to include them.

@MINUTE

@MINUTE is a time @function that you use to extract the minute component of a time number.

Syntax

@MINUTE(*time-number*)

Time-number is a value between .000000 and .999988. Midnight is represented as .000000 and 11:59:59 P.M. is represented as .999988.

Example

If you managed a radio station and wanted to record the exact minutes when you received calls for hourly radio contests, you could use the @MINUTE function. Certain types of contests might generate many calls and immediate winners, whereas other types could be announced throughout the hour before a winner called in with the correct answer. You might want to capture the time of receipt of the calls and record whether the caller was the contest winner. If the times were entered in column C @MINUTE(C3) might extract the minutes from the first time entry.

@MOD

@MOD is a mathematical @function that returns the modulus or remainder from a division operation.

Syntax

@MOD(*x*,*y*)

x is a value used in the division operation *x*/*y*.
y is a value used in the division operation *x*/*y*.

Example

You can use @MOD to determine the number of leftover parts after building the maximum number of complete items from the parts in an inventory. If you are building windmills that each require 12 blades, and you have 750 blades on hand, @MOD(750,12) indicates that you have 6 blades left over. To determine how many complete windmills you can build, use @INT(750/12).

@MONTH

@MONTH is a date @function that extracts a month number from a date number.

Syntax

@MONTH(*date-number*)

Date-number is a serial date number between 1 and 73050.

Example

You could use @MONTH to extract employees' vacation months from historic data, so you could monitor vacation schedules to plan for temporary help. You could use this function to extract the month from the vacation start date. You might enter a formula of @MONTH(D6) if the first vacation start date is in D6.

@N

@N is a string @function that returns the first cell in a specified range as a value.

Syntax

@N(*range*)

Range is an address of either a cell or a range.

Example

If A1 contains 85, @N(A1..B2) returns 85, which is the value in the first cell of the range.

@NA

@NA is a a special @function that can mark the location of data that is not yet available. Since any formula accessing a cell with a value of NA returns the value NA, this is a reminder that the data for the model is not complete.

Tip: Be careful not to confuse the value NA with the label NA. If you type a label of NA in a cell, and reference it with an arithmetic formula, it returns ERR. If you place the value @NA in a cell and reference it in a formula, it returns NA.

Syntax

@NA

This function has no arguments.

Example

The @NA function is useful for recording student grades. All students who missed an exam would have NA, rather than a score. A student with a missing grade will have a grade point average of NA. At the end of the semester, the instructor can change to 0 all grades that are still NA.

@NOW

@NOW is a date @function that returns a date number corresponding to the current system date.

Syntax

@NOW

This function has no arguments.

Example

Enter @NOW to create a date/time stamp in any cell. The format you select will determine the appearance of your entry.

@NPV

@NPV is a financial @function that calculates the net present value of a series of future cash flows.

Syntax

@NPV(*interest*,*range*)

Interest is a value expressed as a percent.
Range is the range address or name of the cells containing the cash flows.

Tip: You can use @NPV even when there is an initial cash outflow by adding the value of this outflow to the result of the @NPV function that references the remaining cash flows.

Example

You might enter expected cash flows in B2..G2 as 5000, 10000, 15000, 10000, 15000, and 5000. If these cash flows are received monthly and the interest rate in D4 is expressed as an annual rate, the interest rate must be changed to a monthly figure. The function argument would be (D4/12) if the interest rate was stored in D4. The formula for the calculation is @NPV(D4/12,B2..G2), which produces a result of $57,396.93. In other words, if the discount rate is 15 percent, you should be willing to pay $57,396.93 for this investment.

@PMT

@PMT is a financial @function that computes a loan payment amount.

Syntax

@PMT(*principal,interest,term*)

Principal is a value that represents the amount borrowed.
Interest is a percent or a reference to a cell containing a percent.
Term is a value representing the duration of the loan.

Example

Figure 9-18 shows a sample payment table. Interest rates are entered across row 3. The first rate is 9 percent, in B3. The rates in C3..G3 are generated with a formula entered in C3 to add 0.005 to B3. This formula is copied across the remaining columns. The entire row is formatted as Percent.

Cells A4..A20 contain the hypothetical principal amounts. The starting point is $100,000, with a $5,000 increment. The last number in A20 is $180,000. These principal amounts are formatted as Currency, with no decimal places.

You only need to enter one payment formula, the rest can be copied. The formula used is

@PMT($A4,B$3/12,240)

The $'s are required to keep part of the cell addresses from changing as the formula is copied. $A4 indicates that the column for the reference is

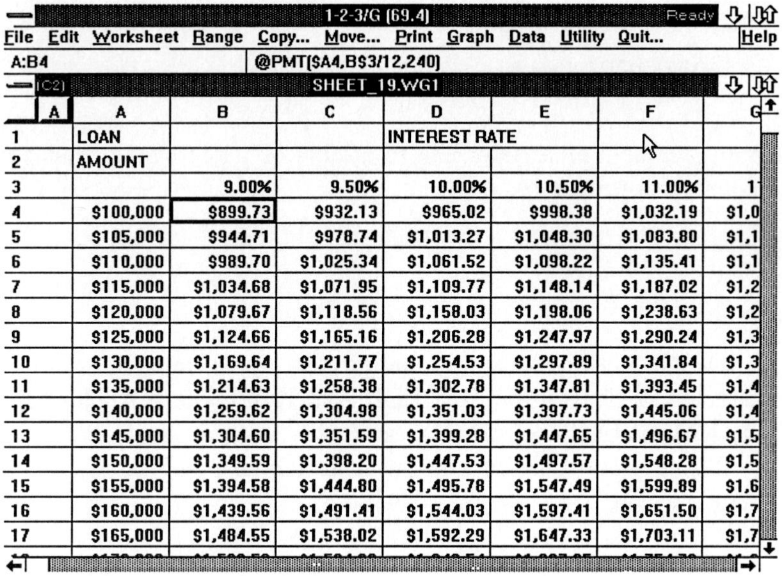

1-2-3/G (69.4) Ready

File Edit Worksheet Range Copy... Move... Print Graph Data Utility Quit... Help

A:B4 @PMT($A4,B$3/12,240)

(C2) SHEET_19.WG1

A	A	B	C	D	E	F	G
1	LOAN			INTEREST RATE			
2	AMOUNT						
3		9.00%	9.50%	10.00%	10.50%	11.00%	1
4	$100,000	$899.73	$932.13	$965.02	$998.38	$1,032.19	$1,0
5	$105,000	$944.71	$978.74	$1,013.27	$1,048.30	$1,083.80	$1,1
6	$110,000	$989.70	$1,025.34	$1,061.52	$1,098.22	$1,135.41	$1,1
7	$115,000	$1,034.68	$1,071.95	$1,109.77	$1,148.14	$1,187.02	$1,2
8	$120,000	$1,079.67	$1,118.56	$1,158.03	$1,198.06	$1,238.63	$1,2
9	$125,000	$1,124.66	$1,165.16	$1,206.28	$1,247.97	$1,290.24	$1,3
10	$130,000	$1,169.64	$1,211.77	$1,254.53	$1,297.89	$1,341.84	$1,3
11	$135,000	$1,214.63	$1,258.38	$1,302.78	$1,347.81	$1,393.45	$1,4
12	$140,000	$1,259.62	$1,304.98	$1,351.03	$1,397.73	$1,445.06	$1,4
13	$145,000	$1,304.60	$1,351.59	$1,399.28	$1,447.65	$1,496.67	$1,5
14	$150,000	$1,349.59	$1,398.20	$1,447.53	$1,497.57	$1,548.28	$1,5
15	$155,000	$1,394.58	$1,444.80	$1,495.78	$1,547.49	$1,599.89	$1,6
16	$160,000	$1,439.56	$1,491.41	$1,544.03	$1,597.41	$1,651.50	$1,7
17	$165,000	$1,484.55	$1,538.02	$1,592.29	$1,647.33	$1,703.11	$1,7

Figure 9-18. Creating a payment table

absolute, although the row can change. The reverse is true of B$3: The column can change, but the row reference is absolute. The function divides B$3 by 12 to convert the annual interest into a monthly interest. The term is 20 years, which amounts to 240 monthly periods. After this cell is formatted as Currency with two decimal places, the formula can be copied to accommodate the remaining places in the table. You will need to widen some of the columns to fit the currency display in the cells.

You can use the Data Table features with @PMT to create a table of payment options. You just need one formula if you use Data Table, which saves both memory and time.

@PROPER

@PROPER is a string @function that alters the case of words within an entry to proper case. Each word begins with a capital letter; other letters are lowercase.

Syntax

@PROPER(*string*)

String is a label or a reference to a label or text formula that you want to convert to proper case.

Example

@PROPER permits you to change the appearance of data without reentering it. Entering @PROPER(A2&"&B3) where A2 contains JOB-BARD MILLING COMPANY and B3 contains east dallas division, combines the two entries and returns Jobbard Milling Company East Dallas Division.

@PV

@PV is a financial @function that calculates the present value of a series of equal future payments.

Syntax

@PV(*payments,interest,term*)

Payments is a value representing the amount of the periodic payment. *Interest* is the periodic interest rate expressed.

Example

As an example, assume that you can either take a one-time cash payment of $500,000 or monthly payments of $5,000 for the next 20 years.

To compare the two options, you must look at the present value of the future cash flows. This means that you must assess the rate of return you would receive for investing the $500,000 lump sum payment today. This example assumes that you could get 12 percent compounded monthly. The present value becomes @PV(5000,1%,240). The result indicates that the best decision, if you are attempting to maximize return, is to choose the lump sum payment, since the present value of the monthly payments, 454097.08, is less than 500000. This comparison of the value of a lump sum payment and periodic payments does not consider tax effects.

@RAND

@RAND is a mathematical @function that generates a random number between 0 and 1. The result of @RAND is recalculated any time the worksheet is recalculated.

Syntax

```
@RAND
```

The @RAND function does not require arguments or parentheses.

Example

If you enter @RAND, a new decimal fraction will be displayed each time the worksheet is recalculated. You can control the range of the random number by multiplying the result by a number or adding a number to @RAND. Multiplying @RAND by a factor raises the upper limit to the number by which you are multiplying. For example, @RAND*100 provides random numbers between 0 and 100. Adding a fixed number to @RAND raises the lower limit. For example, @RAND*100+50 generates random numbers between 50 and 150.

@RATE

@RATE is a financial @ function for the periodic interest rate that allows an investment to grow to a specific value in the future.

Syntax

@RATE(*future-value,present-value,term*)

Future-value is the value your initial investment reaches after compounding.
Present-value is the value of the investment today.
Term is a value representing the number of future periods for compounding.

Example

Suppose that you invested $5,000 in a bond maturing in eight years. You could use the @RATE function to calculate the rate of return. This example assumes that the maturity value is $10,000 and that interest is compounded monthly. The required formula is

@RATE(10000,5000,8*12)

The formula returns .72 percent. To annualize the interest rate, multiply by 12 to obtain 8.7 percent.

@REPEAT

@REPEAT is a string @function that repeats a string a specified number of times in the cell that contains this function.

Syntax

@REPEAT(*string,n*)

String is a label enclosed in quotes, a reference to a cell address or range name containing a label, or a text entry within the @function.
n is an integer indicating the number of times you want to repeat the string in the result.

Example

You can draw lines with the @REPEAT function. Since 1-2-3/G is currently set to display long labels, you can create a long dividing line using some of these entries. You might enter @REPEAT("+ –",36).

Tip: Although the \ (backslash) also repeats a label, it only repeats the entry enough times to fill the cell where the entry is made. @REPEAT is not limited by the width of the column in which it is entered. The results of @REPEAT will carry across cells as required by the entry and the number of duplications requested.

@REPLACE

@REPLACE is a string @function. You can use it to locate a series of characters within a string and replace them with another series of characters.

Syntax

@REPLACE(*original-string*,*start-number*,*n*,*new-string*)

Original-string is the string you start with.
Start-number is an integer indicating the offset position within the original string where you wish to begin the replacement.
n is the number of characters you wish to remove from the old string.

New-string is series of characters you wish to place in the original string.

Example

Sample uses of @REPLACE include the following:

Function	Returns
@REPLACE("Department 100",11,3,"200")	Department 200
@REPLACE("Commissions for: ",17,10,"Mary Brown")	Commissions for: Mary Brown
@REPLACE("AX/1265",2,1,"–")	AX-1265
@REPLACE("AX/1265",0,7,"–")	–

Tip: Use @REPLACE to change text entered incorrectly. First, enter the function in an empty area of the worksheet, referencing the data to be corrected. You need to restructure the data in a different location before copying it back, and want to be sure not to overlay important data while doing so. After the formulas are entered, you can freeze the values in the cells with F2 (Edit) followed by F9 (Calc). You can then transfer them with Move. Alternatively, you can use Range Value to freeze the formulas as values and copy them all in one step. After verifying the accuracy of the data, you can erase the work area that originally contained the @REPLACE formula.

@RIGHT

@RIGHT is a string @function that extracts the specified number of characters from the right side of a character string.

Syntax

@RIGHT(*string*,*n*)

String is a series of text characters.
n is the number of characters you wish to extract from the end of the string.

Example

Some examples of the @RIGHT function are

Function	Returns
@RIGHT("Lotus 1-2-3",5)	1-2-3
@RIGHT("1:30:59",5)	30:59
@RIGHT("ABC COMPANY ",8)	Y with seven trailing spaces

@ROUND

@ROUND is a mathematical @function that alters the internal precision of a number by rounding it to a specified number of decimal places.

Syntax

@ROUND(*x*,*n*)

x is a value that you want to round. You can place a value in the @function. You can enter the value as a formula or you can store the number or formula in a cell. With the latter approach, you can use a cell address or range name to reference the entry.

n is an integer that indicates the place of rounding. *n* can vary between 100 and –100. The number zero indicates rounding to a whole number.

Example

Figure 9-19 shows the number 12345.678123 rounded to varying numbers of decimal places in column B, using the formulas in column C.

@ROWS

@ROWS is a special @function that counts the number of rows in a range.

1-2-3/G [69.4] Ready

File Edit Worksheet Range Copy... Move... Print Graph Data Utility Quit... Help

A:A1 '

SHEET_35.WG1

A	A	B	C	D	E	F
1		Rounded	Formula Used			
2	Number	Number	for Rounding			
3	12345.678123	12345.67812	12345.67812			
4		12345.6781	@ROUND($A$3,4)			
5		12345.678	@ROUND($A$3,3)			
6		12345.68	@ROUND($A$3,2)			
7		12345.7	@ROUND($A$3,1)			
8		12346	@ROUND($A$3,0)			
9		12350	@ROUND($A$3,-1)			
10		12300	@ROUND($A$3,-2)			
11		12000	@ROUND($A$3,-3)			
12		10000	@ROUND($A$3,-4)			
13						
14						
15						
16						
17						

Figure 9-19. Using @ROUND

Syntax

@ROWS(*range*)

Range is a range name or range address.

Example

Here are a few examples:

Function	Returns
@ROWS(A2..H3)	2
@ROWS(EMPLOYEES)	8 when EMPLOYEES refers to the range A3..Z10

@S

@S is a special function that returns the entry in the first cell in a range as a label.

Syntax

@S(*range*)

range is a cell address or a range name.

Example

@S(A3) equals SALES if A3 contains SALES.

@SECOND

@SECOND is a time @function that extracts the seconds number from a time number.

Syntax

@SECOND(*time-number*)

Time-number is a serial representation of a time.

Example

The @SECOND function always returns a value between 0 and 59. If cell A3 contains a serial time number representing 11:08:19, @SECOND(A3) equals 19. Used with @TIME, the @SECOND function might read @SECOND(@TIME(10,15,25)) and would return 25.

@SHEETS

@SHEETS is a special @function that can determine the number of sheets in a range.

Syntax

@SHEETS(*range*)

Range is a range address or range name.

Example

Here are some examples of @SHEETS:

Function	Returns
@SHEETS(A:A1..L:K72)	12
@SHEETS(DIVISION)	20 when the range called DIVISION uses 20 worksheets.

@SIN

@SIN is a mathematical @function that performs a trigonometric calculation. It computes the sine of an angle in a right triangle. It is a ratio of the length of the side of the triangle opposite the acute angle to the hypotenuse of the right triangle.

Syntax

@SIN(*z*)

z is a value representing the measurement of an angle expressed in radians.

Example

The diagram in Figure 9-20 shows a large swampy area that blocks a road crew from traversing the path from point C to point B. They know that the distance from A to C is 100 meters. If they can determine the distance from B to C, they can use that distance in the Pythagorean theorem to determine the distance from A to B. Their entire distance traveled to avoid the swamp is C to A, and then A to B. The angle ACB is 30 degrees.

To calculate the distance from C to B, the crew could use the formula SIN(30) = 100/x. Using the @SIN function to determine the sine of 30, @SIN(30*@PI/180) would return .5. Multiplying 30 by @PI/180 converts the degrees to radians. The distance then is 100/.5, or 200 meters. Using the Pythagorean theorem, $a^2 = b^2 + c^2$, they get $200^2 = 100^2 + s^2$. This means that 40,000 equals 10,000, plus the unknown side squared. The side is thus equal to the square root of 30,000, which they can find with @SQRT(30,000). This function returns 173.2, so the distance from C to B is 173.2 meters.

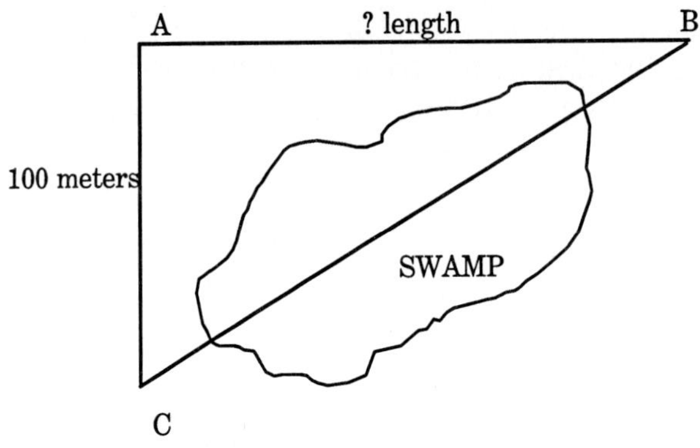

Figure 9-20. Going around the swamp

@SLN

@SLN is a financial @function that computes the straight-line depreciation for an asset. The formula for computing straight-line depreciation is

$$\frac{\textit{cost} - \textit{salvage value}}{\textit{life}}$$

Syntax

@SLN(*cost,salvage,life*)

Cost is a value that represents the price paid for the asset.
Salvage is the value the asset has at the end of its useful life.
Life is the amount of time it will take to depreciate the asset to its salvage value.

Example

As an example, if you purchase a $12,000 machine and estimate its salvage value to be $2,000 at the end of its five-year life, you can use @SLN to calculate its depreciation expense with the formula shown @SLN(12000,2000,5). It will have the same depreciation all five years.

@SOLVER

@SOLVER is a special @function that returns information about the Solver utility. This @function is recalculated whenever the worksheet is recalculated.

Syntax

@SOLVER(*query-string*)

Query-string is a label that specifies the information you need about the Solver utility. Table 9-14 shows the eight options that you can use for *query-string*.

Example

If you open the Solver window and switch to the worksheet before starting Solver, @SOLVER("done") will return 3, indicating that Solver is active but not solving as yet. Your entry might look like @SOLVER("Done").

@SQRT

@SQRT is a mathematical @function that determines the square root of a number.

Syntax

@SQRT(*x*)

x is a positive value or a range name or address where the value is located.

Example

Here are a few examples of the square root function:

Function	Returns
@SQRT(9)	3
@SQRT(64)	8
@SQRT(100)	10

Query String	Return String	Meaning
Consistent	1	All constraints true
	2	One or more constraints false
	ERR	Solver inactive or no answer
Done	1	Done
	2	Solving
	3	Active but not solving
	ERR	Solver inactive
Moreanswers	1	All answers found
	2	More answers possible
	ERR	Solver inactive
Needguess	1	Guess not needed
	2	Guess needed
	ERR	Solver inactive
Numanswers	*n*	Number of answers
	ERR	Solver inactive
Optimal	1	Optimal answer
	2	Best answer
	3	Unbounded problem
	4	Optimal answer not requested
	ERR	Solver inactive
Progress	*n*	Percent complete
	ERR	Solver inactive
Result	1	One or more answers
	2	No answers
	ERR	Solver inactive

Table 9-14. Solver Query Strings

@STD

@STD is a statistical @function that computes the standard deviation of the values in a list. @STD measures the amount of variation from the average of the values. This computation assumes that you are including the data for the entire population and use the following formula. If you are working with a sample, you need to use the @STDS function. @STD uses the following formula:

$$\sqrt{\frac{\sum(x_i - \text{AVG})^2}{n}}$$

Syntax

@STD(*list*)

List can consist of one or more cell addresses, range addresses, or range names referring to individual cells, ranges, or collections. A list can contain a range that spans sheets in a worksheet file.

Example

Suppose that the Commemorative Bronze Company has made 50 replicas of antique bronze cash registers and wants to determine the standard deviation in the weight of these products. The weights of these registers are stored in A3..D15. An entry of @STD(A3..D15) yields a standard deviation of 2.2515142.

@STDS

@STDS is a statistical @function that computes the standard deviation when you have the data from a population sample.

Syntax

@STDS(*list*)

List can consist of one or more cell addresses, range addresses, or range names referring to individual cells, ranges, or collections. A list can contain a range that spans sheets in a worksheet file.

Example

The @STDS function uses the $n - 1$, or unbiased, method. The function performs this formula:

$$\sqrt{\frac{\sum(x_i - \text{AVG})^2}{(n-1)}}$$

where x_i is the ith item in the list and n is the number of items in the list.

The difference between the results of the @STD and @STDS function increases as the number of measurements decreases—making it critical to select the proper function. As an example, suppose you have a worksheet like that in Figure 9-21 containing product survey information. Each of the questions has an answer between 1 and 5. For each question, the worksheet might show the average and the standard deviation. For the first question, the standard deviation is small, it means that most of the responses vary slightly around the average. For questions where the standard deviation is high, such as 1.8, there is significant variation around the average. The size of a standard deviation also varies depending on the size of the values measured.

@STRING

@STRING is a string @function that allows you to convert a value into a label that looks like a value.

1-2-3/G [69.4] Ready

File Edit Worksheet Range Copy... Move... Print Graph Data Utility Quit... Help

A:B4 @STDS(B6..B64)

SHEET_73.WG1

A	A	B	C	D	E	F	G
1	Survey Response						
2	Question	1	2	3	4	5	6
3	Average	3.2711864	2.9322034	3.1186441	2.9152542	3.0338983	3.0169492
4	Std. Dev.	0.8676267	1.8276083	1.3401588	1.417722	1.4259431	1.5479856
5	Responses						
6	1	3	3	4	2	5	5
7	2	4	5	5	2	5	5
8	3	4	1	4	5	1	4
9	4	2	4	3	3	4	5
10	5	5	1	3	1	5	2
11	6	1	2	3	1	1	1
12	7	2	3	3	1	2	5
13	8	5	1	2	4	3	2
14	9	3	2	1	1	1	1
15	10	4	5	2	2	2	2
16	11	3	2	5	2	2	5
17	12	4	1	2	1	4	1

Figure 9-21. Using @STDS to measure the fluctuations in survey responses

Syntax

@STRING(*x*,*n*)

x is a value that you want to convert to a label.
n is an integer value representing the number of decimal places you want to see as the value is made into a label.

Example

Several examples of @STRING are

Function	Returns
@STRING(1.6,0)	the string 2
@STRING(12,4)	the string 12.0000
@STRING(2.3E+04,2)	the string 23000.00

@SUM

@SUM is a statistical @function that totals all values in a list.

Syntax

@SUM(*list*)

List can consist of one or more cell addresses, range addresses, or range names referring to individual cells, ranges, or collections. A list can contain a range that spans sheets in a worksheet file.

Example

You might have a list of accounts and their current balances on a worksheet. The @SUM function can be used to obtain the total, rather than a formula like +B4+B5+B6+B7, and so on. If the account balances are in B4..B11, @SUM(B4..B11) can be entered in B13.

@SUMPRODUCT

@SUMPRODUCT is statistical @function that computes the products of many pairs or larger groups of values and then adds each of the products.

Syntax

@SUMPRODUCT(*list*)

List can consist of range addresses or range names referring to a range. A list can contain ranges that spans sheets in a worksheet file. The list needed for @SUMPRODUCT differs from that of other statistical @functions. The @SUMPRODUCT function must consist of at least two ranges that are the same length.

Example

An example of computing a cross product is shown in Figure 9-22, which lists the products on an order form. The total for the entire order is computed after the last item. @SUMPRODUCT multiplies each item quantity by its price and adds it to the shipping cost. The shipping cost is the quantity times the weight times the shipping cost per pound. Once the cost for each item is computed, @SUMPRODUCT adds the totals for all of the items. Using the @SUMPRODUCT function reduces the number of formulas the worksheet needs to compute the total cost. You can also use this function to double-check worksheets that perform the same computations using multiplication and the @SUM function.

@SYD

@SYD is a financial @function that computes depreciation for an asset using one of the accelerated depreciation methods known as sum-of-the-

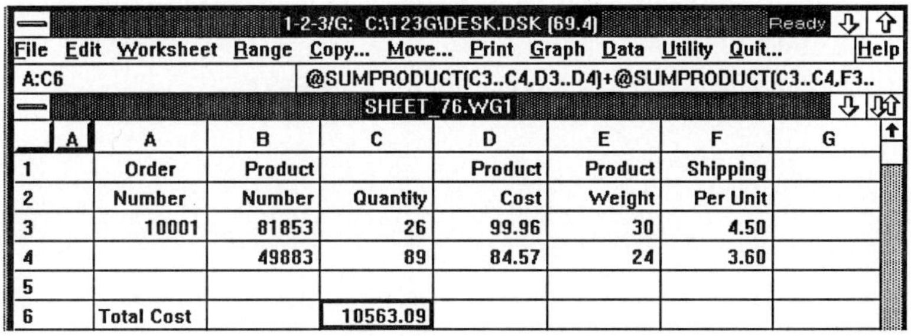

1-2-3/G: C:\123G\DESK.DSK (69.4) Ready

File Edit Worksheet Range Copy... Move... Print Graph Data Utility Quit... Help

A:C6 @SUMPRODUCT(C3..C4,D3..D4)+@SUMPRODUCT(C3..C4,F3..

SHEET_76.WG1

A	A	B	C	D	E	F	G
1	Order	Product		Product	Product	Shipping	
2	Number	Number	Quantity	Cost	Weight	Per Unit	
3	10001	81853	26	99.96	30	4.50	
4		49883	89	84.57	24	3.60	
5							
6	Total Cost		10563.09				

Figure 9-22. Using @SUMPRODUCT to compute order totals

years'-digits depreciation. @SYD uses this formula to compute the depreciation.

Syntax

@SYD(*cost,salvage,life,period*)

Cost is a value that represents the price paid for the asset.
Salvage is the value the asset will have at the end of its useful life.
Life is the amount of time it will take to depreciate the asset to its salvage value.
Period is an integer representing one of the years in the asset's life.

Example

The formula used by the function is

$$\frac{(cost - salvage)*(life - period\ for\ depreciation\ expense + 1)}{(life*(life + 1)/2)}$$

@SYD(12000,2000,5.1) computes the sum-of-the-years'-digits depreciation expense for year 1 for an asset that was purchased for $12,000 and has a $2,000 salvage value and a 5 year life. The depreciation for the 5 years is 3333.33, 2666.67, 2000, 1333.33, and 666.67.

@TAN

@TAN is a mathematical @function that calculates a trigonometric function. @TAN computes the tangent, which is the ratio of the side opposite an acute angle to the side adjacent to the acute angle. You can use this information to determine the length of an angle side.

Syntax

@TAN(*z*)

z is the measurement of the acute angle in radians.

Example

The diagram in Figure 9-23 requires the @TAN function to determine the distance of guide wires for high-tension power lines. The electric company has high-tension wires at the top of a pole 50 feet high, and wants to install guide wires from the top of the pole at a 30-degree angle with the ground. You can use the tangent function to determine the distance away from the high-tension wires that the guide wires should be attached. The tangent of 30 must be calculated, and, since the angle was measured in degrees, it must also be converted to radians. The formula thus becomes

@TAN(30*@PI/180)

The height of 50 feet is divided by the result of .5774 to provide a distance of 87 feet.

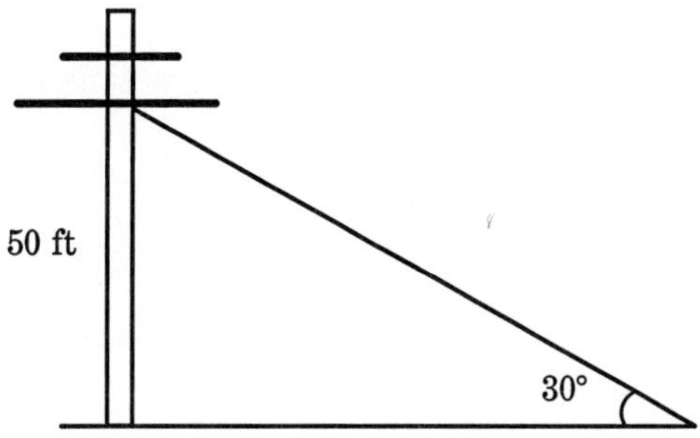

Figure 9-23. Guide wires for high-tension power lines

@TERM

@TERM is a financial @function that computes the payments needed before periodic payments reach a future value.

Syntax

@TERM(*payments,interest,future-value*)

Payments is a value that represents the amount of the equal payments.
Interest is a percentage representing the interest rate earned.
Future-value is a value that represents the accumulated value of an investment.

Example

Assuming that you manage to set aside $350 a month, which is invested at 10.25 percent, how long will it take for you to accumulate the $25,000 that you need for a new car. Compute the answer of 56 months with the formula @CTERM(350,.1025/12,25000).

@TIME

@TIME is a time @function that records a time serial number.

Syntax

@TIME(*hour,minutes,seconds*)

Hour is a value between 0 and 23. The number 0 represents midnight and the number 23 represents 11 P.M.
Minutes is a value between 0 and 59.
Seconds is a value between 0 and 59.

Example

You can sue the @TIME function to record the time that vehicles are brought in for repair, and the time that the work on each vehicle is completed. Entering both sets of numbers makes it easy to perform calculations with the time values, and the Range Format Date Time command allows you to choose a suitable Time display format. For example, to enter 3:15 PM, you would enter @TIME(15,15,0).

Tip: If you forget to apply a Range Format or Worksheet Global Format of Time, the cell will not look like a time. The time number will display as a number using the global format.

@TIMEVALUE

@TIMEVALUE is a time @function that allows you to perform time arithmetic with a time entry initially recorded as a string. It converts the string to a valid time number.

Syntax

@TIMEVALUE(*string*)

String is any label entered in any one of 1-2-3/G's valid time formats.

Example

The times in column B and D of Figure 9-24 are labels. To bill the customer, you need an elapsed time. You cannot subtract the time entries in column B from column D, since they are not time numbers. You can use a formula like this to perform the required computation for elapsed hours:

+@TIMEVALUE(D4)−@TIMEVALUE(B4)

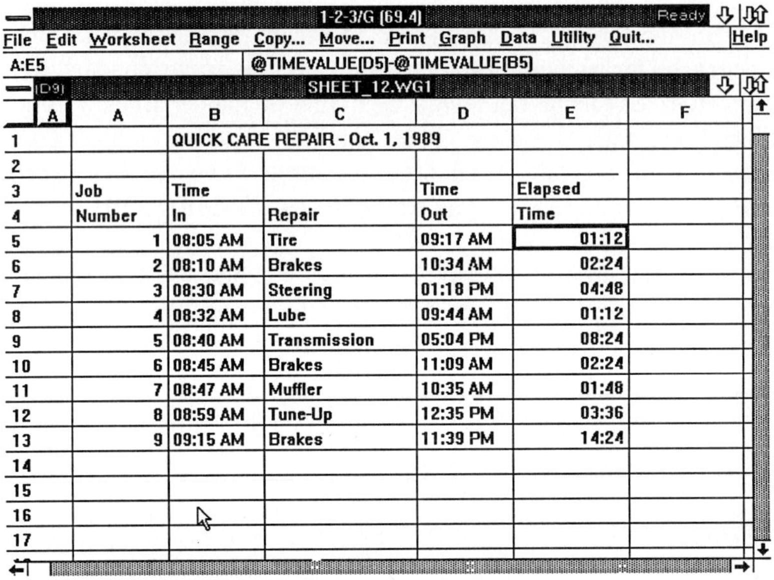

1-2-3/G [69.4] Ready

File Edit Worksheet Range Copy... Move... Print Graph Data Utility Quit... Help

A:E5 @TIMEVALUE(D5)-@TIMEVALUE(B5)

(D9) SHEET_12.WG1

A	A	B	C	D	E	F
1		QUICK CARE REPAIR - Oct. 1, 1989				
2						
3	Job	Time		Time	Elapsed	
4	Number	In	Repair	Out	Time	
5	1	08:05 AM	Tire	09:17 AM	01:12	
6	2	08:10 AM	Brakes	10:34 AM	02:24	
7	3	08:30 AM	Steering	01:18 PM	04:48	
8	4	08:32 AM	Lube	09:44 AM	01:12	
9	5	08:40 AM	Transmission	05:04 PM	08:24	
10	6	08:45 AM	Brakes	11:09 AM	02:24	
11	7	08:47 AM	Muffler	10:35 AM	01:48	
12	8	08:59 AM	Tune-Up	12:35 PM	03:36	
13	9	09:15 AM	Brakes	11:39 PM	14:24	
14						
15						
16						
17						

Figure 9-24. Working with time labels

You should format the result as a time so you can see the result in a format that looks like an elapsed time. In Figure 9-24, the formula in E5 calculates the elapsed time.

If you want to compute a charge based on an hourly rate of $25, you need to calculate the daily rate and multiply by the elapsed time number. You need a daily rate since the elapsed time is expressed as a fractional part of a day, not an hour. The formula for the computation for the worksheet in Figure 9-24 might look something like this: +E5*25*24.

@TODAY

@TODAY is a date @function that records a date number for the current system date in a worksheet cell. This date number can be formatted to look like a date.

Syntax

@TODAY

The @TODAY function does not require arguments.

Example

You could use the @TODAY function to determine if accounts are past due. For example, you could enter the formula

@IF(@TODAY>B3," ","Account is past due")

in C3. After copying the formula down column C, overdue accounts are flagged.

@TRIM

@TRIM is a string @function that removes unneeded spaces from entries. This @function removes spaces at the beginning of an entry (leading) and spaces at the end of an entry (trailing). Individual spaces within the entry are not deleted. Multiple consecutive spaces are reduced to one space. @TRIM retains one space between strings separated by an ampersand (&).

Syntax

@TRIM(*string*)

Example

These examples show how you might use @TRIM:

Function	Returns
@TRIM(" Sales")	Sales
@TRIM("January "&" Fuel Allowance")	January Fuel Allowance.

@TRUE

@TRUE is a logical @function that represents a logical 1.

Syntax

@TRUE

This function has no arguments.

Example

Here is an example:

@IF(A3=10,@TRUE,"A3 is not equal to 10")

For a more sophisticated example of @TRUE you can look to the section for @FALSE earlier in this chapter.

@UPPER

@UPPER is a string @function that converts text to uppercase.

Syntax

@UPPER(*string*)

String is a label or a reference to a label or text formula that you want to convert to uppercase.

Example

@UPPER(A2&" "&B3), where A2 contains Jobbard Milling Company and B3 contains east dallas division, the program returns JOBBARD MILLING COMPANY EAST DALLAS DIVISION. All words in each string are converted to uppercase.

@VALUE

@VALUE is a string @function that converts to a value a number initially entered as a string.

Syntax

@VALUE(*string*)

String is a label or a reference to a label containing nothing but numbers and formatting characters.

Example

Here are a few examples:

Function	**Returns**
@VALUE(" 23.98")	the number 23.98
@VALUE(Z10)	0 if Z10 is blank, and ERR if Z10 contains a label such as abc

@VAR

@VAR is a statistical @function that computes the variance for the values in a population. You must have all the values in a total population to use this method. If you only have a sample of the values, you need to use @VARS. The variance is the square root of the standard deviation. The @VAR function is biased, since it uses a count as part of its calculation. Specifically, it uses the following formula:

$$\frac{\sum(x_i - \mathrm{AVG})^2}{n}$$

where x_i is the ith item in the list and n is the number of items in the list. The number of items is critical in determining whether to use @VAR or @VARS. When n is equal to the total population, use @VAR; when n represents a sample of the population, use @VARS.

Syntax

@VAR(*list*)

List can consist of one or more cell addresses, range addresses, or range names referring to individual cells, ranges, or collections. A list can contain a range that spans sheets in a worksheet file.

Example

As an example, suppose that the Commemorative Bronze Company has made 50 replicas of antique bronze cash registers and wants to determine the variance in their weight. If the weights are stored in A3..B20 and C3..C16, you would enter @VAR(A3..B20,C3..C16).

@VARS

@VARS is a statistical @function that calculates the variance for the values in a population sample. @VARS produces a result equivalent to the following formula:

@COUNT(*list*)/(@COUNT(*list*) − 1)*@VAR(*list*)

This @function makes it easier to work with population sample data.

Syntax

@VARS(*list*)

List can consist of one or more cell addresses, range addresses, or range names referring to individual cells, ranges, or collections. A list can contain a range that spans sheets in a worksheet file.

Example

The variance calculation determines the amount of variation between individual values and the mean. For example, suppose that the companies in a product survey have average sales of $500,000. A variance of 2.5 billion indicates that more of your customers have approximately the same sales volume than a variance of 160 billion. The variance values accentuate the variances among a set of values. You can use this information to target your advertising to the appropriate companies.

The @VARS function uses the $n - 1$, or unbiased, method. The function performs this formula:

$$\frac{\sum(x_i - \text{AVG})^2}{(n - 1)}$$

where x_i is the ith item in the list and n is the number of items in the list.

As with @STD and @STDS, the difference between the results of @VAR and @VARS increases as the number of measurements decreases.

@VDB

@VDB is a financial @function that calculates the variable-rate declining-balance depreciation for an asset. Unlike the other depreciation methods, @VDB allows you to compute depreciation for the fractional part of the year in which you acquired the asset. The formula used in the calculation of variable declining-balance depreciation is as follows:

$$\frac{\textit{book value for the period*depreciation factor}}{\textit{life of the asset}}$$

Syntax

@VDB(*cost,salvage,life,start-period,end-period*[*,depreciation*][*,switch*])

Cost is a value that represents the price paid for the asset.
Salvage is the value the asset will have at the end of its useful life.
Life is the amount of time it will take to depreciate the asset to its salvage value.
Start-period is a value corresponding to the acquisition date for an asset in relation to the beginning of a fiscal year.
End-period is the time when you no longer want to calculate depreciation. If you purchase an asset midway through a year, the start period is 0 and the end period is .5.
Depreciation is an optional argument that allows you to specify the percentage of straight-line depreciation that you want to use. The default is 2.
Switch is another optional argument. The default value is 0, which causes @VDB to switch to straight-line depreciation in the period where straight-line exceeds @VDB. If you enter a 1, @VDB does not switch to straight-line depreciation.

Example

1-2-3/G adjusts the calculations to ensure that total depreciation is exactly equal to the asset's cost minus the salvage value. @VDB automatically switches to straight-line depreciation when that method provides greater depreciation.

Assuming the cost of the asset was $11,000, its salvage value is $1,000, and a 1.5 depreciation factor to calculate depreciation using a 150 percent declining-balance depreciation rate, the entry for year 1 would be @VDB(11000,1000,5,0,1,1.5). Since an argument is not supplied for switch the variable declining-balance depreciation method switches to straight-line depreciation when straight-line is higher. The depreciation for the five years is 3300, 2310, 1617, 1386.50, and 1386.50.

@VLOOKUP

@VLOOKUP is a special @function that allows you to perform a table lookup when the entries you are checking are stored in a vertical column at the left side of the table. This @function returns a value from a specific column of the table determined by the row requested. The only difference between this @function and @HLOOKUP is the arrangement of the data in the table.

Syntax

@VLOOKUP(*x*,*range*,*column-offset*)

x is a value or label that will be compared against the entries in the first column of the table.
Range is a range address or name refers to the table location.
Column-offset is an offset from the beginning of the table that determines which column of table entries the function uses. The column used for comparison with the codes is column 0.

Figure 9-25 shows a table in J7..L9 with codes in J7..J9, and return values in K7..L9. The process 1-2-3/G uses for determining the value to be returned is as follows:

- The specified code is compared against the values in the left column of the table.

- The largest value in the left column of the table that is not greater than the code is considered a match. If the code to be looked up in the table is 2.5, the value adjacent to the 3 is returned.

- Offset is used to determine which value in the column that contains the matching table cell will be returned. If offset is 0, the matching code value itself is returned. If offset is 1, the value to the right of the matching value is returned, and so on.

- A code with a value less than the first value in the left column of the table will return ERR.

- A code value greater than the last value in the first column of the table will be considered to match the last value.

- If you are using label entries for codes and have label entries in the left column of the table, only exact matches will return table values.

1-2-3/G [69.4] Ready

File Edit Worksheet Range Copy... Move... Print Graph Data Utility Quit... Help

A:J6 'LODGING & MEAL/MISC COST LOOKUP

SHEET_65.WG1

A	J	K	L	M	N	O
6	LODGING & MEAL/MISC COST LOOKUP					
7	1	$125.00	$35.00			
8	2	$150.00	$45.00			
9	3	$175.00	$50.00			
10						
11	AIRFARE COST LOOKUP					
12	1	$250.00				
13	2	$300.00				
14	3	$350.00				
15	4	$500.00				

Figure 9-25. Sample vertical tables

When you build a table with numeric codes, they must be in ascending sequence. However, they needn't be consecutive numbers; nor do the gaps between numbers have to be of a consistent size. With label entries, the codes do not have to be in any special sequence within the table.

Tip: When you reference the table location in @VLOOKUP, you will want to use an absolute reference in most applications. Since most applications are working with only one table location, forgetting the $ symbols for an absolute reference causes the copies you make of the original formula to reference cells that are not part of the table.

Example

Figure 9-26 provides a portion of a model to project travel costs. The tables for this model are located in J7..L9 and J12..K15 in Figure 9-25. The tables offer a list of codes that provide an estimate of one night's meal and lodging costs for a travel location on the worksheet, as well as airfare and miscellaneous costs such as taxis, phone calls, and so on.

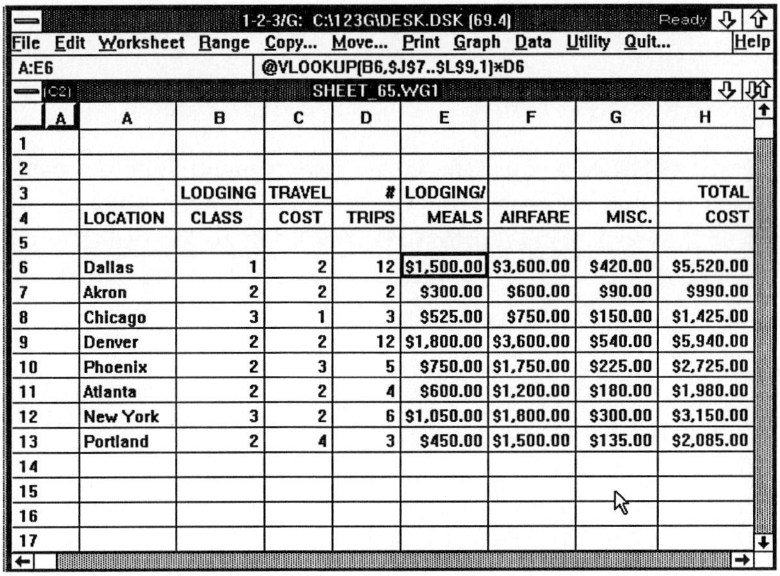

1-2-3/G: C:\123G\DESK.DSK [69.4] Ready

File Edit Worksheet Range Copy... Move... Print Graph Data Utility Quit... Help

A:E6 @VLOOKUP(B6,$J$7..$L$9,1)*D6

(C2) SHEET_65.WG1

A	A	B	C	D	E	F	G	H
1								
2								
3		LODGING	TRAVEL	#	LODGING/			TOTAL
4	LOCATION	CLASS	COST	TRIPS	MEALS	AIRFARE	MISC.	COST
5								
6	Dallas	1	2	12	$1,500.00	$3,600.00	$420.00	$5,520.00
7	Akron	2	2	2	$300.00	$600.00	$90.00	$990.00
8	Chicago	3	1	3	$525.00	$750.00	$150.00	$1,425.00
9	Denver	2	2	12	$1,800.00	$3,600.00	$540.00	$5,940.00
10	Phoenix	2	3	5	$750.00	$1,750.00	$225.00	$2,725.00
11	Atlanta	2	2	4	$600.00	$1,200.00	$180.00	$1,980.00
12	New York	3	2	6	$1,050.00	$1,800.00	$300.00	$3,150.00
13	Portland	2	4	3	$450.00	$1,500.00	$135.00	$2,085.00
14								
15								
16								
17								

Figure 9-26. Vertical tables for the travel-cost model

The model in Figure 9-26 contains city names in column A. Column B contains a numeric code for Lodging Class that categorizes cities according to their relative living costs. Column C contains the numeric code for Travel Cost, assigned on the basis of distance from the origination point. Column D contains the number of trips to the location. This model assumes that all trips are for one night, but you could easily insert another column to show variable numbers of nights.

The next column contains the first lookup formula. From the three arguments in the function, you can see that the formula looks up B6 in the table with the absolute address of $J$7..$L$9. The formula uses an offset of 1, referring to the value in the column right next to the code. As a final step, this formula multiplies the returned value by the number of trips to obtain a total lodging cost for this location. Columns F and G use the @VLOOKUP function to return the airfare and miscellaneous costs per trip, which is multiplied by the number of trips.

The @VLOOKUP and @HLOOKUP functions cannot access multiple worksheets for the lookup tables, but you can bypass this obstacle by combining the @CHOOSE function with the @VLOOKUP and @HLOOKUP function.

@WEEKDAY

The @WEEKDAY function is an undocumented date function that returns a value between 0 and 6, with each number equal to a different day of the week. This function returns 0 for a date occuring on Saturday, and assigns each day a different number finishing with 6 for Friday.

Syntax

@WEEKDAY(*date-number*)

Date-number is a number between 0 and 73050 representing one of the sequential numbers assigned to a date.

Example

You can use this @function to determine the day of the week a date number occurs. A sample formula is @WEEKDAY(33105), which equals 2 for Monday. You can combine this with the @CHOOSE function to create a formula like

```
@CHOOSE(@WEEKDAY(33105),"Sat","Sun","Mon","Tue","Wed",
        "Thur","Fri")
```

which returns Mon.

@YEAR

@YEAR is a date @function that extracts the year component from a date number.

Syntax

@YEAR(*date-number*)

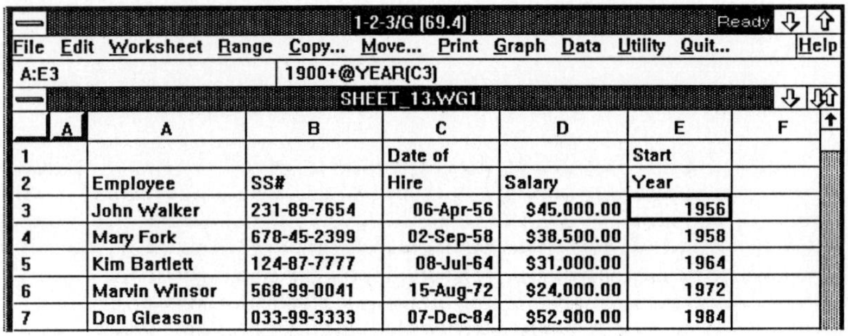

1-2-3/G [69.4] Ready

File Edit Worksheet Range Copy... Move... Print Graph Data Utility Quit... Help

A:E3 1900+@YEAR(C3)

SHEET_13.WG1

A	A	B	C	D	E	F
1			Date of		Start	
2	Employee	SS#	Hire	Salary	Year	
3	John Walker	231-89-7654	06-Apr-56	$45,000.00	1956	
4	Mary Fork	678-45-2399	02-Sep-58	$38,500.00	1958	
5	Kim Bartlett	124-87-7777	08-Jul-64	$31,000.00	1964	
6	Marvin Winsor	568-99-0041	15-Aug-72	$24,000.00	1972	
7	Don Gleason	033-99-3333	07-Dec-84	$52,900.00	1984	

Figure 9-27. Using @YEAR

Date-number is a number between 0 and 73050 representing one of the sequential numbers assigned to a date.

Example

You could use this function to determine the start year for each of a group of employees. You can reference the date of hire and extract the year number, for an easy reference to the anniversary year, as shown in Figure 9-27 where @YEAR extracts the year number.

Using Multiple Windows and Links

TEN

This chapter includes several suggestions for using multiple windows. In addition, it discusses how to create links between files with the Edit Link commands, and contains additional information about external link formulas.

Using Windows Effectively

In Chapter 2, you learned how to change the size and position of any window, including 1-2-3/G's desktop. In subsequent chapters, you discovered different ways to display windows on the desktop. When you create your own applications, several considerations determine how you will display your worksheets on the desktop:

- What other OS/2 applications are you using? How does the other OS/2 application affect your current 1-2-3/G task and vice versa?
- How many worksheet windows do you want open simultaneously?
- How much of each worksheet file do you want to see at once?
- Do you want to see multiple parts of each worksheet file at once?

- Are there some windows that you need open but don't need to see on the desktop?

Answering these questions will help you decide how large you want the 1-2-3/G desktop and the windows inside it, and whether each window uses panes, titles, perspective display, or a smaller font.

As an example, Figure 10-1 shows several worksheets combined. This layout enables you to see how changing the values in the first sheet affects the values in the remaining sheets. These worksheet files have nested formulas, as described in the "Creating External File Links with Formulas" section. In this case, the labels match, so you can align the rows in the three sheets. You should save this desktop so the desktop remembers the size and position of each worksheet window on the desktop. This arrangement lets you quickly see the values in one column of all three sheets. Since the values derived from the final worksheet are

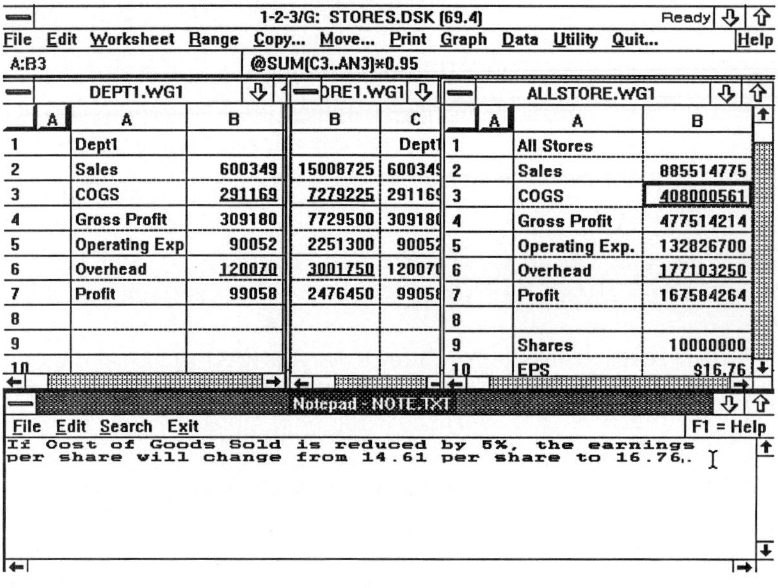

1-2-3/G: STORES.DSK [69.4] Ready

File Edit Worksheet Range Copy... Move... Print Graph Data Utility Quit... Help

A:B3 @SUM(C3..AN3)*0.95

DEPT1.WG1

A	A	B
1	Dept1	
2	Sales	600349
3	COGS	291169
4	Gross Profit	309180
5	Operating Exp	90052
6	Overhead	120070
7	Profit	99058
8		
9		
10		

ORE1.WG1

B	C
	Dept1
15008725	60034
7279225	29116
7729500	30918
2251300	9005
3001750	12007
2476450	9905

ALLSTORE.WG1

A	A	B
1	All Stores	
2	Sales	885514775
3	COGS	408000561
4	Gross Profit	477514214
5	Operating Exp.	132826700
6	Overhead	177103250
7	Profit	167584264
8		
9	Shares	10000000
10	EPS	$16.76

Notepad - NOTE.TXT

File Edit Search Exit F1 = Help

If Cost of Goods Sold is reduced by 5%, the earnings per share will change from 14.61 per share to 16.76..

Figure 10-1. Using the size and position features for multiple 1-2-3/G and OS/2 windows

used in another application, you can make the 1-2-3/G desktop shorter to display the window for the other Presentation Manager application (Borland's Sidekick notepad in this example).

You can also arrange the windows on the desktop when a worksheet uses values from a table on another worksheet file. Figure 10-2 shows a worksheet file where the values in column G are determined by the table in the bottom window. The bottom worksheet window uses the perspective view to display two sheets from this worksheet file. The sheets also use titles so you can constantly see the column and row headings as you move around in the table. Since the worksheet file in the top of the desktop uses the values in the table, you can quickly match the value in the table with the value returned by the formula in column G. As you create your own applications, make sure to consider what information you expect to see in each open worksheet file.

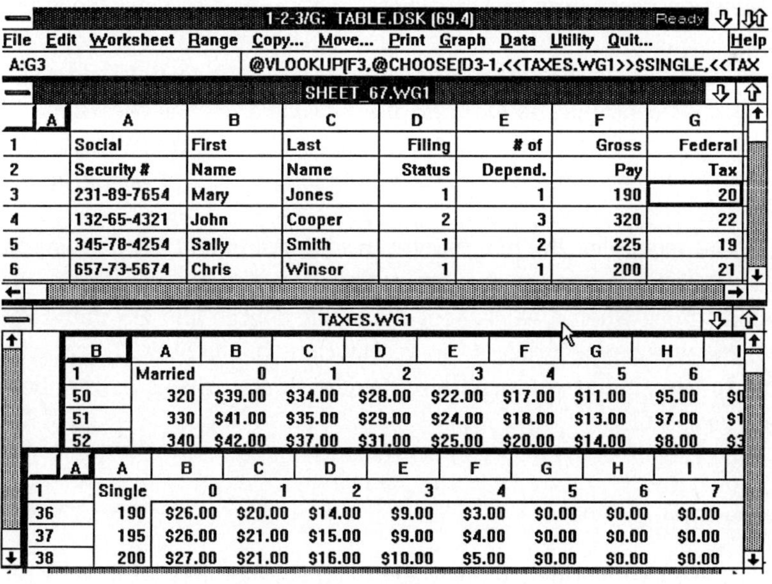

Figure 10-2. Using a separate window to store a table

Creating Links with the Edit Link Commands

External file links are links to another a worksheet or Presentation Manager application. These links let you take data in one worksheet or Presentation Manager application and use it in another worksheet. Chapter 6 introduced external file links created with formulas. You can also use the Edit Link commands to create links. However, if you create a link with a formula, you cannot modify it with Edit Link commands.

You can use the Edit Link commands to create, alter, and delete external file links. Creating a link with the Edit Link commands is much like using a worksheet tool window, graph tool window, or another Presentation Manager application. You can use the Edit Link commands to link the worksheet to data in any Presentation Manager application that supports the Dynamic Data Exchange (DDE).

There are four parts to link between a worksheet file or a Presentation Manager application and a worksheet file: the name of the file the data comes from, where the data is located in the file, the file containing the link, and where the link is stored in the file. The link must know the file and the item for both the worksheet file or Presentation Manager application that contains the original data, and the worksheet that will contain the link. The file is the name of the worksheet file or Presentation Manager application that contains the data to link and the worksheet that contains the external file link. The item is the range of data the link uses from the other worksheet file or Presentation Manager application. This can be a worksheet range, cell, or a paragraph from a text file.

The examples in this chapter use a worksheet as the destination. Since 1-2-3/G supports the Dynamic Data Exchange (DDE), you use similar steps when a worksheet file is the source and another Presentation Manager application is the destination. In Chapter 17, you will learn how to use similar commands to develop links using a graph file as the destination file.

Creating Links

There are two methods of creating external file links with the Edit Link commands. One method uses the Clipboard to supply the source file and item. The other method presents a dialog box so you can supply the source file and item.

The easiest way to create a link is to copy the data to the clipboard and then paste the data as a link to the worksheet. As described in Chapter 8, you can use the Edit Copy and Edit Cut commands to transfer a cell or range from a worksheet to the clipboard. In other Presentation Manager applications, you use these commands to transfer information from the application to the clipboard. Once the data is copied, activate the worksheet window that you want to contain the link and move the cell pointer to the first cell you want to use the link. Select Edit Link Paste Link. This establishes the external file link using the data in the clipboard as the source information for the link.

You can also create a link by supplying the source file, source item, and destination item. Select Edit Link Create to display the dialog box shown in Figure 10-3. The Destination file is the file containing the cell pointer. For the Source file and item, you can select one of the choices in the list box or type the desired information. If the clipboard contains data, the source file and item of this data initially appears in the text box and [from clipboard] appears in the list. Lotus applications and files appear in uppercase while other Presentation Manager applications appear in lowercase. You can select another source file from the list box. When you select a source file, you must supply the item information in

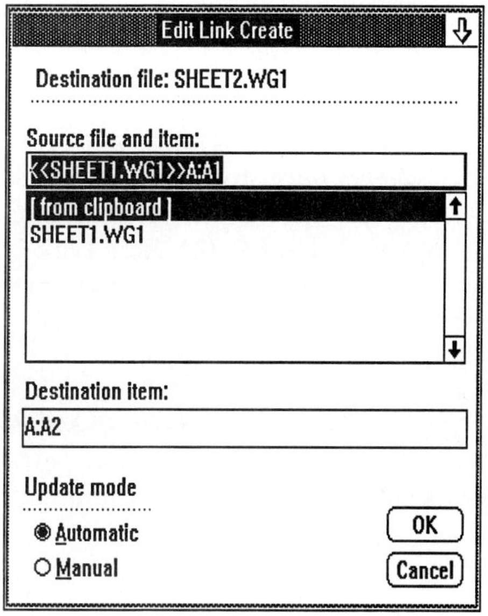

Edit Link Create

Destination file: SHEET2.WG1

Source file and item:

<<SHEET1.WG1>>A:A1

[from clipboard]

SHEET1.WG1

Destination item:

A:A2

Update mode

Automatic

Manual

OK

Cancel

Figure 10-3. Edit Link Create dialog box

the format that 1-2-3/G expects. For example, if the source file is an Excel worksheet, the source item is the range or cell address expressed as the column number and row number. An example is

<< Excel | C:\EXCELOS2\TEMPER.XLS >> R3C2:R3C8

After you select the source file and item, select the destination item if you want to change it from the cell pointer's current position. You can also select whether the link is updated automatically (the default) or manually. If you select Manual, 1-2-3/G only updates the link values when you select Edit Link Update. Selecting the OK command button creates an external file link with the source file and item selected.

Once you create a link, cells that are part of the external file link display L in the window title bar when the cell pointer selects the cell.

In addition, the contents box in the control line displays the value that also appears in the cell. When the source item contains multiple cells or multiple lines and the destination item is defined as a single cell, the link starts at the single cell and continues to use other cells—as when you copy or move a range and only select a single cell as the To range. For example, if you link A:A4..A:A10 from SHEET1.WG1 to A:B1 in BAL.WG1, the linked range uses A:B1..A:B7 in the BAL worksheet file.

If the link is updated manually, you should select Edit Link Update every time you want to check that the worksheet is using the most up-to-date values. 1-2-3/G only updates the values of the open files referenced by links. If the worksheet uses manual recalculation, you should press F9 (Calc) after issuing the Edit Link Update command so that the other worksheet formulas use the updated values.

Tip: When your worksheet includes cells linked to other worksheets and Presentation Manager applications, enable worksheet protection so that you don't accidentally overwrite cells containing linked data.

Tip: If you use the Edit Link commands to link multiple worksheet files, include the worksheet files in a desktop. This way, you can retrieve the desktop and know that all necessary files are open and will be updated.

Altering a Link

There are two ways to alter links in 1-2-3/G. The most common method is to select Edit Link Edit. This presents a dialog box that lists the linked destination items. As the items are highlighted, the Current link information box lists the source file and item and when the link is updated. The Source file and item text box list the source file and item, which you can alter to change the source file and item the link uses. You can also change the update mode to update values automatically when 1-2-3/G updates the external file link, or to update the values through the Edit Link Update command manually. When you select the OK command button, 1-2-3/G uses the updated link information.

You may also want to change the file one or more link uses. For example, if one or more links use BALANCE as the source file, and you rename the BALANCE.WG1 worksheet file to BAL_1990.WG1, you should change every external file link reference to reflect the new worksheet name. Rather than using the Edit Link Edit command for each link to be changed, you can use the Edit Link Move command and change all of the files at once. From the Edit Link Move dialog box, select the source file that contains the links to be changed. Under the New source list box, select an open file that you want to be the source file of all links that use the selected file under Current source. You must select an open file. You can also type the filename of either source in the text box. When both files are selected, choose the Move links command button.

Removing a Link

If you are finished with a link, you can remove it from the worksheet. To delete a link, select Edit Link Delete. You can either select All links or Selected link. Selecting All links removes all links that you created with the Edit Link commands, but does not affect external file links created with formulas. Selecting Selected link and a link from the list box (or typing the destination item in the text box) removes only the specified link. As a destination item is highlighted, its source file and item are displayed at the bottom along with option buttons for selecting Automatic or Manual updating. When you select the OK command button, the L for linked disappears from either the selected linked cell or all linked cells. When you delete the link from one range, you are deleting the links between all cells in the source and destination range. Deleting a link is different than making new entries into a linked cell, since the link is still established between the source and the destination although the cell displays the new entry.

You can also use the Edit Link Move command to delete all links to a single file. For example, if you want to delete all links to BALANCE.WG1, you can use the Edit Link Move command to delete all links to that file rather than deleting each link with Edit Link Delete. From the Edit Link Move dialog box, select from the Current source list box or type in the source file from which you want to delete links. Once this file is selected, choose the Delete links command button. Every external file link in the active worksheet file that uses the selected file as the source file will be deleted. Links that use other source files are not affected. In the same manner, links created with 1-2-3/G formulas do not change, even if they use the selected source file.

Creating External File Links with Formulas

External file links in formulas are similar to external file links you create with the Edit Link commands. The source file and item are described within the file cell formula. The cell containing the formula is the destination item. To change the source file and item, press F2 (Edit) and alter the filename in the double angle brackets or the subsequent cell or range address or name. External file links created with formulas and with Edit Link commands have advantages and disadvantages, which are summarized in Table 10-1.

One advantage of using formula links is that the values you use can be directly included in a formula instead of creating the link in the

	Links Created with Formulas	Links Created with Edit Link Commands
Source file must be open	No	Yes
Command to update manually updated links	File Admin Links Refresh	Edit Link Update
Number of links in a cell	As many as fits in the 512 formula character limit	One per cell
Compatibility with other Presentation Manager applications	Unique to 1-2-3/G	Same steps used in each Presentation Manager Application that supports DDE
Source of data	Other worksheets	Worksheets or other Presentation Manager Applications
Altering links	Press F2 (Edit)	Use Edit Link Edit command
Use Clipboard to select link source and item	No	Yes

Table 10-1. Comparison of External File Links

current worksheet and having the formula refer to the link value. This means that you can include multiple file links in a single formula using different worksheet files. An example is the formula

+ <<SHEET1.WG1>>A:A1*<<SHEET2.WG1>>A:A1

To achieve the same results by using external file links created with the Edit Link commands, you would link one cell (such as A:A1) to A:A1 in <<SHEET1.WG1>>, and another cell (such as A:A2) to A:A1 in SHEET2.WG1. With the two cells linked, you would enter a formula such as +A1*A2 in the current sheet.

In addition, with formulas, you can create external file links to worksheet files that are not open—only the destination file must be open. With the Edit Link commands, in contrast, the source and destination files must be open when you create and use the values of the source file.

If the cell or range in the other worksheet you want a formula to use is named, and that worksheet file is open, you can use the F3 (Name) key to select the cell or range from the other worksheet. When you are ready to add the external file link, type + and then press F3 (Name). The dialog box presented includes all range names in the current worksheet as well as the names of any other open worksheet files. When you select one of the worksheet files, 1-2-3/G lists the range names in the file. When you select one of these range names, 1-2-3/G inserts both the filename and the range name in the formula. When you use a range name, you needn't alter the formula if you move the cell or range in the other worksheet file.

With external file links created with formulas, you must consider whether the source files will always be in the default directory. If not, you must include the path information with the filename in the link formulas.

Tip: If 1-2-3/G cannot determine the file used by the external file link in a formula, the formula evaluates to ERR.

Using External File Links

Using external file links is somewhat different than working with a single worksheet. When you use multiple worksheet files, you can create nested files. For example, you can create an overall balance sheet composed of formulas that use values from other worksheet files. If all of the worksheet files are not open, you may have a problem if some of the files don't have the most up-to-date values. When you use external file links, you must consider if the source file of the link is password protected.

Nested File Links

Nested formulas are as simple as one formula that uses the value of another formula, which uses the value of a third formula, and so on.

With external file links, you can create nested file links where one formula result depends on another, and the values in one file depend on the values in another. As an example, consider the consolidation of a department store where the totals of each department for each store must be added before the stores are consolidated. Figure 10-4 shows an example of nested worksheet files, where the formulas are shown as text. In this example, the value of C2 in STORE1.WG1 depends on B2 in DEPT1.WG1. Also, the cell in C2 in ALLSTORE.WG1 depends on B2 in STORE1.WG1.

With nested external file links, one of the worksheet files may not be using the most up-to-date information. (When all of the information is in a single worksheet file, this is not a problem since 1-2-3/G constantly updates the values in the current worksheet.) When the data for each department and each store is in a separate worksheet file, you may have problem if you try calculating the total for all stores before calculating

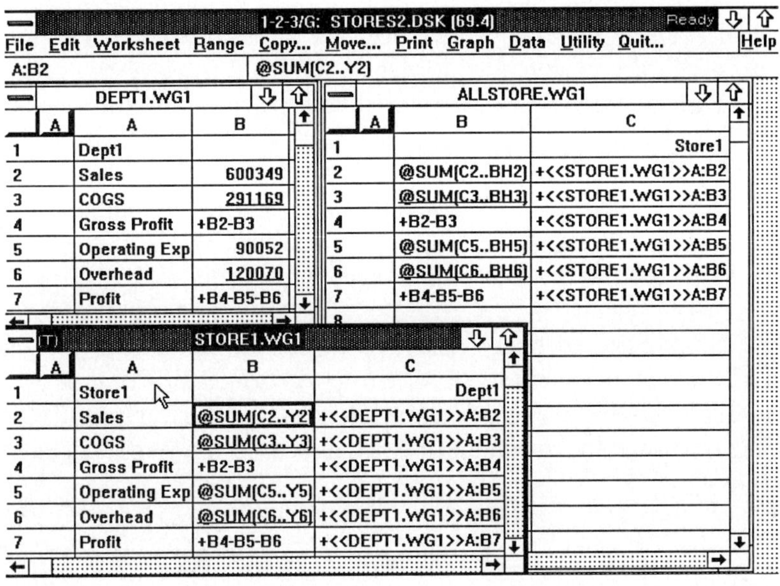

Figure 10-4. Nesting external file link formulas

the total for each store. With external file links in formulas, 1-2-3/G uses the last value of the cell or cells in the saved file when the source file is not open. This means that you must consider the order in which the files are retrieved and saved.

Such nesting problems have two solutions. You can open all the files you are using at once. This way 1-2-3/G is responsible for calculating each of the worksheet files and updating the changed values between worksheet files. In the example shown in Figure 10-4, this would mean loading files DEPT1.WG1, STORE1.WG1, and ALLSTORE.WG1 into memory all at once. While this solution works for three files, it won't work for three hundred. In this case, you would divide the worksheet files into levels. The first level would include the departments in each store. These are the first worksheets that need to be calculated. You would retrieve the departmental worksheets, enter any new values, update all calculations, and save the files for each department separately. Once the department worksheet files were up to date, you would work on the next level—the stores in the example. In this example, you would retrieve each store's worksheet file so that the external file links in the formulas would use the updated values in the department worksheet files. Once the store worksheet files were updated, you could save the files with the new values. Finally, you would retrieve the consolidation worksheet that uses the updated values from the store worksheet files. This step-by-step approach assures that each level of worksheet files uses the most up-to-date values of the previous level. Another approach is to save a small number of related files by opening each of them on the desktop and saving the desktop. When the desktop is opened again, all of the files will be available.

Tip: If you have so many nested external file links that you cannot load all files at once, create a macro as described in Chapter 23, that loads each file from the first level to the top, and recalculates the worksheet using the most up-to-date values of the worksheets in the prior level.

Using a Password Protected File as the Source

When the source file of an external file link is password protected, you must know the password for the file. Both types of external file links will not contain the up-to-date value from the password-protected file. With formulas that use password-protected files, the formula evaluates to ERR until the password-protected file is successfully retrieved.

Printing

ELEVEN

Working with models on the screen is adequate if you want to see the immediate impact of changes you make. However, when you have to reference these same numbers at a meeting, the screen in your office is no help. Fortunately, 1-2-3/G has extensive print features that allow you to create a professional looking multiple-page report. You can decide what portions of the worksheet to print, and can create a worksheet that uses a variety of fonts and even colors if your output device supports these features.

Preparing to use 1-2-3′G's print features begins when you install a printer with OS/2. You can do this before, during, or after you install 1-2-3/G. If you haven't installed your printer yet, review Appendix A for detailed directions on completing this vital step.

This chapter covers all of 1-2-3/G's commands related to printing. With these commands, you can set default parameters, such as margins and page length, that are used every time you print. By the time you finish this chapter, you should have mastered simple printing tasks, and also be familiar with the more advanced print options that 1-2-3/G provides. Since the appearance of a printed worksheet can vary depending on the printer you are using, your printouts may differ from the examples. These examples are created with the Hewlett-Packard LaserJet series II.

How 1-2-3/G Prints in OS/2

Printing in 1-2-3/G is very different than printing in previous 1-2-3 releases—primarily because 1-2-3/G uses the OS/2 operating system instead of DOS. In OS/2 applications, the operating system selects the printer and some of the printer settings. In DOS applications, in contrast, each application requires its own printer selection. With OS/2, you can install the printer and make printer selections with the OS/2's Control Panel Program. When you install a printer, the printer can be used by many applications. You can create a print spooler to store all of your print output until your printer is able to print it.

Since OS/2 selects the printer and makes some of the printer setting selections, many printer options that previously required menus for selection are now located in the OS/2 Control Panel program or the print spooler program. This also means that you no longer use setup strings to communicate with your printer. The printer drivers used by OS/2 are configured for your specific printer settings. When you print a worksheet, 1-2-3/G tells OS/2 what data to print and what fonts and attributes to use. OS/2 intercepts the data going from 1-2-3/G to the printer, and inserts the necessary printer codes.

Unlike earlier releases, 1-2-3/G draws the printed worksheet on the page. OS/2 has to send the information to the printer, so it draws the worksheet as you want to see it. Earlier 1-2-3 releases used the built-in printer characters to print the worksheet, simply telling the printer what characters to type. In 1-2-3/G and OS/2, the printer must be told how to draw every character and line that appears in the worksheet. This means that printing with 1-2-3/G takes longer, since the printed worksheet includes the graphics features of the worksheet. While this may seem a disadvantage, the print spooler that 1-2-3/G uses makes printing with 1-2-3/G quicker since you do not have to wait until the printer is finished to continue using 1-2-3 and the print quality is much better than before.

What Is a Spooler?

A *spooler* is a program that controls the flow of information to the printer. Spooler programs predate OS/2; however, with OS/2, the spooler is an integrated part of the operating system. The advantage of a spooler can be illustrated by comparing how 1-2-3 Release 2.2 and 1-2-3/G print worksheets. When you print using Release 2.2, 1-2-3 sends all of the information to the printer at once. Since most printers can handle only a limited amount of information at a time, you wait while the computer slowly sends information to the printer as fast as the printer can accept it. When you print without a spooler, you must wait until the printer finishes accepting the print information before you can continue using 1-2-3.

In contrast, a spooler program copies the information that you want to print to a temporary file on your hard disk. The spooler can store the print information in a file quicker than a printer can print it. Once the print information is in a file, you can continue working with 1-2-3/G or any other application. While you continue working, the spooler program sends the print information to the printer—this is called *background printing.* The information is sent as fast as the printer accepts it. When all of the information in the file is sent to the printer, the spooler program deletes the temporary file.

Besides making printing faster, a spooler is used when you are working with several applications at once. For example, suppose that you want to print data from two applications. If you enter the commands in the second application before the printer prints the data from the first application, you may have a problem when both applications try sending the data to the printer at the same time. A spooler program instead accepts both sets of print information (each set of print information for a different printing task is a *print job*). Then the spooler keeps track of all print jobs, printing them separately. Since you can perform many applications simultaneously with OS/2, your print jobs can originate from 1-2-3/G and any other application you are running.

When the spooler prints your information, the program makes several assumptions. It assumes that each print job starts on a new page. It also assumes that the paper in the printer is at the top of the page when the operating system is started. This means that the print spooler advances the paper at the end of each job to the next page before printing the next one.

How 1-2-3/G Uses the Spooler

1-2-3/G uses the spooler by not sending information to be printed until it knows all of the printing information be sent. For example, suppose that you are printing two ranges separated with several blank lines. After you select the commands to print the first range, 1-2-3/G doesn't send any information to the spooler because it doesn't have all of the information the printer will need. Not until you select the commands to skip a few lines and print the second range will 1-2-3/G send any information to the printer. The 1-2-3/G print dialog boxes contain a Quit command button. This command button tells 1-2-3/G that you are finished making selections for the current print job and that 1-2-3/G can start sending information to the spooler. It is important to have 1-2-3/G wait until the entire print job is selected, since while you are between selecting commands to print the two ranges you may want to print information from another application. If 1-2-3/G sent the printer information as it received it, the spooler couldn't accept information from other sources.

When you don't use the spooler, 1-2-3/G still does not start printing any information until you select the Quit command button. When you select Quit, 1-2-3/G sends the information to the printer through the operating system. Since the information is sent to the printer rather than to a temporary file, you must wait until the printing is completed. If you are printing a worksheet that uses several pages, you may want to work with another OS/2 application while 1-2-3/G is sending information to the printer.

The Basic Print Procedure

1-2-3/G has two menu paths you can use to print. The pull-down menu and dialog boxes available under Print match the Print menu found in other 1-2-3 releases. Under the File commands, you can select Print to access a similar set of menu options. The File Print pull-down menu and dialog boxes resemble other OS/2 Presentation Manager applications. The File Print and the Print commands can often be used interchangeably, except for a few options. The File Print pull-down menu lets you change the printer that 1-2-3/G uses, combine graphs and worksheets (as described in Chapter 17), select the status of the print jobs, and choose how the colors in the worksheet are translated to patterns in the printed worksheet. The Print pull-down menu includes a File option that is unavailable under File Print. The changes that you make in one print dialog box to print a worksheet also appears in any other print dialog box that prints worksheets for the same worksheet file window.

Print Destination

Before printing, you must first select the destination of your printed output. You must decide whether you want the information sent directly to your printer or written to a disk file. You can send the printed output to the printer, an ASCII file, or an encoded file.

When you send the output to a file, you can select whether or not the file contains formatting codes specific to a printer (an *encoded* file). If you don't have a printer attached to your system, a disk file is naturally your only choice. Likewise, if your printer is broken or you want to use a different printer, you should choose Encoded. If you want to save the output to a file for use by another program, choose File, since it omits the printer codes an encoded file contains.

When 1-2-3/G writes your print file to disk, it assigns to the filename the extension .ENC for encoded files or .PRN for nonencoded files. This distinguishes the print file from the worksheet files on your disk, which have a .WG1 extension. If you want to review the contents of your print file, you can use operating system commands such as TYPE to scroll through the output on your screen. You can also use your word processor to view the print file. If the file is encoded, it contains several special characters that alter the worksheet appearance. To print an encoded file, use the OS/2 COPY or PRINT command to copy the file to the printer (LPT1). With Postscript printers use only the PRINT command, not the COPY command.

You select the print job destination one of two ways. When you select Print from the menu bar, the pull-down menu displays Printer File and Encoded for the print destination. Once you make a selection, a dialog box appears in which you make the remainder of your selections. If you selected Encoded or File, the first item in this dialog box prompts for a filename that the print process will create. If you are using the File Print menus to print, select File Print Destination. From the dialog box, select Encoded and supply a filename if you want to print to an encoded file on disk. Select Printer if you wish to print to the printer. You can choose any printer from the list. The File Print Destination dialog box has no option for printing to an unencoded file. The choice you make in this dialog box determines the destination of the print output chosen with the File Print Print Worksheet command. Regardless of the destination choice, you have the same menu items when you print to the printer or to an encoded file. When you print to an ASCII or unencoded file, some of the options are not available.

When you select the destination with the File Print Destination command, the dialog box includes a Setup command button that you can use to change some of the printer's settings. Selecting Setup changes the settings of the printer highlighted in the printer list box. The dialog box that appears is actually part of OS/2's Control Panel program. You can use the Setup button in the File Print Destination box to access many of the OS/2 Control Panel print options, such as changing the paper size, rotating the printout, and more. (The Control Panel program is described in detail later in this chapter.) The changes that you make here also affect the printing you do using the 1-2-3/G Print command, and apply to all worksheets and OS/2 applications that use the printer name highlighted when you select the Setup command button.

Print Range

Whether printing to your printer or to a disk file, you must decide and specify what worksheet cells you want to print. You can print every cell that contains entries, or just selected cells. These cells can reside on one sheet, or several sheets in a multiple-sheet file. You can even specify several areas in a worksheet file as separate print ranges—all with one Range command.

You specify the cells to be printed through the Range text box in a dialog box for printing worksheets. Figure 11-1 shows one such dialog box. Most of the options are the same whether you select File Print Print Worksheet, Print Encoded, Print File, or Print Printer. To see how to select a range, assume that you want to print the model shown in Figure 11-2. If you have never printed this worksheet before, 1-2-3/G assumes that the starting location for printing is the current cell pointer location. Make sure to position your cell pointer on A1 before selecting Print Printer to tell 1-2-3/G to print to the printer.

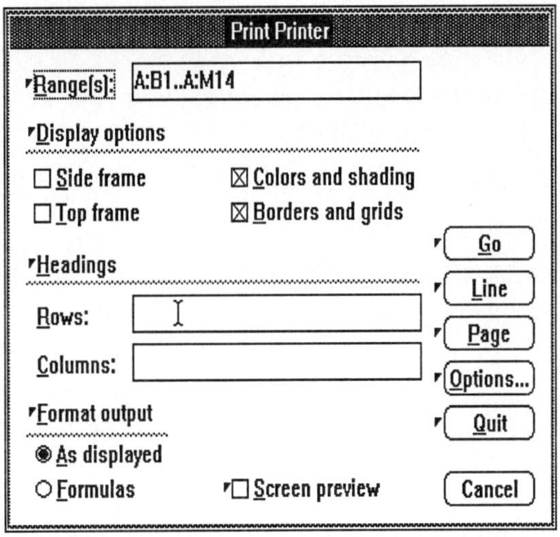

Print Printer

Range(s): A:B1..A:M14

Display options

☐ Side frame ☒ Colors and shading

☐ Top frame ☒ Borders and grids

Headings

Rows:

Columns:

Format output

◉ As displayed

○ Formulas ☐ Screen preview

Go | Line | Page | Options... | Quit | Cancel

Figure 11-1. Dialog box for printing worksheets

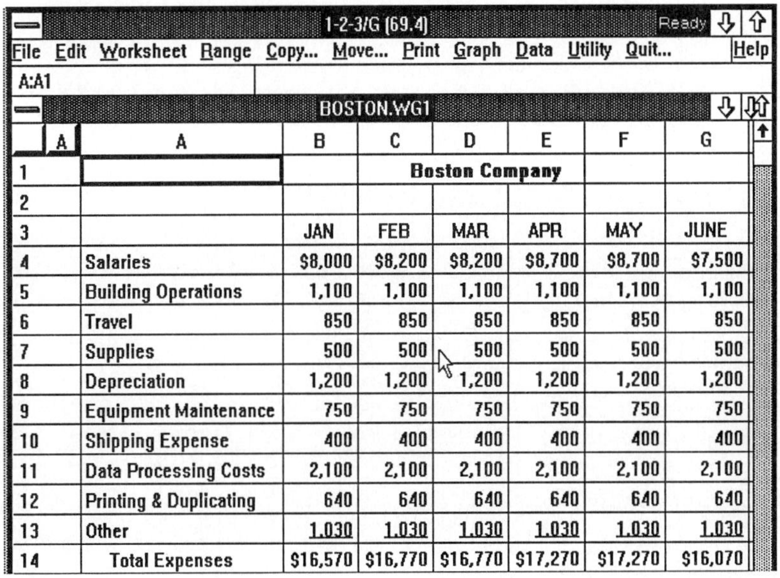

1-2-3/G (69.4) Ready

File Edit Worksheet Range Copy... Move... Print Graph Data Utility Quit... Help

A:A1

BOSTON.WG1

A	A	B	C	D	E	F	G
1			Boston Company				
2							
3		JAN	FEB	MAR	APR	MAY	JUNE
4	Salaries	$8,000	$8,200	$8,200	$8,700	$8,700	$7,500
5	Building Operations	1,100	1,100	1,100	1,100	1,100	1,100
6	Travel	850	850	850	850	850	850
7	Supplies	500	500	500	500	500	500
8	Depreciation	1,200	1,200	1,200	1,200	1,200	1,200
9	Equipment Maintenance	750	750	750	750	750	750
10	Shipping Expense	400	400	400	400	400	400
11	Data Processing Costs	2,100	2,100	2,100	2,100	2,100	2,100
12	Printing & Duplicating	640	640	640	640	640	640
13	Other	1,030	1,030	1,030	1,030	1,030	1,030
14	Total Expenses	$16,570	$16,770	$16,770	$17,270	$17,270	$16,070

Figure 11-2. Worksheet example for specifying print range

To tell 1-2-3/G what range to print, follow these steps:

1. Type **R** to select Range or click the Range text box.

2. Lock the beginning of the range in place at A1 by typing a period. With a mouse, click A1.

3. Move to the end of the model by pressing END-HOME. With a mouse, drag the cell pointer to G14.

4. Press ENTER to tell 1-2-3/G that the range has been selected. If you use a mouse to select the range, you can omit this step.

5. Assuming that all the default settings are acceptable, check that the printer is on and the paper is at the top of the page. Then select Go and Quit from the Print menu. Your printout should look like Figure 11-3.

The default margins and page length are used to produce 1-2-3/G printouts. 1-2-3/G also uses the font and font attributes that match the worksheet display. The number of lines per page varies depending on the size of the font selected to print the worksheet. Options for changing these and other settings that affect the appearance of your printed output are covered later in the chapter. You make changes to the

		Boston Company				
	JAN	FEB	MAR	APR	MAY	JUNE
Salaries	$8,000	$8,200	$8,200	$8,700	$8,700	$7,500
Building Operations	1,100	1,100	1,100	1,100	1,100	1,100
Travel	850	850	850	850	850	850
Supplies	500	500	500	500	500	500
Depreciation	1,200	1,200	1,200	1,200	1,200	1,200
Equipment Maintenance	750	750	750	750	750	750
Shipping Expense	400	400	400	400	400	400
Data Processing Costs	2,100	2,100	2,100	2,100	2,100	2,100
Printing & Duplicating	640	640	640	640	640	640
Other	1,030	1,030	1,030	1,030	1,030	1,030
Total Expenses	$16,570	$16,770	$16,770	$17,270	$17,270	$16,070

Figure 11-3. Printed output from worksheet example

default settings between steps 4 and 5 in the print procedure just described. As with other 1-2-3/G commands that use ranges, you can select the range before you select the command to print the worksheet and 1-2-3/G will include the range in the Range text box.

When the range you are printing requires more than one page, 1-2-3/G divides the printout into pages, determining how much can fit on each page based on the page size, margins, and printer. The first page contains as much of the range as can fit on one page, starting with the range's upper-left corner. If the range can't fit on one page, the next page contains the same columns with the next set of rows. For example, if you are printing A1..P75, the first page might contain A1..J29, the second page might contain A30..J58, the third page might contain A59..J75, the fourth page might contain K1..P29, the fifth page might contain K30..P58, and the sixth page might contain K59..P75.

When the selected range includes long labels that extend beyond their cells, you must include in the range the cells from which the labels borrow space. This keeps the labels from being truncated in the printout. For example, if G4 contains "Date of Report: March 16, 1990" and the cell width is 9, the label borrows G4, H4, and I4 for its display. If you don't include these three cells in the print range, 1-2-3/G doesn't print the part of the label that displays in H4 and I4, only printing the portion of the label that appears in the selected range.

Changing the Print Range

If you have already printed a worksheet, and now want to print a new area from it, the printing procedure may involve an additional step. When you select Range again to print the next range of the worksheet, 1-2-3/G highlights the last selected range. To select a new range, press ESCAPE or BACKSPACE to change the range address to a single cell address. You can then reposition and anchor again before moving to the opposite corner of the range to be printed. Selecting a new range with the mouse automatically replaces the previously selected print range.

Tip: When the Print Printer Range command is executed, 1-2-3/G highlights the last range you printed. To expand and contract the print range, move the cell pointer to different corners of the range. To change the active range corner, press the period; 1-2-3/G then moves the active corner of the range in a clockwise direction. The *active corner* determines the direction in which expansion and contraction of the range occurs. The first cell address is the anchored corner, and the second address is the corner that you can change.

Printing Collections

1-2-3/G can print collections. This feature is ideal when you want to print several different areas on a sheet or when you need to print data from several sheets.

You can select the collection before or after you select the print command. To print more than one range, highlight the first range that you want to print. Then type a comma or semicolon instead of pressing ENTER. 1-2-3/G finalizes the first range and repositions the cell pointer at the current position so you can highlight another range. Once you select all ranges to be printed, press ENTER. With a mouse, select the first range using the left mouse button and subsequent ranges using the right mouse button. 1-2-3/G prints the ranges in the collection in the order in which they are listed. You may want to include some blank cells between ranges to separate the ranges printed in the collection. The next time you select the range to print, 1-2-3/G lists all of the selected ranges and allows you to alter the last range in the collection, if desired. You can edit the other ranges in the collection by pressing F2 (Edit) to edit the range addresses.

You can also print multiple ranges by selecting Range, the first range to print, and then Go. Next, select Range, the second range to print, Go, and Quit. Selecting Go tells 1-2-3/G that you want the currently selected information sent to the printer once you select Quit. By selecting Go several times before you select Quit, you are sending several sets of information to the printer as part of a single print job. If you selected Quit each time, each range would be on a different page.

Tip: To print the notes for cells, use the Table command button in the Note utility window to create a table containing the addresses and notes for all cells containing notes. Once you create this table, you can print the worksheet range as you would print other worksheet ranges.

Monitoring 1-2-3/G During Printing

Once you tell 1-2-3/G to start printing the worksheet, it prints the worksheet in the background. There are commands to stop printing the print jobs, or to change the background printing to printing in the foreground. You can also monitor how many print jobs 1-2-3/G is sending to the spooler or printer. The File Print Status command presents a dialog box that lists the job printing and the filename if a file is the destination of the current print job. This dialog box also lists the number of print jobs in 1-2-3/G's queue.

When you are printing one or more jobs, you may decide not to print the worksheets. You can cancel the print job as 1-2-3/G is sending it to the spooler or printer. To cancel the current print job, select the Delete Current command button. To cancel all print jobs, select the Delete All command button. You can also halt the printing temporarily by selecting Suspend. This changes the command button to Resume. You may want to suspend printing, for example, if you are using a spooler and you want to delete some files from a command prompt window so the disk has enough room for the temporary files created by the spooler. When you select the Resume command button, 1-2-3/G continues printing where it left off. The last command button, Complete, tells 1-2-3/G not to use background printing so the dialog box remains on the screen until 1-2-3/G finishes printing all print jobs in the queue. You can use this option to ensure that the worksheet is printed before you use 1-2-3/G for other tasks. You can use the Cancel command button to return to the Ready mode without using the command buttons you have selected.

Basic Printing Options

Besides the Range, Go, and Quit selections in a dialog box to print worksheets, 1-2-3/G has other choices that provide blank lines, pages numbers, column and row headings. You can also set display options and select whether 1-2-3/G prints the cell formulas or values as they appear in the worksheet.

You can return most print settings to their defaults by pressing the DELETE key. For example, if you select a range for column headings, you can later delete this range by clicking the text box or selecting Headings Columns and pressing DELETE. You should press TAB or click another part of the dialog box to finalize your selection.

Advancing Printer Paper One Line at a Time

The Line command button moves the paper in your printer up one line. This command has the same effect as turning your printer off line and pressing the line feed button. However, the printer's line feed does not alter the internal line count that 1-2-3/G maintains to determine when a new page is needed. The Line command, in contrast, adds one to 1-2-3/G's internal line count, so it stays in sync with the paper. You can select Line to separate ranges that you are printing. This command button is not available from the Print File dialog box.

Advancing Printer Paper One Page at a Time

The Print Printer Page command moves the paper in your printer to the top of the next form. When you select this command, 1-2-3/G tells OS/2 to advance the printer to the next page. The result is similar to pressing form feed with your printer off line, but the Page command can print a footer (if you define one) for the bottom of your page; form feed cannot. When 1-2-3/G prints the worksheet, the page break assumes that you started printing at the top of a form. You don't need to add a page break to make sure that the next print job starts on a new page since 1-2-3/G assumes that you want to advance to the next page when you select Quit. This Page command button is not available from the Print File dialog box.

Exiting the Print Menu

The dialog box that you use to print a worksheet remains on the screen until you select Quit or Cancel. Selecting Quit sends any information to the printer and returns you to Ready mode. Selecting Cancel sends no information to the printer but returns you to Ready mode. Pressing ESCAPE several times or CTRL-BREAK once is another way to select Cancel.

Adding Column and Row Headings

The Headings option in a dialog box for printing worksheets allows you to include column and row heading in your worksheet, on every printed page of a report. This feature is useful if you use the months of the year as column heads across the worksheet, for example, and have more data than can fit on one printed page. You can print the worksheet with these column heads at the top of each page, if you specify the row containing the months as a heading.

Similarly, if your report is wider than it is long, you can print row heading on the far left of every page of your report. This information could be account names or other descriptions. You can use both options at once to identify each column and row that you print.

The range of worksheet cells that you specify for printing are then printed either to the right of or below the headings information. Lotus calls *column headings* the columns that appear on the left of every page and *row headings* the rows that appear at the top of every page. Rules for headings are summarized in the "Headings Rules" box. Headings are available with all dialog boxes that print worksheets except File Print.

Tip: When you specify a print range for a worksheet, do not include the heading rows and columns in the print range, since 1-2-3/G will print them twice.

Column Headings

You use column headings when you have more columns than will fit across one page, and there are labels or other information in a column or columns on the left side of the worksheet that identify data printed on subsequent pages of your report. If you select these columns as headings, they print in the first columns on each page of the report.

For example, consider the expense worksheet containing monthly figures shown in Figure 11-4. If you use the print range A1..M16, the

Heading Rules

The Headings option allows you to print descriptive information on each page of a multiple-page report. The descriptive information may be in columns, rows, or both. To include a row or column in a heading, just select one cell from a row or column to select the entire row or column. When 1-2-3/G prints the range, it prints the rows and columns that apply to the rows and columns for the print range. For example, a worksheet can have a print range of A:B2..M:L24 and use column A and row 1 as the heading. When 1-2-3/G prints B:B2..B:H24 (the portion of the worksheet in worksheet B that can fit across the page) it prints B:A1..B:A24 as the column heading and B:A1..B:H1 as the row heading.

1-2-3/G [69.4] Ready

File Edit Worksheet Range Copy... Move... Print Graph Data Utility Quit... Help

A:A1

BOSTON.WG1

A	A	B	C	D	E	F	G	
1			Boston Company					
2								
3		JAN	FEB	MAR	APR	MAY	JUNE	JU
4	Salaries	$8,000	$8,200	$8,200	$8,700	$8,700	$7,500	$7
5	Building Operations	1,100	1,100	1,100	1,100	1,100	1,100	1
6	Travel	850	850	850	850	850	850	
7	Supplies	500	500	500	500	500	500	
8	Depreciation	1,200	1,200	1,200	1,200	1,200	1,200	1
9	Equipment Maintenance	750	750	750	750	750	750	
10	Shipping Expense	400	400	400	400	400	400	
11	Data Processing Costs	2,100	2,100	2,100	2,100	2,100	2,100	2
12	Printing & Duplicating	640	640	640	640	640	640	
13	Other	1,030	1,030	1,030	1,030	1,030	1,030	1
14	Total Expenses	$16,570	$16,770	$16,770	$17,270	$17,270	$16,070	$16

Figure 11-4. Worksheet data to use with column headings

descriptive account names will only appear with the first months printed. However, if you specify these account names as a column heading, you can print them on each page. To do this, select Headings Columns from a dialog box to print worksheets. In response to the prompt for columns, select the range A1..A1. Then, when you print the worksheet, begin your print range with B1. (If you begin it with A1, the account name column information is printed twice, as shown in Figure 11-5.) The correct multiple-page printout should look like Figure 11-6.

Row Headings

You use row headings when the identifying data you want repeated on each page is located in rows at the top of your worksheet. Use this option if there are more rows of data than will fit on one page. First, select Headings and Row or click the Row text box. Select a range containing one cell from each row you want to use as a row heading. Once you have defined the heading, check that the print range does not include the heading rows.

The example shown in Figure 11-7 has a set of row headings in column 1, and many rows of data below the headings. Assuming that the model uses the rows 1 through 76, when 1-2-3/G prints the second page, the second page will omit any identifying labels at the top of each

			Boston Company						
		JAN	FEB	MAR	APR	MAY	JUNE	JULY	AUG
Salaries	Salaries	$8,000	$8,200	$8,200	$8,700	$8,700	$7,500	$7,500	$10,000
Building Operations	Building Operations	1,100	1,100	1,100	1,100	1,100	1,100	1,100	1,100
Travel	Travel	850	850	850	850	850	850	850	850
Supplies	Supplies	500	500	500	500	500	500	500	500
Depreciation	Depreciation	1,200	1,200	1,200	1,200	1,200	1,200	1,200	1,200
Equipment Maintenance	Equipment Maintenance	750	750	750	750	750	750	750	750
Shipping Expense	Shipping Expense	400	400	400	400	400	400	400	400
Data Processing Costs	Data Processing Costs	2,100	2,100	2,100	2,100	2,100	2,100	2,100	2,100
Printing & Duplicating	Printing & Duplicating	640	640	640	640	640	640	640	640
Other	Other	1,030	1,030	1,030	1,030	1,030	1,030	1,030	1,030
Total Expenses	Total Expenses	$16,570	$16,770	$16,770	$17,270	$17,270	$16,070	$16,070	$18,570

Figure 11-5. Columns printed twice

	NOV	DEC
Salaries	$10,000	$10,000
Building Operations	1,300	1,300
Travel	850	850
Supplies	500	500
Depreciation	1,200	1,200
Equipment Maintenance	750	750
Shipping Expense	400	400
Data Processing Costs	2,100	2,100
Printing & Duplicating	640	640
Other	1,030	1,030
Total Expenses	$18,770	$18,770

		Boston Company								
	JAN	FEB	MAR	APR	MAY	JUNE	JULY	AUG	SEPT	OCT
Salaries	$8,000	$8,200	$8,200	$8,700	$8,700	$7,500	$7,500	$10,000	$10,000	$10,000
Building Operations	1,100	1,100	1,100	1,100	1,100	1,100	1,100	1,100	1,300	1,300
Travel	850	850	850	850	850	850	850	850	850	850
Supplies	500	500	500	500	500	500	500	500	500	500
Depreciation	1,200	1,200	1,200	1,200	1,200	1,200	1,200	1,200	1,200	1,200
Equipment Maintenance	750	750	750	750	750	750	750	750	750	750
Shipping Expense	400	400	400	400	400	400	400	400	400	400
Data Processing Costs	2,100	2,100	2,100	2,100	2,100	2,100	2,100	2,100	2,100	2,100
Printing & Duplicating	640	640	640	640	640	640	640	640	640	640
Other	1,030	1,030	1,030	1,030	1,030	1,030	1,030	1,030	1,030	1,030
Total Expenses	$16,570	$16,770	$16,770	$17,270	$17,270	$16,070	$16,070	$18,570	$18,770	$18,770

Figure 11-6. Two pages of print using column headings

column if you don't use row headings. The following steps show how to select row 1 in Figure 11-7 for a row heading:

1. Move your cell pointer to A1.
2. Select Print Printer Headings Rows.

1-2-3/G: DESK1.DSK [69.4] Ready

File Edit Worksheet Range Copy... Move... Print Graph Data Utility Quit... Help

A:A1 'Description

INV_PRNT.WG1

A	A	B	C	D	E	F	G
1	Description	Life	Cost	Dept	Type	Inv Code	
2	IBM Selectric Typewriter	5	$980	Accounting	Office	54301	
3	Royal Typewriter	5	$950	Training	Office	54455	
4	Swivel Chair	10	$345	Check	Furniture	54789	
A	A	B	C	D	E	F	G
73	TI Calculator	7	$100	Audit	Office	54177	
74	Walnut Desk	15	$1,200	Cash	Furniture	54138	
75	Xerox Copier	3	$2,500	Cash	Processing	54392	
76	Xerox Copier	3	$2,800	Accounting	Processing	54999	
77							

Figure 11-7. Purchases worksheet for multiple-page printout

3. You only need to select one cell in the row you want to use as a heading. Using the mouse, click any cell in row 1. Using the keyboard, press RIGHT ARROW and then press ENTER. (If you want to use more than one row in your heading, specify a range that includes one cell in each heading row.)

4. Finally, select Range to tell 1-2-3/G what range to print. In this case, specify A2 to F100, carefully excluding the heading row so it does not print twice.

5. Select Go and Quit to print the two pages. The beginning of both pages includes the row headings shown in Figure 11-8.

Setting Display Options

1-2-3/G has several display options that are available with all dialog boxes that print worksheets except File Print. These choices let you include a side frame, a top frame to display column letters, use the colors and shading, and include borders and grids. Initially, 1-2-3/G

Description	Life	Cost	Dept	Type	Inv Code
TI Calculator	7	$100	Audit	Office	54177
Walnut Desk	15	$1,200	Cash	Furniture	54138
Xerox Copier	3	$2,500	Cash	Processing	54392
Xerox Copier	3	$2,800	Accounting	Processing	54999

Description	Life	Cost	Dept	Type	Inv Code
IBM Selectric Typewriter	5	$980	Accounting	Office	54301
Royal Typewriter	5	$950	Training	Office	54455
Swivel Chair	10	$345	Check	Furniture	54789

Figure 11-8. Printout using row headings

assumes that you want to print the worksheet using the colors and shading selected in the worksheet and to separate each cell with borders and grids. You can also change the patterns 1-2-3/G uses to distinguish worksheet colors when you are printing using only one color.

You can add incremental row numbers and column labels as a frame around the range of print data, as shown in Figure 11-9. You add the

A:	A	B	C	D	E	F	G	H	I	J	K
1				Boston Company							
2											
3		JAN	FEB	MAR	APR	MAY	JUNE	JULY	AUG	SEPT	OCT
4	Salaries	$8,000	$8,200	$8,200	$8,700	$8,700	$7,500	$7,500	$10,000	$10,000	$10,000
5	Building Operations	1,100	1,100	1,100	1,100	1,100	1,100	1,100	1,100	1,300	1,300
6	Travel	850	850	850	850	850	850	850	850	850	850
7	Supplies	500	500	500	500	500	500	500	500	500	500
8	Depreciation	1,200	1,200	1,200	1,200	1,200	1,200	1,200	1,200	1,200	1,200
9	Equipment Maintenance	750	750	750	750	750	750	750	750	750	750
10	Shipping Expense	400	400	400	400	400	400	400	400	400	400
11	Data Processing Costs	2,100	2,100	2,100	2,100	2,100	2,100	2,100	2,100	2,100	2,100
12	Printing & Duplicating	640	640	640	640	640	640	640	640	640	640
13	Other	1,030	1,030	1,030	1,030	1,030	1,030	1,030	1,030	1,030	1,030
14	Total Expenses	$16,570	$16,770	$16,770	$17,270	$17,270	$16,070	$16,070	$18,570	$18,770	$18,770

Figure 11-9. Printout with a row and column frame

frame by selecting the Side frame and Top frame check boxes under Display options. You can also use one or the other option by selecting only one check box. You can use this option to display the formulas of your worksheet by changing the default format to Text and then printing the worksheet with a frame. To remove the frame, unselect the appropriate check boxes.

The two other display options determine whether 1-2-3/G prints the worksheet with some of the features that you see in the worksheet window. If you select the Colors and shading check box, the worksheet is printed using the colors selected with the Range Attribute Color and Worksheet Global Screen Attributes commands. When this check box is selected and you are using a noncolor printer, 1-2-3/G prints the different colors as different patterns. You can change the pattern that 1-2-3/G prints for each color. If you unselect this check box, 1-2-3/G prints the worksheet as black letters on white text.

The Borders and grids check box determines whether 1-2-3/G prints the range borders and grid lines. The range borders are added with the Range Attribute Border command and the grid lines are displayed with the Worksheet Global Screen Attributes command. When this check box is selected, 1-2-3/G prints both grid and border lines. If the worksheet does not display grid lines and/or border lines, they don't appear in the printout. When this check box is unselected, 1-2-3/G doesn't print grid lines and lines added with Range Attributes Border.

Setting the Patterns 1-2-3/G Uses To Print Colors

When you print a worksheet that displays colors to a noncolor printer, 1-2-3/G automatically substitutes patterns for the colors. Figure 11-10 shows part of a worksheet that displays some cells as white text on a red background (it appears as black in the figure). When 1-2-3/G prints the worksheet, the printout looks like Figure 11-11. You can change the patterns 1-2-3/G uses to represent each color with the File Print Color Map command. In the command's dialog box, 1-2-3/G indicates the patterns that it will substitute for various different colors. The right side of the dialog box displays the 16 patterns available. To change the pattern for a specific color, select a color from the left side of the dialog box and then choose the pattern from the right side of the dialog box. With a mouse, you can quickly alternate between selecting colors and their associated patterns. Select the OK command button when you are finished. If you are using a keyboard to select colors and patterns,

1-2-3/G: DESK1.DSK [69.4] Ready

File Edit Worksheet Range Copy... Move... Print Graph Data Utility Quit... Help

A:A4 'Customer-id

COLORPRT.WG1

A	A	B	C	D	E	F	G
1			Every Rental Videos				
2							
3			Checked	Checked	Amount		
4	Customer-id	Video	Out	In	Due		
5	21-876	350	30-Aug-89	01-Sep-89	$4.50		
6	23-765	610	30-Aug-89	01-Sep-89	$4.50		
7	34-651	212	01-Sep-89	02-Sep-89	$2.25		
8	11-223	443	01-Sep-89	05-Sep-89	$9.00		
9	56-675	551	02-Sep-89	03-Sep-89	$2.25		
10	77-990	215	02-Sep-89	06-Sep-89	$9.00		
11	11-983	623	03-Sep-89	05-Sep-89	$4.50		

Figure 11-10. Worksheet using colors for ranges

		Every Rental Videos		
		Checked	Checked	Amount
Customer-id	Video	Out	In	Due
21-876	350	30-Aug-89	01-Sep-89	$4.50
23-765	610	30-Aug-89	01-Sep-89	$4.50
34-651	212	01-Sep-89	02-Sep-89	$2.25
11-223	443	01-Sep-89	05-Sep-89	$9.00
56-675	551	02-Sep-89	03-Sep-89	$2.25
77-990	215	02-Sep-89	06-Sep-89	$9.00
11-983	623	03-Sep-89	05-Sep-89	$4.50

Figure 11-11. Printed worksheet using patterns instead of colors

select the color by typing a letter or by moving the dotted outline to the color you want and pressing the SPACEBAR, then select the pattern by moving the dotted outline to the pattern you want and pressing the SPACEBAR. To select the next color, press TAB. When you are ready to select the last pattern, you can type the letter of the pattern you want, which also selects the OK command button. The changes you make in this menu apply to printing any range in the current worksheet file, whether you print the worksheet using the File Print Print Worksheet command or one of the print commands. Changing one worksheet file does not affect other worksheet files.

Selecting the Format of the Output

The two options under Format output in a dialog box to print worksheets allow you to decide whether information is printed with or without formatting that has been added to the text. You can also choose to print formulas rather than the information displayed on your screen.

Printing What You See on the Screen

The default setting under Format output, As displayed, causes your printed report to contain the same information you see on the screen. This means that the results of formulas are printed as values, just as they display on the screen. The formats in effect on your screen display are used for the printout, as are the column widths, row heights, and fonts. In short, you have an exact duplicate of the worksheet portion of the screen display, except that you are not restricted to the size of the screen for your printout range. However, you are restricted to the limitations of the established print page size.

Printing Cell Formulas

In Chapter 7, you learned how to display formulas in cells by using the Range Format Text command. To print a Text format worksheet like the one described in Chapter 7, you can use the As displayed option, since the formulas are already displayed in the example. Alternatively, you can use 1-2-3/G's built-in formula printing option. With this option, you don't have to change the format and width of cells because the package doesn't print the formulas according to the widths of the worksheet columns. Instead, it prints the formulas one per line down the page.

If an entire large worksheet is involved, this approach may produce quite a long list of documentation. However, this is an excellent way to print the formulas for a smaller range of cells, because it involves so little work on your part. You just select your print range and choose Format output and Formulas. Selecting the Go and Quit command buttons then produces a formula listing like the one in Figure 11-12. The formulas print according to the column they are in, with the order being A1, A2, A3, B1, B2, B3, and so on. When you select the Formulas option button, the Display options check boxes and the column and row headings options dim to indicate that they are not available.

The Preview Utility

The first time you print your worksheet, you may not obtain exactly what you want. Fortunately, you can preview the printed worksheet using the Preview utility. The Preview utility creates a Preview window that displays the printout as it will look when printed. If the printout looks right, you can tell 1-2-3/G to print the contents of the Preview window. If the printout is not what you want, you can close the Preview window and try again. Like other 1-2-3/G windows, the Preview window

```
A:A2: [W 15.75] 'Alpen, Pat
A:A3: [W 15.75] 'Arbor, Jim
A:B2: (C2) [W 10.5] 35000
A:B3: (C2) [W 10.5] 23000
A:C2: [W 7.125] 10
A:C3: (F0) [W 7.125] 4
A:D2: (P2) [W 6.625] 0.04
A:D3: (P2) [W 6.625] 0.07
A:E2: (C2) [W 10.25] ((C2-1)*(B2/12))+((12-(C2-1))*(1+D2)*(B2/12))
A:E3: (C2) [W 10.25] ((C3-1)*(B3/12))+((12-(C3-1))*(1+D3)*(B3/12))
A:F2: (C2) [W 9.75] +E2*0.14
A:F3: (C2) [W 9.75] +E3*0.14
```

Figure 11-12. Cell-formulas printout

has a window control menu that you can use to minimize, maximize, position, size, and close the window. You can also perform the same tasks with the mouse.

1-2-3/G redirects output to the Preview window when you select the Screen preview check box in any dialog box that prints worksheets except the Print File dialog box. Figure 11-13 shows a Preview window that contains a worksheet. Notice that each page is represented as a small drawing of what the page will look like. The control line displays the page the mouse is pointing to and the worksheet range that the page is part of. Using the mouse or keyboard, you can expand a page to see it up close. The mouse pointer in a Preview window changes to a magnifying glass. When a Preview window contains multiple pages, their layout depends on the size of the worksheet range printed. The Preview window displays columns of preview pages with each column of preview pages containing the same columns of worksheet data and each row of preview pages containing the same rows of worksheet data. As an example, if you print A1..P75, you should see a window like the one shown in Figure 11-14. The first column of pages corresponds to the

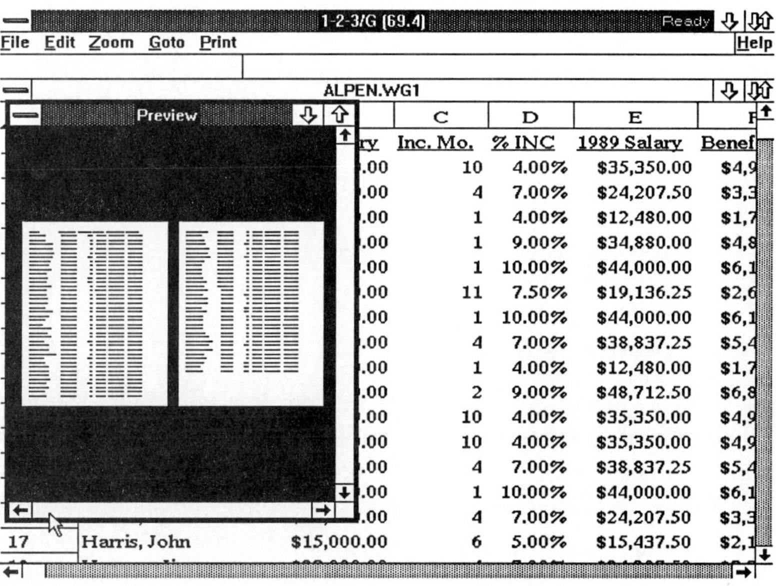

Figure 11-13. Worksheet printed to Preview window

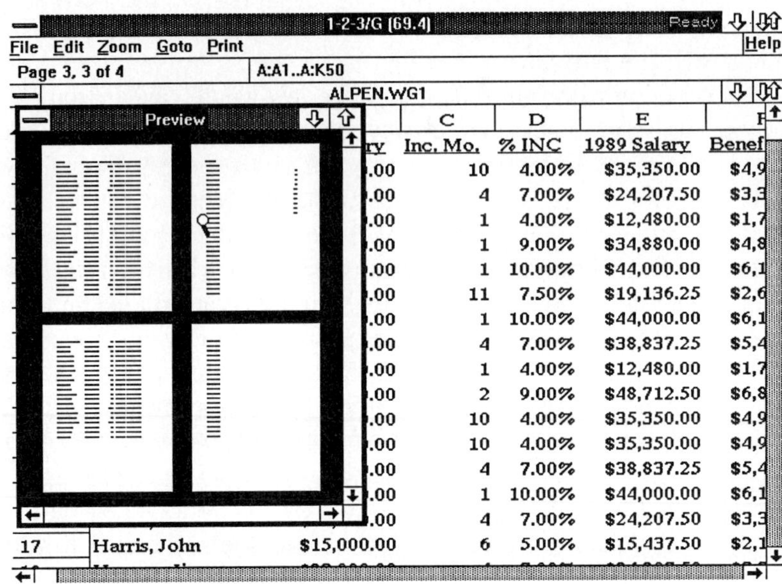

Figure 11-14. Printing a large worksheet

pages that contain columns A through J of worksheet data and the second column of pages corresponds to printing columns K through P. The first row of pages corresponds to the worksheet rows 1 through 38 and the second row of pages corresponds to printing rows 39 through 75. If 1-2-3/G has to split a column or row, a dotted line marks the split.

Using the Preview Window

The Preview utility has its own menu that lets you select the portion of the previewed printout to view and the size of the pages. If you are using a mouse, these changes are easy. With a keyboard, you will use the Preview utility menu commands to perform the same features.

With a mouse, it's easy to change the magnification of one or many pages. Each time you press the left mouse button, you are zooming in one level of magnification. Each time you press the right mouse button, you are zooming out one level of magnification. The number of magnification levels depends on the number of pages in the Preview window. You can zoom out to see all of the pages, as in Figure 11-14, or zoom in to look closely at one page, as in Figure 11-15. The mouse icon, the magnifying glass, selects the page or area of the sheet that you want to be in the center of the window as you zoom in or out. You can also use the scroll bars on the right side and the bottom of the window to change the part of the previewed printout that appears in the window.

With a keyboard, you change the magnification by using the Preview utility commands. The Zoom command changes the level of magnification. Selecting In magnifies the page one level of magnification. Selecting Out contracts the window one level of magnification. Selecting Closest magnifies the screen so that you can read the contents, as in Figure 11-15. Selecting Farthest reduces the magnification so that you can see small versions of every page, as in Figure 11-14. Selecting Page changes the magnification to display an entire page in the Preview window. As with a mouse, the number of magnification levels depends on

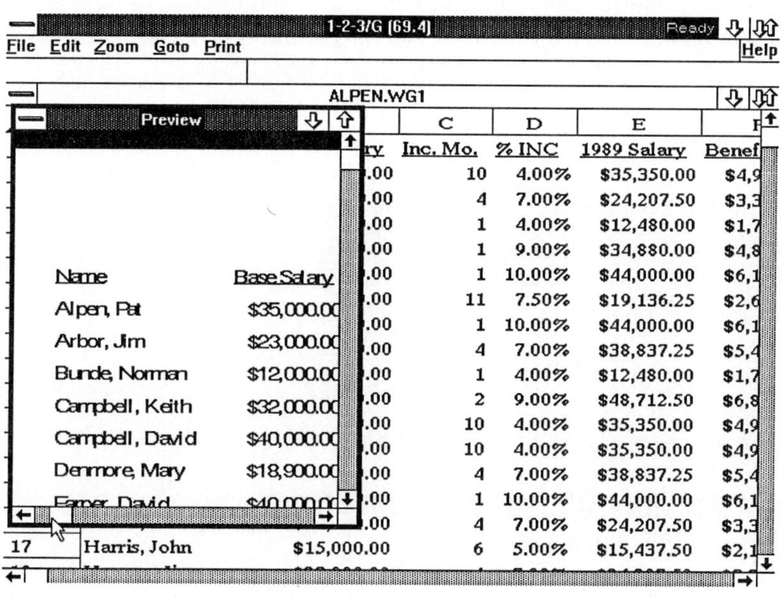

Figure 11-15. Zooming in to see a printout closely

the number of pages in the Preview window. The center of the window remains the same after each magnification change.

With the keyboard, you can use a combination of commands and keys to change what appears in the Preview window. When you are displaying part of a page in the Preview window, pressing HOME moves to the upper-left corner of the page and pressing END moves to the lower-right corner of the page. At other magnification levels when you are displaying more than one page, pressing HOME moves to the first page and pressing END moves to the last page. The Goto Home and Goto End commands also move you to the first and last page. Selecting Goto and Left, Right, Down, or Up moves the previewed output to a different page in the selected direction. Pressing PGUP and PGDN changes the display of the printed output one page at a time. The LEFT ARROW, RIGHT ARROW, DOWN ARROW, and UP ARROW keys shift the part of the page displayed on the screen.

The preview window has three menu commands that do not have mouse equivalents. The Print Printer and File Print Print Preview commands tell 1-2-3/G to start printing the information. This sends the information to the printer or an encoded file. If 1-2-3/G cannot print the information, you may see error messages. When you use the File Print Destination command to select an encoded file for the destination, 1-2-3/G asks if you want to overwrite the file if a file with the same name already exists. When the information is transferred to the printer or the encoded file, 1-2-3/G closes the Preview window. You can also close the Preview window with CTRL-F4 (Close Tool) or with Close from the window control menu, which closes the window without printing the data. You can close the windows if the previewed printout contains data that you don't want. You can also use the Edit Undo command for this purpose. The Edit Undo command removes one range at a time from the Preview window. If one of the printed selections is a collection, 1-2-3/G removes one range at a time from the collection.

Using a Preview Window to Print from Many 1-2-3/G Sources

The Preview utility can combine ranges from other 1-2-3/G sources. While Chapter 17 will show you how to do this with worksheets and graphs, you can use the Preview utility window to print ranges from multiple worksheet files as if they were part of a single worksheet file. For example, suppose that you want to print the worksheet data in the two worksheet files shown in Figure 11-16. You can print the data on one sheet rather than on two separate sheets. First, in the UNITSOLD worksheet file, select Print Printer Range, the range A1..B17, Screen preview, Go, and Quit. Once the worksheet data appears in the Preview window, switch to the UNITSALE worksheet and select Print Printer Range, the range A1..B17, Screen preview, Line, Go, and Quit. The Preview window displays both ranges, as shown in Figure 11-17. When you select Print Printer, 1-2-3/G prints the page as shown in the Preview window. If you hadn't used the Preview window to continually store information, the range from each worksheet would be a separate print job, and the two ranges would print on separate pages.

1-2-3/G [69.4] Ready

File Edit Worksheet Range Copy... Move... Print Graph Data Utility Quit... Help

A:B2 15918.27

UNITSOLD.WG1

A	A	B
1	Units Sold	
2	Product 1	1,376
3	Product 2	983
4	Product 3	9,680
5	Product 4	2,514
6	Product 5	2,039
7	Product 6	9,792
8	Product 7	8,254
9	Product 8	7,073
10	Product 9	9,637
11	Product 10	4,390
12	Product 11	6,347
13	Product 12	2,725
14	Product 13	5,861
15	Product 14	2,821
16	Product 15	1,927
17	Product 16	6,042

(C2) UNITSALE.WG1

A	A	B
1	Sales By Product	
2	Product 1	$15,918.27
3	Product 2	$16,181.22
4	Product 3	$64,893.94
5	Product 4	$19,226.06
6	Product 5	$60,707.34
7	Product 6	$40,075.47
8	Product 7	$15,919.96
9	Product 8	$47,690.83
10	Product 9	$8,473.68
11	Product 10	$12,504.52
12	Product 11	$57,374.21
13	Product 12	$79,227.74
14	Product 13	$5,364.52
15	Product 14	$63,036.44
16	Product 15	$43,439.41
17	Product 16	$43,781.17

Figure 11-16. Two worksheet files to print from

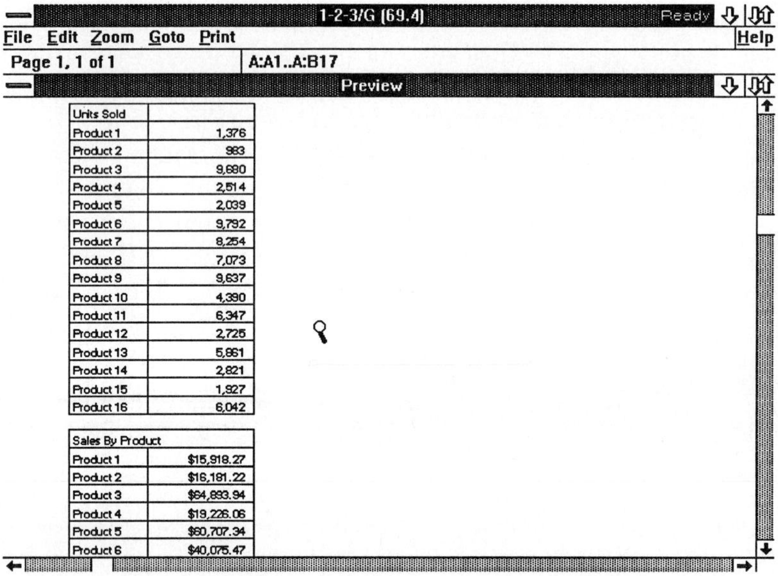

1-2-3/G (69.4) Ready
File Edit Zoom Goto Print Help
Page 1, 1 of 1 A:A1..A:B17
Preview

Units Sold	
Product 1	1,376
Product 2	983
Product 3	9,680
Product 4	2,514
Product 5	2,039
Product 6	9,792
Product 7	8,254
Product 8	7,073
Product 9	9,637
Product 10	4,390
Product 11	6,347
Product 12	2,725
Product 13	5,861
Product 14	2,821
Product 15	1,927
Product 16	6,042

Sales By Product	
Product 1	$15,918.27
Product 2	$16,181.22
Product 3	$64,893.94
Product 4	$19,226.06
Product 5	$60,707.34
Product 6	$40,075.47

Figure 11-17. Printed worksheet files in a Preview window

Additional Printing Options

You have already explored some of the default print settings. In this section you will learn how to tailor printing to the task at hand, making changes that affect only the current worksheet file. You can implement these changes by using the Options dialog box like the one shown in Figure 11-18. This dialog box appears when you select File Print Options or select the Options command button from the File Print Print Worksheet, Print File, Print Encoded, or Print Printer dialog boxes.

Headers and Footers

Headers and *footers* are lines printed at the top and bottom of every page of your report. For example, a header or footer can be a date, company name, report name, department, page number, or a combination of these elements. Except for page numbers, they are the same for each page. When 1-2-3/G prints a header or footer, it advances down the page for the top margin and then prints the header, the worksheet,

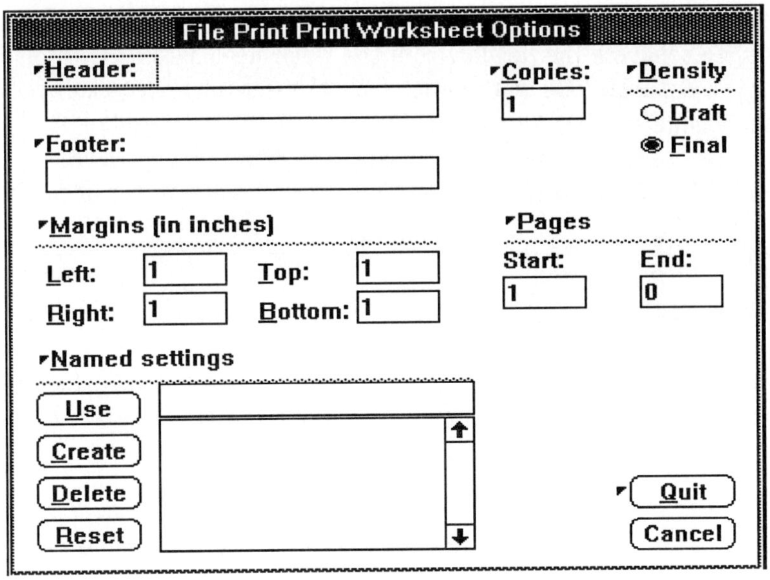

Figure 11-18. Dialog box for supplying printing options

and the footer. It doesn't skip blank lines between the header or footer and the worksheet data. If you omit a header and/or footer, 1-2-3/G uses the area to print more worksheet data.

1-2-3/G allows you to use up to 512 characters for a header or footer. You can split a header or footer into multiple lines, each of which can be divided into thirds. This permits you to include more than one element in a header or footer. Rules for setting up headers and footers are summarized in the "Header and Footer Rules" box.

You specify headers and footers through the Options dialog box for printing. When you select Header or Footer, or click one of the text boxes, 1-2-3/G prompts for the text to appear at the top or bottom of each page. In the text you type for the header or footer, type a tilde (~) where you want to divide the text into lines. For example, to place the company name of Adams & Associates on one line, and the report number 1234 in the next line, enter

Adams & Associates~Rpt. No. 1234

While 1-2-3/G does not limit the number of lines you can use for a header or footer, you are restricted by the 512-character maximum.

Also, the more lines the header and/or footer uses, the fewer lines remain for your worksheet data. You can use the tilde to include blank lines to separate the header from the worksheet data.

To separate the information you are entering into each section of the header or footer, use the vertical bar character (|). Any spaces included between the vertical bars are counted as characters to be included in the header or footer, and affect the alignment of the heading

Header and Footer Rules

Several characters are essential to creating headers and footers: the tilde (~), the vertical bar (|), the at sign (@), the pound sign (#), and the cell reference (\).

~	Splits the header or footer into lines.
|	Divides the three sections of a line in a header or footer (right, left, and center). For example, if you enter the header Accounting Department|Texas Company|Rpt: 8976 the department name prints at the left, the company name in the center, and the report identification at the right. The heading ||Rpt 4356 places the report identifier on the far right; the left and center portions of the header are empty.
@	Incorporates the current system date anywhere in a header or footer. You can also combine it with a character string, such as Today's Date:
#	Incorporates the current page number in a header or footer. You can also combine it with a character string, such as Page Number:
\	Allows you to change header and footer information quickly. Place \ in a header or footer, followed by a cell address or range name (1-2-3/G uses the first cell of the named range). 1-2-3/G then uses the header or footer stored in the cell referenced. For

Header and Footer Rules (Continued)

example, if cell A3 contains

Acme Company~Toy Division|Page #|@

the header entry \A3 places Acme Company on the first line, Toy Division on the left side, the page number in the middle section, and the date at the far right of the second line.

sections. For example, to place the company name of Adams & Associates on the left, and the report number 1234 on the right of a heading, make the following entry in the Header text box:

Adams & Associates || Rpt. No. 1234

When you print the worksheet containing the equipment data, the beginning of the report should look like Figure 11-19. To place a heading only at the right of each page, precede the header information with two vertical bars (||). You can also omit one or both vertical bars. Omitting the second indicates that the line in the header or footer has no right-aligned text. Omitting both vertical bars indicates that all header or footer text is left aligned. You can also use vertical bars in each line of the text to divide each line of the header or footer into left, center, and right segments.

Using Special Characters in a Header or Footer

You can include two special characters in headers and footers to have 1-2-3/G add the page number and date. Use # to indicate where you

Adams & Associates Rpt. No. 1234

Description	Life	Cost	Dept	Type	Inv Code
IBM Selectric Typewriter	5	$980	Accounting	Office	54301
Royal Typewriter	5	$950	Training	Office	54455
Swivel Chair	10	$345	Check	Furniture	54789

Figure 11-19. Printed output with a header

want 1-2-3/G to add a page number. 1-2-3/G begins with 1 and automatically increments the number for each page. In three situations, 1-2-3/G does not start numbering pages with 1. When you are printing to an open Preview window, 1-2-3/G numbers the pages according to the order in which they appear in the Preview window. If you select the Go command button several times before selecting Quit, the pages are numbered according to the order in which they are printed. In other words, if you are printing a range and select Go, Page, Go, and then Quit, 1-2-3/G prints the first part of the print job starting with page 1, and the second part of the print job starting where the first part left off. Finally, you can supply a double number sign followed by the page number on which you want 1-2-3/G to start numbering pages. An example is ##10, which starts numbering pages with 10. You can use this special character to ensure that 1-2-3/G starts numbering on page 1 by including ##1 in the header or footer text.

Use @ to indicate where you want 1-2-3/G to place the current date. 1-2-3/G uses the system date, which is stored in your computer's memory. You can only change this date by accessing the DATE command from a DOS or OS/2 command prompt window, entering a new date, and returning to 1-2-3/G.

The #, ##, and @ characters can be entered in any header or footer segment and can be combined with other text, as in

Adams & Associates~Today's Date: @|Page No: #|Rpt. No. 1234~

The finished product appears at the top of the report in Figure 11-20. While these examples use headers, you have the same results with footers, but the text is at the bottom of the page.

Tip: To date stamp every page of output automatically, use the @ to represent the current date in either a header or footer on every worksheet printed.

Adams & Associates
Today's Date: 04/06/90 Page 1 Rpt. No. 1234

Description	Life	Cost	Dept	Type	Inv Code
IBM Selectric Typewriter	5	$980	Accounting	Office	54301
Royal Typewriter	5	$950	Training	Office	54455
Swivel Chair	10	$345	Check	Furniture	54789

Figure 11-20. Printed output with the date and page number

Storing Headers and Footers in Worksheet Cells

If you need to use different headers and footers when printing different sections of a worksheet, it's easiest to store the complete header or footer in a worksheet cell. Rather than typing the long header or footer entry into the Options menu with each change, you can instead reference the cell address for the appropriate header or footer after selecting the menu option. Type \ and a cell address or range name to represent the referenced cell's contents. If you supply a range name that includes multiple cells, 1-2-3/G uses only the contents of the first cell in the range. The cell or range name can be in any open worksheet file.

Since 1-2-3/G updates the information in the header each time it uses a header, referencing a cell instead of retyping the contents provides the current contents of the cell. An example of the backslash in a footer entry is \A28. In this example, each time 1-2-3/G prints the footer, it checks the current contents of cell A28 and uses the cell's contents in the footer. The referenced cell can include the header and footer special characters. If you use a backslash to reference a cell for a header or footer, you cannot include text other than the backslash plus the cell address in the Header or Footer text box.

Margins

The Margins text boxes in a printing dialog box control the amount of white space at the top, bottom, and sides of your printed document. Figure 11-21 shows a graphic representation of the page layout, including margins. If you are printing a narrow range of cells, for example, you might want to increase the side margin settings to center the output on the paper, as shown in Figure 11-22. On the other hand, if you want to include a great deal of data across a page, you might want to use very small side margin settings, like those in Figure 11-23.

The four Margins options are Left, Right, Top, and Bottom. These values are measured in inches or millimeters, according to the option button chosen under Measurement in the Utility User Settings International dialog box.

The default setting for the margins is 1 inch on all sides, but you can change each margin by selecting Margins and the side, or clicking the appropriate text box and then typing the distance you want for a margin on the selected side. Once you set the margin for one side, you can switch to a different text box to change another margin by pressing TAB or SHIFT-TAB, or clicking the desired text box.

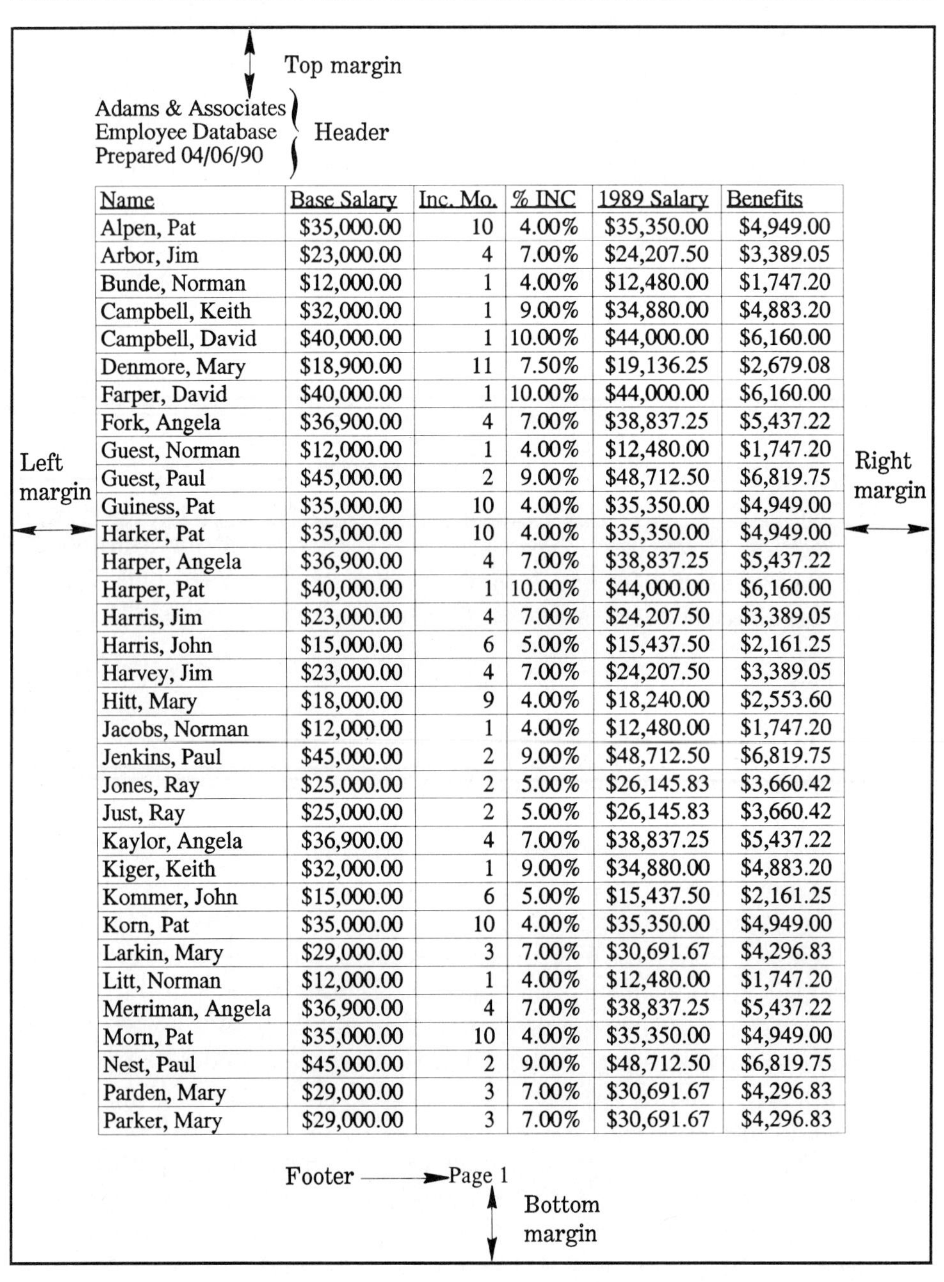

Adams & Associates
Employee Database
Prepared 04/06/90

Name	Base Salary	Inc. Mo.	% INC	1989 Salary	Benefits
Alpen, Pat	$35,000.00	10	4.00%	$35,350.00	$4,949.00
Arbor, Jim	$23,000.00	4	7.00%	$24,207.50	$3,389.05
Bunde, Norman	$12,000.00	1	4.00%	$12,480.00	$1,747.20
Campbell, Keith	$32,000.00	1	9.00%	$34,880.00	$4,883.20
Campbell, David	$40,000.00	1	10.00%	$44,000.00	$6,160.00
Denmore, Mary	$18,900.00	11	7.50%	$19,136.25	$2,679.08
Farper, David	$40,000.00	1	10.00%	$44,000.00	$6,160.00
Fork, Angela	$36,900.00	4	7.00%	$38,837.25	$5,437.22
Guest, Norman	$12,000.00	1	4.00%	$12,480.00	$1,747.20
Guest, Paul	$45,000.00	2	9.00%	$48,712.50	$6,819.75
Guiness, Pat	$35,000.00	10	4.00%	$35,350.00	$4,949.00
Harker, Pat	$35,000.00	10	4.00%	$35,350.00	$4,949.00
Harper, Angela	$36,900.00	4	7.00%	$38,837.25	$5,437.22
Harper, Pat	$40,000.00	1	10.00%	$44,000.00	$6,160.00
Harris, Jim	$23,000.00	4	7.00%	$24,207.50	$3,389.05
Harris, John	$15,000.00	6	5.00%	$15,437.50	$2,161.25
Harvey, Jim	$23,000.00	4	7.00%	$24,207.50	$3,389.05
Hitt, Mary	$18,000.00	9	4.00%	$18,240.00	$2,553.60
Jacobs, Norman	$12,000.00	1	4.00%	$12,480.00	$1,747.20
Jenkins, Paul	$45,000.00	2	9.00%	$48,712.50	$6,819.75
Jones, Ray	$25,000.00	2	5.00%	$26,145.83	$3,660.42
Just, Ray	$25,000.00	2	5.00%	$26,145.83	$3,660.42
Kaylor, Angela	$36,900.00	4	7.00%	$38,837.25	$5,437.22
Kiger, Keith	$32,000.00	1	9.00%	$34,880.00	$4,883.20
Kommer, John	$15,000.00	6	5.00%	$15,437.50	$2,161.25
Korn, Pat	$35,000.00	10	4.00%	$35,350.00	$4,949.00
Larkin, Mary	$29,000.00	3	7.00%	$30,691.67	$4,296.83
Litt, Norman	$12,000.00	1	4.00%	$12,480.00	$1,747.20
Merriman, Angela	$36,900.00	4	7.00%	$38,837.25	$5,437.22
Morn, Pat	$35,000.00	10	4.00%	$35,350.00	$4,949.00
Nest, Paul	$45,000.00	2	9.00%	$48,712.50	$6,819.75
Parden, Mary	$29,000.00	3	7.00%	$30,691.67	$4,296.83
Parker, Mary	$29,000.00	3	7.00%	$30,691.67	$4,296.83

Page 1

Figure 11-21. Page layout

		Bo
	JAN	FEB
Salaries	$8,000	$8,200
Building Operations	1,100	1,100
Travel	850	850
Supplies	500	500
Depreciation	1,200	1,200
Equipment Maintenance	750	750
Shipping Expense	400	400
Data Processing Costs	2,100	2,100
Printing & Duplicating	640	640
Other	1,030	1,030
Total Expenses	$16,570	$16,770

Figure 11-22. Wide margins

Other Printing Options

The Options dialog box for printing includes three options that control the printing process. One option selects the number of copies, a second selects whether the printer uses the highest resolution, and the third selects which pages 1-2-3/G prints. In the Copies text box, you can change the default so that 1-2-3/G prints more than one copy. You can also do this via the print spooler program.

		Boston Company										
	JAN	FEB	MAR	APR	MAY	JUNE	JULY	AUG	SEPT	OCT	NOV	DEC
Salaries	$8,000	$8,200	$8,200	$8,700	$8,700	$7,500	$7,500	$10,000	$10,000	$10,000	$10,000	$10,000
Building Operations	1,100	1,100	1,100	1,100	1,100	1,100	1,100	1,100	1,300	1,300	1,300	1,300
Travel	850	850	850	850	850	850	850	850	850	850	850	850
Supplies	500	500	500	500	500	500	500	500	500	500	500	500
Depreciation	1,200	1,200	1,200	1,200	1,200	1,200	1,200	1,200	1,200	1,200	1,200	1,200
Equipment Maintenance	750	750	750	750	750	750	750	750	750	750	750	750
Shipping Expense	400	400	400	400	400	400	400	400	400	400	400	400
Data Processing Costs	2,100	2,100	2,100	2,100	2,100	2,100	2,100	2,100	2,100	2,100	2,100	2,100
Printing & Duplicating	640	640	640	640	640	640	640	640	640	640	640	640
Other	1,030	1,030	1,030	1,030	1,030	1,030	1,030	1,030	1,030	1,030	1,030	1,030
Total Expenses	$16,570	$16,770	$16,770	$17,270	$17,270	$16,070	$16,070	$18,570	$18,770	$18,770	$18,770	$18,770

Figure 11-23. Narrow margins

The Density option determines whether 1-2-3/G prints the worksheet using final or draft quality. Selecting Draft omits the grid lines, range borders, multiple fonts, and colors. Selecting Final, the default, includes these features and also prints more dots (or more densely) per inch, which creates sharper looking images. Figure 11-24 shows the beginning of the same document printed using Final on the top and Draft on the bottom.

The third choice, Pages, determines which pages 1-2-3/G prints. A start page of 1 and an ending page of 0 prints every page of the printout. When you change the value in the Start or End text box, you are telling 1-2-3/G not to print some of the beginning pages or some of the final pages. For example, if you enter 2 in the Start text box and 3 in the End text box, and then print a range that normally takes four pages, 1-2-3/G prints the data that would appear on pages 2 and 3. This feature lets you print only a section of a worksheet range.

Saving Print Settings

When a worksheet file is saved, the print settings associated with it are also saved. This ensures that you don't have to reenter these settings the next time you use the file. You can also assign a name to a group of print settings. These print settings names are also saved with the file. You can have more than one set of print settings, which you can switch between.

Boston Company						
	JAN	FEB	MAR	APR	MAY	JUNE
Salaries	$8,000	$8,200	$8,200	$8,700	$8,700	$7,500
Building Operations	1,100	1,100	1,100	1,100	1,100	1,100

Boston Company

	JAN	FEB	MAR	APR	MAY	JUNE
Salaries	$8,000	$8,200	$8,200	$8,700	$8,700	$7,500
Building Operations	1,100	1,100	1,100	1,100	1,100	1,100

Figure 11-24. Printed worksheet using final and draft quality

To save the current worksheet's print settings, you must first assign a print settings name. Select Named settings and Create from an Options dialog box for printing worksheets, and provide a name of up to 15 characters. To use a named set, select Named ranges Use and a name from the list. This replaces the current print settings with the print settings associated with the print settings name.

To modify the settings associated with a print settings name, select Named ranges Use to activate the print settings, modify the desired settings, and save the print settings again using the same name. To remove a single print settings name, select Named ranges Delete and choose a print settings name to remove from the list. To remove all print settings names, select Named ranges Reset.

Other 1-2-3/G Commands that Affect Printing

1-2-3/G has several additional commands that affect how it will print your worksheet. These commands include formatting commands such as fonts, numeric formats, colors, column widths, and row heights. You can also use the Worksheet Page command to insert page breaks. You can use other worksheet commands to hide columns, rows, and sheets so that they don't appear in the printed worksheet.

Choosing the Font for Printing

Generally, you should use the font in which you display the worksheet to print the worksheet. Because the display is correct, this ensures that all of the columns are wide enough to display the formatted numbers. You can also change the font that you use for printing with either the Range Attributes Font or the Worksheet Global Attributes Font command. When you select the Setup command button from either dialog box, you change the fonts that 1-2-3/G uses for the worksheet file. You can select a different font from the list. When you select a font from the list box, you can then select whether to change the screen or printer font. In this way, you can use one font for printing and another font for displaying the information on the screen. Once you select Screen or Printer, you can select the font type and size. When you select Change, 1-2-3/G updates the font list to include your selection. Selecting OK updates the font list and returns you to the previous dialog box.

Unless you change the fonts in the list box, 1-2-3/G uses font A, initially set to 8-point Helvetica. You can change the worksheet global font with the Worksheet Global Attributes Font command. Ranges can have their fonts altered with the Range Attributes Font command. 1-2-3/G does not adjust column widths and row heights if the printing font is different than the display font. Headers and footers use font C, which by default is set for 8-point Helvetica.

Other Worksheet Formatting Commands

Most worksheet and range commands that change the worksheet appearance change both the way the worksheet appears on the screen and the way it is printed. These changes include borders, colors, font attributes, numeric format, column width, and row height. Font attributes such as boldface, underlining, strikeout, and italics are included whether or not 1-2-3/G uses the same font for printing and displaying the worksheet. You can remove borders and colors from the printout by unselecting the appropriate check boxes under Display options in a dialog box that prints a worksheet. If the column width is set for a specified number of characters, 1-2-3/G adjusts the column width to the global worksheet font used for printing. If the column width is set for an absolute number of inches or millimeters, 1-2-3/G does not change the column width to fit the font being used for printing. 1-2-3/G adjusts the row height to match the height of the characters printed. If the row height is adjusted to use more or less space, the row height in the printout will also use more or less space to match the worksheet display.

Inserting a Page Break in the Printed Worksheet

A worksheet with many separate sections was a printing nightmare in the past. You could either request each section separately, using Page during print requests, or set up a print macro to automate the printing commands. Neither process was easy.

The Worksheet Page Break command enables you to split the printing of your reports wherever you want. Worksheet Page Break causes 1-2-3/G to insert a blank line, adding a page indicator (::) at the cell pointer location. You can add a page break manually by placing |:: on a blank row. (The Range Erase or Worksheet Delete Row commands can erase an unwanted page break.) 1-2-3/G ignores anything in the row after the page break when printing the page

Figure 11-25 shows a worksheet with a page break inserted. When you select A1..G16 as the print range, the output shown on the two pages in Figure 11-26 is produced. The page break indicator causes the page break to occur before the first page is filled.

Hiding Columns, Rows, and Sheets to Affect Print Range

If you want to print more than one range from a worksheet, you can select the ranges and print them. The second range will print immediately after the first range, as shown in Figure 11-27. Notice that the columns in the second range don't have descriptive information to the left identifying each row.

1-2-3/G (69.4) Ready

File Edit Worksheet Range Copy... Move... Print Graph Data Utility Quit... Help

A:A8 |::

ASSUME.WG1

A	A	B	C	D	E	F	G
1							
2		ASSUMPTIONS					
3		Sales Growth					
4		Product A	10.0%				
5		Product B	12.0%				
6		Product C	9.0%				
7							
8	::						
9	Sales		1991	1992	1993	1994	1995
10	Product A		100,000	110,000	121,000	133,100	146,410
11	Product B		50,000	56,000	62,720	70,246	78,676
12	Product C		45,000	49,050	53,465	58,276	63,521
13	Cost of Goods Sold		87,750	96,773	106,733	117,730	129,873
14	Profit		107,250	118,278	130,451	143,892	158,734
15							
16							
17							

Figure 11-25. Worksheet with page break

Sales	1991	1992	1993	1994	1995
Product A	100,000	110,000	121,000	133,100	146,410
Product B	50,000	56,000	62,720	70,246	78,676
Product C	45,000	49,050	53,465	58,276	63,521
Cost of Goods Sold	87,750	96,773	106,733	117,730	129,873
Profit	107,250	118,278	130,451	143,892	158,734

ASSUMPTIONS	
Sales Growth	
Product	10.0%
Product	12.0%
Product	9.0%

Figure 11-26. Printout using Worksheet Page Break

In many instances, you can't fit all the information in your worksheet across one printed page. You can solve this problem by using the Worksheet Column Hide feature, discussed in Chapter 3, to choose which columns to print, effectively extending the print features. Figure 11-28 presents part of a worksheet, the result of using Worksheet Column Hide to eliminate columns C and D. Selecting Print Printer Range A1..I16, Go, and then Quit creates the printed report shown in Figure 11-29. Hiding columns is one way to print a second range with

Name	Base Salary
Alpen, Pat	$35,000.00
Arbor, Jim	$23,000.00
Bunde, Norman	$12,000.00
Campbell, Keith	$32,000.00

1989 Salary	Benefits
$35,350.00	$4,949.00
$24,207.50	$3,389.05
$12,480.00	$1,747.20
$34,880.00	$4,883.20

Figure 11-27. Two print ranges printed consecutively

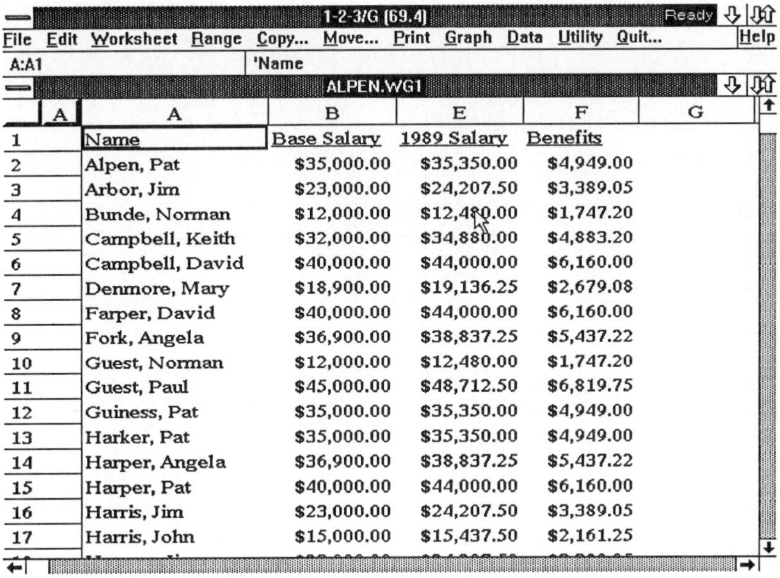

1-2-3/G [69.4] Ready

File Edit Worksheet Range Copy... Move... Print Graph Data Utility Quit... Help

A:A1 'Name

ALPEN.WG1

	A	B	E	F	G
1	Name	Base Salary	1989 Salary	Benefits	
2	Alpen, Pat	$35,000.00	$35,350.00	$4,949.00	
3	Arbor, Jim	$23,000.00	$24,207.50	$3,389.05	
4	Bunde, Norman	$12,000.00	$12,480.00	$1,747.20	
5	Campbell, Keith	$32,000.00	$34,880.00	$4,883.20	
6	Campbell, David	$40,000.00	$44,000.00	$6,160.00	
7	Denmore, Mary	$18,900.00	$19,136.25	$2,679.08	
8	Farper, David	$40,000.00	$44,000.00	$6,160.00	
9	Fork, Angela	$36,900.00	$38,837.25	$5,437.22	
10	Guest, Norman	$12,000.00	$12,480.00	$1,747.20	
11	Guest, Paul	$45,000.00	$48,712.50	$6,819.75	
12	Guiness, Pat	$35,000.00	$35,350.00	$4,949.00	
13	Harker, Pat	$35,000.00	$35,350.00	$4,949.00	
14	Harper, Angela	$36,900.00	$38,837.25	$5,437.22	
15	Harper, Pat	$40,000.00	$44,000.00	$6,160.00	
16	Harris, Jim	$23,000.00	$24,207.50	$3,389.05	
17	Harris, John	$15,000.00	$15,437.50	$2,161.25	

Figure 11-28. Worksheet with hidden columns

descriptive information. This method is also useful when some columns contain data that you don't need in your report.

You can also hide rows and sheets to prevent 1-2-3/G from printing them. Figure 11-30 shows the beginning of a worksheet that has several hidden rows (hidden with the Worksheet Row Hide command) and the

Name	Base Salary	1989 Salary	Benefits
Alpen, Pat	$35,000.00	$35,350.00	$4,949.00
Arbor, Jim	$23,000.00	$24,207.50	$3,389.05
Bunde, Norman	$12,000.00	$12,480.00	$1,747.20
Campbell, Keith	$32,000.00	$34,880.00	$4,883.20
Campbell, David	$40,000.00	$44,000.00	$6,160.00

Figure 11-29. Printed output with hidden columns

Preview window zoomed to show how 1-2-3/G will print the data. Since rows 6 through 8 are hidden, they do not appear in the printout. Hiding sheets works the same way. For example, if you are printing A:A1..C:G20 and hide sheet B with Worksheet Hide, 1-2-3/G prints A:A1..A:G20 and C:A1..C:G20.

OS/2 Programs that Affect Printing

OS/2 has two programs that affect how you print: the Control Panel program and the printer spooler program. The Control Panel program selects the default settings used, including screen display colors, time, date, and country. This program also installs printers, fonts, and queues. The printer spooler program controls how OS/2 prints your printouts that are temporarily stored in the spooler. In OS/2 version 1.1, you use the Control Panel program to change the printer settings. In OS/2 version 1.2, these printer selections are in the Print Manager program.

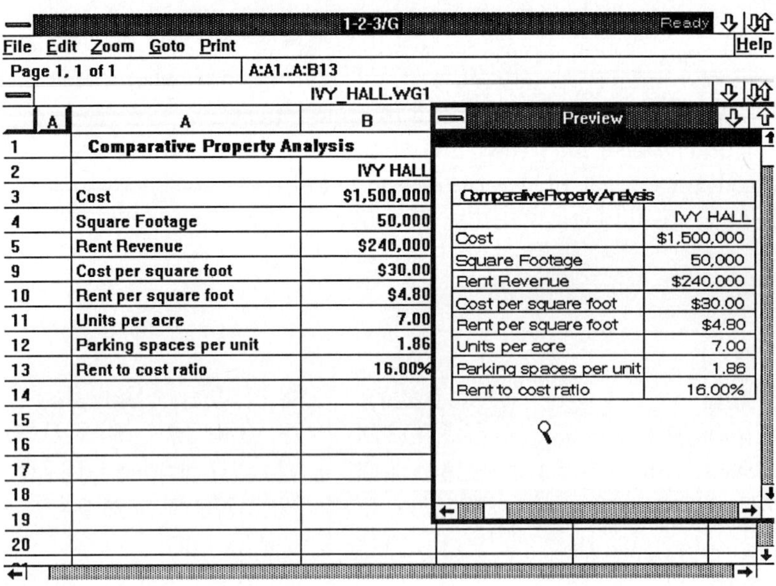

Figure 11-30. Worksheet printed with hidden rows

It's easy to use the Control Panel and printer spooler programs, since they employ the same selection methods that you use in 1-2-3/G. However, to move from one part of a dialog box to another, you will usually use the TAB and SHIFT-TAB keys rather than typing an underlined letter. The following discussion focuses on how you will use these OS/2 programs to print worksheet files, but you use the same programs to print other OS/2 applications. The choices you make depend on whether you are using OS/2 version 1.1 or version 1.2. For both versions, the print spooler has several features for controlling how your worksheets are printed.

The Control Panel Application

The Control Panel Application program controls many settings that all applications, including 1-2-3/G, use. In OS/2 version 1.1, you start this application by activating the Start Programs window, selecting Group and 2. Utility Programs, and selecting Control Panel from the list. To start the Control Panel application in OS/2 version 1.2, activate the Group-Utilities window and select Control Panel from the list. Figure 11-31 shows the Control Panel application for OS/2 version 1.2. In OS/2 version 1.1, the menu bar contains Preferences, Setup, Installation, and Exit. From the Control Panel, you can change the date and time the computer uses by changing the entries in the text boxes. You can also change how quickly the cursor blinks and how quickly you must double-click an item to select it. The menu items in the Options or Preferences pull-down menu let you select whether the computer makes sounds, the colors the screen uses, the width of the border around each Presentation Manager application, whether to switch the mouse buttons so the left button performs the task assigned to the right button, how long OS/2 displays logos and the default country setting which selects how dates, times, currency values and numbers are presented. The Installation pull-down menu is covered in Appendix A which describes how to install 1-2-3/G and a printer. When you are finished with the Control Panel program you can exit the program using the Exit pull-down menu, pressing ALT-F4 or F3, or selecting Close from the system menu icon (the window control box).

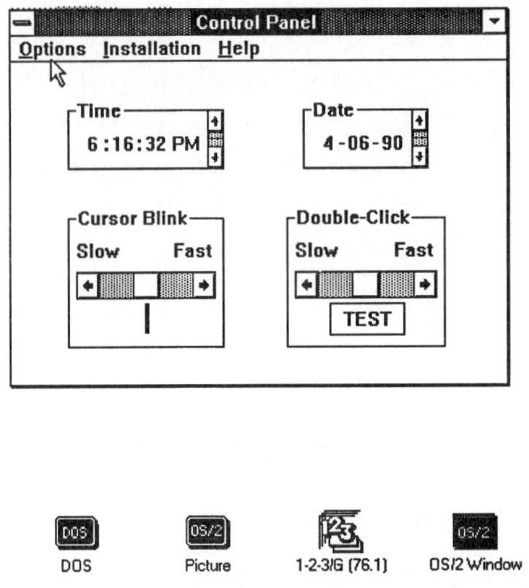

Figure 11-31. Control Panel program for OS/2 version 1.2

The Printer Spooler Program

The printer spooler, when enabled, allows you to control the way OS/2 prints your data. The menu lets you change the order in which OS/2 prints your data, the number of copies OS/2 prints, and lets you cancel one or more print jobs. To activate the printer spooler program (called Spooler Queue Manager in OS/2 version 1.1 and Print Manager in OS/2 version 1.2), select it from the list in the Task Manager or Task List window, or double-click the spooler icon (which looks like a small printer printing a page) from the bottom of the screen or the Group-Main menu in OS/2 version 1.2. Figure 11-32 shows the Print Manager window. The Queue and Job pull-down menus in the Print Manager and the Spooler Queue Manager perform the same functions. Each printer spooler used by the computer is listed, followed by any printing jobs printed to the spooler. Each job has a name, date, and time. From the list, you can highlight a job and change how it is printed or highlight a queue name to change how all jobs in a queue are printed.

When a job is selected and you select Job from the menu bar, you can change how OS/2 prints the job. Selecting Job details displays a

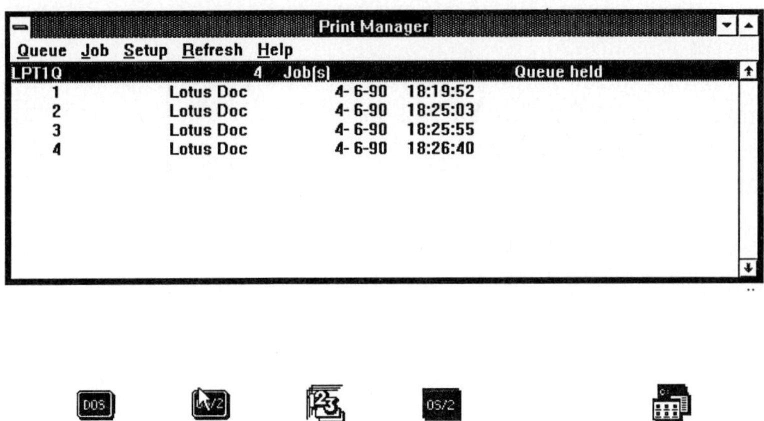

Figure 11-32. Print Manager window for OS/2 version 1.2

dialog box that lists the document's name, its job number, the printer it will be printed on, its job priority number, the queue processor name, any forms code, any processor or networking parameters, and the date and time the print job was added to the queue. You can only change the priority number. When you enter a higher priority number, the print job is printed before print jobs with lower priority numbers. When the list includes several print jobs with the same priority level, they are printed in the order in which they were added to the print spooler. You can also stop a job by selecting Cancel job. When the highlighted job is not the one OS/2 is currently printing, you can select Print Job next to make it the next print job printed. You can also repeat a print job by selecting Repeat job, which is the same as printing two copies by entering **2** in the Copies text box of the Options dialog box for printing a worksheet. If you use both methods of printing multiple copies, your results are multiplied. For example, if the number of copies in the Options dialog box is three and you select Repeat job from the Job pull-down menu, you will have six copies. You can also stop the current job and start it over by selecting Start job again. You would use this option if the paper jammed. You can also temporarily prevent OS/2 from printing a job by selecting Hold job; select Release job when you want a suspended job printed. Use these commands when you have a lengthy print job in the queue that you want to postpone printing so that OS/2 can print some shorter jobs first.

With a queue highlighted, you can use the Queue pull-down menu to change how OS/2 prints all jobs in the queue. The options in the Queue pull-down menu are like the options in the Job pull-down menu, but they apply to every job in the queue.

The Special pull-down menu in OS/2 version 1.1 and Refresh in OS/2 version 1.2 control when OS/2 updates the list in the window. When Auto refresh is selected (a check appears next to it), OS/2 constantly updates the list in the printer spooler program. When Auto refresh is not selected, OS/2 only updates the list when you select Refresh now from the Special or Refresh pull-down menu or press F5.

Selecting Printer Features in OS/2 Version 1.1

The Control Panel program in OS/2 version 1.1 sets many of the printer settings. Selecting Setup from the menu bar lets you change the printer settings.

If you select Printer communications from the Setup pull-down menu, you can select most of the printer settings that you will want to change. This dialog box associates a printer name with a communications port that connects the computer to the printer. You can associate only one printer name with a specific communications port. You can select the printer name from the list box and then select the communications port that the printer uses. The Names command button lets you add, change, and delete printer names. Selecting the Drivers command button displays another dialog box that lets you select the printer driver that the printer name uses. From this dialog box, select a printer name and a printer driver name from each list box. If you select a printer name and the Setup command button, you should see a dialog box customized to match the features of the printer, which allows you to change the default settings of printer. Figure 11-33 shows a dialog box displayed by this selection after the Hewlett-Packard LaserJet series II printer has been selected. This is the dialog box you see when you select File Print Destination from 1-2-3/G and select the Setup command button. As this example dialog box shows, you can often choose the print quality, paper feeding options, orientation, and page size. To change the page size, you must select or create a form—a description of what the page looks like. The dialog box that appears when you add a form usually prompts you for the height and width of the page or form. The exact entries vary by printer. If you select the Comms command button under Port, you can make the same selections for serial ports that you can make by selecting Setup Communications port as described next.

The other menu items in the Setup pull-down menu let you change other settings that 1-2-3/G and other applications use for printing. By selecting Setup and Communications port, you can select the print settings a printer uses if it is using one of the serial ports. These serial ports are called COM1, COM2 and COM3. A serial port uses information such as baud rate, word length, parity, stop bits, and handshake protocol. To determine the specific settings to use with your printer, consult your printer manual. By selecting Printer Defaults, you can select the default printer and the printer timeout times. The default printer that you select in this dialog box is the printer used unless you select a different printer with the File Print Destination command. Under Device not selected, you can enter the number of seconds the printer driver continues sending information to a printer before the OS/2 printer driver decides if the printer is not connected or is off line.

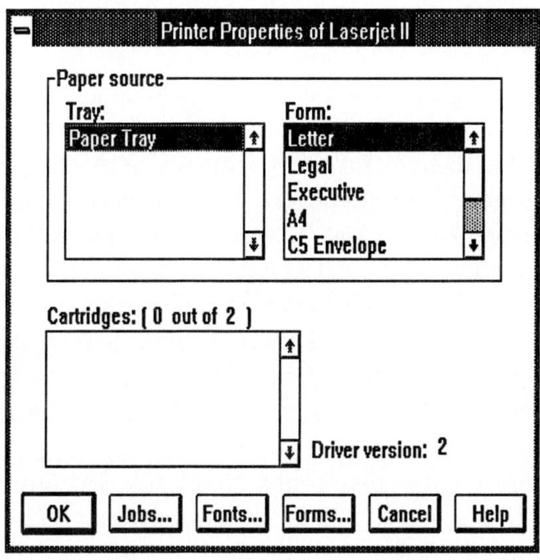

Figure 11-33. Dialog box to select printer settings

Transmission retry is the number of seconds before the printer driver determines that a packet of data needs to be sent to the printer again because the printer is not connected, is off line, or already has all of the data it can process and store. Selecting Queue connections lets you associate a queue with a printer driver name. Selecting Spooler options lets you select if the spooler is enabled, and the directory that contains the temporary spooler files. To disable the spooler, unselect the Spooler enabled check box.

Selecting Printer Features in OS/2 Version 1.2

The Print Manager window controls the settings that you can change for the printer in OS/2 version 1.2. From the Setup pull-down menu, you can change the printer and queue settings.

You will make most changes by selecting Printers from the Setup pull-down menu. The dialog box that appears lists the installed printer drivers. You can add, delete, and change printer drivers. When you add or change a printer driver, the first dialog box lets you select the name, description, device (how the computer connects with the printer), the transmission timeouts, and the default printer driver that the printer name uses. The device is the communications port that connects the computer to the printer. Only one printer name can be associated with a specific communications port. If the communications port is a serial port (COM1, COM2, or COM3), you may need to change the serial port settings by selecting Options and Communications port from the Control Panel program. You need to provide the baud rate, word length, parity, stop bits and handshake protocol (consult your printer manual). The transmission timeout selections are Device not selected and Transmission retry. Under Device not selected, you can enter the number of seconds the printer driver continues sending information to a printer before the driver decides if the printer is not connected or is off line. Transmission retry is the number of seconds before the printer driver determines that a packet of data needs to be sent to the printer again because the printer is not connected, is off line, or already has all of the data it can process and store.

The Change Printer dialog box also has a Printer Properties command button. If you select this command button, OS/2 displays a dialog box that is customized to match the features of the printer. As you saw in Figure 11-33, a dialog box is displayed by this selection after the

Hewlett-Packard LaserJet series II printer has been selected. This is the dialog box you see when you select File Print Destination from 1-2-3/G and select the Setup command button. As this example shows, you can often choose the form or page size and other printing options such as cartridges. To change the page size, you must select or create a form. The dialog box that appears when you add a form usually prompts you for the height and width of the page or form. The exact entries vary depending on the printer.

Selecting Queues lets you add, delete, and change a queue. Each queue has a name, description, and printer associated with it. When you select the Add or Change command button, you can also select a Job Properties command button from the second dialog box. The next dialog box that appears lets you select other printer features such as number of copies, orientation, form size, resolution, and paper feeding mechanism. Selecting Spooler lets you determine whether the spooler is enabled, and the directory that contains the temporary spooler files. Choosing Application defaults selects the default queue and printer that 1-2-3/G and other OS/2 applications use.

Disabling the Printer Spooler

As mentioned, you can disable the spooler. There are several reasons for disabling the print spooler. First, a spooler does not run well with several Epson printer drivers. In addition, if you are using 1-2-3/G on a network, the network has its own spooler, which will control the print jobs sent to the network printers. When the spooler is disabled, 1-2-3/G sends the printing information to the printer instead of the spooler. You should also make sure that you don't try printing from another application when you are printing from 1-2-3/G. When the printer spooler is disabled, you don't have access to the Presentation Manager spooler options for changing how OS/2 prints your data.

Building Advanced Worksheet Applications

TWELVE

In previous chapters, you learned to develop worksheet models by creating formulas and using menu commands. 1-2-3/G has several special commands that you can use to build advanced worksheet applications. While these features are not used in every worksheet model you build, they provide significant time savings when you can use them.

This chapter covers the advanced worksheet model building commands from 1-2-3/G's Data menu. These commands perform sensitivity analysis, data regression, matrix operations, splitting long labels, and sorting. You may not use these features immediately in your own models, but after reading this chapter, you will be able to apply them when your data analysis needs require more advanced operations.

All of the commands introduced in this chapter return values. Since the command results are values, 1-2-3/G does not update the results as the worksheet changes. For example, when you multiply a matrix and then change the values in the matrix, 1-2-3/G does not recalculate the multiplied matrix. With all of these commands, if you want to update the results you must reissue the command.

Performing Statistical Analysis with Data Commands

The statistical options that are part of the data commands allow you to perform sophisticated data analyses. You can do a regression analysis, create a frequency distribution, or prepare a sensitivity analysis.

Sensitivity Analysis

The Data Table options allow you to substitute a range of values in one or two cells referenced by formulas and to record the results of worksheet calculations at the same time. In other words, Data Table automates the what-if analysis you may have been doing as you plugged in new individual variable values and tried to remember the results from previous iterations. The advantage of this automated approach is that 1-2-3/G does all the work, inserts the different values you specify, and remembers the results for you. As you might guess, these results are recorded in a table.

The Data Table command provides five options: a one-way table, a two-way table, a three-way table, a labeled table, and a Reset option that eliminates settings you have made through any of the other choices.

One-Way Data Tables

A *one-way data table* allows you to choose a set of values for one variable and record the results of worksheet formulas in the table's column. The variables are located in the first column of the table. The formulas to evaluate for each value of the variable are located in the row above the first input variable, starting with the next column in the table. The formula results are recorded below the formulas to form a complete table.

What follows are two examples of a one-way table. The first uses the worksheet data shown in Figure 12-1. This worksheet computes commissions using the quarterly sales figure for each salesperson times the commission percentage in D1. If you are considering changing the commission percentage, you might want to know what you would have paid if the different percentage existed in prior periods. You could plug

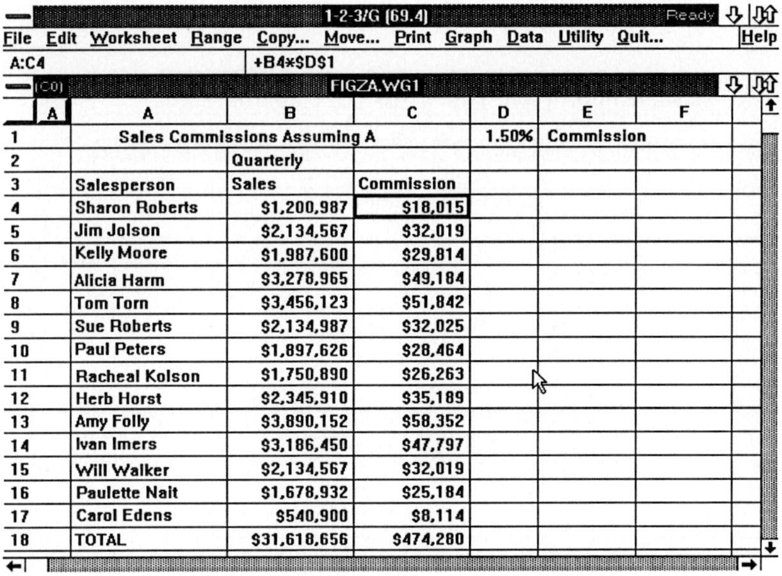

	A	B	C	D	E	F
1	Sales Commissions Assuming A			1.50%	Commission	
2		Quarterly				
3	Salesperson	Sales	Commission			
4	Sharon Roberts	$1,200,987	$18,015			
5	Jim Jolson	$2,134,567	$32,019			
6	Kelly Moore	$1,987,600	$29,814			
7	Alicia Harm	$3,278,965	$49,184			
8	Tom Torn	$3,456,123	$51,842			
9	Sue Roberts	$2,134,987	$32,025			
10	Paul Peters	$1,897,626	$28,464			
11	Racheal Kolson	$1,750,890	$26,263			
12	Herb Horst	$2,345,910	$35,189			
13	Amy Folly	$3,890,152	$58,352			
14	Ivan Imers	$3,186,450	$47,797			
15	Will Walker	$2,134,567	$32,019			
16	Paulette Nait	$1,678,932	$25,184			
17	Carol Edens	$540,900	$8,114			
18	TOTAL	$31,618,656	$474,280			

Figure 12-1. Commission schedule

individual values into D1 one by one and monitor the effect on the total commission calculation in C20. However, it is faster to have 1-2-3/G do the work for you.

Before you select Data Table, you need to set up the framework for the table. Record the values you want to substitute for D1 in a column. The example in Figure 12-2 uses I3..I17, but you can use any empty location. If you are using values in even increments, you can have Data Fill generate these values for you. Next, record the formula or formulas you wish to evaluate, placed one column to the right of and one row above the values. In this example, a reference to C19 suffices to evaluate total commission. This entry is made in J2. After entering **+C19**, you can format the cell as text to display the formula. At this time, the table looks like the display in Figure 12-2. After completing these two preliminary steps, you are ready to use the Data Table command.

Tip: If your data table input values are evenly spaced, use the Data Fill command to generate the values. This makes it easier to set up a data table.

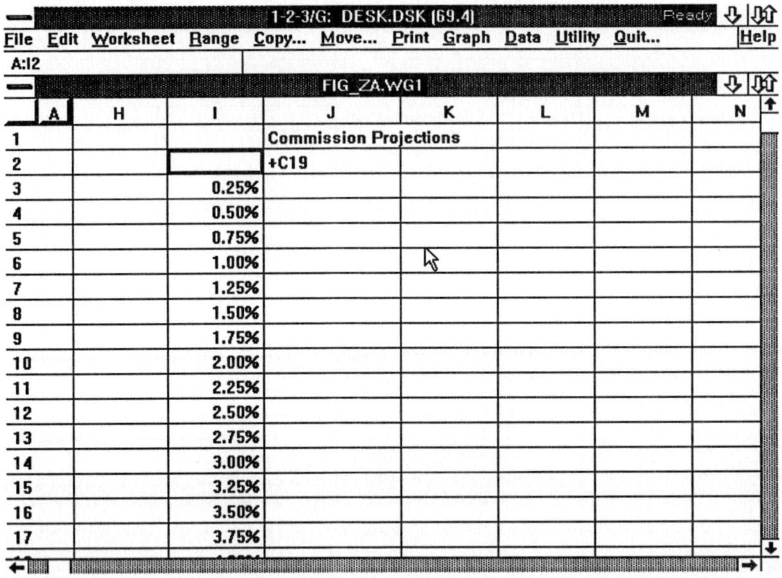

1-2-3/G: DESK.DSK [69.4] Ready

File Edit Worksheet Range Copy... Move... Print Graph Data Utility Quit... Help

A:I2

FIG_ZA.WG1

A	H	I	J	K	L	M	N
1			Commission Projections				
2			+C19				
3		0.25%					
4		0.50%					
5		0.75%					
6		1.00%					
7		1.25%					
8		1.50%					
9		1.75%					
10		2.00%					
11		2.25%					
12		2.50%					
13		2.75%					
14		3.00%					
15		3.25%					
16		3.50%					
17		3.75%					

Figure 12-2. Framework of one-way table

Move your cell pointer to I2, the blank cell to the left of the formulas and immediately above the values. If you want, select the range containing the table before you choose the command. Select Data Table and select 1 for a one-way table. 1-2-3/G displays any range that you selected before choosing this command. Select the range I2..J17 for the table range location. You can select the range by dragging the mouse, typing the range address or name, selecting the range with the arrow keys, or pressing F3 (Name) to select a range name from a list.

1-2-3/G's next prompt is for the input cell. This is the cell into which you want to plug the values from the commission percentage column, one by one. For the example, this is D1. When you click the OK command button or press ENTER, 1-2-3/G takes the first value in the input column and plugs it into D1 in the model. After the first calculation is completed, 1-2-3/G records the result in the table and repeats the process for each of the remaining values. Figure 12-3 shows the level of total commissions at a variety of percentages. Remember, if you change the formulas in your model, the table is not updated to reflect these changes. To update the table values, re-issue the Data Table command.

1-2-3/G: DESK.DSK [69.4] Ready

File Edit Worksheet Range Copy... Move... Print Graph Data Utility Quit... Help

A:J3 79046.64

(C0) FIG_ZA.WG1

	A	H	I	J	K	L	M	N
1				Commission Projections				
2				+C19				
3			0.25%	$79,047				
4			0.50%	$158,093				
5			0.75%	$237,140				
6			1.00%	$316,187				
7			1.25%	$395,233				
8			1.50%	$474,280				
9			1.75%	$553,326				
10			2.00%	$632,373				
11			2.25%	$711,420				
12			2.50%	$790,466				
13			2.75%	$869,513				
14			3.00%	$948,560				
15			3.25%	$1,027,606				
16			3.50%	$1,106,653				
17			3.75%	$1,185,700				

Figure 12-3. Commission table output

Since you are using the same settings, just press F8 (Table) and 1-2-3/G recalculates the last data table you calculated.

Tip: Use F8 (Table) to recalculate tables instead of executing the Data Table command each time you want to update the values of the formulas. Pressing F8 re-executes the last Data Table command.

The second example one-way table uses more than one formula. Figure 12-4 shows the model and the completed table. The model projects sales, cost of goods sold, and profit through 1996, using a 9 percent fixed growth rate for sales, and 45 percent as the cost of goods sold percentage. Suppose you want to consider the impact on sales, costs, and profits of variations in the sales growth factor. Place the variable values in A8..A17. References to the cells containing the formulas to be evaluated are placed in B7..D7, as +G4, +G2, and +G3. Select Data Table and then 1 to define the table as A7..D17 and the input cell as H7. The table range must include the formulas in the top row and the input values in the leftmost column. The results are shown in cells B8..D17 of the figure.

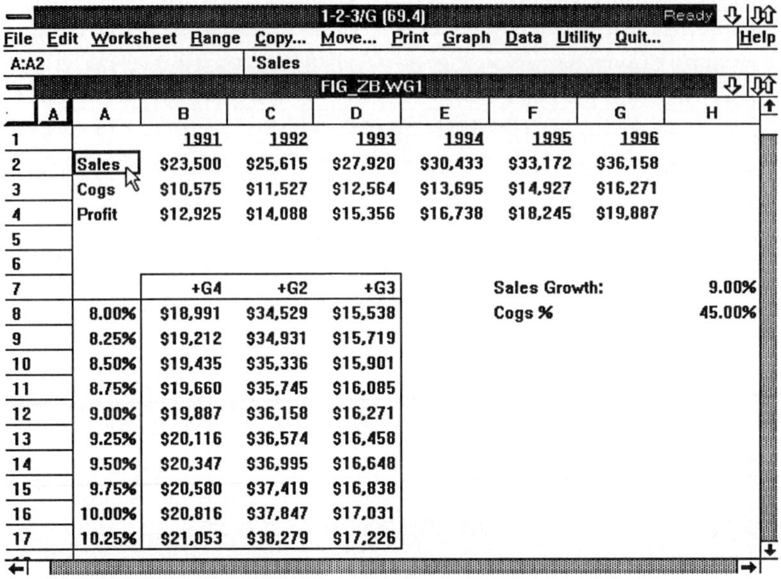

1-2-3/G (69.4) Ready

File Edit Worksheet Range Copy... Move... Print Graph Data Utility Quit... Help

A:A2 'Sales

FIG_ZB.WG1

	A	B	C	D	E	F	G	H
1		1991	1992	1993	1994	1995	1996	
2	Sales	$23,500	$25,615	$27,920	$30,433	$33,172	$36,158	
3	Cogs	$10,575	$11,527	$12,564	$13,695	$14,927	$16,271	
4	Profit	$12,925	$14,088	$15,356	$16,738	$18,245	$19,887	
5								
6								
7		+G4	+G2	+G3		Sales Growth:		9.00%
8	8.00%	$18,991	$34,529	$15,538		Cogs %		45.00%
9	8.25%	$19,212	$34,931	$15,719				
10	8.50%	$19,435	$35,336	$15,901				
11	8.75%	$19,660	$35,745	$16,085				
12	9.00%	$19,887	$36,158	$16,271				
13	9.25%	$20,116	$36,574	$16,458				
14	9.50%	$20,347	$36,995	$16,648				
15	9.75%	$20,580	$37,419	$16,838				
16	10.00%	$20,816	$37,847	$17,031				
17	10.25%	$21,053	$38,279	$17,226				

Figure 12-4. One-way table with multiple formulas

Two-Way Data Tables

The Data Table 2 command allows you to build a *two-way table* in which you supply input values for two variables. 1-2-3/G then applies these values when recalculating the worksheet and recording the result of one of the worksheet formulas in the table. Two-way tables differ from one-way tables in that they use two sets of variable values and can record the results of only one formula. Data Table 2 allows you to see which variable the formula being evaluated is most sensitive to.

Like one-way tables, two-way tables require a significant amount of preliminary work. The example uses a two-way table with the model in Figure 12-5 for payment calculations. The payment calculation is dependent on the amount borrowed, the interest rate, and the term of the loan. The amount borrowed may vary, since it is equal to the cost of the new home minus the equity from the sale of the existing home. While holding the loan term constant, you can use Data Table 2 to vary both interest rate and equity received from the sale of an existing home.

Values for the first input variable (the interest rate) are stored in one column of the worksheet. Values for the second input value (equity)

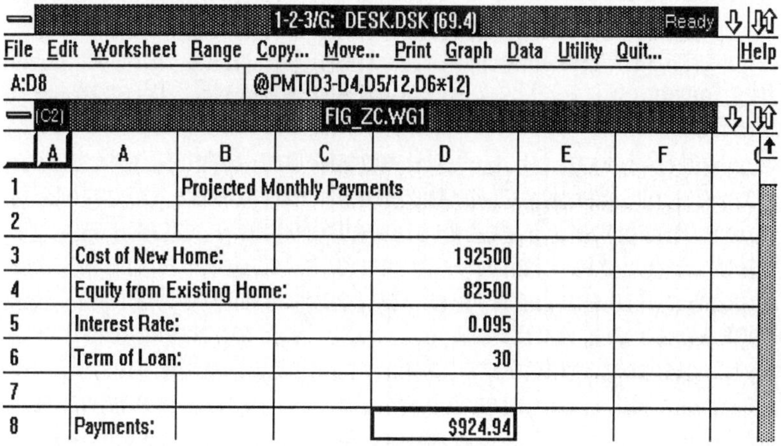

1-2-3/G: DESK.DSK (69.4) Ready

File Edit Worksheet Range Copy... Move... Print Graph Data Utility Quit... Help

A:D8 @PMT(D3-D4,D5/12,D6*12)

(C2) FIG_ZC.WG1

A	A	B	C	D	E	F
1		Projected Monthly Payments				
2						
3	Cost of New Home:			192500		
4	Equity from Existing Home:			82500		
5	Interest Rate:			0.095		
6	Term of Loan:			30		
7						
8	Payments:			$924.94		

Figure 12-5. Model used in two-way table

are placed one row above and one cell to the right of the top value for input variable 1. The values for the second input variable are placed across the row. A formula or a reference to a formula is then placed in the cell at the top of the column used for input variable 1.

The payment example in Figure 12-6 uses column H for the values

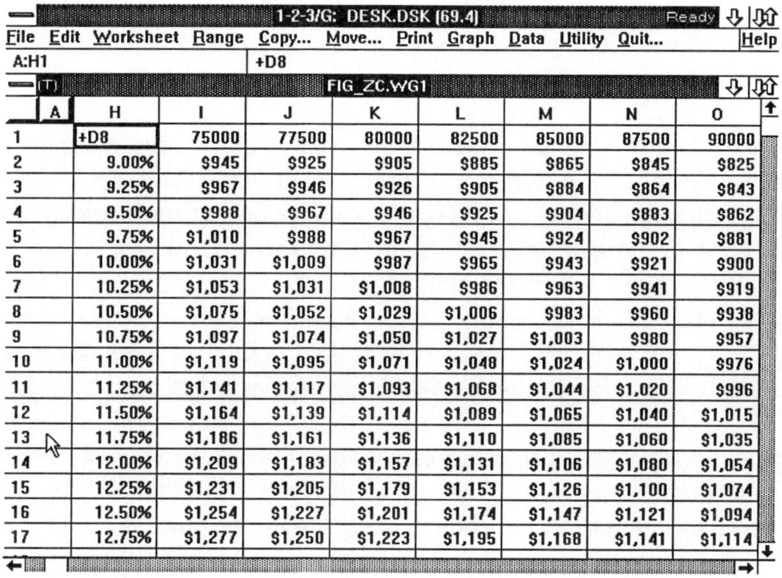

1-2-3/G: DESK.DSK (69.4) Ready

File Edit Worksheet Range Copy... Move... Print Graph Data Utility Quit... Help

A:H1 +D8

(T) FIG_ZC.WG1

A	H	I	J	K	L	M	N	O
1	+D8	75000	77500	80000	82500	85000	87500	90000
2	9.00%	$945	$925	$905	$885	$865	$845	$825
3	9.25%	$967	$946	$926	$905	$884	$864	$843
4	9.50%	$988	$967	$946	$925	$904	$883	$862
5	9.75%	$1,010	$988	$967	$945	$924	$902	$881
6	10.00%	$1,031	$1,009	$987	$965	$943	$921	$900
7	10.25%	$1,053	$1,031	$1,008	$986	$963	$941	$919
8	10.50%	$1,075	$1,052	$1,029	$1,006	$983	$960	$938
9	10.75%	$1,097	$1,074	$1,050	$1,027	$1,003	$980	$957
10	11.00%	$1,119	$1,095	$1,071	$1,048	$1,024	$1,000	$976
11	11.25%	$1,141	$1,117	$1,093	$1,068	$1,044	$1,020	$996
12	11.50%	$1,164	$1,139	$1,114	$1,089	$1,065	$1,040	$1,015
13	11.75%	$1,186	$1,161	$1,136	$1,110	$1,085	$1,060	$1,035
14	12.00%	$1,209	$1,183	$1,157	$1,131	$1,106	$1,080	$1,054
15	12.25%	$1,231	$1,205	$1,179	$1,153	$1,126	$1,100	$1,074
16	12.50%	$1,254	$1,227	$1,201	$1,174	$1,147	$1,121	$1,094
17	12.75%	$1,277	$1,250	$1,223	$1,195	$1,168	$1,141	$1,114

Figure 12-6. Two-way table for payment calculation

for input variable 1. Values are in H2..H17, beginning with 9 percent, adding increments of 0.25 percent, and ending with 12.75 percent. The equity figures start in I1 with 75000 and proceed at increments of 2500, ending with 90000 in O1. Cell H1 contains the formula reference, +D8, that represents the payment calculated. If you want this cell to display as a formula, format the cell as text with Range Format Text.

Now, select Data Table and choose 2 from the submenu. The first prompt asks for the location of the table, which is H1..O17. The next prompt asks for the cell to use for the first input value, which is D5. Answer the third prompt by typing or pointing to **D4**, the second input cell. You can enter all of these locations as a range, as a range name, or by pointing with the arrow keys or the mouse. After you click the OK command button or press ENTER, 1-2-3/G provides the results shown in Figure 12-6.

You can use this table of results to determine the monthly payment assuming the amount borrowed is $192,500 less the amount in row 1. In column H, locate the interest rate that you think you can obtain for a loan. Then use that row to determine your payments at different levels of borrowing. Similarly, you can use the column for any given borrowing level and determine your payments, based on one of the interest rates in column H.

Three-Way Data Tables

Selecting Data Table and then 3 allows you to build a three-dimensional, or *three-way* table in which you supply input values for three variables. 1-2-3/G then applies these values when recalculating the worksheets and recording the result of one of the worksheet formulas in the table. Three-way tables use three sets of variable values and can record the results of only one formula. Also, three-way tables use a separate worksheet for each value of the third input variable. Data Table 3 lets you see which variable the formula being evaluated is most sensitive to.

Like two-way tables, three-way tables require a significant amount of preliminary work. The example uses a three-way table with the model in Figure 12-7 for present value of an annuity calculations. The present value of an annuity is dependent on the amount paid each period, the interest rate, and the number of periods. By adding the annuity length as a third variable, you can use Data Table 3 to vary the periodic payment, the interest rate, and the number of periods (annuity length).

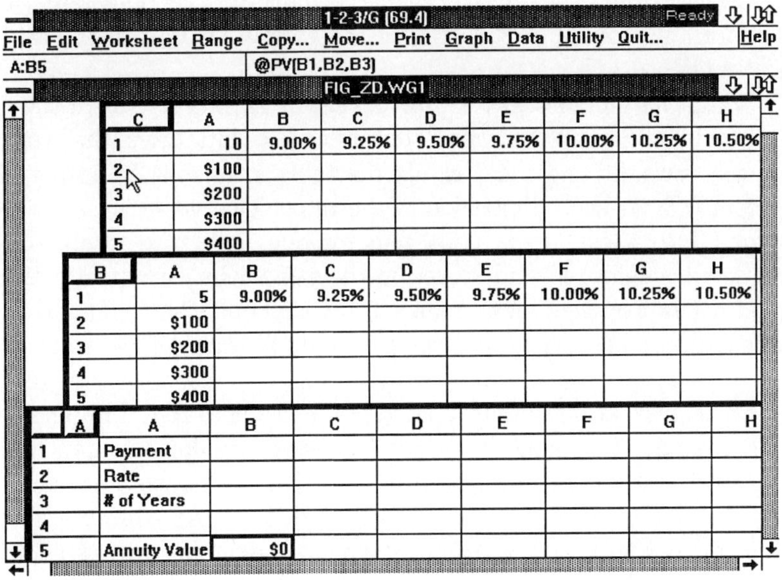

1-2-3/G [69.4] Ready

File Edit Worksheet Range Copy... Move... Print Graph Data Utility Quit... Help

A:B5 @PV(B1,B2,B3)

FIG_ZD.WG1

C	A	B	C	D	E	F	G	H
1	10	9.00%	9.25%	9.50%	9.75%	10.00%	10.25%	10.50%
2	$100							
3	$200							
4	$300							
5	$400							

B	A	B	C	D	E	F	G	H
1	5	9.00%	9.25%	9.50%	9.75%	10.00%	10.25%	10.50%
2	$100							
3	$200							
4	$300							
5	$400							

A	A	B	C	D	E	F	G	H
1	Payment							
2	Rate							
3	# of Years							
4								
5	Annuity Value	$0						

Figure 12-7. Preliminary work for a three-way table

Values for the first input variable are stored in one column of the data table, as in Column A of Figure 12-7. Values for the second input value are placed one row above and one cell to the right of the top value for input 1. In Figure 12-7, the values for the second input value start at B1 and continue across the row.

Once the first and second input variables are stored in the usual way in the first data table worksheet, you create the data tables in the other sheets. Each worksheet must use the same rows and columns for the data table. You may want to use the Copy command to copy the data table setup from the first sheet to the other sheets. You can also supply different input values for the first and second input variables in the subsequent sheets. Finally, all of the third variables are entered in the upper corner of the data table in separate worksheets, at the intersection of the column and row of data values already entered for the first two variables.

Unlike Data Table 1 and Data Table 2, Data Table 3 places the worksheet formula or a reference to one in a cell outside the data table. This formula supplies the table entries as the values of the variables change. Other formulas can exist on the worksheet, but one formula is singled out, and its results provide the entries within the table. This formula does not include references to values in the data table, but to other formulas or input cells where the variable values in the table are substituted.

When the table is set up, you can select Data Table 3. In the dialog box, you must supply the range containing the data table, the input cells for each variable, and the formula the table evaluates. You must define an input cell for each dimension of the table. The values in the table are plugged into these input cells one by one, and the results of each iteration are captured and stored in the table cells. Systematically, each input cell is assigned new values from the table shell, and the Data Table command returns the formula results for each of the values of the three variables.

Look back at the annuity example in Figure 12-7. The first worksheet contains the input variables cells and the formula for the data table. The formula is stored in A:B5. The data table is located in B:A1..F:K6. For each sheet in the data table, A2..A6 contains the input values for variable 1 (the periodic payment) beginning with $100, adding increments of $100, and ending with $500. B1..K1 in each worksheet is for the input values for variable 2 (the interest rate) beginning with 9 percent, adding increments of 0.25 percent, and ending with 11.25 percent. A1 in each worksheet is for the input values for variable 3 (the number of periods) beginning with 5, adding increments of 5, and ending with 25. In this example, variable 3 is the only value that is different in each worksheet.

With these preliminaries accomplished, select Data Table 3. The first prompt asks for the location of the table; select B:A1..F:K6. Click the next text box or press ENTER or TAB. A text box asks for the cell containing the formula to evaluate for each set of values in the data table. In the annuity example, select A:B5. In the next text box, 1-2-3/G prompts for the input cell to use for the first input variable. In this example, the input cell is A:B1, which you can point to with the mouse or arrow keys or type as a range name or address. The same procedure works for A:B2, the second input cell, and A:B3, the third input cell. After you respond to this last prompt, 1-2-3/G provides the results shown in Figure 12-8.

You can use this table of results to determine the present value of annuities for various payment amounts, interest rates, and payment periods. Move to the worksheet with the desired number of years in the upper-left corner, and look down the column with the desired interest rate to determine what the annuity is worth. You can also look across

1-2-3/G: DESK.DSK (69.4) Ready

File Edit Worksheet Range Copy... Move... Print Graph Data Utility Quit... Help

A:B5 @PV(B1,B2,B3)

FIG_ZD.WG1

C	A	B	C	D	E	F	G	H
1	10	9.00%	9.25%	9.50%	9.75%	10.00%	10.25%	10.50%
2	$100	$642	$635	$628	$621	$614	$608	$601
3	$200	$1,284	$1,270	$1,256	$1,242	$1,229	$1,216	$1,203
4	$300	$1,925	$1,904	$1,884	$1,863	$1,843	$1,824	$1,804
5	$400	$2,567	$2,539	$2,512	$2,484	$2,458	$2,432	$2,406

B	A	B	C	D	E	F	G	H
1	5	9.00%	9.25%	9.50%	9.75%	10.00%	10.25%	10.50%
2	$100	$389	$386	$384	$382	$379	$377	$374
3	$200	$778	$773	$768	$763	$758	$753	$749
4	$300	$1,167	$1,159	$1,152	$1,145	$1,137	$1,130	$1,123
5	$400	$1,556	$1,546	$1,536	$1,526	$1,516	$1,507	$1,497

A	A	B	C	D	E	F	G	H
1	Payment							
2	Rate							
3	# of Years							
4								
5	Annuity Value	$0						

Figure 12-8. Three-way table

the row for a particular payment amount and determine the present value at various interest rates.

Tip: When you are selecting variables for a three-way table, use the variable with the fewest values as the third input variable. Since each third input cell value creates a table on a different worksheet, using a third variable with many values can fill the computer's memory quickly.

Using Labeled Data Tables in Sensitivity Analysis

The fourth type of data table is a labeled data table. A labeled data table uses the intersection of the table's values to select where 1-2-3/G returns the values of one or more formulas. A labeled data table circumvents the limits presented by the other Data Table commands. For example, Data Table 1 requires that the input values be stored in the first column of the data table. With Data Table Labeled, you can create one-way tables with the input values in a column, a row, or on multiple worksheets. The Data Table Labeled command also allows you to:

- Include blank rows, columns, and worksheets between the input values and the results, and among the results
- Include more labels to document the table and make it easier to understand
- Evaluate multiple formulas
- Include formulas within the data table that operate on the results. This feature can add some numbers generated by the table
- Include more than three variables by having multiple variables for a column, row, or worksheet that are assigned different input values
- Use sets of input variables rather than one variable value that is unique for each column, row, or sheet

The Data Table Labeled command requires more preliminary work than the other Data Table commands. The following paragraphs show you how to create a simple one-way labeled table, and a more complicated three-way table. The steps for creating a labeled table are summarized in the "Creating a Labeled Table" box.

Creating a Simple Labeled Table

You can use the Data Table Labeled command to create one- and two-way tables that have a different orientation than Data Table 1 and Data Table 2 tables. The Data Table Labeled command can also create tables that manipulate more values than the other tables. Figure 12-9 shows the preliminary work of a labeled table that uses these features. This table computes the net profit and the after-tax profit using assumptions about the sales growth rate, the cost of goods sold (COGS) percentage, and operating expenses. The formulas (A16..B18) and the income statement (A10..B14) appear using the Text format. The data in rows 3 and 4 is formatted using the Percent format; and row 5 is formatted as Currency.

Creating a Labeled Table

You must follows these steps to create a labeled table:

1. Select the input cells you want to use for the labeled input variables and enter labels next to them.
2. Enter the formulas that you want evaluated in the table. List the formula name label on one row and the formula itself in the cell below.
3. Select an area in the worksheet file that you want to use for the data table.
4. Enter the values that you want plugged in as column variable values. Place them above or below where you want 1-2-3/G to fill in the values. If you have multiple-column variable values, they must be in adjacent rows.
5. Enter the values that you want plugged in as row variable values. Place them to the right or to the left of where you want 1-2-3/G to fill in the values. If you have multiple-row variable values, they must be in adjacent columns.
6. Enter the values that you want plugged in as sheet variable values. They must be in the same cell in each sheet, but can be anywhere on each sheet.
7. Enter the formula labels (entered in Step 2) above or below column variable values, or to the left or right of the row variable values. The formula labels must be on the opposite side of the column or row input variables as the values that this command generates. You can use the label fill character (a hyphen) to let a formula label extend its display across multiple columns.
8. Select Data Table Labeled Formulas. Select the formula range created in Step 2; then select the formula label range selected in Step 7.

Creating a Labeled Table (Continued)

9. Select the Across option if you have entered column variable values. Specify the cells entered in Step 4. For each row in the column variable values, 1-2-3/G prompts for confirmation and the input cell.

10. Select the Down option if you have entered row variable values. Specify the cells entered in Step 5. For each column in the column variable values, 1-2-3/G prompts for confirmation and the input cell.

11. Select the Sheets option if you have entered worksheet variable values. Specify the cells entered in Step 6. For each cell in the worksheets, 1-2-3/G prompts for confirmation and the input cell.

12. Choose Go to create the table.

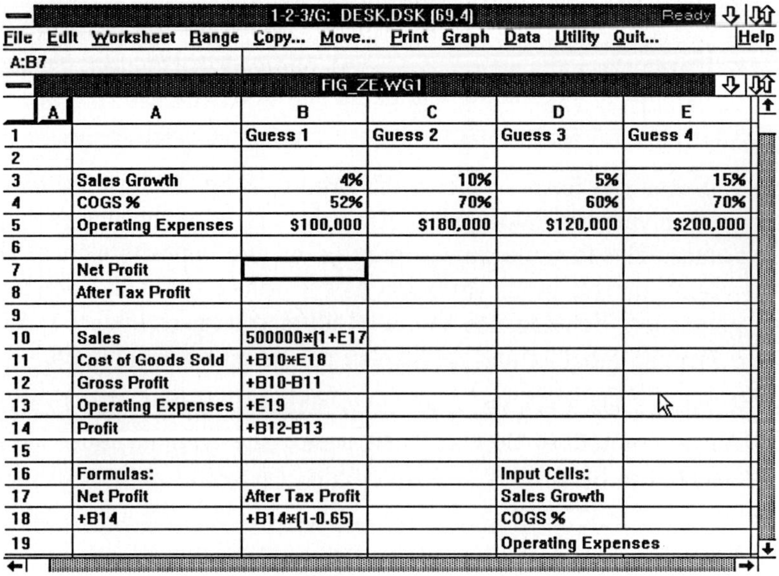

1-2-3/G: DESK.DSK (69.4) Ready

File Edit Worksheet Range Copy... Move... Print Graph Data Utility Quit... Help

A:B7

FIG_ZE.WG1

A	A	B	C	D	E
1		Guess 1	Guess 2	Guess 3	Guess 4
2					
3	Sales Growth	4%	10%	5%	15%
4	COGS %	52%	70%	60%	70%
5	Operating Expenses	$100,000	$180,000	$120,000	$200,000
6					
7	Net Profit				
8	After Tax Profit				
9					
10	Sales	500000*(1+E17			
11	Cost of Goods Sold	+B10*E18			
12	Gross Profit	+B10-B11			
13	Operating Expenses	+E19			
14	Profit	+B12-B13			
15					
16	Formulas:			Input Cells:	
17	Net Profit	After Tax Profit		Sales Growth	
18	+B14	+B14*(1-0.65)		COGS %	
19				Operating Expenses	

Figure 12-9. Preliminary work for a labeled table

Figure 12-9 is like a one-way table. The resulting table substitutes the input values in each column in the input cells. With the input values temporarily in place, the table returns the values of two formulas—one called Net Profit and the other called After Tax Profit. Unlike a one-way table, however, this table uses formula names instead of the actual formulas. Also, instead of substituting one value from the table into an input cell, this table substitutes three input values in three input cells.

For you to use this table with the Data Table Labeled command, the table must have several additional features, which are shown in Figure 12-9. First, you must select the input cells, in this case, E17..E19. Titles for each of these input cells are located in D17..D19. While the input cells could be directly part of the calculations, putting them on the side creates a better documented worksheet.

Next, you must create and label the formulas. This table has two formulas: Net Profit and After Tax Profit. Above the actual formulas in A18..B18 are the formula names. The formulas plus their names make up the *formula range.* 1-2-3/G uses the names of the formula in the formula range to match with the formula names that appear in the labeled data table. In Figure 12-9, the table uses the Net Profit formula to compute row 7, and the After Tax Profit formula to compute row 8. The formulas in rows 7 and 8 are called the *formula label range,* which appears above or below the table to indicate which formulas the columns use, or to the left or right of the table to indicate which formulas the rows use. The formulas can reference any cell outside of the data table. As the figure shows, you can add blank rows to a labeled table.

At this point, you are ready to create the table with the Data Table Labeled command. 1-2-3/G presents the dialog box that is shown in Figure 12-10.

1. Select Formulas and Formula range. 1-2-3/G prompts for the formula range, which is A17..B18. This includes the formula name in the first row and the formula in the second.

2. Then 1-2-3/G prompts for the formula label range, which is A7..A8. This is the formula name that tells 1-2-3/G which formula to use for each row.

3. Since this table has input variables stored across columns, select Across next. When 1-2-3/G prompts for the column variable range, enter B3..E5.

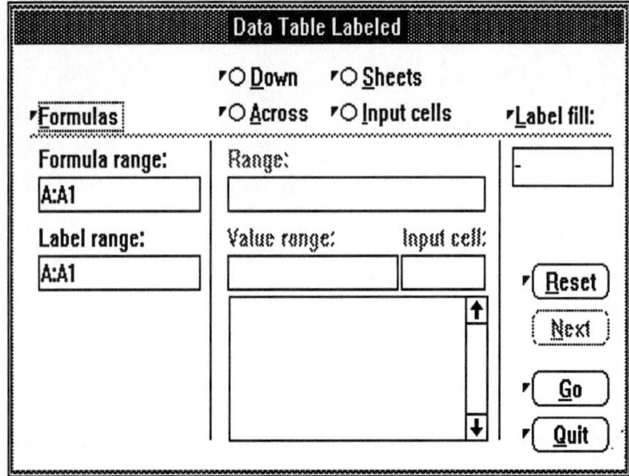

Figure 12-10. Data Table Labeled dialog box

4. Once 1-2-3/G knows the column variable range, it prompts for confirmation of each row in the column range, and wants to know the input cell for this row. For the Sales Growth variables, 1-2-3/G displays B3..E3; the input cell is E17.

5. Next, 1-2-3/G prompts for confirmation of B4..E4 as the second row in the column range (COGS percentage), and wants to know the input cell, which is E18.

6. Then 1-2-3/G asks you to confirm that B5..E5 is the third row in the column range (Operating Expenses), and prompts for the input cell, which is E19.

7. Since this finishes your selections, select Go to have 1-2-3/G generate the table.

The results are shown in Figure 12-11. You don't need to define a data table range, since this command assumes that the data table uses every cell in the rows with the Net Profit and After Tax Profit formulas that have across variable values in rows 3..5. Since 1-2-3/G knows that any cell that does not intersect with the parts of the table is not part of the table, you can enter any type of data in these other cells. For example, if you enter a formula that calculates earnings per share in B6..E6, 1-2-3/G knows that it is not part of the table to calculate, since there is no formula name in A6 that matches a formula in the formula range.

1-2-3/G: DESK.DSK (69.4) Ready

File Edit Worksheet Range Copy... Move... Print Graph Data Utility Quit... Help

A:B7 149600

(C0) FIG_ZE.WG1

A	A	B	C	D	E
1		Guess 1	Guess 2	Guess 3	Guess 4
2					
3	Sales Growth	4%	10%	5%	15%
4	COGS %	52%	70%	60%	70%
5	Operating Expenses	$100,000	$180,000	$120,000	$200,000
6					
7	Net Profit	$149,600	($15,000)	$90,000	($27,500)
8	After Tax Profit	$52,360	($5,250)	$31,500	($9,625)
9					
10	Sales	500000*(1+E17			
11	Cost of Goods Sold	+B10*E18			
12	Gross Profit	+B10-B11			
13	Operating Expenses	+E19			
14	Profit	+B12-B13			
15					
16	Formulas:			Input Cells:	
17	Net Profit	After Tax Profit		Sales Growth	
18	+B14	+B14*(1-0.65)		COGS %	
19				Operating Expenses	

Figure 12-11. Table after Data Table Labeled command

Tip: Use Copy or Range Transpose to copy the formula names into formula label ranges. Since the Data Table Labeled command does not calculate formulas properly if the formula name is misspelled, use Copy or Range Transpose to copy the exact formula names from the formula range to the data table.

Creating a Three-Way Labeled Table

You can create more advanced tables with the Data Table Labeled command, for example, you can calculate costs for a house. Figure 12-12 shows the beginning of a worksheet that calculates some of the expenses associated with a house. Like the previous example, the table has data stored across columns that use several rows. This labeled data table uses multiple sheets—each sheet uses different years that a mortgage is outstanding. A three-way table was created in Figure 12-12, allowing

1-2-3/G (69.4) Ready

File Edit Worksheet Range Copy... Move... Print Graph Data Utility Quit... Help

B:E5 @SUM(B5..D5)

FIG_ZO.WG1

C	A	B	C	D	E	F	G	H
1	20 Yr Mtg	Payment	Taxes	Repairs	Total	Payment	Taxes	Repai
2	House Cost	80,000	80,000	80,000		100,000	100,000	100,0
3	Tax Rate	1.5%	1.5%	1.5%		2.0%	2.0%	2.0
4	Age	35	35	35		25	25	
5	9%				$0			
6	10%				$0			

B	A	B	C	D	E	F	G	H
1	15 Yr Mtg	Payment	Taxes	Repairs	Total	Payment	Taxes	Repairs
2	House Cost	80,000	80,000	80,000		100,000	100,000	100,000
3	Tax Rate	1.5%	1.5%	1.5%		2.0%	2.0%	2.0%
4	Age	35	35	35		25	25	25
5	9%				$0			
6	10%				$0			

A	A	B	C	D
1	Input 1 - House Cost		Row Input - Interest Rate	
2	Input 2 - Tax Rate		Sheet Input - Years of Mortgage	
3	Input 3 - Age of House			
4	Payment	Taxes	Repairs	
5	@PMT(B1-20000,D1/12,D2*12)	+B1*B2	+B3*20	

Figure 12-12. Preliminary work for a three-way labeled table

you more labeled data features. For example, the formula in column E computes the total payment, repairs, and taxes to be spent on the house.

Setting Up the Input Cells and Formulas

First, you must label the input cells that the table uses. The five input cells the table uses are in A:B1..A:B3 and A:D1..A:D2. Each of these input cells is labeled. In this example, all of this information is contained in the first worksheet to keep it separate from the data table. Having multiple worksheets in perspective also enables you to see the results of two of the worksheets in the data table, as well as the formula and input cells.

Once you have chosen and labeled the input cells, you must add the formula range, entering the formula name and, below it, the formula. The formula must reference cell values outside the labeled table. The first formula, Payment, assumes that a $20,000 down payment is made on the house, so the amount borrowed is $20,000 less than the house cost. The second formula, Taxes, multiplies the house cost by the tax rate. The third formula, Repairs, calculates the repair cost assuming that for each year of a house's age, $20 is spent on repairs.

Setting Up the Data Table

After you enter the input cells and the formulas, you can create the labeled data table. For the example in Figure 12-12, the table uses sheets B through E. Cell A1 in each worksheet contains the number of years the monthly payment calculation uses, formatted with a user-defined format N99 Yr Mtg. Unlike three-way data tables, values for input cells that span worksheets can be in any cell; they just have to be in the same cell in each sheet. For the data values stored across columns in the table, as in the previous example, the table has sets of three values. In this table, the sets are repeated three times each for a different formula. The first input range across the column stores the house cost, the second range contains the tax rate, and the third range contains the age. This information is considered a group, since each house you are considering has a unique price, age, and tax rate. The percentages in column A make up the third part of input values for this table. These are the potential interest rates the table uses.

The columns in Figure 12-12 look different from other Data Table commands because the formula label range is combined with the column variable values. The labels in row 1 determine the formulas of which 1-2-3/G returns the value. The formula results (using the data values in the column) are returned to the table on the opposite side of the data values in the table. Total is not a formula, but 1-2-3/G will recognize that it doesn't match the formula names in the formula range and will ignore the column. 1-2-3/G ignores data table columns that contain blank cells, labels that do not match formula names and values. This lets you enter formulas such as the formula in B:E5, which adds the monthly house payment, taxes, and repair cost for the 35 year old house that costs $80,000 and has a property tax of 1.5 percent. Like the table created earlier, this table provides three sets of input values across the column. The three sets of values provide the different sets of assumptions you are using for the house cost, tax rate, and age of the house. This example also demonstrates how you can use a formula name repeatedly. The formula and input values can also be below the data table, as long as the formula label is below the input values. The table's values are placed on the opposite side of the input variables that the formula names are on.

Once you enter the input variables and labels for the first sheet, you can copy the sheet to the other sheets in the labeled data table. To duplicate this table, the Copy command uses B: as the From range and

C:..E: as the To range. Before the Copy command is finalized, the Copy Options dialog box is displayed and the All attributes copied check box selected so that 1-2-3/G copies column widths and other attributes of the columns, rows, and sheet. Once the table is copied, the sheet input values in A1 of each sheet are edited.

Using the Data Table Labeled Command

You have worked hard but the payoff is here. 1-2-3/G will now supply all the calculations for the tables.

1. Select Data Table Labeled.

2. Select Formulas and Formula range. 1-2-3/G prompts for the formula range, which is A:A4..A:C5. This includes the formula name in the first row and the formula in the second. Then 1-2-3/G prompts for the formula label range, which is B:B1..E:B1. You only need to select one cell in each sheet, since 1-2-3/G knows that the remaining cells in the same row of each sheet that match the formula names are part of the formula label range.

3. Since this table uses input values stored in a column, select Down. When 1-2-3/G prompts for the row variable range, enter **B:A5..E:A7**. Once 1-2-3/G knows the row variable range, it wants to know the input cell for the only column in the row variable range. In this example, the input cell is A:D1.

4. Since this table has input values stored in several rows, select Across. When 1-2-3/G prompts for the column variable range, enter **B:B2..E:L4**. 1-2-3/G ignores columns E and I, since the cell in the formula label range does not match the formula names in the formula range, and since columns E and I don't have input values. 1-2-3/G divides this range into three value ranges: B:B2..E:L2, B:B3..E:L3, and B:B4..E:L4. Next 1-2-3/G displays each value range in the value range text box and, after confirmation, prompts for an input cell. The three input cells are A:B1, A:B2, and A:B3, respectively.

5. Since this table has input variable values that span worksheets, select Sheets. When 1-2-3/G prompts for the worksheet variable

range, enter **B:A1..E:A1**. Then, after confirming the value range, select A:D2 as the input cell.

6. Now you can select Go to generate the table. The results are shown in Figure 12-13.

After you create a labeled table, you may want to perform the table calculations again if you change a variable value. For example, you may want to change the first interest rate to 8 percent. To make this change, enter .08 in B:A5 and copy it from B:A5 to C:A5..E:A5. To recompute the table, use the Data Table Labeled Go command, or press F8 (Table).

If you want to change one of the input cells that the table uses, select the Data Table Labeled and then select Input cells command. When you execute this command, 1-2-3/G displays each values range and its input cell in the two text boxes. You can accept the value range and accept or edit the input cell. With a mouse, you can also select a different input range and input cell from the list by clicking it or clicking the Next command button.

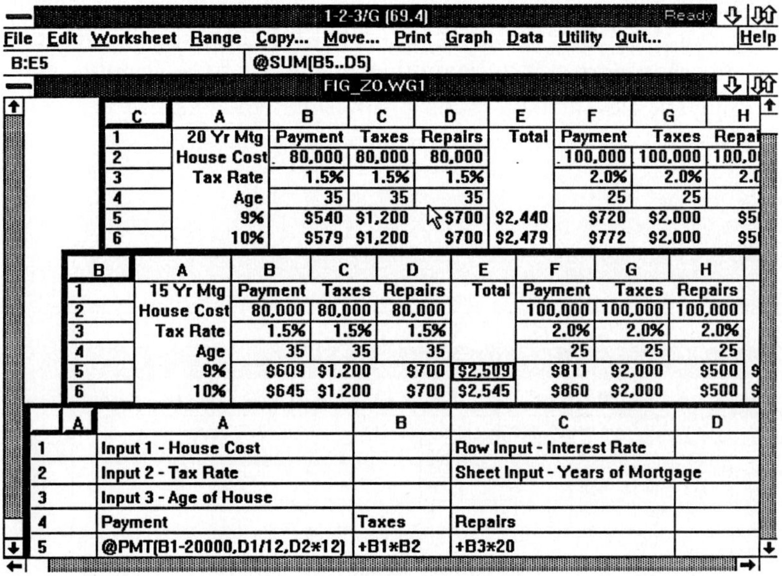

Figure 12-13. Three-way labeled table

Adding Blank Columns, Rows, and Worksheets to the Data Table

The Data Table Labeled command allows you to insert blank columns, rows, and worksheets into the data table. You can use this feature to improve the way your table looks. To insert a blank row in a data table, skip the row when you are entering the row variable range. Follow the same procedure to skip columns and worksheets. In Figure 12-13, you omit columns E and I from the table by omitting input values in rows 2 though 4. While this example used the column to contain formulas, you can also use the column to provide blank space to divide the table into sections. You can achieve the same affect by omitting input cells from rows and sheets. For example, if C:A1 were blank, 1-2-3/G would omit this worksheet from the labeled data table. Similarly, if you deleted the 10%, 1-2-3/G would ignore row 6 in sheets B through F in the data table.

Extending Formulas Across Columns

In Figure 12-13, the data table stores the formula name at the top of each column. Using the same formula for multiple columns results in an unexciting labeled table. An alternative is to extend the formula name over several columns by using the label fill character. If you place the label fill character at the beginning and end of the formula name, you are applying the formula name to multiple columns. An example, using the same type of application, is a table setup like this:

1-2-3/G (69.4) Ready

File Edit Worksheet Range Copy... Move... Print Graph Data Utility Quit... Help

B:A1 15

FIG_Z02.WG1

B	A	B	C	D	E	F	G	H	I
1	15 Yr Mtg		Payment		Total		Taxes		Total
2	House Cost	80,000	100,000	135,000		80,000	100,000	135,000	
3	Tax Rate	1.5%	2.0%	2.5%		1.5%	2.0%	2.5%	
4	Age	35	25	10		35	25	10	
5	9%	$609	$811	$1,166	$2,586	$1,200	$2,000	$1,166	$4,366
6	10%	$645	$860	$1,236	$2,740	$1,200	$2,000	$1,236	$4,436
7	12%	$720	$960	$1,380	$3,060	$1,200	$2,000	$1,380	$4,580

In this table, columns B through D calculate the monthly payment for three houses. The columns use the same formula. B1 contains the formula label '----------------Payment---------------. This uses display space for columns B, C, and D so 1-2-3/G knows to use the same formula for the three columns. In the same worksheet, the Taxes formula is stretched over columns F, G, and H using the label fill character. The label fill character is a hyphen by default, but you can change it to another character by selecting Data Table Labeled and then selecting Label fill and supplying a different character.

Using Data Table with Database Statistical Functions

You can also use the Data Table command effectively with the database statistical functions covered in Chapter 9. For example, you can use the command's variable values to supply different criteria values to be used with the database functions. These values may be numeric or label entries, depending on the search criteria you are using. For more on creating criteria to use with databases, see Chapter 19.

Another example of the Data Table command uses the database shown in Figure 12-14. This database contains employee records for a variety of locations and job codes. You will use the Data Table 2 command to vary the values for these two variables systematically, and to obtain an employee count for each job code at each location.

The table is created in H2..K8, as shown in Figure 12-15. In H2..H8, job code values 12, 14, 15, 17, 21, and 23 are listed. Locations are in I2..K2 as 2, 4, and 10. The formula is @DCOUNT(A1..F17,0,G10..H11). The first argument references the database. The second argument references the first column of the database, which contains last name (a good choice because it is unlikely to be missing from any record). The third argument references the criteria area shown below the table. While these input cells are blank, as the Data Table 2 command executes, it supplies values for criteria to compute the selective counts of database records.

With all the preliminary work accomplished, select Data Table 2 and specify the table location as H2..K8, the first input cell as **G11**, and

1-2-3/G (69.4) Ready

File Edit Worksheet Range Copy... Move... Print Graph Data Utility Quit... Help

A:A1 'Last Name

FIG_ZG.WG1

A	A	B	C	D	E	F
1	Last Name	First Name	SS#	Job Code	Salary	Location
2	Larson	Mary	543-98-9876	23	$12,000	2
3	Campbell	David	213-76-9874	23	$23,000	10
4	Campbell	Keith	569-89-7654	12	$32,000	2
5	Stephens	Tom	219-78-8954	15	$17,800	2
6	Caldor	Larry	459-34-0921	23	$32,500	4
7	Lightnor	Peggy	560-55-4311	14	$23,500	10
8	McCartin	John	817-66-1212	15	$54,600	2
9	Justof	Jack	431-78-9963	17	$41,200	4
10	Patterson	Lyle	212-11-9090	12	$21,500	10
11	Miller	Lisa	214-89-6756	23	$18,700	2
12	Hawkins	Mark	215-67-8973	21	$19,500	2
13	Hartwick	Eileen	313-78-9090	15	$31,450	4
14	Smythe	George	560-90-8645	15	$65,000	4
15	Wilkes	Caitlin	124-67-7432	17	$15,500	2
16	Deaver	Ken	198-98-6750	23	$24,600	10
17	Kaylor	Sally	312-45-9862	12	$32,900	10

Figure 12-14. Employee database

1-2-3/G: DESK.DSK (69.4) Ready

File Edit Worksheet Range Copy... Move... Print Graph Data Utility Quit... Help

A:H2 @DCOUNT(A1..F17,0,G10..H11)

(T) FIG_ZG.WG1

A	G	H	I	J	K
1				Location	
2		@DCOUNT(A1..F17,0,G10..H11)	2	4	10
3		12			
4	C	14			
5	J O	15			
6	O D	17			
7	B E	21			
8		23			
9					
10	Job Code	Location			
11					

Figure 12-15. Table range selected

the second input cell as **H11**. 1-2-3/G will produce the output in Figure 12-16. From this table, you can tell how many employees from each job code work at each location.

Regression Analysis

The Data Regression command performs a simple regression with one independent variable, or a multiple regression with as many as 16 independent variables. You can have up to 8192 observations (that is, values) for each of your variables. All variables must have the same number of observations. For example, you cannot have 8192 values for one independent variable, and 50 values for the dependent variable or another independent variable.

This statistical technique determines whether changes in the independent variables can predict changes in the dependent variable. This potential interrelationship is described quantitatively with *regression analysis*. For details on the theory of regression analysis, consult any book about statistics.

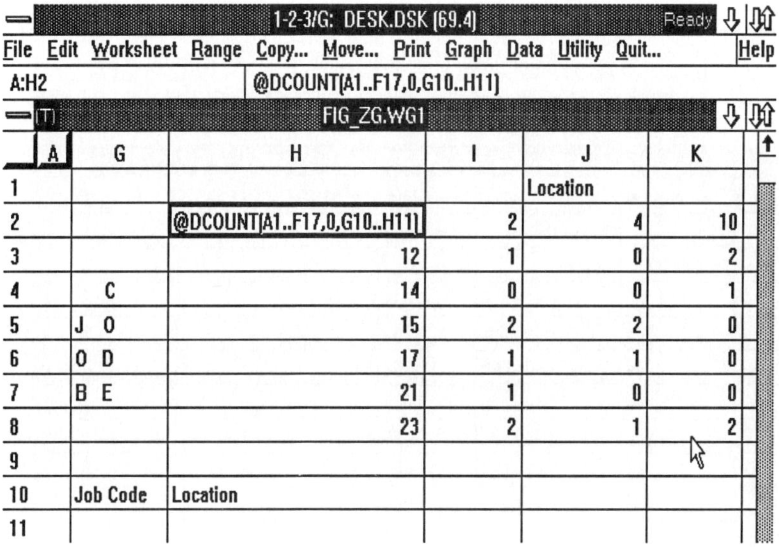

1-2-3/G: DESK.DSK [69.4] Ready

File Edit Worksheet Range Copy... Move... Print Graph Data Utility Quit... Help

A:H2 @DCOUNT(A1..F17,0,G10..H11)

[T] FIG_ZG.WG1

A	G	H	I	J	K
1				Location	
2		@DCOUNT(A1..F17,0,G10..H11)	2	4	10
3		12	1	0	2
4	C	14	0	0	1
5	J O	15	2	2	0
6	O D	17	1	1	0
7	B E	21	1	0	0
8		23	2	1	2
9					
10	Job Code	Location			
11					

Figure 12-16. Table created using database table

When using regression analysis, you must first record the values for the dependent and independent variables in columns on your worksheet. Figure 12-17 shows the dependent variable—the sales of Product A—in column A. You can use regression analysis to see whether the independent variables had an impact on the sales figures for the same period. If these variables seem to have a relationship to the values for sales, you may be able to use this information to predict sales for future periods—if you know the values for the other independent variables during the future periods.

Suppose that the two independent variables selected are disposable income and advertising expense. Disposable Income is in column B, and Advertising Expense is in column C.

You can now select Data Regression. 1-2-3/G will display a dialog box from which you select the data the regression uses. You must make a number of selections, which are summarized in the "Creating a Regression Analysis" box. First, select the range containing the independent variables values with the X-range text box. You can specify up to 16 adjacent columns of values, with as many as 8192 total entries in each of the columns. This example uses B3..C10. You cannot select the columns as the range address, as in A:B..A:C. You can use a range name, cell addresses, or the pointing method with a mouse or arrow keys to make your choice.

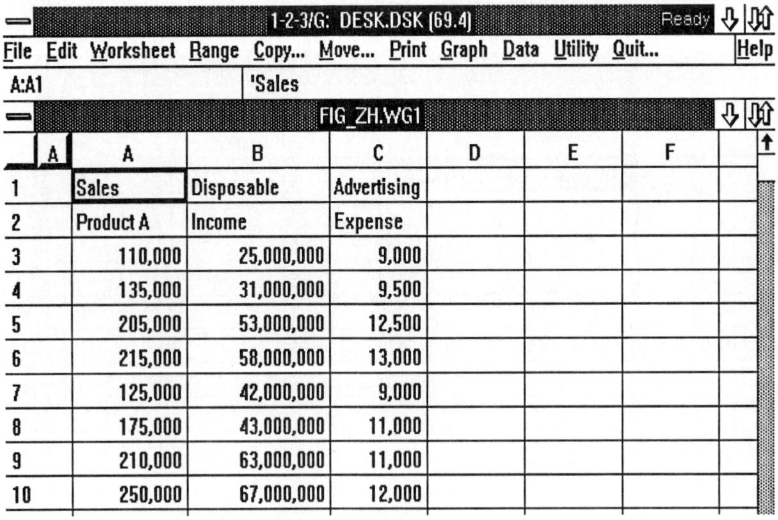

1-2-3/G: DESK.DSK (69.4) Ready

File Edit Worksheet Range Copy... Move... Print Graph Data Utility Quit... Help

A:A1 'Sales

FIG_ZH.WG1

A	A	B	C	D	E	F
1	Sales	Disposable	Advertising			
2	Product A	Income	Expense			
3	110,000	25,000,000	9,000			
4	135,000	31,000,000	9,500			
5	205,000	53,000,000	12,500			
6	215,000	58,000,000	13,000			
7	125,000	42,000,000	9,000			
8	175,000	43,000,000	11,000			
9	210,000	63,000,000	11,000			
10	250,000	67,000,000	12,000			

Figure 12-17. Regression variables

Creating a Regression Analysis

You must follow these steps to create a regression analysis:

1. Enter values for the dependent and independent variables in worksheet columns.
2. Select Data Regression.
3. Choose the X-range option to select the range containing the independent variables.
4. Choose the Y-range option to select the range containing the dependent variable.
5. Choose an output range of nine rows and at least four columns. The number of columns should be equal to the number of independent variables plus two.
6. Select Intercept and choose Zero for a zero intercept, or Compute if you want 1-2-3/G to compute the intercept. If you haven't done a regression with a 0 intercept during the current session, omit this entry if you want the intercept to be computed (Compute is the default).
7. Choose Go to create the regression output.

Your next selection is Y-range. This selection, used to specify the dependent variable, is A3..A10 in the example. You can specify a range name or cell addresses by pointing a mouse or using arrow keys.

Output range is the third text box. You can specify the upper-left cell in the range or the complete range. If you specify the range explicitly, keep in mind that it must be at least nine rows from top to bottom, and two columns wider than the number of independent variables, with a minimum width of four columns. If you specify only the left corner, be sure that the space under and to the right of that cell is free, or 1-2-3/G overwrites existing data with your regression results. The example uses A21 as the first cell of the range. Since only the first cell is selected, 1-2-3/G uses as much space as necessary.

The fourth choice is Intercept. If you want 1-2-3/G to compute the Y intercept, you can leave this choice blank, since Compute is the default. If you want the intercept set to zero, select Zero rather than Compute.

At this stage, you can select Go to have 1-2-3/G tabulate the regression statistics. Figure 12-18 shows the result of the regression for the two variables when 1-2-3/G computes the intercept. When you later perform a second regression analysis, you can use the Reset option to remove the existing settings in the dialog box.

In general, the higher the R value returned by the regression analysis, the greater the correlation. The more the observations and the less the degree of freedom, the more reliable the results. For more details, refer to any book on statistics. The results shown in the example include a computed intercept of -60493.6; a standard error of the estimated Y values; R squared (to find out what R is, use @SQRT with R squared as the argument); the number of observations for your variables; the coefficients or slopes for the independent variables; and the standard error for the X coefficients.

You can use the same variable values to do two simple regressions. The variable with the highest R squared value has the closest relationship to the dependent variable. Figure 12-19 presents two regression output areas. The upper one is for disposable income, and the lower one is for advertising dollars. The R squared value for disposable income is

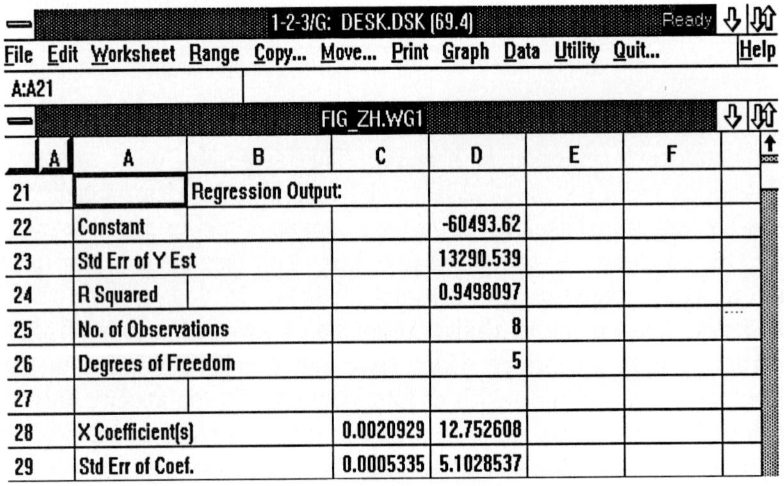

1-2-3/G: DESK.DSK [69.4] Ready

File Edit Worksheet Range Copy... Move... Print Graph Data Utility Quit... Help

A:A21

FIG_ZH.WG1

A	A	B	C	D	E	F
21		Regression Output:				
22	Constant			-60493.62		
23	Std Err of Y Est			13290.539		
24	R Squared			0.9498097		
25	No. of Observations			8		
26	Degrees of Freedom			5		
27						
28	X Coefficient(s)		0.0020929	12.752608		
29	Std Err of Coef.		0.0005335	5.1028537		

Figure 12-18. Multiple regression analysis

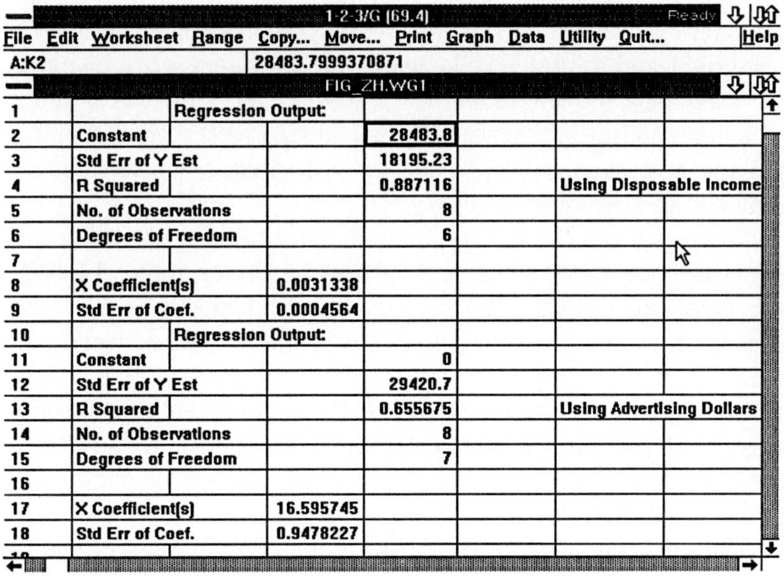

1-2-3/G [69.4] Ready

File Edit Worksheet Range Copy... Move... Print Graph Data Utility Quit... Help

A:K2 28483.7999370871

FIG_ZH.WG1

1		Regression Output:				
2	Constant			28483.8		
3	Std Err of Y Est			18195.23		
4	R Squared			0.887116		Using Disposable Income
5	No. of Observations			8		
6	Degrees of Freedom			6		
7						
8	X Coefficient(s)		0.0031338			
9	Std Err of Coef.		0.0004564			
10		Regression Output:				
11	Constant			0		
12	Std Err of Y Est			29420.7		
13	R Squared			0.655675		Using Advertising Dollars
14	No. of Observations			8		
15	Degrees of Freedom			7		
16						
17	X Coefficient(s)		16.595745			
18	Std Err of Coef.		0.9478227			

Figure 12-19. Two simple regression analyses

higher, which indicates that disposable income is a better predictor of sales than advertising dollars. Since the R squared value in Figure 12-18 is higher than either output in Figure 12-19, you can assume that both variables together are stronger predictors than either one individually.

You can also use the regression output to determine estimated Y values and the best fitting regression line. You would use this formula to estimate the Y values:

$$\text{Constant} + \text{Coefficient of X1} * \text{X1} + \text{Coefficient of X2} * \text{X2}$$

You can use this formula to project sales values, assuming that historic relationships are being maintained.

Frequency Distribution

A *frequency distribution* allows you to count the number of values that fall within specific categories. With 1-2-3/G's Data Distribution command, you can set up any intervals (bins) for categorizing your data. 1-2-3/G will then count the number of entries that fall within each of these intervals.

You can set up the frequency distribution table before using the command by positioning the value categories such that both the column to the right and the table cells below the last interval are blank. You can also use a separate worksheet to store the bins. The cells to the right of and below the last bin value must be blank to record frequencies greater than the largest specified frequency. All category entries must be numeric and in ascending sequence.

When you select Data Distribution and tell 1-2-3/G the locations of the data to be categorized and of the frequency table, 1-2-3/G places each data entry within the selected range into the smallest category equal to or greater than the value in your data. In other words, it adds 1 to the frequency count for that bin. With bin values of 3, 7, and 10, a value of 4 would be counted in bin 7. Each time a value is counted for a category, it increments that category's counter by 1. 1-2-3/G ignores labels and blank cells in the values range. @NA is counted in the first bin and @ERR in the last.

The worksheet in Figure 12-20 contains commission data in C3..C19. The categories for the frequency count are located in E3..E12. These are arbitrary settings and could be any set of ascending numbers. The area

1-2-3/G Ready

File Edit Worksheet Range Copy... Move... Print Graph Data Utility Quit... Help

A:C3 +B3*0.015

(C0) FIG_ZI.WG1

A	A	B	C	D	E	F
1		Quarterly			Frequency Distribution	
2	Salesperson	Sales	Commission			
3	Sharon Roberts	$1,200,987	$18,015		10000	
4	Jim Jolson	$2,134,567	$32,019		15000	
5	Kelly Moore	$1,987,600	$29,814		20000	
6	Alicia Harm	$3,278,965	$49,184		30000	
7	Tom Torn	$3,456,123	$51,842		35000	
8	Sue Roberts	$2,134,987	$32,025		40000	
9	Paul Peters	$1,897,626	$28,464		45000	
10	Racheal Kolson	$1,750,890	$26,263		50000	
11	Herb Horst	$2,345,910	$35,189		55000	
12	Amy Folly	$3,890,152	$58,352		60000	
13	Ivan Imers	$3,186,450	$47,797			
14	Will Walker	$2,134,567	$32,019			
15	Paulette Nalt	$1,678,932	$25,184			
16	Carol Edens	$540,900	$8,114			
17	Abe Avens	$1,235,243	$18,529			
18	Jane Linhurst	$5,612,900	$84,194			
19	Vern Venn	$2,134,750	$32,021			

Figure 12-20. Commission data

to the right of these categories is blank, as are cells E13 and F13 immediately below the category area. Since C3..C17 is selected, 1-2-3/G uses this range as the range of values requiring categorization when you select Data Distribution. When you click the Bins range prompt or press ENTER, 1-2-3/G prompts you for the location of the frequency table or bin range. You can select just the bin values, as in E3..E12, or the entire table area as your range, as in E3..F13. Click the confirm icon or press ENTER, and the completed table in Figure 12-21 should appear. The first entry in the table means that there is one entry less than or equal to 10,000. The last 1, in F13, indicates that there is one entry greater than the largest bin of 60,000.

Data Distribution provides a quick way to condense data. This method is ideal when you want an overall picture of the data within a category. You can also very effectively show the result of a frequency distribution in a bar chart or line graph.

You can perform frequency distribution for a category of numeric values, or on the results of a formula calculation, as in the example. However, the frequency count is not updated as changes occur in the

1-2-3/G Ready

File Edit Worksheet Range Copy... Move... Print Graph Data Utility Quit... Help

A:E3 10000

FIG_ZI.WG1

A	A	B	C	D	E	F
1		Quarterly			Frequency Distribution	
2	Salesperson	Sales	Commission			
3	Sharon Roberts	$1,200,987	$18,015		10000	1
4	Jim Jolson	$2,134,567	$32,019		15000	0
5	Kelly Moore	$1,987,600	$29,814		20000	2
6	Alicia Harm	$3,278,965	$49,184		30000	4
7	Tom Torn	$3,456,123	$51,842		35000	4
8	Sue Roberts	$2,134,987	$32,025		40000	1
9	Paul Peters	$1,897,626	$28,464		45000	0
10	Racheal Kolson	$1,750,890	$26,263		50000	2
11	Herb Horst	$2,345,910	$35,189		55000	1
12	Amy Folly	$3,890,152	$58,352		60000	1
13	Ivan Imers	$3,186,450	$47,797			1
14	Will Walker	$2,134,567	$32,019			
15	Paulette Nait	$1,678,932	$25,184			
16	Carol Edens	$540,900	$8,114			
17	Abe Avens	$1,235,243	$18,529			
18	Jane Linhurst	$5,612,900	$84,194			
19	Vern Venn	$2,134,750	$32,021			

Figure 12-21. Frequency output

data that is categorized. If the data is changed, you must execute Data Distribution again to update the frequency table.

Tip: If the bins are the same interval apart, use Data Fill to create the bins the Data Distribution command uses.

Matrix Arithmetic

Another type of data analysis is matrix arithmetic. Matrices can solve problems of econometric modeling, market share, and population study. The word *matrix* indicates a tabular arrangement of data—something that is quite easy to arrange on a worksheet. 1-2-3/G enables you to perform matrix multiplication and matrix inversion, both of which allow you to perform sophisticated calculations on the data in these tabular arrangements, without complicated formulas.

Matrix Multiplication

You can use matrix multiplication to streamline formulas where you must multiply one set of variables by another and add the results of each multiplication. For example, consider four different products for which you are trying a number of advertising spots. Each advertising option has a price, and you have placed varying numbers of ads for each of the products, in various time slots.

With conventional formulas, determining the total advertising costs for one product would involve multiplying the cost of advertising in time slot 1 by the number of slots purchased. You would have to repeat this process for each of the advertising slots, each time multiplying the number of slots for the product by the cost per slot. After determining the cost for each advertising slot, you add the values to determine a total advertising cost for the first product. You must repeat this process for each product—a cumbersome process, even when the number of products and potential advertising slots is small.

Matrix multiplication can provide a solution if you can construct your problem according to the rules for matrix operations.

Matrix Multiplication Rules

You must follow a few rules before you perform matrix multiplication. These restrictions combine the rules of matrix algebra and the limitations of matrix use in 1-2-3/G.

- Matrix multiplication involves multiplying the values in one matrix by the values in a second matrix. The order in which the multiplication is expressed is critical. Multiplying matrix A by matrix B is *not* equivalent to multiplying matrix B by matrix A.

- Matrix order is determined by the number of rows and columns in the tabular arrangement of the matrix entries. A matrix with x rows and y columns is an x-by-y matrix. When you multiply matrices, the number of columns (the y) for the first matrix must be equal to the number of rows in the second matrix (the x). The easiest way to test this rule is to write the order of the matrices next to each other, as in 5-by-4 and 4-by-6. When the two inner numbers are the same, as in this example, the matrices are compatible and can be multiplied. Rewriting this as 4-by-6 and 5-by-4 produces an incompatible set of matrices, which demonstrates that the order in which the two matrices are multiplied is critical.

- The maximum matrix that 1-2-3/G can multiply is 256 rows by 256 columns.

- Matrices cannot have blank cells. You must insert a zero in any cell that is blank before you invoke the matrix command.

- Matrices can include multiple sheets. Both matrices must have the same number of sheets. 1-2-3/G multiplies the first sheet in the first matrix by the first sheet in the second matrix then continues for each sheet in the matrix.

Entering the Advertising Matrix

In the advertising problem, there are four different products and five different advertising spots. The advertising spots for each product are arranged in a 4-by-5 matrix in B11..F14 of the worksheet shown in Figure 12-22, which also shows the Data Matrix Multiply dialog box. The costs of the spots are arranged in a 5-by-1 matrix in A2..A6. For the two matrices to be compatible, the data must be arranged in a 5-by-1 table rather than a 1-by-5 table. It is expected that results are stored in B17..B20, and appropriate labels are entered around the worksheet to label all the entries.

The Data Matrix Multiply command is invoked and the first matrix is highlighted, as shown in Figure 12-22. The next prompt is for the second matrix in A2..A6. The results are placed in B17..B20, as shown in Figure 12-23. The $21,500 represents the total advertising cost for the Vectra product, which is obtained as the matrix operation multiplies B11*A2, C11*A3, D11*A4, E11*A5, and F11*A6, and then adds each of these products. A similar process occurs for Xandu, Koala, and Retter. All of this is accomplished without a formula.

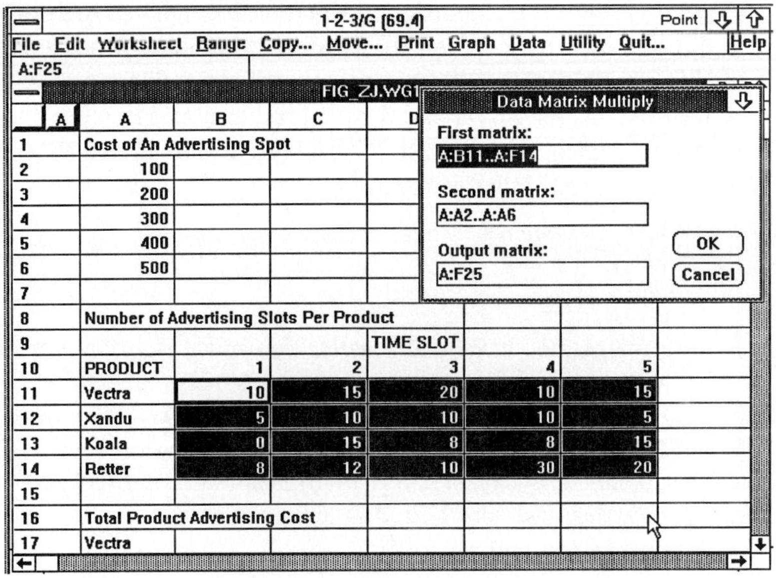

1-2-3/G [69.4] Point

File Edit Worksheet Range Copy... Move... Print Graph Data Utility Quit... Help

A:F25

FIG_ZJ.WG1

Data Matrix Multiply

First matrix: A:B11..A:F14

Second matrix: A:A2..A:A6

Output matrix: A:F25

OK Cancel

A	A	B	C	D	E	F
1	Cost of An Advertising Spot					
2	100					
3	200					
4	300					
5	400					
6	500					
7						
8	Number of Advertising Slots Per Product					
9				TIME SLOT		
10	PRODUCT	1	2	3	4	5
11	Vectra	10	15	20	10	15
12	Xandu	5	10	10	10	5
13	Koala	0	15	8	8	15
14	Retter	8	12	10	30	20
15						
16	Total Product Advertising Cost					
17	Vectra					

Figure 12-22. Matrices to multiply

1-2-3/G [69.4] Ready

File Edit Worksheet Range Copy... Move... Print Graph Data Utility Quit... Help

A:A20 'Retter

FIG_ZJ.WG1

A	A	B	C	D	E	F	G
4	300						
5	400						
6	500						
7							
8	Number of Advertising Slots Per Product						
9				TIME SLOT			
10	PRODUCT	1	2	3	4	5	
11	Vectra	10	15	20	10	15	
12	Xandu	5	10	10	10	5	
13	Koala	0	15	8	8	15	
14	Retter	8	12	10	30	20	
15							
16	Total Product Advertising Cost						
17	Vectra	$21,500					
18	Xandu	$12,000					
19	Koala	$16,100					
20	Retter	$28,200					

Figure 12-23. Result of Data Matrix Multiply in B17..B20

Matrix multiplication is a real time-saver if it fits your application. The Data Matrix Multiply command uses less memory to obtain multiplication results than formulas that calculate the same results. One drawback is that the Data Matrix results are not automatically updated when a value in either matrix changes. To do this updating, you must reissue Data Matrix Multiply. A second potential drawback is that matrices are more difficult to document than formulas—most business users are less likely to understand them. Despite the drawbacks, matrices are a great tool for many applications.

Matrix Inversion

Matrix inversion is more difficult than matrix multiplication, but has even greater potential. In essence, it involves creating a matrix that, when multiplied by your original matrix, results in an identity matrix.

In an *identity matrix,* all of the elements are zeros (0), except one element in each row, which is a 1. The 1 is in a different location in each row. It's easy to remember the location of the 1 for each row: In row 1, the 1 is in the first element; in row 2, the 1 is in the second element; and so on. You can only invert square matrices (matrices with the same number of columns and rows). 1-2-3/G lets you invert matrices of up to 80 columns by 80 rows.

A traditional application for matrix multiplication also uses matrix inversion. These are the product-mix problems that are common in college algebra. Product-mix problems come in all flavors. Normally, there is a limited amount of certain resources, and you have to decide how much of each product to produce. In the sample problem, you must determine how much Green Slime and Red Goo should be produced. Green Slime requires two units of resource A, and six units of resource B. Red Goo takes eight units of resource A, and five units of resource B. There are 50 units of A available and 100 units of B. The matrix operations allow you to optimize your use of these two raw materials.

First, the data of Green Slime and Red Goo are entered in a 2-by-2 matrix, as in C3..D4 in Figure 12-24. This matrix is inverted to create another 2-by-2 matrix, which is used in the solution. A7..B8 contains the inverted matrix. This matrix is created by selecting Data Matrix Invert, and then selecting C3..D4 as the From range and A7 as the To range.

The resulting (2-by-2) inverted matrix is multiplied by a 2-by-1 matrix (F3..F4 in Figure 12-24), which contains the available units of each resource. The result is a new matrix, which is stored in A11..A12 and contains the Optimal Production for each of the products. Since the profit from Green Slime is $10 a unit and the profit from Red Goo is $20 a unit, the whole units produced for each product are multiplied by their respective unit profit figures. The formula in A15 uses the @INT function to use the whole units of Green Slime and Red Goo for the final formula, which is placed in A15. All of the arbitrary locations used in this example are shown in Figure 12-24, which includes the results.

If you want to in learn more about matrix inversion, look for a reference on linear programming. If you already use linear programming, you should be delighted that these handy techniques are incorporated into 1-2-3/G. If you don't need this type of problem-solving tool, keep it in mind in case you need it later.

Splitting Long Labels Into Individual Cell Entries

The File Import command can bring information from an ASCII text file into your 1-2-3/G worksheet, as described in Chapter 6. However, it

1-2-3/G (69.4) Ready

File Edit Worksheet Range Copy... Move... Print Graph Data Utility Quit... Help

A:A15 @INT(A11)*10+@INT(A12)*20

(C0) FIG_ZK.WG1

A	A	B	C	D	E	F	G
1			Product Requirements			Available	
2			Goop	Gunk			
3	Green Slime		2	6		50	
4	Red Goo		8	5		100	
5							
6	Inverted Matrix						
7	-0.131579	0.1578947					
8	0.2105263	-0.052632					
9							
10	Optimal Production						
11	9.2105263						
12	5.2631579						
13							
14	Profit						
15	$190						
16							
17							

Figure 12-24. Matrix inversion solving simultaneous equations

imports this information as a column of long labels, which may not be what you want. Fortunately, the Data Parse command allows you to split these long labels into various cell components— labels, numbers, or serial time or date numbers.

Using Data Parse involves several steps, which are summarized in the "Splitting Text Entries Into Cell Values" box. To use Data Parse, place your cell pointer on the first cell in the column to be parsed and select Data Parse. From the dialog box that appears, select Format line and Create. 1-2-3/G then inserts a blank row above your cell pointer and creates a format line that shows how it will split the label. 1-2-3/G also displays the format line and the lines to be parsed in a monospace font

Splitting Text Entries into Cell Values

After importing text into your worksheet, you may need to use Data Parse to split long labels into individual entries. Follow these steps to parse long labels:

1. Move your cell pointer to the top of the column containing the labels to parse, and select Data Parse.
2. Choose the Format line option, and then select Create to have 1-2-3/G generate a suggested format line.
3. If the generated format line requires changes, choose Format line Edit and make your changes.
4. Select the Input column option and choose the column of labels to parse; include the format line in the range.
5. Select the Output range option, and choose the upper-left cell in a blank area large enough to hold the output, or else specify a range large enough to hold each of the parsed entries. The width of this area is determined by the number of individual fields in the output. The length is the same as the number of labels being parsed.
6. Select Go.

(each character occupies the same amount of space), as shown in Figure 12-25.

The characters used in the format line are as follows:

D	Marks the first character of a date block
L	Marks the first character of a label block
S	Marks the first character of a block to be skipped during the parse operation. This character is never generated by 1-2-3/G, but you can enter it manually through the Edit option
T	Marks the first character of a time block

V Marks the first character of a value block

> Indicates the continuation of a block of the type specified by the previous letter.

* Represents a blank space immediately below the character. This position can become part of the block that precedes it.

The pattern established in the format line is followed in the parsing operation to determine where to split the labels and what type of data is needed for each block. Although you can generate a format line in multiple locations within your column of labels, you need some consistency in the format of the column for this command to be useful.

If you are not pleased with the format line generated by 1-2-3/G, you can edit it by selecting Data Parse, then Format line, and then Edit. You can add, replace, or delete any part of the format line after entering the Edit option. 1-2-3/G only accepts valid format line characters while you are editing a format line.

Once the format line is established, choose Input column, and then either select the range of cells to parse with the arrow keys or mouse,

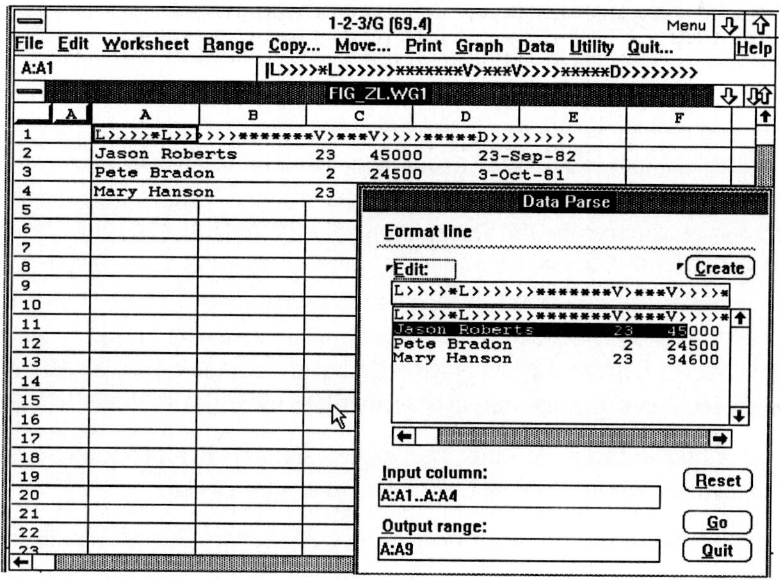

Figure 12-25. Data Parse dialog box

or type in the address of this column of label entries. Be sure to include the format line in the range. Then select Output range and select either the upper-left cell or the complete range of cells required. If you supply only the upper-left cell, 1-2-3/G determines the space requirements, overwriting data if necessary. If you select a complete range that isn't large enough, 1-2-3/G produces an error message rather than overwriting data beyond the range. With the first three menu options set, select the Go command button to have 1-2-3/G restructure the long labels into individual cell entries according to the pattern established by the format line.

The other two options in the Parse menu are Reset and Quit. Reset eliminates all settings in the dialog box. Quit leaves the dialog box and returns you to Ready mode.

In the following illustration, the entries in A1..A3 are long labels.

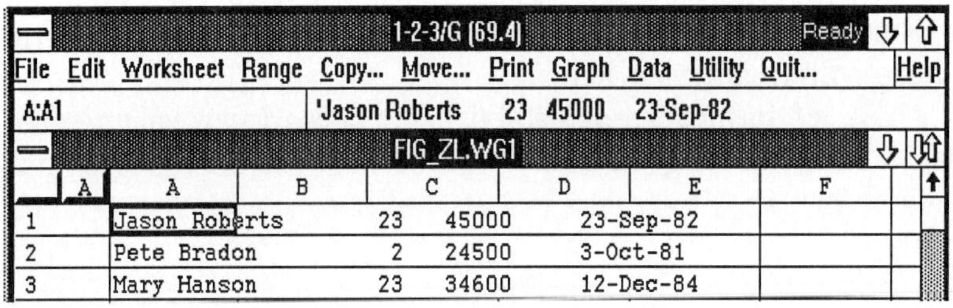

```
1-2-3/G [69.4]                                                  Ready
File Edit Worksheet Range Copy... Move... Print Graph Data Utility Quit...  Help
A:A1            'Jason Roberts   23  45000   23-Sep-82
FIG_ZL.WG1
 A |    A     |    B    |    C    |    D    |    E    |    F
 1 | Jason Roberts         23     45000       23-Sep-82
 2 | Pete Bradon            2     24500       3-Oct-81
 3 | Mary Hanson           23     34600       12-Dec-84
```

Although the components of each line may appear to be in separate cells, the menu bar shows that each line is in fact a single label entry. The entries are displayed using the 10-point Courier font. Using a monospace font means that the characters in the cells to be parsed align with the characters in the format line. To parse these labels,

1. Move the cell pointer to A1 and select Data Parse, then Format line, and then Create. 1-2-3/G generates a format line like the entry in A1 in Figure 12-25. Notice that first names and last names are treated as separate entries because of the space between them.

2. Choose Input column and select A1..A4. 1-2-3/G includes these labels in the list box in the Data Parse dialog box.

3. To duplicate this example, choose A9 as the Output range.

4. Select Go, and the output shown in Figure 12-26 will be produced.

1-2-3/G (69.4) Ready

File Edit Worksheet Range Copy... Move... Print Graph Data Utility Quit... Help

A:A1 |L>>>>*L>>>>>>>*******V>***V>>>>*****D>>>>>>>>

FIG_ZL.WG1

A	A	B	C	D	E	F
1	L>>>>*L>>>>>>>*******V>***V>>>>*****D>>>>>>>>					
2	Jason Roberts 23 45000 23-Sep-82					
3	Pete Bradon 2 24500 3-Oct-81					
4	Mary Hanson 23 34600 12-Dec-84					
5						
6						
7						
8						
9	Jason	Roberts	23	45000	30217	
10	Pete	Bradon	2	24500	29862	
11	Mary	Hanson	23	34600	31028	

Figure 12-26. Output from Data Parse

If you don't want the two name components treated as separate entries, choose Format line and then Edit. Then change the format line to match the one in Figure 12-27, and issue Go. Notice that the entry Jason Roberts is now in A9. The display is initially truncated due to the column width, but you can change this easily with Worksheet Column Set-Width.

1-2-3/G (69.4) Ready

File Edit Worksheet Range Copy... Move... Print Graph Data Utility Quit... Help

A:A9 'Jason Roberts

FIG_ZL.WG1

A	A	B	C	D	E	F
1	L>>>>>>>>>>>>*******V>***V>>>>*****D>>>>>>>					
2	Jason Roberts 23 45000 23-Sep-82					
3	Pete Bradon 2 24500 3-Oct-81					
4	Mary Hanson 23 34600 12-Dec-84					
5						
6						
7						
8						
9	Jason Rob	23	45000	30217		
10	Pete Brad	2	24500	29862		
11	Mary Hans	23	34600	31028		

Figure 12-27. Output after editing format line

1-2-3/G's Solver and Backsolver

PART THREE

Getting Started with Solver

THIRTEEN

Solver is a new utility that is part of 1-2-3/G. The Solver utility can analyze data and present the values for multiple solutions to problems, reducing the need to build complex worksheet formulas. You can create your worksheets just as you have always done. To use Solver, you must develop a model, specify any constraints that will limit acceptable problem solutions, and invoke the Solver utility. Solver can find as many as 999 solutions at one time, and then allow you to look at each of them individually or as part of a report.

To explore Solver's features, you will build a model to compute the profitability from various staffing levels. You could substitute different numbers for each staff position to determine the profit with four different staff classifications—the possibilities are almost endless. You can ask Solver to find the solution that optimizes your profit or some other variable, and the solution is presented in a matter of minutes.

Creating the Basic Model

First you will determine the profitability for each staff classification. These computations are based on an average hourly rate of pay, an average billable rate, and an average number of hours worked annually. The entries are shown in Figure 13-1, with the profitability calculated in column E. You can either follow these steps, or make all the entries except those in column E, and then use the directions in step 4 for the formulas.

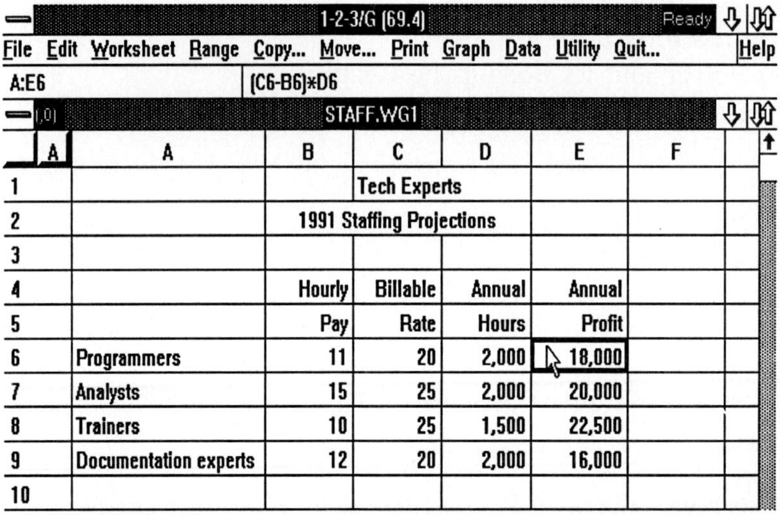

1-2-3/G [69.4] Ready

File Edit Worksheet Range Copy... Move... Print Graph Data Utility Quit... Help

A:E6 (C6-B6)*D6

STAFF.WG1

A	A	B	C	D	E	F
1			Tech Experts			
2		1991 Staffing Projections				
3						
4		Hourly	Billable	Annual	Annual	
5		Pay	Rate	Hours	Profit	
6	Programmers	11	20	2,000	18,000	
7	Analysts	15	25	2,000	20,000	
8	Trainers	10	25	1,500	22,500	
9	Documentation experts	12	20	2,000	16,000	
10						

Figure 13-1. Model for calculating profitability

Follow these steps to complete the model:

1. Enter the following labels:

Cell Address	Contents
A:C1	Tech Experts
A:B2	' 1991 Staffing Projections
A:B4	"Hourly
A:B5	"Pay
A:C4	"Billable
A:C5	"Rate
A:D4	"Annual
A:D5	"Hours
A:E4	"Annual
A:E5	"Profit

A:A6	Programmers
A:A7	Analysts
A:A8	Trainers
A:A9	Documentation experts

2. Select Worksheet Column Fit Largest with the cell pointer in column A.

3. Enter the following values:

Cell Address	Contents
A:B6	11
A:B7	15
A:B8	10
A:B9	12
A:C6	20
A:C7	25
A:C8	25
A:C9	20
A:D6	2000
A:D7	2000
A:D9	1500
A:D10	2000

4. Select Range Format , Comma with 0 decimal places for the range A:D5..A:E9.

5. Enter the following formulas to compute profitability for each person within the classifications:

Cell Address	Contents
A:E6	(C6-B6)*D6
A:E7	(C7-B7)*D7
A:E8	(C8-B8)*D8
A:E9	(C9-B9)*D9

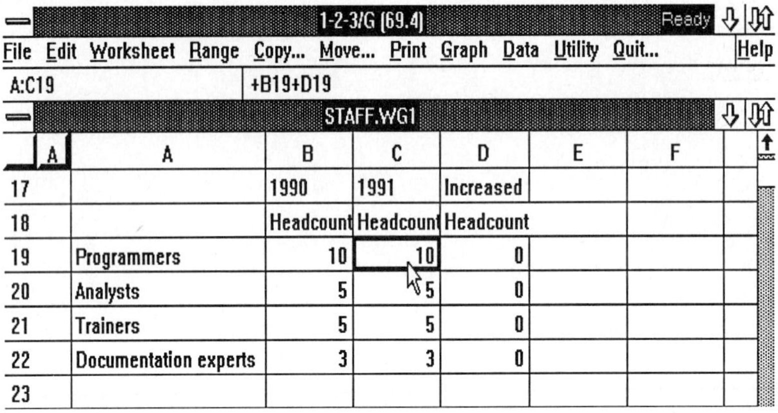

	A	B	C	D	E	F
17		1990	1991	Increased		
18		Headcount	Headcount	Headcount		
19	Programmers	10	10	0		
20	Analysts	5	5	0		
21	Trainers	5	5	0		
22	Documentation experts	3	3	0		
23						

Figure 13-2. Model for calculating headcount

The second section of the model contains current and projected headcounts. The current numbers are entered with an initial entry of zero for each of the increases. You can adjust increases in headcount for each of the four staff classifications to see the effect on profit. Although you might have some defined limits for various staffing levels, there remain a large number of possibilities. The increases for each category are defined as zero initially, since Solver doesn't accept a blank in an adjustable cell that is supposed to be changed. Later Solver will explore alternative profit levels by supplying values for these adjustable cells. Follow these steps to complete the initial entries shown in Figure 13-2:

1. Type the following labels:

Cell Address	Contents
A:B17	'1990
A:B18	'Headcount
A:C17	'1991

A:C18	'Headcount
A:D17	'Increased
A:D18	'Headcount
A:A19	Programmers
A:A20	Analysts
A:A21	Trainers
A:A22	Documentation experts

2. Type the following initial values:

Cell Address	**Contents**
A:B19	10
A:B20	5
A:B21	5
A:B22	3
A:D19	0
A:D20	0
A:D21	0
A:D22	0

3. Formulas are entered to compute the 1991 staff levels as follows:

Cell Address	**Contents**
A:C19	+B19+D19
A:C20	+B20+D20
A:C21	+B21+D21
A:C22	+B22+D22

The next section of the model computes the 1990 and 1991 profitability. The total profit for each classification is determined by multiplying the profit for one staff member in the class by the projected number of staff members. Initially, 1990 and 1991 formulas produce the same

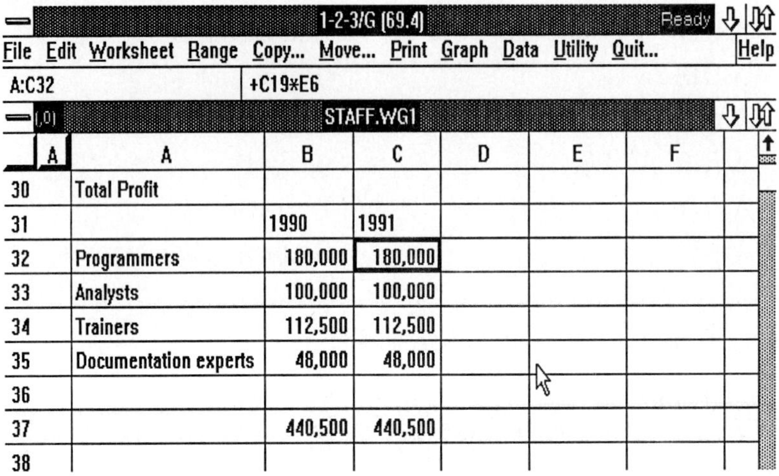

1-2-3/G [69.4] Ready

File Edit Worksheet Range Copy... Move... Print Graph Data Utility Quit... Help

A:C32 +C19*E6

(,0) STAFF.WG1

A	A	B	C	D	E	F
30	Total Profit					
31		1990	1991			
32	Programmers	180,000	180,000			
33	Analysts	100,000	100,000			
34	Trainers	112,500	112,500			
35	Documentation experts	48,000	48,000			
36						
37		440,500	440,500			
38						

Figure 13-3. Model for calculating total profit

results as the model defines a zero increase in staff levels by default. Follow these steps to complete the entries shown in Figure 13-3:

1. Enter the following labels:

Cell Address	Contents
A:A30	Total Profit
A:A32	Programmers
A:A33	Analysts
A:A34	Trainers
A:A35	Documentation experts
A:B31	'1990
A:C31	'1991

2. Enter the following formulas:

Cell Address	Contents
A:B32	+B19*E6
A:B33	+B20*E7
A:B34	+B21*E8
A:B35	+B22*E9
A:B37	@SUM(A:B32..A:B35)
A:C32	+C19*E6
A:C33	+C20*E7
A:C34	+C21*E8
A:C35	+C22*E9
A:C37	@SUM(A:C32..A:C35)

Defining the Constraints

If you attempt to solve this model with your own entries in the increased headcount field, your entries are guided by certain assumptions. You might not be able to absorb more than three new staff members assigned to documentation, or your might want to maintain the same ratio between the number of programmers and analysts. Since you want Solver to find a solution, you must enter these constraints on the worksheet as logical formulas. Figure 13-4 shows one set of constraints, entered as logical formulas in column D, described in column A, and displayed in column E. Use the figure to complete your entries, or follow these detailed steps:

1. Enter the following labels to describe your constraints:

Cell Address	Contents
A:A44	At least two trainers
A:A45	At least two analysts

A:A46	At least 1 documentation expert
A:A47	Less than 3 documentation experts
A:A48	Less than 8 programmers
A:A49	Total increase less than 20
A:A50	'1991 profit projections less than $750,000
A:A51	'1991 Profit > = 1990 Profit

2. The formulas entered in column D (and which are displayed in column E, as shown in Figure 13-4) are shown here:

Cell Address	**Contents**
A:D44	+D21>=2
A:D45	+D20>=2

1-2-3/G Ready

File Edit Worksheet Range Copy... Move... Print Graph Data Utility Quit... Help

A:D44 +D21>=2

STAFF.WG1

A	A	B	C	D	E	F
44	At least two trainers			0	+D21>=2	
45	At least two analysts			0	+D20>=2	
46	At least 1 documentation expert			0	+D22>=1	
47	Less than 3 documentation experts			1	+D22<=3	
48	Less than 8 programmers			1	+D19<8	
49	Total Increase less than 20			1	@SUM(D19..D22)<20	
50	1991 profit projections less than $750,000			1	+C37<750000	
51	1991 Profit >= 1990 Profit			1	+C37>=B37	

Figure 13-4. Constraints for Solver application

A:D46	+D22>=1
A:D47	+D22<=3
A:D48	+D19<8
A:D49	@SUM(D19..D22)<20
A:D50	+C37<750000
A:D51	+C37>=B37

You don't need to complete the entries in column E, since they just document the formulas in column D.

Invoking Solver and Exploring the Results

You can invoke Solver from any location on the worksheet. First, complete the problem definition in the Solver window. Once the problem is defined, you can wait for Solver to find the answer, or minimize Solver and continue to work on other activities while Solver runs in the background looking for solutions. Follow these steps to invoke Solver and complete the definition:

1. Select Utility Solver.

2. Press ENTER to accept the current worksheet name.

3. Select cells A:D19..A:D22 with the mouse or type the appropriate range address for the adjustable cells. The cells contain the headcount increases.

4. If you are using a mouse, click the constraint box. If you typed the range for the adjustable cells, you can press ENTER to activate the box for the constraint cells.

5. Select cells A:D44..A:D51 as the constraint cells, or type the appropriate address.

6. Activate the optimal cell box by clicking it with a mouse or pressing ENTER if you typed the range address.

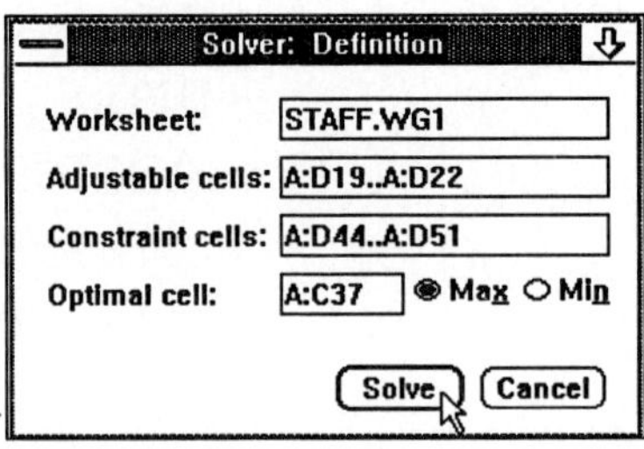

Figure 13-5. Solver: Definition window with entries for worksheet

7. Select A:C37 to maximize the 1991 profit.

8. Click the Max command button or press ENTER to select it. The entries will match Figure 13-5.

9. Click Solve or press ENTER again. Solver begins checking for solutions immediately.

When Solver completes its problem-solving tasks, it displays the number of answers found in the Solver window. In Figure 13-6, you can see that nine answers are found. This window also indicates that the initial values are still displayed for the adjustable cells and resulting calculations. Follow these steps to look at some of the answers and determine their effects on the worksheet.

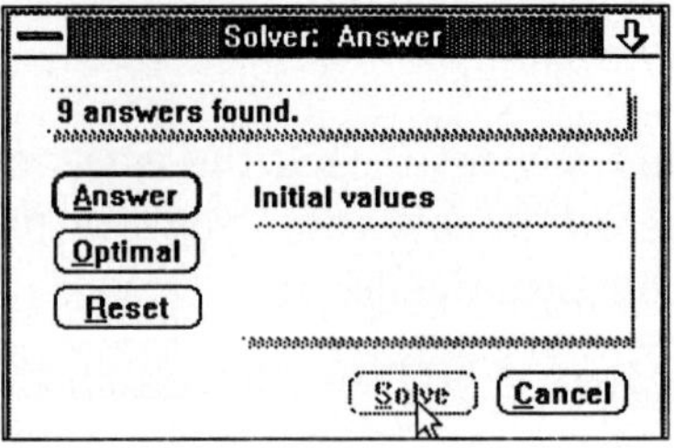

Figure 13-6. Initial Solver: Answer window

1. Activate the worksheet by clicking it with the mouse or pressing ALT-SPACEBAR and selecting Window and the worksheet window.

2. Scroll down in the worksheet to display the headcount.

3. Repeat step 1, substituting the Solver window for the worksheet.

4. Click Optimal or type an **O** to display the headcounts for optimal profit levels, as shown in Figure 13-7.

   You could use either @ROUND, @INT, or a format with zero places to show whole numbers. You could also add additional constraints to restrict the result to whole numbers.

5. Click Answer or type an **A** to display the second answer, as shown in Figure 13-8.

6. Reactivate the worksheet window by repeating step 1.

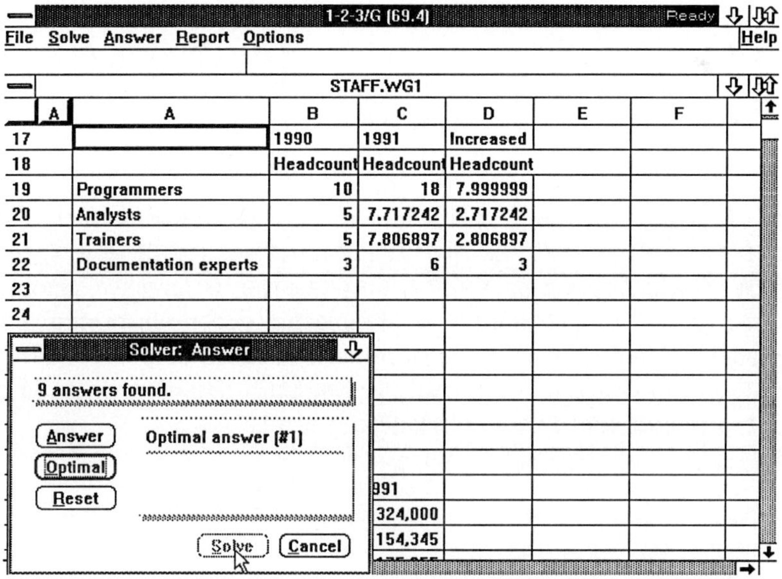

	A	B	C	D
17		1990	1991	Increased
18		Headcount	Headcount	Headcount
19	Programmers	10	18	7.999999
20	Analysts	5	7.717242	2.717242
21	Trainers	5	7.806897	2.806897
22	Documentation experts	3	6	3

Figure 13-7. Displaying optimal answers with Solver

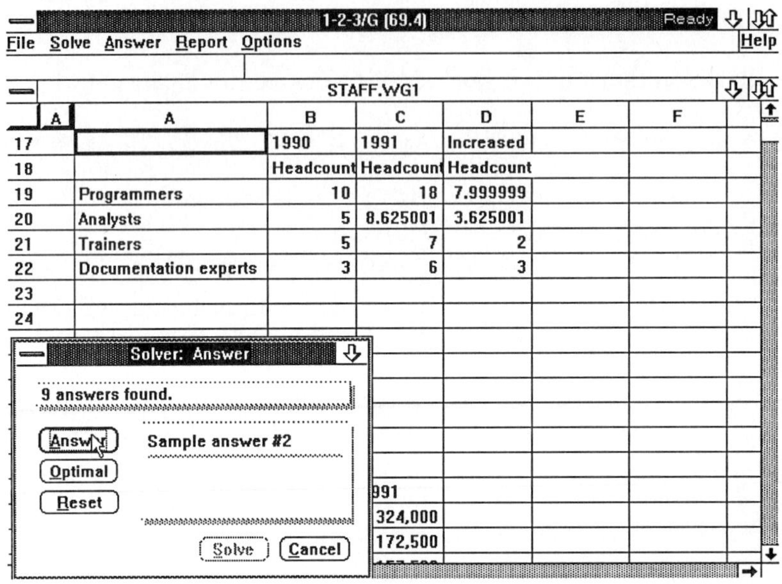

Figure 13-8. Using Solver to display additional answers

7. Scroll to display the Total Profit section.
8. Reactivate the Solver window by repeating step 3.
9. Click Optimal or type **O** so answer 1 displays. Notice the 750,000 profit figure in Figure 13-9.
10. Click Answer or type **A** until answer 9 displays again. This result, shown in Figure 13-10, displays a decline in profitability for some classifications since headcount is reduced below 1990 levels for some classifications. You could prevent this situation with additional constraints that maintain headcount levels.

Producing an Answer Report

Solver also enables you to search for additional solutions or produce reports. The reports examine aspects of the problem or its solutions.

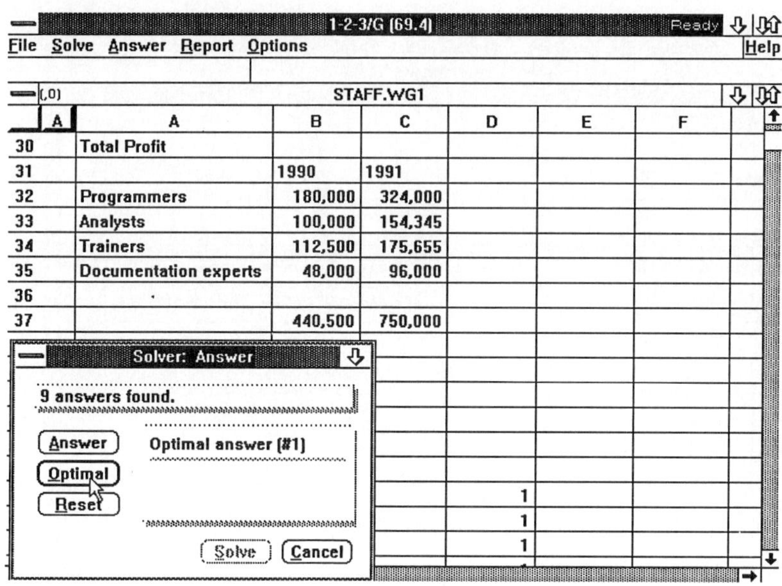

Figure 13-9. Optimal answer generated with Solver

1-2-3/G (69.4) Ready

File Solve Answer Report Options Help

(,0) STAFF.WG1

	A	B	C	D	E	F
30	Total Profit					
31		1990	1991			
32	Programmers	180,000	79,000			
33	Analysts	100,000	140,000			
34	Trainers	112,500	157,500			
35	Documentation experts	48,000	64,000			
36						
37		440,500	440,500			

Solver: Answer

9 answers found.

Answer
Optimal
Reset

Sample answer #9

Solve
Cancel

Figure 13-10. Displaying the worksheet using the last answer generated

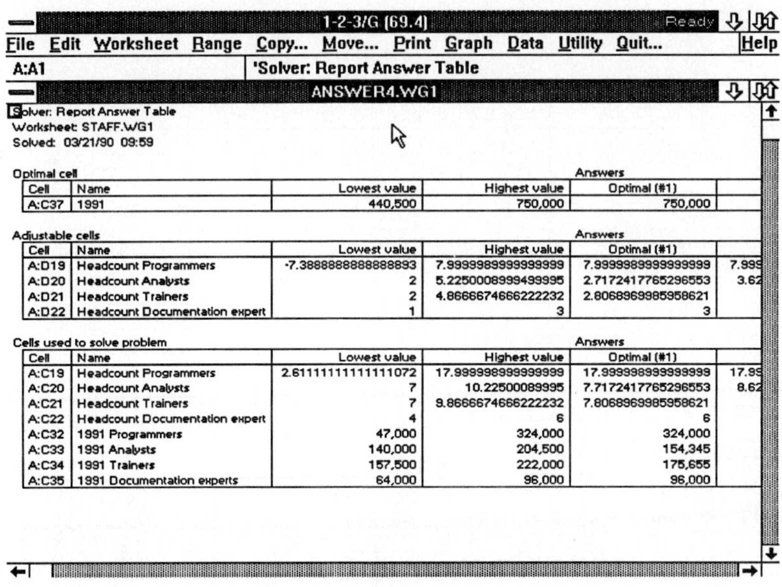

1-2-3/G (69.4) Ready

File Edit Worksheet Range Copy... Move... Print Graph Data Utility Quit... Help

A:A1 'Solver: Report Answer Table

ANSWER4.WG1

Solver: Report Answer Table
Worksheet: STAFF.WG1
Solved: 03/21/90 09:59

Optimal cell — Answers

Cell	Name	Lowest value	Highest value	Optimal (#1)
A:C37	1991	440,500	750,000	750,000

Adjustable cells — Answers

Cell	Name	Lowest value	Highest value	Optimal (#1)	
A:D19	Headcount Programmers	-7.3888888888888893	7.9999989999999999	7.9999989999999999	7.999
A:D20	Headcount Analysts	2	5.2250008999499995	2.7172417765296553	3.62
A:D21	Headcount Trainers	2	4.8666674666222232	2.8068969985958621	
A:D22	Headcount Documentation expert	1	3	3	

Cells used to solve problem — Answers

Cell	Name	Lowest value	Highest value	Optimal (#1)	
A:C19	Headcount Programmers	2.6111111111111072	17.999998999999999	17.999998999999999	17.99
A:C20	Headcount Analysts	7	10.22500089995	7.7172417765296553	8.62
A:C21	Headcount Trainers	7	9.8666674666222232	7.8068969985958621	
A:C22	Headcount Documentation expert	4	6	6	
A:C32	1991 Programmers	47,000	324,000	324,000	
A:C33	1991 Analysts	140,000	204,500	154,345	
A:C34	1991 Trainers	157,500	222,000	175,655	
A:C35	1991 Documentation experts	64,000	96,000	96,000	

Figure 13-11. Report created with Solver

For a look at the answer report, follow these steps:

1. Select Report from the menu.
2. Select Answer Table from the Report menu.
3. Press ENTER or click OK to accept the defaults in the dialog box.

The answer table is displayed in a worksheet like the one shown in Figure 13-11.

The Solver and Backsolver Utilities

FOURTEEN

Chapter 13 presented a quick example of the Solver and Backsolver utilities. You can use these new features with all types of 1-2-3 models. Solver lets you determine many alternate solutions to analyze models, working with product constraints that you define. Besides finding answers to your problems, you can create reports with these answers, helping you to analyze your results.

Backsolver essentially solves backwards, starting with an answer and telling you what variable value is required to achieve the specific results you desire. This chapter explores all the features of both utilities, helping you to apply these new techniques in your model building.

1-2-3/G's New Solver Technology

Solver is a flexible utility that will assist you in problem-solving activities. You can use it in place of linear programming utilities that find the optimal solution to a series of equations involving only addition and subtraction. You can also use it to find many alternative solutions to problems that are nonlinear and contain multiplication, division, exponentiation, square roots, and many of the @functions. Since Solver supports a wide variety of acceptable formulas, it is useful in most what-if analysis models that you can create with a spreadsheet. The box "Steps for Using Solver" summarizes how to define a Solver problem and how to use Solver to locate problem solutions.

Once you invoke Solver and indicate the location of the entries in your problem, Solver uses a combination of algebraic (symbolic equations) and numeric techniques to find solutions. Solver relies on symbolic techniques, which can fill the application with hundreds of algebraic rules that are too complex to build with formulas. If the problem is too complex for Solver, it switches to a trial and error method for testing and locating acceptable values for adjustable cells in the problem. Al-

Steps for Using Solver

1. Enter your model, including all formulas, numbers, and labels.
2. Define your constraints on the worksheet, using logical formulas.
3. Leave a place on the worksheet for adjustable cells entries.
4. If you plan to select a range for adjustable cells that includes blank cells, unprotect the cells where Solver can make entries, and select Worksheet Global Protection Enable.
5. Select Utility Solver to invoke Solver.
6. Accept the name of the active worksheet or enter the name of another worksheet used in the current Solver problem.
7. Select the adjustable cells. You cannot select blank cells as part of a range unless they are unprotected and worksheet protection is enabled.
8. Select the cells containing the constraints.
9. If you want to look for an optimal solution, specify a cell to optimize and then select Minimize or Maximize.
10. Select Solve.

though you don't need to know specifically how Solver works, note that Solver stores your answers first in memory and, if the problem is big enough, in a disk file named SWAPPER.DAT.

Classes of Suitable Problems

Because Solver is flexible, it is the ideal tool for analyzing a variety of problems. These are only some of the areas where you will find it useful:

- **Marketing** Solver can help you decide what mix of promotional activities would be the most effective. It can also help you decide what mix of advertising media would reach the greatest number of potential customers.

- **Sales** Solver can help you decide what combination of new sales and existing customer increases will enable you to meet your sales quotas. It can also help you decide which commission structure will yield the greatest sales increase.

- **Financial** Solver can assist with tasks such as structuring a loan portfolio to minimize risk. It can help you construct a diverse investment portfolio with set maximums in each investment category. Solver can help with budgeting decisions, indicating what cost increases you might need to delay in order to stay within budget projections.

- **Production** Solver can handle standard product mix problems involving limited resources—problems typically solved with a linear programming package. You can use Solver to schedule customized jobs on several production lines. You can also use it to assist in decisions involving the repair versus the purchase of equipment.

- **Personnel** Solver can help you evaluate a variety of bonus programs. You can also use it for hiring decisions when you plan large staff increases. Solver allows you to establish constraints, maintaining certain ratios between different personnel categories, and ensuring that staff levels do not increase faster than new employees can be absorbed into the existing structure. It also allows personnel to work with operating units to match increases to revenue projections and time the new hirings appropriately.

Limitations of Solver

Solver's only limitation is problems that are too large for your personal computer memory and disk space, or problems that use @functions that are not currently supported with Solver. Lotus recommends that the combined total of adjustable cells that Solver can change in finding answers, constraints which define acceptable answers, and other formulas used to determine values the Solver needs not exceed 1,000 cells.

@Functions that can be used in Solver Problems are

@ABS	@IRR
@ACOS	@ISNUMBER
@ASIN	@LN
@ATAN	@LOG
@ATAN2	@MAX
@AVG	@MIN
@CHOOSE	@MOD
@COLS	@NOW
@COS	@NPV
@COUNT	@PI
@CTERM	@PMT
@DDB	@PV
@EXP	@RATE
@FALSE	@RAND
@FV	@ROUND
@HLOOKUP	@ROWS
@IF	@SHEETS
@INDEX	@SIN
@INT	@SLN

@SQRT	@TERM
@STD	@TODAY
@STDS	@VAR
@SUM	@VARS
@SUMPRODUCT	@VDB
@SYD	@VLOOKUP

Although Solver allows you to use all these @functions just mentioned, many of the more complex @functions slow Solver's answer finding process. Additionally, you shouldn't use some of the functions in this table in the same worksheet as the Solver problem. Certain functions cause 1-2-3/G to recalculate and change worksheet values, which causes Solver to discard existing answers. These include database statistical functions that refer to an external table, @@, @CELL, @CELLPOINTER, @INFO, @ISNAME, @NOW, @RAND, @SOLVER, and @TODAY. This is because, as the equations for your problem become more complex, Solver must use numeric rather than symbolic techniques. Numeric solutions require iteration to try many values in adjustable cells and thus take longer than symbolic techniques. If you combine and nest @functions in one formula, it becomes less likely that Solver will be able to find a solution. Also, as you use more @functions, more memory is required to obtain solutions.

In addition, @functions in Solver models cannot use the value of an adjustable cell for an argument. Moreover, logical formulas in constraint cells cannot refer either directly or indirectly to cells that contain @functions.

Increasing the number of adjustable cells requires additional solution time. It may also mean that Solver does not have enough memory to solve a problem. If Solver determines that a problem has too many adjustable or constraint cells to find a solution, it displays a message informing you of the problem. You can reduce the adjustable cells or constraints and try again for a solution.

Entering the Basic Problem

Unlike the add-in programs that performed calculations in previous releases, Solver is not restricted to linear programming problems.

Solver works with your existing model layout; it doesn't require that you repeat entries. Because it is a part of 1-2-3/G, Solver is also easier to use than an add-in: You use 1-2-3/G's commands and features to construct the problem you will use Solver to handle.

You must complete all of your worksheet entries before invoking Solver. You construct your model with familiar 1-2-3/G entries—the only limitation is that you can't use certain @functions. Solver specifically needs adjustable cells that it can change, and constraints that place limits on its solutions.

Besides making your entries, you can add range names. For example, you can name the ranges or collections used for constraint and adjustable cells. This will make it easier to define these cells to Solver. If you are defining a collection of nonadjacent cells as adjustable cells, you might want to unprotect the cells you want Solver to adjust and enable worksheet protection. This allows you to specify a range of cells that include some where entries should be made. The nonadjustable cells in this range should be protected.

Tip: Range names offer another important advantage when you start creating Solver reports. These names will appear to label important cells in the report. If you choose not to use range names, place label entries on the worksheet. 1-2-3/G will use these labels to identify report entries.

Model Entries

You can use as many as 15 worksheet files when setting up a model to use with Solver. This is the limit because you must have an open window for Solver and 1-2-3/G allows a maximum of 16 open windows at one time.

You will build your model with the same techniques used to construct any model. Organize your entries to create a model that is easy to work with, and group similar types of entries. You can choose any formats for your entries, including the predefined options and custom reports. Selecting fonts and other presentation attributes won't affect being able to obtain workable solutions and won't require any more computing time than unformatted data. You should create a model that is esthetically pleasing and is not set up differently just because you're using Solver.

Figure 14-1 shows some worksheet entries that are used to project how a sales quota is met. Since sales consist of sales to an existing customer base plus sales to new customers, both must be a factor in sales projections. An increase percent is applied to the current sales for existing customers and a projection is made for the total merchandise that will be sold to new customers. The formulas in C7..C12 look like +B7*(1+D7), and the sales projection formula in C3 contains @SUM(C7..C12,C14). There are many possibilities for achieving this sales level, although some may be more realistic than others. Next you must define the adjustments that Solver can make and tell Solver what are realistic options.

Adjustable Cells

In addition to the formulas and data values that you supply in the model definition, you should define data that Solver can change as it locates acceptable answers. The cells in which Solver will place these answer values are called adjustable cells. They are the same cells that you

1-2-3/G (69.4) Ready

File Edit Worksheet Range Copy... Move... Print Graph Data Utility Quit... Help

A:A1

A:\QUOTA2.WG1

A	A	B	C	D
1				
2	**Sales Quota**		975,600	
3	**Projected Sales**		964,994	
4				
5	**Existing Customer Sales**			
6	**Company**	**1990 Sales**	**1991 Sales**	**Increase**
7	ABC Alliance	125,694	125,694	0.00%
8	Deaver & Sons	175,900	175,900	0.00%
9	Nelson Brothers	235,000	235,000	0.00%
10	Pritchard Manufacturing	75,000	75,000	0.00%
11	Richards Stone Company	105,900	105,900	0.00%
12	Weaver, Inc.	87,500	87,500	0.00%
13				
14	**New Customer Sales**		160,000	
15				

Figure 14-1. Sales quota worksheet

would change if you manually performed a series of what-if calculations that affected the model.

The adjustable cells in the sales model are located in D7..D12 and C14, as shown in Figure 14-1. Solver can alter the percentages indicating the difference between 1990 and 1991, as well as the total sales predicted for new customers. If you don't define solution constraints, there are an infinite number of possible answers.

Tip: Disable the protection for adjustable cells with Range Unprotect and then enable worksheet protect with Worksheet Global Protection Enable. At this point, you can select the entire column or sheet that includes the adjustable cells and the Solver utility will only alter unprotected cells.

Constraints

Constraints define the range for adjustable cells and place limits on acceptable solutions. Every constraint must be expressed as a logical formula that can be evaluated as true or false. For example, you might enter +D2=.05. You can use any of the logical operators discussed in Chapter 5. The objective is for Solver to identify answers where all of the constraints evaluate as a 1 for true. If a particular answer does not meet all of Solver's constraints, the Solver answer window displays a message to this effect.

You cannot use compound logical formulas when entering constraints. If you need to indicate that the value in C5 is greater than zero and less than 5000, you must use two separate constraints: +C5>0 and +C5<5000. Solver won't accept +C5>0#AND#C5<5000. Often you'll need more than one constraint to control values for adjustable cells, since you will want to control both upper and lower limits. All of the constraint entries must be recorded on the worksheet before you invoke Solver.

Make sure that constraints do not contradict each other. For example, you should not indicate that sales will increase by 10 percent, yet be between 0.75 and 0.85 of what they were in the previous period. Solver couldn't find an acceptable solution meeting both constraints, and would provide a message indicating inconsistent constraints. Figure 14-2 shows a description of the constraints for the sales problem. Each entry is recorded as a formula in columns E and F. The descriptive information in column A serves as documentation.

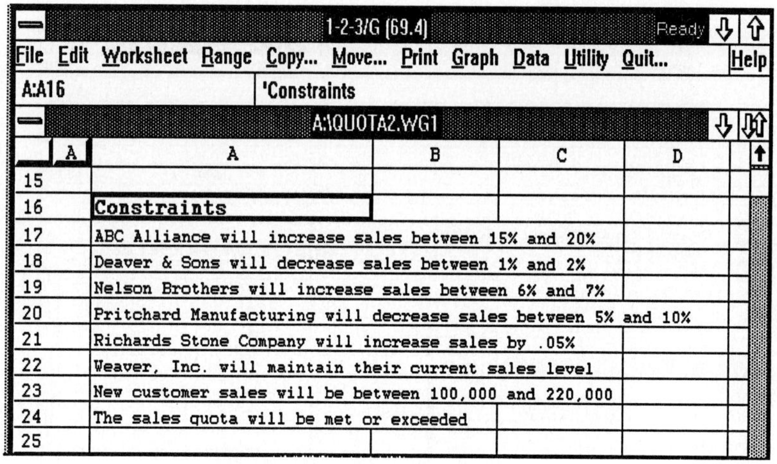

1-2-3/G [69.4] Ready

File Edit Worksheet Range Copy... Move... Print Graph Data Utility Quit... Help

A:A16 'Constraints

A:\QUOTA2.WG1

A	A	B	C	D
15				
16	Constraints			
17	ABC Alliance will increase sales between 15% and 20%			
18	Deaver & Sons will decrease sales between 1% and 2%			
19	Nelson Brothers will increase sales between 6% and 7%			
20	Pritchard Manufacturing will decrease sales between 5% and 10%			
21	Richards Stone Company will increase sales by .05%			
22	Weaver, Inc. will maintain their current sales level			
23	New customer sales will be between 100,000 and 220,000			
24	The sales quota will be met or exceeded			
25				

Figure 14-2. Constraints for the sales quota model

Tip: If you want the adjustable values to be positive numbers, make sure to include a constraint that prevents the calculated values from being less than zero. Examples of these types of constraints are +D7>0 and +D8>0.

Invoking Solver

To activate Solver, select Utility Solver. You should see the Solver: Definition window shown in Figure 14-3. This window displays the worksheet name, text boxes for both adjustable and constraint cells (required entries), options for finding an optimal solution that minimizes or maximizes a value (optional entries).

Defining the Data Locations

You define all of the data Solver needs in a problem definition box like the one in Figure 14-3. If you save the worksheet with entries specified in the definition box after Solver completes its calculations, the current definition contained in the box is saved.

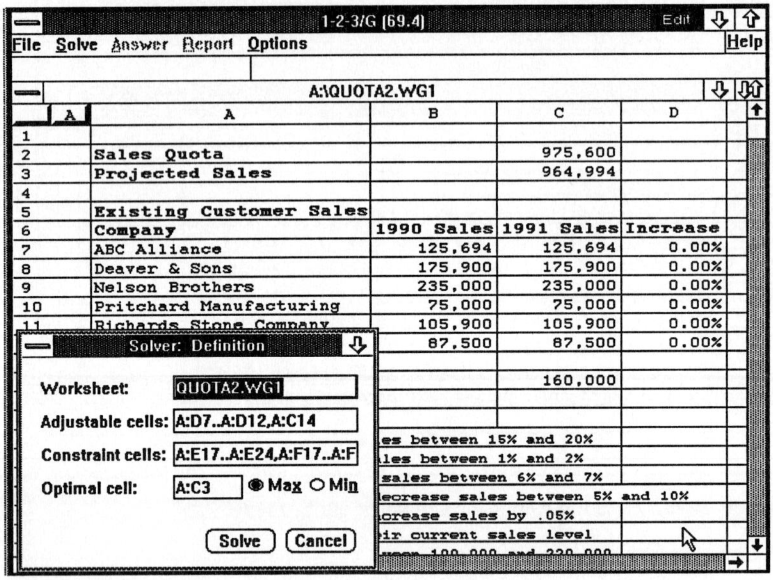

Figure 14-3. Solver: Definition window

Specifying a Worksheet The Solver Definition window displays the active worksheet file in the Worksheet text box. You can accept this file by pressing ENTER or clicking another text box in the window. You can change the worksheet reference with 1-2-3/G's standard entry or editing techniques.

The file specified in this box will contain your definition of the adjustable and constraint cells used in the Solver definition when the worksheet is saved. If you later retrieve this worksheet and start Solver, Solver's definition window will contain all of the entries you made in the previous session. If you use more than one worksheet file in a Solver problem, you can use File Save to choose which one you want to use to store Solver's definition.

Defining Adjustable Cells In the Adjustable cells text box, you should specify a range containing the cells that Solver can change. The

Solver utility ignores blank cells, cells containing labels, and cells containing formulas. The cells that you want Solver to alter must contain numbers. You will want to enter 0's in adjustable cells that do not yet contain numbers. If worksheet protection is enabled, the adjustable cells must be unprotected.

You can enter as many as 512 characters in the Adjustable cells text box. References to cells in worksheets other than the one specified in the Worksheet box in the definition window require full external file path entries. When you specify a collection of entries, commas must separate each entry.

Tip: To make the entries in the Solver: Definition window easier to understand, consider using range or collection names.

Defining Constraints You use the Constraint cells text box to indicate the logical formulas that will guide Solver in finding problem solutions. Solver has satisfied all constraints with a solution when the values of all the cells specified in the Constraint cells box change to a 1.

Constraints also cannot exceed 512 characters. You can type the address of the constraints, or select them by pointing after activating the Constraints cells text box.

An entry in a constraint cell that is not a logical formula is ignored. Other unacceptable constraint entries are conflicting constraints, constraints that don't depend on adjustable cells, and constraints with compound logical operators like #OR#.

Specifying an Optional Optimal Cell You select an optimal cell when you want Solver to find either the highest or lowest value that meets all the constraints. This cell can be an adjustable cell or a cell that depends on an adjustable cell. You can choose only one optimal cell, which you can specify either with a cell address, a range name, or by pointing.

After you select Optimal, the Min and Max choices are available. If you choose Max, Solver will find the highest value for the optimal cell; if you choose Min, Solver will find the lowest value.

Waiting for a Solution

After you complete the Solver definition entries and select Solve, Solver analyzes your problem and begins its search for answers. There are several ways to begin the solution process. Instead of selecting Solve from the definition window, you can press F9 (Solve) or choose Solve Problem from the menu. Solver searches for up to ten answers unless you change the default value with Options Number Answers.

You can minimize the Solver box to an icon by clicking the minimize box while you are solving problems. You can resume activities on other worksheets while Solver operates in the background by activating a window not used in the problem definition for Solver. You can use the standard ALT-SPACEBAR method for activating the desktop control menu to select another window. If you prefer, you can also work on another Presentation Manager application.

Function-Key Options

Some function keys have new uses when Solver is active. Table 14-1 shows the function-key assignments that help you review Solver's answers and attempts. All of these keys have corresponding menu selections that also allow you to choose the selections.

Resolving Problems

When Solver resorts to numeric techniques to finding a solution, it may pause to ask you to supply a guess. It uses your guess to verify that its guesses are getting closer rather than farther away from a viable solution.

Function Key	Action
F7	First answer. Also optimal or best answer if Optimal is selected
SHIFT-F7	Last answer
F8	Next answer
SHIFT-F8	Previous answer
SHIFT-F9	Reset to original values

Table 14-1. Function-Key Assignments for Solver in the Answer Window

Inconsistent constraints may also prevent Solver from locating solutions. When the inconsistent constraints message appears in Solver's Answer window, some of the constraint conditions are in conflict with each other, usually due to a mistake in the constraint definitions. You must correct the problem and request Solve again.

When Roundoff appears in the Solver: Answer window, this usually means that one or more constraints are false after rounding occurs. You can use the Report Inconsistent Constraints features for a closer look at the cause of the result.

If Solver cannot find any answers that meet your constraints, it displays the word "Attempt" in the Solver: Answer window. You can select the Answer box to review these attempts.

If you change an entry in a worksheet used in the Solver problem definition, Solver beeps and discards all of its answers. Your change may affect the answers and cause Solver to recalculate them.

Solver's Answers

When Solver finishes its search for solutions, the initial model values still display on your screen. If Solver can find a solution, as many as ten answers are available for review if you use the default setting. If Solver can't find a solution, it provides information about its attempt to find an answer. You can cycle through the answer values on your screen, or you can select a current cell or table report.

Exploring the First Group

To explore the answers Solver finds, you can select Answer from the Solver: Answer window shown in Figure 14-4. If you requested an optimal solution, the first answer represents either the optimal answer or the best answer. When there are additional solutions, Solver is not always able to determine whether the best answer is also optimal. You can request Solve again to get the next group of answers. Then select the best answer in the next group of answers to choose the optimal answer yourself.

Each time you select Answer from the Solver: Answer window, the next answer is displayed. After the last answer is displayed, selecting Answer again displays the first answer. Selecting Optimal causes Solver

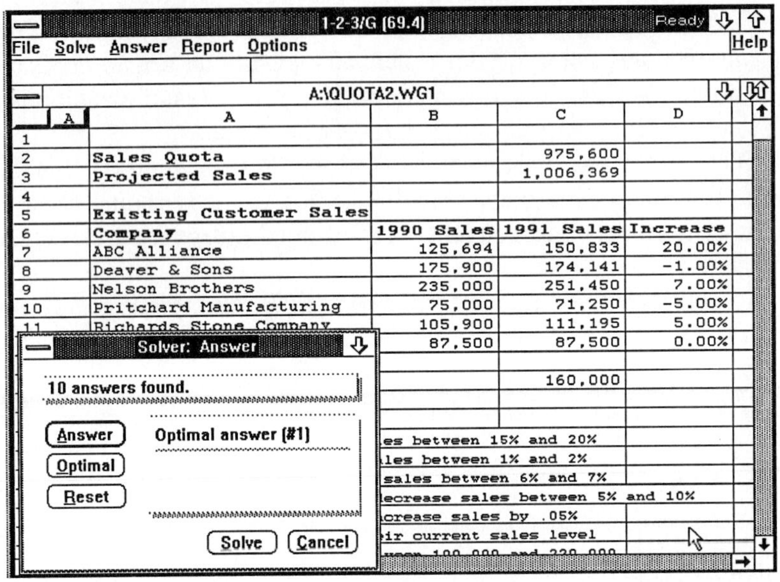

Figure 14-4. Solver Answer window

to display the optimal or best answer. To advance to the next answer, you can press F8 or select Answer Next from the Solver menu that you can activate with F10.

The menu and functions keys offer additional selections that can speed your review of specific answers. Selecting Answer First from the menu or pressing F7 displays the first answer. If you selected Optimal, this is also the optimal answer or the best answer in the group of solutions presented. To go to the last answer you can select the Answer Last command or press SHIFT-F7. To select the previous answer, select the Answer Previous command or press SHIFT-F8. To redisplay the values on the worksheet before Solver was last activated, select the Answer Reset command, press SHIFT-F9, or use the Edit Undo command.

If Solver can't find an answer you can use the Solver: Answer window to review attempts at a solution. The buttons available in this window depend on the results Solver obtains. An attempt at an answer returns a false value for at least one of the constraint cells. When this occurs, you can select the Inconsistent button at the bottom of the box to see which constraints evaluate as false (0).

Requesting More Answers

Unless Solve is grayed after the first group of answers are returned, you can select Solve in the Solver window or Solve Continue from the menu to explore another group of answers. If you need to review answers in the previous group again, you should create an Answer report of these values before looking at another group.

If Solver displays the message "Optimal answer," the optimal answer is in the first answer group. If Solver reports "Best answer," you might find a better answer in a different group of answers.

Supplying Guesses

Occasionally, Solver will prompt you to supply guesses for adjustable cells to help it locate a solution. You can choose Guess in the Solver Guess window or select Solver Guesses from the menu. Follow this procedure to enter your guesses for adjustable cells:

1. Display the attempt that seems closest to a viable solution.

2. Choose Solve: Guesses from the Desktop Control menu or Guess from the Solver window. Solver displays a Guess window with the address of an adjustable cell, its initial value, and its current value used in the attempt.

3. Type a new guess in the New Guess box.

4. Select Next to enter information for the next adjustable cell requiring a guess. The window will not change if no additional guesses are required.

5. Select Solve to attempt a solution using the value of the new guess.

Increasing the Size of the Answer Group

Solver is set to find a maximum of ten answers. If there are fewer than ten solutions for a problem, Solver will find them all before continuing.

You can increase or decrease the number of answers Solver searches for using the Options Number Answers setting. If you want Solver to find only the optimal answer, try setting this option to 1. If you want more than ten, increase the setting to something larger. Don't make this number too large, since if you do, Solver will take a long time to return and allow you to examine the requested set of answers.

Interrupting the Search for Solutions

You can monitor Solver's progress from the Solver Progress window. This window displays the elapsed time and Solver's estimate of its percent completion. You can work on other tasks while you wait, as long as you don't change values in the worksheets that Solver uses. If you change the values, Solver must discard the current answers and start over. You can also switch to another OS/2 window and work on another application.

If you want to check Solver's progress more closely, you can stop and then restart Solver. To suspend Solver's progress temporarily, select Cancel from the Solver Progress window or Solve Stop from the Desktop Control menu. If you choose Solve Continue after stopping Solver, Solver continues finding the current group of answers. If you choose Solve Continue and you haven't stopped Solver, it looks for a new group of answers.

Solver Report Options

You can use Solver's report options to obtain additional information about answers or attempts that Solver makes to find answers. There are seven reports:

- Answer
- How Solved
- What-if Limits
- Differences

- Inconsistent Constraints
- Unused Constraints
- Cells Used

You can create an abbreviated current cell report within a small screen window, or a table report in a worksheet. The answer report is only available in a table format. Since you can create each Solver report as a table in a separate worksheet file, it is easy to print, graph, or store these reports. The current cell reports are summary offerings available in a report window for specific cells on the worksheet. Figure 14-5 shows a current cell report for an inconsistent constraint. The remaining reports in this chapter are discussed in their table form.

The Answer Report

The Answer report provides information on the answers or attempts. This report is useful when you want an overview of all answers in a group. It has either two or three sections depending on whether or not you selected an optimal cell. The three sections are:

- **Optimal cell** Displays the range of values for the optimal cells in the answers or attempts. Displays the value of the optimal cell in each answer.

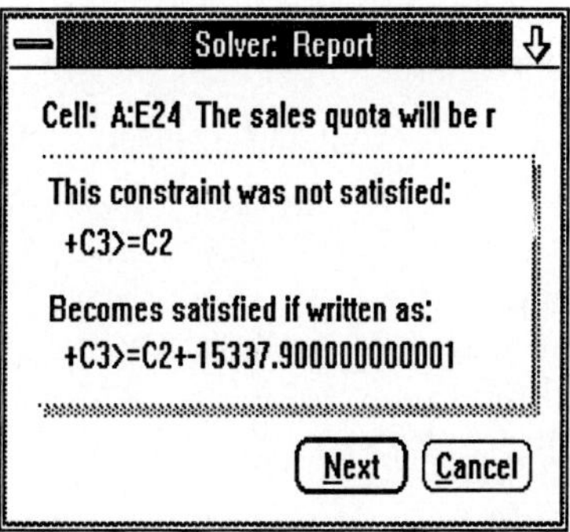

Figure 14-5. Current cell report for inconsistent constraints

- **Adjustable cells** Displays the range of values for the adjustable cells as well as the value of each adjustable cell in every answer.
- **Cells used to solve** Reports the range of values used in all other cells in the problems. Provides the range of values and each answer for each cell.

The answer report is available in a worksheet named ANSWER*n* where *n* is the next sequential number that is not in the current directory. Figure 14-6 shows part of an answer report.

Solver: Report Answer Table
Worksheet: QUOTA2.WG1
Solved: 03/26/90 12:12

Optimal cell — ***Answers***

Cell	Name	Lowest value	Highest value	Optimal (#1)	2	3
A:C3	Projected Sales	992,225	1,006,369	1,006,369	1,002,619	1,000,860

Adjustable cells — ***Answers***

Cell	Name	Lowest value	Highest value	Optimal (#1)	2	3
A:D7	Increase ABC Alliance	15.00%	20.00%	20.00%	20.00%	20.00%
A:D8	Increase Deaver & Sons	−2.00%	−1.00%	−1.00%	−1.00%	−2.00%
A:D9	Increase Nelson Brothers	6.00%	7.00%	7.00%	7.00%	7.00%
A:D10	Increase Pritchard Manufacturi	−10.00%	−5.00%	−5.00%	−10.00%	−10.00%
A:D11	Increase Richards Stone Compan	5.00%	5.00%	5.00%	5.00%	5.00%
A:D12	Increase Weaver, Inc.	0.00%	0.00%	0.00%	0.00%	0.00%
A:C14	1991 Sales New Customer Sales	160,000	160,000	160,000	160,000	160,000

Cells used to solve problem — ***Answers***

Cell	Name	Lowest value	Highest value	Optimal (#1)	2	3
A:C7	1991 Sales ABC Alliance	144,548	150,833	150,833	150,833	150,833
A:C8	1991 Sales Deaver & Sons	172,382	174,141	174,141	174,141	172,382
A:C9	1991 Sales Nelson Brothers	249,100	251,450	251,450	251,450	251,450
A:C10	1991 Sales Pritchard Manufactu	67,500	71,250	71,250	67,500	67,500
A:C11	1991 Sales Richards Stone Comp	111,195	111,195	111,195	111,195	111,195
A:C12	1991 Sales Weaver, Inc.	87,500	87,500	87,500	87,500	87,500

Figure 14-6. Answer Table report

The How Solved Report

The How Solved report provides a summary of the solution process. It covers guess cells, the optimal cells, binding constraints, inconsistent constraints, and adjustable cell values. It is available for the current answer or attempt, and shows the following information:

Cell	Provides a cell address
Name	Provides the name of the cell specified as Cell
Value	Provides the value of Cell for the current answer or attempt
Optimal answer	Reports the optimal answer if one is found
Optimal cell	Provides the optimal cell's address, name, and value
Adjustable cells	Reports on all adjustable cells in the current answer or attempt
Binding constraints	Reports on constraints that affect the current answer or attempt
Formula	Displays the logical formula for each constraint
Becomes binding	Shows how to change the logical formula to make it binding
Unused constraints	Reports on cells that don't affect the answer
Becomes satisfied	Displays the change needed in a constraint cell to make it true

Guessable cells	Reports on cells where a guess is needed
Unsatisfied constraints	Reports on cells where the constraints are false

The How Solved report is available in a worksheet file named HOW*n*.WG1, where *n* is the next sequential number not in the current directory. Figure 14-7 shows part of a How Solved report.

What-If Limits

The What-If Limits report option is grayed until you display an answer. If you select the table version, Solver lists the range of highest and lowest values for all answers in a group as well as the range for a particular answer, assuming that the other variables in the answer remain constant. You can use this report to determine how much you can change one adjustable cell without affecting the answer. The table version of a What-If report provides the following information:

Cell	Address of cell
Name	Range name or closest labels
Range for all answers	Range of values across answers
What-if limits	Range within which you can change values and not affect the current answer

This report is available in a worksheet file named WHATIF*n*.WG1, where *n* is the next unused sequential number. Figures 14-8a and 14-8b show parts of this report.

Solver: Report How Solved
Worksheet: SLSQUOTA.WG1
Solved: 03/26/90 19:05

Sample attempt #1

Attempt #1 is one of 1 which satisfies some, but not all, constraints.

For this attempt, the optimal cell attained the following value:

Optimal Cell

Cell	Name	Value
A:C3	Projected Sales	960,262

For this attempt, Solver changed the values in the following adjustable cells:

Adjustable cells

Cell	Name	Value
A:D7	Increase ABC Alliance	0
A:D8	Increase Deaver & Sons	(0)
A:D9	Increase Nelson Brothers	(0)
A:D10	Increase Pritchard Manufacturi	(0)
A:D11	Increase Richards Stone Compan	(0)
A:D12	Increase Weaver, Inc.	(0)
A:C14	1991 Sales New Customer Sales	150,000

These values make the following constraints binding:

Binding constraints

Cell	Name	Formula
A:F17	ABC Alliance will increase sal	+D7< =0.15
A:F18	Deaver & Sons will decrease sa	+D8< = −0.02
A:F19	Nelson Brothers will increase	+D9< = −0.02
A:F20	Pritchard Manufacturing will d	+D10< = −0.02
A:F21	Richards Stone Company will in	+D11< = −0.02
A:F22	Weaver, Inc. will maintain the	+D12< = −0.02
A:F23	New customer sales will be bet	+C14< =150000

However, the following constraints could not be satisfied:

Unsatisfied constraints

Cell	Name	This constraint was not satisfied	Becomes satisfied if written as
A:E24	The sales quota will be met or	+C3> =C2	+C3> =C2+ −15337.9

The following constraints are not binding for this answer:

Unused constraints

Cell	Name	Formula	Becomes binding if written as
A:E17	ABC Alliance will increase sal	+D7> =0.1	+D7> =0.1+0.05
A:E18	Deaver & Sons will decrease sa	+D8> = −0.04	+D8> = −0.04+0.02
A:E19	Nelson Brothers will increase	+D9> = −0.04	+D9> = −0.04+0.02
A:E20	Pritchard Manufacturing will d	+D10> = −0.04	+D10> = −0.04+0.02
A:E21	Richards Stone Company will in	+D11> = −0.04	+D11> = −0.04+0.02
A:E22	Weaver, Inc. will maintain the	+D12> = −0.04	+D12> = −0.04+0.02
A:E23	New customer sales will be bet	+C14> =100000	+C14> =100000+50000
A:E24	The sales quota will be met or	+C3> =C2	+C3> =C2+ −15337.9

Figure 14-7. How Solved report

Solver: Report What-if Limits
Worksheet: QUOTA2.WG1
Solved: 03/28/90 10:49

Answer #1

		Range of values found for all answers	
Cell	**Name**	**Lowest value**	**Highest value**
A:D7	Increase ABC Alliance	15.00%	20.00%
A:D8	Increase Deaver & Sons	–2.00%	–1.00%
A:D9	Increase Nelson Brothers	6.00%	7.00%
A:D10	Increase Pritchard Manufacturi	–10.00%	–5.00%
A:D11	Increase Richards Stone Compan	5.00%	5.00%
A:D12	Increase Weaver, Inc.	0.00%	0.00%
A:C14	1991 Sales New Customer Sales	160,000	160,000

Figure 14-8a. What-if report

Differences

The Differences report allows you to focus on the differences in any two answers that exceed a tolerance amount. After choosing the report, you

What-if for answer #1

Lowest value	**Highest value**
15.00%	20.00%
–2.00%	–1.00%
6.00%	7.00%
–10.00%	–5.00%
5.00%	5.00%
0.00%	0.00%
129,231	160,000

Figure 14-8b. What-if report

can select any two answers and specify the difference amount. The fields presented in the report are

Cell	The address of a cell
Name	The range name for the cell or the closest labels
Answer #	The cell values for the answers or attempts
Difference	The amount of difference between the two answers
Difference %	The percent difference between the two answers

Figure 14-9 shows part of a Differences report stored in a worksheet file named DIFFS*n*.WG1, where *n* is the next sequential number.

Solver: Report Differences
Worksheet: QUOTA2.WG1
Solved: 03/26/90 19:13

Comparing answers 1 and 10
For differences > =0

Cell	Name	Answer 1	Answer 10	Difference	Difference %
A:C3	Projected Sales	1,006,369	992,225	14,144	1%
A:C7	1991 Sales ABC Alliance	150,833	144,548	6,285	4%
A:C8	1991 Sales Deaver & Sons	174,141	172,382	1,759	1%
A:C9	1991 Sales Nelson Brothers	251,450	249,100	2,350	1%
A:C10	1991 Sales Pritchard Manufactu	71,250	67,500	3,750	6%
A:C11	1991 Sales Richards Stone Comp	111,195	111,195	0	0%
A:C12	1991 Sales Weaver, Inc.	87,500	87,500	0	0%
A:C14	1991 Sales New Customer Sales	160,000	160,000	0	0%
A:D7	Increase ABC Alliance	20.00%	15.00%	5.00%	33%
A:D8	Increase Deaver & Sons	–1.00%	–2.00%	1.00%	–50%
A:D9	Increase Nelson Brothers	7.00%	6.00%	1.00%	17%
A:D10	Increase Pritchard Manufacturi	–5.00%	–10.00%	5.00%	–50%
A:D11	Increase Richards Stone Compan	5.00%	5.00%	0.00%	0%
A:D12	Increase Weaver, Inc.	0.00%	0.00%	0.00%	

Figure 14-9. Differences report

The Inconsistent Constraints Report

The Inconsistent Constraints report provides information on why Solver could not find an answer. It highlights how you would need to change constraints to find an answer and lists all the constraints that return false, providing the following fields:

Cell	Address of a constraint cell
Name	Range name or closest labels
This constraint was not satisfied	Current formula that returns false
Becomes satisfied if written as	Formula for the constraint that would return true

The Inconsistent Constraints table reports are stored as INCONS*n* .WG1, where *n* is the next sequential number. Figure 14-10 shows part of this report.

The Unused Constraints Report

The Unused Constraints report provides information on constraints that Solver didn't use in finding an answer. This means that the constraint is not currently binding on the problem solution. This situation often arises when the upper or lower limits established for a variable are unrealistic given other constraints in the problem. For example, you might have a

Solver: Report Inconsistent Constraints
Worksheet: SLSQUOTA.WG1
Solved: 03/26/90 19:04

Attempt #1

Cell	**Name**	**This constraint was not satisfied**	**Becomes satisfied if written as**
A:E24	The sales quota will be met or	+C3>=C2	+C3>=C2+−15337.9

Figure 14-10. Inconsistent Constraints report

customer discount shown as a maximum of 50 percent, but find that constraint to be unrealistic if you also expect to make a profit. Solver makes a suggestion for how you might change the constraint to make it binding. Fields shown in the Unused Constraints report include:

Cell	Address of the unused constraint
Name	Range name or nearest labels for the unused constraint
This constraint was not used	Logical formula used for the constraint
Becomes binding if written as	Rewritten constraint that would become binding

Figure 14-11 shows a portion of an Unused Constraints report. These reports are written in worksheets named UNUSED*n*.WG1, where *n* is the next sequential number.

The Cells Used Report

The Cells Used report indicates the cells that Solver uses. If these cells are not what you expected, there may be a flaw in your problem

Solver: Report Unused Constraints
Worksheet: SLSQUOTA.WG1
Solved: 03/26/90 19:08

Attempt #1

Cell	**Name**	**This constraint was not used**	**Becomes binding if written as**
A:E17	ABC alliance will increase sal	+D7>=0.1	+D7>=0.1+0.05
A:E18	Deaver & Sons will decrease sa	+D8>=−0.04	+D8>=−0.04+0.02
A:E19	Nelson Brothers will increase	+D9>=−0.04	+D9>=−0.04+0.02
A:E20	Pritchard Manufacturing will d	+D10>=−0.04	+D10>=−0.04+0.02
A:E21	Richards Stone Company will in	+D11>=−0.04	+D11>=−0.04+0.02
A:E22	Weaver, Inc. will maintain the	+D12>=−0.04	+D12>=−0.04+0.02
A:E23	New customer sales will be bet	+C14>=100000	+C14>=100000+50000
A:E24	The sales quota will be met or	+C3>=C2	− +C3>=C2+ −15337.9

Figure 14-11. Unused Constraints report

definition. The data shown in the report is

Optimal cell	The address and name of the optimal cell, if one exists
Adjustable cells	Addresses and names of adjustable cells
Constraint cells	Addresses and names of constraint cells

Solver creates a worksheet named CELLS*n*.WG1, where *n* is the next sequential number. Figure 14-12 shows part of this report.

The Backsolver Utility

The Backsolver utility can solve backwards from the answer to the value that you need to achieve this result. Given an affordable monthly payment, Backsolver can tell you the price of the house you can buy and still meet this payment. Given that your goal is to break-even, Backsolver can tell you how many units you must sell to achieve this aim. Although Backsolver's application is more limited than Solver's, you may often want to proceed backward from the final result to find a value that you need to achieve a known result.

As with Solver, you enter Backsolver problems directly on the worksheet, without special techniques. After you invoke Backsolver, the location of the required information is defined and Backsolver goes to work.

When you select Backsolver, a dialog box appears. You need to make three entries before asking for a solution:

Make cell	The address of the formula that you want to evaluate to a specific value. The restrictions of @functions that evaluate to a value apply to Backsolver as well as Solver. You can use only the functions listed earlier in this chapter. You can supply Make cell with a cell address or range name. This cell must be directly or indirectly affected by the cell referenced in By changing cell.

Equal to value	The number that you want the cell specified as Make Cell to evaluate to
By changing cell	This is the cell whose value can be changed to affect the cell specified as Make cell

---

Solver: Report Cells Used
Worksheet: QUOTA2.WG1
Solved: 03/26/90 19:14

Optimal cell:

Cell	**Name**
A:C3	Projected Sales

Adjustable cells:

Cell	**Name**
A:D7	Increase ABC Alliance
A:D8	Increase Deaver & Sons
A:D9	Increase Nelson Brothers
A:D10	Increase Pritchard Manufacturi
A:D11	Increase Richards Stone Compan
A:D12	Increase Weaver, Inc.
A:C14	1991 Sales New Customer Sales

Constraint cells:

Cell	**Name**
A:E17	ABC Alliance will increase sal
A:E18	Deaver & Sons will decrease sa
A:E19	Nelson Brothers will increase
A:E20	Pritchard Manufacturing will d
A:E21	Richards Stone Company will in
A:E22	Weaver, Inc. will maintain the
A:E23	New customer sales will be bet
A:E24	The sales quota will be met or
A:F17	ABC Alliance will increase sal
A:F18	Deaver & Sons will decrease sa
A:F19	Nelson Brothers will increase
A:F20	Pritchard Manufacturing will d
A:F23	New customer sales will be bet

Figure 14-12. Cells Used report

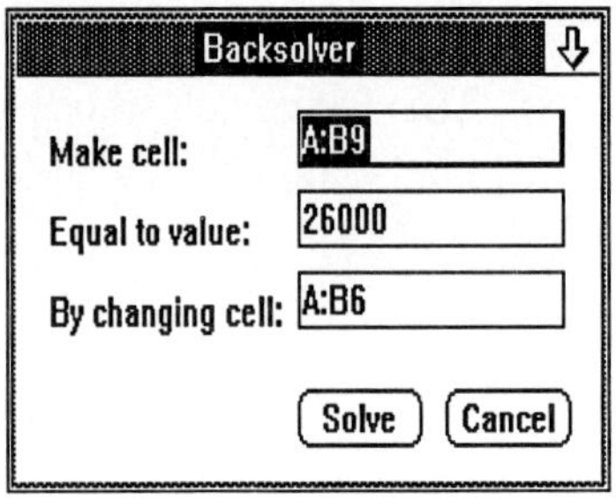

Backsolver

Make cell: A:B9

Equal to value: 26000

By changing cell: A:B6

Solve Cancel

Figure 14-13. Backsolver window

Figure 14-13 shows the entries made in the Backsolver window for the model in Figure 14-14, which shows the number of units that must be sold to make a profit of $26,000. After completing the three entries, you can select Solve. If Backsolver succeeds, it removes the Backsolver dialog box from the screen and displays the value for the changed cell

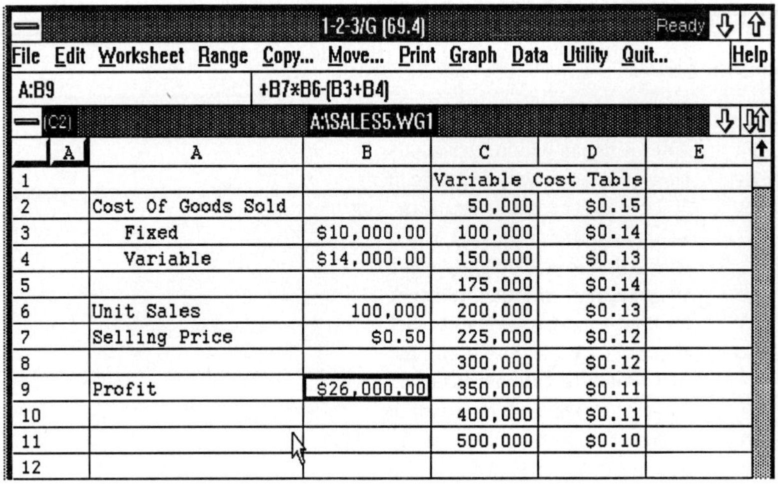

1-2-3/G [69.4] Ready

File Edit Worksheet Range Copy... Move... Print Graph Data Utility Quit... Help

A:B9 +B7*B6-(B3+B4)

(C2) A:\SALES5.WG1

A	A	B	C	D	E
1			Variable Cost Table		
2	Cost Of Goods Sold		50,000	$0.15	
3	Fixed	$10,000.00	100,000	$0.14	
4	Variable	$14,000.00	150,000	$0.13	
5			175,000	$0.14	
6	Unit Sales	100,000	200,000	$0.13	
7	Selling Price	$0.50	225,000	$0.12	
8			300,000	$0.12	
9	Profit	$26,000.00	350,000	$0.11	
10			400,000	$0.11	
11			500,000	$0.10	
12					

Figure 14-14. Profit model used with Backsolver

on the worksheet. For the model in Figure 14-14, the units sold changes to 100,000 as the solution, which will produce a profit of $26,000.

Tip: You can return your model to its initial values by using Edit Undo.

1-2-3/G's Graphs

PART FOUR

Getting Started with Graphs

Creating a Quick Graph
Changing Graph Objects
Changing the Graph Type
Using the Gallery to Preview a Type or Style Selection
Printing a Chart

FIFTEEN

1-2-3/G can create a graph quicker than you ever thought possible. In this chapter you will explore some of 1-2-3/G's shortcuts to graph creation. With an investment of approximately 20 minutes, you will create and modify several types of graphs. You will not learn all the features 1-2-3/G's graphics have to offer since those details are reserved for Chapter 16, "Creating and Printing Basic Graphs," and Chapter 17, "Advanced Graph Techniques." Instead, you will focus on some of the highlights from these chapters as you learn by creating a few graphs. If you have already created graphs with 1-2-3/G you will want to skip to Chapter 16 and focus on the specific commands you may not be familiar with.

The exercises in this chapter require worksheet data before you can create a graph. The entries required for your first graph can be placed in any new worksheet file. They are shown in Figure 15-1 and are listed here:

Location	Entry
B1:	Have-It-All Office Supply
A3:	Salaries
A4:	Benefits
A5:	Travel
A6:	Rent
A7:	Supplies
B3:	100000
B4:	10000
B5:	22000
B6:	18500
B7:	4500

Creating a Quick Graph

The data that you entered is all within the range A1..B7. You can create an instant graph from this data by placing the cell pointer in any of these cells. 1-2-3/G limits the graph data by looking in all four directions from the cell pointer. It defines the range for the graph as stopping at a

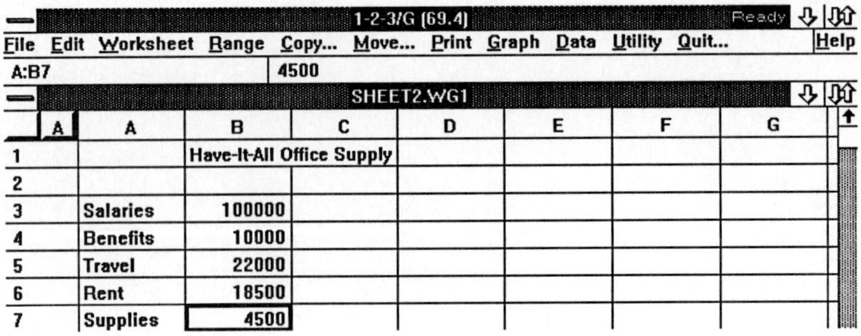

1-2-3/G [69.4] Ready
File Edit Worksheet Range Copy... Move... Print Graph Data Utility Quit... Help
A:B7 4500
SHEET2.WG1

A	A	B	C	D	E	F	G
1		Have-It-All Office Supply					
2							
3	Salaries	100000					
4	Benefits	10000					
5	Travel	22000					
6	Rent	18500					
7	Supplies	4500					

Figure 15-1. Worksheet data entries for graph

worksheet boundary of two blank rows or columns. For the data you entered, 1-2-3/G will use A1..D9. Follow these steps to create the graph:

1. Check to be sure your cell pointer is within the range for the graph data and relocate it if necessary.
2. Select Graph from the main menu.

   The pull-down menu displays all the graph options available from the worksheet window.
3. Select View.

1-2-3/G displays the graph window shown in Figure 15-2. Notice that the window has the same name as the worksheet window although it uses a .GPH rather than a .WG1 extension. Initially, the graph window is placed on the desktop, where it partially obscures the worksheet data. Later you will learn how to reposition it to see both the worksheet data and the graph. The individual objects that make up the graph are labeled in this window to familiarize you with graph terminology. You will notice that such words as "Title" and "Series: A" are used as labels for information on the graph. You will learn how to customize this descriptive information.

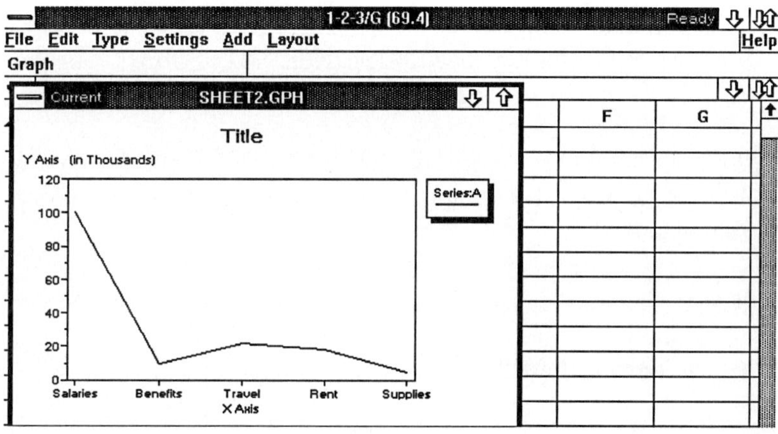

Figure 15-2. Line graph created from the worksheet data

1-2-3/G automatically assigned the data values within the range to a series. When there are more rows than columns in the data, 1-2-3/G assigns the entries in the first column as X-axis labels. So in this example, the entries in column A were used for the X axis. The data in the second column will be assigned to the first data range, Series A. When there are more columns than rows, series are assigned by row rather than by column.

Changing Graph Objects

One of 1-2-3/G's advantages over earlier worksheets is the ability to move, change, or delete graph objects, the individual elements that make up a graph, such as the labeled components in Figure 15-2. In the steps that follow you will delete the legend and change the graph title.

Deleting an Object

On a line graph, a legend supplies the meaning of the different lines. You can use the legend to identify which line corresponds to which data series. In the current graph, there is only one series so the legend is not needed. To delete this object, follow these steps:

1. If you are using a mouse, click the legend that reads Series A. If you are using the keyboard select Edit Select Object Legend Label A. 1-2-3/G marks the legend with small boxes called handles.

2. Press DELETE to remove the legend label and the frame around it. 1-2-3/G redraws the graph to use the space formerly occupied by the legend.

Modifying a Text Object

The default text for the top-line title is Title. Obviously, this doesn't offer descriptive information, so you'll want to change it. Follow these steps to make the change:

1. If you are using a mouse, click Title. If you are using the keyboard, select Edit Select Object Title First.

   Handles surround the title after your actions.

2. Type **Have-It-All Office Supply**.

3. Press ENTER or click the check box when you are finished.

   The handles remain until you select another object or the entire graph. To select the entire graph, click the background of the graph or select Edit Select Object Graph from the menu.

Changing the Graph Type

A line graph is the default graph type that is created from a quick graph. A line graph is a good way to show a trend in sales but is not particularly well suited for the breakdown of budget expenses shown in the current graph. You can change the graph type to a pie graph easily. A pie graph can only display one series of values since each slice of the pie is sized based on its relationship to the total of all the values in the series. To change the current graph to a pie graph follow these steps:

1. Select Type from the menu.

2. Select Pie.

   1-2-3/G redraws the current graph as a pie graph.

You will notice that a legend is added to the graph again. A pie graph legend allows you to distinguish what each pie slice represents.

Using the Gallery to Preview a Type or Style Selection

The Gallery command on the Type menu allows you to preview different graph styles for the current graph type. Pie graph options include exploding (pulling out) a pie slice and eliminating the legend box while adding additional descriptive information to the graph. Follow these steps to look at the various gallery options for a pie graph:

1. Select Type Gallery.
   A dialog box with six different pie-graph styles appears on screen as shown in Figure 15-3.
2. If you are using the mouse, double-click the bottom-left box to explode a section from the pie. If you are using the keyboard, press TAB twice then press the DOWN ARROW twice followed by ENTER.
   The pie graph is redrawn with the graph type selected from the gallery.
   The display doesn't match the gallery display because the section exploded in the gallery display is a smaller portion of the pie than in this example.
3. Select Type Gallery again and pick one of the other six styles for the pie chart using the mouse or keyboard as described in step 2.

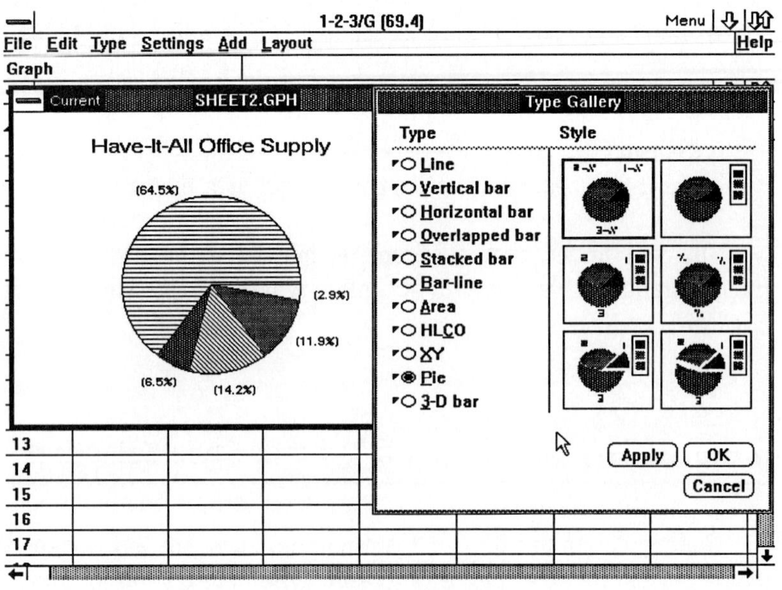

Figure 15-3. Gallery options for a pie graph

Printing a Chart

You can use the File Print command from the Graph window to print the current graph. The graph can be printed on a full, half, or quarter page, or at a custom size, and you can position the graph on the page. You'll also want to take advantage of the Preview feature to look at the printed output on screen before sending it to the printer. To preview and print the graph follow these steps:

1. Select File Print from the graph menu.

2. Select Print Graph.

3. If you are using a mouse, click Half Page. If you are using the keyboard, press TAB followed by DOWN ARROW and the SPACEBAR to select Half Page.

4. With a mouse, click Screen Preview. With the keyboard, press TAB until Screen Preview is the current item in the dialog box and then press SPACEBAR to select.

5. Press TAB to move to Print and then press ENTER or click the Print box.

   The current graph will display in the Preview window.

6. Maximize the Preview window by clicking the maximize box in the upper-right corner of the window or by pressing ALT-MINUS to activate the window control menu and selecting maximize.

   Your screen will look like Figure 15-4. The mouse cursor changes to look like a magnifying glass when it is moved to the Preview window.

7. Zoom in for a closer look at the graph by clicking the left mouse button or by selecting Zoom Closest from the Preview window menu.

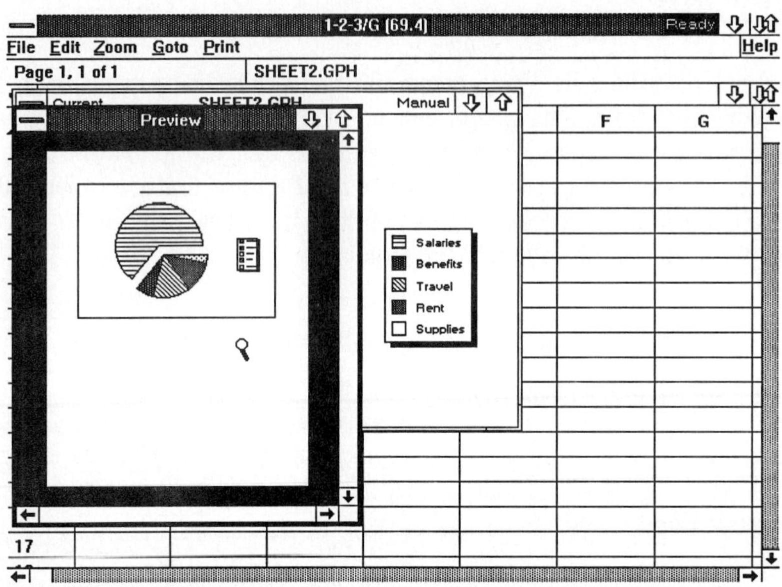

Figure 15-4. Creating a pie graph

8. Zoom back out by clicking the right mouse button or by selecting Zoom Farthest from the Preview menu.
9. Select Print Printer from the Preview menu to print the graph.

Creating and Printing Basic Graphs

Creating Instant Graphs
Displaying Graphs and Worksheets Simultaneously
Creating Graphs
Storing and Using Graphs
Printing Graphs
Adding Simple Enhancements
Using Undo with Graphs

SIXTEEN

1-2-3/G's graphics features let you display worksheet information in a format that is easy to interpret. Rather than presenting all the specific numbers, graphs summarize the essence of your data, focusing on general patterns and trends. When you notice something that warrants further analysis, you can return to the supporting worksheet numbers and review them more closely. If you completed the exercises in Chapter 15, "Getting Started with Graphs," you already know how easy it is to create a professional looking graph. In this chapter, you will learn the details of basic graph creation.

1-2-3/G's graphics features don't require that you reenter data. Indeed, you can use unaltered worksheet data, and you don't need to transfer this data to another program or learn a new system to print a graph. 1-2-3/G's graphics menus are just like the other 1-2-3/G menus, so you only need to learn a few new 1-2-3/G commands in order to use the graphics features. They are an integral part of 1-2-3/G, available from the worksheet and graph menus. After creating your worksheet model, you simply make a few more menu selections to project the data onto a graph.

If you have worked with character-based releases of 1-2-3, you will notice 1-2-3/G's marked increase in graph clarity and detail. 1-2-3/G lets you select and modify individual graph objects such as legends and titles. The separate graph tool windows provide additional flexibility when you are displaying multiple graphs.

With 1-2-3/G, you can create an instant graph by positioning the cell pointer on the worksheet data for the graph and selecting Graph View. You can change the type and style of the graph by clicking one of 1-2-3/G's gallery of graph options. These gallery selections also provide different selections and placement for labels, titles, and other graph objects. Without understanding the commands needed to create a particular gallery option, you can select the option and 1-2-3/G will make all the required changes.

This chapter explores basic graph options. You will learn the several ways to supply data for a graph. You will also learn about various graph objects and ways to move and change them. Finally, you will learn how to print graphs and save them for future use.

Creating Instant Graphs

You can create an instant graph using the data around the cell pointer on the current worksheet. Data from rows or columns is assigned to series, or data values that are plotted on the graph. An instant graph is a good solution as long as your data is grouped together on the worksheet, arranged in the desired sequence for series assignments. 1-2-3/G creates an automatic graph when you select Graph View and the current worksheet file does not already have a graph (unless your cell pointer is not located in an area where there is data). When you select Graph View, 1-2-3/G creates an instant graph from the range containing the cell pointer. 1-2-3/G defines the range separated from other worksheet data by two rows and two columns. If you want 1-2-3/G to use a different range, select the desired range before selecting Graph View.

Rowwise and Columnwise Instant Graphs

1-2-3/G creates two types of instant graphs: Rowwise and Columnwise. Rowwise and Columnwise refer to the way the data in the range for the graph are assigned to the various graph ranges. When a Columnwise graph is created, the first column in the range is assigned to the X range used to label X-axis data points. The second column of entries is assigned to the A range used to display the first range on the graph. Legends which distinguish multiple graph ranges are obtained from the first row in the range if it contains label entries.

Assignments are reversed with a Rowwise graph. The first row is used for the X range and the second for the A range. Legends are obtained from the entries in the first column.

1-2-3/G determines whether to create a columnwise or rowwise instant graph by the relative number of rows and columns. If the range 1-2-3/G selects to graph contains more rows than columns, a columnwise instant graph is created. If the range 1-2-3/G selects to graph contains more columns than rows, a rowwise instant graph is created. If the number of rows and columns in the range are identical, 1-2-3/G creates a columnwise graph.

You can also use columns and rows to separate the data to be graphed from other worksheet data. 1-2-3/G stops using the worksheet data for the graph when it selects the twenty-fourth data range (the twenty-four ranges consisting of an X range for X axis labels and graph data ranges A through W) or when it encounters two blank rows or columns that mark the end of the worksheet data to be graphed. Once you create an instant graph, 1-2-3/G keeps the instant graph data ranges in the current graph settings, which permits you to add enhancements to the instant graph without reentering settings.

Tip: You can add blank rows and columns to the worksheet to separate out the data for an instant graph. Use Worksheet Columns Hide or Worksheet Row Hide if you do not want these rows or columns displayed.

Creating a Columnwise Graph

In a columnwise instant graph, each of the columns of values are assigned to a series. 1-2-3/G defaults to this type of assignment when there are more rows than columns, as in the worksheet in Figure 16-1. The worksheet data to be graphed must have two blank rows and columns on all sides to isolate it from the remaining worksheet data. The edges of the worksheet can serve as one or two of these borders.

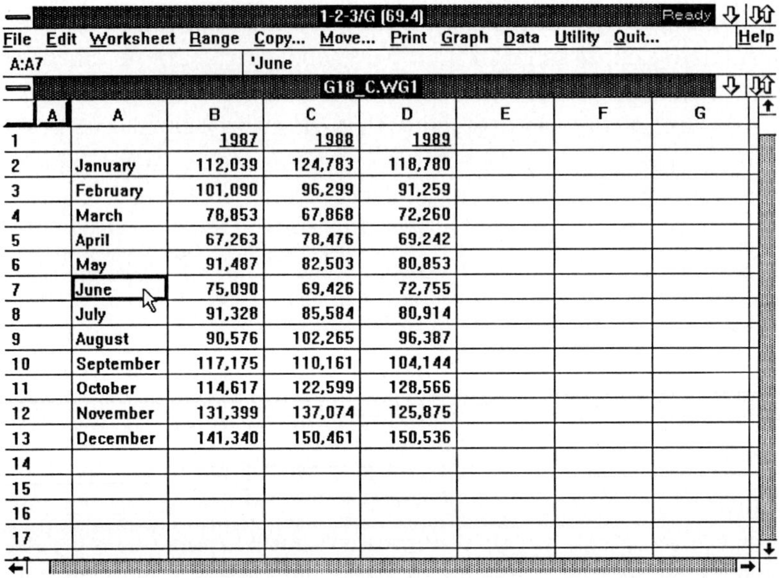

A	B	C	D	E	F	G
1		1987	1988	1989			
2	January	112,039	124,783	118,780			
3	February	101,090	96,299	91,259			
4	March	78,853	67,868	72,260			
5	April	67,263	78,476	69,242			
6	May	91,487	82,503	80,853			
7	June	75,090	69,426	72,755			
8	July	91,328	85,584	80,914			
9	August	90,576	102,265	96,387			
10	September	117,175	110,161	104,144			
11	October	114,617	122,599	128,566			
12	November	131,399	137,074	125,875			
13	December	141,340	150,461	150,536			

Figure 16-1. Data for columnwise instant graph

An instant graph created from the data in Figure 16-1 will use the labels in the first column, A2..A13, as the X-axis labels. Each column to the right of the labels will become an additional data range. 1-2-3/G will use the years (entered as labels in B1..D1) for the legend text. Since the years were entered as labels instead of values, 1-2-3/G will use these entries for legends instead of including them in the graph data. To display this data as an instant graph, move the cell pointer to any cell in the range A1..D13 and select Graph View. Figure 16-2 shows the instant line graph for the worksheet in Figure 16-1. 1-2-3/G creates the default graph type, a line graph, since another graph type was not selected.

Creating a Rowwise Graph

A rowwise instant graph divides the worksheet data into data ranges by rows instead of columns. As with columnwise instant graphs, place the cell pointer on any cell in the worksheet range containing the graph data.

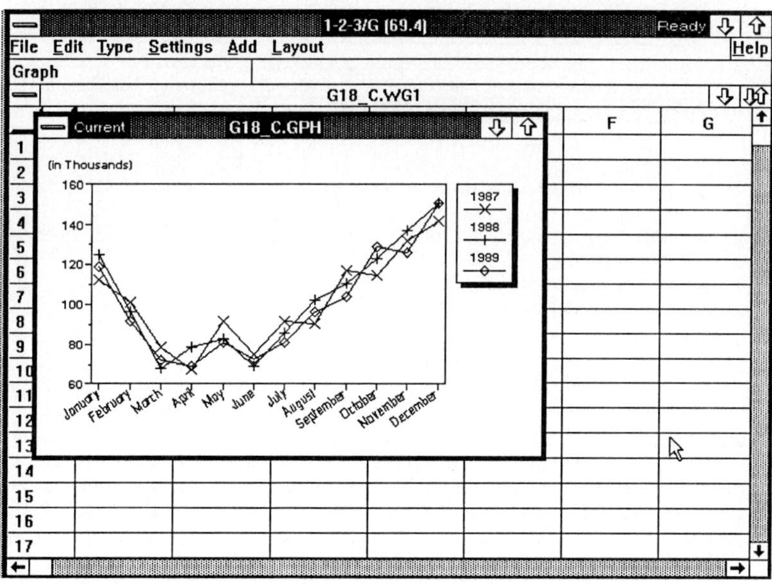

Figure 16-2. Instant columnwise graph

A rowwise instant graph uses the first row for the values along the X axis, and the subsequent rows as the other data ranges. To display the data as an instant graph, select Graph View. Figure 16-3 shows the instant graph for the worksheet in Figure 16-4. The labels in A3..A6 are the legend text that identifies the data ranges automatically drawn by 1-2-3/G.

Instant graphs use the currently selected graph type. Since a line graph is the default, creating an instant graph without selecting a graph type results in a line graph, as in Figures 16-2 and 16-3. If you select a graph type, 1-2-3/G uses your selection when creating the instant graph.

Displaying Graphs and Worksheets Simultaneously

1-2-3/G's graphs are always stored in a separate window from worksheet data. In fact, a separate graph tool handles the display and

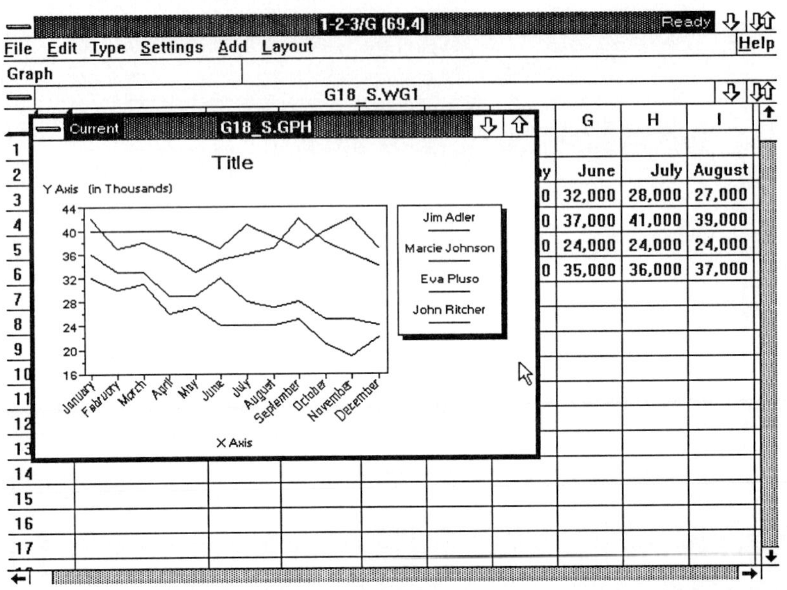

Figure 16-3. Instant rowwise graph

1 2 3/G (69.4) Ready

File Edit Worksheet Range Copy... Move... Print Graph Data Utility Quit... Help

A:D6 38000

(,0) G18_S.WG1

A	A	B	C	D	E	F	G	H	I
1	Sales								
2		January	February	March	April	May	June	July	August
3	Jim Adler	36,000	33,000	33,000	29,000	29,000	32,000	28,000	27,000
4	Marcie Johnson	40,000	40,000	40,000	40,000	39,000	37,000	41,000	39,000
5	Eva Pluso	32,000	30,000	31,000	26,000	27,000	24,000	24,000	24,000
6	John Ritcher	42,000	37,000	38,000	36,000	33,000	35,000	36,000	37,000
7									
8									
9									
10									
11									
12									
13									
14									
15									
16									
17									

Figure 16-4. Data for rowwise instant graph

modifications for a graph. This feature allows you to have multiple graph and worksheet windows on the 1-2-3/G desktop.

When you are using graph and worksheet windows, you can use the same window sizing and positioning commands used for other windows. With the desktop control menu, you can tile windows, as in Figure 16-5, and stack windows. You can change the size of any window with the sizing options that you either access through the tool control menu or by dragging a window border with the mouse. As you change the size of a graph window, 1-2-3/G redraws the graph in the window, using the new window size.

1-2-3/G updates your graph as the data that it draws upon changes. For example, if you enter **501** in A:B5 in the G11_M worksheet window, the graph changes so the area used for the Dallas region sales of Product 1 decreases. In a worksheet window, you can change your worksheet and watch as 1-2-3/G applies these changes to the graph in the graph window. This also lets you spot problems—for example, the data ranges you have selected may be too dispersed to be shown on one

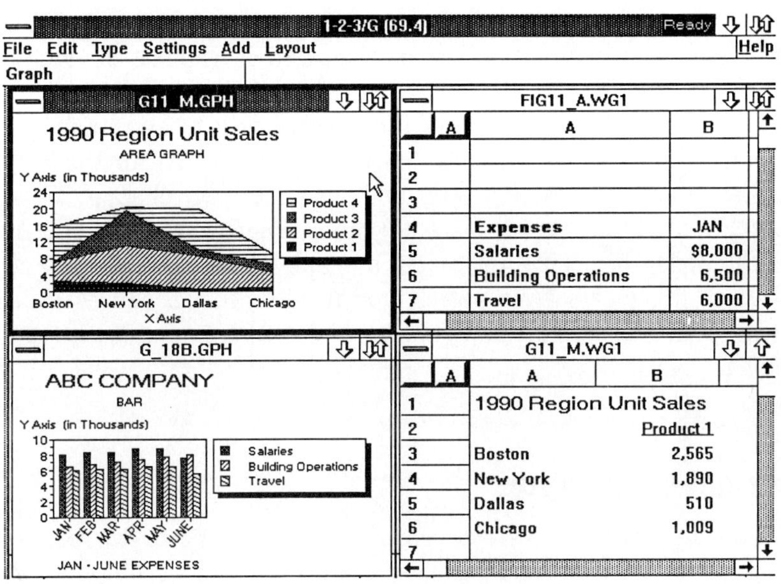

Figure 16-5. Tiled graph and worksheet windows

graph. An extreme example would be a pie chart where one section was 99 percent of the total and several other sections split the remaining 1 percent. In a bar or line graph showing multiple data sets, you would encounter a similar problem if one data set had values in the hundreds and others had values in the millions.

Creating Graphs

1-2-3/G offers more than one method of selecting graph options. You can create and modify graphs through the commands in the Graph menu within the worksheet window. The menu in the Graph Tool offers another option and in some cases commands that are not available from the Graph menu in the worksheet window. Although most graphs are initially created from the worksheet window, the dual selection options are a real convenience—they eliminate the need to switch continuously between the graph and the worksheet windows. The Graph commands in the worksheet menu are for selecting basic features as you initially create a graph. Once you have created a graph, you will probably use the graph tool menu to make subsequent changes.

Most of the commands for creating graphs are in the Graph menu in a worksheet menu. When you select Graph, you see the menu shown in Figure 16-6. Under Type, you can select the graph type displayed in the graph window. You access the specific data to appear in the graph through Add Ranges. Options lets you select the text for the legend and titles. Setup creates a graph, and also lets you change the settings 1-2-3/G would use in an instant graph. When you select OK from the Setup dialog box, 1-2-3/G creates a graph using the chosen data range. Various other selections permit you to view, name, and reset a graph. Some of the choices in the Graph menu are also available in a graph tool menu.

Selecting a Graph Type

To create a regular (versus instant) graph for the first time, you must make several selections. First, select the type of graph you want. You can select Type to display the dialog box in Figure 16-7 or Setup to display the dialog box in Figure 16-8. Both dialog boxes let you select

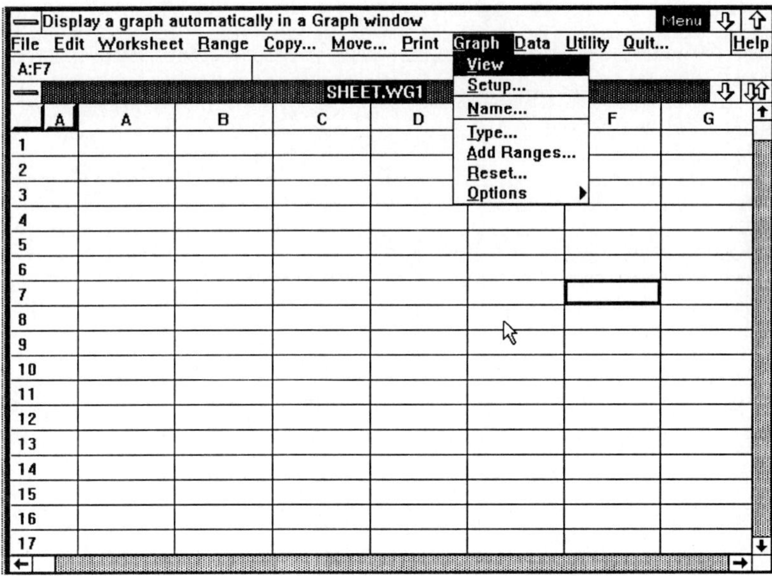

Figure 16-6. Graph menu from a worksheet window

Figure 16-7. Graph Type dialog box

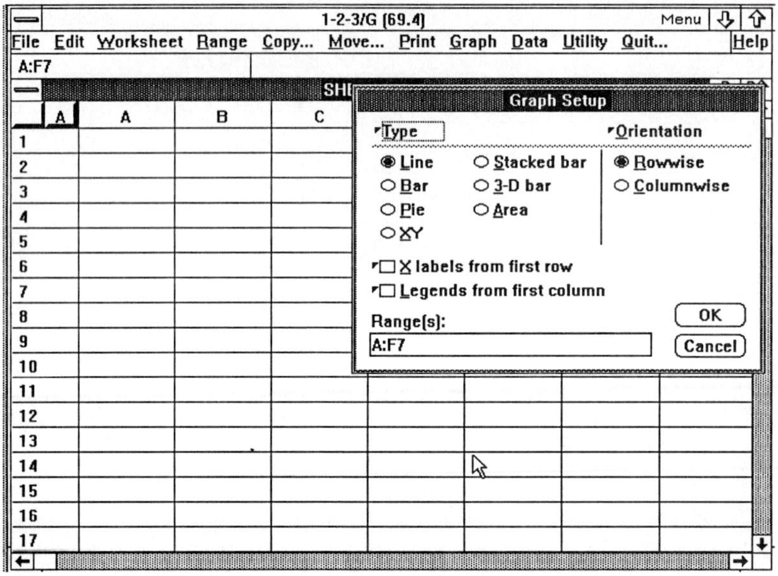

Figure 16-8. Graph Setup dialog box

from seven basic graph types. The Graph Setup dialog box initially displays settings 1-2-3/G would choose for an instant graph. The first set of option buttons let you select one of the graph types that are also listed in the Graph Type dialog box.

You can easily change from one type of presentation to another by returning to the Graph Type dialog box and choosing another graph. The two dialog boxes include basic graph types like line and bar, as well as additional options through the graph window. 1-2-3/G has other graph types that you can select from a graph window, allowing you to view and display your data in a number of presentation formats. Figure 16-9 provides examples of the graph types.

A description of each graph type along with some suggested uses follows:

Area An area graph is a variant of a line graph that stacks the values in each series for any one point on the X axis and fills the area between the series with different hatch mark patterns. The total height of the area represents the total values in all the series. An area graph effectively shows the contribution each series makes to the total. For example, an area graph can illustrate contributions to total company profit of the various subsidiaries.

Bar A bar graph represents the data points in your series with bars of different heights. Although you can plot any data on a bar graph, this graph type is especially appropriate for comparing the values in several series. 3-D and vertical bar graphs are variations of a regular bar graph.

Line A line graph shows the points of your data range or ranges plotted against the Y axis. The points may be connected with a line, shown as symbols, or both. The line graph is an excellent choice for plotting trend data over time, such as sales, profit, or expenses.

Stacked Bar A stacked bar graph places the values in each series on top of each other for any one point on the X axis. The total height of a bar represents the total values in all the series plotted for any given point. Use a stacked bar graph when you want to see both total levels and components' levels. Contribution to total company profit of the various subsidiaries could be shown effectively on a stacked bar graph, for example.

Overlapped Bar An overlapped bar graph overlaps the values of several series for any one point on the X axis, with the first series in front. An overlapped bar is more appropriate than a bar graph when you want to emphasize the values of the first series.

Pie A pie chart shows one range of values, representing each value's percentage of the total by the size of its pie wedge. A pie chart works well when you need to see the relative size of different components. Pie charts are effective for analyzing different kinds of expenses, or the contribution to profit from different product lines, for example.

XY An XY graph plots the values in one series against those in another. For example, you could use an XY graph to plot age against salary, machine repairs by age, or time against temperature.

HLCO A HLCO chart shows the high, low, close, and open values. For each set of data values for each X-axis value (such as each day you are recording stock prices), the HLCO graph has a line from the high to the low value. A projection to the left indicates the opening value and a projection to the right indicates the closing value. Additional ranges can appear as a bar graph below the high, low, close, and open values, and as a line graph shown with the high, low, close, and open values. This graph type is normally used to graph financial commodities or statistical results.

Mixed A mixed graph combines features from bar, line, area, stacked bar, and overlapped bar graphs. Each series can use one of these graph types. You use this graph type to combine different types of data such as market share percentage and profits.

Expanding Type Options Through the Graph Window

When you select Type from a graph window, you can also select the graph type. 1-2-3/G offers four graph type options that are not available in the Graph Type or Graph Setup dialog box—two additional graph types and the ability to display the X axis horizontally or vertically.

Two New Graph Types

In the Type menu in a graph window, you can select overlapped bar and high-low-close-open graphs. The overlapped bar graph is like a bar graph with the bars clustered around X axis data points. In a clustered bar graph, all except the first data range overlap the previous bar, as shown in the overlapped graph in Figure 16-9. The values in the first series are emphasized since they are not overlapped.

The high-low-close-open, or HLCO, graphs were developed for tracking stock market performance. As shown in the HLCO graph in Figure 16-9, the graph draws a line from the high to the low value for each data point on the X axis. The opening value is drawn as a line to the left and the closing value is drawn as a line to the right of the vertical line reflecting the high and low values. This graph can also include a series drawn as a bar graph that you might use to graph volume. Additional series you might add are line graphs, which can include averages of competitors' prices.

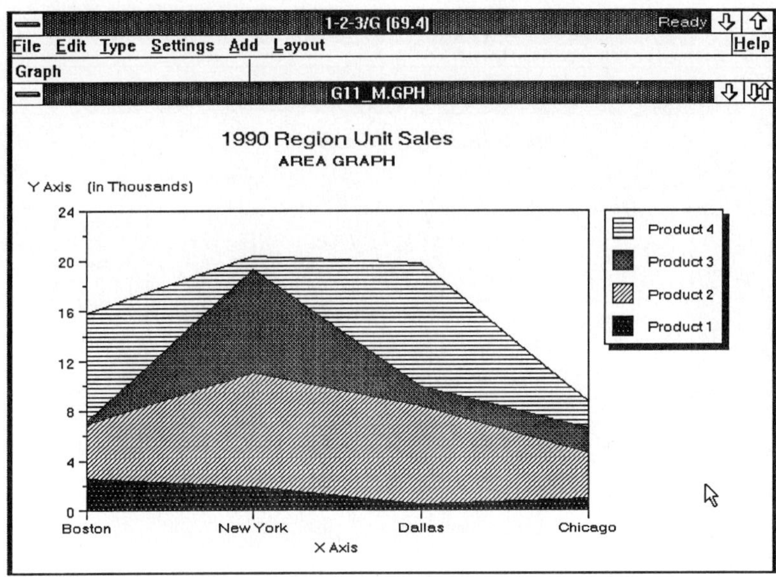

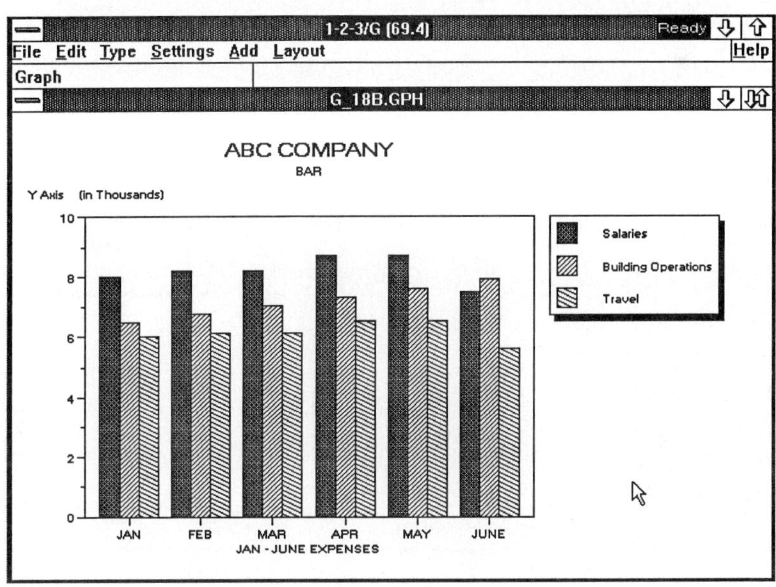

Figure 16-9. Examples of different graph types (*continued on following pages*)

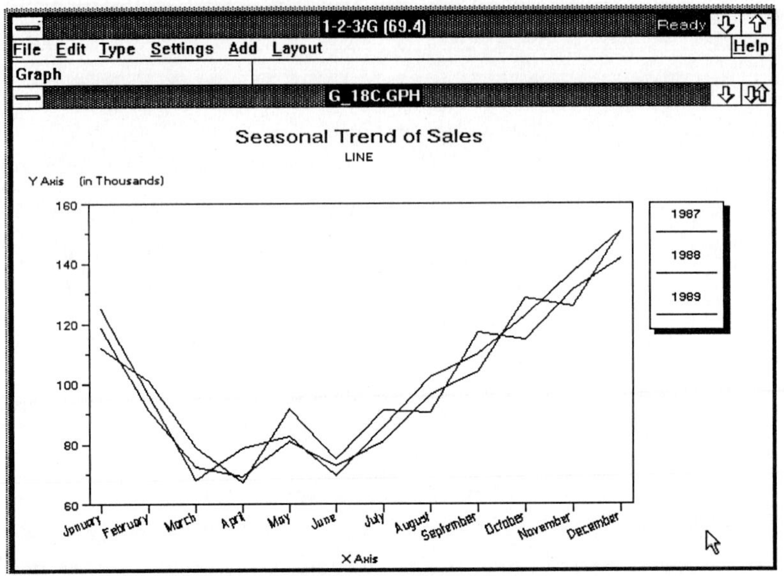

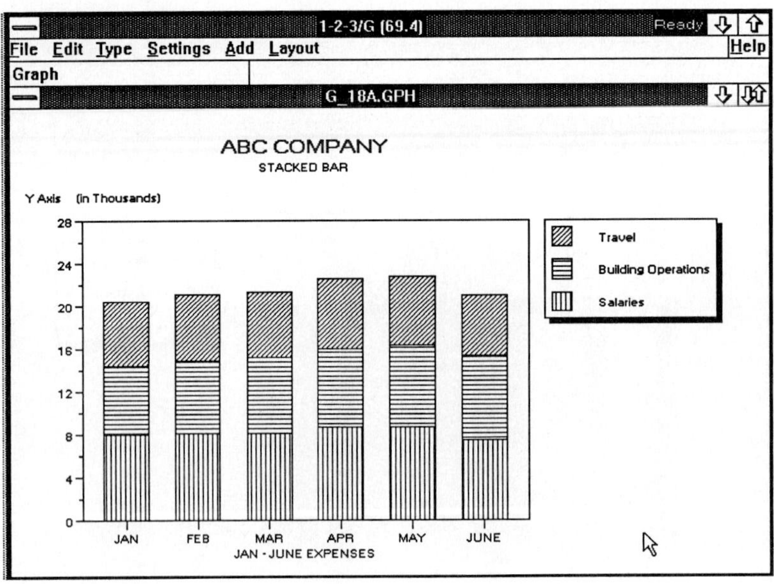

Figure 16-9. Examples of different graph types (*continued*)

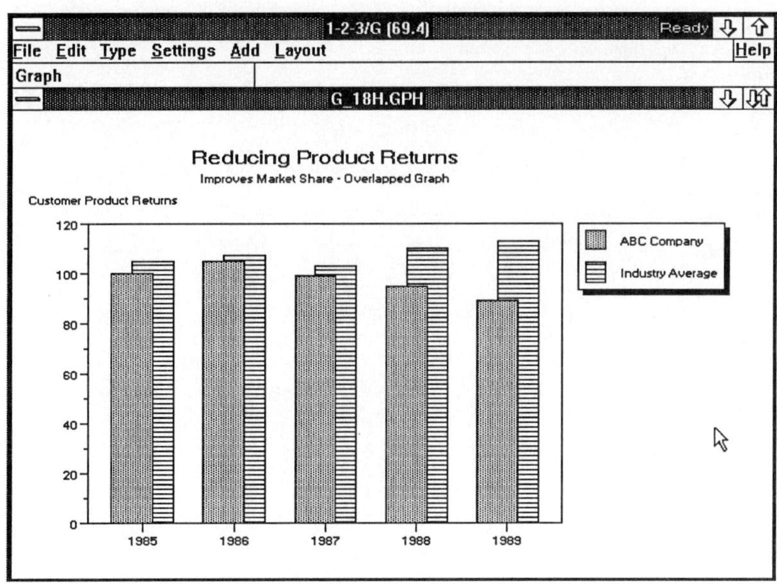

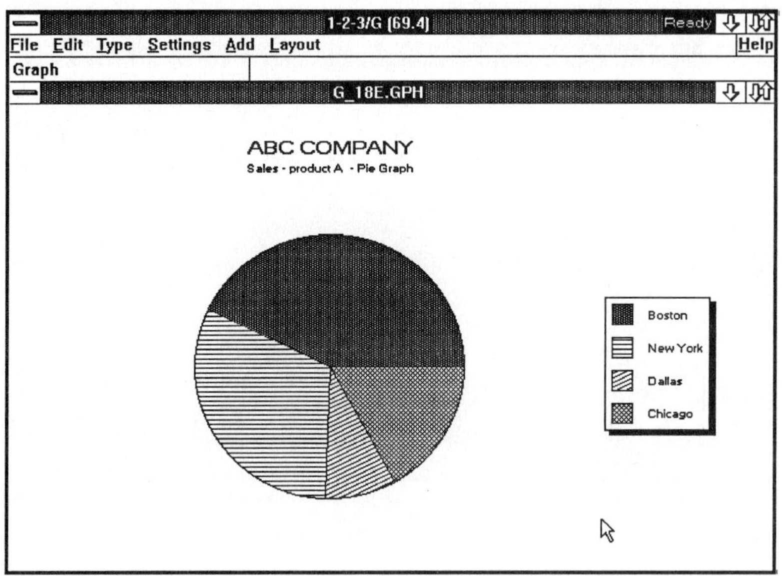

Figure 16-9. Examples of different graph types (*continued*)

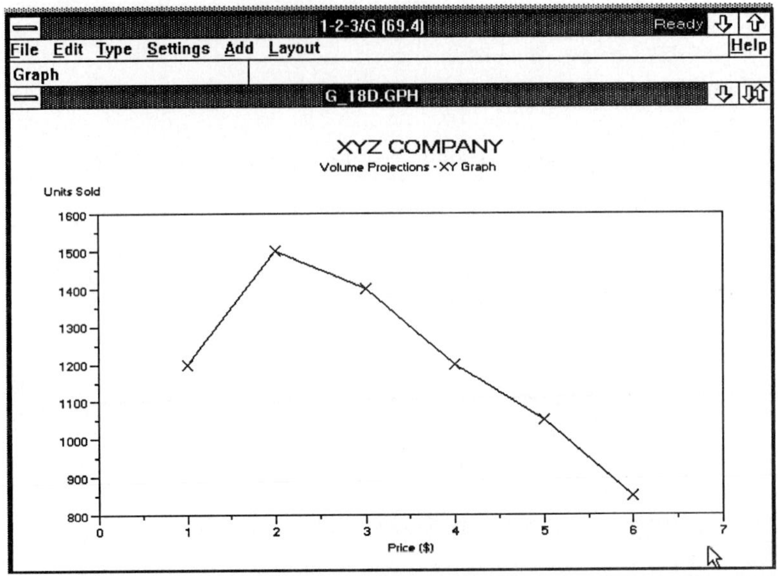

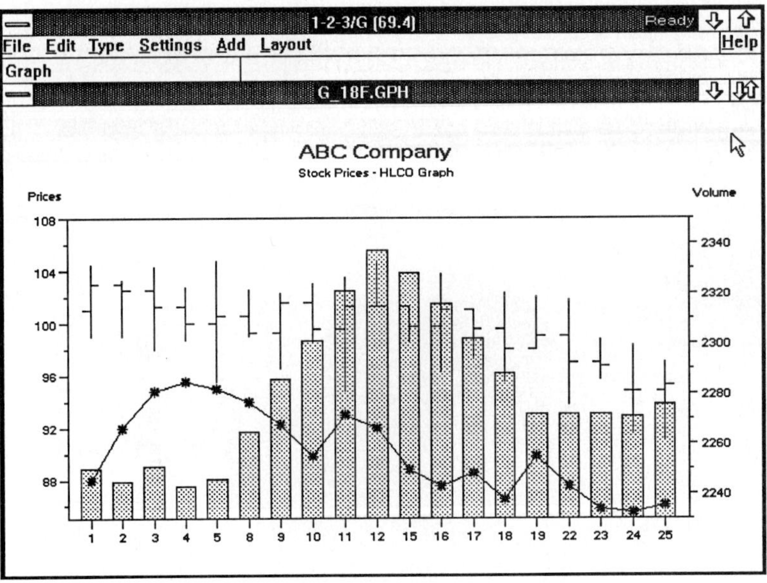

Figure 16-9. Examples of different graph types (*continued*)

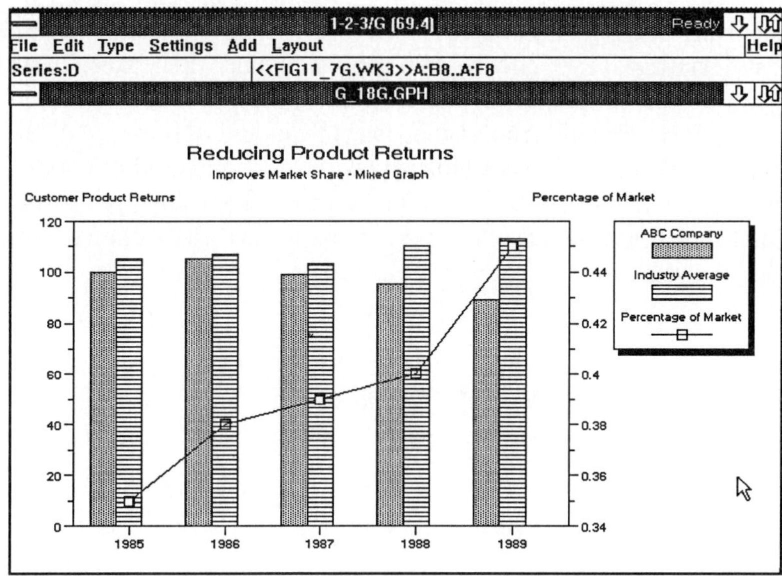

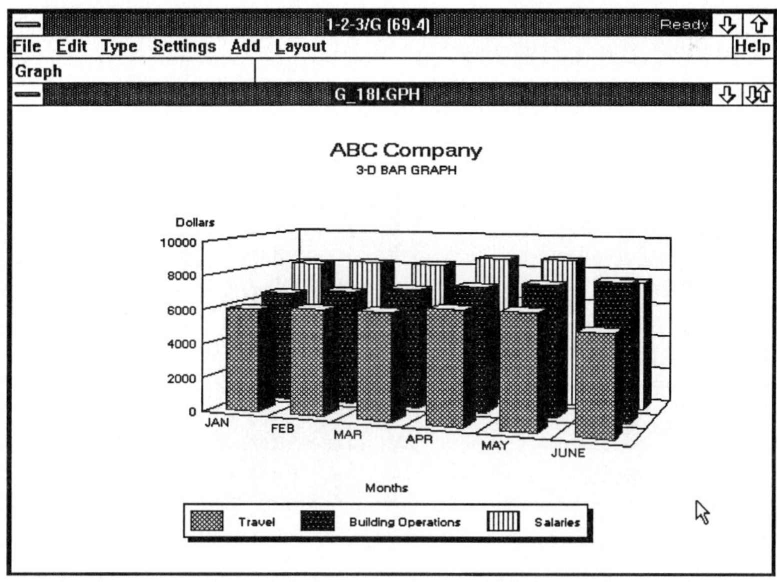

Figure 16-9. Examples of different graph types

Vertical Versus Horizontal Axes

The Horizontal and Vertical choices in the Setup menu available in a graph window direct how certain graphs display their axes. In all graph types except pie graphs, by default the X axis is horizontal and the Y axis vertical. For all graph types except Pie and 3-D bar, you can rotate the axes. When you select Horizontal, 1-2-3/G makes the X axis vertical and the Y axis horizontal. Selecting Vertical from the Type menu makes X axis horizontal and the Y axis vertical. Figure 16-10 shows two graphs with the same data but reversed axes.

A Gallery of Type and Style Choices

The gallery available though the graph windows lets you change graph types and styles with a minimal time investment. The gallery features

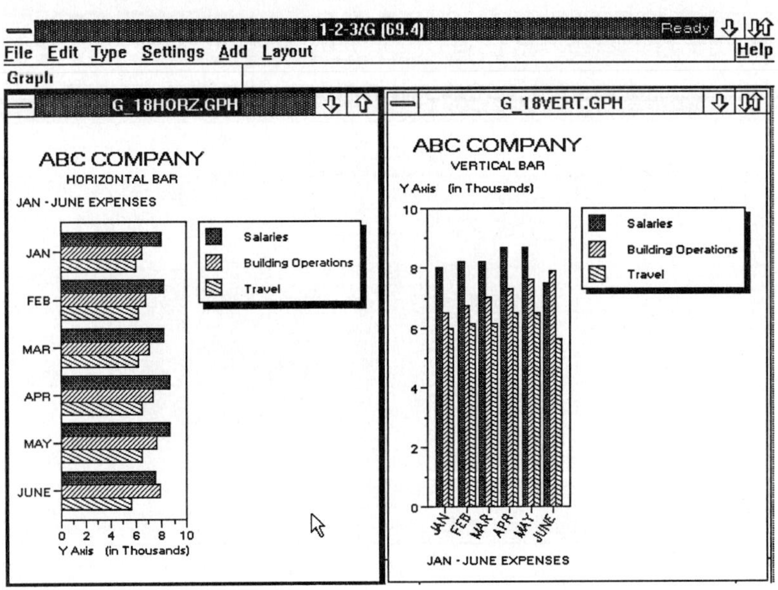

Figure 16-10. Graphs with different axis rotations

provide an alternative method to select a graph type. Although you can create any gallery graph with a series of commands, if you see an image in the gallery you like you don't need to know the commands required to complete the changes. By choosing the screen image you like best you can affect settings such as titles and location as well as graph type.

After selecting Type Gallery from the graph window, you can select a graph type from the option buttons. In the right side of the dialog box, you can select a graphic image that combines style options with the basic graph type you selected.

The Bar-Line choice displays the first series as a line graph and the remaining series as bars. The style boxes offer features such as legend placement, axis orientation, and labels for data points. While these features are covered in more detail in Chapter 17, "Advanced Graph Techniques," you can quickly try out a variety of options by selecting a graphic image that displays the features the way you wish to present them.

Assigning X-Axis Labels

Unless you use the instant graph features, you must define the data to be shown on your graph. You might want to define X-axis labels for your graph—labels placed along the X axis, for all graphs except XY and pie charts. These labels are stored in a range on the worksheet and can mark the points of the graph as years, months, or other data values. For the example in Figure 16-11, the cells containing the words "JAN" through "JUNE" are selected as the X range. The words in the X range are placed along the X axis, as shown in Figure 16-12.

For pie charts, the X range is used to label the sections of the pie. It might list regions, expense categories, and so on. X-range data for a pie chart must be in the same sequence as the data you provide for the A range, which gives the values for the chart.

For XY charts, the X-range data is plotted against corresponding Y values provided by the data ranges. For an XY graph, the entries should be values rather than labels. If an XY type is selected for an automatic graph, 1-2-3/G uses the worksheet data differently. The XY graphs skip rows or columns containing labels and use the first numeric row or column as the first data range (the X axis).

To select an X data range using 1-2-3/G's menus, choose Add Ranges from the Graph menu in a worksheet window. Then, from the

1-2-3/G [69.4] Ready

File Edit Worksheet Range Copy... Move... Print Graph Data Utility Quit... Help

A:A5 'Salaries

FIG11_A.WG1

A	A	B	C	D	E	F	G
1				ABC Company			
2							
3							
4	**Expenses**	JAN	FEB	MAR	APR	MAY	JUNE
5	Salaries	$8,000	$8,200	$8,200	$8,700	$8,700	$7,500
6	Building Operations	6,500	6,760	7,030	7,312	7,604	7,908
7	Travel	6,000	6,150	6150	6,525	6,525	5,625
8	Supplies	500	500	500	500	500	500
9	Depreciation	1,200	1,200	1,200	1,200	1,200	1,200
10	Equipment Maintenance	750	750	750	750	750	750
11	Shipping Expense	400	400	400	400	400	400
12	Data Processing Costs	2,100	2,100	2,100	2,100	2,100	2,100
13	Printing & Duplicating	640	640	640	640	640	640
14	Other	1,030	1,030	1,030	1,030	1,030	1,030
15	**Total Expenses**	$27,120	$27,730	$28,000	$29,157	$29,449	$27,653
16							
17							

Figure 16-11. Worksheet data for graph

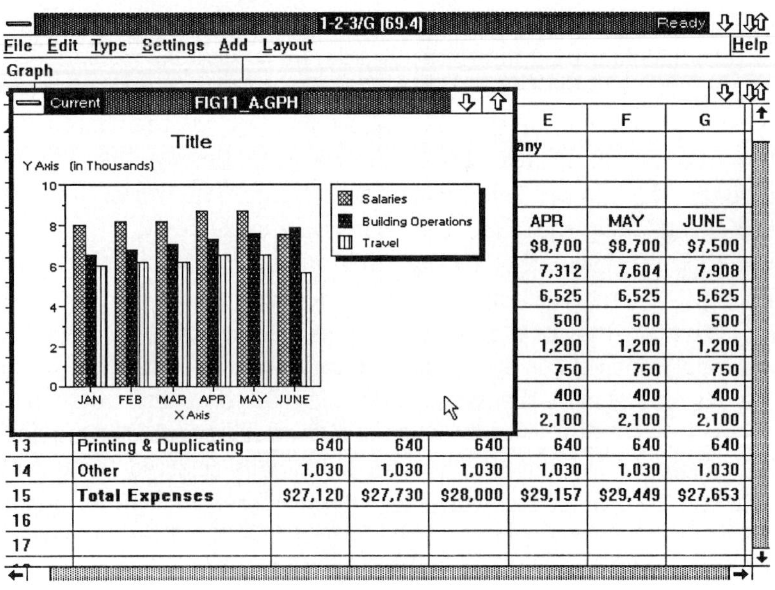

Figure 16-12. Using a range as X-axis labels

dialog box shown in Figure 16-13, select X and the range containing the worksheet cells to use as the X-axis labels. You can also select X-axis labels by choosing Graph Setup. From the Graph Setup dialog box, you can tell 1-2-3/G to take the first row or column from the range by selecting the X labels from the first column/row selection box. You can indicate that the X axis and the other data ranges are stored in separate columns by selecting the Columnwise option button. You can indicate that the X axis and the other data ranges are stored in separate rows by selecting the Rowwise option button.

The Y axis

In contrast to the X axis, the Y axis is labeled automatically once you select the data for your graph. 1-2-3/G determines whether it needs to represent your data values in thousands, millions, and so on, and labels the Y axis appropriately. This label is called the *scale indicator.* In an XY graph, both axes can use a scale indicator.

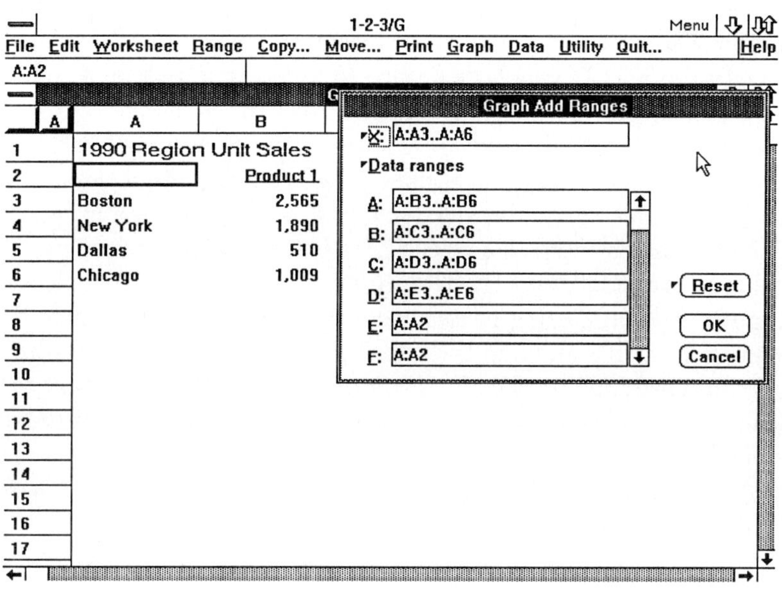

Figure 16-13. Graph Add Ranges dialog box

Selecting Graph Data

1-2-3/G lets you show up to 23 sets of data values on all graph types except the pie graph. A set of data values might represent the sales of a product for a period of months or years, or the number of rejects on a production line for each of the last 16 weeks. You can use any series of values, as long as they all pertain to the same subject, and are organized according to the points labeled on the X axis. The 23 different sets of data values are specified for the chart in data ranges A through W.

Since pie graphs show what percentage each value is of the total, they are not appropriate for multiple sets of data. With a pie graph, you use only the A data range for your data values. As mentioned in "Assigning X-Axis Labels," you use the X range to label the sections of the pie. 1-2-3/G can use the B and C data ranges to change the appearance of the pie slices, as discussed in the next chapter.

The high-low-close-open (HLCO) graph automatically decides how different ranges are treated. As mentioned, it is designed for financial applications, such as following the price of a stock. A HLCO graph expects a high-to-low range for each value of X. The A data range is the high value for each X value; the B data range is the low value for each X value. The C data range is the closing value, and the D data range is the opening value for the X values. The E data range is graphed as a bar graph. The remaining data ranges are graphed as a line graph.

In the HLCO graph in Figure 16-9, the X data range contains the dates for which you are tracking the stock price, as in 1 through 25 in the graph. The A data range contains the highest sell values for the stock during each day; the B data range contains the lowest sell values. In Figure 16-9, the high price for day 1 is 104.5 and the low price is 99. A bar connects these two prices. The C data range contains the closing value of the stock, and the D data range contains its opening value. In Figure 16-9, the closing price for day 1 is marked with a bar to the right representing 103 and and the opening price is marked with a bar to the left representing 101. The E data range contains the numbers of shares traded, as in 2250 for day 1, and the F data range contains the average stock price for the industry, as in 88 for day 1. HLCO graphs allow you to focus on trends in stock prices. The next chapter discusses these HLCO graphs in more detail.

Choosing the Data Ranges

Earlier character-based releases of 1-2-3/G limited data assignments to six different ranges on one graph. 1-2-3/G supports as many as 23 different series through range assignments A through W. The Graph Add Ranges dialog box displays the possible ranges of data values to be shown on a graph. If you plan to show only one set of data values, choose A and specify the range of cells containing the numeric values to plot on the graph. You can include cells from other worksheets and other Presentation Manager application files. To show other sets of data in the graph, select as many range letters as are appropriate, and specify the range of data to be assigned to each. Remember that you don't have to show all your worksheet data on a graph; you can select just the most important data ranges. For example, you may have sales, cost of goods sold, and profit data on your worksheet, but you may elect to graph just the Profit data.

Figure 16-14 shows the unit sales of four products for the Boston, New York, Dallas, and Chicago regions of a company. To create a graph from this data, select Graph to invoke the Graph menu, and then select Type. If you want to see the data for Product 1 as a pie chart, choose Pie. Next, select Graph and Add Ranges. Select A for the first data range and specify B3..B6 as the range containing the data. You can specify this range by selecting a range from the worksheet, or by typing the range reference. Now, select X, and specify A3..A6 as the X-axis range.

Choosing Data Ranges with the Cell Pointer

When creating an instant graph or using Graph Setup, you can select the cells the graph uses with the cell pointer. If you use these methods, 1-2-3/G makes several assumptions about the cells to use for graph ranges based on the cell pointer's location. When you select Graph Setup, or select Graph View without defining a graph, 1-2-3/G selects the range the cell pointer is located in, splitting the range into individual series assignments. 1-2-3/G selects a range of nonblank cells; it defines this range as separated by other worksheet data on the same sheet by

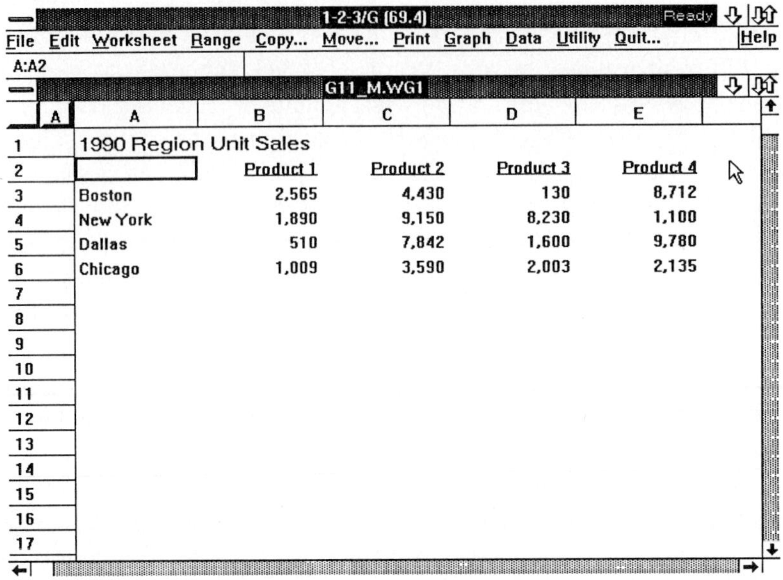

1-2-3/G (69.4) Ready

File Edit Worksheet Range Copy... Move... Print Graph Data Utility Quit... Help

A:A2

G11_M.WG1

	A	B	C	D	E
1	1990 Region Unit Sales				
2		Product 1	Product 2	Product 3	Product 4
3	Boston	2,565	4,430	130	8,712
4	New York	1,890	9,150	8,230	1,100
5	Dallas	510	7,842	1,600	9,780
6	Chicago	1,009	3,590	2,003	2,135
7					
8					
9					
10					
11					
12					
13					
14					
15					
16					
17					

Figure 16-14. Sales data for four locations

two columns and two rows. For example, if your cell pointer is in A5 andthe Worksheet contains entries in A1..D13, 1-2-3/G will use A1..D13 for the graph, assuming the Worksheet has at least two empty columns to the right of A1..D13 and at least two blank rows below A1..D13. The edge of a worksheet can count as two blank rows. 1-2-3/G looks at the first row and column of the range to see if they contain labels. If they do, these labels are prospective X-axis labels and legends.

1-2-3/G also looks at the number of rows and columns in the range. Unlike an instant graph, in a graph created with Graph Setup you can change the assumptions 1-2-3/G automatically makes about your data range. From the Graph Setup dialog box, you can change the graph type, whether 1-2-3/G divides the range by rows or columns, whether 1-2-3/G uses the labels in the first row or column for X-axis labels or legends, and the range 1-2-3/G uses for the graph data. If you select Area for the graph type with the data in Figure 16-14, the result will look like Figure 16-15.

You can select the range the graph uses before selecting Graph View or Graph Setup; 1-2-3/G will use the selected range for the graph, instead of the range that it would automatically select. You can also select collections to skip rows or columns; 1-2-3/G will only use the selected data.

Adding Data Ranges Through Links

You can also assign data ranges for a graph by establishing links. When you select data ranges with Graph Add Ranges, you are using 1-2-3/G to create the links for you. The links between the worksheet and the graph files are updated only while both files are open.

You can establish new links to a graph. You will want to establish links when you are combining data from multiple worksheets. For example, suppose you want to graph the data in the GDIV_1 and GDIV_2 worksheets shown in Figure 16-16. You can only use the Graph Add Ranges command with one worksheet. To select the graph data range

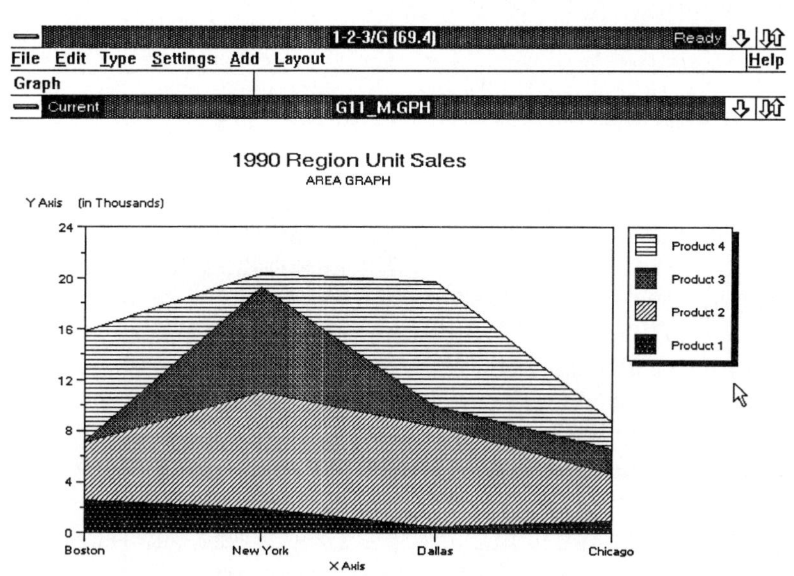

Figure 16-15. Area graph

from the other worksheet, you must link the second worksheet to the graph. You can also link the graph to other Presentation Manager applications. For instance, you could create a graph in 1-2-3/G that uses data stored in other applications. Links are covered in more detail in Chapters 10 and 17.

The easiest way to create a link is to copy the data that you want to link to the Clipboard and then use the clipboard data as the source of the link. For example, with the worksheets shown in Figure 16-16, you can copy the range A:B2..A:B5 in the GDIV-2 worksheet file to the Clipboard. Then, from the graph window containing the graph you are developing, select Edit Link Create to obtain the dialog box shown in Figure 16-17. The clipboard information is shown as the source file and item. If you did not copy the range to the Clipboard, you can also select the filename from the list of open 1-2-3/G worksheet files and other Presentation Manager applications files that a graph can potentially use. Lotus applications are shown in uppercase and other applications are shown in lowercase.

1-2-3/G [69.4] Ready

File Edit Worksheet Range Copy... Move... Print Graph Data Utility Quit... Help

A:B2 336633

GDIV_1.WG1

A	A	B	C
1	Division 1	Sales	
2	1st Qtr	336633	
3	2nd Qtr	217996	
4	3rd Qtr	302211	
5	4th Qtr	378678	
6			
7			
8			
9			
10			
11			
12			
13			
14			
15			
16			
17			

GDIV_2.WG1

A	A	B	C
1	Division 2	Sales	
2	1st Qtr	360915	
3	2nd Qtr	247741	
4	3rd Qtr	355673	
5	4th Qtr	313015	
6			
7			
8			
9			
10			
11			
12			
13			
14			
15			
16			
17			

Figure 16-16. Two worksheets with data for one graph

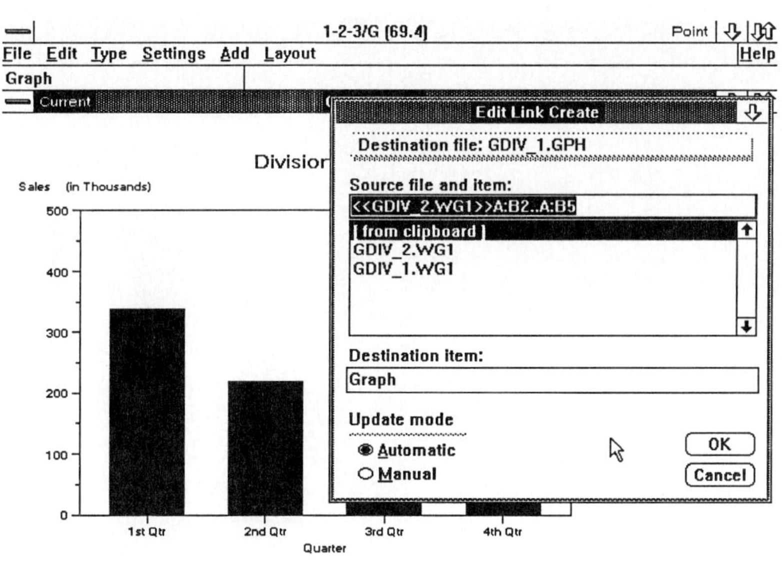

Figure 16-17. Edit Link Create dialog box

Under Destination item is the graph object name for which the link will be created. To establish a link to a new series, press F3 (Name) and select Series or type **Series.** 1-2-3/G assigns the link to the next unused series. Under Update mode, selecting Automatic updates the links as the values in the links change; selecting Manual only updates the links when you select Edit Link Update. In both cases, the file with the source must be open.

If you later want to change the data range, select the object by choosing Edit Select Object Series and the letter for the data range. Then select Edit Link Edit to display the Edit Link Edit dialog box, which contains the same settings you entered in the Edit Link Create dialog box. Change these settings to change the link information.

Adding Descriptive Labels

Figure 16-18 shows a bar graph. This graph has been enhanced with titles at the top, labels for the X and Y axes, and legends. With these

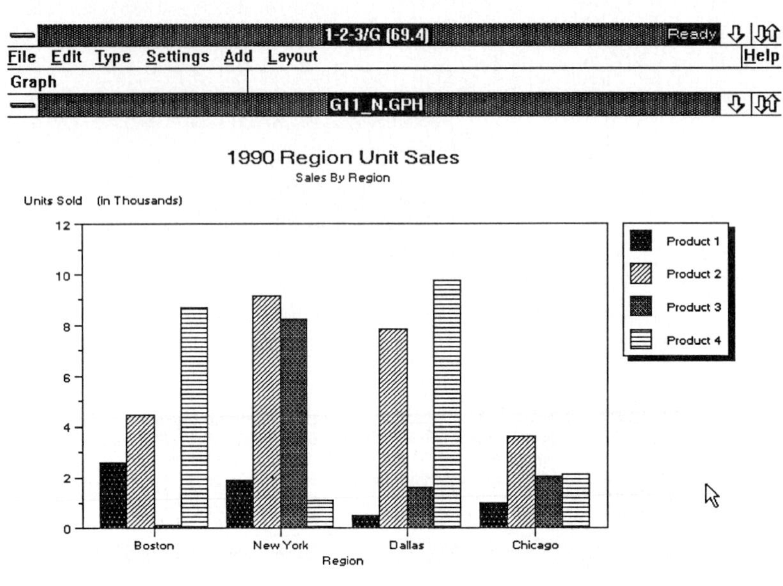

Figure 16-18. Bar graph using titles and legends

extras, a graph conveys your message more effectively. You can also select the color, font, and size of the text, as well as the color, font, and size of any object in the graph containing text.

Adding Legends

A *legend* provides a description for each of the ranges shown on a graph (see the box on the upper-right side of the graph window in Figure 16-18). In a pie graph, 1-2-3/G uses the legend to display the X-axis labels. If you create a line graph, the legend defines the color of the line connecting the data points and the markers each data range uses, if any. If you create a graph with bars, the legend defines the color and pattern each data range uses. You saw how instant graphs use worksheet data for legends. A graph created with Graph Setup also uses worksheet data as text if you select the Legends from the first row/column box. If you define a graph with the Graph Add Ranges command, you must select or enter the text you want for the legend for each data range.

You add legends via the Graph Options Legend command. In the dialog box shown in Figure 16-19, select Data ranges and the letter corresponding to the data range for which you want to specify a legend. If the data range you want is not visible, type its letter. If you are not certain which letter to type, use the arrow or the scroll bar to view. You can also display the desired choice and click the mouse to select it. Select Range if the text that you want for all of the legends is predefined in a range in the worksheet.

When you select a data range, 1-2-3/G prompts you for its legend description. The legends in Figure 16-19 are Product 1 through Product 4 for the A, B, C, and D ranges, respectively. If the desired legend appears in a worksheet cell, you can merely type a backslash (\) and the address of the cell containing the legend data. For example, typing **\A:D2** tells 1-2-3/G to use the text in cell A:D2 as the legend for the C data range. When you complete the dialog box, 1-2-3/G will convert the cell address to a range address as shown in the figure. 1-2-3/G accepts up to 512 characters for the legend, but lengthy legend text reduces the space used for the graphed data. Later, you will learn how to split such text into several lines.

If you select Range, 1-2-3/G prompts you for the worksheet range containing the predefined legends. After you select the range containing the legend text, 1-2-3/G assigns the first cell as the A range legend, the

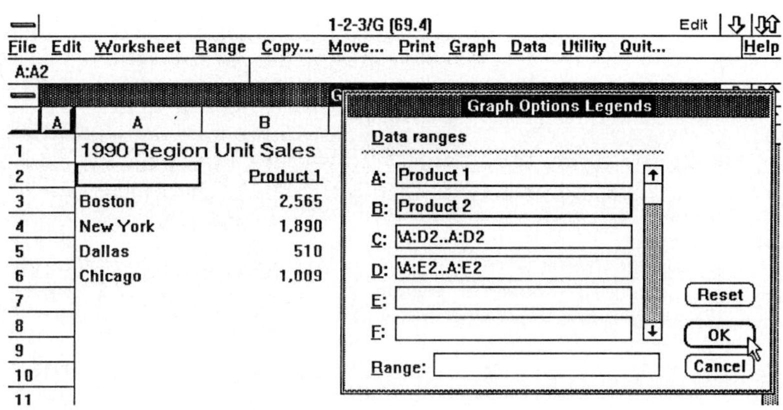

Figure 16-19. Graph Options Legends dialog box

second cell as the B range legend, and so on, until it runs out of cells or graph data ranges. For example, for the legends in Figure 16-19, you could have selected Range and then selected B2..E2.

Adding Titles

Titles are descriptive text placed in defined locations on a graph. 1-2-3/G has five title options, four of which you can access through the Graph Options Titles command. Titles can appear at the top of the chart, below the first title, or along the X or Y axis—the default titles for these are Title, Second Title, X Axis, and Y Axis. Second Title is the only one of these that doesn't appear automatically on an instant graph. You can change any of the default titles by selecting the option and entering new text. If you use Edit Select Object from the graph tool, you can also add a title for the second Y axis which is used when one axis is not adequate for displaying all the data ranges.

When you select Graph Options Titles, you see the dialog box shown in Figure 16-20. The first title appears at the top of the graph. For example, the first line title of the graph in Figure 16-18 was generated by typing **1990 Region Unit Sales** in the First title box. A line for a second label is also reserved at the top of the graph. To place an entry in this location, type **Sales By Region** in the Second title box.

You can also give titles to the X or Y axis. These titles normally describe the quantities being measured. The Y-axis title might be Dollars and the X-axis title might be Sales, for example. By default, 1-2-3/G

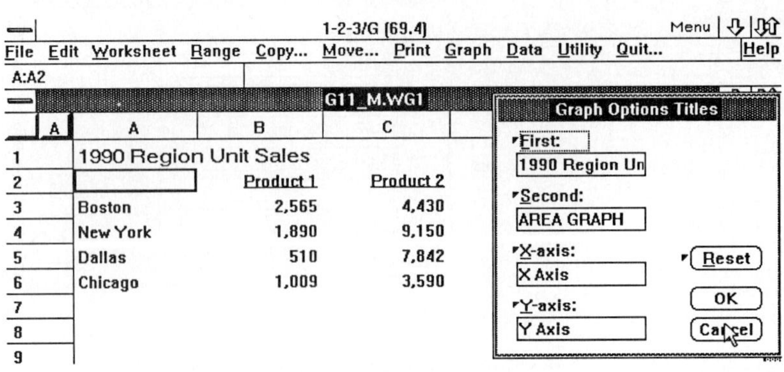

Figure 16-20. Graph Options Titles dialog box

places the Y-axis title horizontally above the Y axis and the X-axis title horizontally below the X axis. A graph containing a second Y axis can also have a second Y-axis title, but you must select the text for the title from the graph window.

1-2-3/G lets you enter up to 512 characters for all titles. Your graph will show fewer characters depending on the size of the text. Like legends, you can assign titles from cell entries by typing a backslash followed by the cell address.

Resetting Graphs

After specifying particular options for a graph, you might change your mind. You can erase individual text entries by reentering the appropriate command and deleting the existing text entry from the prompt. As an example, if you wish to remove a first line title of ABC COMPANY, select Graph Options Title First and delete the title ABC COMPANY from this entry. If you used a cell reference to supply the text entry, just delete the cell reference and backslash from the entry. Several dialog boxes include a Reset command button to quickly reset all entries in the displayed dialog box.

However, if you want to eliminate all the graph settings, you should use Graph Reset. This command eliminates all graph settings, including ranges. It lets you redefine a new graph from the beginning. You will need to select the Yes command button to confirm that you want to remove the graph settings.

Storing and Using Graphs

The graphs created so far have been current graphs for the worksheet file. 1-2-3/G limits the worksheet file to one current graph at a time. To include multiple graphs in your worksheet, you must name a current graph before you create a new one. Once you name a graph, it can become the current graph later.

Naming Graphs for Later Use

1-2-3/G uses all the graph settings you make to define the current graph. Since you can only have one current graph in a graph window at a time, you will lose the original settings if you choose different settings for a new graph. To retain the definition of the current graph while you begin a new graph, first save the current graph with Graph Name Create or create a new graph window with a different name.

If you name the current graph settings, 1-2-3/G prompts you for the name of the graph to create. You can type any name up to 15 characters in length, or you can select one from the list. To eliminate all current settings after saving the graph, use Graph Reset. You can then start defining a new graph, which you can name when the definition is complete. When you save your worksheet, all the graph names and definitions are saved along with the other file data.

You can reuse a graph whose settings you have saved. To do so, select Graph Name Use and specify the graph name. The settings that were current when the graph was saved are activated, and the graph you named will be the current graph in the graph window.

1-2-3/G's ability to name and save graphs lets you create a number of graphs on one worksheet file. You can define and name all the graphs you need for a single application. Then, when you update your worksheet figures, you can create an up-to-date slide show of graphic results by using and viewing each of the named graphs. You don't have to recreate the graphs, because the graph settings are saved with the worksheet.

Tip: 1-2-3/G doesn't retain the changes that you make to a graph unless you save it again with the Graph Name Create command. This command saves the named graph with the other worksheet data. To use this graph in another 1-2-3/G session, save the worksheet file.

Deleting Graphs

The Graph Name Delete command lets you eliminate stored graph settings that you no longer need. 1-2-3/G displays a list of all existing graph names when you select this command. Selecting a name from the list or typing in a name eliminates all the settings for that graph. Now, if you decide to reproduce the graph, you must reenter all the graph options.

Saving a Graph Window

The graphs displayed in a graph window are connected to the worksheet. You can save the graph window, and the last graph displayed in the window will appear when you open the graph file in a graph window. You can also create several graph windows using one worksheet as the basis of the graph data. This is an alternative to naming the settings of each graph you want to use. 1-2-3/G only updates the data in a graph window when you open both the graph and the worksheet containing the data in the graph.

To save a graph window, select File Save. You can save the graph window alone or as part of the graph type. You can also enter a graph filename different than the name of the worksheet file. The graph file uses a .GPH file extension. When you select Graph View from a worksheet file, 1-2-3/G always displays the graph window with the same filename as the worksheet file.

Printing Graphs

You can print your graphs directly from the 1-2-3/G program by using the File Print menus. You just need to use a few different options in the dialog boxes, since you will use the same commands for printing graphs that you used for printing worksheets. In Chapter 17, "Advanced Graph Techniques," you will learn how to print worksheet text and graphs on the same page. Besides printing directly to the printer, you can print to an encoded file. However, 1-2-3/G cannot print graphs to a text file.

If your printer only prints in one color, 1-2-3/G will convert the colors into patterns for you. The File Print Color Map command selects the patterns 1-2-3/G will use to print each color. You can also change the pattern and color 1-2-3/G uses in the graph.

Selecting Graphs to Print

When printing a graph, first activate the graph window that displays the graph to be printed. If you want to print several graphs, you may want to create multiple graph windows, displaying each graph that you want to print in a separate window. This way, you can switch rapidly between the graphs that you want to print.

Tip: Preview your graph before printing it. The preview displays the graph as it will print, giving you a last chance to check its appearance.

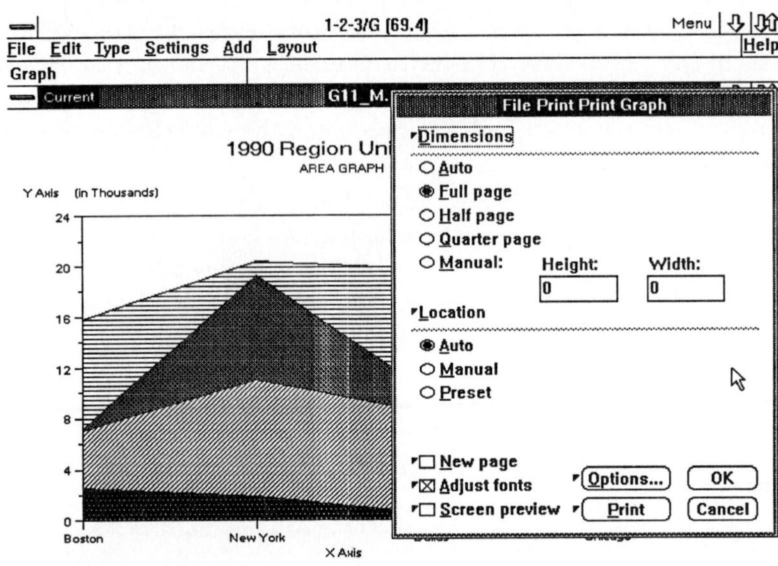

Figure 16-21. File Print Print Graph dialog box

Print Menu Commands for Graphs

When you select File Print Print Graph from a graph window, 1-2-3/G displays the dialog box shown in Figure 16-21. This dialog box contains options for selecting the size and position of the graph. You can also determine whether the graph appears on a new page, adjust the font size, and display the output in a preview screen. Selecting Options displays a dialog box for choosing margins, headers, footers, and other settings that you use to print worksheets.

From the File Print Print Graph dialog box, selecting New page makes 1-2-3/G advance to the next page before printing the graph. Selecting Adjust fonts tells 1-2-3/G to reduce or expand the font size as the graph size is reduced or expanded. You may want to keep the font sizes that you selected in the graph window if you are printing a small graph. Selecting Screen preview sends the output to the screen preview window instead of to the printer or the encoded file.

The remaining File Print menu commands are identical to the options with the same name that came up when you select File Print from a worksheet window. For example, by selecting Destination and Setup you can change the printer's setup to print in landscape, rotating the output 90 degrees. By selecting Color Map, you can change the patterns that 1-2-3/G prints for the different colors. When you are ready to print, select the Print command button and 1-2-3/G prints the graph to the printer, encoded file, or screen preview window. As when you print worksheets, select Print when you wish to display the graph as formatted output in the screen preview window.

Selecting the Graph Size

Under Dimensions are the options for selecting the size of the graph. By default, 1-2-3/G selects Full page, which uses an entire page to print the graph. You can also select Half page or Quarter page. You may want to adjust the graph so it fits on the same page with other print ranges. The Auto option makes the graph fit the largest remaining area on the current page. The Manual option lets you enter the number of inches or millimeters (depending on the Measurement setting in the Utility User Settings International dialog box) of the graph's height and width. The size of the resulting graph for all options except Manual depends on the page size selected for the print driver and margins chosen.

Selecting the Graph Position

Under Location are the options that select the position of the graph on the page. By default, 1-2-3/G selects Auto, which starts the graph in the upper-left corner of the page. Selecting Manual lets you enter the vertical distance between the top margin and the top of the graph, as well as the horizontal distance between the left margin and the left side of the graph. These numbers are inches or millimeters, depending on the Measurement setting in the Utility User Settings International dialog box. Selecting Preset lets you select from one of three preset horizontal and three preset vertical positions for the distance between the graph and the top and left margins. For vertical orientation, you can choose between Top, Center, or Bottom. For horizontal orientation, you can choose either Left, Center, or Right.

Adding Simple Enhancements

Once you know how to create, save, and print a basic graph, you are ready to add enhancements that turn your simple graph into a professional looking product. You can change the colors that 1-2-3/G uses for an object in a graph, and you can also change the appearance of the text. Both of these changes are easy.

Selecting A Graph Object

Before you can change a graph, you need to select a graph object so that 1-2-3/G knows what graph object is to be changed. You can select an object using the menu, a mouse, or the keyboard. 1-2-3/G only lets you select one object at a time. When an object is selected, 1-2-3/G marks it with either white or black handles. Figure 16-22 shows the C data range selected. You can also tell that an object is selected by the

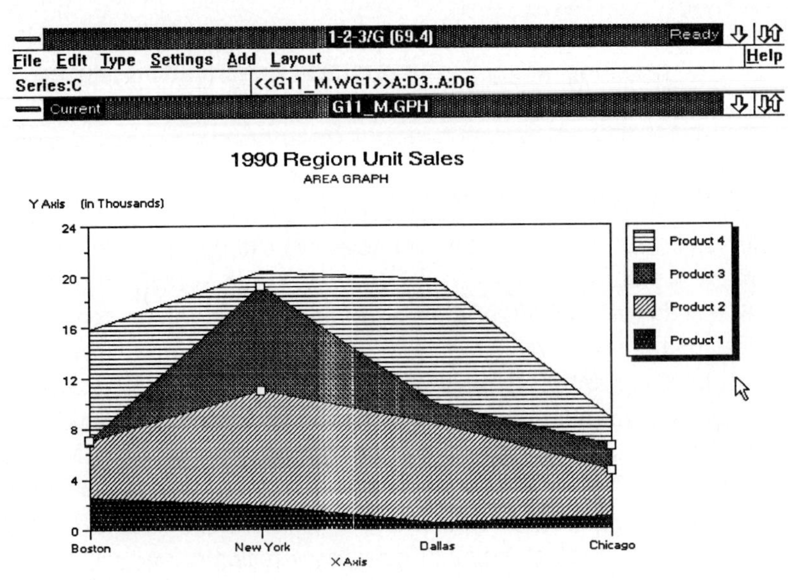

Figure 16-22. Graph object marked with handles

object name that appears in the control line—in this example, series C. With several objects, the link to the object or the text in the object also appears in the control line.

To select an object with the menu, choose Edit Select Object. From the menu, pick the description of the object, such as Legends to change a part of the legend. For objects except Plot Frame and Graph, you must refine your object selection by making additional selections from other menus or dialog boxes. For example, after selecting Series, you would select the letter of the series you want from the dialog box.

To select an object with a mouse, point to it and click. To select an object with the keyboard, press TAB or SHIFT-TAB until the name of the desired object appears in the control line and the object has handles.

Changing the Text Appearance

A graph contains many text objects. Text objects include titles, legends, scale indicators, and the axis values. In the next chapter, you will learn how to add data labels and text notations. For each of these text objects, you can change the font, boldface and italics, justification, and color. You can also split the text object into several lines if you entered the text directly rather than using a backslash and cell address to develop a link between a worksheet and the graph.

Splitting Text into Lines

With some text objects, you will want to use several lines of text. As an example, you may want to use several lines for the legend text or as a second title. You can split a long line into several smaller lines but still treat all of the lines as a single object. You can only split titles, legend text, and text notations into multiple lines.

To split a text object into several lines, select the title or legend text. Press F2 or click the object again to edit the text in the object. When the I-beam is where you want to split the text, press CTRL-ENTER. Figure 16-23 shows a legend where the text for several series is divided into two lines. You can split the first title into four lines, text notations (see Chapter 17) into five lines, and legends, axis titles, and the second title into two lines. Since all of the lines for a particular object are treated together, all changes you make to the text will change all lines of text in the object.

Selecting a Font

You can choose a particular font for a text object. To change the font and attributes of the selected text object, choose Settings Font. This presents a dialog box identical to the one you used to select fonts with the Range Attribute Font command for worksheets. From this dialog box, you can select the font the text uses and whether the font is bold, italicized, struck out, or underlined. By default, the first title uses 14-point Helvetica and the remaining text uses 8-point Helvetica.

Selecting the Text Color and Justification

By default 1-2-3/G uses black text with a white background. You can enhance the graph by changing the colors of the letters. To choose the text color, select Settings Text Style and then choose the color of the letters. Next you will learn how to change the background color of any objects, including text objects.

From the same dialog box, you can change the justification of text. This is like the label alignment you select for worksheet cells. You can

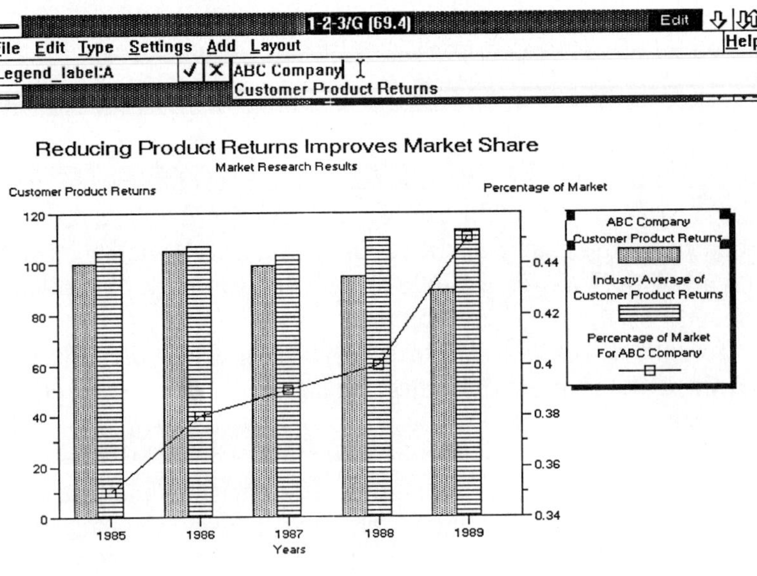

Figure 16-23. Legend with text divided into several lines

change the justification of the first and second titles and the justification of multiline entries. After selecting the object and Settings Text Style, you can choose whether the text is left-aligned, centered, or right-aligned. If you choose Settings Text Style for an object that cannot have the justification altered, the dialog box side for Justify is grayed.

Choosing Colors and Patterns

1-2-3/G automatically displays the graphs in color. You can choose the color for every object except grid lines. You can also change the pattern 1-2-3/G uses for every object except grid lines. Initially, the pattern is solid, but 1-2-3/G has 15 other patterns that you can use. You can change the color and pattern of the selected objects by selecting Settings Area Style. From the dialog box shown in Figure 16-24, you can choose a color and pattern. (On a monochrome screen, your options will appear as gray shades similar to the display shown here.) When you use this command on a text object, you are changing the color behind the

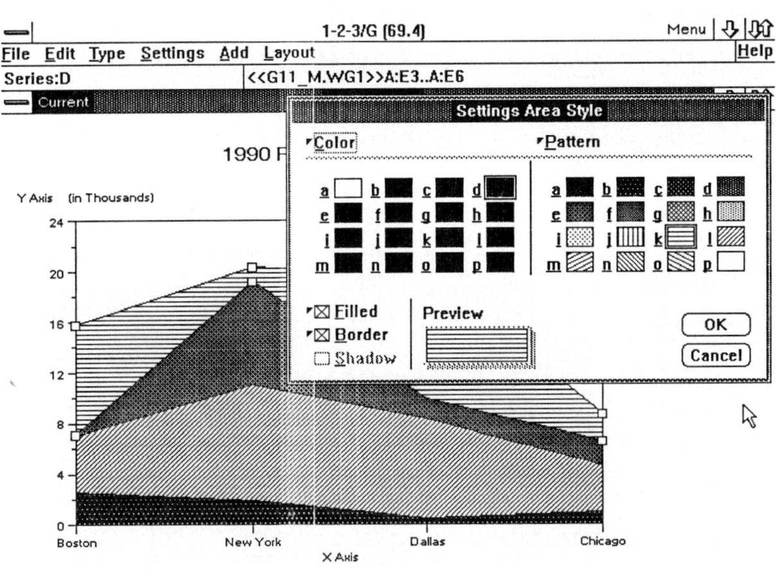

Figure 16-24. Settings Area Style dialog box

text. If Graph is the object for this command, the command changes the background color and pattern of all objects that don't have their color and pattern selected for them.

When you choose a new color and pattern you want to check how the graph looks. For example, if you choose bold and bright colors for one series and cool subdued colors for the other series, the first series will dominate the other series visually. The patterns you select also greatly affect the appearance of your graphs. In Figure 16-25, the lines don't seem straight—an illusion caused by the direction of the patterns.

The three selection boxes (Filled, Border, and Shadow) determine how the area is filled. If you select Filled, the object is filled with the selected color and pattern shown in the preview box. If you don't select Filled, the object uses the color and pattern of the graph. If you select Border, 1-2-3/G draws a line around the object. The legend automatically has a border, but you can use this option to add borders to titles, data values, and other objects in the graph. Selecting Shadow adds a shadow or three-dimensional effect to the border, and also selects Filled. This option is only available for legends and titles.

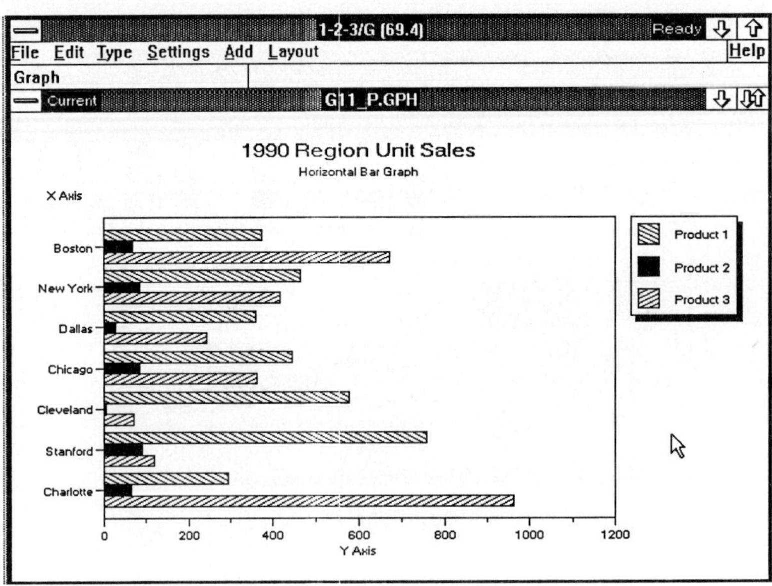

Figure 16-25. Horizontal bar graph creating visual illusion

Tip: When you choose graph colors and patterns, look at the graph from a distance to check how the colors work together and make sure the graph doesn't create any illusions.

Choosing Line Styles

All of the lines in the graph have certain features such as color, line width, and line style. This includes lines that represent each series as well as borders that you draw around objects. 1-2-3/G lets you change the line style for any object except grid lines. You can change the line style after selecting the object by choosing Settings Line/Edge Style. If you can't change the line style of the selected object, Line/Edge Style appears grayed in the Settings menu.

From the dialog box shown in Figure 16-26, you can choose whether a line is solid or divided. You can also make the line thicker. For the two thicker lines, the only line style is solid. You can choose which of the 16 colors or shades of gray to use. The Border selection box lets you decide

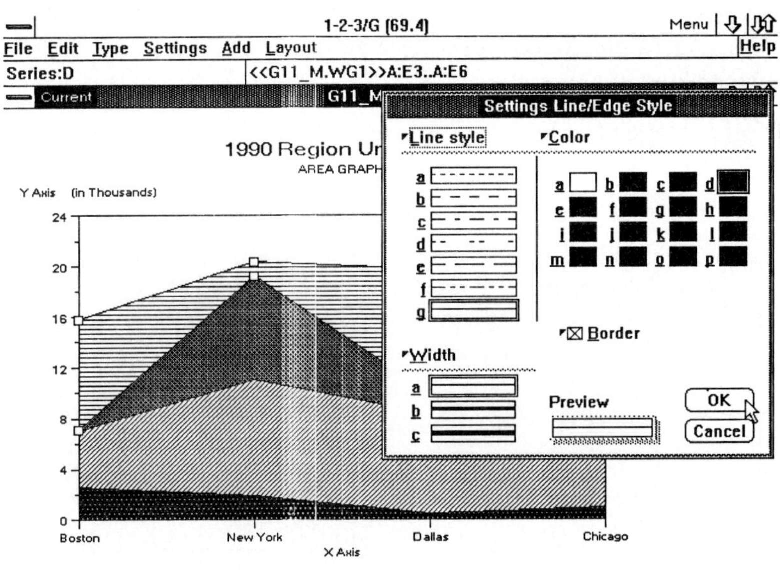

Figure 16-26. Settings Line/Edge Style dialog box

whether the object should have a border. This border will use the line displayed in the Preview box. While you can add a border with the Area Style dialog box, you must use the Setting Line/Edge Style command to change the appearance of the border.

Using Undo with Graphs

The Undo feature works differently with graphs than it does with worksheets. In a worksheet window, the Edit Undo command has no effect on graphs. For example, if you selected Graph Reset Yes without first naming the graph, you cannot use Edit Undo to restore the graph. In addition, in a graph window, 1-2-3/G only remembers the last change you made to the window, and you can only use the Edit Undo command to remove the effect of this last change. In contrast, the Edit Undo command can remove the effect of the last 20 actions from a worksheet. The Edit Undo command cannot remove the effect of Edit Link, Edit Select Object, and any File commands except File Print Print Graph. Also, you cannot undo the File commands in a graph window. If you perform one of these commands, Undo in the Edit menu is grayed.

Advanced Graph Techniques

Enhancing the Graph
Using Two Graph Types in One Graph
Changing an Object's Appearance
Using Different View Modes
Adding Notations
Advanced Linking in Graphs
Using the Clipboard in a Graph
Printing Graphs and Worksheets Together
Creating Graph Templates

SEVENTEEN

Chapters 15 and 16 covered the basic features for graphs. In this chapter, you will build on these basics by changing various graph objects such as lines, markers, axes, and scale indicators. You will learn how to move, size, and delete various graph objects. You will also discover how to add text or arrows to your graphs. In addition, you will learn how to work with graph links, clipboard data, and how to combine text and graphs on a single printed page.

Enhancing the Graph

Once you are sure that you have selected the appropriate graph type, you may want to refine your graph's appearance. 1-2-3/G offers a wide range of enhancement options, from exploding a section of pie graph to adding labels to the data ranges in the graph. The changes that you can make depend on the object you select.

1-2-3/G lets you alter an object's features quickly. Clicking a graph object selects that object. Double-clicking an object produces a dialog box that allows you to change the selected object. The dialog box varies with the object selected, as shown in Table 17-1.

Object	Dialog Box Displayed
Series	Settings Series Options
Legend frame	Settings Position Legend
Plot frame	Settings Grid/Frame
Data labels	Settings Data Labels
Titles	Edit mode for the title
Scale indicator for an axis	Settings Scale for the axis

Table 17-1. Dialog Box Displayed When You Double-Click an Object

Choosing Line and Marker Options

1-2-3/G allows you to show line graphs and XY graphs in a variety of formats. You change the lines and markers for these graphs by selecting from the right half of the Settings Series Options dialog box shown in Figure 17-1. If you select Connectors under Line format, you can show the one or more data ranges as smooth lines connecting the points. If you select Markers, you can mark the data points with one of ten different markers. If you select both, 1-2-3/G marks the data points with markers and connects them with a line. You have to select a data range before you select Settings Series Options unless you want to change all series.

After selecting the line object, you can change the color and pattern of the connecting line with the Settings Line/Edge Style command. You can use this command to change the style of any line in a graph. You change markers with the Settings Markers Style command. In the Settings Markers Style dialog box, you can choose the style and color of the selected marker. You can only use this command after selecting a series to change.

Using Data to Label Your Graph

You can use the contents of worksheet cells to label the points or bars in a graph. 1-2-3/G lets you assign data labels to any one of the data ranges in your graph. You can use the range of cells that supplies the data values for the graph, or you can use another range.

You can add the data labels to the entire graph or to a single series. Select the graph to add data labels for all series or select a specific

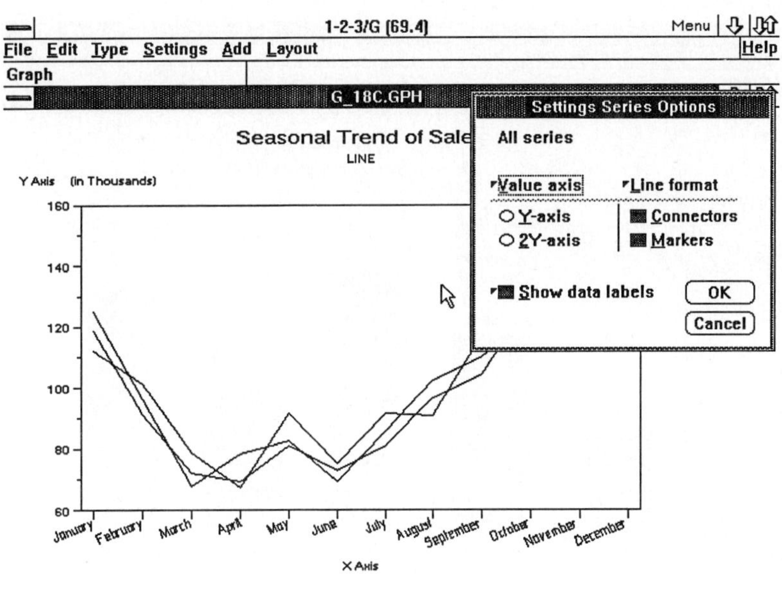

Figure 17-1. Settings Series Options dialog box

series to change just one range. Next, select Settings Series Options and the Show data labels selection box. These selections use the same data ranges that the graph uses for data points for the data labels. If you want to use a different range for data labels, edit the link that 1-2-3/G establishes for the data labels. (You will learn more about links later in this chapter.) The data labels for a series are different than the series itself. For example, if you want to change the font of some data labels, you must select the data labels and not the series the data labels represent.

After adding data labels, you can change their position relative to your data points. To do so, select Settings Data Labels. Your options are Center, Left, Above, Right, and Below. Figure 17-2 presents a bar graph with labels above the data points to indicate clearly the height of each bar.

When you add data labels to some bar graphs, you will need to change the text and background color of the data labels to make them stand out. In stacked bar, overlapped bar, and area graphs, the data labels may overlap the colors or patterns used for other series. For

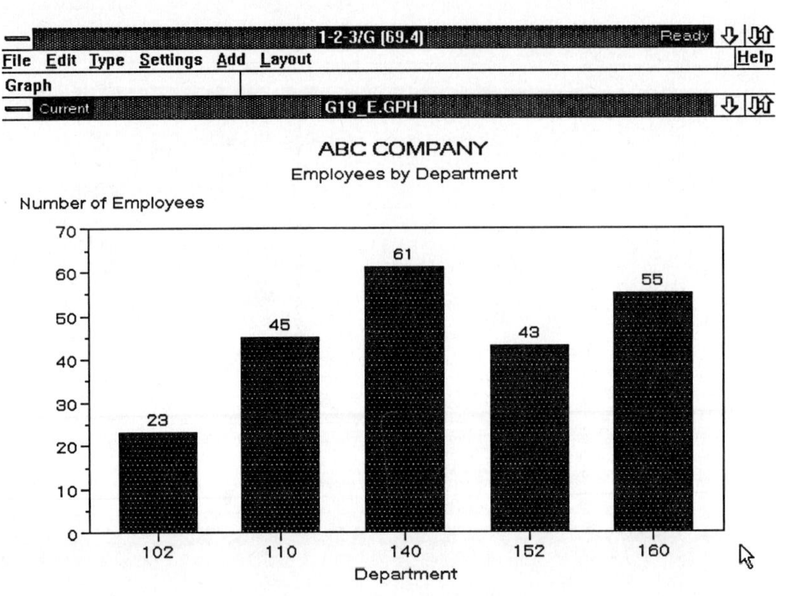

Figure 17-2. Graph using data labels

instance, a color change improved the graph in Figure 17-3, which displays the data labels below the data point in the stacked bar. The data labels are visible on both color and monochrome versions of this graph, since the Settings Text Style command set the text color to white and the Settings Area Style command set the text background color to black.

To use data labels as the only marker on a graph, create a line or XY graph. Next, select the graph and the command Settings Series Options. In the dialog box, unselect Connectors and Markers and select Show data labels. Then select the Center position for the data labels to center them on the data points. Your graph should resemble the one shown in Figure 17-4.

Using Two Y Axes

Initially, most graphs use a single Y range. However, if you are graphing different types of data, you may want to include two Y axes—one for

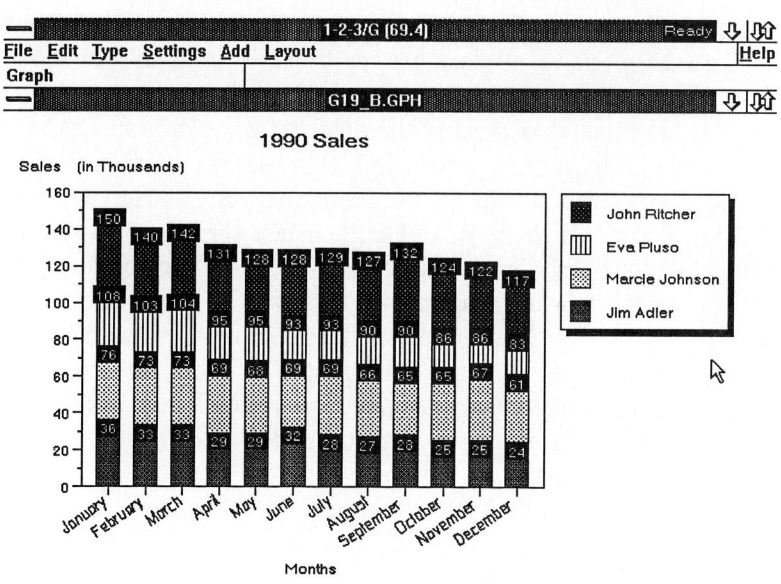

Figure 17-3. Displaying data labels below data points

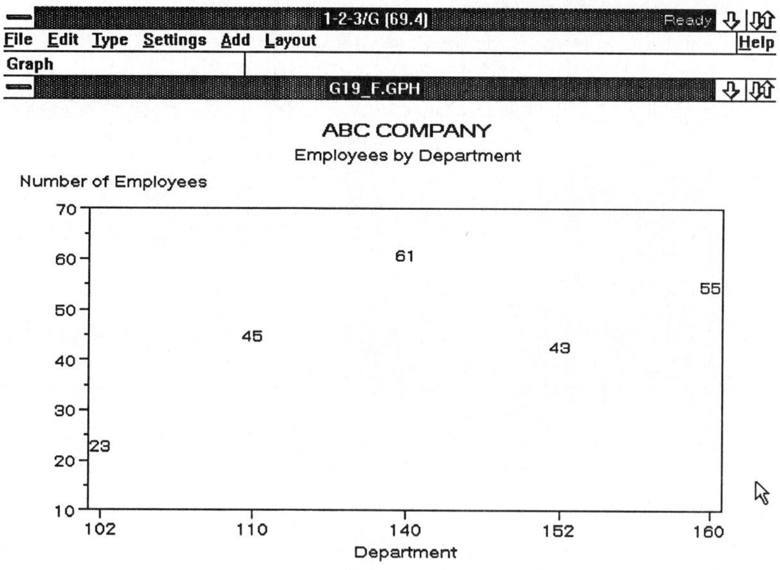

Figure 17-4. Displaying data labels in place of data points

each measurement. Creating a second Y axis is simple, since 1-2-3/G automatically creates the second axis when you assign data ranges to it.

To assign one or all data ranges to the second axis, select Settings Series Options and choose 2Y-axis under Value axis. If only one data range is selected, this assigns the selected data range to the second Y axis. If the Graph object is selected, this assigns all data ranges to the second Y axis. After assigning all the series, you can reassign a range to the first Y axis. To make this change, select the range to reassign, and then select Settings Series Options and choose Y-axis under Value axis.

If a graph has no ranges assigned to a Y axis, the axis does not appear even if you have defined it. A second Y axis has the same features as the first Y axis, and you can use the same commands to change its appearance. Once you use a second Y axis, 1-2-3/G adds the text 2Y Axis for the axis title. You can select this object and enter more appropriate text for the axis title.

Figure 17-5 shows a mixed graph with two axes. A mixed graph

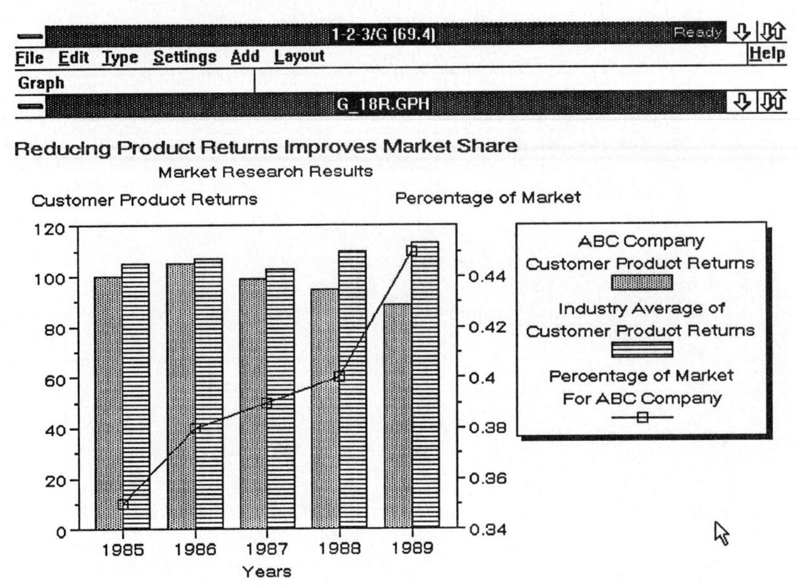

Figure 17-5. Bar/line graph

frequently uses one graph type for one Y axis and another graph type for the other Y axis.

Sometimes 1-2-3/G automatically assigns data to the second Y axis. An HLCO graph, described in the previous chapter, automatically assigns the E range to the second Y axis. Selecting Bar-Line from the Type Gallery dialog box automatically assigns the A range to the first Y axis and the other data ranges to the second Y axis.

Setting the Number Format

From within the graph tool, you can choose the format for many of the numbers that appear on a graph. You can format the axes values, the data labels, pie values (described later), or all of the values. To change the format for values, select Settings Number Format. Next, choose the type of values you want to format. If you select All, all values (except the percentages in a pie graph) will use the selected format.

Formatting graph numbers is much like formatting worksheet cells, where you can use global and range formatting options. You can choose a format for the graph and override that format for a particular group of values. To override the global format, invoke the command again and select the axis, data labels, or pie values to be changed. Then select the format to be used. The formats available are the same as ones you use with worksheet cells with the Range Format or Worksheet Global Format command. You can also develop your own user-defined formats by using the user format definition characters described in Chapter 7.

Selecting Scaling Options

Scaling refers to the range of values shown on the axes and the intervals between these values. In most cases, you will want to use the automatic scaling values that 1-2-3/G provides for you. Occasionally, however, you may want to change the upper or lower limits for the scaling to convey your message better. You can override 1-2-3/G's default scaling selections.

You can change the scaling for the X, first Y, or second Y axis, or specify a skip factor for X-axis data labels. The selections you make for the X axis only affect XY graphs. You can also change the scale indicator and the type of axis 1-2-3/G uses. Specify the scale to be changed by choosing Settings Scale followed by X, Y, or 2Y. You should see a dialog box like the one in Figure 17-6, except when the X axis contains labels.

Setting the Scale Limits

If the X axis contains data labels, you can choose the skip factor. This allows you to skip some X-axis labels, leaving room for others. Selecting Auto after choosing Settings Scale X lets 1-2-3/G decide the appropriate skip factor based on the space available for the X-axis labels. If you select Manual and enter a skip factor in the text box, 1-2-3/G will skip some of the labels in the range. If you choose a skip factor of 3, every third label in the X range will be displayed on the graph.

For the numerical axes, you can select Manual and enter the upper or lower limit. Auto, the default lets 1-2-3/G select the upper and lower

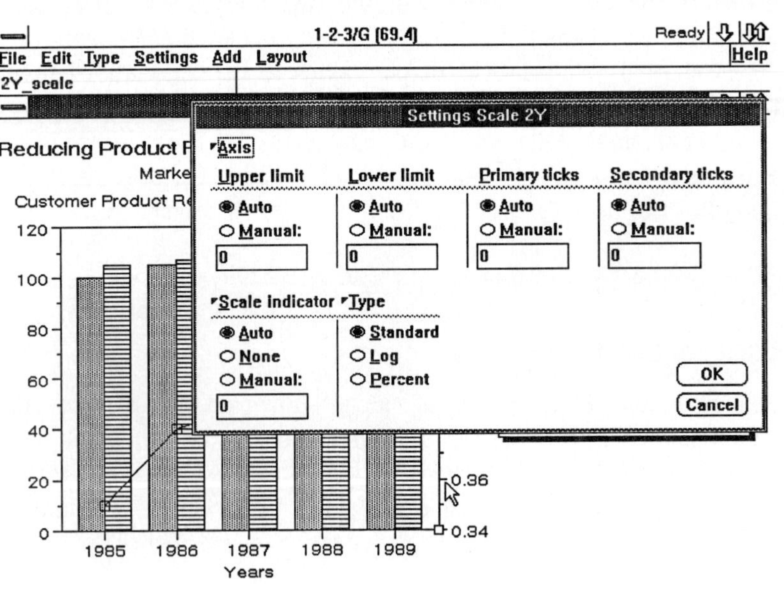

Figure 17-6. Dialog box for setting scale options

limit based on the data. Under Primary ticks, select Auto to have 1-2-3/G determine the numerical difference between each tick. (Primary ticks are the notches in the axis that have a value displayed next to them.) If you select Manual, you must indicate the increment you want between primary ticks. Under Secondary ticks, you can select Auto to let 1-2-3/G determine the numerical difference between each tick. (Secondary ticks are the notches in the axis that do not have a value displayed next to them.) If you choose Manual, you have to specify the increment you want between secondary ticks. If you select Manual for any of the preceding settings, the lower limit must be lower than the upper limit, the secondary tick mark must be less than the primary tick mark, and the primary tick mark must be less than the difference between the upper and lower limits.

HLCO graphs often need the scale limits changed. Figure 17-7 shows a HLCO graph in which the bars for the prices overlap the diagrams representing the different stock volumes. By changing the lower limit of the first Y axis to 80, and the upper limit of the second Y axis to 2500, you can make the graph look like Figure 17-8.

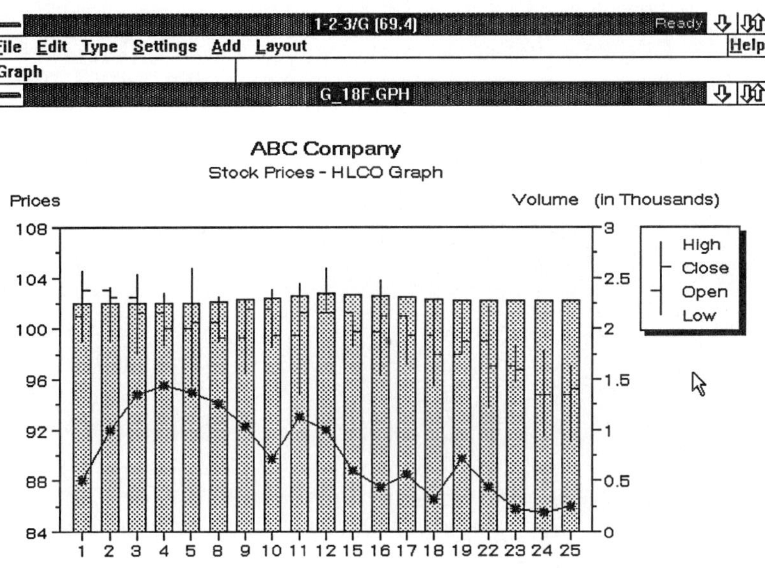

Figure 17-7. Original HLCO graph

Tip: If the graph uses two Y axes, you may need to set the upper or lower limits of each axis so the data for the two axes does not overlap, as it did in Figure 17-8.

Setting the Scale Indicator

The scale indicator specifies the order of magnitude for the numbers on the graph. It might read thousands or millions to indicate that each of the scale numbers would be multiplied by this factor. By default 1-2-3/G generates a correct indicator based on your data values, unless the data in your worksheet is already scaled. For instance, if you used numbers on your worksheet to represent thousands, 1-2-3/G would not know to adjust the scale indicator accordingly.

Under Scale indicator, you can remove the label indicator, display the label indicator 1-2-3/G provides, or tell 1-2-3/G to use a different power of 10 for the indicator. As an example, suppose that you are showing sales in thousands of dollars, and 1-2-3/G generates the label

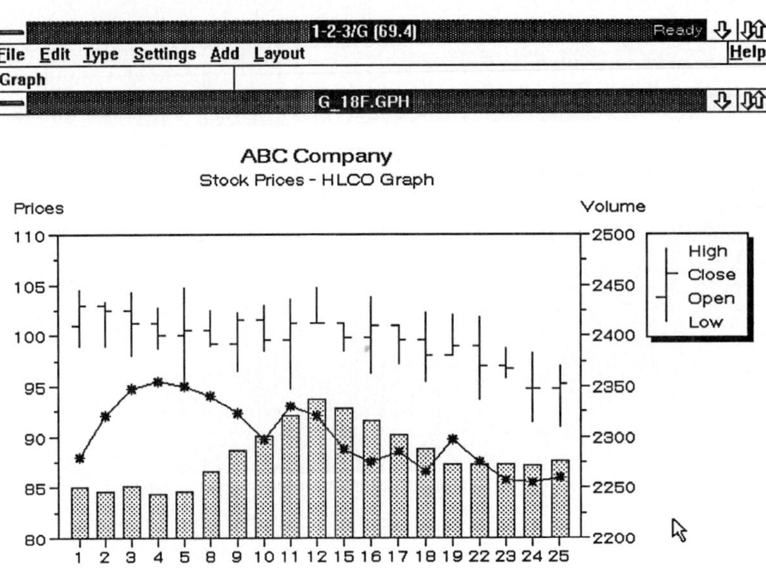

Figure 17-8. HLCO graph with scales altered

(in thousands) along the Y axis. To delete the label, select None. To use a different power of 10 for the axis scaling, select Manual and enter a number between 0 and 500 representing the power of ten; 1-2-3/G will convert the number into the appropriate scale indicator. For example, to change the scale of the axis to millions, select Manual and enter 6. 1-2-3/G will add the label (in millions) next to the axis title. To use different text for the scale indicator, add the text to the axis title and select None under Scale indicator. Auto is the default setting for this option.

Setting the Axis Scaling

You can use the Type option to select the type of scaling used for the axes. The three choices are Standard, Log, and Percent. Standard is the default; a standard scale means that the interval between each primary tick mark is the same. A logarithmic scale increases the difference between tick marks by powers of 10. You may want to use this type of scaling to emphasize a trend. For example, Figure 17-9 shows a graph with the standard scaling. Since the numbers grow so rapidly after 1989,

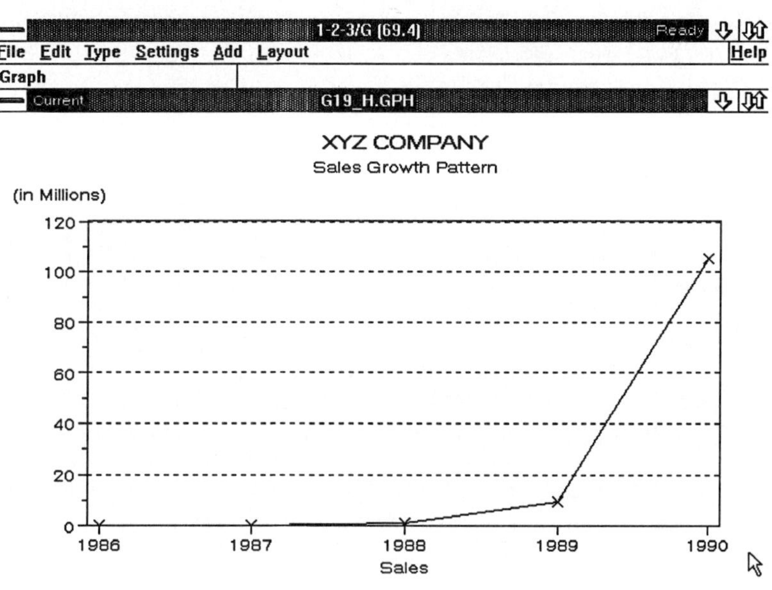

Figure 17-9. Graph using standard Y-axis scale

it is difficult to see any trend. Figure 17-10 shows the same graph with logarithmic scaling. This graph shows a more definite trend.

You can also create an area or bar graph to show the proportion of each value to the total. This is like a pie graph using several series. To use this special display for any graph except HLCO, XY, Pie, and 3-D bar graphs, select Settings Scale Y Type Percent. Figure 17-11 shows a bar graph that illustrates the percentage each region sells of a product.

Pie Graph Options

Normally, you use the B graph data range to specify a second set of data for your graph. With a pie graph, however, you can use the B data range to specify the color for the individual slices of the pie. You can also use the C data range to display percentages. Select Settings Pie Choices to display the Settings Pie Choices dialog box in Figure 17-12. Choosing Show values displays the values of the pie slices next to the percentage of the total that each value represents.

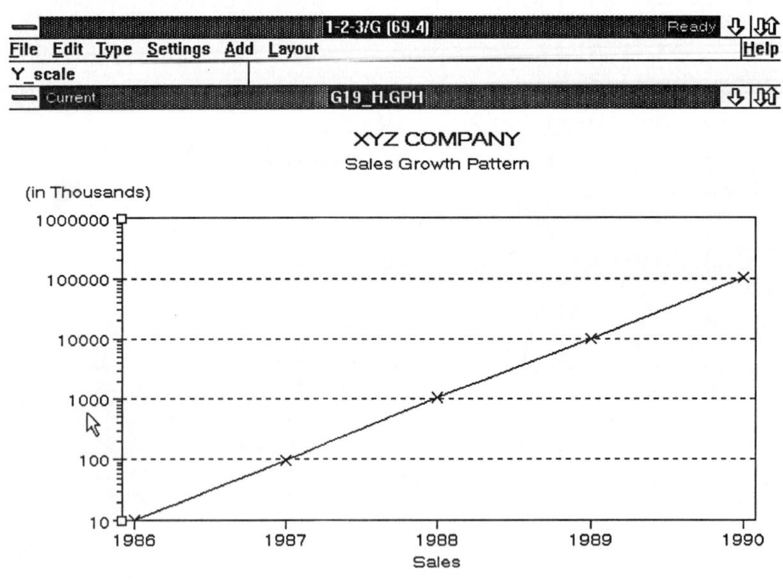

Figure 17-10. Graph using logarithmic Y-axis scale

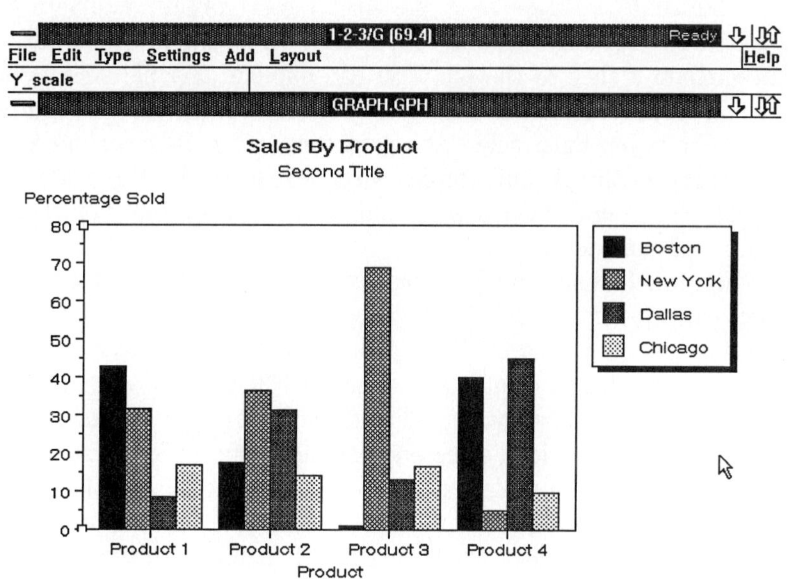

Figure 17-11. 100% graph

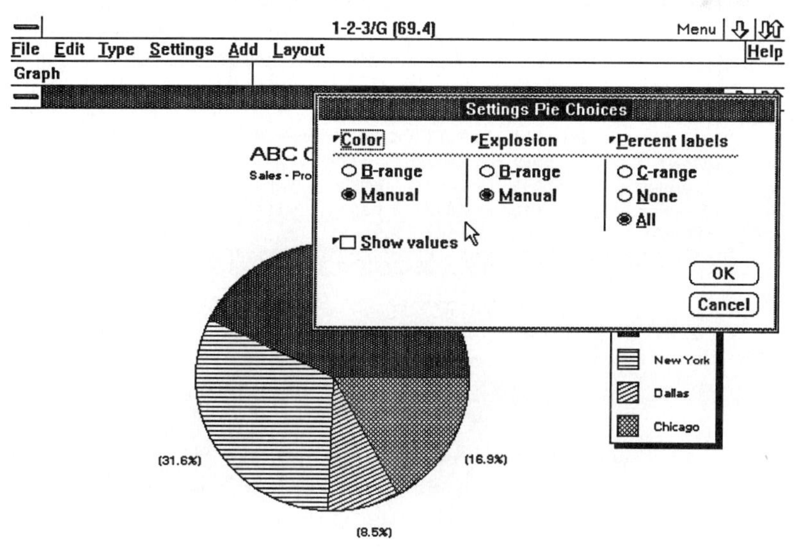

Figure 17-12. Settings Pie Choices dialog box

The B data range in a pie graph can contain numbers from 1 through 16 representing different colors. In addition, the B data range can explode a slice of the pie. You can explode any pie slice by adding 100 to the color code number for the slice. Either process requires two steps. First, you must select the data containing the color and/or explosion codes as the B data range. Next, select Settings Pie Choices and select B-range under Color or Explosion to indicate that you want to set colors and explode slices.

Figure 17-13 shows a pie graph and worksheet data that includes an extra column for the color codes to be specified as the B data range. These codes are stored in F3..F6; each set of data values to be shown in the pie graph has a color code. When A:F3..A:F6 is selected as the B data range and B-range is selected for color and explosion, the pie graph adopts the colors selected with the color codes. Notice that the section for Dallas is pulled away from the center, or exploded; This is accomplished by using 103 for the B range value for this pie slice.

You can also select whether 1-2-3/G displays the percentages for each pie slice. To display percentages for all pie slices, select All under

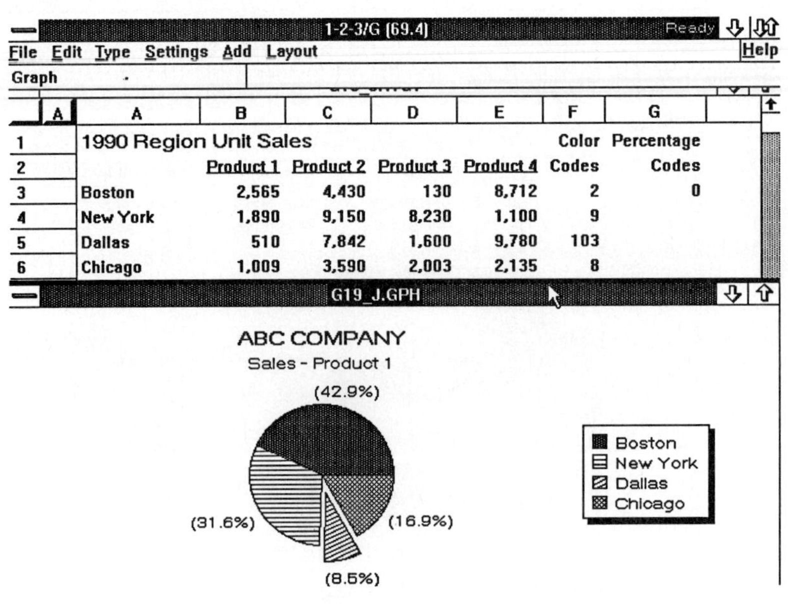

Figure 17-13. Worksheet and graph using ranges for data colors

Percent labels in the Settings Pie Choices dialog box. To hide percentages for all pie slices, select None. To display percentages for some pie slices, select C-range and assign a range of worksheet cells to the C data range. In the cells for the C data range, put a zero in the data range for those segments where you do not want percentages displayed. Leave the other cells in the C range blank. For example, using the data and graph in Figure 17-13, define a C range as G3..G6 and put a 0 in G3, leaving G4 through G6 blank. When 1-2-3/G displays the graph, the percentage for Boston will not appear.

Tip: If you use B and C ranges in pie graphs, hide the values in the worksheet so as not to confuse users. You can also put the B and C data ranges away from the A data range on the worksheet, so the values for the B and C data ranges don't interfere with other worksheet data.

Enhancing an XY Graph

Data for the volume projections for XYZ Company is shown in Figure 17-14. You can use an XY graph to plot the unit sales at different prices. To produce such a graph, first select Graph Type XY from a worksheet window or select XY from the Graph Setup dialog box. Then select Graph Add Ranges and specify B6..G6 as the X-axis values and B5..G5 as the A data range.

You might want to add titles like the ones shown in Figure 17-15. Select Graph Options Titles, and use the mouse or the TAB key to move to the next text box. Enter **\A1** in the first title text box, **\A2** in the second title text box, **Price ($)** in the X-axis title text box, and **Units Sold** in the Y-axis title text box. Once you have an XY graph, you can alter the X axis the same way you alter the Y axis. Since the X axis contains values, selecting Settings Scale X produces the same dialog box that you see when you select Settings Scale Y.

Adding Grid Lines and Frames

If you have a number of points on a graph, it may be difficult to identify the exact X and Y values for each point on the line. For this reason, 1-2-3/G allows you to add vertical and horizontal lines that originate at the axis markers and extend upward and to the right. These lines are

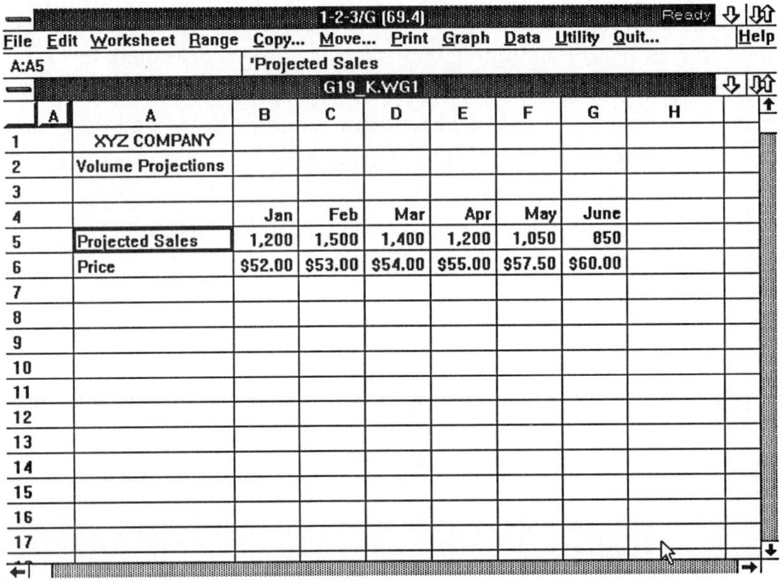

1-2-3/G [69.4] Ready

File Edit Worksheet Range Copy... Move... Print Graph Data Utility Quit... Help

A:A5 'Projected Sales

G19_K.WG1

A	A	B	C	D	E	F	G	H
1	XYZ COMPANY							
2	Volume Projections							
3								
4		Jan	Feb	Mar	Apr	May	June	
5	Projected Sales	1,200	1,500	1,400	1,200	1,050	850	
6	Price	$52.00	$53.00	$54.00	$55.00	$57.50	$60.00	
7								
8								
9								
10								
11								
12								
13								
14								
15								
16								
17								

Figure 17-14. XY graph worksheet data

called *grid lines,* since using them in both directions forms a grid pattern across your graph. You can also change the frame that 1-2-3/G draws around the graphed data. By default, the graph frame is on all four sides.

To access the dialog box for choosing grids and frames, select Settings Grid/Frame. You can use the grid options with all graph types except the pie graph. Select the X-axis, Y-axis, or 2Y-axis to add grid lines starting from the selected axis. X-axis grid lines are best used in XY graphs. Y- and 2Y-axis grid lines are used most frequently. You can select Solid, Dotted, or Gray to choose the appearance of the grid lines. Solid draws black solid lines, Dotted draws black dotted lines, and Gray draws gray solid lines. The grid lines start from the primary tick marks on the selected axes.

The grid lines start at a specific axis. If you rotate the axes, the grid lines rotate as well. For example, if you rotate a graph with horizontal grid lines starting at the first Y axis, the rotated graph will have vertical

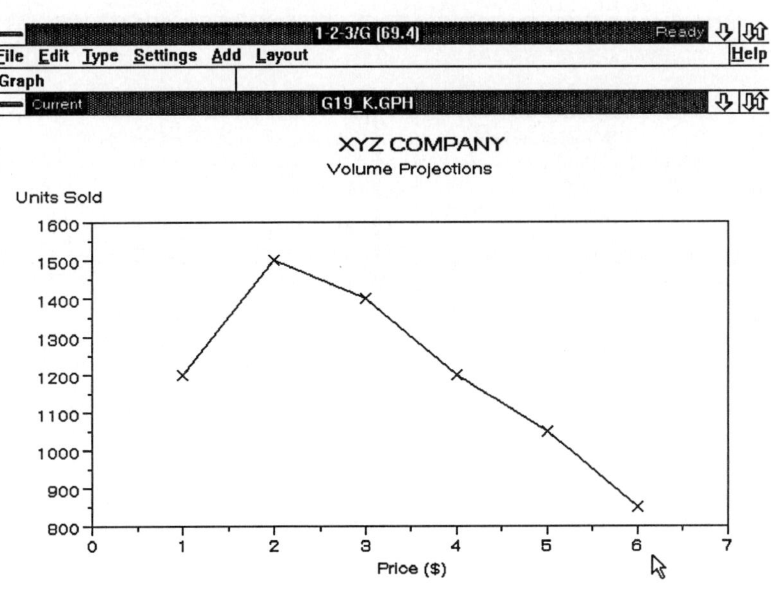

Figure 17-15. XY graph

lines starting from the first Y axis. To remove any grid lines, select Settings Grid/Frame and unselect the selection boxes under Grid.

For the graph frame, you can choose the part of the graph containing the grid. You can choose X-axis to draw a line for the graph frame only along the X axis. Choosing Y-axis draws a line for the graph frame along the first and second Y axes. Selecting Both draws lines along the X and Y axes. Selecting All, the default, draws a four-sided graph frame. Selecting None removes any graph frame. Figure 17-16 shows several graphs with different frame and grid options. You can change the line drawn for the frame with the Settings Line/Edge Style command that you use to change any line in a graph. This command will not change grid lines.

Tip: Be careful when using grid lines from both the first and second Y axis: This can potentially create a cluttered and difficult to read graph. In a graph using two axes, you will probably add grid lines to one axis.

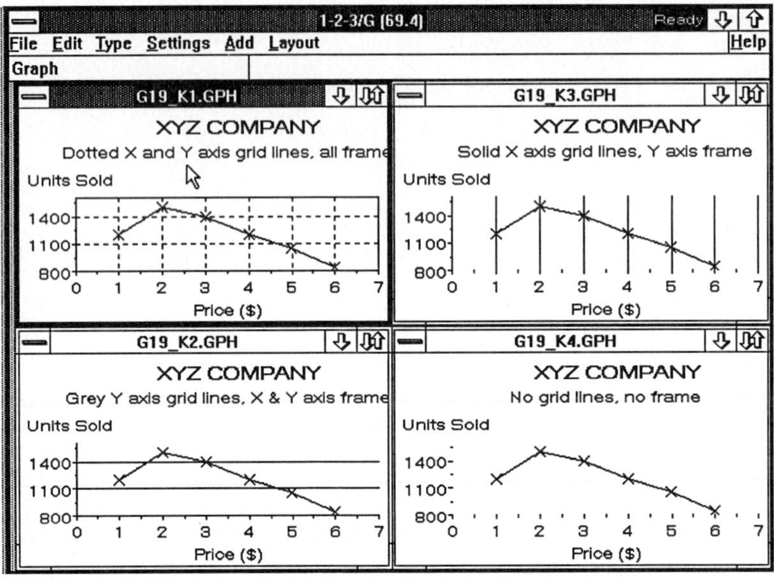

Figure 17-16. Sample grid options

Using Two Graph Types in One Graph

With combined graph types, you can combine the features of line, bar, overlapped bar, stacked bar, and area graphs. You can combine the graph types with two Y axes so that the different graph types use different Y axes. A combination graph adds variety to a presentation and allows you to separate different types of information on a graph.

If you want to use more than one type of graph, the basic graph type must be a line, bar, overlapped bar, stacked bar, or area graph. In a worksheet window, a subset of the basic graph types are available through the Graph Type or Graph Setup command. In a graph window, use the Type Gallery command to select the basic graph type. If something other than a series is the selected object, selecting Type and a graph type changes the graph type for the entire graph. If you select a series before selecting Type, the graph type you select only applies to the selected series. For example if the basic graph type is Line and you select the B data range, selecting Type Bar displays the B data range as a bar graph and the remaining series as a line graph. When you select Type to change the graph type of the selected series, only the graph types listed in black are available. The graph types that cannot be mixed are grayed. As you change the graph type for a data range, the data range continues to use the same Y axis. To change the Y axis, use the Settings Series Options command.

As an example, you might want to graph the worksheet data in Figure 17-17 with the ABC Company and industry average returns graphed as overlapping bars and the percentage of market graphed as a line graph. To do so, you must be in the graph tool where the full set of type options are available. First, select Overlapped bar as the basic graph type. Next, select the C data range and Type Line. To assign the C data range to the second Y axis, select Settings Series Options and then select 2Y-axis for the Value axis. The final graph is shown in Figure 17-18.

If you select Type Gallery, you can quickly select a mixed bar-line graph. In the gallery, the A data range is graphed as a line graph and the remaining series appears as bars. You can use the gallery to create

1-2-3/G (69.4) Ready

File Edit Worksheet Range Copy... Move... Print Graph Data Utility Quit... Help

A:B3 1985

G19_G.WG1

A	A	B	C	D	E	F	G	H	I
1	Customer Product Returns								
2	per thousand								
3		1985	1986	1987	1988	1989	1990		
4	ABC Company	100	105	99	95	89	87		
5	Industry Average	105	107	103	110	113	112		
6									
7	Percentage of Market	0.35	0.38	0.39	0.4	0.45	0.47		
8									
9									
10									
11									
12									
13									
14									
15									
16									
17									

Figure 17-17. Data for graph in Figure 17-18

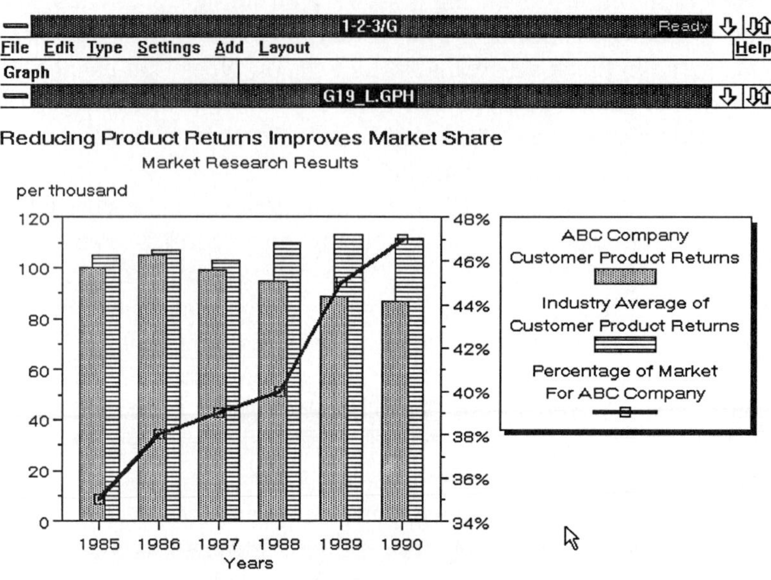

Figure 17-18. Combining two graph types

mixed graphs or use the options in the Type menu. Once you select this type, you can change which series 1-2-3/G displays using different graph types.

Tip: When you create a mixed graph, combine a line type with a bar, overlapped bar, stacked bar, or area type. Do not combine bar, overlapped bar, stacked bar, or area graph types since the resulting graphs are difficult to understand.

Changing an Object's Appearance

Being able to work with individual graph objects allows you to customize your graphs. 1-2-3/G offers many choices for moving objects through menus. In addition, you can move objects using the keyboard or the mouse. You can resize and delete objects. You can also add titles, legends, and X-axis labels.

1-2-3/G has two composition modes. The graph uses Auto Compose mode by default. This mode lets 1-2-3/G adjust the graph as you make changes. 1-2-3/G automatically prevents objects from overlapping and evenly distributes the space among objects in the graph. This lets you focus on the features of your graph rather than the position of the existing graph objects. When you move or resize an object, however, the graph switches to Manual mode. In this mode, Manual appears on the title bar and 1-2-3/G doesn't adjust the position of objects in the graph as you make changes. In a manual composition mode graph, you must check that objects do not unintentionally overlap. You can switch back to Auto Compose mode by selecting Layout Auto Compose.

Positioning Objects with the Menu

1-2-3/G decides where most of the objects in the graph are placed. Nevertheless, you can position legends, axis labels, tick marks, and titles. The Settings Position command in the graph tool menu lets you reposition various objects in the graph. The Settings Position command selections let you move objects that you cannot move manually.

Moving the Legend

You can reposition the legend, and 1-2-3/G will adjust the graph to reflect the legend's new position. To move the legend, select Settings Position Legend. From the dialog box, you can select the legend's position relative to the graph; the choices are Left, Right, and Bottom. You can also choose whether the legend is inside or outside the plot frame. Figure 17-19 shows the four graphs using different combinations of these choices.

Tip: When you position the legend inside the graph frame, you may need to change the upper or lower limit of a Y axis so there's enough room to display the legend without overlapping the graphed data.

Tip: When you position the legend inside the graph frame, you may want to hide the legend frame by selecting Settings Area Style and unselecting Border, Shadow, and Filled.

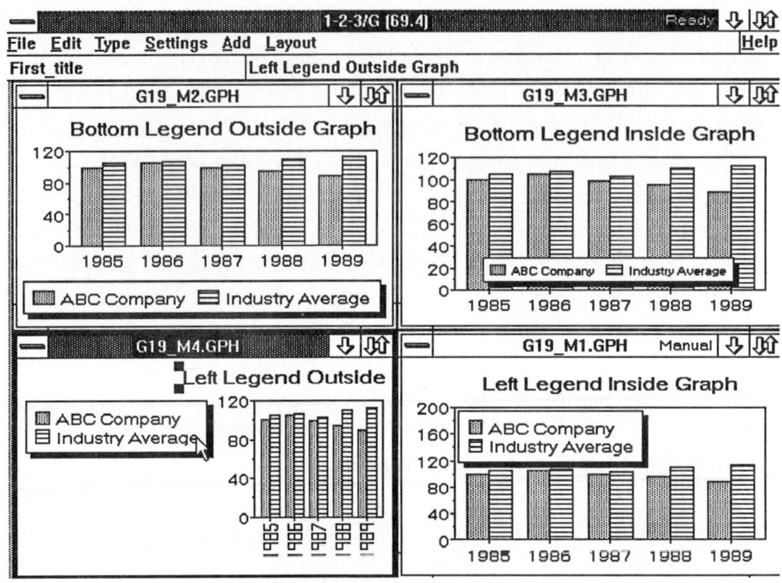

Figure 17-19. Sample legend positions

Moving the Axis Title

You can place the axis titles in several locations. When you select Settings Position Titles and the axis to be changed, you can choose whether the axis title is horizontal (the default) or vertical. You can also choose whether the scale indicator appears after (appended) or below the axis title. Parts of the dialog box are grayed when the axis title doesn't include a scale indicator and when the axis title is for the horizontal axis. The axis letter is grayed after you select Settings Position Titles if the axis is horizontal and doesn't include a scale indicator. Changing the orientation of any vertical axis title sets the orientation for all vertical axis titles in the graph. In other words, if you rotate the axis, the X axis uses the orientation you chose for the Y axis.

Positioning the Y Axis

When you have one Y axis, you can select the side on which the axis appears. Initially, the Y axis appears on the left or bottom of the plot frame. To change the Y-axis location, select Settings Position and then select Y if the graph uses the first Y axis or 2Y if the graph uses the second Y axis. For either choice, you can select whether to put the Y axis on the left, right, or both. If the X axis is the vertical axis, you can select whether to put the Y axis on the top, on the bottom, or both. In a graph using two Y axes, the first Y axis is always on the left or bottom, and the second Y axis is always on the right or top.

Positioning Tick Marks

By default, the tick marks that 1-2-3/G creates are on the outside of the plot frame; but you can alter this setting. To change the tick marks, select Settings Position Tick Marks and then select X, Y, or 2Y for the axis to be changed. For an X axis containing label data, you can position the tick marks inside the plot frame, outside the plot frame, or across the plot frame. You can also choose to have no tick marks. For the Y axes and an X axis that contains values, you have the same choices, but you can also select different options for the primary and secondary ticks.

Positioning Axis Labels

When the horizontal axis contains labels but there is not enough space to display them horizontally, you have several options. To change the length of axis labels, select Settings Position Axis Labels and X, Y, or 2Y for the axis to be changed. You can choose to have the X-axis labels staggered, shown at an angle, or displayed vertically. If you select a setting for one axis, this setting applies to any horizontal axis in the graph.

Moving Objects Manually

If you are not satisfied with the fixed location options 1-2-3/G provides for graph objects, you can move many of them with the keyboard or mouse. You can manually move objects to refine the position for the legend, relocate titles, and explode pie slices. Moving objects manually gives you more control over their placement. However, the graph will change from Auto Compose to the Manual mode. 1-2-3/G won't automatically prevent overlapping objects unless you reselect Auto Compose mode from the Layout menu.

To move an object, you must select the desired object before moving it with the keyboard or mouse. You can click the object with the mouse or select Edit Select Object and pick the object you want to work with. Once the object is selected, you can move it by dragging the mouse or pressing the arrow keys in the appropriate direction. As you move the object, 1-2-3/G draws a dotted outline to represent the object's new position. When you either press ENTER or lift the mouse button, 1-2-3/G redraws the graph using the position you have just selected.

When you select a pie slice, moving it manually explodes the slice. You can also use various arrow keys, depending on the direction of the pie slice handle relative to the pie center. You can also move the legend frame. When you move the legend frame, 1-2-3/G will move both the legend frame and all objects inside the frame. If you move the first or second title, both titles will be moved. Moving an axis title also moves the axis's scale indicator. Moving the plot frame moves the plot frame, the graphed data, the axis, and the axis titles.

Tip: If you want to move objects manually, wait until the very end so the graph window will remain in Auto Compose mode as long as possible. This lets you focus on the graph instead of continually checking that objects don't overlap unintentionally.

Tip: Switching back to Auto Compose mode after working in Manual mode undoes all changes made to object locations in Manual mode, except notations.

Sizing Objects

You can also change the size of the plot frame and line and arrow notation, as discussed in the section "Adding Notations" later in the chapter. You will want to change the size of objects when you are in Manual mode and need to adjust the size of the plot frame or notation to adjust for objects you have moved. To change the size of text objects, use the Settings Font command to change the font size of the object. You can change the size of the plot frame or notations using the keyboard or mouse.

To resize an object such as the plot frame, select the plot frame or line or arrow notation. Using a keyboard, type a period to indicate that you want to resize an object that is not linkable. Then press the arrow keys in the direction that you want the object expanded or contracted. The corner that changes position uses a different handle, as shown in Figure 17-20. If the object is not linkable and cannot be edited, you can only change the corner by typing a period. When the dotted outline is the right size, press ENTER. To change the size of an object with a mouse, drag one corner of the plot frame or line or arrow notation to the new corner position and lift the mouse button when the outlined box is the desired size.

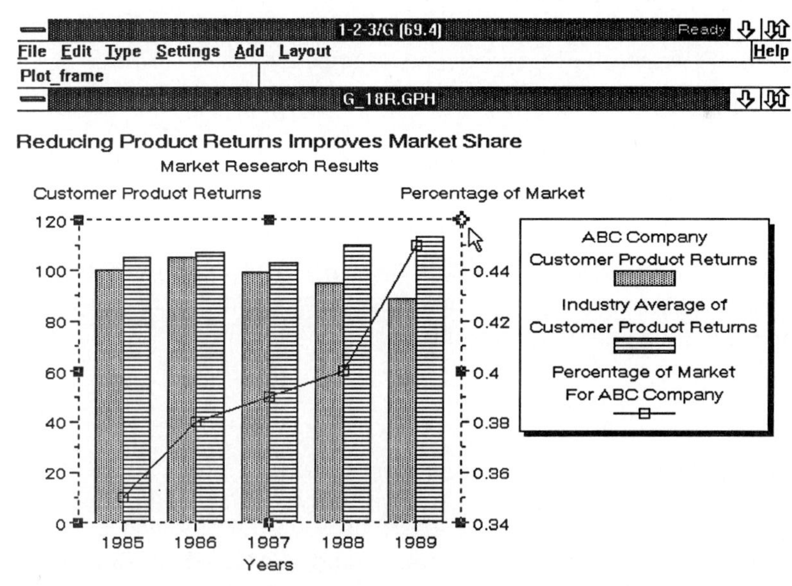

Figure 17-20. Handle indicating object to resize

Deleting Objects

To delete objects in a graph, just select the object to delete and press DELETE. You can delete series, X-axis labels, legend labels, legend frames, titles, the graph, and data labels. Deleting objects with DELETE is the same as selecting the Edit Clear command. If you delete the wrong object, you can undelete it by pressing ALT-BACKSPACE or selecting Edit Undo. When you delete an object that is a link between a worksheet and a graph, you are deleting the link but not changing the worksheet data that the link uses. For example, if you delete the A data range, you are deleting the link that describes the data that the A data range uses. However, you are not deleting the worksheet cells containing the data that the graph used for the A data range.

When you delete an object, 1-2-3/G redraws the graph accordingly. When you delete a series, 1-2-3/G removes the series from the graph and the legend label and symbol from the legend frame. If the deleted series is the only one assigned to a Y axis, the Y axis also disappears. Deleting the X-axis labels in a pie graph also deletes the legend frame that contains the X-axis labels. When you delete the legend frame, 1-2-3/G removes the legend frame, the legend label, and the symbols. If you don't want the legend frame to appear, select Settings Area Style and unselect the Border and Shadow selection boxes. Deleting the legend frame in a pie graph moves the X-axis labels to the pie slice labels. Deleting the legend label deletes only the legend label and the symbol associated with it. The legend label and symbols for the other series remain intact. When you delete an axis title, the axis retains the scale indicator. When you delete the Graph object, the entire graph is deleted, as if you selected Graph Reset Yes from the worksheet file with the same filename as the graph file.

Adding Objects

You can add new objects to a graph or add objects that were previously deleted. You can add titles, legends, and X-axis labels to a graph. You can also add notations (additional lines, arrows, and text objects, as described in the section "Adding Notations" later in the chapter). Title, Legend, and X Labels, are grayed in the Add menu when the graph already contains these objects.

To add a title, select Add Title and then select First, Second, X-axis, Y-axis, or 2Y-axis to indicate the specific title you wish to add. 1-2-3/G adds the title to the graph with the default text of Title, Second Title, X-axis, Y-axis, or 2Y-axis in the title's default location. Once the title is added to the graph, you can edit it just as you edit any other graph text.

To add a legend or legend label for a series, select Add Legend. If you select Frame from the next menu, 1-2-3/G adds a legend frame and fills it with legend labels for each series in the graph. A HLCO graph is an exception, since it displays four series in the legend frame. If you select Label and a series displayed in black, 1-2-3/G adds the legend label for the series in the legend frame, adding a legend frame if necessary. The default legend label for any series is Series: followed by the data range letter. You can select the legend label object and replace the legend label with a more appropriate description.

To add X-axis labels, select Add X Labels. 1-2-3/G adds numbers starting with 1 for each point on the X axis. Use this command when you have not supplied a data range for the X axis and you want to number the points along the X axis.

Using Different View Modes

1-2-3/G has three view modes—Window View, Printer View, and Link View. The mode affects the appearance of your graph. By default, the graph appears in the Window View mode, as in Figure 17-21. The Window View mode displays the entire graph inside the graph window, displaying text in the selected point size. You can also preview the graph, to see what it will look like when printed or when displayed in other Presentation Manager applications. To change the graph appearance, select Layout. Choose Printer View to display the second view mode and see the graph as it will appear with the selected printer, as in Figure 17-22. By default, the graph will use the settings in the File Print Print Graph dialog box, including the graph size and whether fonts are adjusted. The graph in Figure 17-22 is a half page but the fonts are not adjusted so they seem large in the smaller graph. However, 1-2-3/G will display the graph using colors instead of the patterns chosen with File Print Color Map. Choose Layout Link View to see the third view

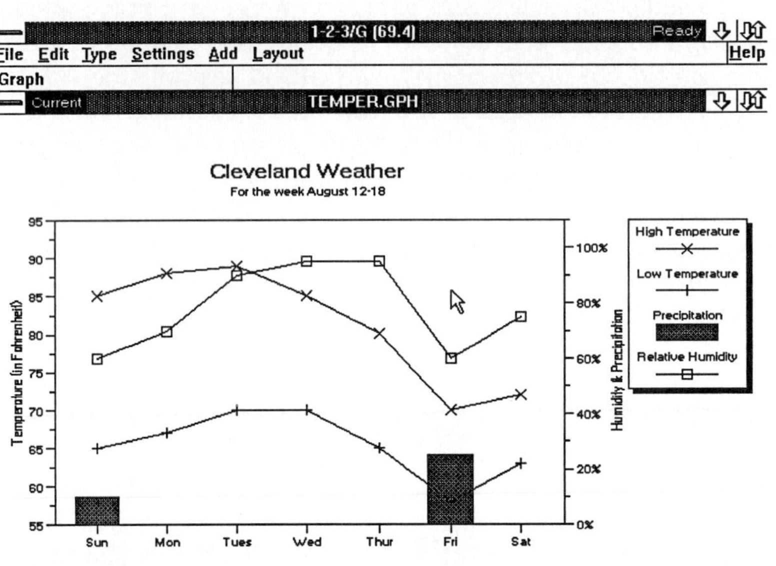

Figure 17-21. Window View display mode

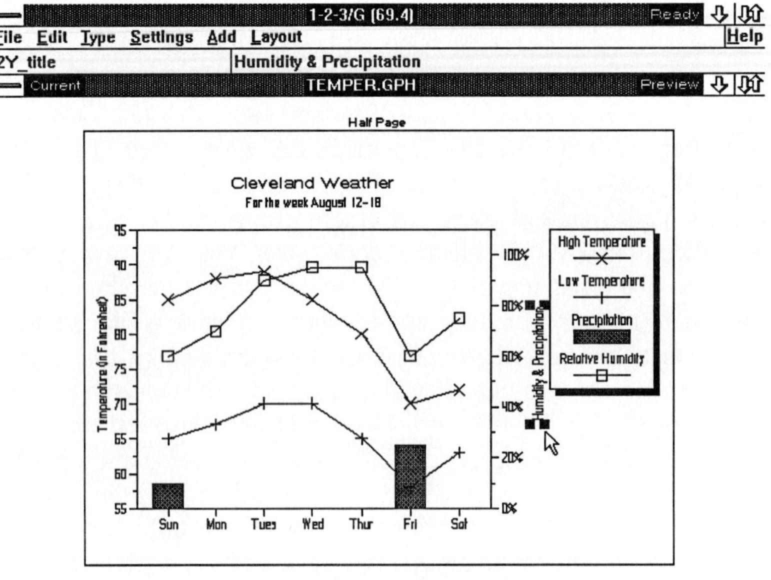

Figure 17-22. Printer View display mode

mode and display a dialog box that lets you select another Presentation Manager application. Once you select the Presentation Manager application, 1-2-3/G displays the graph as it would appear in that application. Text in a graph in the Link View mode uses the fonts used in other Presentation Manager applications. For both Printer View and Link View mode, the Preview status indicator appears in the title bar. While in Printer View mode or Link View mode, you can alter the graph just as you can in the Window View mode. To return to Window View mode, select Layout Window View.

Tip: To see how the graph will appear when printed with a single color printer, use the Preview window available through the File Print Print Graph dialog box.

Adding Notations

Besides the basic graph objects already discussed, there are additional objects that you can add to a graph. These objects are called *notations,* and consist of text, lines, and arrows. You can use notations to enhance the graph. For example, you can use arrows to point out data points and text to describe special data points and add footnotes to a graph. In an HLCO graph, you can add notations to identify the data ranges. When you add notations to a graph, 1-2-3/G adds the default text, line, or arrow, which you can then edit and reposition. For text notations, you have the same customizing options as for titles, data labels, and other text objects. You can alter the appearance of lines and arrows with Settings Line/Edge Style, just as you alter border lines and plot frame lines.

To add a notation, select Add Notation, and then select Text, Line, or Arrow. 1-2-3/G adds the default text line or arrow in the upper-right side of the graph window. Each notation object has the object name Notation: followed by a number. Added notations have the same settings as the previous notation object. For example, if you create a red text object using the 12-point Times Roman font, the next text object you create in the graph is red and 12-point Times Roman by default. You can also delete any type of notation object using the DELETE key. Figure 17-23 shows a text and arrow notation object added by selecting Add Notation Text and then Add Notation Arrow.

After you add a notation, it is still the selected object. At this point, you can change its position. Moving a notation object is like moving an object such as a legend. You can also change the size of and rotate lines and arrows. Changing the size of a line or arrow is just like changing the size of the plot frame. With a mouse, you drag one corner. With a keyboard, press a period, move the selected object corner to a new position with the arrow keys, and press ENTER. You also rotate a line or arrow using the same keystrokes or mouse actions. For example, Figure 17-23 shows an arrow that needs to point to the next to last data point for the last data range. First, move the arrow so that it points to the next to last data point for the last data range. Next, drag the opposite corner to directly above the data point or press a period and then press

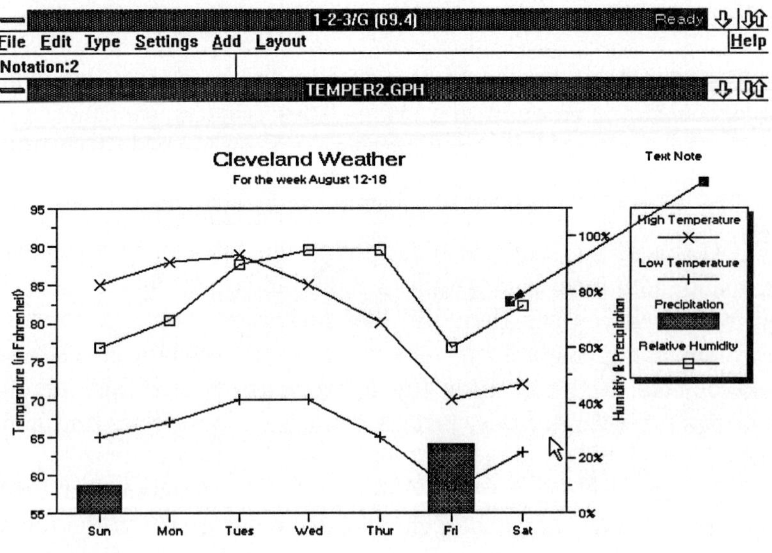

Figure 17-23. Text and arrow annotation added to graph

the RIGHT ARROW key until the arrow is pointing down. As you move one corner of an arrow or line notation, the arrow or line rotates to use the new position and the stationary corner.

Arrows offer a unique customization option. When you select Settings Arrow Heads, 1-2-3/G presents a dialog box from which you can choose the pointed side of the arrow. You can choose between Start, End, Both, and None. Selecting None makes the arrow appear as a line.

Advanced Linking in Graphs

In the previous chapter, you learned how 1-2-3/G establishes links between a graph and worksheets. These links are created for the series, legend labels, and titles. You can also delete links, add links, move links, and edit links. Links are updated either automatically or manually. Both updating choices require that the source of the link be in an open file. If not, the graph file uses the values the source had the last time the link was updated.

Deleting Links

Sometimes you will want to delete a link. For example, if you no longer want to use a worksheet cell for a title or legend label, you must delete the link before you can enter the new text.

To delete a link, select Edit Link Delete. You can delete all links or a selected link. If you delete a selected link, you can choose a linked object from the list. By default, 1-2-3/G selects the current object. As a linked object is highlighted, the bottom of the dialog box lists the source of the link and when the link is updated. Once you select OK, the link is deleted. If you delete a link to a text object such as an axis title or a legend label, 1-2-3/G replaces the link with the text that exists when the link is deleted. If you delete a link to a series, 1-2-3/G replaces the data range link with a series of numbers that match the data point values when the data link is broken.

Adding Links

The links that you have created so far are for the data ranges and titles. You can also create links to other objects. For example, you could add a link that would display different data labels than the data point values. You can also link the graph with other Presentation Manager applications, as long as the Presentation Manager application supports the Dynamic Data Exchange (DDE).

As mentioned in the previous chapter, you can create links by selecting Edit Link Create. In the dialog box, you must supply the worksheet file or Presentation Manager application to use as the source and the object to use as the destination. You can only create links from open files. If the clipboard contains data, the source of the clipboard data initially appears for the link source. Under destination, you can select the graph object that will use the link. You can press F3 (Name) to list all potential objects. In addition, you can link a range of worksheet cells to the legend labels displayed in a legend frame. This is the same as selecting Graph Options Legends Data Range from a worksheet window. Linking a graph establishes links for the data series, legend, and X-axis labels. This is similar to selecting a range for an instant graph.

Some objects cannot be linked—including the plot frame, pie slices, and text notation—and are not included in the list that appears when you press F3 (Name). In addition, you cannot link an object that is already linked. You also cannot link related objects. For example, if the graph has a link, you cannot link the data series, legend frame, legend label, or X-axis labels. If the legend frame, a legend label, the X-axis labels, or a data series is linked, you cannot link the graph. If the legend frame is linked, you cannot link the legend label. If the legend label is linked, you cannot link the legend frame.

As an example, to use worksheet data for the data labels in Figure 17-24, you would establish links to the C data range labels. From the worksheet, you would select the range A:B7..A:H7 and then select Edit Copy. In the graph, you would select Edit Link Create. For the source, you would accept <<TEMPER.WG1>>A:B7..A:H7. After moving to the destination item, you could press F3 and select Data_Labels, and then type :C and select OK. Figure 17-25 shows the graph after you add the data labels.

Tip: If you link to an Excel application, the item will appear as the row and column number. For example, if you are using the range B3..H3

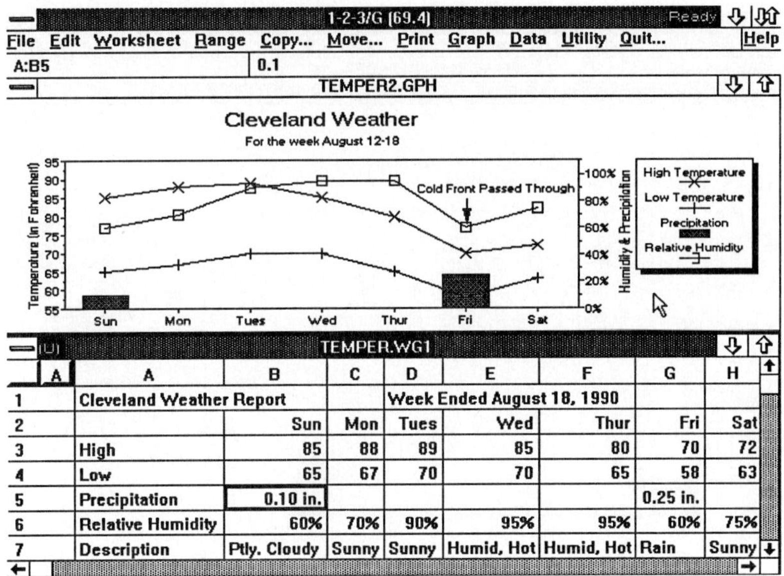

Figure 17-24. Worksheet and graph to link for series data labels

from the Excel worksheet TEMPER.XLS, the link appears as <<Excel| C:\EXCELOS2\TEMPER.XLS>> R3C2:R3C8. When pasting a link from Excel, the receiving range selected for the paste must be the same size as the originating range in Excel.

Tip: If you don't use the clipboard to select data to use for the Edit Link Create command, name the worksheet cells and use the range names instead of the address. The range name is easier to remember as you switch between windows, and the graph window will continue using the same values if you move the cells.

Using Links to Select Colors and Patterns

Earlier you learned how you can use the Settings Area Style to select colors and patterns of bars and areas in a graph. You can also select colors and patterns for data ranges by creating a link with a worksheet range that contains color or pattern numbers. This feature enables you to use different colors or patterns for each data point.

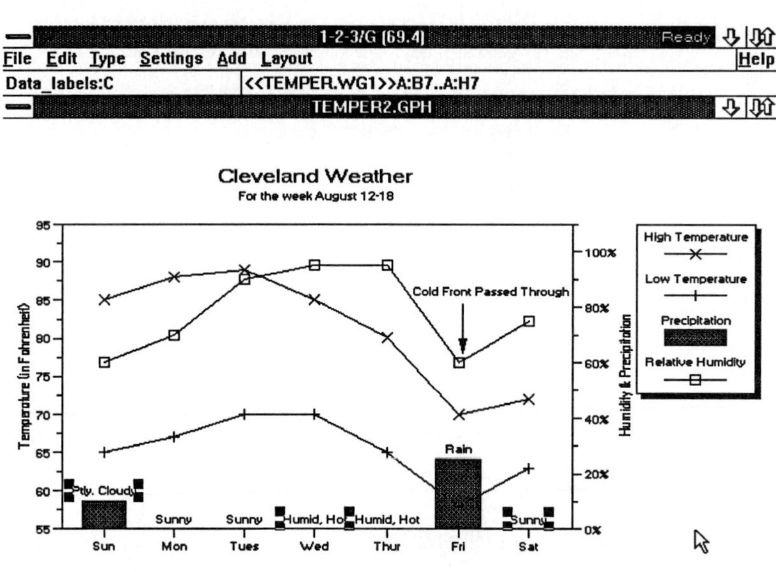

Figure 17-25. Using a link to display different data labels

The worksheet range for the colors or patterns must contain the same number of cells as the number of data points in the data range. These cells contain numbers 1 through 16, corresponding to the colors listed in Table 17-2 and the patterns shown in Figure 17-26. Once you have the values in the worksheet range, you can copy this range to the clipboard and then switch to the graph window. In the graph window, you can select Edit Link Create. For the destination item, select a color or pattern from the list of graph objects that appears when you press F3 (Name). If you want the color or pattern numbers to apply to a specific series, add a colon and the series letter. If you don't supply a series letter, 1-2-3/G uses the color or pattern codes for the first series that does not already have a range assigned for color or pattern. The legend will continue using the color and pattern selected for the series with Settings Area Style.

The graph in Figure 17-27 shows how you can use colors and patterns. This graph uses the pattern codes in rows 13 and 14 of the worksheet shown in Figure 17-28. These pattern codes are determined by a formula that compares the day's high or low temperature with the

Number	Color
1	White
2	Blue
3	Red
4	Magenta
5	Green
6	Cyan
7	Yellow
8	Black
9	Dark Gray
10	Dark Blue
11	Dark Red
12	Dark Magenta
13	Dark Green
14	Dark Cyan
15	Dark Yellow
16	Gray

Table 17-2. Color Codes

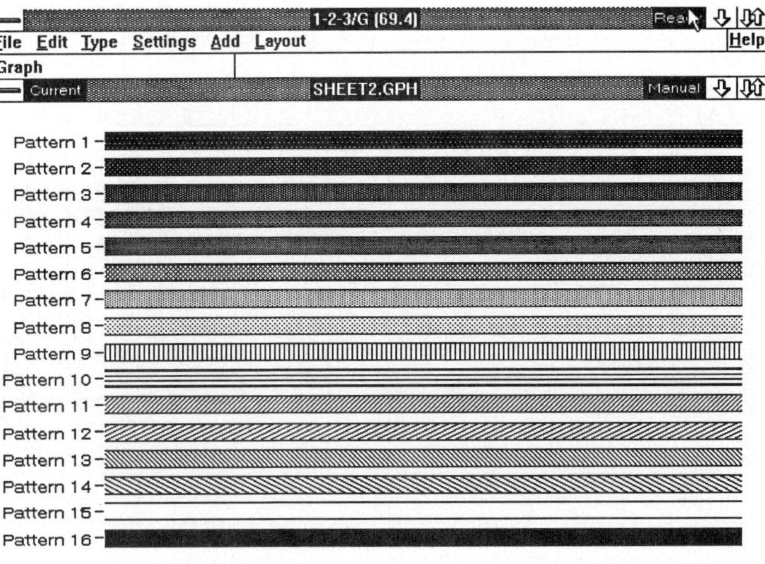

Figure 17-26. Available patterns

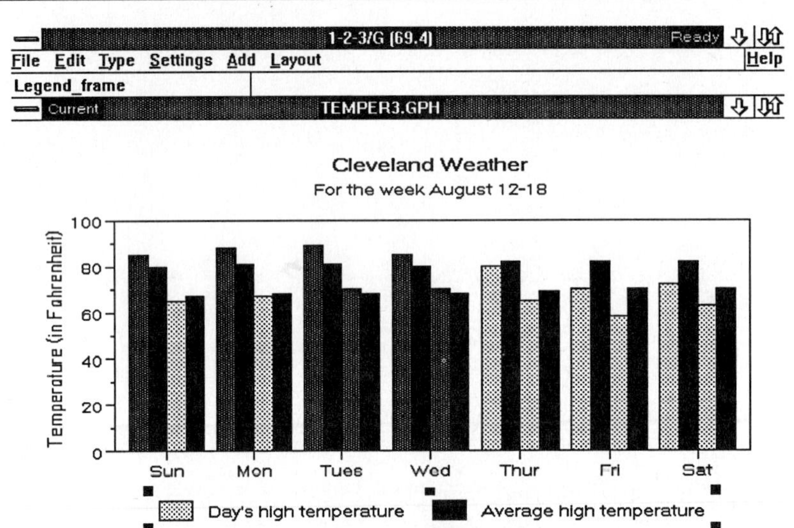

Figure 17-27. Graph using linked values for patterns

1-2-3/G [69.4] Ready

File Edit Worksheet Range Copy... Move... Print Graph Data Utility Quit... Help

A:B13 @IF(B3>B10,3,8)

TEMPER3.WG1

A	A	B	C	D	E	F	G	H
3	High	85	88	89	85	80	70	72
4	Low	65	67	70	70	65	58	63
5	Precipitation	0.10 in.					0.25 in.	
6	Relative Humidity	60%	70%	90%	95%	95%	60%	75%
7	Description	Ptly. Cloudy	Sunny	Sunny	Humid, Hot	Humid, Hot	Rain	Sunny
8								
9	Average Temperature							
10	High	80	81	81	80	82	82	82
11	Low	67	68	68	68	69	70	70
12	Pattern Codes:							
13	High	3	3	3	3	8	8	8
14	Low	8	8	3	3	8	8	8
15								
16								
17								
18								
19								

Figure 17-28. Worksheet with pattern codes for two series

average. The graph uses the same gray shade for each data range, so it's easy to see which data points are assigned to each series. To assign the pattern codes, copy the worksheet range (B13..H13) to the clipboard. Then switch to the graph window and select Edit Link Create. Select the clipboard data for the source file and item, and enter **Pattern:A** for the destination item. For the low temperatures, copy the worksheet range A:B14..A:H14 to the clipboard. Next, switch to the graph window and select Edit Link Create. Select the clipboard data for the source file and item and enter **Pattern:B** for the destination item. This graph also shows how you can hide the legend frame by selecting Settings Area Style and unselecting the Filled, Border, and Shadow selection boxes. You may want to hide the legend frame to display a legend box title or, as in this example, to add explanatory text.

Changing Links

After you create the links, you will occasionally need to edit them. For example, if you move the values used by a link, the link does not update the range address to use.

To alter a link, select Edit Link Edit. From the dialog box, you can select the destination item, which is the graph object to alter the link. 1-2-3/G lists the selected object by default. With the destination item selected, you can change the source file and item (cell or range address for a worksheet source file) and whether 1-2-3/G updates the link automatically or only when you enter Edit Link Update.

You may also want to change the filename that one or more links in the graph uses. For example, if you rename the worksheet file a graph uses, you also need to update all filenames in the link sources. You can use the Edit Link Move command to do this. When you select Edit Link Move, you can select a source file used by one or more linked graph objects. Once the old source file is selected, you can select a new source file from the list of open 1-2-3/G worksheet files and other Presentation Manager applications. When you select Move links, 1-2-3/G replaces every link that uses the current source file and replaces the filename in the link with the new source file. The item for each link, usually the cell or range address, remains the same.

The Edit Link Move command also lets you globally delete links to a file. When you select a filename from the Current source list and select the Delete links command button, 1-2-3/G deletes every link that uses the selected source file. This is just like using Edit Link Delete for every link with the same source file.

Using the Clipboard in a Graph

1-2-3/G also uses the Clipboard to store graph objects. The commands for copying and pasting objects with the clipboard are the same as in a worksheet window. You can use the clipboard to copy objects between graphs. You can also use the clipboard to paste data from a worksheet file, another graph, or another Presentation Manager application that supports the dynamic data exchange. A clipboard stores the graph objects in a Desktop text format, as a series of entries containing labels and values. The clipboard does not store attributes such as color, font, or numeric format. When you copy an entire graph to the clipboard, the graph is stored in a Metafile, bitmap, and Desktop format. This allows the clipboard to store all graphical attributes such as fonts and color. The capabilities of the package that supports the Dynamic Data Exchange (DDE) depends on the specific attributes that appear in the other software package when the information is copied.

To copy graph objects to the clipboard, you can use the Edit Copy or Edit Cut command. You can use these commands to copy titles, text notations, one or all legend labels, data labels, X-axis labels, data series values, and the graph. Copying the graph to the clipboard copies the X-axis labels, data series values, and legend labels. When the clipboard stores a graph object, it stores the values or labels of the object rather than the link that provided the values. If you use the clipboard to copy graph objects, the new copy of the graph objects will use the labels and values but will not have the link that updates the labels and values. The clipboard does not store attributes.

To paste most objects to the graph, select the object to be replaced with data in the clipboard. Then select Edit Paste. The selected object will be replaced with the clipboard data. If you select a title, text notation, or single legend label, 1-2-3/G replaces the text with the contents of the upper-left cell or first item as a label. If you select a legend frame, 1-2-3/G replaces all legend labels with the series of entries in the clipboard. If you select a data range's data labels, 1-2-3/G replaces the data labels with the entries stored in the clipboard. If you select the X-axis labels, 1-2-3/G replaces them with the entries stored in the clipboard. If you select a data range, 1-2-3/G replaces it with the values in the range stored in the clipboard. If you select the graph, 1-2-3/G replaces the X-axis labels, data ranges, and legend labels with the range stored in the clipboard, as if using the entries in an instant graph.

You can paste worksheet data from the clipboard to the graph by using Edit Paste Special. The differences between Edit Paste and Edit Paste Special are much like the differences between an instant graph and a graph created with Graph Setup. As with Graph Setup, the Edit Paste Special dialog box lets you choose if the worksheet data stored in the clipboard is divided into series according to columns or rows. You can also choose whether the graph uses the first row and column for the X-axis labels and the legend labels.

Printing Graphs and Worksheets Together

1-2-3/G can print worksheets and graphs on the same page. This is much like printing a separate worksheet or graph, but you display the output in the Preview window before printing. This lets you select the worksheet data and graphs to print before sending all of the output to the printer. Each print request will be treated as a separate print job.

To print graphs and worksheets together, activate the graph or worksheet that you want to print. Then select File Print and Print Graph or Print Worksheet. For either the worksheet or graph, make the selections to be used to print the worksheet or graph. Make sure that you select the Screen preview selection box. When you are finished making selections, either select Go from the File Print Print Worksheet dialog box or Print from the File Print Print Graph dialog box. 1-2-3/G will open a preview window containing the graph or worksheet that you have just selected. Next, go to the worksheet or graph that you want to appear after the text or graph shown in the preview window, and perform the steps for printing the graph or worksheet in the preview window. You can continue printing worksheets and graphs in the preview window until you have accumulated the graphs and worksheet data that you want to print. At this point, select Print Printer from the preview window. By printing worksheets and graphs in the preview window instead of directly to the printer, 1-2-3/G groups all of the information in the preview window so that the graphs and worksheets are printed together.

Tip: Select Line from the File Print Print Worksheet dialog box several times to insert blank lines between the printed worksheets and graphs.

Tip: To print text and graphs side by side, another strategy is to place the graph on the left side and select a very wide right margin to place the text on the right side.

Creating Graph Templates

In Chapter 6, you learned how to create a template file for a worksheet. You can also create a graph template file to store all of the graph settings in the graph file, including fonts, text, attributes, and scaling options. When you create a graph template, you may want to delete the data ranges. You may also want to return the titles to the default so that the template file does not contain graph-specific information.

To create a graph template file, save the graph as a template; for instance, C:\123G\TEMPLATE\DEFAULT.GPH. You can save it under another name as long as you save it to the C:\123G\TEMPLATE directory. The template called C:\123G\TEMPLATE\DEFAULT.GPH is used every time that you delete the entire graph or when you use the File New command to create a new graph window. To use a different template file with the File New command, move to the template name text box, press F3 (Name), and select the graph template filename from the list.

1-2-3/G's Data Management Features

Getting Started with Data Management
Basic Data Management Operations
Advanced Data Management Features

PART FIVE

Getting Started with Data Management

Building the Database
Changing the Sequence of Records
Working with the Data Query Features

EIGHTEEN

Data management offers new commands that allow you to focus more on the storage and management of information than on computations. With the data management features, you can record data and then organize it in many different sequences in only minutes. You can put 1-2-3/G in charge of maintaining the information while you define exactly what you need to know. 1-2-3/G will search through a large database table quickly and return only the information of interest. You can create one or more database tables in worksheet files. You can also work with external databases and bring information from them directly into 1-2-3/G. This chapter focuses on the basics. It provides an exercise that gets you started with both Data Sort and Data Query within a single worksheet database table.

Building the Database

In 1-2-3/G, a database table is a tabular arrangement of data composed of fields and records. A *field* is one piece of information. A *record* is all the information for one entity in the database, and consists of a potential entry for each database field.

Each column in the table stores information for a different field in the database. A field might consist of a name, an invoice number, or an amount. You must choose a unique name for each of these fields and use it throughout your data management activities. A record is one row in the database table. It can have a maximum of one entry for each field, although some fields within a record may be blank. Figure 18-1 shows a database table that contains four fields and nine records. Although this is a very small database, it will illustrate 1-2-3/G's data management commands.

Manage Files Menu

File Edit Worksheet Range Copy... Move... Print Graph Data Utility Quit... Help

A:A1 "Invoice

A:\INVOICE.WG1

	A	B	C	D	E	F
1	Invoice	Client	Date	Amount		
2	36900	Allied Construction	06/15/90	$784.50		
3	36901	Norris Supplies	06/16/90	$325.99		
4	36902	Allied Construction	06/17/90	$802.95		
5	36903	Jacobs Brothers	06/18/90	$502.50		
6	36904	Norris Supplies	06/18/90	$125.99		
7	36905	Allied Construction	06/20/90	$95.54		
8	36906	Jacobs Brothers	06/22/90	$1,200.85		
9	36907	Norris Supplies	06/23/90	$54.50		
10	36908	Allied Construction	06/25/90	$1,450.00		
11						
12						
13						
14						
15						
16						
17						

Figure 18-1. Database records

Follow these steps to enter the database records:

1. Enter the following field names:

Cell	**Entry**
A1	Invoice
B1	Client
C1	Date
D1	Amount

2. Select Range Attribute Font Attributes Bold for the range A1..D1. This sets the field names apart from the entries beneath them.

3. Move the cell pointer to column B. Select Worksheet Column Set width, and specify 16 as the cell width.

4. Select Range Label Labels Right and then specify the collection A1,C1..D1.

5. Select Range Format Date 4 for the range C2..C10.

6. Select Range Format Currency 2 for the range D2..D10.

7. Select Data Fill. Select the range A2..A10 to have 1-2-3/G generate the invoice numbers for you. Type **36900** as the Start number, **1** as the increment, and **99999** as the Stop value.

8. Enter the following client names in the cells shown:

Cell	**Entry**
B2	Allied Construction
B3	Norris Supplies
B4	Allied Construction
B5	Jacobs Brothers
B6	Norris Supplies
B7	Allied Construction
B8	Jacobs Brothers
B9	Norris Supplies
B10	Allied Construction

9. Type the following dates in the cells shown:

Cell	**Entry**
C2	6/15/90
C3	6/16/90
C4	6/17/90
C5	6/18/90
C6	6/18/90
C7	6/20/90
C8	6/22/90
C9	6/23/90
C10	6/25/90

1-2-3/G converts these dates into serial numbers but uses the date format to display the desired dates.

10. Enter the amounts as shown:

Cell	Entry
D2	784.5
D3	325.99
D4	802.95
D5	502.5
D6	125.99
D7	95.54
D8	1200.85
D9	54.5
D10	1450

1-2-3/G automatically formats your entries due to the Range Format applied in step 6.

Changing the Sequence of Records

The records in the database were entered in invoice number sequence. Even with a four-field database like the one shown, you might need other record sequences at times. You may want to group the records by client name to see the total amount outstanding for a particular client or to identify your repeat customers. You might want to sequence the records by amount to focus collection attempts on the largest outstanding invoices.

The primary sort sequence establishes the main order for the records. If the field selected for the primary sequence contains duplicates, you can choose a secondary sort field that is used as a tie breaker for the duplicate entries in the primary field. In Chapter 19, you will learn how to establish extra sort keys beyond a secondary key.

To establish a primary sequence of client with a secondary sequence of amount, follow these steps:

1. Select Data Sort to display the Data Sort dialog box. Then select Data range.

2. Use the mouse to select this range, or type **A2..D10** and then press ENTER. Note that the field names at the top of each column are not selected. If you accidentally select the row of field names, 1-2-3/G will sort these entries as if they were data values.

3. Select Primary.

4. Select B2 as the primary sort key, or type **B2** and then press ENTER.

5. Select Ascending with the mouse or type an **A**.

6. Select Secondary.

7. Select D2 as the secondary key, or type **D2** and then press ENTER.

8. Select Descending or type a **D**.

The completed Data Sort dialog box should look like the one shown in Figure 18-2.

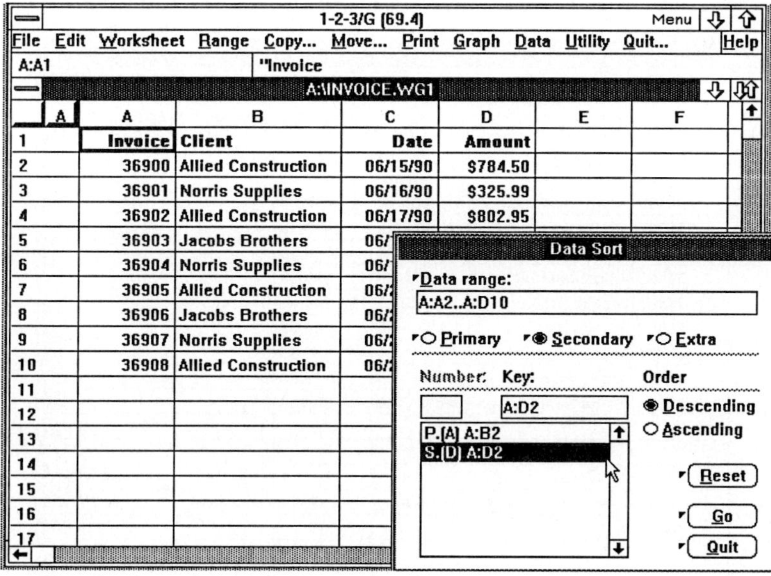

Figure 18-2. Data Sort dialog box

9. Select Go to sort the records. The sorted records will match Figure 18-3.

Working with the Data Query Features

The Data Query feature can gather important information in the database for you. Rather than having to scan records to find the right ones, you can tell 1-2-3/G the records you want. 1-2-3/G can then highlight the records that match your needs, or write them to an output area. You can use this information to answer a customer phone inquiry or produce a quick report that you just defined.

1-2-3/G [69.4] Ready

File Edit Worksheet Range Copy... Move... Print Graph Data Utility Quit... Help

A:A1 "Invoice

A:\INVOICE.WG1

A	A	B	C	D	E	F
1	Invoice	Client	Date	Amount		
2	36908	Allied Construction	06/25/90	$1,450.00		
3	36902	Allied Construction	06/17/90	$802.95		
4	36900	Allied Construction	06/15/90	$784.50		
5	36905	Allied Construction	06/20/90	$95.54		
6	36906	Jacobs Brothers	06/22/90	$1,200.85		
7	36903	Jacobs Brothers	06/18/90	$502.50		
8	36901	Norris Supplies	06/16/90	$325.99		
9	36904	Norris Supplies	06/18/90	$125.99		
10	36907	Norris Supplies	06/23/90	$54.50		
11						
12						
13						
14						
15						
16						
17						

Figure 18-3. Sorted records

Finding Matching Records

To locate records that meet your needs, enter your specifications on the worksheet and then invoke Data Query Find. You can look for an exact match on label or value entries, or use a formula to perform a logical test. When searching for label entries, you can even use wildcards to increase the matching potential of an entry. (You will learn about wildcards in Chapter 19.) Follow these steps to locate records for Jacobs Brothers and then look for records in which the amount exceeds $1,000:

1. Press CTRL-PGUP to move to sheet B in the current worksheet file.
2. Type **Client** in A1.
3. Type **Jacobs Brothers** in A2.
   The criteria area looks like this:

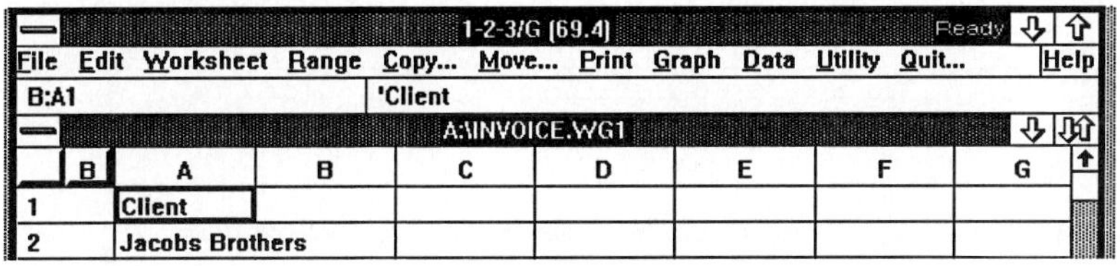

1-2-3/G [69.4] Ready
File Edit Worksheet Range Copy... Move... Print Graph Data Utility Quit... Help
B:A1 'Client
A:\INVOICE.WG1

B	A	B	C	D	E	F	G
1	Client						
2	Jacobs Brothers						

4. Press CTRL-PGDN and then press HOME.
5. Select Data Query. 1-2-3/G presents a dialog box that allows you to specify the location of the database table with Input, the location of the criteria with Criteria, and an Output area if you plan to extract records. This dialog box also permits you to indicate the query operation to be performed.
6. Select Input and then select A1..D10 with the mouse, or type **A1..D10** and then press ENTER.
7. Select Criteria and then press CTRL-PGUP and select B:A1..B:A2 with your mouse. If you are using the keyboard, type **B:A1..B:A2** and then press ENTER to finalize your selection.
8. Select Find. 1-2-3/G highlights the first matching entry, as shown in Figure 18-4, and allows you to use the UP ARROW and DOWN ARROW keys to move to other records that match the criteria. You can use the RIGHT ARROW and LEFT ARROW keys to view other fields in a matching record if the entire record does not display on your screen. You cannot use the mouse to move from record to record or view other fields because the mouse does not function in Find mode.

1-2-3/G (69.4) Ready

File Edit Worksheet Range Copy... Move... Print Graph Data Utility Quit... Help

A:A6 36906

A:\INVOICE.WG1 Find

A	A	B	C	D	E	F
1	Invoice	Client	Date	Amount		
2	36908	Allied Construction	06/25/90	$1,450.00		
3	36902	Allied Construction	06/17/90	$802.95		
4	36900	Allied Construction	06/15/90	$784.50		
5	36905	Allied Construction	06/20/90	$95.54		
6	36906	Jacobs Brothers	06/22/90	$1,200.85		
7	36903	Jacobs Brothers	06/18/90	$502.50		
8	36901	Norris Supplies	06/16/90	$325.99		
9	36904	Norris Supplies	06/18/90	$125.99		
10	36907	Norris Supplies	06/23/90	$54.50		
11						
12						
13						
14						
15						
16						
17						

Figure 18-4. First matching record for Jacobs Brothers

9. Press ESCAPE to return to the Data Query dialog box, and then select Quit to return to Ready mode.

Now you want to try a formula to locate records that meet a condition. To find records in which the amount field contains an entry greater than $1,000, follow these steps:

1. Press CTRL-PGUP to move to sheet B in the current worksheet file.
2. Type **Amount** in B:A1.
3. Type **+A:D2>1000** in B:A2. The criteria area looks like this:

1-2-3/G (69.4) Ready

File Edit Worksheet Range Copy... Move... Print Graph Data Utility Quit... Help

B:A2 +A:D2>1000

A:\INVOICE.WG1

B	A	B	C	D	E	F	G
1	Amount						
2	1						

By referring to the first cell containing the data you want the criteria to use, 1-2-3/G knows to apply the criteria to every record in the database.

1-2-3/G always displays logical formulas as a 1 or a 0 depending on whether the condition test is true or false for the first record in the database table. If you would prefer to see the logical formula, you can apply a format of Text to the cell.

4. Press CTRL-PGDN and then press HOME.
5. Press F7 (Query).

   Since Input and Criteria are in the same location as the last query, you don't need to invoke the menu to perform another Data Query Find. 1-2-3/G uses the new entries in the Criteria area and displays the first matching record, as shown in Figure 18-5.
6. Use the arrow keys to move between records that meet your criteria. Press ESCAPE to return to Ready mode when finished.

You don't need to select Quit from the Data Query dialog box since you used the F7 shortcut to activate the Find feature this time.

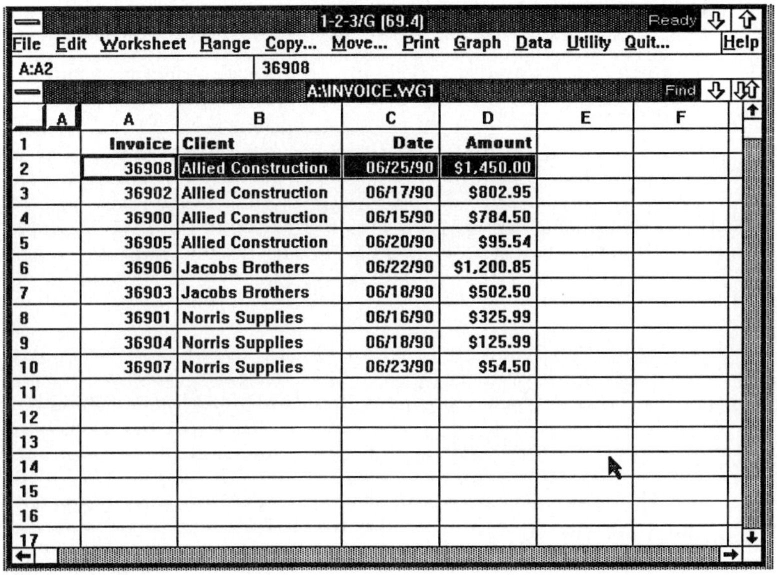

1-2-3/G [69.4] Ready

File Edit Worksheet Range Copy... Move... Print Graph Data Utility Quit... Help

A:A2 36908

A:\INVOICE.WG1 Find

A	A	B	C	D	E	F
1	Invoice	Client	Date	Amount		
2	36908	Allied Construction	06/25/90	$1,450.00		
3	36902	Allied Construction	06/17/90	$802.95		
4	36900	Allied Construction	06/15/90	$784.50		
5	36905	Allied Construction	06/20/90	$95.54		
6	36906	Jacobs Brothers	06/22/90	$1,200.85		
7	36903	Jacobs Brothers	06/18/90	$502.50		
8	36901	Norris Supplies	06/16/90	$325.99		
9	36904	Norris Supplies	06/18/90	$125.99		
10	36907	Norris Supplies	06/23/90	$54.50		
11						
12						
13						
14						
15						
16						
17						

Figure 18-5. First record with amount greater than $1,000

Extracting Records that Meet Your Needs

Besides highlighting records that match your needs, 1-2-3/G can write them out in another table. You can define which fields to include in this table and the order in which they occur. As with Data Query Find, your criteria entries define which records are selected from the database table. Follow these steps to copy the records for invoices dated after 20/Jun/90:

1. Press CTRL-PGUP to move to sheet B.

2. Type "**Date** in B:A1.

3. Type **+A:C2>@DATE(90,6,20)** in B:A2 and press ENTER. The criteria entry looks like this:

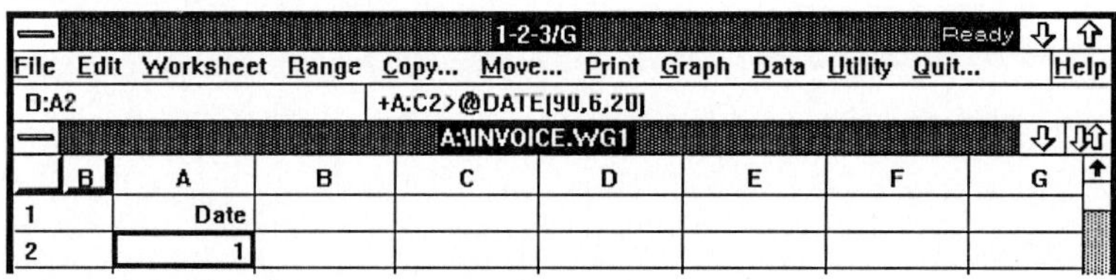

4. Press CTRL-PGUP to move to sheet C.

5. Complete the following entries to lay out the order of the fields in the Output area:

Cell	**Cell Entry**
A1	Client
B1	"Amount
C1	"Date
D1	"Invoice

Notice that the Output area contains the fields in a different order than the original database.

6. Click the mouse pointer on A1 or press HOME to place the cell pointer in column A.

7. Select Worksheet Column Set Width and type **16** for the width.

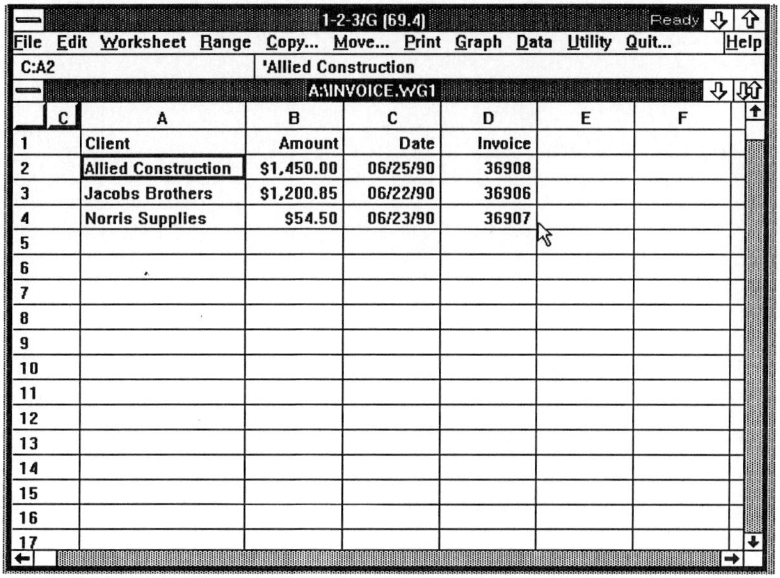

1-2-3/G [69.4] Ready

File Edit Worksheet Range Copy... Move... Print Graph Data Utility Quit... Help

C:A2 'Allied Construction

A:\INVOICE.WG1

C	A	B	C	D	E	F
1	Client	Amount	Date	Invoice		
2	Allied Construction	$1,450.00	06/25/90	36908		
3	Jacobs Brothers	$1,200.85	06/22/90	36906		
4	Norris Supplies	$54.50	06/23/90	36907		
5						
6						
7						
8						
9						
10						
11						
12						
13						
14						
15						
16						
17						

Figure 18-6. Extracted data for invoices after 20-Jun-90

8. Select Data Query.
9. Select Output.
10. Use the mouse to select C:A1..C:D1, or type **C:A1..C:D1** and press ENTER.
11. Select Extract. 1-2-3/G extracts all records with dates after 20/Jun/90.
12. Select Quit to return to Ready mode. With the Data Query dialog box removed, you can see the extracted records, as shown in Figure 18-6. Notice that the extracted data is formatted just as it is in the original database.

Basic Data Management Operations

The 1-2-3/G Database
Setting Up a Database
Sorting Your Data
Searching the Database

NINETEEN

In one sense, all the work you've done so far with 1-2-3/G has been data management, because it has involved managing information recorded on the worksheet. However, *data management*, as defined by 1-2-3/G, refers to the formalized process of designing, entering, and retrieving information from a database.

The world of data management has its own terminology. A *database*, for example, is a collection of the information you have about a set of things. These things can be customers, orders, parts in inventory, employees, or just about anything else. If you create a database of employee information, for instance, you want it to contain information about each of your employees. All the information about one employee would be one record in the database. A record is composed of all the pieces of information you have about one thing in the set, such as one employee. These individual pieces of information in a record are referred to as fields. In each record in an employee database, you might want to include fields for name, address, job classification, date of hire, social security number, department, benefits, and salary. When you design a new database, you need to decide what fields to include in each record.

This chapter describes how you can set up databases in 1-2-3/G. When your database is established, you can use the program's Data Query commands to review the records. By setting up criteria for querying your database, you can select the records that you will use. This chapter covers the most frequently used data query commands. The next chapter covers the remaining data query commands, and other advanced techniques that you can use with databases.

1-2-3/G (69.4) Ready

File Edit Worksheet Range Copy... Move... Print Graph Data Utility Quit... Help

A:A1 'Last Name

EMPLOYEE.WG1

A	A	B	C	D	E	F
1	Last Name	First Name	SS#	Job Code	Salary	Location
2	Larson	Mary	543-98-9876	23	$12,000	2
3	Campbell	David	213-76-9874	23	$23,000	10
4	Campbell	Keith	569-89-7654	12	$32,000	2
5	Stephens	Tom	219-78-8954	15	$17,800	2
6	Caldor	Larry	459-34-0921	23	$32,500	4
7	Lightnor	Peggy	560-55-4311	14	$23,500	10
8	McCartin	John	817-66-1212	15	$54,600	2
9	Justof	Jack	431-78-9[illegible]3	17	$41,200	4
10	Patterson	Lyle	212-11-9090	12	$21,500	10
11	Miller	Lisa	214-89-6756	23	$18,700	2
12	Hawkins	Mark	215-67-8973	21	$19,500	2
13	Hartwick	Eileen	313-78-9090	15	$31,450	4
14	Smythe	George	560-90-8645	15	$65,000	4
15	Wilkes	Caitlin	124-67-7432	17	$15,500	2
16	Deaver	Ken	198-98-6750	23	$24,600	10
17	Kaylor	Sally	312-45-9862	12	$32,900	10

Figure 19-1. Portion of an employee database

The 1-2-3/G Database

A 1-2-3/G database is a range of cells on a worksheet. It can be in any area of the worksheet, but the field names (the names that you use to categorize data) must run across the top row of the range. The records in the database that contain data for each field are placed in the rows immediately following the row of field names. Figure 19-1 shows a section of an employee database in A1..F17. The field names are located in A1..F1, and the first database record is located in A2..F2.

As a database manager, 1-2-3/G differs from other packages in the following ways:

- The data in your 1-2-3/G database is all stored in memory while you are working with the database. Unlike other packages that must read data from the disk when you need it, 1-2-3/G provides quick response to requests for resequencing records and finding those that match specific criteria. However, this feature requires that your computer have sufficient memory to hold your entire database at once. You need a large memory capacity, a fairly small database, or both.

• 1-2-3/G's data management commands are similar to its worksheet commands, which makes them easy for you to learn. By contrast, it may take you a long time to master the command structure of other packages.

• Most data management packages create formatted screens to enter or review one record at a time. With macros (as covered in Chapter 23) you can now easily design a formatted screen for use when inputting or viewing information in your database.

• 1-2-3/G lets you enter up to 8191 records in one database table in a worksheet. You can create multiple database tables in a file by putting them on different worksheets. You can combine these database tables when you use 1-2-3/G functions and database commands. The practical limit to a database size is the amount of memory available, since the entire database resides in memory. These limits are sufficient for many applications, but some other products do allow an unlimited number of records.

• 1-2-3/G can accommodate up to 256 fields in one database. Some packages allow more and others less.

• 1-2-3/G permits each field to have up to 512 characters. Some packages allow more and others less.

Setting Up a Database

When designing a 1-2-3/G database, you must first create a list of fields the database will contain. Once you have recorded all the field names, estimate the number of characters that each field will require for storage and the number of records in your database. Determine the number of characters for each field, and then multiply by the number of records. You should include a few extra characters for each field, since each cell uses additional space for formatting information. If the potential number of records exceeds 1-2-3/G's limits, you should find another alternative, such as splitting your file into two sections.

Choosing a Location for the Database

Next, you need to select an area of the worksheet for storing the database. It's easiest to put a database on its own spreadsheet. This allows the database to expand and contract without affecting other data in the worksheet. If you put the database on a worksheet with other worksheet data, make sure that there's enough room below the bottom of the database and to the right of the database to add new records and fields. A problem with storing database and other worksheet data on the same sheet is that you may add or delete rows in the database or other worksheet data without realizing how the rest of the worksheet is affected. Separating the database from other worksheet data makes the database easier to find and prevents damage to the database or other worksheet data.

Entering Field Names

Record your selected field names across the top row of the database area. Following these rules for field names will help you create a workable database:

- Make sure that you record field names in the order in which they appear in the form you plan to use for data entry. This will minimize the time required for entry.
- Each field name is placed in one cell and must be unique.
- The field names that you choose are used with some of the other database features. Therefore, choose meaningful names, but not names so long that reentry in other places will lead to misspellings.
- Don't enter spaces at the end of field names. You cannot see that you included these spaces, and the names will not match with later entries that don't include trailing spaces.

A layout of field names for an employee database might look like this:

1-2-3/G [69.4] Ready

File Edit Worksheet Range Copy... Move... Print Graph Data Utility Quit... Help

A:A1 'Last Name

EMPLOYEE.WG1

A	A	B	C	D	E	F
1	Last Name	First Name	SS#	Job Code	Salary	Location
2						

Entering Information

The first database record should begin immediately beneath the row of field names. Don't leave blank lines or use special symbols as divider lines. If you want to use additional column headings for the database, enter them above the field names. When you want to use the headings, hide the row containing the field names with the Worksheet Row Hide command. You can also use formatting commands such as borders and underlining on the field names without affecting how they work.

All entries in corresponding fields of like records should be of the same type. For example, if a field contains numeric data, the value for that field should be numeric in every record in the database. If you mix numeric values and labels in a single field, the two types of data will be separated when records are sorted and when you attempt to select a subset of the records. However, you can leave a field blank within a particular record if you lack data. You can also construct user-defined formats to display the values differently—you could display the label "Not Available" in place of a 0 value. Figure 19-2 presents an employee database with the first ten records entered.

As your database grows larger, the field names will scroll off the screen, making data entry more difficult. You can prevent this by using the Worksheet Titles Horizontal command to lock the field names in place on your screen. If you have forgotten how this command works, go back to Chapter 7 for a quick review.

Tip: To ensure that the data in each field is of the same type, use the Worksheet Window Map mode Enable command. 1-2-3/G shows the data type of each of the cells. To return the display to normal, use the Worksheet Window Map mode Disable command. If you have forgotten how this command works, refer to Chapter 7.

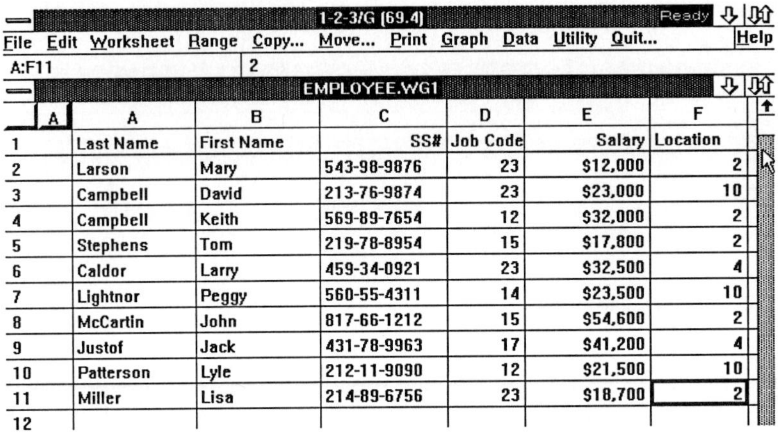

1-2-3/G [69.4] Ready

File Edit Worksheet Range Copy... Move... Print Graph Data Utility Quit... Help

A:F11 2

EMPLOYEE.WG1

A	A	B	C	D	E	F
1	Last Name	First Name	SS#	Job Code	Salary	Location
2	Larson	Mary	543-98-9876	23	$12,000	2
3	Campbell	David	213-76-9874	23	$23,000	10
4	Campbell	Keith	569-89-7654	12	$32,000	2
5	Stephens	Tom	219-78-8954	15	$17,800	2
6	Caldor	Larry	459-34-0921	23	$32,500	4
7	Lightnor	Peggy	560-55-4311	14	$23,500	10
8	McCartin	John	817-66-1212	15	$54,600	2
9	Justof	Jack	431-78-9963	17	$41,200	4
10	Patterson	Lyle	212-11-9090	12	$21,500	10
11	Miller	Lisa	214-89-6756	23	$18,700	2
12						

Figure 19-2. Employee database with first ten records completed

If a database becomes too large for a single worksheet, you can split the records into multiple database tables in different worksheets. For example, if a customer database doesn't fit on one worksheet, you can place customers with last names beginning with "A" through "L" in the first worksheet's data table, and customers with last names beginning with "M" through "Z" in the second worksheet's data table. Be sure to keep the field names and order consistent when using databases that span sheets.

Making Changes

You can change entries in a database with any of the techniques you have used on regular worksheets. You can retype an entry to replace its current value. You can press F2 (Edit) to insert, delete, and replace characters within an entry.

You can use Worksheet Insert to add a blank row for a new record or add a blank column for another field. The Worksheet Delete command can remove records or fields. However, keep in mind that the entire worksheet is affected by both of these commands; it is important to assess the effect that these commands have, which can potentially damage areas outside the database. This is not a problem if the database is the only information on the worksheet. A good strategy is to save the file before using insertion or deletion commands. Then, if you have a problem, you can restore the file from disk. Also note that the Copy command can copy field values only from other database records.

Sorting Your Data

1-2-3/G sorts very quickly because the entire database is stored in RAM. Any change in sequence can take place at the speed of transfer within RAM, which is considerably faster than sorting records from disk.

The Data Sort dialog box shown in Figure 19-3 contains all the options you need to specify the records to sort, specify the sort sequence, and initiate the sort. This dialog box displays when you select Data Sort. The steps for resequencing your data using the various Sort options are summarized in the "Steps for Sorting Your Data" box.

Determining What Data to Sort

You can sort all the records in your database or just some of them, depending on the range you specify. Be sure to include all of the

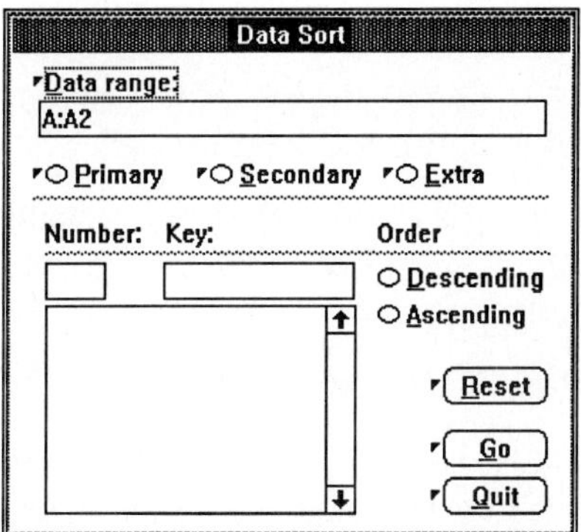

Figure 19-3. Data Sort dialog box

records' fields in the sort. If you exclude some fields, those fields will remain stationary while the rest of the record is moved during the sort. If you ever plan to return your records to their original entry sequence

Steps for Sorting Your Data

Sorting is a quick and easy process, but it requires the following sequence of commands from the Data Sort menu:

1. Select Data Sort and choose Data range.
2. Highlight (specify) all records and fields to be sorted, but don't include the field names within the range.
3. Select Primary from the Sort menu.
4. Highlight any data value within the column of entries you wish to use to control the sort sequence.
5. If you expect duplicate primary keys within your database, choose Secondary from the Sort menu.
6. Highlight any data value within the column that you wish to use as the tie breaker if there are duplicate primary keys.
7. If you expect duplicate primary and secondary keys within your database, choose Extra from the Sort menu.
8. Enter the number of the extra key, or accept 1-2-3/G's default value and press ENTER.
9. Highlight any data value within the column that you wish to use as the tie breaker if there are duplicate primary and secondary keys.
10. Repeat steps 7 through 9 for each extra key that you want to use.
11. Select Go from the Sort menu to have 1-2-3/G resequence your data.

after a sort, you must include a field for record number in the record. A sequential number can be placed in this field at the time of entry.

To set the range for the sort, select Data Sort Data range. Then specify the range for the database, as shown in Figure 19-4. As with other commands that use ranges, you can select the range to sort before you select Data Sort and 1-2-3/G will display the selected range in the Data range text box. Be sure *not* to include the row of field names. If you do, they are sorted along with the record values. In Figure 19-4, notice that the selected range includes all of the records and all of the fields, but omits the field names in the first row.

When sorting, you can also select a range containing multiple sheets. If you do, 1-2-3/G sorts each worksheet separately. When you use 1-2-3/G's sort features, records are not moved between worksheets.

Specifying the Sort Sequence

You can specify multiple sort keys. In all cases, the primary key will control the sequence of the records. The additional keys are ignored except where duplicate examples of the primary key occur. In this situation, the secondary key is used to break the tie. When records contain the same data for the primary and secondary keys, 1-2-3/G uses the extra keys to break the tie. 1-2-3/G can use up to 253 extra keys to

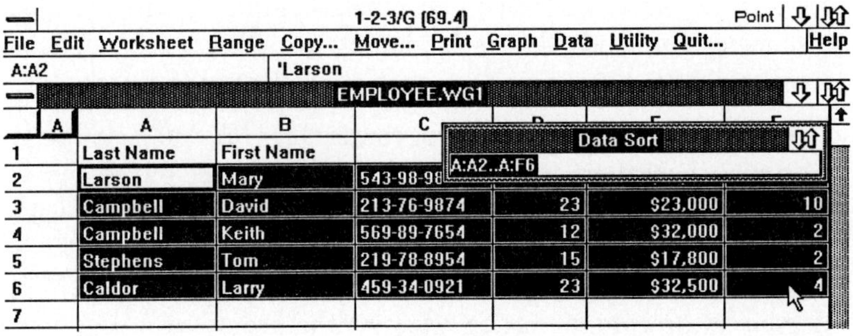

Figure 19-4. Sort range selected

sort your data. For all sort keys, you can select whether the values are sorted in ascending or descending order.

The sort order is also affected by the Sort order setting, which is in the Utility User Settings International dialog box. As discussed in Chapter 7, 1-2-3/G has three options for a collating sequence: Numbers First, Numbers Last, and ASCII. The "Effect of Sort Order on Sorting" box also describes these options in further detail. To make a change, select Utility User Settings International Sort order and choose the option button for the desired sort order.

Choosing a Primary Sort Key

To specify a primary key, select Primary in the Data Sort dialog box and point to a cell containing data for a particular field within the database.

Effect of Sort Order on Sorting

The order of your data after a sort partly depends on the sort order you choose with the Utility User Settings International command. The three possibilities for ascending sequence are as follows:

- *Numbers last* Blank cells; label entries beginning with letters in alphabetical order; label entries beginning with numbers in numeric sequence; labels beginning with special characters; values.
- *Numbers first* Blank cells; labels beginning with numbers in numeric sequence; labels beginning with letters in alphabetical order; labels beginning with special characters; values.
- *ASCII* Blank cells; labels containing letters, numbers, and special characters according to the ASCII value of the characters in the label; values. Capitalization affects the sort order with this choice.

Sorting in descending order reverses the order.

This field (column) becomes your primary sort key. If you prefer, you can type the cell address instead of pointing. In either case, you are prompted to choose the sort order. When you choose Ascending, the sort order you selected with Utility User Settings International is used. When you choose Descending, the sequences are reversed. Either type the underlined letter or click the option button to select the sort order. Note that a default sort order may already be present on your screen. This is the order you chose for your previous sort.

Setting the sort sequence does not automatically resequence your data. You also have to specify the data range and then select Go from the Data Sort dialog box.

Choosing a Secondary Sort Key

The secondary sort key serves as a tie breaker. For example, in an employee file where last name is the primary sort key, you may wish to use first name as the secondary key in case more than one employee has the same last name. Within the group of duplicate last names, records will be sorted by first name.

Set the secondary key by selecting Secondary in the Data Sort dialog box. Then either point to a cell containing a data value for the field you want to sort, or type the cell address. Next, specify Ascending or Descending, as you did with the primary key. Again, the default sequence is the last order you selected.

Choosing Extra Sort Keys

The extra sort keys serve as additional tie breakers when records contain identical data in both their primary and secondary sort key fields. Since 1-2-3/G permits up to 253 extra keys, you can select up to 255 different sort keys, although you will usually use only a few sort keys for most of your databases.

In a large employee database, you may have more than one employee with the same first and last name. You may want to add the social security number as an extra key. In another example, suppose you need to sort expense data that is coded by division, region, branch, and expense code. The data for this example is shown in Figure 19-5. The

1-2-3/G (69.4) Ready

File Edit Worksheet Range Copy... Move... Print Graph Data Utility Quit... Help

A:A1 'Expense Code

EXPENSES.WG1

A	A	B	C	D	E	F
1	Expense Code	Division	Region	Branch	Amount	
2	RF-1265	1	2	200	$6,785.00	
3	ST-1100	2	2	500	$7,500.00	
4	RX-1254	2	1	110	$1,200.00	
5	ST-1100	3	1	110	$560.00	
6	RT-1000	1	1	300	$998.00	
7	ST-8978	1	2	200	$1,050.00	
8	RF-1265	3	2	610	$2,341.00	
9	RX-1254	3	1	100	$1,208.90	
10	ST-8978	2	1	110	$2,341.00	

Figure 19-5. Expense data

division can be the primary key, the region can be the secondary key, the branch can be the first extra key, and the expense code can be the second extra key. Once you sort the records, they will look like Figure 19-6.

Specify an extra key by selecting Extra in the Data Sort dialog box. 1-2-3/G prompts for the extra sort key number by displaying the lowest unselected extra sort key number. You can either accept this number or

1-2-3/G (69.4) Ready

File Edit Worksheet Range Copy... Move... Print Graph Data Utility Quit... Help

A:A1 'Expense Code

EXPENSES.WG1

A	A	B	C	D	E	F
1	Expense Code	Division	Region	Branch	Amount	
2	RT-1000	1	1	300	$998.00	
3	RF-1265	1	2	200	$6,785.00	
4	ST-8978	1	2	200	$1,050.00	
5	RX-1254	2	1	110	$1,200.00	
6	ST-8978	2	1	110	$2,341.00	
7	ST-1100	?	2	500	$7,500.00	
8	RX-1254	3	1	100	$1,208.90	
9	ST-1100	3	1	110	$560.00	
10	RF-1265	3	2	610	$2,341.00	

Figure 19-6. Sorted expense records

enter your own. If you type a number of a sort key that is already selected, you can modify the selections for the extra key. Next, 1-2-3/G prompts for the field (column) containing the extra sort key. Either point to a cell containing a data value for the field by which you want to sort, or type the cell address. Once you supply an address, 1-2-3/G asks whether the values in the selected key should be sorted in ascending or descending order. Figure 19-7 shows a Data Sort dialog box filled to use several extra keys. The list box contains the sort keys that are already selected. The list box uses a P for the primary sort key, an S for the secondary key, and a number for the extra keys. After the period, the sort keys display an (A) for ascending order and a (D) for descending order. Finally, the sort key description lists the cell that you chose for the key. With a mouse, you click the sort key that you want to change and then click the text box or option button that you want to change.

Starting and Stopping the Sort

With the data range and (at a minimum) a primary key selected, you are ready to resequence your data. Simply select Go from the Data Sort dialog box, and your data is sorted in the specified order. 1-2-3/G sorts quickly. With a small database, the sort is complete as soon as you lift your finger after selecting Go.

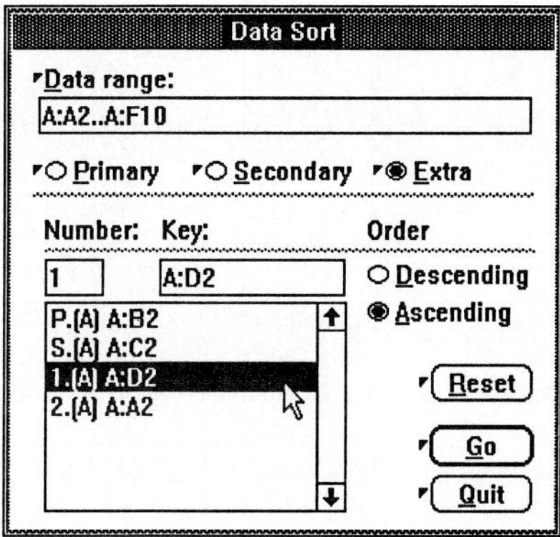

Figure 19-7. Data Sort dialog box using many sort keys

Figure 19-8 presents an employee database with the records in random sequence. Suppose that you select the data range as A2..H20 by using Data Sort Data range. Next, you select the Last Name field (A2) as the primary key using an ascending sort order. Then choose a secondary key of First Name (B2) using an ascending sort order. Once you select Go from the Data Sort dialog box, the records are placed in the new sequence shown in Figure 19-9. Notice that the two records with a last name of Campbell are sequenced by first name.

If you decide to leave the Data Sort dialog box without completing the sort operation, you can select Quit. You don't need to select Quit after selecting Go to sort, since selecting Go automatically returns you to Ready mode after the data is sorted.

Starting Over

Once you have made choices for a sort, 1-2-3/G uses these settings as a default. Making a new selection for the data range or either of the sort

1-2-3/G [69.4] Ready
File Edit Worksheet Range Copy... Move... Print Graph Data Utility Quit... Help
A:A1 'Last Name
EMPLOYEE.WG1

A	A	B	C	D	E	F
1	Last Name	First Name	SS#	Job Code	Salary	Location
2	Larson	Mary	543-98-9876	23	$12,000	2
3	Campbell	David	213-76-9874	23	$23,000	10
4	Campbell	Keith	569-89-7654	12	$32,000	2
5	Stephens	Tom	219-78-8954	15	$17,800	2
6	Caldor	Larry	459-34-0921	23	$32,500	4
7	Lightnor	Peggy	560-55-4311	14	$23,500	10
8	McCartin	John	817-66-1212	15	$54,600	2
9	Justof	Jack	431-78-9963	17	$41,200	4
10	Patterson	Lyle	212-11-9090	12	$21,500	10
11	Miller	Lisa	214-89-6756	23	$18,700	2
12	Hawkins	Mark	215-67-8973	21	$19,500	2
13	Hartwick	Eileen	313-78-9090	15	$31,450	4
14	Smythe	George	560-90-8645	15	$65,000	4
15	Wilkes	Caitlin	124-67-7432	17	$15,500	2
16	Deaver	Ken	198-98-6750	23	$24,600	10
17	Kaylor	Sally	312-45-9862	12	$32,900	10

Figure 19-8. Employee records in random sequence

keys will replace the default. If you want to eliminate your settings, select the Reset command button in the Data Sort dialog box. This option eliminates current settings for data range, primary sort key, secondary sort key, and extra sort keys.

Adding Record Numbers for Sorting Records

Unless you use Edit Undo or retrieve the file again, 1-2-3/G does not have an "unsort" feature. Once you change the sequence of your records, you can't automatically restore them to their original sequence. However, if you plan ahead, you can add to each record a record number field containing a sequential number based on when the records are added to the database. To return sorted records to their original entry order, you could then simply resort based on record number.

You can have 1-2-3/G assign sequential record numbers by using Data Fill, which is covered in Chapter 5. This command can generate any series of numbers that have even increments, if you specify the start, stop, and increment values to be used. You can use this command to generate record numbers within a field in your database.

1-2-3/G [69.4] Ready

File Edit Worksheet Range Copy... Move... Print Graph Data Utility Quit... Help

A:A3 'Campbell

EMPLOYEE.WG1

A	A	B	C	D	E	F
1	Last Name	First Name	SS#	Job Code	Salary	Location
2	Caldor	Larry	459-34-0921	23	$32,500	4
3	Campbell	David	213-76-9874	23	$23,000	10
4	Campbell	Keith	569-89-7654	12	$32,000	2
5	Deaver	Ken	198-98-6750	23	$24,600	10
6	Hartwick	Eileen	313-78-9090	15	$31,450	4
7	Hawkins	Mark	215-67-8973	21	$19,500	2
8	Justof	Jack	431-78-9963	17	$41,200	4
9	Kaylor	Sally	312-45-9862	12	$32,900	10
10	Larson	Mary	543-98-9876	23	$12,000	2
11	Lightnor	Peggy	560-55-4311	14	$23,500	10
12	McCartin	John	817-66-1212	15	$54,600	2
13	Miller	Lisa	214-89-6756	23	$18,700	2
14	Parker	Dee	659-11-3452	14	$19,800	4
15	Patterson	Lyle	212-11-9090	12	$21,500	10
16	Preverson	Gary	670-90-1121	21	$27,600	4
17	Samuelson	Paul	219-89-7080	23	$28,900	2

Figure 19-9. Resequenced employee records

For example, consider the employee database from previous examples. Suppose that you inserted a blank column at the left of the employee database for record sequence numbers, and entered the field name, Sequence, in A1. You can use record numbers in this field to keep track of the original entry order for the employee records. To make Data Fill supply the numbers, follow these steps:

1. Move the cell pointer to A2, the upper-left cell in the range where the numbers are generated.

2. Select Data Fill and specify the fill range as A2..A20, either by pointing or by typing the range reference.

3. At the prompt, type **1** for the start value.

4. The next prompt is for the step or the amount to add to each value to generate the next number. Press ENTER or click the Stop text box to accept the default of 1.

5. The last prompt is for the stop value. You could enter a 19, since this will be the last value in the range. However, since the default stop value is greater than the stop value you want, you can let 1-2-3/G generate the exact stop value, based on the range and increment you have supplied. To do this, accept the default of 8192 in the dialog box by pressing ENTER or clicking the OK command button. 1-2-3/G stops generating numbers when it fills the last cell in the selected range. The result of the Data Fill operation is shown in Figure 19-10.

Searching the Database

As your database grows large, it becomes increasingly important to review its information selectively. 1-2-3/G's data query commands enable you to work selectively with information in your database. These commands can bring to your attention information considered to be outside an established norm, such as finding purchases in an expense journal that exceed a specified amount or are negative amounts. You can also use the selective review feature to clean up your database, or to create reports in response to unexpected requests.

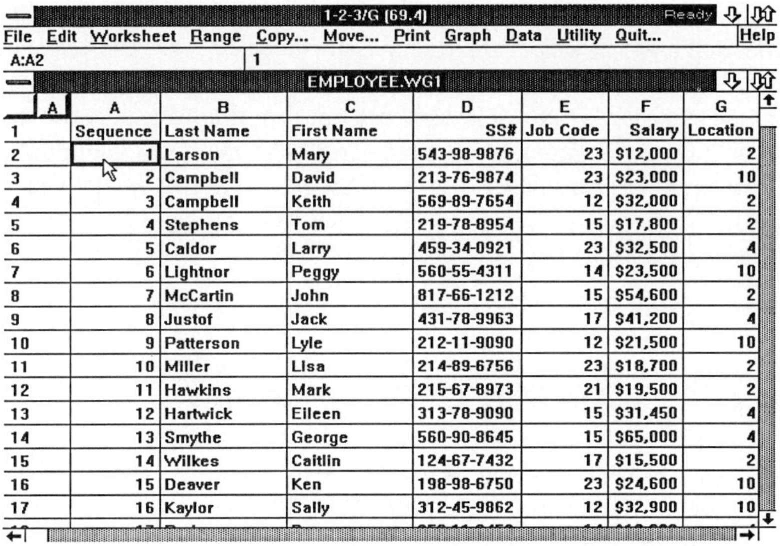

1-2-3/G [69.4] Ready
File Edit Worksheet Range Copy... Move... Print Graph Data Utility Quit... Help
A:A2 1
EMPLOYEE.WG1

A	A	B	C	D	E	F	G
1	Sequence	Last Name	First Name	SS#	Job Code	Salary	Location
2	1	Larson	Mary	543-98-9876	23	$12,000	2
3	2	Campbell	David	213-76-9874	23	$23,000	10
4	3	Campbell	Keith	569-89-7654	12	$32,000	2
5	4	Stephens	Tom	219-78-8954	15	$17,800	2
6	5	Caldor	Larry	459-34-0921	23	$32,500	4
7	6	Lightnor	Peggy	560-55-4311	14	$23,500	10
8	7	McCartin	John	817-66-1212	15	$54,600	2
9	8	Justof	Jack	431-78-9963	17	$41,200	4
10	9	Patterson	Lyle	212-11-9090	12	$21,500	10
11	10	Miller	Lisa	214-89-6756	23	$18,700	2
12	11	Hawkins	Mark	215-67-8973	21	$19,500	2
13	12	Hartwick	Eileen	313-78-9090	15	$31,450	4
14	13	Smythe	George	560-90-8645	15	$65,000	4
15	14	Wilkes	Caitlin	124-67-7432	17	$15,500	2
16	15	Deaver	Ken	198-98-6750	23	$24,600	10
17	16	Kaylor	Sally	312-45-9862	12	$32,900	10

Figure 19-10. Output from Data Fill

All the commands for reviewing information selectively are located in the Data Query dialog box shown in Figure 19-11. You must use at

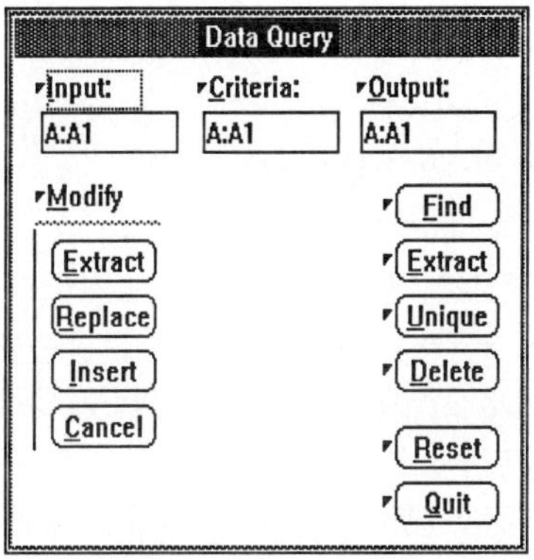

Figure 19-11. Data Query dialog box

least three data query commands to make a selection. You must specify your database with Data Query Input, and you must identify your selection criteria with Data Query Criteria before you can pick a specific action for the Query command to perform. In addition, you must enter database records and selection criteria on the worksheet before you enter a Query command that uses them. The steps for using data query commands are summarized in the "Steps for Using Query Commands" box.

Steps for Using Data Query Commands

1
2
3
G

The Data Query commands allow you to access selected records in your database. Obtaining the desired results involves some preliminary work, as well as a number of Data Query options. The required steps are as follows:

1. Enter the query criteria on your worksheet.
2. If you plan to use the Extract, Unique, or Modify options, enter the field names you are copying in the output area of your worksheet.
3. Select Data Query Input and specify the range for your database, including field names.
4. Select Criteria from the Data Query dialog box and specify the location of your criteria.
5. If you plan to use Extract, Unique, or Modify, select Output from the Data Query dialog box and specify the location of your output area.
6. Select the Data Query option you wish to use: Find, Delete, Extract, Unique, or Modify.
7. If you choose Find, press ESCAPE after you have finished browsing through your file, and then select Quit to exit the Query menu.

Telling 1-2-3/G Where Your Data Is Located

When you use the Query options, 1-2-3/G must know where your field names and data records are located. Unlike Data Sort, you *must* include the field names when you specify the database range to query. These field names are matched against the field names placed in the selection criteria area to ensure that selections are correct.

You specify the location of the database range to query with Data Query Input. After you select this command, you can point to your data range or type the required cell references. As with the Data Sort command, you can select the database range before you select Data Query and 1-2-3/G uses the selected range for the database queries. Using the data in Figure 19-8, you would select Data Query Input and the range A1..F20. By including row 1 in the range, you let 1-2-3/G know the name of each field that the database uses. 1-2-3/G lets you select input ranges that are in active files, inactive files, and external tables (see the next chapter). If you plan to insert or replace records with the data query commands, you must use an active file for the input range.

Specifying the Desired Records

To determine what records from the database will fill your query request, 1-2-3/G checks the criteria you specify against each record in the selected database range. Records that don't meet the criteria are not used.

When entering criteria on the worksheet, keep in mind that they must be positioned in a location that does not interfere with the expansion of the database. One option is to put the database and its criteria on separate sheets. You must enter the criteria in the worksheet before you select Data Query, since once you select Data Query, you cannot make entries on the worksheet. In addition, you need to indicate where the criteria are stored by using the Data Query Criteria command.

Location of Criteria

When you use one of the data query commands, you must use the Data Query Criteria command to tell 1-2-3/G the location of the criteria. (Remember that you must enter the criteria themselves before you select Data Query.) Entering criteria and telling 1-2-3/G where they are located with Data Query Criteria does not find the matching records, however. Once you select the input range and the criteria, you can select a command button in the Data Query dialog box to work with database records that match the criteria. The effect of each command button is explained later in this chapter and the next, according to the task they perform.

You can choose any location for your search criteria. A popular location is to the right of the database—this allows the criteria area to be expanded to the right, and does not interfere with the downward expansion of your database records. If your database occupies columns A through M, for example, you may wish to begin your criteria in column R. This allows for the expansion of the database by four new fields before the criteria would have to be moved.

With 1-2-3/G, you can put your criteria on a separate worksheet or a separate file. This means that you don't have to plan for expansion or modifications. The only limitation is that the range containing the criteria is on a single sheet that must be open on the desktop when the query is performed.

Types of Criteria

You can specify which records in the database you wish to query in a variety of ways. You can use values that match your database entries exactly; you can use 1-2-3/G's wildcard characters to specify only a portion of the entry type you are looking for; or you can specify formulas. For matches other than formula format, the name of the field in the database you are searching must appear above the specific entry you are searching for. For formula matches, you can include the field name in the criteria entry. For documentation purposes, it is best to record the name of the field referenced in the formula.

For example, if you want to search the last name field in an employee database to find all records with a last name of Smith, your criteria area might look like this:

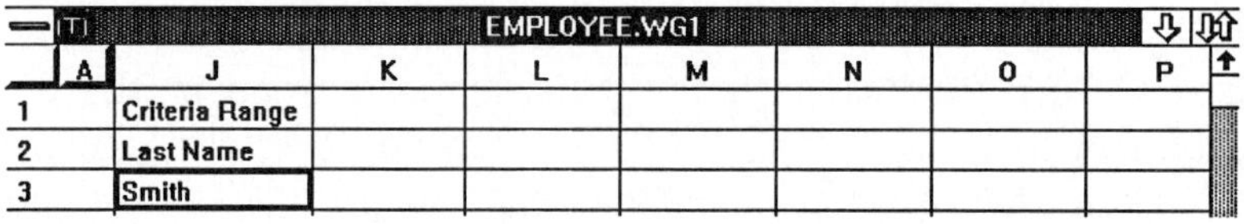

EMPLOYEE.WG1

A	J	K	L	M	N	O	P
1	Criteria Range						
2	Last Name						
3	Smith						

For this example, the criteria area is J2..J3. The entry in J1 is documentation. The search value is placed immediately underneath the field name in the criteria area. The field name in J2 of the criteria area must match the field name in your database exactly. A space at the end of one or the other can cause a problem. The safest approach is to copy the field name from its location above the database records to the criteria area where you wish to use it.

In 1-2-3/G, you can now leave blank criteria areas without jeopardizing query operation results. In previous releases, if your criteria area included blank columns or rows, the criteria would match every record in the database. Now, you can include columns with field names but no criteria beneath them. 1-2-3/G will only use the fields in the criteria range with entries below the field names to find the matching records. If the criteria area has blank rows, they are ignored. However, if all of the field names in the criteria don't have entries below them, the criteria matches with all database records.

Tip: Copy database field names from the database table to the criteria range, so the spacing and spelling of the field names in the criteria match the database table. Mistakes such as misspelling or extra spaces in the field name can cause 1-2-3/G to respond as if the criteria match every database record.

Values To search for numeric values in your records, record the desired field name in the criteria area. Underneath this field name, enter the value for which you are searching. The criteria value need not have the same format as the values you are looking for. In a search based on the following criteria area, only records for job code 23 would match:

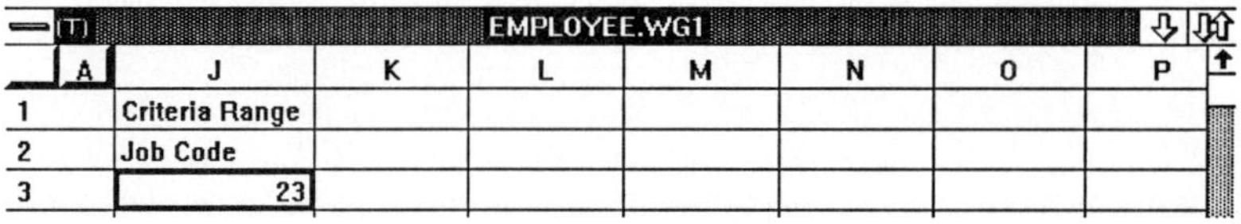

(T) EMPLOYEE.WG1

A	J	K	L	M	N	O	P
1	Criteria Range						
2	Job Code						
3	23						

Labels If you want to match label entries, you can enter them in the criteria exactly as they appear in your database, under the name of the field you wish to search. For example, if you enter Last Name in the criteria area and Jones beneath, 1-2-3/G selects records that contain Jones in the last name field.

1-2-3/G has two special wildcard characters that are useful when specifying label criteria: the asterisk (*) and the question mark (?).

The * that appears at the end of a criteria entry indicates that if the first part of the criteria entry matches a database record, any characters from the location of the * to the end of the database entry should be accepted in the match. For example, the following criteria would search the Last Name field for all records beginning with Sm:

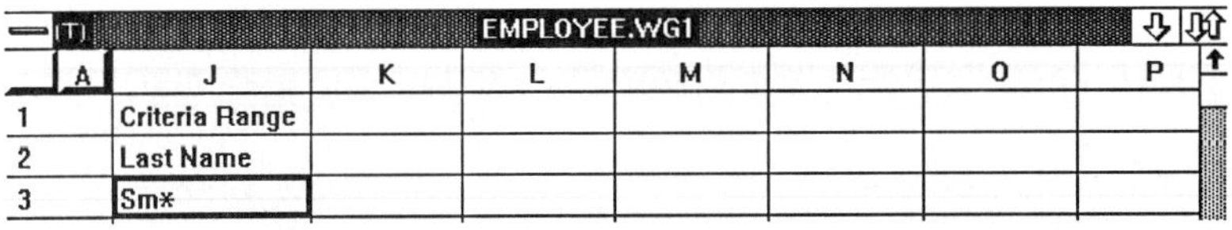

EMPLOYEE.WG1

A	J	K	L	M	N	O	P
1	Criteria Range						
2	Last Name						
3	Sm*						

Smith would match, as would Smithfield, Smothers, and Smeltman.

The ? replaces any one character in an entry only—all the other characters must match exactly. The following criteria tells 1-2-3/G that any character can be located in the second position of the Last Name field, as long as "B" is the first character, and "tman" the third through the sixth characters of the database entry:

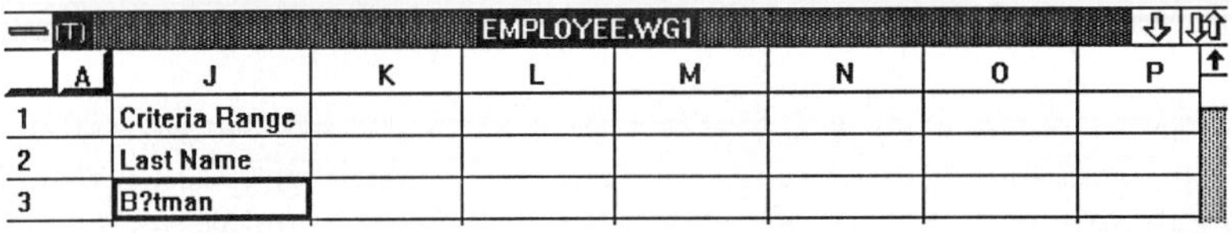

EMPLOYEE.WG1

A	J	K	L	M	N	O	P
1	Criteria Range						
2	Last Name						
3	B?tman						

Bitman, Butman, Batman, Botman, and Betman would be among the matching entries if records containing these names were in the database. All entries longer than six characters, such as Bitmanson, would be rejected.

Formulas You can also create formulas to serve as search criteria. You can use formula comparisons to check for records that contain values with a specific range. You can even use string formulas in your criteria. When you enter a formula as a criteria, the formula will display as 0 or 1, depending on whether it evaluates to true or false for the first

1-2-3/G [69.4] Ready

File Edit Worksheet Range Copy... Move... Print Graph Data Utility Quit... Help

A:A1 'Last Name

EMPLOYEE.WG1

A	A	B	C	D	E	F
1	Last Name	First Name	SS#	Job Code	Salary	Location
2	Larson	Mary	543-98-9876	23	$12,000	2
3	Campbell	David	213-76-9874	23	$23,000	10
4	Campbell	Keith	569-89-7654	12	$32,000	2
5	Stephens	Tom	219-78-8954	15	$17,800	2
6	Caldor	Larry	459-34-0921	23	$32,500	4
7	Lightnor	Peggy	560-55-4311	14	$23,500	10
8	McCartin	John	817-66-1212	15	$54,600	2
9	Justof	Jack	431-78-9963	17	$41,200	4
10	Patterson	Lyle	212-11-9090	12	$21,500	10
11	Miller	Lisa	214-89-6756	23	$18,700	2
12	Hawkins	Mark	215-67-8973	21	$19,500	2
13	Hartwick	Eileen	313-78-9090	15	$31,450	4
14	Smythe	George	560-90-8645	15	$65,000	4
15	Wilkes	Caitlin	124-67-7432	17	$15,500	2
16	Deaver	Ken	198-98-6750	23	$24,600	10
17	Kaylor	Sally	312-45-9862	12	$32,900	10

Figure 19-12. Employee database

database record. You may want to format the cell of the criteria area as Text so it will display as the formula you entered.

When you create formulas as search criteria, the field name used in the criteria area needn't match the field referenced in the formula. As you construct your formulas to compare values in the database against a specific value, always reference the first value for the field in the database, or the field name. For clarity, it is always best to use the proper field name.

In the example in Figure 19-12, to find all values greater than $25,000 in a Salary field in column E, you might use this criteria formula:

(T) EMPLOYEE.WG1

A	J	K	L	M	N	O	P
1	Criteria Range						
2	Salary						
3	+E2>25000						

The cell referenced is E2, since that contains the first value in the salary field. Always use a relative reference when referring to database fields. When you format criteria cells as Text, the formulas will display as you enter them. You could also enter the previous formula as +SALARY>25000, since 1-2-3/G will substitute the field values for the field name.

If you need a criteria formula that compares a database field against a value located elsewhere in the worksheet, use an absolute reference as the reference outside the database. Suppose that you want to compare the salaries in Figure 19-12 to the average salary amount stored in L2. The criteria might look like this:

A:L2 @AVG(E2..E20)

(C2) EMPLOYEE.WG1

A	J	K	L	M	N	O
1	Criteria Range		Average Salary			
2	Salary		$28,528.95			
3	+E2>$L$2+3000					

This criteria will identify all records where the salary exceeds the average by $3,000.

Tip: You may need to start a criteria with a less than (<) symbol. When you type a less than symbol in the Ready mode, 1-2-3/G activates the menus. This feature accommodates foreign language keyboards, where the slash (/) is in an awkward position. To start a formula for a criteria range with a less than symbol, type a label prefix before typing the <.

You can also use the complex operators #AND#, #OR#, and #NOT# in formula criteria. For example, suppose that you want to determine whether a salary is less than or equal to $25,000 or greater than or equal to $50,000. The proper criteria formula to use is shown here:

(T) EMPLOYEE.WG1

A	J	K	L	M	N	O
1	Criteria Range					
2	Salary					
3	+E2<=25000#OR#E2>=50000					

If you use the #AND# operator, the conditions on both sides of the operator must be true for the record to be selected. If you use #OR#, either condition may be true for the record to be selected. #NOT# negates the condition that follows it. When you use a complex operator, you must include the field names or the cell address for the first record. In the previous example, you couldn't use the criteria < =25000#OR#> =50000 in that location. This criteria would look for the string < =25000#OR#> =50000 in the salary column.

Compound Criteria Whenever you use more than one field in the criteria area, you are using *compound criteria.* 1-2-3/G allows you to use up to 256 fields for search criteria at one time. These criteria must be joined by implied "and's" and "or's."

If two criteria values are placed on the same line beneath their separate field names, they are joined by an implied "and." The following criteria, for example, will select records where the job code is equal to 23 *and* the salary is less than $16,000:

A:K3 23

EMPLOYEE.WG1

A	J	K	L	M	N	O	P
1	Criteria Range						
2	Salary	Job Code					
3	+E2<16000	23					

Notice that the field names in the criteria area are in the same row, with their criteria in the rows below. Note also that the criteria types don't have to be the same; one criterion is a formula, and the other a value. A database record must meet both criteria to be selected.

If one criteria value is placed one row below the other, the two criteria are joined by an implied "or." Perhaps you want records with a job code of 23 or a salary of less than $16,000. The criteria shown here will select records meeting either or both of these conditions:

A:K4 23

EMPLOYEE.WG1

A	J	K	L	M	N	O	P
1	Criteria Range						
2	Salary	Job Code					
3	+E2<16000						
4		23					

Highlighting Selected Records

Once you have defined your search area and criteria, 1-2-3/G's Data Query Find command will highlight records that match the defined criteria. The records are highlighted one at a time, beginning at the top of the database. Table 19-1 lists the keys that you can use to move through the selected records.

Finding records requires a few preliminary steps. You must have defined your database, including the field names, with Data Query Input. You must also have entered your search criteria on the worksheet or in a separate area before requesting the query commands, and then defined this range as criteria using Data Query Criteria. Figure 19-13 shows a database that has been defined with Data Query Input as

Key	Action
DOWN ARROW	Moves to the next record in the input range that meets the criteria. If the cell pointer is on the last record that meets the criteria, 1-2-3/G beeps.
UP ARROW	Moves to the previous record in the input range that meets the criteria. If the cell pointer is on the first record that meets the criteria, 1-2-3/G beeps.
LEFT ARROW	Moves one field to the left in the selected record. If the cell pointer is on the first field, 1-2-3/G beeps.
RIGHT ARROW	Moves one field to the right in the selected record. If the cell pointer is on the last field, 1-2-3/G beeps.
HOME	Moves to the first record in the input range that meets the criteria.
END	Moves to the last record in the input range that meets the criteria.
ESCAPE	Ends the Data Query Find operation and returns to the Data Query menu.
ENTER	Ends the Data Query Find operation and returns to the Data Query menu.
F2 (Edit)	Switches to Edit mode for the current field in the selected record. Pressing F2 (Edit) again or ENTER saves your edits and returns to the Data Query Find operation. Pressing ESCAPE cancels the edits and returns to the Data Query Find operation.
F7 (Query)	Ends the Data Query Find operation and returns to Ready mode.

Table 19-1. Cell Pointer Movement Keys for Use with Data Query Find in Database Records

1-2-3/G [69.4] Ready

File Edit Worksheet Range Copy... Move... Print Graph Data Utility Quit... Help

A:A1 'Description

ASSETS.WG1

A	A	B	C	D	E
1	Description	Life	Cost	Dept	Type
2	FTY Computer	5	$980	Accounting	Office
3	Dover Typewriter	5	$950	Training	Office
4	Swivel Chair	10	$345	Check	Furniture
5	KL Calculator	7	$100	Audit	Office
6	Walnut Desk	15	$1,200	Cash	Furniture
7	Lanver Copier	3	$2,500	Cash	Processing
8	Lanver Copier	3	$2,800	Accounting	Processing
9	Computer Table	5	$300	Training	Furniture
10	File Cabinet	10	$450	Audit	Furniture

Figure 19-13. Asset records

A1..E10. The following criterion is established in J1..J3 to locate records for the Accounting Department:

A:J3 'Accounting

ASSETS.WG1

A	J	K	L	M	N	O	P
1	Criteria Range						
2	Dept						
3	Accounting						

Figure 19-14 shows the first record matching the criterion highlighted on the screen. While you are in Find mode, you can only move to the matching database records. When you are finished, press ESCAPE, ENTER, or F7 (Query).

The Data Query Find option works well if you need quick answers about data you have stored in your database. However, all the matching records are not listed at once and cannot be printed. If you need to do either of these things, you should use the Data Query Extract command.

Writing Selected Records on the Worksheet

1-2-3/G provides three commands that copy selected records and fields from your database to another area of the worksheet. You can add

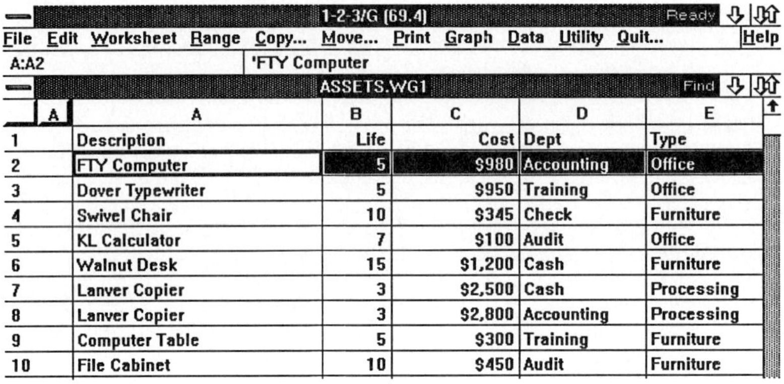

1-2-3/G [69.4] Ready

File Edit Worksheet Range Copy... Move... Print Graph Data Utility Quit... Help

A:A2 'FTY Computer

ASSETS.WG1 Find

A	A	B	C	D	E
1	Description	Life	Cost	Dept	Type
2	FTY Computer	5	$980	Accounting	Office
3	Dover Typewriter	5	$950	Training	Office
4	Swivel Chair	10	$345	Check	Furniture
5	KL Calculator	7	$100	Audit	Office
6	Walnut Desk	15	$1,200	Cash	Furniture
7	Lanver Copier	3	$2,500	Cash	Processing
8	Lanver Copier	3	$2,800	Accounting	Processing
9	Computer Table	5	$300	Training	Furniture
10	File Cabinet	10	$450	Audit	Furniture

Figure 19-14. Finding records for a specific department

headings to these new areas to create an instant report that you can share with others. Before you copy database information, however, prepare an output location that will store the copy of the database records.

Defining an Output Area

First decide on a location and prepare it to receive data. The bottom of the existing database is often used, but could present a problem as your database expands. Since 1-2-3/G overwrites all data below the output area, make sure that your worksheet does not have data below the output area. One good solution is to place your output on a separate worksheet or a separate file. This allows both the input and output areas to be as large as 8191 records, and lets you place your output where a growing database will not interfere with it.

With the location selected, enter the names of the fields you wish to copy from matching records. They need not be in the same sequence as the fields in your database, and you don't have to include every field. You also needn't include fields used as criteria in the output area.

Tip: Use the Copy command to copy the range of field names from the database table directly to the output range, so the spacing and case of the field names in the criteria match the database table exactly. Once you have copied all of the field names, you can delete the names of fields you do not want to include in the output range.

Once you place the field names in the output area, you are ready to define its location to 1-2-3/G with Data Query Output. If you define the output area as only the row containing the headings, 1-2-3/G will use columns of cells from the heading area to the bottom of the worksheet to write records that match, erasing data stored below the output area.

You can also specify the range for the output area to include a number of blank rows beneath the row of field names. If you use this approach, 1-2-3/G will stop copying matching database records when the specified output area becomes full. For example, if you select B:A1..B:F10 as the output range, 1-2-3/G only copies the first nine records that it finds (it uses the first line for the field names). Any data below row 10 in the columns used by the output range is not affected. If 1-2-3/G cannot fit the selected records into the output range, it displays an error message on the status line.

Extracting All Matches

To extract matching records, set up the criteria and output areas on your worksheet, and define the database, criteria, and output to 1-2-3/G. Then select Data Query Extract. Every time you select the Extract option, 1-2-3/G erases the output area before writing the newly selected records to it. The many preliminary steps you must do before using this command are reviewed here, using the database in Figure 19-13:

1. Add selection criteria to the worksheet, as shown here:

1-2-3/G [69.4] Ready

File Edit Worksheet Range Copy... Move... Print Graph Data Utility Quit... Help

A:J1 'Criteria Range

ASSETS.WG1

A	J	K	L	M	N	O	P
1	Criteria Range						
2	Dept	Cost					
3	Training	+C2>500					

2. 1-2-3/G will only extract the fields of matching records that appear in the output range. Set up the output area on the worksheet to look like this:

1-2-3/G [69.4] Ready

File Edit Worksheet Range Copy... Move... Print Graph Data Utility Quit... Help

A:A21 'Description

ASSETS.WG1

A	A	B	C	D	E
21	Description	Cost	Dept		
22					
23					

3. Select Data Query Input and range A1..E10 as database location.
4. Select Criteria and the range J2..K3.
5. Define the output area by selecting Output and specifying A21..C21.
6. Select Extract to extract matching records.
7. Select Quit to see the following output:

ASSETS.WG1

A	A	B	C	D	E
21	Description	Cost	Dept		
22	Dover Typewriter	$950	Training		
23					

If you want to create a report using extracted records, you just need to add a report title at the top of the extract area and print the worksheet range containing the heading and the extract.

Resetting Selection Options

You can eliminate all of the Query specifications with the Data Query Reset command. This includes the Input, Criteria, and Output specification if you made one. To change only one of the ranges, select Input, Criteria, or Output, press ESCAPE or BACKSPACE to convert the range address to a single cell address, and select the new range.

Quitting the Query Menu

When you want to leave the Data Query operation, choose Quit from the Query menu to return to Ready mode. This allows you to make new entries for criteria and perform other tasks. To return to Data Query after making changes, you can use the Data Query menu. Alternatively, if you wish to use the same choices for Input, Criteria, and Output ranges and want to perform the same query operation as before (Find, Unique, Delete, or Extract), you can simply press F7 (Query) to execute another query. In between queries, you can change the criteria in the criteria range—this way, 1-2-3/G will use the new criteria for the query operation when you press F7 (Query).

Advanced Data Management Features

Advanced Data Query Commands and Functions
Using Two Databases
Using External Databases

TWENTY

In Chapter 19, you learned how to create and use databases. However, 1-2-3/G has more advanced data management features, including additional data query commands, using formulas in an output range, using multiple databases, and using external databases. If you are not familiar with the basic features in Chapter 19, review the sections on creating a database and using the Data Query features before experimenting with the material in this chapter.

Its ability to use external databases is what differentiates 1-2-3/G from many of the other spreadsheet products. *External databases* are databases that 1-2-3/G can work with but that have been created with another database package. You can use 1-2-3/G to work with the database records without bringing the data into 1-2-3/G. You can create, modify, and delete external databases. You can also use 1-2-3/G to generate reports based on the data in the external database.

Advanced Data Query Commands and Functions

1-2-3/G has advanced Data Query commands that weren't discussed in Chapter 19. You can use these commands to extract a unique list of values found in a particular field or set of fields, extract and then replace records, and delete records. You can also use formulas in the output range to make calculations and to create summary statistics on the database.

Extracting and Replacing Records

You already know how to use the Data Query Find command to find records that match a set of criteria. Once these records are located, you can change the original copies by typing replacement entries for the fields or editing the existing entries. However, the Data Query Find command won't work if you want to modify the records in a different location. 1-2-3/G's Data Query Modify commands let you extract matching records from a database, modify the records, and then return the records to their original position. Data Query Modify enables you to cancel the modification request and maintain a separate copy of the modified data, rather than replace the original entries. When you use Data Query Modify, 1-2-3/G remembers the position of each record within the database.

To use the Data Query Modify commands, select Data Query Modify Extract once you set up the criteria and output areas on your worksheet, and define the database, criteria, and output. Every time you select Data Query Modify Extract, 1-2-3/G erases the output area before writing the newly selected records to it. 1-2-3/G only copies the fields for each record that are in the first row of the output range. Since several

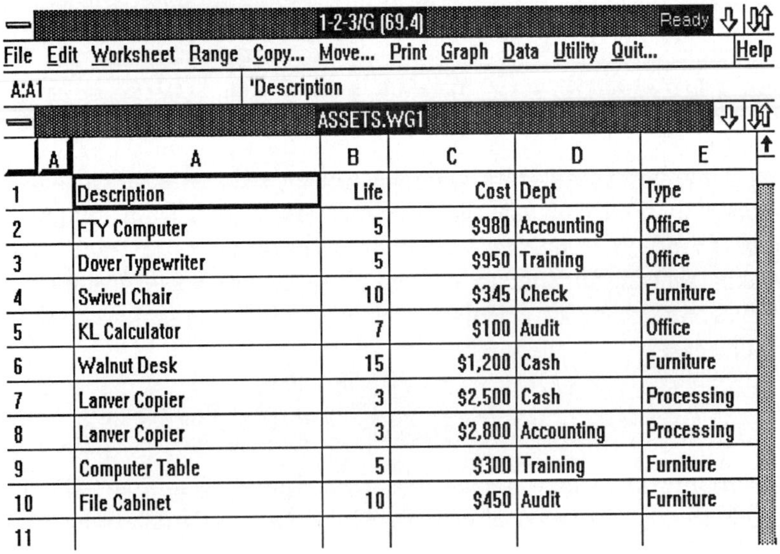

1-2-3/G [69.4] Ready

File Edit Worksheet Range Copy... Move... Print Graph Data Utility Quit... Help

A:A1 'Description

ASSETS.WG1

A	A	B	C	D	E
1	Description	Life	Cost	Dept	Type
2	FTY Computer	5	$980	Accounting	Office
3	Dover Typewriter	5	$950	Training	Office
4	Swivel Chair	10	$345	Check	Furniture
5	KL Calculator	7	$100	Audit	Office
6	Walnut Desk	15	$1,200	Cash	Furniture
7	Lanver Copier	3	$2,500	Cash	Processing
8	Lanver Copier	3	$2,800	Accounting	Processing
9	Computer Table	5	$300	Training	Furniture
10	File Cabinet	10	$450	Audit	Furniture
11					

Figure 20-1. Database used for record extraction process

steps are required to extract and replace records, you can use the data in Figure 20-1 as you review the order of each step:

1. Add criteria to the worksheet, as shown here :

ASSETS.WG1

A	J	K	L	M	N	O	P
1	Criteria Range						
2	Dept	Cost					
3	Training	+C2>500					

If you have never done this before, review Chapter 19.

2. Set up the output area on the worksheet to look like this:

A:A21 'Description

ASSETS.WG1

A	A	B	C	D	E
21	Description	Cost	Dept		
22					

3. Select the Data Query Input command to define the database as located in A1..E10.

4. Select Criteria and the range J2..K3 so only records for the Training department with a cost greater than 500 match the criteria.

5. Next, define the output area by selecting Output, and specifying its location of A21..C21 at the prompt.

6. Select Modify Extract to extract the matching records. 1-2-3/G then returns to the Data Query menu.

7. Select Quit to return to Ready mode. The output area now looks like this:

ASSETS.WG1

A	A	B	C	D	E
21	Description	Cost	Dept		
22	Dover Typewriter	$950	Training		
23					

8. Edit the data in the extract; change the cost of the typewriter to $850.

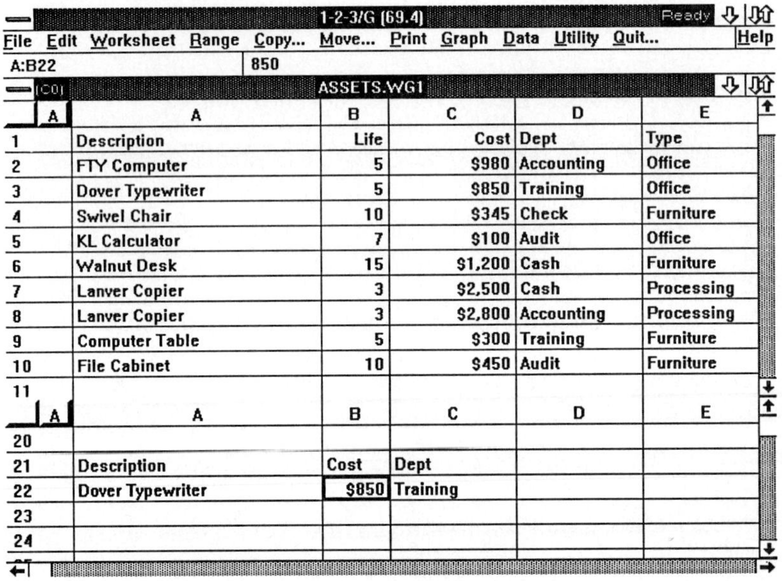

1-2-3/G [69.4] Ready

File Edit Worksheet Range Copy... Move... Print Graph Data Utility Quit... Help

A:B22 | 850

(C0) ASSETS.WG1

A	A	B	C	D	E
1	Description	Life	Cost	Dept	Type
2	FTY Computer	5	$980	Accounting	Office
3	Dover Typewriter	5	$850	Training	Office
4	Swivel Chair	10	$345	Check	Furniture
5	KL Calculator	7	$100	Audit	Office
6	Walnut Desk	15	$1,200	Cash	Furniture
7	Lanver Copier	3	$2,500	Cash	Processing
8	Lanver Copier	3	$2,800	Accounting	Processing
9	Computer Table	5	$300	Training	Furniture
10	File Cabinet	10	$450	Audit	Furniture
11					

A	A	B	C	D	E
20					
21	Description	Cost	Dept		
22	Dover Typewriter	$850	Training		
23					
24					

Figure 20-2. Database after Modify Replace process

9. Select Data Query Modify Replace. The database should now look like Figure 20-2.

10. Select Quit to return to Ready mode.

If you decide not to replace the records, use the Data Query Modify Cancel command. This cancels the current modify command and instructs 1-2-3/G to disregard the original positions the extracted records had in the database.

Adding Selected Records to the Database

The Data Query Modify Insert command copies records from one database to another. When you use this command, be careful that the area below the database is empty. The records overwrite any data below the database as they are added. The Data Query Modify Insert command requires that the output range contain both the field names and the records to add, rather than the single row range you can use when

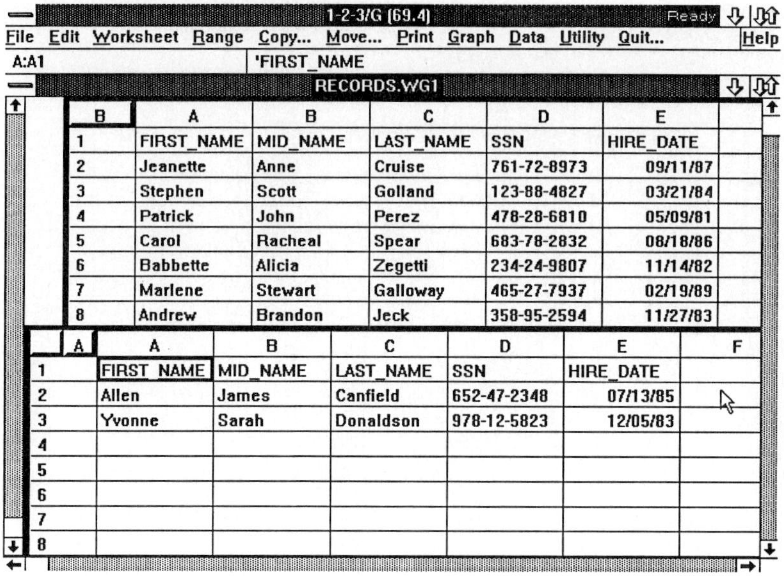

1-2-3/G [69.4] Ready

File Edit Worksheet Range Copy... Move... Print Graph Data Utility Quit... Help

A:A1 'FIRST_NAME

RECORDS.WG1

B	A	B	C	D	E
1	FIRST_NAME	MID_NAME	LAST_NAME	SSN	HIRE_DATE
2	Jeanette	Anne	Cruise	761-72-8973	09/11/87
3	Stephen	Scott	Golland	123-88-4827	03/21/84
4	Patrick	John	Perez	478-28-6810	05/09/81
5	Carol	Racheal	Spear	683-78-2832	08/18/86
6	Babbette	Alicia	Zegetti	234-24-9807	11/14/82
7	Marlene	Stewart	Galloway	465-27-7937	02/19/89
8	Andrew	Brandon	Jeck	358-95-2594	11/27/83

A	A	B	C	D	E	F
1	FIRST_NAME	MID_NAME	LAST_NAME	SSN	HIRE_DATE	
2	Allen	James	Canfield	652-47-2348	07/13/85	
3	Yvonne	Sarah	Donaldson	978-12-5823	12/05/83	
4						
5						
6						
7						
8						

Figure 20-3. Using Modify Insert to add records

extracting records. This command adds all records in the selected output area to the bottom of the input area. Blank rows are excluded in this copy operation. If you don't want all the records added, you must remove unwanted records from the selected output area. You should use a range name for the input area; this way, 1-2-3/G will automatically expand the range used by the range name when new records are inserted. Using the same range name in other Data Query commands and database statistical functions ensures that other Data Query commands access the same expanded database.

As an example, suppose you have the database tables in Figure 20-3. You can add the records in the second database table to the first one with the Data Query Modify Insert command. Define the input range as A:A1..A:E3 and the output range as B:A1..B:E8. When you perform the Data Query Modify Insert command, 1-2-3/G copies all of the output range to the database (the input range). Figure 20-4 shows the first five records added to the input range. Only the data in the fields common to both the input and output range are copied.

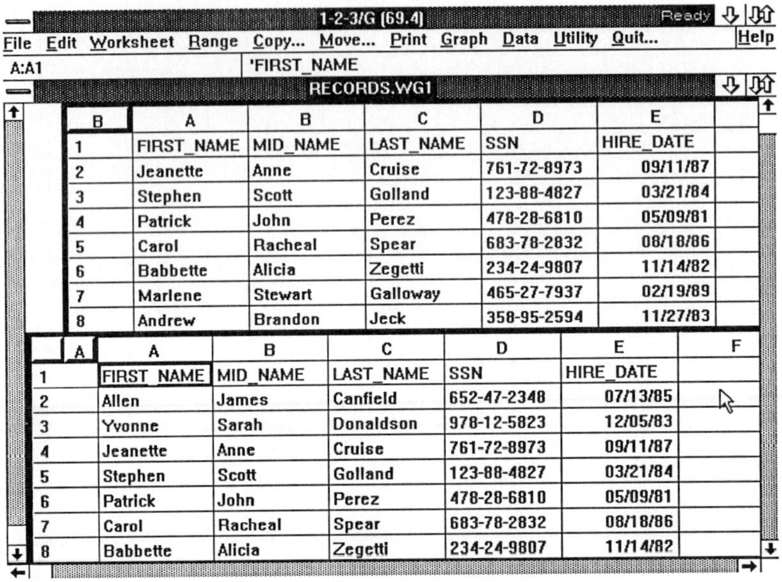

1-2-3/G [69.4] Ready

File Edit Worksheet Range Copy... Move... Print Graph Data Utility Quit... Help

A:A1 'FIRST_NAME

RECORDS.WG1

B	A	B	C	D	E
1	FIRST_NAME	MID_NAME	LAST_NAME	SSN	HIRE_DATE
2	Jeanette	Anne	Cruise	761-72-8973	09/11/87
3	Stephen	Scott	Golland	123-88-4827	03/21/84
4	Patrick	John	Perez	478-28-6810	05/09/81
5	Carol	Racheal	Spear	683-78-2832	08/18/86
6	Babbette	Alicia	Zegetti	234-24-9807	11/14/82
7	Marlene	Stewart	Galloway	465-27-7937	02/19/89
8	Andrew	Brandon	Jeck	358-95-2594	11/27/83

A	A	B	C	D	E	F
1	FIRST_NAME	MID_NAME	LAST_NAME	SSN	HIRE_DATE	
2	Allen	James	Canfield	652-47-2348	07/13/85	
3	Yvonne	Sarah	Donaldson	978-12-5823	12/05/83	
4	Jeanette	Anne	Cruise	761-72-8973	09/11/87	
5	Stephen	Scott	Golland	123-88-4827	03/21/84	
6	Patrick	John	Perez	478-28-6810	05/09/81	
7	Carol	Racheal	Spear	683-78-2832	08/18/86	
8	Babbette	Alicia	Zegetti	234-24-9807	11/14/82	

Figure 20-4. Database after record insertion

Deleting Selected Records from the Database

Data Query Delete is a powerful yet dangerous command. In one easy process, it can purge outdated records from your database. However, if you enter your search criteria incorrectly, it can also purge records that you still need. For this reason, it's prudent to test your criteria with Find or Extract before selecting the Delete option. When you select Data Query Delete, 1-2-3/G deletes all database records that match the defined criteria.

If you specified the criteria

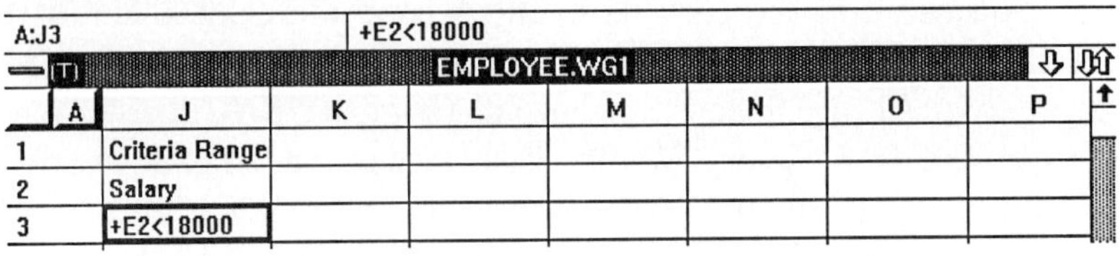

A:J3 +E2<18000

(T) EMPLOYEE.WG1

A	J	K	L	M	N	O	P
1	Criteria Range						
2	Salary						
3	+E2<18000						

for the database in Figure 20-5, and then chose the Delete command, only the following records would remain in the database:

1-2-3/G [69.4] Ready

File Edit Worksheet Range Copy... Move... Print Graph Data Utility Quit... Help

A:A1 'Last Name

EMPLOYEE.WG1

A	A	B	C	D	E	F
1	Last Name	First Name	SS#	Job Code	Salary	Location
2	Larson	Mary	543-98-9876	23	$12,000	2
3	Stephens	Tom	219-78-8954	15	$17,800	2
4	Wilkes	Caitlin	124-67-7432	17	$15,500	2
5						

Tip: Look at database records before you delete them. Use Data Query Find or Data Query Extract to view records that the Data Query Delete command will delete. This step prevents you from accidentally deleting records that you want to keep.

1-2-3/G [69.4] Ready

File Edit Worksheet Range Copy... Move... Print Graph Data Utility Quit... Help

A:A1 'Last Name

EMPLOYEE.WG1

A	A	B	C	D	E	F
1	Last Name	First Name	SS#	Job Code	Salary	Location
2	Larson	Mary	543-98-9876	23	$12,000	2
3	Campbell	David	213-76-9874	23	$23,000	10
4	Campbell	Keith	569-89-7654	12	$32,000	2
5	Stephens	Tom	219-78-8954	15	$17,800	2
6	Caldor	Larry	459-34-0921	23	$32,500	4
7	Lightnor	Peggy	560-55-4311	14	$23,500	10
8	McCartin	John	817-66-1212	15	$54,600	2
9	Justof	Jack	431-78-9963	17	$41,200	4
10	Patterson	Lyle	212-11-9090	12	$21,500	10
11	Miller	Lisa	214-89-6756	23	$18,700	2
12	Hawkins	Mark	215-67-8973	21	$19,500	2
13	Hartwick	Eileen	313-78-9090	15	$31,450	4
14	Smythe	George	560-90-8645	15	$65,000	4
15	Wilkes	Caitlin	124-67-7432	17	$15,500	2
16	Deaver	Ken	198-98-6750	23	$24,600	10
17	Kaylor	Sally	312-45-9862	12	$32,900	10

Figure 20-5. Employee database before record deletion process

Writing Only Unique Records

Like Extract, the Unique option writes records to the output area. However, it writes only unique records to this area—if two selected entries are an exact match, only one will be written. Uniqueness of records is determined by the fields written to the output area.

The number of records written to the output area can be affected by the number of fields you include. If two records contain matching data in only five of the six selected fields, they are unique; however, if you selected those five matching fields, the two records would no longer be considered unique, and only one of them would be copied to the output area.

For instance, consider the following criteria:

BILLINGS.WG1

A	I	J	K	L	M	N	O
1	Criteria Range						
2	Rate						
3	+F4>60						

and the database records shown in Figure 20-6. 1-2-3/G will produce the following output if you select Unique from the Data Query menu. Note that the Tower College record appears only once, even though several qualifying records for it exist in the database.

1-2-3/G [69.4] Ready

File Edit Worksheet Range Copy... Move... Print Graph Data Utility Quit... Help

A:A22 'STR Rentals

BILLINGS.WG1

A	A	B	C	D	E	F	G
21	Customer	Phone	Location				
22	STR Rentals	231-4567	Dallas				
23	Tower College	431-9092	New York				
24							

Every time you use the Unique option, the output area is cleared so that the newly selected records can be written to it.

Using Formulas in an Output Range

All of the output examples in the previous chapter used only field names in the output range. However, 1-2-3/G also lets you use formulas in the

	A	B	C	D	E	F	G
1		CLIENT BILLINGS - SEPTEMBER 1990					
2							
3	Customer	Type	Phone	Location	Hours	Rate	
4	STR Rentals	5	231-4567	Dallas	10.5	75	
5	XCV Company	3	341-4545	Chicago	5	60	
6	Tower College	5	431-9092	New York	15	85	
7	Lower Rentals	3	498-2123	Dallas	20	60	
8	Nelson Products	4	213-9845	Albany	3	60	
9	Tower College	5	431-9092	New York	30	85	
10	Lower Rentals	3	498-2123	Dallas	2	60	
11	Nelson Products	4	213-9845	Albany	14	60	
12	XCV Company	3	341-4545	Chicago	15	60	
13	Tower College	5	431-9092	New York	22	85	
14	Lower Rentals	3	498-2123	Dallas	7	60	
15							
16							
17							

Figure 20-6. Database used with Data Query Unique

output range. The formulas you enter in the output range can provide calculations on the values in the matching records copied to the extract range. All you need to do is place the desired formula in the top row in the output range. In addition, they can calculate statistical values without entering the formulas and the criteria each formula uses directly to individual cells.

Figure 20-7 shows how you can use a formula in the output range. In this example, the output range lists all employees with a job code of 23. The last column calculates the effect of increasing each salary by 5 percent. This formula is entered as it appears in Figure 20-7 and formatted as text. Rather than referring to specific cells or ranges, the formula uses database field names to indicate which values it evaluates. If the formula uses any values stored in cells that are not part of the record, it refers to these cells using the cell address. This type of formula can use any valid 1-2-3/G formula, but cannot include @AVG, @COUNT, @MAX, @MIN, or @SUM. These @functions are reserved for use by aggregate columns in the output area.

1-2-3/G (69.4) Ready

File Edit Worksheet Range Copy... Move... Print Graph Data Utility Quit... Help

A:R1 +SALARY*1.05

(T) EMPLOYEE.WG1

A	O	P	Q	R	S	T	U
1	Last Name	First Name	Salary	+SALARY*1.05		Job Code	
2	Larson	Mary	$12,000	$12,600		23	
3	Campbell	David	$23,000	$24,150			
4	Caldor	Larry	$32,500	$34,125			
5	Miller	Lisa	$18,700	$19,635			
6	Deaver	Ken	$24,600	$25,830			
7	Samuelson	Paul	$28,900	$30,345			

Figure 20-7. Output range using a formula

An aggregate column in an output area calculates the values of every record that matches the other fields listed in the output range. As an example, suppose you wanted to total the salaries for each combination of job code and location. Rather than creating a data table, you can use an aggregate column. An output area using an aggregate column is shown in Figure 20-8. In this case, the criteria is empty to match with every record. The first two columns list every combination of job code and location in the employee database. In the third column, the @SUM function totals the salary for each employee that has the job code and location combination shown in the first two columns.

Using Two Databases

You can also combine the data in two databases into a single database. For example, with the employee database you may also have a database that includes the benefit information for each employee. While you will usually use one database or the other, you may want to use both databases simultaneously. For example, you may want to know the

1-2-3/G [69.4] Ready

File Edit Worksheet Range Copy... Move... Print Graph Data Utility Quit... Help

A:X1 @SUM[SALARY]

EMPLOYEE.WG1

A	V	W	X	Y	Z	AA	AB
1	Job Code	Location	@SUM[SALARY]		Criteria:	Job Code	
2	12	2	32000				
3	12	10	54400				
4	14	4	19800				
5	14	10	23500				
6	15	2	72400				
7	15	4	96450				
8	17	2	15500				
9	17	4	41200				
10	21	2	19500				
11	21	4	27600				
12	23	2	59600				
13	23	4	32500				
14	23	10	47600				
15							
16							
17							

Figure 20-8. Output range containing aggregate column

names and job codes of the employees who include life insurance in their benefits. To do this, you must indicate the databases to use and how the records in one database connect with the other. When you combine databases, each database is a table within the larger database.

To work with multiple databases, you use the Data Query Input command to select the collection address containing the databases to be used. For example, using the employee database in Figure 20-5 and the employee benefits database table in Figure 20-9, you would select Data Query Input and enter A:A1..A:G20, B:A1..B:F20 as the input range. To make using multiple databases easier, these ranges are named EMPLOYEE and BENEFITS. Using the range name also allows you to use the F3 (Name) key to select the database's name. The databases can be in any open file or external database. To tell how the database records in the employee and benefits database tables are related, you must include another criteria in the criteria range. For example, to find employees who have a job code of 23 and who participate in the company's life insurance plan, you would use these criteria:

B:I2 +SS#=SOC_SEC_NUM

(T) EMPLOYEE.WG1

B	I	J	K	L	M	N
1	Join Formula	Employee.Job Code	Life			
2	+SS#=SOC_SEC_NUM	23	1			

The last two parts of the criteria look like other criteria you have created, except they are from different databases. The first part of the criteria, +SS#=SOC_SEC_NUM, tells 1-2-3/G how to match a record from the first database with a record from the second database. If these field names were both SS#, you would precede the field names with the database name and periods to distinguish them, as in +EMPLOYEE.SS#=BENEFITS.SS#. As the preceding example shows, you can join databases with the same field name or with different field names, as long as the fields contain the same data.

Once you've selected the criteria and input range, you can use the Data Query Extract or Data Query Unique commands just as you would with a single database. The output range is created the same way, but the field names common to both databases and used in the extract

1-2-3/G (69.4) Ready

File Edit Worksheet Range Copy... Move... Print Graph Data Utility Quit... Help

B:B1 'Life

EMPLOYEE.WG1

B	A	B	C	D	E	F	G	H
1	Soc_Sec_Num	Life	Accident	Health	Profit_Sharing	Job Code		
2	543-98-9876	1	1	1	1	23		
3	213-76-9874	0	0	0	1	23		
4	569-89-7654	1	1	0	1	12		
5	219-78-8954	0	0	0	1	15		
6	459-34-0921	1	0	1	0	23		
7	560-55-4311	1	0	1	1	14		
8	817-66-1212	1	0	1	0	15		
9	431-78-9963	1	0	0	1	17		
10	212-11-9090	1	1	0	1	12		
11	214-89-6756	0	1	0	0	23		
12	215-67-8973	1	0	0	0	21		
13	313-78-9090	0	1	0	0	15		
14	560-90-8645	1	0	0	0	15		
15	124-67-7432	0	0	0	1	17		
16	198-98-6750	1	0	0	1	23		
17	312-45-9862	1	1	1	0	12		

Figure 20-9. Benefits database

criteria must be preceded with the database table name and a period, as in this output area that includes the extracted records:

EMPLOYEE.WG1

C	A	B	C	D	E	F	G
1	Last Name	First Name	Soc_Sec_Num	Life	Employee.Job Code		
2	Deaver	Ken	198-98-6750	1	23		
3	Caldor	Larry	459-34-0921	1	23		
4	Larson	Mary	543-98-9876	1	23		

Using Two Databases with Multiple Matching Records

In the previous example, only one record from the first database matched one record from the second database. This is a *one-to-one* relationship. Not all databases are like this, however. For example, the weekly payroll records for each employee will contain many records for the same employee. When you combine the employee database with the payroll database, each record in the employee database will match multiple records in the payroll database. This is a *one-to-many* or a *many-to-one* relationship. When you join two databases using criteria, 1-2-3/G checks every record in the combined database against the criteria. For example, suppose you have the criteria and the beginning of the database named PAYROLL stored in the EMPLOYEE database shown in Figure 20-10. When you join the PAYROLL and the EMPLOYEE databases, the combined database contains 12 records. The combined database that 1-2-3/G uses has four records for Mary Larson with a social security number of 543-98-9876, four records for David Campbell with a social security number of 213-76-9874, and four records for Keith Campbell with a social security number of 569-89-7654. As an example, the record for Mary Larson in the EMPLOYEE database matches with the first, fourth, seventh, and tenth records in the PAYROLL database, so the combined database that the query uses has four records for Mary Larson.

Using External Databases

While 1-2-3/G fulfills many of your data processing needs, you may want to continue using a data management package for your data manage-

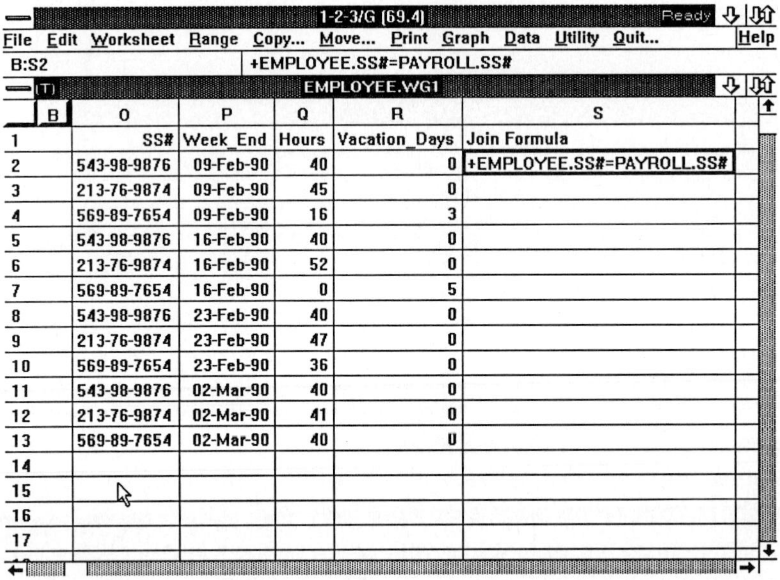

1-2-3/G [69.4] Ready

File Edit Worksheet Range Copy... Move... Print Graph Data Utility Quit... Help

B:S2 +EMPLOYEE.SS#=PAYROLL.SS#

(T) EMPLOYEE.WG1

B	O	P	Q	R	S
1	SS#	Week_End	Hours	Vacation_Days	Join Formula
2	543-98-9876	09-Feb-90	40	0	+EMPLOYEE.SS#=PAYROLL.SS#
3	213-76-9874	09-Feb-90	45	0	
4	569-89-7654	09-Feb-90	16	3	
5	543-98-9876	16-Feb-90	40	0	
6	213-76-9874	16-Feb-90	52	0	
7	569-89-7654	16-Feb-90	0	5	
8	543-98-9876	23-Feb-90	40	0	
9	213-76-9874	23-Feb-90	47	0	
10	569-89-7654	23-Feb-90	36	0	
11	543-98-9876	02-Mar-90	40	0	
12	213-76-9874	02-Mar-90	41	0	
13	569-89-7654	02-Mar-90	40	U	
14					
15					
16					
17					

Figure 20-10. Payroll database

ment needs. For example, you may already have a customer processing application developed with another data management program. Rather than bringing the application into 1-2-3/G, you can use the data management application in the application's format and use 1-2-3/G to access its database in the external database. You can use a special facility known as DataLens to link to databases from other packages while you are using 1-2-3/G.

You can use DataLens to access data from another database that you don't want to retrieve into 1-2-3/G—for example, databases that are much too large to bring into a worksheet file. In such cases, 1-2-3/G's Data External commands let you manipulate the external file like a database table in an active 1-2-3/G file.

Figure 20-11 shows an external database created with dBASE III (Lotus' Magellan package is used to display the database since it allows you to examine the contents of many types of files). This external database has similarities to the databases you create in 1-2-3/G. Like 1-2-3/G databases, external databases are divided into records and fields. Each field contains a specific type of data and has a name. Each external database package has its own rules for database field names and field types. When you use external databases in 1-2-3/G, you must use the field names as created in the external database.

To use an external database, 1-2-3/G must have a DataLens driver for the external package. 1-2-3/G includes a sample DataLens driver file for dBASE III. Other drivers are available through Lotus or the database program manufacturers. The steps for accessing the database are summarized in the "Steps for Using an External Database" box.

1-2-3/G provides a database driver for dBASE III. You can also use this driver for a dBASE IV database if none of the fields are memo or floating field types. Other database drivers are provided by the company that makes the data management package. The sample dBASE III driver that 1-2-3/G provides has some limitations. It cannot delete or modify records in the external database table with Data Query Delete or Data Query Modify Replace, delete external database tables with Data External Delete, or use the Data External Other Command or the @DQUERY function.

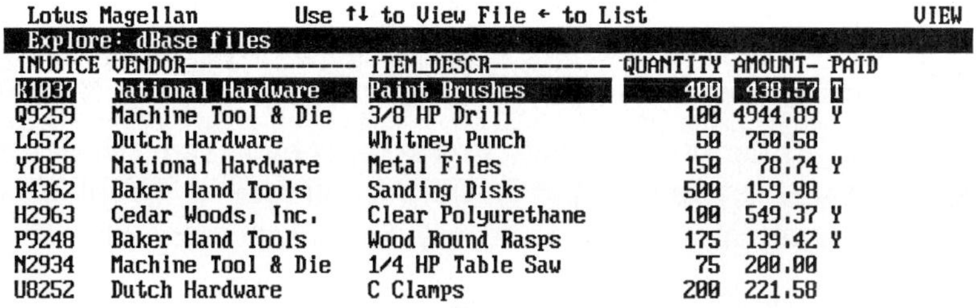

```
Lotus Magellan         Use ↑↓ to View File ← to List                    VIEW
 Explore: dBase files
INVOICE VENDOR--------------- ITEM_DESCR---------- QUANTITY AMOUNT- PAID
K1037   National Hardware     Paint Brushes             400  438.57 T
Q9259   Machine Tool & Die    3/8 HP Drill              100 4944.89 Y
L6572   Dutch Hardware        Whitney Punch              50  750.50
Y7858   National Hardware     Metal Files               150   78.74 Y
R4362   Baker Hand Tools      Sanding Disks             500  159.98
H2963   Cedar Woods, Inc.     Clear Polyurethane        100  549.37 Y
P9248   Baker Hand Tools      Wood Round Rasps          175  139.42 Y
N2934   Machine Tool & Die    1/4 HP Table Saw           75  200.00
U8252   Dutch Hardware        C Clamps                  200  221.50
```

Figure 20-11. INVOICES.DBF file from dBASE III PLUS

Steps for Using an External Database

The Data External commands let you access records in external database tables. Before you can use an external database table, you must create a link between 1-2-3/G and the external database table. You must also use the sample driver to set the directory to the directory containing the driver file (in this case C:\123G) before executing commands. These are the required steps:

1. Select Data External Use.
2. Double-click or highlight the driver name from the list box and press ENTER. The driver name is normally the name of the database management program.
3. Double-click or highlight the database name and press ENTER. (For dBASE III, this is the path to the dBASE files.)
4. Double-click or highlight the connection table name and press ENTER. (For dBASE III, this is the database filename.)
5. Enter a range name, or accept the default range name that 1-2-3/G uses to refer to the external database table. The default is the name from Step 4, unless the table name starts with a $ or !, contains a period, or could be interpreted as a cell address. Press ENTER or click the OK command button. The screen should now display the worksheet in Ready mode.
6. Select Data Query Input. Press F3 (Name) and select the range name entered in Step 5, which is followed by "(Table)," to use the external database table in Data Query commands.

Opening an External Database

To use an external database, you first need to open the file from 1-2-3/G:

1. To open the file, select Data External Use.
2. 1-2-3/G prompts you for the driver name. This is normally the name of the other database management program. 1-2-3/G lists the selections it uses.

3. 1-2-3/G prompts you for the database name. (For dBASE III, you must provide the path to the dBASE file and the database name.) 1-2-3/G displays the default directory for the database name. You can either accept the default, select another listed directory, or press ESCAPE and type a directory.

4. \1-2-3/G prompts you for the table name. You can select a listed table or database filename, or press ESCAPE and type a table or database filename.

5. Finally, 1-2-3/G prompts you for the range name for the external database table. 1-2-3/G displays a list of the table name, unless the name starts with a $ or !, contains a period, or could be interpreted as a cell address. You can accept the default or type a new range name before pressing ENTER.

6. If the external program requires that you enter a password or user name, 1-2-3/G prompts you for a password or user name before establishing the connection to a worksheet file.

If you have 1-2-3/G and the proper DataLens driver on your system, you don't need a copy of the other database management program on your system to access its files. This means that you can use databases that have been created on other machines. If you are primarily using an external database with 1-2-3/G, consider placing the external database file in the 1-2-3/G default directory.

As an example, suppose that you want to use the data in the dBASE III file shown in Figure 20-11. Assume that this file is called INVOICES.DBF and is in the C:\123G\WORK directory. First select Data External Use. Then select Sample as the driver in the list box. Next, select C:\123G\WORK before pressing ENTER. When 1-2-3/G lists the dBASE files in the C:\123G\WORK directory, select INVOICES. The dialog box should look like this:

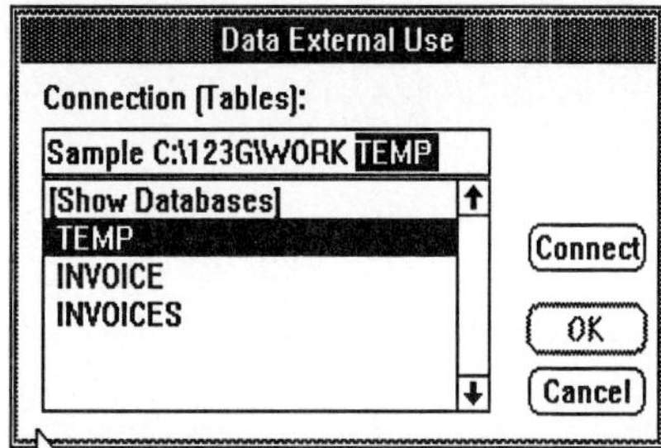

When you highlight INVOICES and double-click or press ENTER, 1-2-3/G prompts for a range name to assign to the table, and displays INVOICES as the default range name. Press ENTER or click the OK command button to accept the range name. As you make selections, 1-2-3/G marks with a double arrow choices made for other connected external databases. If the database requires a password or user ID, 1-2-3/G displays a dialog box in which you must enter the information. The password or user ID must match the requirements of the other data management package. If you don't have the password or user ID information, you cannot access the database. Especially when using a database on a network, you may need to consult the network or database administrator to obtain the appropriate password and user ID.

Once you establish a connection between a table in an external database and a worksheet file, you can apply 1-2-3/G Data Query commands, formulas, and database @functions to the table. To refer to the external database in 1-2-3/G, use the range name assigned by the Data External Use command. The number of links you can create to external databases is limited by your computer's memory.

If your external databases are in a different directory, you can add the directory containing the database files to the directory list 1-2-3/G displays in step 3. To do this, edit the LOTUS.BCF file in a text editor such as the OS/2 System Editor (available from the Start Programs or Group-Utilities window) and add this line to the end of the file:

```
DB="database files path" DN="Driver name that uses this path";
```

For example, to add the C:\DBASE directory, add

```
DB="C:\DBASE" DN="Sample"
```

This displays the directory C:\DBASE in step 3 when you select the Sample DataLens driver in step 2. You can also add a description by appending DD="message" to the line. The LOTUS.BCF file also lists the DataLens drivers with a line such as:

```
DN="Sample" DL="LTSDBASE"
DD="Lotus sample dBASE III DataLens Driver Version 1.0";
```

The text in quotes after DN lists the driver name, the text in quotes after DL lists the DataLens driver filename, and the text in quotes after the DD lists the DataLens description. The semicolon is used to end the driver and provide a separator for the directory descriptions when one is provided.

If the external database contains characters that aren't displaying correctly, such an accented "A" appearing as a graphics character, 1-2-3/G is not using the correct translation character set. To change the translation character set, use the Data External Other Translation command. 1-2-3/G displays the available character sets.

Listing Information About External Databases

Once you create links to an external database, you can obtain information about the database with the Data External List Tables and Data External List Fields commands.

The Data External List Tables command lists the tables that you can use with a DataLens driver. You must select the driver and directory for the external databases to list. The table lists the table names in one column, and the table descriptions or NA in a second column. When you execute this command, 1-2-3/G first prompts for a range in which to write the list. Figure 20-12 shows such a list of external tables.

Data External List Fields lists a table definition of an external database. You must select the DataLens driver, and the directory and filename or table name of the external database to list the fields. You can use this feature to create a database similar to an existing database. Data External List Fields lists the field names, types, widths, column labels, descriptions, and field creation strings. If a field lacks any of this information, 1-2-3/G displays NA. When you execute Data External List Fields, 1-2-3/G prompts for the first cell to use for recording the fields list. The list uses as many rows as the external database has fields. Figure 20-13 shows such a list of fields in the INVOICE database.

Tip: Use Data External List Fields to list the field names in the external database table that you want to use with data query commands. Once you have the table definition, you can use the Copy or the Range Transpose command to copy the field names to the criteria range. Then you can erase the table definition. This ensures that the field names in the search criteria are correct.

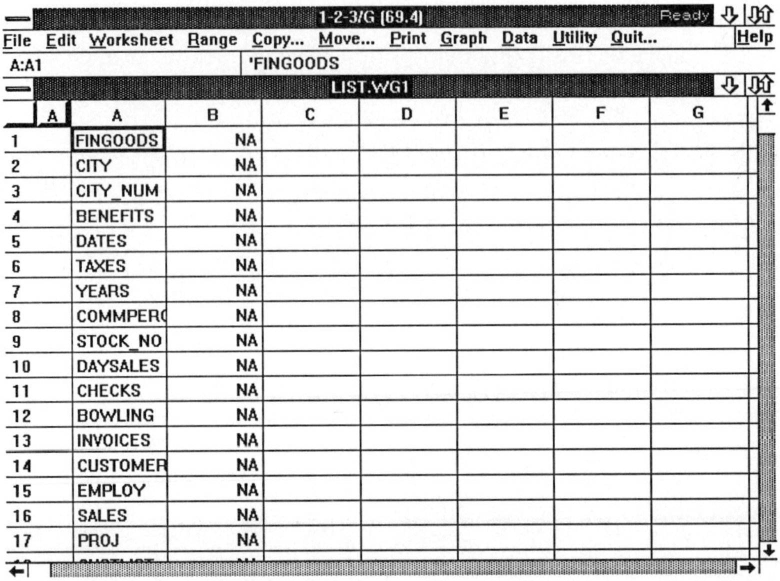

1-2-3/G [69.4] Ready

File Edit Worksheet Range Copy... Move... Print Graph Data Utility Quit... Help

A:A1 'FINGOODS

LIST.WG1

A	A	B	C	D	E	F	G
1	FINGOODS	NA					
2	CITY	NA					
3	CITY_NUM	NA					
4	BENEFITS	NA					
5	DATES	NA					
6	TAXES	NA					
7	YEARS	NA					
8	COMMPER(	NA					
9	STOCK_NO	NA					
10	DAYSALES	NA					
11	CHECKS	NA					
12	BOWLING	NA					
13	INVOICES	NA					
14	CUSTOMER	NA					
15	EMPLOY	NA					
16	SALES	NA					
17	PROJ	NA					

Figure 20-12. List of external database tables

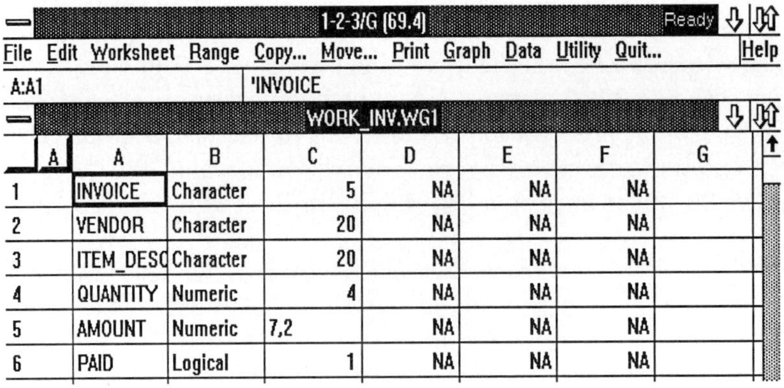

1-2-3/G [69.4] Ready

File Edit Worksheet Range Copy... Move... Print Graph Data Utility Quit... Help

A:A1 'INVOICE

WORK_INV.WG1

A	A	B	C	D	E	F	G
1	INVOICE	Character	5	NA	NA	NA	
2	VENDOR	Character	20	NA	NA	NA	
3	ITEM_DESC	Character	20	NA	NA	NA	
4	QUANTITY	Numeric	4	NA	NA	NA	
5	AMOUNT	Numeric	7,2	NA	NA	NA	
6	PAID	Logical	1	NA	NA	NA	

Figure 20-13. Table definition for INVOICES.DBF

Accessing External Databases

Once you create a link to an external database, you can start using its data in 1-2-3/G commands. In Data Query commands, you can specify an external database as an input range by entering its name as assigned by the Data External Use command. To look at the database's records, use the Data Query Extract, Data Query Modify Extract, and Data Query Unique commands to copy the records to a worksheet. To copy records from an external database table, specify it as the input range name. To copy records to the external database table, specify it as the output range name.

1-2-3/G can also perform some commands in the other database management program if you are familiar with the program's required command syntax. To do this, use Data External Other Command. 1-2-3/G prompts for the database driver, the external database directory, and the database management command.

When you include the external database values in @functions and formulas, 1-2-3/G updates their values according to the Worksheet Global Manual Recalc command and the Data External Other Refresh command. When both of these commands are set to automatic, 1-2-3/G reexecutes the last issued Data Query and Data Table commands, updates worksheet formulas, and updates database @functions at the interval selected with Interval set in the Data External Other Refresh dialog box. This command sets the number of seconds between 1-2-3/G external database updates. When Data External Other Refresh is set to manual, Data Query and Data Table commands are updated each time the commands are executed or F7 (Query) or F8 (Table) is pressed. If worksheet recalculation is set to manual, you must also press F9 (Calc) to update the @functions that use an external database table.

The Data External Use command establishes a connection between the external database and the currently active worksheet file. The other open worksheet files don't have a connection to the external database. You must establish the connection for each worksheet file that uses the external database.

Copying Records to the New Database Table

Once you create an external database table, you can copy records to it. Define the new table range name as the output range with the Data Query Output command. Then you can copy in all desired records using

Data Query Extract. To limit which records 1-2-3/G copies, specify criteria with the Data Query Criteria command. The criteria you select must follow all of the criteria rules discussed earlier. Figure 20-14 shows the database (sheet B) and the criteria (sheet C) that the Data Query Criteria and Data Query Extract commands use to copy records to the EMPLOYEE external database table. The criteria range is C:A7..C:E8, which selects records with a HIRE_DATE on or after January 1, 1985. The Data Query Extract command copies the first, fourth, sixth, eighth, and ninth records.

Closing an External Database

After you finish using an external database, you should close it with the Data External Reset command. This breaks the connection between the worksheet file and the database. 1-2-3/G lists the table names (dBASE filenames) to which the active worksheet file is connected. Double-click the table name you want or highlight it and press ENTER.

1-2-3/G [69.4] Ready

File Edit Worksheet Range Copy... Move... Print Graph Data Utility Quit... Help

C:E8 '>=31048

RECORDS.WG1

C	A	B	C	D	E	F
1	FIRST_NAME	Character	10	NA	NA	NA
2	MID_NAME	Character	10	NA	NA	NA
3	LAST_NAME	Character	15	NA	NA	NA
4	SSN	Character	11	NA	NA	NA
5	HIRE_DATE	Date	8	NA	NA	NA
6						
7	FIRST_NAME	MID_NAME	LAST_NAME	SSN	HIRE_DATE	
8					>=31048	

B	A	B	C	D	E	F
1	FIRST_NAME	MID_NAME	LAST_NAME	SSN	HIRE_DATE	
2	Jeanette	Anne	Cruise	761-72-8973	09/11/87	
3	Stephen	Scott	Golland	123-88-4827	03/21/84	
4	Patrick	John	Perez	478-28-6810	05/09/81	
5	Carol	Racheal	Spear	683-78-2832	08/18/86	
6	Babbette	Alicia	Zegetti	234-24-9807	11/14/82	
7	Marlene	Stewart	Galloway	465-27-7937	02/19/89	
8	Andrew	Brandon	Jeck	358-95-2594	11/27/83	

Figure 20-14. Worksheet containing information to extract to an external database table

For example, suppose that you want to close the database table in INVOICES.DBF that you have established with the Data External Use command. First, select Data External Reset. Then select INVOICES in the list box by double-clicking it or highlighting it and pressing ENTER. 1-2-3/G breaks the connection to the INVOICES.DBF file.

Creating an External Database

You can create an external database rather than storing all your database information within 1-2-3/G. This feature is frequently used for transferring information between external databases, or for transferring information from 1-2-3/G database tables to external databases. You can also use this feature to transfer 1-2-3/G data to another database package.

To create an external database, you must create a table definition, create the structure in the external table, and copy information to the external table. The following examples use the data in the 1-2-3/G worksheet shown in Figure 20-15.

Selecting Records for the New External Database Table

Before copying records to an external database, select the desired records with the Data Query Input command. These records determine the structure of the new database table. The input range can be a database table in an active worksheet file or in an external database. For the data in Figure 20-15, the input range is A:A1..A:E10.

Creating a Table Definition

When creating an external table, you first need to create a table definition—defining the database structure that the new external database uses. The format of the table definition is identical to the fields listing created by the Data External List Fields command. The steps for creating a table definition vary depending on which external database product you are using. The following discussion focuses on dBASE III; for other DataLens drivers, you should refer to the specific DataLens documentation.

1-2-3/G (69.4) Ready

File Edit Worksheet Range Copy... Move... Print Graph Data Utility Quit... Help

B:A1 'FIRST_NAME

RECORDS.WG1

B	A	B	C	D	E	F
1	FIRST_NAME	MID_NAME	LAST_NAME	SSN	HIRE_DATE	
2	Jeanette	Anne	Cruise	761-72-8973	09/11/87	
3	Stephen	Scott	Golland	123-88-4827	03/21/84	
4	Patrick	John	Perez	478-28-6810	05/09/81	
5	Carol	Racheal	Spear	683-78-2832	08/18/86	
6	Babbette	Alicia	Zegetti	234-24-9807	11/14/82	
7	Marlene	Stewart	Galloway	465-27-7937	02/19/89	
8	Andrew	Brandon	Jeck	358-95-2594	11/27/83	
9	Mark	Paul	Jones	324-87-1369	02/28/89	
10	Karen	Allen	Smith	484-62-1669	04/01/88	

Figure 20-15. Employee database

Creating a Table Definition in a 1-2-3/G Worksheet If the external database that you want to create is unlike other external database structures or 1-2-3/G database tables, perform these steps:

1. Move to an empty area in a worksheet that has at least six columns and as many rows as the new database table has fields.

2. Put the field name in the first column, field type in the second column, field width in the third column, field label in the fourth column, field description in the fifth column, and field creation string in the sixth column. The last three columns are optional. The format of the data must match what the database driver expects.

3. Repeat step 2 for each field that you want in the created external table, using a new row for each field. An example table definition is shown in Figure 20-16.

4. Select Data External Create Name, and specify the database driver and external database you want to create. You can use the list that 1-2-3/G supplies to make your selection. Then type the new table name and press ENTER. Supply a new range name or accept 1-2-3/G's suggestion and select Connect. If the database driver requires an owner name or password for the database, enter the owner's name or password in the dialog box.

5. Enter any table creation string in the appropriate text box. Some database packages, such as dBASE, do not use them.

6. Select Definition Use and select the table definition that you created. For the table in Figure 20-16, the range is C:A1..C:E5.

7. Select Go to create the new table. This creates the external database table but does not add any records to it. Because creating a database establishes a link to it, you can use the Data Query commands to copy data into the database.

Tip: Use the Data External List Fields command to create a sample table definition to refer to as you create another table definition. This prevents errors due to lack of information or inappropriate format.

Using an Existing Database To Create a Table Definition The Data External Create Definition Create command can create a table definition from a 1-2-3/G database table or an external database table. First name the new table with Data External Create Name. Supply the database driver, external database, table name, and range name for the table. Supply any user identification or password if necessary.

To create the table definition that the new external database will use, select Definition Create. Then select the 1-2-3/G database table or enter the range name of the database that 1-2-3/G uses as the basis for the table definition. Select a range in which to place the table definition. This area must have at least six columns, and as many rows as the 1-2-3/G database table or external database table has fields. If you want

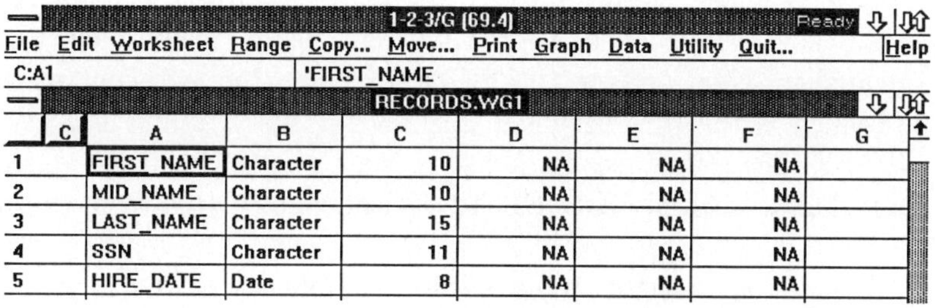

1-2-3/G [69.4] Ready

File Edit Worksheet Range Copy... Move... Print Graph Data Utility Quit... Help

C:A1 'FIRST_NAME

RECORDS.WG1

C	A	B	C	D	E	F	G
1	FIRST_NAME	Character	10	NA	NA	NA	
2	MID_NAME	Character	10	NA	NA	NA	
3	LAST_NAME	Character	15	NA	NA	NA	
4	SSN	Character	11	NA	NA	NA	
5	HIRE_DATE	Date	8	NA	NA	NA	

Figure 20-16. Employee database table definition

to alter the table's contents, you must select Quit and then reexecute the Data External Create command later.

When you create a table by using a database table in 1-2-3/G as a model, 1-2-3/G uses the field names in the top row as the table definition field names, the data types in the second row as the table definition field types, and the column widths as the field widths. When you create a table using an external database table, 1-2-3/G uses the field names, field types, and field widths from the external database table. In both cases, 1-2-3/G may not assign field widths to fields containing values, depending upon the database driver selected by the Data External Create command. Figure 20-16 showed a table created with this command.

Once you create a table definition, you can create an external database by selecting Go to return to Ready mode. This creates the external database but does not add any records to it. Since selecting Go establishes a link to the new database, you can use the Data Query commands to copy data to it. If you need to return to Ready mode before creating the table, select Quit. When you are ready to create the table, you must select the Data External Create Name and Use Definition commands again. Edit the table definition from Ready mode.

Deleting External Database Tables

Just as you can create external database tables, you can also delete them permanently from the disk. To delete an external database table, use Data External Delete. This command does not require a connection between 1-2-3/G and the external database table. 1-2-3/G will prompt for driver name, database name (or directory containing the database file), and table name (filename of external database). In each case, 1-2-3/G lists possibilities to select or type in the text box.

As an example, suppose you want to delete the INVOICES.DBF database table. First, select Data External Delete. Then select dBASE as the driver. Next, select C:\123G\WORK for the external database name (which is the directory for dBASE III files). When 1-2-3/G lists the dBASE files, select the database name INVOICES. Once you press ENTER or double-click INVOICES, 1-2-3/G deletes the file from the disk.

Tip: 1-2-3/G deletes the table without confirmation. Once you have deleted the table, you cannot retrieve it from 1-2-3/G or the database program that it is designed for.

1-2-3/G's Macro Features

Getting Started with Macros
Keyboard Alternative Macros
Command Language Macros

PART SIX

Getting Started with Macros

TWENTY ONE

Macros are stored instructions that allow you to execute repetitive tasks quickly. Macros can contain keystrokes that are equivalent to the keystrokes needed to make menu selections. This type of macro is called a *keyboard equivalent macro.* Macros can also contain special macro commands that allow you to program 1-2-3/G to complete a complex series of tasks. These macros are called *command language macros.* In this chapter, you will create a few simple keyboard alternative macros that are equivalent to selections you can make from 1-2-3/G's menus. You will create, name, and execute these macros. You will also try the Keystroke Editor that records keystrokes as you make them. The Keystroke Editor can take much of the work out of macro creation because it automatically captures the keystrokes you need rather than requiring that you type them into a cell. After you learn a few of the basics, you can explore the complete world of keyboard equivalent macros in Chapter 22, or the more complex command language macros in Chapter 23.

Entering the Macro Keystrokes

To record a macro on the worksheet, you can type the keystrokes in one or more cells in a column of the worksheet. Normally, you will choose a sheet that is not used for other data. In this exercise, however, the data and macro will be entered on the same sheet so you can see both entries at once.

Your macro keystrokes must always be entered as text. This means that you must type a label indicator if 1-2-3/G does not recognize the first character you type as a label entry.

The first macro you enter only uses one worksheet cell for the keystrokes. If you need to enter a large number of keystrokes, you can use several cells in consecutive rows in any column of a sheet.

Follow the steps listed next to create a macro that formats the current cell as currency with zero decimal places. You record the keystrokes by entering the letter you would type to select each menu or dialog box option. The only unusual character in these entries is the tilde (~), which is used every time you want to represent ENTER.

1. Move the cell pointer to B1 and then type **'/rfc0~~**. The apostrophe in the first position prevents 1-2-3/G from activating the menu immediately. Lowercase letters were used for the underlined letters in each menu or dialog box selection (uppercase would produce the same results). Thc first tilde finalizes the entry of the number of decimal places. The second tilde represents the ENTER that you would use to accept the range of the current cell as the location where the format should bc applied.

2. Press ENTER to finalize your entry, which will look like this:

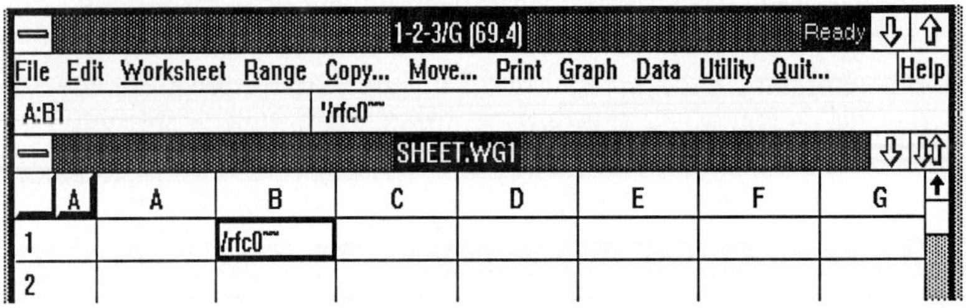

You cannot use a tilde to finalize your entry. Remember, you are finalizing the entry of the keystrokes in the cell rather than trying to get the macro to generate an ENTER.

Documenting the Macro

Documentation is text that reminds you of the name and purpose of a macro. Entries documenting the meaning of each line in a macro are useful if you modify the macro later. It is also a good idea to place the name you use for the macro in a cell to the left of the first macro instruction in case you forget the range name that you assign to the macro. Follow these steps to document your macro:

1. Move the cell pointer to A1.
2. Type **'\c**, then press ENTER to finalize your entry, which should look like this:

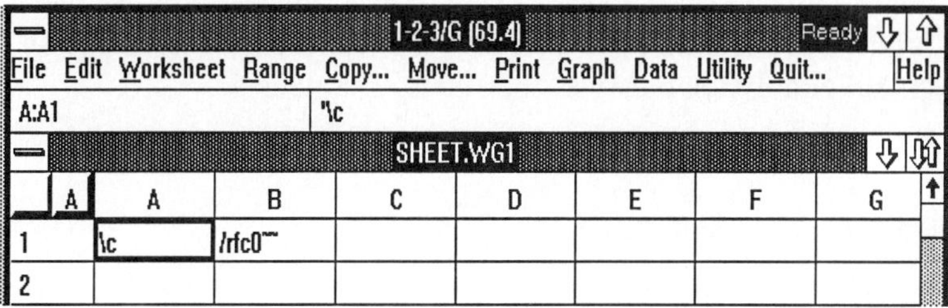

Since this macro will soon be assigned the name \c, this name is being documented on the worksheet. Entering \ without an apostrophe would cause 1-2-3/G to regard the \ as a request for a repeating label, which would fill the cell with the letter c.

3. Move the cell pointer to C1 by pressing RIGHT ARROW twice.
4. Type **Formats as currency with 0 decimals** and press ENTER. This entry documents the macro's task and serves as a reminder when you look at the macro keystrokes later. After you move the cell pointer back to B1, the macro should look like this:

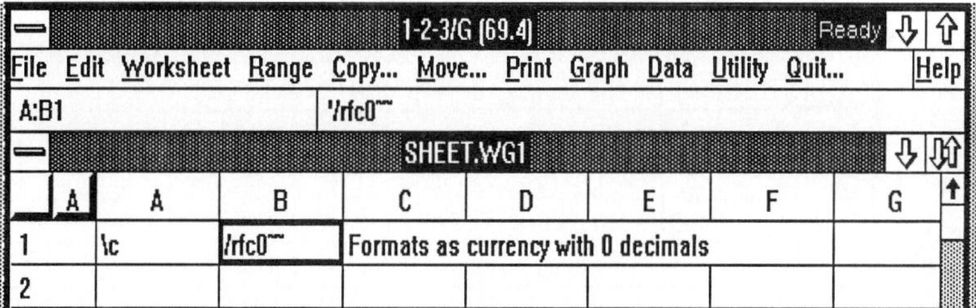

Naming the Macro for Quick Execution

You can assign macro names with the Range Name Create command. There are two basic styles for names. You can use either a backslash and a single letter; for example, \a, or you can use a longer name. Your choice will control the ease with which you can execute the macro. The backslash and letter combination offers a shortcut, since you can execute the macro by pressing CTRL and the letter. You can use this approach for assigning a macro name by following these steps:

1. Move the cell pointer to B1.
2. Select Range Name Create.
3. Type **\c** and press ENTER to finalize the name.
4. Press ENTER to assign the name to the top cell in the macro.

The worksheet does not change its appearance in any way. The command simply enables you to execute the macro.

Executing the Macro

Macros that you name with the backslash and letter combination are easy to execute. If you need to position the cell pointer before starting the macro, you should complete that step first. Next, use a simple key combination to start the macro. Follow these steps to execute the \a macro you just created:

1. Move the cell pointer to A3, type **9**, and press ENTER. Your entry should look like this:

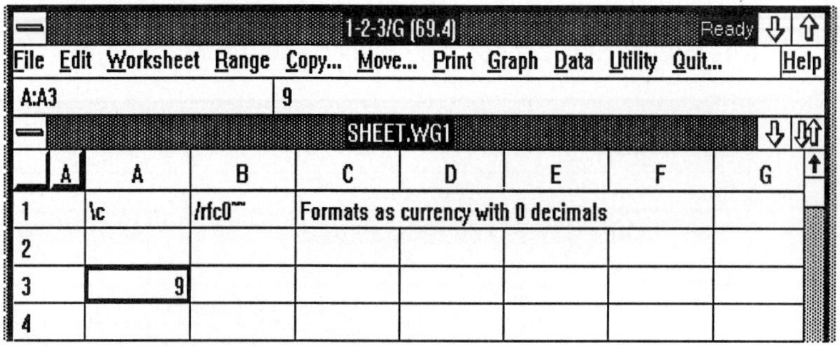

1-2-3/G [69.4] Ready

File Edit Worksheet Range Copy... Move... Print Graph Data Utility Quit... Help

A:A3 9

SHEET.WG1

A	A	B	C	D	E	F	G
1	\c	/rfc0~	Formats as currency with 0 decimals				
2							
3	9						
4							

Make sure to relocate the cell pointer if you want it in a specific location when the macro starts.

2. Hold down CTRL and type **C**. This causes 1-2-3/G to execute the instructions stored in the \c macro. Your entry is formatted as currency with 0 decimal places and should look like this:

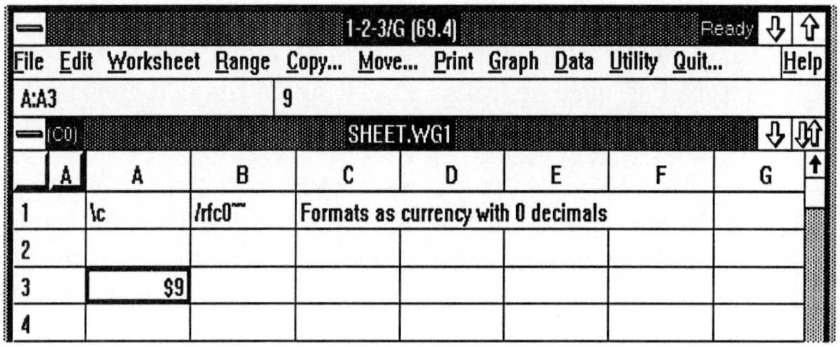

1-2-3/G (69.4) Ready

File Edit Worksheet Range Copy... Move... Print Graph Data Utility Quit... Help

A:A3 9

(C0) SHEET.WG1

A	A	B	C	D	E	F	G
1	\c	/rfc0~~	Formats as currency with 0 decimals				
2							
3	$9						
4							

Entering a Macro that Uses More than One Cell

Since 1-2-3/G can store a label entry of up to 512 characters in a cell, a macro could contain 512 characters before you needed a second cell. However, it is best to split macro entries into many short entries rather than one long entry that is difficult to follow. Short entries display one command and are easier to understand. Follow these steps to create a macro that will print the current worksheet entries:

1. Move the cell pointer to B5. Any location other than B2 on this worksheet would be fine. You cannot use B2 since executing the first macro would cause 1-2-3/G to execute the keystrokes in the \c macro and the macro instructions that start in B2. This is because 1-2-3/G doesn't stop executing macro keystrokes until it encounters a blank cell.

2. Type **'/pp** and press the DOWN ARROW key to move to B6.

3. Type **ra1.f8~** and press the DOWN ARROW key to move to B7.

4. Type **gpq** and press ENTER.

5. Move the cell pointer to A5.

6. Type **'\p** and then press the RIGHT ARROW key twice to move the cell pointer to C5.

7. Type **Invokes print & requests printer** and then press the DOWN ARROW key to move to C6.

8. Type **Specifies range of A1..F8** and then press the DOWN ARROW key to move to C7.

9. Type **Prints, form feeds, & quits** and then press ENTER.

10. Move the cell pointer to A5 and then select Range Name Labels Right. This command allows you to apply the name that you have entered as documentation in cell A5 to the cell directly to the right (B5).

11. Press ENTER to accept the suggested range. Although you cannot tell by the appearance of the screen, cell B5 is now named \p. You will know that your actions worked when you execute the macro in the next step. At this point, your two macros should look like this:

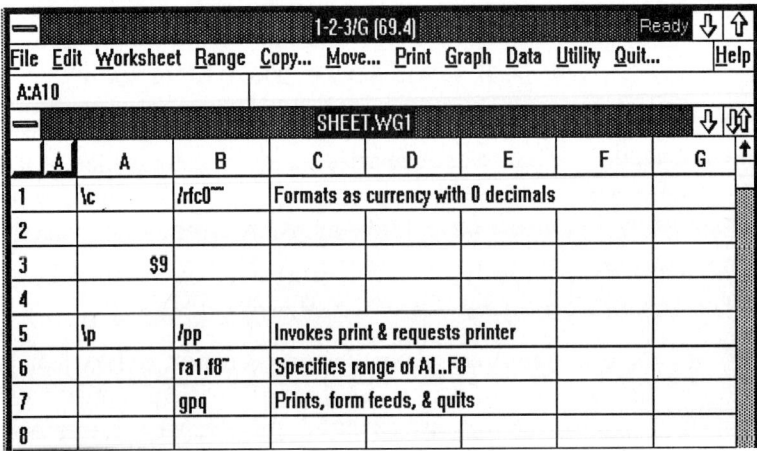

1-2-3/G (69.4) Ready

File Edit Worksheet Range Copy... Move... Print Graph Data Utility Quit... Help

A:A10

SHEET.WG1

A	A	B	C	D	E	F	G
1	\c	/rfc0~~	Formats as currency with 0 decimals				
2							
3	$9						
4							
5	\p	/pp	Invokes print & requests printer				
6		ra1.f8~	Specifies range of A1..F8				
7		gpq	Prints, form feeds, & quits				
8							

12. Check your printer to be sure that it is on before starting the macro.

13. Hold down CTRL and type **P**.

Modifying a Macro

You can edit macro instructions just as you can edit any entry made to a cell on the worksheet. You can also append new instructions to a macro as long as there will still be a blank cell between the macro and the next macro on the sheet. You don't need to rename the macro, since the name just needs to be applied to the first cell in the macro. You can change the macro that formats as currency to format the current cell and the cell immediately beneath it. Your change will require a cell pointer movement key to expand the range when the macro requests the range to format. Follow these steps to modify the macro and try it again:

1. Move the cell pointer to B1.
2. Press F2 (Edit) and then press BACKSPACE once to delete the ending tilde (~).
3. Press the DOWN ARROW key to finalize the entry.
4. Type **{DOWN}~** in B2 and then press the RIGHT ARROW key.
   This tells 1-2-3/G that you want the range extended down by one cell.
5. Type **Expands the range by one cell** in C2 and press ENTER.
6. Move the cell pointer to F3.
7. Type 4 and then press the DOWN ARROW key.
8. Type 8 and press ENTER.
9. Press the UP ARROW key to move to F3.
10. Press the CTRL-C combination. Both entries are formatted as currency when the macro ends.

Using the Keystroke Editor

1-2-3/G's Keystroke Editor constantly records the keystrokes that you type. These keystrokes include the first letters of menu selections, but also include keys that relocate the cell pointer, correct errors, or make entries in worksheet cells. Mouse actions are not recorded—it's important not to use the mouse if you want to record all of your actions in a macro automatically. The keystrokes stored by the Keystroke Editor are placed in a special storage area with a capacity of 16K. When this storage area fills, the oldest keystroke is deleted to make room for each new keystroke that you type. You can copy keystrokes from this storage area onto your worksheet at any time to create a macro. Once the keystrokes are copied, you just need to name the top cell in the macro. Follow these steps to erase the Keystroke Editor's storage area and capture keystrokes for a macro:

1. Select Utility Macros Keystroke Editor to place the Keystroke Editor window on the screen.

2. Press ALT-MINUS to activate the window control menu.

3. Select Maximize.

If you made entries before starting this chapter, your window may be full of keystrokes. This illustration shows the entries for this chapter:

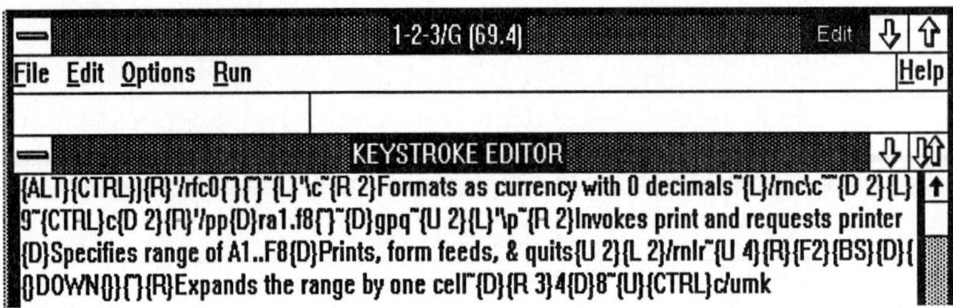

4. Select Edit Clear to clear all the keystrokes from the editor.

5. Press ALT-MINUS to activate the window control menu and select Close. When you close the Keystroke Editor window, 1-2-3/G continues recording your keystrokes.

6. Press HOME to move to A1. Next, press PGDN and then press RIGHT ARROW.

You will be in column B, one screen down from the top of the sheet. Your exact row location will depend on the font size selected and the size of the worksheet window. With System Proportional 10-point font and a maximized desktop and worksheet window, these actions would place you in B17. Move the cell pointer to B17 if you are in another location. Remember, if you complete any of the cell pointer movement actions with a mouse, the Keystroke Editor will not record them.

7. Select Worksheet Global Format Comma 0.

Since mistakes are recorded along with correct entries, be extremely careful as you experiment with the tasks in the steps listed next. Each keystroke you type is recorded in the storage area. You will need to delete extraneous entries after you are through recording the keystrokes.

Copying the Keystrokes to the Worksheet

All the keystrokes you entered to set the global format to Comma are stored in the Keystroke Editor. Any other keystrokes you typed since you cleared the Keystroke Editor window also appear. To copy them to the worksheet and apply a name to them:

1. Select Utilities Macros Keystroke Editor.

   The Keystroke Editor window appears at the bottom of the screen, as shown in Figure 21-1. Your initial cell pointer movement keys are displayed at the top of the window. The Keystroke Editor uses entries like {HOME} to represent the HOME key and {R} to represent the RIGHT ARROW key. Your request for the menu is represented as / or {F10}, depending on whether you use / or F10 to invoke the menu.

2. Use the mouse to drag the Keystroke Editor window to the upper-right corner of your screen.

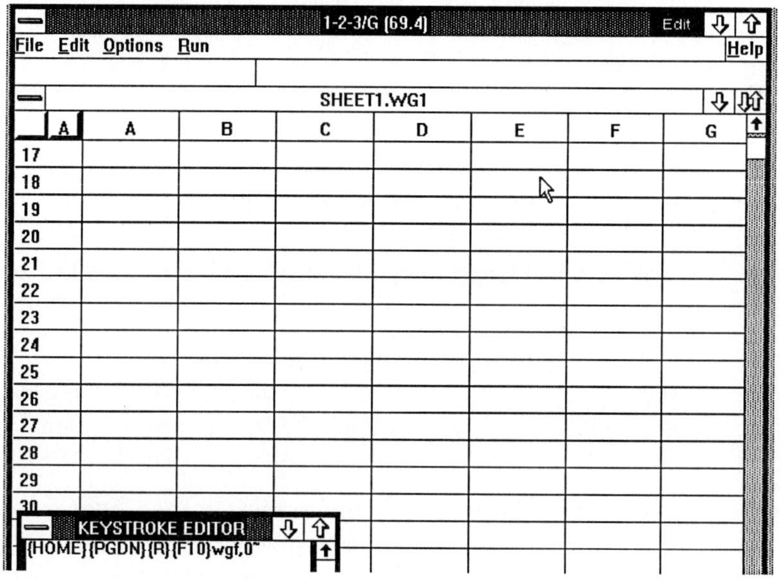

Figure 21-1. Keystroke Editor window listing keystrokes

3. Use the mouse to select the keystrokes that precede / or {F10} by clicking the mouse and then dragging it to the first keystroke you want to remove. You can also hold down the SHIFT key while you press HOME. Since you are in Edit mode when you are in the Keystroke Editor window, keys such as HOME and END behave as they do when you edit worksheet cells.

4. Press F10 to activate the Keystroke Editor window menu.

You cannot type a slash (/), since this would add a / to the captured keystrokes instead of activating the menu. You can use the mouse to activate the menu if you wish.

5. Select Edit Clear to delete the highlighted keystrokes.

The window should look like this:

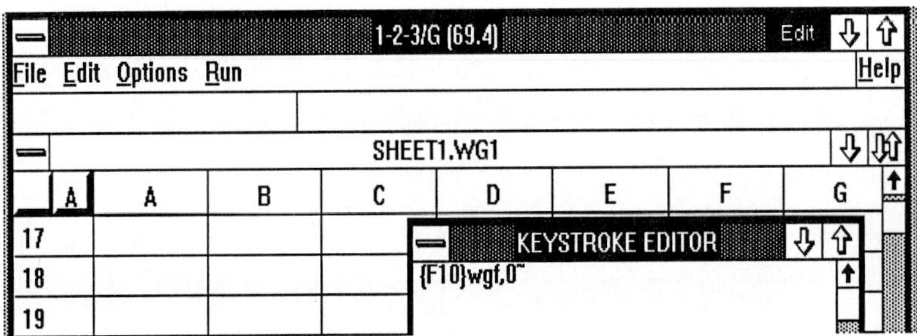

6. Highlight the remaining keystrokes in the Keystroke Editor window either by dragging the mouse or by pressing SHIFT-HOME or SHIFT-END, depending on the insertion point's position.

7. Select Edit Copy to copy the highlighted keystrokes to the Clipboard.

8. Click B17 on the worksheet to activate this cell. If you aren't using a mouse, press ALT-SPACEBAR to activate the desktop control menu, select Window, and type the number next to your worksheet file.

9. Select Edit Paste to copy the entries on the Clipboard to B17 and B18. {F10} is placed in B17 and wgf,0 is placed in B18. Now you just need to name the macro and add documentation.

10. Move the cell pointer to A17 and type **GLOBAL_COMMA**.

11. Move the cell pointer to C17 and type **Activates menu**.

12. Move the cell pointer to C18, type **Select global format comma 0 decimals**, and press ENTER.

Using a Longer Range Name for a Macro

Macros can have names other than the backslash letter combinations used so far. Longer names can be more meaningful and easier to remember. However, you cannot use the CTRL-letter sequence to execute longer names. Instead, you must use the ALT-F3 (Run) key sequence and then type or select the name of the macro from the list. Follow these steps to create a macro with a longer name:

1. Move the cell pointer to A17 and then select Range Name Labels Right and press ENTER. Even though the name is longer, Range Name Labels Right is used to name the top cell in the macro.

2. Press ALT-F3 to activate the Run a Macro dialog box.

3. Highlight GLOBAL_COMMA and press ENTER to execute the macro. With a mouse, you can double-click GLOBAL_COMMA from the list.

This macro would be useful if you frequently change the global format, since it provides a quick way to change it back again.

Keyboard Alternative Macros

Many people are intimidated by macros. However, macros are a powerful and time-saving 1-2-3/G feature. They can be quite simple to master if you use a step-by-step approach and learn the most basic macros before attempting the more sophisticated ones. The keystroke recorder feature and other macro enhancements make it easier than ever to master macros. You can also create macros successfully by following the procedures outlined in this and the next chapter.

Types of Macros

1-2-3/G's keyboard alternative macros can automate printing, formatting, or any other task that is accomplished with menu selections. This type of macro provides an alternative to typing from the keyboard. Keyboard macros are a good place to start if you are new to macros, since they contain familiar keystroke commands. If you follow the instructions in this chapter, you should be able to create keyboard alternative macros that work on the first try.

The second type of macro uses commands that are not available as menu selections. These commands are available as keyword options from 1-2-3/G's macro command language. With command language macros, you can read and write records to a file, create your own menus, use iterative loops, and alter the order in which commands are processed. 1-2-3/G's command language is a full programming language that allows you to develop complete applications. With new 1-2-3/G macro commands, you can position, size, and activate windows as well as pause a macro while a dialog box is used. Chapter 23 covers all the features of 1-2-3/G's command language.

Both types of macros can be stored in the worksheet file where they are used, or in a separate file if you want to create a library of macros for use with many worksheets. It's a good idea to place macros on a separate sheet of the file. This makes it less likely that they'll be changed when you alter the remainder of the worksheet entries. With 1-2-3/G, you can easily build macro library files that support many applications. Since 1-2-3/G can access macros in any sheet in memory, you can open a macro library at the beginning of a session and use it throughout your session and various worksheet files.

Keyboard Macros

Like all macros, a keyboard alternative macro is nothing more than a column of label entries that have a name assigned to them. The contents of the labels are the sequence of keystrokes that you want 1-2-3/G to execute. Macros perform keystrokes rather than selections that you make with a mouse. You cannot use a mouse to provide instructions for a macro.

After all your label entries are stored in a column, you name the top cell in the column with the Range Name Create command. You can give a macro any name that conforms to the rules of range names and falls within the 15-character limit. 1-2-3/G can use special names that consist of a backslash and a single letter, enabling you to execute a keyboard macro by pressing the CTRL key in combination with the letter. The drawback is that these letters are not very descriptive.

The steps for creating and executing keyboard macros are summarized in the box "The ABC's of Keyboard Macros."

The ABC's of Keyboard Macros

1. Plan the task you want the macro to perform.
2. Erase the keystroke recorder by activating the Keystroke Editor window and selecting Edit Clear All.
3. Activate the worksheet window to be used for the macro and execute the steps required for your task. Don't use the mouse, since the Keystroke Editor cannot record these actions.
4. Copy the keystrokes to your macro. Activate the Keystroke Editor window, select the keystrokes to transfer to the worksheet, and select Edit Copy or press CTRL-INS. Switch to the worksheet in which you want to store the macro, move to the first cell where you want to place the macro keystrokes, and select Edit Paste or press SHIFT-INS. An alternative to steps 2 through 4 involves typing the macro keystrokes you want as a series of label entries in a column of worksheet cells.
5. Review the label entries in the macro column and make any required changes.
6. Type the macro name one cell to the left of the top cell in the macro column. Use the backslash key and a single letter if you want to execute the macro with a single key combination. Or you can use any valid range name.
7. Use Range Name Labels Right to apply the name to the macro.
8. Add text to the right of the macro to document the tasks the macro performs.
9. Save the worksheet containing the macro.
10. Execute the macro using the CTRL key plus the macro letter name, as in \s. If you used a longer range name, use ALT-F3 (Run), highlight the name, and select the OK command button.

To execute a macro without the special backslash-letter combination name, press ALT-F3 (Run) and highlight the macro name in the list or type the name. In this dialog box, you must press ENTER, and click the OK command button or double-click the macro name to start macro execution.

Figure 22-1 shows a macro. The entries in column B are the macro instructions that 1-2-3/G will perform. The entry in A1 is the macro name. The entries in column C are documentation for each macro instruction in column B.

Tip: Avoid macro names that duplicate cell addresses, existing range names, and keywords—that is, stay away from macro names like A10, @SUM, and {DOWN}, which may cause confusion.

Recording the Keystrokes

There are several options for storing macro keystrokes in 1-2-3/G. You can type them in a cell as label entries, or you can use the entries in

1-2-3/G [69.4] Ready

File Edit Worksheet Range Copy... Move... Print Graph Data Utility Quit... Help

A:A1 'Salary

MAC_SAL.WG1

A	A	B	C
1	Salary	{HOME}	Move cell pointer to A1 of current sheet
2		Last Name{RIGHT}	Enter Last Name & move right
3		First Name{RIGHT}	Enter First Name & move right
4		"SS#{RIGHT}	Enter "SS# & move right
5		Job Code{RIGHT}	Enter Job Code & move right
6		"Salary{RIGHT}	Enter "Salary & move right
7		Location~	Enter Location & press ENTER
8		{GOTO}C19~	Move to C19~
9		TOTAL SALARIES{RIGHT 2}	Enter TOTAL SALARIES & move right
10		@SUM(E2..E17)~	Enter @SUM formula
11		/RFC0~E2..E19~	Format salaries as currency
12		{HOME}	Move to A1
13			
14			
15			
16			
17			

Figure 22-1. Macro to add labels to a worksheet

1-2-3/G's buffer, which records your keystrokes. To use any of the characters that 1-2-3/G records in the Keystroke Editor, you must first copy them to a cell or play them back directly from the buffer.

Typing the Required Keystrokes

When you want to store a menu request in a macro, begin the sequence with a single quotation mark, so it is treated as a label. This prevents 1-2-3/G from executing a menu request immediately. Then enter the keystrokes. Indicate the request for a menu command with a slash or {MENU}, and record each of the menu commands by entering the underlined letter of the menu choice. For instance, to enter the keystrokes for viewing a Worksheet Status screen, type **'/ws** or **'/WS** in the cell (case is not important).

Tip: If you make a mistake repeatedly throughout a long macro, the quickest correction method is the Replace option of Range Search.

Besides specifying menu selections, you may have to indicate an ENTER key press. The ENTER key is represented in a macro by the tilde mark (~).

Filenames or range names should be entered in full. As an example, to store the characters for retrieving a file named SALES from the default drive, enter **'/FRSALES~** or **'/FRsales~** in the macro cell. Although you can use all upper- or lowercase letters for the keystroke entries, a consistent combination can help to distinguish range names, filenames, cell addresses, and menu selections.

Tip: Beware of missing tildes—the single most frequent cause of mistakes in macros. After recording the correct menu selections, it is easy to forget that you press ENTER at certain points when executing a command sequence from the keyboard. Even one missing tilde can cause the macro to malfunction.

To correct a macro once it is entered, you can use the F2 (Edit) key with the cell pointer on the cell containing the macro code. Since the macro code is nothing more than a label entry, you don't need to use special techniques to make changes.

Tip: Use the {TAB} macro command to represent the TAB key to switch from one part of the dialog box to another. In many instances, you cannot use ENTER to switch to another part of the dialog box since pressing ENTER selects the OK command button.

Recording Special Keys

There are a number of special keyboard keys—like the function keys and cell-pointer movement keys—that you will want to include in your macros. These keys and the macro keywords that represent them are listed in Table 22-1. Note that all the keywords are enclosed in curly braces ({ }). Whether you type in your macros or use the keystroke recorder, you need to know the effect of each of these keys in order to make intelligent modifications to existing macros.

There is no keyword for the NUM LOCK and SCROLL LOCK keys, which must be requested from outside a macro. CAPS LOCK is not represented either, since cell entries are typed right into a macro and you can type either uppercase or lowercase letters. Case is also unimportant in operator entries made while a macro is executing, unless you are storing these entries on the worksheet and have a personal preference. In these cases, you may want to use the @UPPER, @PROPER, and @LOWER pfunctions to convert cell entries. Other keys not supported are PRINT-SCREEN and ALT-BACKSPACE for the Edit Undo command. As mentioned, 1-2-3/G has no macro commands for mouse movements.

Tip: Carefully check the spelling of the special-key names. In a macro, your entries must be exact since 1-2-3/G only recognizes entries that match the defined set of options exactly.

Cursor Movement Keys

In a macro, movement of the cell pointer to the right is represented by {RIGHT}. Movement to the left is {LEFT}, movement down is {DOWN}, and movement up is {UP}. These can be abbreviated as {R}, {L}, {D}, and {U}, respectively. If you want to move the cell pointer up three times, use {UP}{UP}{UP} or either of the shortcut entries {UP 3} or {U3}.

Specifying {HOME} for a worksheet or a cell has a different effect depending on whether the macro is in Ready or Edit mode. In Ready mode, {HOME} returns you to A1. In Edit mode, it moves you to the

Cell Pointer Movement Keys	Keywords
UP ARROW	{UP} or {U}
DOWN ARROW	{DOWN} or {D}
RIGHT ARROW	{RIGHT} or {R}
LEFT ARROW	{LEFT} or {L}
HOME	{HOME}
END	{END}
PGUP	{PGUP}
PGDN	{PGDN}
CTRL-RIGHT	{BIGRIGHT}
TAB	{TAB}
CTRL-LEFT	{BIGLEFT}
SHIFT-TAB	{BACKTAB}
CTRL-PGUP (next sheet)	{NEXTSHEET} or {NS}
CTRL-PGDN (prev sheet)	{PREVSHEET} or {PS}
CTRL-HOME (first cell)	{FIRSTCELL} or {FC}
END, CTRL-HOME (last cell)	{LASTCELL} or {LC}
Editing Keys	**Keywords**
DELETE	{DELETE} or {DEL}
INSERT	{INSERT} or {INS}
ESCAPE	{ESCAPE} or {ESC}
BACKSPACE	{BACKSPACE} or {BS}
Function Keys	**Keywords**
F1 (Help)	{HELP}
F2 (Edit)	{EDIT}
F3 (Name)	{NAME}
F4 (Abs)	{ABS}
F5 (Goto)	{GOTO}
F6 (Window)	{WINDOW}
F7 (Query)	{QUERY}
F8 (Table)	{TABLE}
F9 (Calc)	{CALC}
F10 (Menu)	{MENU}
F11 (Help Index)	{F11}
ALT-F1 (Compose)	{COMPOSE}
ALT-F2 (Step)	{STEP}
ALT-F3 (Run)	{RUN}

Table 22-1. Keys in Macro Commands (*continued on next page*)

Function Keys	Keywords
SHIFT-F2 (Trace)	{TRACE}
SHIFT-F3 (Options)	{OPTIONS}
SHIFT-F4 (Bound)	{BOUND}
SHIFT-F6 (Hide)	{HIDE}
SHIFT-F7 (Group)	{GROUP}
SHIFT-F8 (Detach)	{DETACH}
SHIFT-F11 (Help Main Index)	{SHIFT}{F11}
Special Keys	**Keywords**
ENTER	~
~ (Tilde)	{~}
{	{{}
}	{}}
/	/ or {MENU}
ALT	{ALT}
CTRL	{CTRL}
SHIFT	{SHIFT}
SHIFT-SPACEBAR	{SELECT}
Desktop Control menu	{DESKMENU}
Window Control menu	{TOOLMENU}
CTRL-BREAK	{BREAK}
CTRL-. (Anchor)	{ANCHOR}

Table 22-1. Keys in Macro Commands

beginning of your entry. In other words, the movement keys work just as they do when you perform the keystrokes yourself.

{BIGLEFT} and {BIGRIGHT} shift you one whole screen to the left or the right, respectively. To page up or down, use the entries {PGUP} and {PGDN}. Unlike {BIGLEFT} and {BIGRIGHT}, {TAB} and {BACKTAB} (pressing SHIFT-TAB) are often used to move among selections in dialog boxes.

1-2-3/G also supports key combinations such as pressing END and an arrow key. You can enter {END}{RIGHT} to move the cell pointer to the last occupied cell entry on the right side of the worksheet. {NEXTSHEET} or {NS} performs the same function as CTRL-PGUP and {PREVSHEET} or {PS} performs the same function as CTRL-PGDN. {FIRSTCELL} or {FC} performs the same function as CTRL-HOME, which moves the cell pointer to A:A1. {LASTCELL} or {LS} performs the same function as END, CTRL-HOME, which moves the cell pointer to the last column row and sheet used by the entries in a worksheet file.

Function Keys

All the function keys can be represented by special macro keywords. To represent a function key, you can use {F#}, where # represents the number—as in {F1} or {F2}. Another option is to enclose the key name in braces—as in {HELP} or {EDIT}. The macro instructions for function keys include the function keys by themselves and the function keys used with other keys such as SHIFT, CTRL, and ALT. These function keys are represented in macros with either a combination of the key names, as in {SHIFT}{F2}, or with their name, as in {TRACE}.

Edit Keys

F2 (Edit) places you in the Edit mode. In addition, you are in Edit mode on several other occasions, such as when you enter the header text in a report. When you are in Edit mode, you can use several special keys when making and correcting entries. The ESCAPE key can remove an entry from a cell and delete a menu default so you can make a new entry. The ESCAPE key is represented as {ESC} or {ESCAPE} in macros.

You can also use {CLEARENTRY} or {CE} to remove existing data from the Edit mode. Although {CE} is similar to {ESC}, there are important differences. {CE} is the only keystroke command that does not have a keyboard equivalent. When there is one entry in the Edit line or an entry in a dialog's text box, {CE} functions like {ESC}, eliminating the entry. When a cell is empty or the dialog box's text box is already empty, one {CE} instruction eliminates any entry without leaving Edit mode. On the other hand, if you press ESCAPE in a cell without an entry during Edit mode or while in an empty text box, 1-2-3/G returns to Ready mode if you editing a cell or Menu mode if you are in a dialog box.

To delete the character in front of the cell pointer while in Edit mode, or to delete the last character entered, you can use the BACKSPACE key when making your entries from the keyboard. To represent this key in a macro, use {BS} or {BACKSPACE}.

The DELETE key deletes the character above the cell pointer while you are in Edit mode. This is represented in a macro as {DEL} or {DELETE}. As an example, you can change a label prefix to center justification with the following sequence of macro entries:

```
{EDIT}{HOME}{DEL}^~
```

You can also use the repeat factors with the editing keys. {DELETE 4} deletes the character above the cursor and the next three characters. {BACKSPACE 7} deletes seven characters to the left of the cursor. You can even use a range name, as in {DELETE *rows*}, where *rows* controls the number of rows deleted. You can also use {DELETE} to remove a cell or selected range.

Other Special Keys

As mentioned, the tilde represents ENTER. To use a macro to place an actual tilde in a cell, type **{~}**. To use a macro to place curly braces in a cell, enter either **{{}** or **{}}**. These features can be useful in a macro that builds another macro. A macro can also use the ALT, CTRL, and SHIFT keys with the {ALT}, {CTRL} and {SHIFT} macro instructions. These three macro instructions are usually combined with other keys, as in {SHIFT}{F2}.

You can use the symbol {?} in a macro to indicate that you want the operator to input something from the keyboard. 1-2-3/G then waits for the use to make the entry and press ENTER. Chapter 23 covers additional methods for indicating keyboard input, including how to present a message to the user regarding the data to be entered.

1-2-3/G has special keystrokes that are new to 1-2-3. These include activating the desktop control menu with ALT-SPACEBAR and activating the window control menu with ALT-MINUS. In a macro, you select these key combinations with {DESKMENU} and {TOOLMENU}. You can use these menus to position and size the windows and the 1-2-3/G desktop.

Typing a Keyboard Macro

Typing is not the fastest way to enter a macro. However, this method should more than pay for itself in time savings during the testing and debugging phase, as you are trying to get your macro to execute correctly.

• When creating a keyboard macro, you must first plan the task that you wish to accomplish. Without a plan, you are not likely to create a well organized and successful macro.

• After you have made your plan, test it by entering the proposed keystrokes for immediate execution by 1-2-3/G. As you enter each keystroke directly (without using a mouse) into the menus, record it on a sheet of paper. Later, you will learn how to turn these written entries into the macro code. For now, you should type at least a few keystrokes for a firsthand look at what each keystroke represents.

• If the menu selections handled your task correctly, use your sheet of paper as a script when you record the keystrokes as labels in the macro cells.

• Choose a location on your worksheet or a macro library worksheet to record your macro. You might want to use a separate worksheet in the current file, or even a separate file. 1-2-3/G can access all the macros in memory as long as they each have a unique name.

• Where possible, use range-name references rather than cell addresses as you build your macro. 1-2-3/G uses the most up-to-date range addresses that are assigned to a range name when you execute a macro, but 1-2-3/G does not adjust the range address entered directly in a macro.

• You can record up to 512 keystrokes in one label cell, but it's inadvisable to do so, since you could never read the entire entry at one time without editing the cell. At the other extreme, you can enter each single keystroke of the entry in a separate cell of the column. However, this second approach is also not advisable because you would need so many cells to create even a short macro. The best approach is to select some reasonable upper limit for the number of characters to be entered in one macro cell, and then, within that limit, move down to a new cell whenever you reach a logical breaking place in your keystroke entries.

• Use file references if you need to refer to cells or ranges outside the current worksheet.

Tip: Remember to enter all of your macro instructions as labels. Start them with a label indicator if the first character is a number or one of these characters: / + – @ . # $.

Naming Your Macro

Once you have entered or copied all of the macro keystrokes, you are ready to name your macro. Before doing this, position your cell pointer on the top cell in the macro, since this is the only cell that is named. Then select Range Name Create. At the range-name prompt, enter a backslash and any single letter before pressing ENTER if you want to be able to execute the macro with a single key combination. An alternative is to type any valid range name. The second type of macro is executed using the ALT-F3 (Run) key combination. Since you positioned your cell pointer before requesting the Range command, simply press ENTER in response to the prompt for the range address. When you save the worksheet, the macro and its name is saved as well and is available whenever you retrieve the worksheet.

You can also name your macro with the Range Name Labels Right command. To use this command, enter the macro name in the cell to the left of the first macro instruction. Next, select Range Name Labels Right and the range containing the macro names. This command is better when you have several macros that you want to name. For example, if you enter the macro names in column A and the instructions in column B, you can select Range Name Labels Right and select A: as the range containing the range names.

You can create an unlimited number of macros. You can also create 26 unique macro names using the backslash and the letters of the alphabet (such as \t). These macros can be executed with the CTRL key in combination with the letter used in the macro name (as in CTRL-T). 1-2-3/G does not distinguish between upper- and lowercase characters in a macro name.

Tip: Choose a special character or letter as the first entry in all macro names. When you use the F3 (Run) option, 1-2-3/G displays a list of all valid range names. To help distinguish macro names from other range names, start all of them with the same character. Using a special symbol like % places the macros at the front of the list.

You can obtain a list of all your current macro names and the range addresses to which they are assigned with the Range Name Table command. Select Range Name Table and respond to the table range prompt by entering the address of the upper-left cell in any blank section of the worksheet in which 1-2-3/G can write the macro name assignments. This command is described more fully in Chapter 5.

Documenting Your Macro

As you create a macro, you are aware of the name you have assigned to it and the function of each of its steps. A month from now, however, you may not remember what you wanted to accomplish. It is therefore wise to document information like the macro name and the function of each step on the worksheet as you create the macro.

It's a good documentation strategy to place the macro name in the cell immediately to the left of the top macro cell. If the macro is named Currency, type **currency** in the cell immediately to the left of the top macro cell. If the macro is named \a, you would enter **'\a** in the name cell. The ' prevents 1-2-3/G from interpreting the backslash as the repeating label indicator and filling your cell with the letter "a." If you have already placed the macro name in the cell to the left of your top macro cell before actually naming the macro range, you can use the Range Name Labels Right command to name the macro cell without typing the name again to define the macro name.

A column of cells to the right of the instructions is a good place for documenting macro instructions. Depending on the length of your macro entries, you can widen the column containing the macro instructions or move several cells to the right of the macro column for the documentation entries. A brief description of every command will clarify the function of each step and will save much time if you need to modify the macro later. In Figure 22-1 you saw a macro with documentation entries for the individual macro instructions.

Executing Your Macro

Once you have entered and named a macro, you can use it any time. 1-2-3/G supports macro execution from Ready mode or within a command. Macros can supply entries like graph titles or print headers. If your macro needs the cell pointer to be in a certain cell, position the cell pointer before executing the macro. The cell pointer needn't be on the macro cell for you to execute the macro.

If you name the macro with a backslash-letter combination, you can execute it in several ways. You can hold down the CTRL key and press the appropriate letter key. Alternately, you can press the ALT-F3 (Run) key, and 1-2-3/G displays all of the range names in active files, including macro names. This approach works for macros with any name. You can select a macro by typing the name in the text box and pressing ENTER, by highlighting the name you want to use and pressing ENTER, or by double-clicking the macro name in the list box. If you want to execute a macro that is stored in another file, select the filename from the list and 1-2-3/G will list the range and macro names in the selected file. If the macro is in the macro library, you can enter the macro name in the text box without supplying a filename.

Once the macro starts executing, 1-2-3/G continues executing macro instructions until it encounters a blank cell or a cell containing a value in the macro. You can stop a macro while it is executing by pressing CTRL-BREAK—this stops the macro and displays an error message. Once you select OK, 1-2-3/G returns to Ready mode, and you can return to editing your macro.

If you must start the macro at a specific location, consider adding to the macro the keystrokes that bring you to the desired location. For example, if a macro must start in A:A1, add {FIRSTCELL} or {FC} as the first macro instruction.

Tip: Save the worksheet in which you recorded the macro before trying it. If the macro contains mistakes, testing it will prevent you from losing your work if the macro writes over its own instructions or locks up your system. If the macro sheet contains other entries, you might want to use the File Save Backup feature to maintain the integrity of the existing file until after you've tested the macro.

Using the Keystroke Editor

1-2-3/G's Keystroke Editor can speed up macro entry. The Keystroke Editor automatically records your keystrokes. This feature means that you can use the keystrokes recorded to the buffer to define your macro actions. The Keystroke Editor records the entries required to represent keys and commands, so you don't have to record this information manually. The Keystroke Editor automatically records your keystrokes from the beginning of your 1-2-3/G session, whether or not the Keystroke Editor window is open. When you open the Keystroke Editor window, you can use the keystrokes 1-2-3/G is recording.

You open the Keystroke Editor using the desktop control menu or the Utility pull-down menu from a worksheet window. Using the desktop control menu, select Keystroke Editor. Using the worksheet tool menu, select Utility Macros Keystroke Editor. When the Keystroke Editor utility window is opened, it initially appears in the lower-left corner, as in Figure 22-2. You can use the Keystroke Editor's window control menu or the mouse equivalents to change the size and position or close the window. Figure 22-3 shows a Keystroke Editor window that is enlarged and repositioned to show more of the recorded keystrokes. The Keystroke Editor has its own menu. The File and Edit pull-down menus contain many of the same commands as in the File and Edit

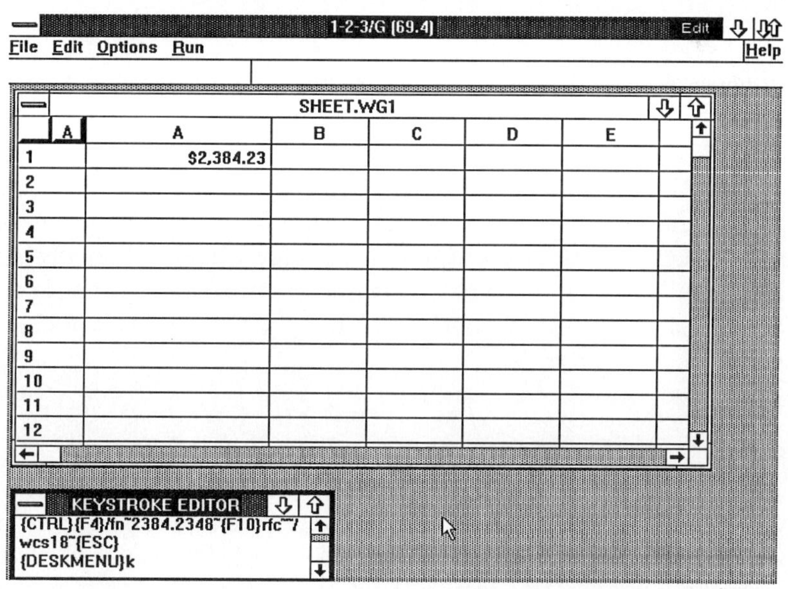

Figure 22-2. Keystrokes stored with the Keystroke Editor

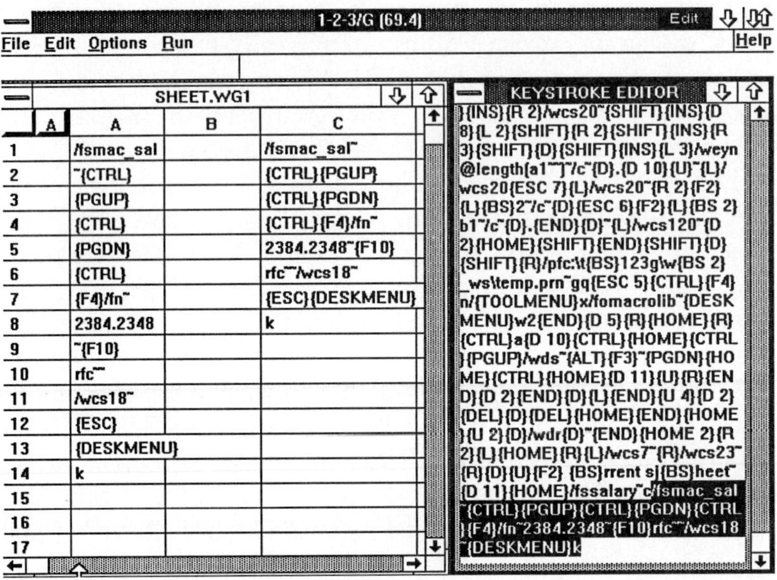

Figure 22-3. Recorded keystrokes copied to a worksheet

pull-down menus in graph and worksheet windows. The Edit menu includes a Clear All, which you can use to remove the keystrokes from 1-2-3/G's memory.

1-2-3/G uses 16K as a buffer to store your keystrokes. When the buffer is full, 1-2-3/G removes characters from the beginning of the recorded keystrokes. If the Keystroke Editor window is open when the buffer is full, 1-2-3/G removes 128 characters at a time. If the Keystroke Editor is closed when the buffer is full, 1-2-3/G removes one character for every character added.

Copying Keystrokes to the Worksheet

You can transfer keystrokes from the Keystroke Editor to a worksheet as the basis for your macro. You just select the keystrokes in the Keystroke Editor, copy them to the Clipboard, switch to the worksheet window, and paste them from the Clipboard to the worksheet. More information about using the Clipboard is included in Chapter 8. Once the keystrokes are in your worksheet, you can use them for macros, just as if you had entered the keystrokes yourself.

As an example, make a few entries so you have at least a few keystrokes recorded, even if you just started your 1-2-3/G session. First, select Range Format Currency and press ENTER twice. Next, select Worksheet Column Set width 18 and press ENTER. As you know, these entries format the current cell as Currency with two decimal places and widen the current column to 18. Notice that these instructions don't use the mouse. The Keystroke Editor records keystrokes, not the actions you perform with the mouse.

To work with these entries in the keyboard buffer, activate the Keystroke Editor window to see the window in Figure 22-2. The window may include additional entries, depending on your previous keystrokes. Notice that the Keystroke Editor window displays your entries exactly as you make them. Function keys and other special keys use the macro key names listed in Table 22-1. The Keystroke Editor uses the abbreviated form for the keyword wherever possible—such as {R} for {RIGHT} or {F2} instead of {EDIT}. Table 22-2 lists the keys you can use in the Keystroke Editor. As you can tell by the mode indicator, you are in Edit

Keystroke	Action
BACKSPACE	Deletes character to the left of the insertion point
CTRL-INSERT	Copies selected keystrokes to the Clipboard. Same as Edit Copy
DELETE	Deletes selected characters or, if no characters are selected, deletes the character to the right of the insertion point
SHIFT-DELETE	Copies selected keystrokes to the Clipboard, removing them from the Keystroke Editor window. Same as Edit Cut
SHIFT-END	Selects all characters to the right of the insertion point
SHIFT-HOME	Selects all characters to the left of the insertion point
SHIFT-INSERT	Copies the Clipboard contents to the insertion point's location. Same as Edit Paste
SHIFT-LEFT ARROW	Selects one character to the left starting at the insertion point
SHIFT-RIGHT ARROW	Selects one character to the right starting at the insertion point
SHIFT-UP ARROW	Selects one line above starting at the insertion point
SHIFT-DOWN ARROW	Selects one line down starting at the insertion point

Table 22-2. Editing Keys in the Keystroke Editor

mode when you use the Keystroke Editor. Edit mode changes how keys such as HOME and END behave in the Keystroke Editor window.

Despite any entries you have already made, you can see an entry like /rfc~ ~/wcs18~ or {F10}rfc~ ~{F10}wcs18~, which represents the Range and Worksheet commands you just entered. Move the insertion point before the / or {F10} that precedes the "r" representing the Range command (the second / or {F10} from the end). Use the keys listed in Table 22-2 to highlight the keys that you want to copy. For this example, you can either press SHIFT-END or SHIFT-DOWN ARROW. To use a mouse to select keys in the Keystroke Editor window, click the beginning of the keystrokes to highlight and then drag the mouse to thelast keystroke to highlight. You may also want to edit the keystrokes using DELETE and BACKSPACE to remove characters from the window—for example, if you make the wrong selection and have to press ESCAPE. To copy these keystrokes to the Clipboard, select Edit Copy or press CTRL-INSERT. Once the keystrokes are in the Clipboard, switch to the worksheet window and move the cell pointer to the first cell in which you want to store the macro keystrokes. From the worksheet window, select Edit Paste or press SHIFT-INSERT. 1-2-3/G copies the keystrokes to the worksheet.

1-2-3/G uses the column's width to divide the keystrokes into different cells. Figure 22-3 shows a keystroke window and the highlighted keys copied to A1 and C1. Since column A is narrower than column C in the example, column A uses more cells to store the keystrokes than column C.

Keywords in a macro are easier to understand when they are spelled out. Use Range Search with the Replace option to locate entries like {D} and change them to {DOWN}. You can even develop a macro to handle this task if you specify the search range to be used.

Use the Range Justify command to shift keystrokes from one cell to another.

Tip: When you are using the Keystroke Editor to record the keystrokes for a macro, move the mouse out of reach so that you aren't tempted to use it to make selections that the Keystroke Editor cannot record.

Executing Keystrokes in the Keystroke Editor

When you want to repeat a sequence of keystrokes without saving them, you can execute the highlighted keystrokes without copying them to a worksheet. This allows you to repeatedly tailor the format of cells, change the width settings for columns, or alter the Protection status of ranges of cells—all without saving the set of instructions as named macro instructions. You can also test that the keystrokes perform the intended task before you copy them to the worksheet.

To execute keystrokes in the Keystroke Editor, select Run Go. 1-2-3/G reactivates the previously active window and performs the appropriate keystrokes. If keystrokes are highlighted, 1-2-3/G performs the selected keystrokes. If no keystrokes are highlighted when you select Run Go, 1-2-3/G performs all of the keystrokes in the buffer.

As an example, try these directions to format selected columns that are evenly spaced on a worksheet:

1. Move to the top of the first column that you want to format in a worksheet window. Select Range Format Currency, type a **0** for the number of decimal places, and press ENTER. When prompted for a range, press END and then press DOWN ARROW. Finally, select the OK command button or press ENTER.

2. Press RIGHT ARROW to move to the top of the next column to be formatted.

3. Activate the Keystroke Editor either by pressing ALT-SPACEBAR and selecting Keystroke Editor, or by selecting Utility Macros Keystroke Editor.

4. Highlight the keystrokes that look like /rfc0~{END}{D}{R} or {F10}rfc0~{END}{D}{R}.

5. Select Run Go. 1-2-3/G formats the column and moves to the next column to be formatted.

Using the Keystroke Editor to Undo Mistakes

In Chapter 5, you learned how to use Edit Undo to remove the effect of up to the last 20 actions. If you realize later that you have made a mistake, you can use the Keystroke Editor to remove the effect of the mistake. You can use the Keystroke Editor to remove some of the changes you have made since you saved the file. To do this, retrieve the previously saved version of the file. Next, activate the Keystroke Editor window and remove the keystrokes that caused the mistake. For example, if you accidentally delete a row, find and delete /wdr~. You should also remove the keystrokes that you made working with a different worksheet file and the keystrokes that retrieved the previous version of the file you are using. Once the desired keystrokes are deleted, select Run Go. This performs all of the keystrokes in the buffer on the current file. While this solution does not always work (especially if you use the mouse to make your selections), it can save a great deal of time. For example, you can remove the effect of a mistake you made in the beginning of the session yet retain your other changes.

Other Recorder Menu Options

1-2-3/G has other commands that you can use in the Keystroke Editor window. One command is the Edit Clear All command, which empties the buffer. You may want to clear the keystroke buffer when you are beginning to record a substantial set of keystrokes you want to incorporate into a macro.

Under Options, you can activate several options. By selecting Options Debug, you can activate the Step mode and open a Trace window. This produces the same results as pressing ALT-F2 (Step) and SHIFT-F2 (Trace), which are discussed later with debugging macros. By selecting Options Minimize on Run, you can select whether 1-2-3/G reduces the Keystroke Editor to an icon when you select Run Go. This is a toggle. When the check mark appears next to Minimize on Run in the Options pull-down menu, the Keystroke Editor window changes to an icon when you select Run Go. When the check mark does not appear, the Keystroke Editor window does not change to an icon when you select Run Go. Selecting Options Pause Recording halts the recording of keystrokes. Like Options Minimize on Run, Options Pause Recording is a toggle that places a check next to Pause Recording to indicate that 1-2-3/G is not recording keystrokes.

Creating a Macro Library

A macro library is simply a worksheet file that contains several macros. With 1-2-3/G, you can use this concept effectively, since the macros and the files they work on can be different (as long as the macros are in an open worksheet window). A macro library is designed to hold the macros that you use with multiple files. When you select a macro to execute (unless you specifically select the file containing the macro to execute), 1-2-3/G first checks for a macro with the selected name in the current worksheet file, and then checks the macro library worksheet file.

A macro library file is any worksheet file called MACROLIB.WG1. This allows you to create one macro library worksheet file in each directory. Your separate macro library file can be in any worksheet in the file. You might want to start in sheet A at the beginning of the file, since the file does not contain other types of data. You can also group the macros, using different sheets to group a single type of macros. For example, you can group formatting macros, data-entry macros, and print and graph macros. This makes it easier to find macros when you need them. If you decide to create some specialized macros in a worksheet file with a model or a database, you may want to store them on a separate sheet. This minimizes the risk of damage to the macro when you change the application area of the file.

If you use macro libraries to store macros that you will use with many files, you must load the library into memory before using any of its macros. If your application file is already in memory, you can use the File Open command. You may want to minimize the macro library so it occupies less desktop space (the macros will still be available).

When you want to add a new macro to your library file, make the macro library file the current file. Enter the new macro; it will be available for use with your other active files. Save the macro library file under its original filename. To add a macro to the library from another worksheet, use the Copy command to copy the macro from the original worksheet file to the macro library worksheet file. Once the macro is copied, name it in the MACROLIB.WG1 worksheet file, since the Copy command does not copy range names. You can also use the Clipboard to transfer macros between worksheet files. This method also allows you to paste keystrokes from the Keystroke Editor window.

When you want the macro in the MACROLIB.WG1 worksheet file to use a cell in the MACROLIB.WG1 worksheet file, *make sure to include* <<MACROLIB.WG1>> before the cell address or range name. If you omit the filename, 1-2-3/G uses the current worksheet.

Tip: Start each macro in the macro library with a character such as ! or %. This distinguishes the macros in the macro library from the macros in other worksheet files. When both the macro library and the current worksheet file contain macros with the same name, 1-2-3/G will perform the macro in the current worksheet file.

Debugging Macros

The debugging process involves testing and correcting macros to ensure that you obtain the desired results. With keyboard macros, it's easy to forget to enter the tilde mark to represent each press of the ENTER key. 1-2-3/G has two aids that help you find errors in your macro. You can use a Trace window to follow the macro instructions visually, and you can use Step mode to slow the execution of the macro. You activate both of these debugging aids with the Utility Macros Debug command or the equivalent function keys.

A Trace window displays the macro instructions that 1-2-3/G is executing, which can help you find errors. You can add the Trace window by pressing SHIFT-F2 (Trace) or selecting the Trace check box in the Utility Macros Debug dialog box (this key is a toggle).

In Step mode, a macro is executed one keystroke at a time so you can follow its progress and spot any area of difficulty. You can switch to Step mode by pressing ALT-F2 (Step) or selecting the Single Step check box in the Utility Macros Debug dialog box. (Step mode is a toggle operation.) When step mode is on, Step displays in the desktop title bar.

When the Step indicator is on, any macro you invoke is executed one instruction at a time. Press SPACEBAR whenever you are ready for the next instruction. You can use a Trace window to display the macro commands being executed. While the macro is executing, SST appears in place of Step in the desktop title bar.

Tip: If you have a lengthy macro that has an error in the middle, you can add a {STEP} macro instruction before the macro reaches the error to change to Step mode. This way, 1-2-3/G can quickly perform the beginning of the macro, and can slow the macro where you think the problem is occurring so you can debug the macro.

Automatic Macros

1-2-3/G allows you to create an automatic macro for a worksheet. Every time you retrieve a worksheet that contains an automatic macro, 1-2-3/G immediately executes this macro. This feature is generally used with the advanced macro commands discussed in Chapter 23. However, you may want to execute a File Combine or a Range Erase command as soon as a worksheet is retrieved, as an example. You can also suspend execution of automatic macros.

Creating an Automatic Macro

The only difference between creating an automatic macro and a normal executable macro is in the macro name. There can be only one automatic macro on a worksheet, and it must have the name \0 (backslash zero).

Figure 22-4 shows an automatic macro designed to erase a range of input cells in the worksheet in Figure 22-5 every time the worksheet is retrieved. This lets each new operator enter new values for the principal, monthly or yearly payments, and term. To create this macro, place your instructions into a column of worksheet cells on the worksheet file that will trigger its execution, and assign the name \0 to the name cell. Then save the worksheet file with File Save. The next time the worksheet is retrieved, the macro executes immediately.

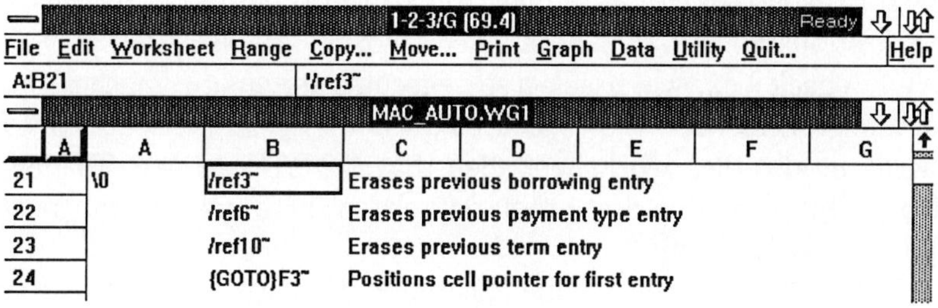

1-2-3/G (69.4) Ready

File Edit Worksheet Range Copy... Move... Print Graph Data Utility Quit... Help

A:B21 '/ref3~

MAC_AUTO.WG1

A	A	B	C	D	E	F	G
21	\0	/ref3~	Erases previous borrowing entry				
22		/ref6~	Erases previous payment type entry				
23		/ref10~	Erases previous term entry				
24		{GOTO}F3~	Positions cell pointer for first entry				

Figure 22-4. Automatic macro to erase worksheet cells

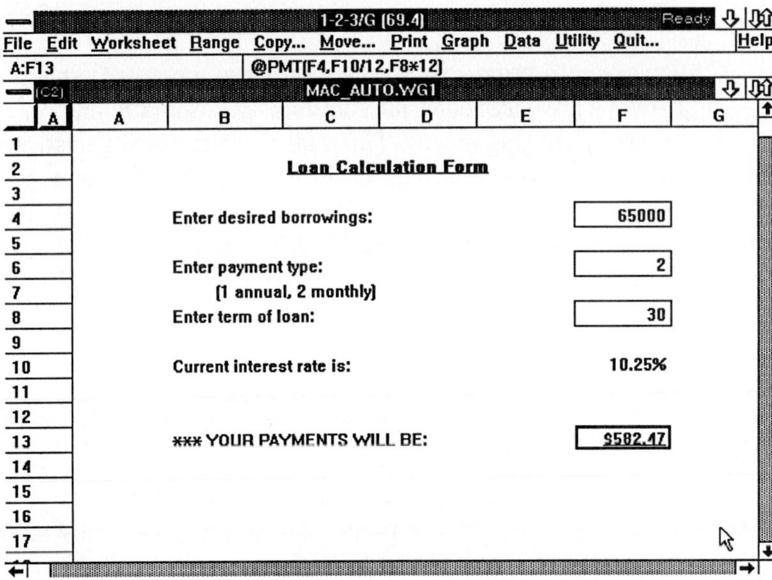

Figure 22-5. Worksheet example with cells that macro erases

Tip: An automatic macro in a macro library worksheet executes when you retrieve the macro library worksheet. You must store an automatic macro in the file in which you want the macro to execute automatically.

Disabling Automatic Macros

If you unselect the check boxes below Autoexec in the Worksheet Global Default dialog box, 1-2-3/G does not execute automatic macros. When you first install 1-2-3/G, both check boxes are selected. The Native (.WG1) check box, when selected, executes automatic macros in .WG1 worksheet files. The Other check box, when selected, executes automatic macros in all other worksheet files that 1-2-3/G can use. To make the changes made to this and other default settings permanent, select the Update command button.

With 1-2-3/G's multiple file capabilities, you can have macros executing other automatic macros. For instance, if a macro in file A contains an instruction that opens file B, and file B contains an automatic macro, the setting for Worksheet Global Default Autoexec determines which macro 1-2-3/G executes after opening Worksheet B. If the check box appropriate for the file type of Worksheet B is not selected, the automatic macro in File A will continue. If the check box appropriate for the file type of Worksheet B is selected, the automatic macro in File B will begin execution once 1-2-3/G opens file B.

Ready-to-Use Macros

The macros in the following sections are ready to use; they are complete macros designed to perform the tasks described. Since your data is probably located in files, sheets, or cells different from the data on the worksheets used to create these examples, you will have to modify the cell addresses referenced in the macros. Each macro description includes guidelines for its use, and a section on potential modifications.

All macro names are in A1 to the left of the top cell in the macro. The macro is written in column B as label entries. A description is placed in widened column C. The macros use uppercase characters to indicate cell addresses, filenames, and special keys indicators such as {TOOLMENU} and {END}. Lowercase letters indicate menu selections and range names.

Worksheet Macros

Many repetitive worksheet tasks are candidates for macros. Examples are changing the global format, checking the worksheet status, moving between worksheets or between files, and changing default settings like the printer interface. You can even have a macro do some of your typing in worksheet cells. For example, you can create a date macro that enters the repetitive keystrokes while you supply the essential year, month, and day information. You can have a macro change an entry to enhance it or to cover up existing errors.

A Macro to Display Formulas

1-2-3/G prints the formulas behind your worksheet results when you specify Print Printer Format Formulas, but it creates one line of printed output per cell. If you want to display or print out formulas while maintaining the integrity of your worksheet design, you have to change the format of each formula cell to Text. You can use a macro to simplify the task.

```
     A      B             C
1    \t     /wgft         Request global format as text
2           /rfr          Request range format reset
3           A:~           Specify range A: as range to reset
4           /wcca:{TAB}f  Widen columns where needed
```

The instructions in the first line request Worksheet Global Format Text. If there are no range formats for your worksheet cells, you could end the macro at this point. Since most worksheets do use a range format to override the global setting, this macro is designed to work with these established settings. It uses Range Format Reset to make all the cells conform to the global format setting of Text. This command is recorded in B2. Next, the range A: removes the format from every cell in sheet A. With the cells formatted as Text, the Worksheet Column Column range Fit largest command adjusts each column's width to display the entries formatted as Text.

Guidelines for Use You must save your worksheet before executing this macro. You shouldn't save your worksheet afterward, since all your regular formats are removed and displayed as text.

Modifying the Macro You may want to add an instruction at the beginning of the macro to save your current worksheet file, so that you do not lose your established formats. The only risk is that you might execute the macro a second time and overlay your existing file with the Text formatted version.

You can also add the commands necessary to print the file. You could place these instructions at the end of the macro. You can alter the macro to select the range to print with a specification of {HOME}..{END}{HOME}. This approach selects A1 as the first cell in the range, and the last cell in the sheet is used as the last cell in the range. You could add a Worksheet Erase command after the Print commands so that the version displaying the worksheet formulas is not saved to disk when the macro ends.

A Macro to Insert Blank Rows

1-2-3/G prevents you from leaving blank rows between column headings and data if you wish to perform Data Query operations on a database. You can, however, create macros that add and delete blank rows. When you use the worksheet for calculations and printed reports, use the macro that inserts blank rows. When you perform a query, you can invoke the macro that deletes blank rows and forms the required database structure. In fact, you could make this macro a part of a Data Query macro.

This macro inserts blank rows:

```
     A        B           C
1    insert   /wi         Request worksheet insert
2             r           Specify rows
3             {DOWN 2}~   Move down to insert 3 rows
```

The macro as shown adds three blank rows, but you can easily modify it to add any number you choose. The first macro instruction, in B1, selects Worksheet Insert. The next instruction specifies that rows rather than columns should be inserted. The third instruction expands the insertion to three rows. B3 uses the shortcut approach for moving the cell pointer by writing this instruction as {DOWN 2}~.

Guidelines for Use This macro requires that you place your cell pointer where you want to insert the blank rows, since they are added at the cell pointer's position. When you invoke the macro, the cell-pointer row is shifted down to make room for the new rows. As with a keyboard entry of the same command, your formulas are adjusted to reflect the addition, but insertions at the top or bottom of a range don't expand the range.

Modifying the Macro By changing the entry in B2, you could create a macro that inserts columns or sheets. If you choose to add sheets, you need to indicate that you want the sheets inserted either before or after the current sheet by including a "B" or an "A" after the "S" in B2 that would replace the "R" for Rows. You may also wish to modify the last instruction, to allow for the addition of extra rows, columns, or sheets. You could also end the macro after line 2 and allow the operator to specify the number of rows, columns, or sheets to be added. You can use a range name and use the range name's size to specify the number of rows.

A Macro to Change the Global Default Directory

When you are working with completed worksheet models, you may want your directory set at drive C if all of your completed models are stored on the hard drive. If you have a number of new models to create and wish to store them on a floppy disk, you may want the directory set at drive B. You may also wish to change the directory if you use 1-2-3/G for two different sets of applications. Changing the drive with a macro eliminates the need to remember the path required with certain 1-2-3/G commands.

The following macro changes the existing directory to drive B:

```
     A         B         C
1    CHG_Dirb  /uu       Request worksheet global change
2              d         Specify a directory change
3              w         Select Working directory
4              B:\~      Set new directory
```

The first instruction selects Utility User Settings. You can also write this macro instruction as {DESKMENU}u. The next two specify a directory change and the working directory. The instruction in B4 generates and finalizes the new directory setting, and returns to Ready mode.

Guidelines for Use When you change the directory, both the old and the new directories must be available on the system you are using to change the settings. If you are changing the directory to a floppy drive, place a data disk in the drive before executing the macro, since 1-2-3/G attempts to read the directory for the selected device. You can also use this macro to change the subdirectory for model storage and retrieval if you are using a hard disk.

Modifying the Macro B4 contains the instruction you may want to modify in this macro. B4 should contain the path name of the device and directory you plan to use for data storage. As an example, if you are currently using C:\123G\WORK and want to change to a subdirectory, you might change this instruction to read C:\123G\DALLAS\SALES\.

A Macro to Set the Window to Perspective and Move to the First Sheet

When you are working with multiple sheets, the Worksheet Window Perspective command makes it easier to work with your data. If you change frequently from a consolidation sheet to one of the detail sheets, you might want several macros to handle some of these changes for you. For example, this macro creates a perspective view and then moves to the first sheet:

```
     A       B             C
1    \w      /wwp          Use perspective window
2            {FIRSTCELL}   Move to A:A1 in the first sheet
```

The consolidated sheet might look something like Figure 22-6 before you invoke the macro. The first instruction sets the screen to a three-window perspective, and the second instruction moves the cell pointer to the first sheet in the current file, providing the display in Figure 22-7. Although the macro only saves a few keystrokes, it can still save time if you need to execute the task frequently. In addition, using a macro frees you from having to remember the commands.

Guidelines for Use You can use this macro to see a perspective view, regardless of the sheet you are on. You can combine this macro with other macros so it does more than display the worksheet in a perspective view.

Modifying the Macro You can modify the macro to generate a Map window, or a horizontally or vertically split screen. You can also activate a sheet other than the first sheet.

A Macro to Change the Global Printer Default Setup

With OS/2, you can install more than one printer. You can have both a dot matrix and a letter-quality printer attached to your system or

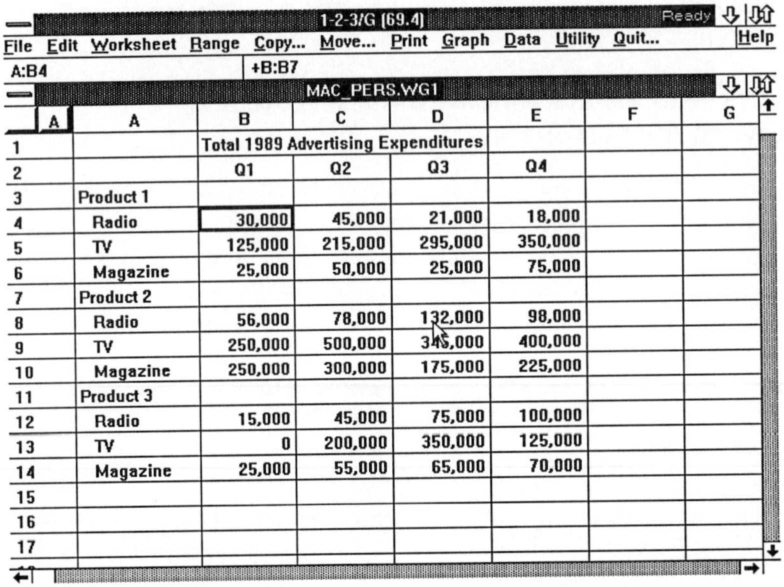

1-2-3/G [69.4] Ready

File Edit Worksheet Range Copy... Move... Print Graph Data Utility Quit... Help

A:B4 +B:B7

MAC_PERS.WG1

	A	B	C	D	E	F	G
1		Total 1989 Advertising Expenditures					
2		Q1	Q2	Q3	Q4		
3	Product 1						
4	Radio	30,000	45,000	21,000	18,000		
5	TV	125,000	215,000	295,000	350,000		
6	Magazine	25,000	50,000	25,000	75,000		
7	Product 2						
8	Radio	56,000	78,000	132,000	98,000		
9	TV	250,000	500,000	345,000	400,000		
10	Magazine	250,000	300,000	175,000	225,000		
11	Product 3						
12	Radio	15,000	45,000	75,000	100,000		
13	TV	0	200,000	350,000	125,000		
14	Magazine	25,000	55,000	65,000	70,000		
15							
16							
17							

Figure 22-6. Worksheet before macro is performed

network. You may want to use the letter-quality printer to print most worksheets, and the dot matrix printer to print graphs or quick drafts of a model.

If you want to change the default printer used when you request Print, you can create a macro to make the switch. This way, the macro selects the correct printer and you don't even have to know the printer's name. Here is a macro for changing the default printer:

```
     A        B            C
1    \s       /fpd         Select File Print Destination
2             p            Choose printer
3             PRINTER1~    Enter the printer name in text box
```

The first line selects File Print Destination. The next line selects Printer. The third line enters the printer name PRINTER1 in the text box below Printer.

A printer can use several settings, including changing the margins and printer quality. You can use a macro to change the printer settings

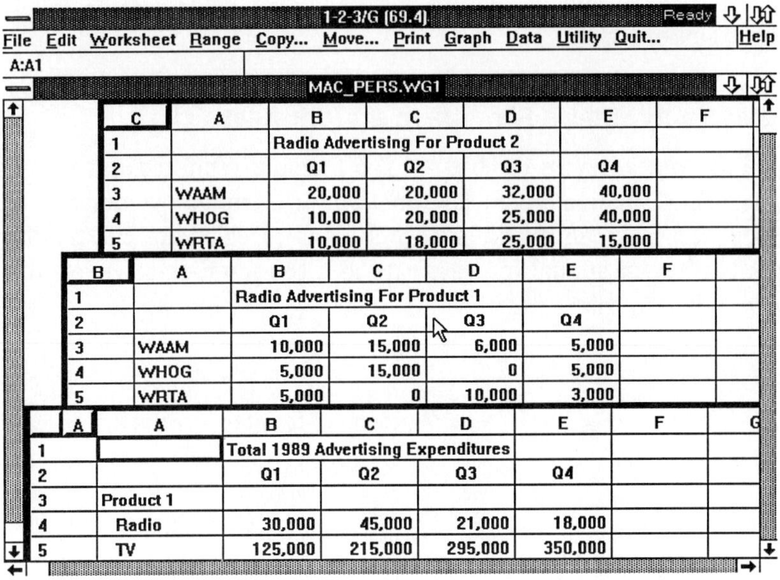

1-2-3/G [69.4] Ready

File Edit Worksheet Range Copy... Move... Print Graph Data Utility Quit... Help

A:A1

MAC_PERS.WG1

C	A	B	C	D	E	F
1		Radio Advertising For Product 2				
2		Q1	Q2	Q3	Q4	
3	WAAM	20,000	20,000	32,000	40,000	
4	WHOG	10,000	20,000	25,000	40,000	
5	WRTA	10,000	18,000	25,000	15,000	

B	A	B	C	D	E	F
1		Radio Advertising For Product 1				
2		Q1	Q2	Q3	Q4	
3	WAAM	10,000	15,000	6,000	5,000	
4	WHOG	5,000	15,000	0	5,000	
5	WRTA	5,000	0	10,000	3,000	

A	A	B	C	D	E	F
1		Total 1989 Advertising Expenditures				
2		Q1	Q2	Q3	Q4	
3	Product 1					
4	Radio	30,000	45,000	21,000	18,000	
5	TV	125,000	215,000	295,000	350,000	

Figure 22-7. Macro setting a Perspective window display

available through the File Print Options dialog box. However, you can't use a macro to change the printer settings available through Setup in the File Print Destination dialog box. When you select the Setup command button, you are switching from 1-2-3/G to OS/2, and 1-2-3/G macros cannot change settings recorded within OS/2.

Guidelines for Use Before creating and executing this macro, you need to know the name of the printer the macro will select. You can view a list of printer names set up for your system by selecting File Print Destination. The text box below Printer lists the available printer names. If you want to change the printers available in the list, you must use the Control Panel program (OS.2 version 1.1) or the Print Manager program (OS/2 version 1.2).

Modifying the Macro You must modify the entry in B3 to match a printer named installed on your system. You could also expand this macro to include a change to the default settings for other print features, such as margins and display options available through the File Print Options menu.

A Macro to Enter a Formula in a Worksheet Cell

You can use a macro to help enter a formula. You just have to start the macro and then supply the function or formula arguments that the macro uses. As an example, if you want to calculate the monthly payment using an annual interest rate and the number of years, the macro may look like this:

```
     A        B           C
1    \f       @PMT(       Enter @PMT in current cell
2             {?}         Wait for operator to enter principal
3             ,           Enter comma after principal
4             {?}         Wait for operator to enter interest
5             /12,        Add /12, after interest
6             {?}         Wait for operator to enter term
7             *12)~       Add *12) and finalize
8             /rfc2~~     Format as Currency, two decimals
9             /wcs9.5~    Set column width to 9.5
```

This macro is designed to make its entries in the current cell and begins by entering the keystrokes @PMT(.

When the macro executes the first input instruction, {?}, it waits for you to make an entry and stores your keystrokes in the cell. Then it adds a comma to the cell and waits for additional input. After the second input, the macro adds /12 to convert the annual interest rate to a monthly interest rate, and adds another comma to separate the second function argument from the third. After the third input instruction is executed, the macro adds *12 to convert the number of years to the number of months. The cell entry is completed with an entry of the closing parenthesis.

B8 contains the Range Format request for the cell in which the entry is just made. The column containing the cell is set to a width of 9.5 via a request for Worksheet Column Set width 9.5. Figure 22-8 shows the result of using the macro three times in different worksheet cells.

Guidelines for Use The {?} method of input does not provide a message prompt. However, the operator should know to enter the principal and press ENTER, then the interest rate and press ENTER, and then

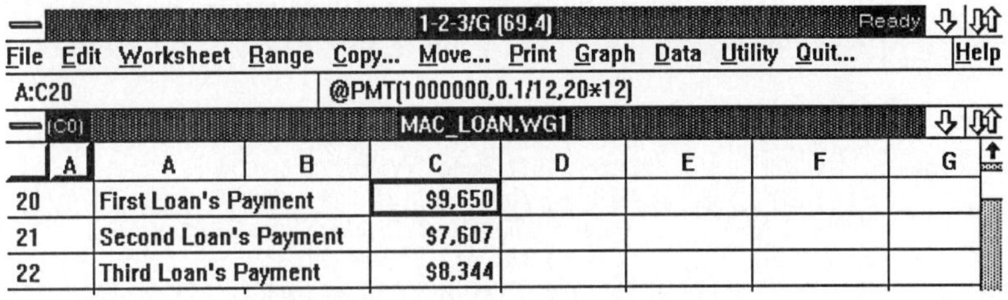

	A	B	C	D	E	F	G
20	First Loan's Payment		$9,650				
21	Second Loan's Payment		$7,607				
22	Third Loan's Payment		$8,344				

Figure 22-8. Worksheet with loan payments entered

the number of years and press ENTER, since the @PMT function requires this argument order. In Chapter 23, you will learn how to use the {GETLABEL} macro command to create prompts for the user.

Modifying the Macro You can modify this macro to use any of 1-2-3/G's built-in @functions. Just begin the macro with a different keyword. The number of input statements depend on the number of arguments used in the particular @function.

In Chapter 23, you will learn how to make a macro like this one display prompts as it fills a complete column of cells. With the current macro, you would have to move to another cell and reexecute the macro if you wished to enter additional dates.

A Macro to Round Formulas

When you format worksheet cells, you may choose a format that displays less than the full number of decimal places in a number. 1-2-3/G will round the displayed number to the specified number of decimal places. However, the internal storage of the number still retains its full accuracy. Calculations will use the stored number, not the displayed one. This can result in a total that seems not to agree with the figures in the cells above it. The two alternatives to this problem are to use the @ROUND function or to use the Range Attributes Precision command.

The @ROUND function rounds the internally stored number to the number of decimal places you specify. However, you have to enclose your numbers or formulas in the @ROUND function arguments, and supply the position in the entry at which rounding should take place. When a number of formulas are involved, this can be a tedious process. You can create a macro like this to make most of the entries for you:

```
     A        B           C
1    round    {EDIT}      Enter Edit mode for current cell
2             {HOME}      Move to the front of the entry
3             @ROUND(     Insert @ROUND( at beginning of entry
4             {END}       Move to the end of the entry
5             ,0)~        Specify 0 decimal places and finalize
```

The first instruction enables the Edit mode for the current cell. The cell pointer is moved to the front of the entry. Next, the keystrokes @ROUND(are added at the front of the entry. The pointer is then moved to the end of the entry with the instruction in B4. The keystrokes ,0) are placed at the end of the entry to complete the arguments for @ROUND, and the entry is finalized with the tilde (~).

Guidelines for Use This macro is position dependent. It rounds only the formula or number at the cell pointer location to the specified number of decimal places (in this example, 0). You must move the cell pointer and reexecute the macro to round additional cells.

Modifying the Macro You can easily modify the macro to round to any number of decimal places. Simply change the number in B5 to reflect the desired number of decimal places. The places for rounding are described under the @ROUND function in Chapter 9.

You could also change this macro to allow the operator to enter the place of rounding. The operator types the number and presses ENTER to include it in the instruction.

In Chapter 23, you will learn how to create a loop with the macro instructions; you can modify this macro to round a whole column of numbers with one execution of the macro.

A Macro to Handle Data Entry Errors

Macros can correct a variety of data input errors. They are especially valuable since 1-2-3/G gives you access to all the string @functions.

For example, suppose employees' names are entered in proper case in your database:

Jeff Jones

Some string @functions are case sensitive, such as @EXACT, @HLOOKUP, and @VLOOKUP. If someone enters names as BOB BROWN or bill smith in your database, you may have trouble using these @functions to match or locate database entries. It can be time consuming to make all the entries match. However, you can create a macro like this that will change any entry into proper case:

```
    A       B              C
1   proper  {EDIT}         Enter Edit mode for current cell
2           {HOME}{DEL}    Delete label indicator
3           @PROPER("      Enter @PROPER @function
4           {END}          Move to the end of the entry
5           "){CALC}~      Add " & ), calculate then finalize
```

The macro begins by preparing to edit the current cell. It then moves to the Home position (A1) and deletes the label indicator in the first position. The @PROPER function is entered, followed by (and ", since the string entry from the current cell must be enclosed in double quotes. The instruction in B4 moves the cell pointer to the end of the entry. The last instruction adds the " at the end and follows it with a). Before finalizing the entry, the macro recalculates the formula so it can be stored in the cell as a label rather than a formula.

Guidelines for Use This macro is position dependent. It only changes proper case the label entry at the cell pointer location. You must move the cell pointer and reexecute the macro to change additional cells.

Modifying the Macro If you want your data in uppercase, you can use the @UPPER function in place of @PROPER. For lowercase, use @LOWER.

A Macro to Enter a Worksheet Heading

If you need to create a whole series of worksheets that use the same heading, you can place the heading instructions in a macro and use them in each worksheet. Since the macro begins the heading at the cell pointer location, the headings need not start in the same position in each worksheet.

The following macro places headings for the quarters of the year across a worksheet:

```
     A        B              C
1    heading  ^QTR1{RIGHT}   Enter QTR1 and move 1 cell right
2             ^QTR2{RIGHT}   Enter QTR2 and move 1 cell right
3             ^QTR3{RIGHT}   Enter QTR3 and move 1 cell right
4             ^QTR4{RIGHT}   Enter QTR4 and move 1 cell right
5             ^TOTAL~        Enter TOTAL and press ENTER
6             {LEFT 4}       Move to the left four cells
7             {DOWN}         Move down 1 cell
```

Each of the first four macro instructions center justifies one of the quarter headings in a worksheet cell, and moves one cell to the right. The instruction in B5 places the heading TOTAL in a cell and finalizes the entry with ENTER. The cell pointer is then moved to the cell containing ^QTR1. The last instruction moves the cell pointer down one cell.

Guidelines for Use The macro places the first heading at the cell pointer location and moves to the right with subsequent entries. It is important that you position your cell pointer in the first cell where you want the headings before executing thc macro.

Modifying the Macro You can modify the macro to create any series of headings, like the months of the year, weeks of the month, multiple years, or account numbers. You just need to change are the headings themselves. You can easily modify the label prefix that begins each heading entry as well, if you want to use different justification.

You can modify this macro to create account names down a column. The only difference is that the cell pointer would be moved down after each entry, and the caret symbol (^) for center justification would not be used.

Range Macros

You can create macros for all the Range commands that you use frequently. They can be either open-ended macros or closed ones. An open-ended macro returns control to the operator before the range is selected. For example, if you want a macro to format cells as Currency with zero decimal places, you would record the following keystrokes:

/rfc0~

If you end the macro at this point, it is open-ended, since the operator can complete the range specification.

The macro would be closed if you supplied the range as part of the formula, for example:

/rfc0~{DOWN 5}~

or

/rfc0~a1..d12~

Closed macros are more limited in their application, since they function only under one defined set of circumstances.

If you are developing macros for yourself, open-ended macros add flexibility. If you are developing them for someone else and want to maintain as much control over the application as possible, try closed macros.

A Macro to Create a Range Name Table

The Range Name Table command lists all of the range names and their cell addresses in a table on your worksheet. However, this table is not refreshed automatically as you add new range names; you must execute the command sequence again to update the table.

The following short macro can easily handle this task:

	A	B	C
1	\z	{GOTO}G5~	Position cursor at range table
2		/rnt~	Request range name table

The first instruction positions the cell pointer in the upper-left corner of the area in which you want your table to appear—cell G5, in this example. The second instruction is a request for the Range Name Table command.

Guidelines for Use Before executing this macro, make sure the area to the right and below G5 (or wherever you send the cell pointer) is empty, since the macro overwrites any data that is stored there with the Range Table list. If you plan to print the table of range names, you should execute this macro before printing to ensure that your table of names is current.

Modifying the Macro You can modify the macro to supply a complete range address or range name for the table. 1-2-3/G uses as many cells as necessary for the table, whether you specify a cell address or a range address or range name. When the table of range names is built, the first column always contains the range names, the second column contains the address defined for the range names, and the third column displays the type of range name.

File Macros

You can automate any of the File commands with a macro. Although File Save and File Retrieve don't require many keystrokes, you can still make macros for them because they are used so frequently. You can also automate other File commands, such as Combine and Xtract. This may cut down on typing errors, since the same keystrokes are executed each time.

A Macro to Save Files

A File Save does not require many keystrokes, but you should do it frequently to prevent data loss. You can create a macro to save your file with one keystroke, as follows:

```
    A       B          C
1   \s      /fs        Request file save
2           ~          Specify existing file name
3           r          Replace file
```

The first line of the macro invokes the File Save command. The tilde (~) in line 2 indicates that you want to retain the file's existing name. The final line tells 1-2-3/G to replace the file on disk with the current contents of memory.

Guidelines for Use This macro saves a file that has been saved previously. You cannot use it if you want to use a new name for the file.

Modifying the Macro You can easily modify the macro to allow your input of the filename. Simply use an input statement between line 1 and line 2 of the macro. If you prefer, you can place a predetermined filename in the macro in the same location. In Chapter 23, this macro is enhanced using the @CELLPOINTER function so you can save the macro in the macro library. This way, you can use the macro with any open file. The @CELLPOINTER function will adjust the filename that the macro uses to match the current file name.

A Macro to Retrieve Files

The following File Retrieve macro calls a new file into memory. The worksheet containing the macro may no longer be resident in memory when the retrieve operation is completed. Such a macro is normally used as part of a larger macro that chooses the task you want to have performed and retrieves the appropriate file.

A Retrieve macro might look like this:

```
     A      B          C
1    \r     /fr        Request file retrieve
2           SALES~     Specify SALES file
```

The first line of the macro issues the request to retrieve a file. The second line contains the filename and the tilde (~) to finalize the filename entry.

Guidelines for Use The macro erases the worksheet in the worksheet window that is current when the macro is executed. If you changed the current worksheet file, 1-2-3/G asks if you want to save the worksheet file before retrieving the selected file. In contrast, the File Open or File New command would retain the current worksheet file on the desktop.

Modifying the Macro You can modify the macro to add a File Save before the File Retrieve. You can also change the name of the file being saved.

If you want, you can modify the macro so it has a name of \0. This causes 1-2-3/G to retrieve the second file as soon as the first one is retrieved. In this situation, you will probably want to add some other macro instructions at the beginning, to perform a few tasks in the current file before retrieving the new file.

A Macro to Extract Files

The File Xtract command saves a section of a worksheet in a separate worksheet file. You can use this command to transfer end-of-period totals to a new worksheet for the next period, for example. If you need to extract data from files frequently, consider the time-saving features of the following macro:

```
     A          B                C
1    extract    /fxv             Request value extract
2               TOTALS~~         Specify filename TOTALS
3               year_end_total~  Enter range name to extract
4               r                Specify replace
```

The first line contains a request to perform a File Xtract Values operation to save the values from the original file. The next step contains the name of the file in which you want the new material saved. The second tilde is to omit entering a file description. In this macro, the filename is TOTALS. The next instruction tells 1-2-3/G what to place in the new file; you can specify a range address or a range name. This macro uses the range name YEAR_END_TOTAL. The R in the last instruction tells 1-2-3/G to replace the TOTALS file with the current contents of YEAR_END_TOTAL.

Guidelines for Use This macro operates on two assumptions. First, it assumes that the range name YEAR_END_TOTAL is already created. Second, it assumes that the file TOTALS has already been created, since it requests that 1-2-3/G replace it.

Modifying the Macro You can modify the macro to use a range address rather than a range name for the extract area. You can also modify the filename used and add a description. The operator can enter either of these while the macro is executing if you use an input instruction.

A Macro to Combine Files

The File Combine command allows you to add data from files on disk to the current worksheet, without erasing the current worksheet as a File Retrieve operation would do. A macro that can combine the four worksheet files in Figure 22-9 is shown here:

```
     A         B              C
1    combine   {HOME}         Move to A1
2              /fcaeREGION1~  Select File Combine Add for Region1
3              /fcaeREGION2~  Select File Combine Add for Region2
4              /fcaeREGION3~  Select File Combine Add for Region3
5              /fcaeREGION4~  Select File Combine Add for Region4
```

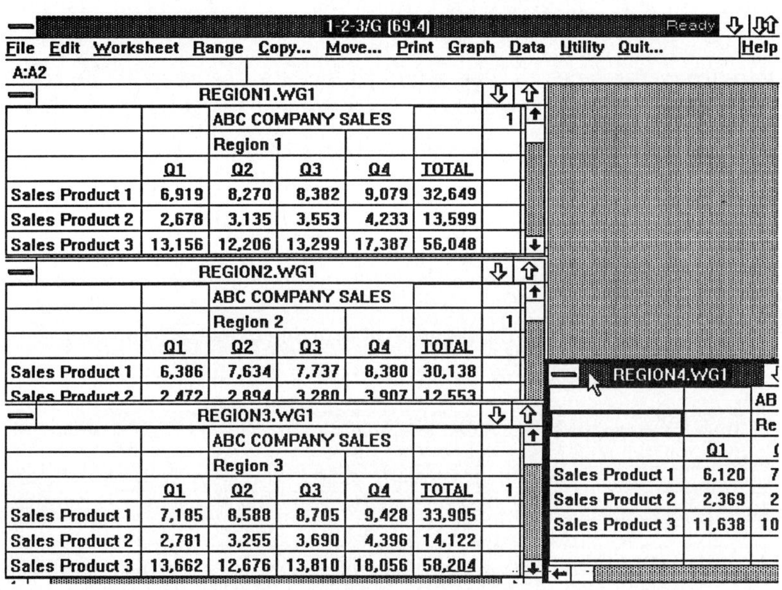

Figure 22-9. Sections from worksheets that will be combined

The final product of the macro is shown in Figure 22-10, where each figure represents the combined totals of each of the four company regions.

Each of the detail worksheets contains a 1 in column G in the row number that corresponds to the region number. After the macro has added all four regions to the consolidated company template, the four cells in column G should each contain a 1, as they do in Figure 22-10. These 1's confirm that each detail sheet is combined with the total worksheet only once, since each detail sheet has a 1 in a different location. In addition to saving keystrokes, this macro ensures that the combining process is handled consistently and accurately. When you are entering File Combine commands from the keyboard to consolidate many worksheets, it is easy to forget which combining operations have been completed.

After moving to the Home position to ensure correct cell pointer placement, the macro executes the File Combine instructions that follow. The four Combine instructions are the same except for the filenames being combined. Each requests a File Combine Add Entire file operation for the appropriate region file.

Guidelines for Use The region files are assumed to be in the current directory when you execute this macro. Each of the region files is also assumed to have a format identical to that of the file in memory. The region file should contain a 1 in column G in the row that corresponds to the region number (rows 1 through 4). As noted, these

1-2-3/G [69.4] Ready

File Edit Worksheet Range Copy... Move... Print Graph Data Utility Quit... Help

B:A1

TRY_MAC.WG1

B	A	B	C	D	E	F	G
1			ABC COMPANY SALES				1
2							1
3		Q1	Q2	Q3	Q4	TOTAL	1
4	Sales Product 1	26610	31807	32239	34918	125574	1
5	Sales Product 2	10301	12057	13666	16281	52305	
6	Sales Product 3	50600	46948	51149	66874	215571	

Figure 22-10. Worksheet after combining files

indicate that each region is combined into the total worksheet. This is a good strategy to use with Combine Add even when you are not using a macro.

Modifying the Macro You can modify the macro to combine any number of files. Although each of the region files is combined with the Add option in this case, you can easily change the macro to use another option instead.

After you learn to create more complex macros in Chapter 23, you may want to return to this macro and make it check for the 1's in column G using the {IF} and {BRANCH} instructions. You could also load the detail for each region on a separate sheet in the file and use formulas that span sheets to create the consolidation report.

Print Macros

Since 1-2-3/G can retain only one set of print specifications at a time, and since many worksheets contain more than one printed report, you may find that you are reentering print specifications each month as you print your worksheet reports. This wastes time and can lead to errors that might require the reprinting of a report.

You can avoid such problems by using macros to record the commands needed to print your reports. Once you have worked out the details, a macro can print as many reports as you like with one keystroke. Also, since the macro is tested, you will not have to reprint reports because of errors in print specifications.

A Macro to Create Printed Reports

You probably send most of your reports directly to the printer. The margins, header, and other specifications for the printed page may differ for two reports printed from the same worksheet. If you store the different print specifications in a macro, you need only position your paper at the top of a form and turn your printer on. 1-2-3/G can handle everything else.

The macro shown here prints two different reports from one worksheet file:

```
     A      B                      C
1    \p     /pp                    Request print
2           rA1..C15~              Specify range
3           oml2{TAB}              Select Options and left margin of 2"
4           2{TAB}                 Set right margin to 2"
5           1.5~                   Set top margin to 1.5"
6           h||Today's Date : @~   Create header with date
7           q                      Quit options
8           gp                     Print and advance to next page
9           rA1..H20~              Specify range
10          oml.5{TAB}             Set left margin to .5"
11          .5~                    Set right margin to .5"
12          q                      Quit options
13          gp                     Print and advance to next page
14          q                      Quit print
```

The first instruction in the macro tells 1-2-3/G that you want the Print commands and would like your output sent directly to the printer. The first print range, A10..C15, is requested in B2.

The Options changes come next. The first request is to change the left margin to 2 inches, the right margin to 2 inches, and the top margin to 1.5 inches. Using {TAB} moves between the margin text boxes while ~ leaves the margin text boxes. B6 specifies the header to appear at the top of each page of the report. There is no entry on the left or in the center of the header, so the line contains two vertical bars to right align the header. The rightmost portion of the header contains the constant Today's Date:. It also contains an @ sign, which will cause 1-2-3/G to substitute the current date. Since this is the last change made in the Options dialog box, a Q selects Quit. Printing is requested with the G for Go in the next cell and a P to advance the paper to the next page.

B9 contains the first instruction for the second report. Since the Print Printer dialog box remains on the screen until you choose Quit, there is no new request for this dialog box. The first Options request for the second report is found in B10. The left and right margins are set at /.5 inches. B12 quits the Options dialog box. The second report is printed by the G in B13. Page is issued again to advance the paper to the next page, and the Print Printer dialog box is exited with the Q in the last macro instruction.

Guidelines for Use Of course, the printer must be installed correctly. Then you just need to position your paper before turning on your printer. The position of your paper when you turn on your printer is where OS/2 assumes the top of the form to be.

Modifying the Macro You will want to modify this macro to conform to the specific ranges you need to print your report. These instructions are found in B2 and B9; you can edit them to supply a new range. Depending on the range you select and your exact printing requirements, you may need to modify Options parameters such as margins and headers. You may also wish to add print options besides those listed in this macro. If you have additional reports to create, you can insert their specifications on new lines before line 14. This way, you can have one macro print all your reports.

A Macro to Store Print Output in a File

There are several good reasons for printing to a file. First, your printer may be out for repair, and you may want to save the printed output until later. Or, you may simply want to continue with your current task and wait until later to print.

The following macro writes worksheet formulas to a file with one formula per line:

```
     A          B             C
1    formulas   /pf           Request print to file
2               FORMULAS~     Write to file FORMULAS.PRN
3               rA1..C20~     Specify range A1..C20
4               ff            Select Format output Formulas
5               g             Write requested file
6               q             Quit print dialog box
```

The first line requests the Print File dialog box. B2 contains the filename that is supplied in response to 1-2-3/G's prompt. The range to be printed is shown next and includes the cells in A1..C20. The macro selects Format output Formulas to print each cell in the range on a line by itself and print the formulas. The next instruction writes the output to a disk file. The Print File dialog box is exited via the Q in B10.

Guidelines for Use Since 1-2-3/G does not start printing until you select Quit, be sure to quit the Print File dialog box with Quit rather than ESCAPE. Also, if you are printing to a file on a floppy disk, make sure that you leave your disk in the drive until after quitting, to ensure that all your data is in the file.

Modifying the Macro This macro will work for any set of reports. You should eliminate the request for Format output Formulas from B6 if you want the worksheet printed as displayed rather than as the formulas the macro requests. You can modify the range in B3 to print other reports.

If you want to print multiple reports to one file, you can begin the range specification process again after B2 or B3, depending on whether or not you want the existing print parameters cleared. If you want the output in a second file, place your second request after B6, and begin again with Print File so you can request a new filename.

Graph Macros

Graphs normally require numerous settings. You have to add titles, data labels, grid lines, legends, and other options to create appealing and informative graphs. You can save time and reduce errors by capturing the required keystrokes in a macro and making it available for use with departmental budgets or other worksheets where a number of managers are using the same formats.

A Macro to Create a Bar Graph

The following macro works with the sales worksheet used with the File Combine macro example shown in Figure 22-10. It can be used for any of the regional budgets or the total company worksheet. You may wish to change the first line title. The macro looks like this:

```
     A        B                   C
1    graph    /gry                Reset any existing graph
2             /gtb                Select bar type graph
3             /gax                Select Graph Add Ranges
4             B:B3..B:E3{TAB}     X range for labels below axis
5             B:B4..B:E4{TAB}     First data range
6             B:B5..B:E5{TAB}     Second data range
7             B:B6..B:E6~         Third data range
8             /gotf\C1            First line title from C1
9             {TAB 3}$ Sales~     Y axis title
10            /goldaProduct 1     Legend for first product
11            {TAB}Product 2      Legend for second product
12            {TAB}Product 3~     Legend for third product
13            /gv                 View graph
14            /sggy~              Add horizontal grid lines
```

The macro begins in line 1 by removing any existing graph settings. Next, the macro selects a bar graph type, and then specifies the ranges for the different series used to create the graph. The labels below the X axis are the entries in cells B3..E3. The next three instructions assign values to data ranges A, B, and C.

The next two instructions add ABC Company, which is stored in C1 as the first graph title and $ Sales as the Y-axis title. After the titles are added, the next three instructions add legend text for each series. With all of the initial graph settings made, the Graph View command displays the graph in the graph window with the same name as the worksheet when the macro is executed. The Graph View also makes the graph window the active window so further macro instruction use the Graph Tool menu. In this macro, the macro instruction in B14 uses the Graph Tool menu to add horizontal grid lines.

Guidelines for Use You can use this macro every time you update your worksheet. This macro is useful when you are in a new 1-2-3/G session and find that someone else has been using the graphics features and has deleted the definition of your graph.

Modifying the Macro You can modify this macro to save the graph specifications under a graph name. Once the settings are named, a second, shorter macro could issue a Graph Name Use command to make the specifications current at a later time. Later, you can add window commands covered in Chapter 23, which allow you to size and position the windows being used and to select the active window. As this window shows, the macro must be run from the worksheet menu. You cannot start running this macro from a graph tool window, since the graph tool menu is different from the worksheet tool menu.

You can also modify the macro to specify settings for any type of graph. Use as many options as you need to enhance your basic data.

Data Macros

Macros can also save you time by automating functions in the data environment. Most of the Data commands require that you make a number of selections before you complete your task. Some, like Data Table, require that you complete preliminary steps before requesting the command. Also, since you must reissue the Data commands if you want to repeat a sort, Data Table, frequency analysis, regression analysis, or Data Fill operation, you could be executing these commands frequently. With the macro approach, you can enter them once, check their accuracy, and then store them in worksheet cells and use them when needed.

A Macro to Create a Data Table

A data table can perform a sensitivity analysis for you by systematically plugging values into your input variables. Before you ask 1-2-3/G to perform this analysis, you must build a table shell on the worksheet. Since a macro to do this is more complicated than the other macros, review the worksheet in Figure 22-11 before you study the next macro listing. Projections for Products A and B use the growth rates in B8 and B9 and the previous years' sales to project future periods. Product C is calculated as a percentage of sales of Products A and B. The completed table is shown in Figure 22-12.

The rules for working with tables are covered in Chapter 12; go back to this chapter if you are not familiar with the Data Table command. The table in the macro is calculated by substituting the values in

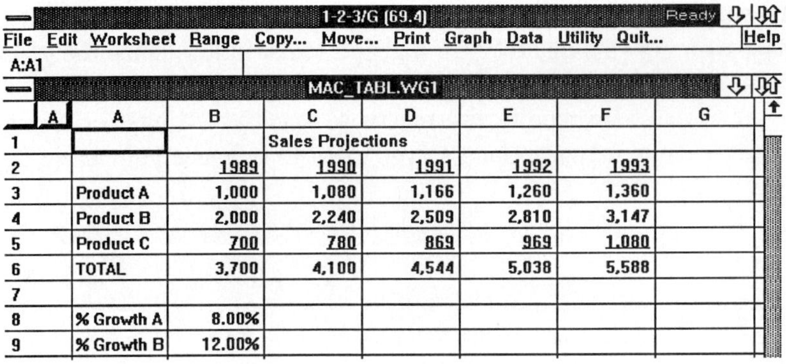

1-2-3/G (69.4) Ready

File Edit Worksheet Range Copy... Move... Print Graph Data Utility Quit... Help

A:A1

MAC_TABL.WG1

A	A	B	C	D	E	F	G
1			Sales Projections				
2		1989	1990	1991	1992	1993	
3	Product A	1,000	1,080	1,166	1,260	1,360	
4	Product B	2,000	2,240	2,509	2,810	3,147	
5	Product C	700	780	869	969	1,080	
6	TOTAL	3,700	4,100	4,544	5,038	5,588	
7							
8	% Growth A	8.00%					
9	% Growth B	12.00%					

Figure 22-11. Worksheet for use with Data Table

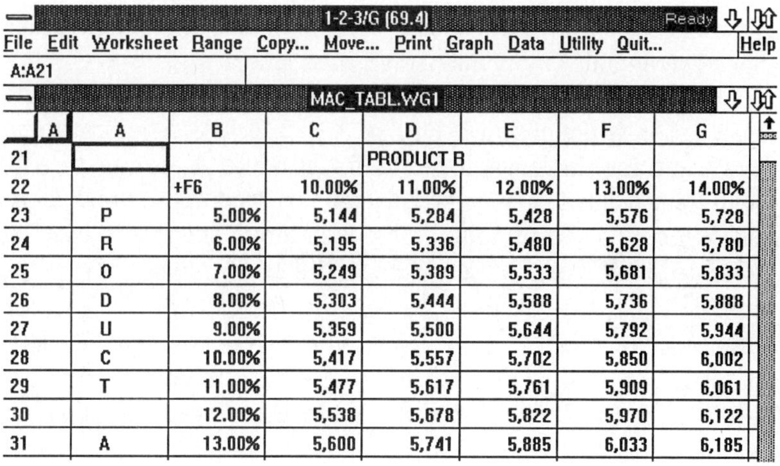

1-2-3/G (69.4) Ready

File Edit Worksheet Range Copy... Move... Print Graph Data Utility Quit... Help

A:A21

MAC_TABL.WG1

A	A	B	C	D	E	F	G
21				PRODUCT B			
22		+F6	10.00%	11.00%	12.00%	13.00%	14.00%
23	P	5.00%	5,144	5,284	5,428	5,576	5,728
24	R	6.00%	5,195	5,336	5,480	5,628	5,780
25	O	7.00%	5,249	5,389	5,533	5,681	5,833
26	D	8.00%	5,303	5,444	5,588	5,736	5,888
27	U	9.00%	5,359	5,500	5,644	5,792	5,944
28	C	10.00%	5,417	5,557	5,702	5,850	6,002
29	T	11.00%	5,477	5,617	5,761	5,909	6,061
30		12.00%	5,538	5,678	5,822	5,970	6,122
31	A	13.00%	5,600	5,741	5,885	6,033	6,185

Figure 22-12. Completed table

column B for the growth of Product A in B8 each time the table performs a new calculation. The percentages in row 22 are substituted as new growth factors for Product B. The table will contain the result of the formula in F6, which is the total sales in 1990.

The first macro instruction is found in B:B1, as shown here:

```
     A      B              C
1    \t     /df            Request Data Fill
2           A:B23..A:B31~  Set fill range
3           .05~           Enter start value
4           .01~~          Enter increment and accept stop value
5           /df            Request Data Fill
6           A:C22..A:H22~  Set fill range
7           .09~           Enter start value
8           .01~~          Enter increment and accept stop value
9           /dt2           Request Data Table 2
10          A:B22..A:H31~  Set range
11          A:B8~          Set input value 1
12          A:B9~          Set input value 2
13          {GOTO}A:A21~   Move cell pointer to view table
```

This first instruction requests Data Fill to start building the shell for the table. A fill range is established with the second instruction. Then a start value of .05 and an increment of .01 are specified. The second tilde in B:B4 accepts the default in the Stop text box, since it is greater than the stop value needed.

The second Data Fill operation supplies the values across row 22. A start value of .09 is used, along with the same increment as the first range. The default stop value is accepted again.

The request for the Data Table 2 command is made in B:B9. The table location is defined in B:B10 as A:B22..A:H31. The first input value is the value for the growth factor for Product A, stored in A:B8. The second input value is the growth factor for Product B, which is stored in A:B9. When this second input value is entered, the macro calculates the new values for F6 and places them in the table.

Guidelines for Use This macro is designed to handle most of the table setup, as well as the call for Data Table to do the calculations. It doesn't enter the formula in cell B22 on the sheet containing the table or format the table cells, ensuring that the values you want are placed in the table as input values. Do not store information in the range the table uses, since executing the macro would overlay these cells.

Modifying the Macro You can modify the macro to create a table of a different size or with different input values generated by the Data Fill operation. You could also modify the instructions in B3, B4, B7, and B8 to contain {?}, so that the operator can enter the fill parameters, and therefore the input values, every time the macro is executed.

You can also modify the macro to handle the remaining preliminary steps for preparing the table. You could include instructions for the entry of the formula in B22 on the table sheet and the Range Format statements required to display the table as shown.

A Macro to Sort a Database

To sort a database you must define the data range. You don't have to do this every time you sort, but you must do it if you have added a new field or new records to your database. A macro can handle this precautionary step to ensure that you do not sort just a section of your database.

The database this example uses is shown in Figure 22-13. Notice that the names are listed in random sequence. The macro sorts the file by last name and uses the first name as a secondary key. Figure 22-14 shows the result of using the macro.

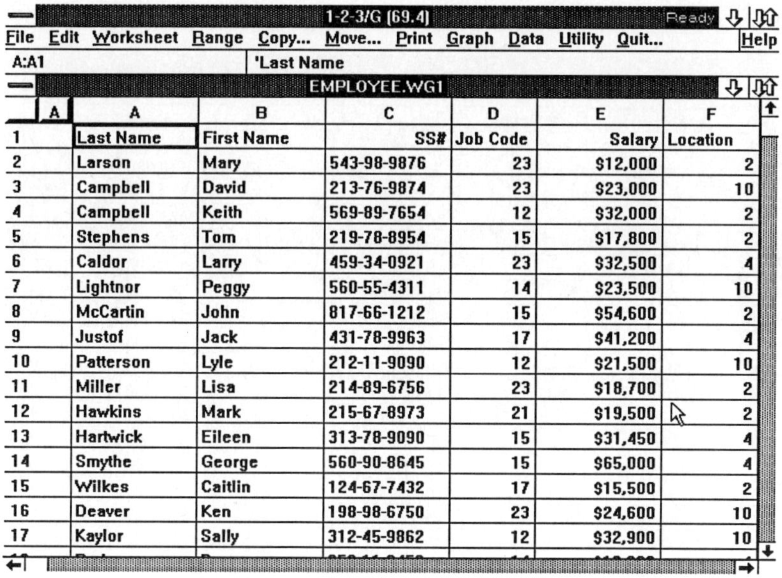

1-2-3/G (69.4) Ready

File Edit Worksheet Range Copy... Move... Print Graph Data Utility Quit... Help

A:A1 'Last Name

EMPLOYEE.WG1

A	A	B	C	D	E	F
1	Last Name	First Name	SS#	Job Code	Salary	Location
2	Larson	Mary	543-98-9876	23	$12,000	2
3	Campbell	David	213-76-9874	23	$23,000	10
4	Campbell	Keith	569-89-7654	12	$32,000	2
5	Stephens	Tom	219-78-8954	15	$17,800	2
6	Caldor	Larry	459-34-0921	23	$32,500	4
7	Lightnor	Peggy	560-55-4311	14	$23,500	10
8	McCartin	John	817-66-1212	15	$54,600	2
9	Justof	Jack	431-78-9963	17	$41,200	4
10	Patterson	Lyle	212-11-9090	12	$21,500	10
11	Miller	Lisa	214-89-6756	23	$18,700	2
12	Hawkins	Mark	215-67-8973	21	$19,500	2
13	Hartwick	Eileen	313-78-9090	15	$31,450	4
14	Smythe	George	560-90-8645	15	$65,000	4
15	Wilkes	Caitlin	124-67-7432	17	$15,500	2
16	Deaver	Ken	198-98-6750	23	$24,600	10
17	Kaylor	Sally	312-45-9862	12	$32,900	10

Figure 22-13. Unsorted database

This macro begins in B:B1 with request for Data Sort Reset:

```
     A       B               C
1    sort    /dsr            Request Data Sort Reset
2            d               Select Data range
3            {FC}{DOWN}      Set A:A2 as beginning of the range
4            .               Lock beginning of range
5            {END}{DOWN}     Move to last entry in first field
6            {END}{RIGHT}~   Move to last field on right
7            pA:A2~a         Set Last Name as primary key
8            sA:B2~a         Set First Name as secondary key
9            g               Complete sort
10           {FC}            Move to A:A1 to view sorted records
```

Since the range is set from previous use, Reset removes all previous settings. The cell pointer is moved to A:A1 with the {FC} or {FIRSTCELL} macro keystroke (equivalent to pressing CTRL-HOME), then down one row to A:A2. This cell is locked in place as the beginning of the sort range by typing a period. The cell pointer is moved to the last

1-2-3/G (69.4) Ready

File Edit Worksheet Range Copy... Move... Print Graph Data Utility Quit... Help

A:A1 'Last Name

EMPLOYEE.WG1

A	A	B	C	D	E	F
1	Last Name	First Name	SS#	Job Code	Salary	Location
2	Caldor	Larry	459-34-0921	23	$32,500	4
3	Campbell	David	213-76-9874	23	$23,000	10
4	Campbell	Keith	569-89-7654	12	$32,000	2
5	Deaver	Ken	198-98-6750	23	$24,600	10
6	Hartwick	Eileen	313-78-9090	15	$31,450	4
7	Hawkins	Mark	215-67-8973	21	$19,500	2
8	Justof	Jack	431-78-9963	17	$41,200	4
9	Kaylor	Sally	312-45-9862	12	$32,900	10
10	Larson	Mary	543-98-9876	23	$12,000	2
11	Lightnor	Peggy	560-55-4311	14	$23,500	10
12	McCartin	John	817-66-1212	15	$54,600	2
13	Miller	Lisa	214-89-6756	23	$18,700	2
14	Parker	Dee	659-11-3452	14	$19,800	4
15	Patterson	Lyle	212-11-9090	12	$21,500	10
16	Preverson	Gary	670-90-1121	21	$27,600	4
17	Samuelson	Paul	219-89-7080	23	$28,900	2

Figure 22-14. Sorted database

entry in the column, then across to the last column to complete the specification.

A2 is defined as the primary key, on which the records are sorted in ascending sequence. The secondary key is B2, the first name, also applied in ascending sequence. The G in B9 requests that the sort begin. The macro ends by moving to A:A1 so you can review your results.

Guidelines for Use The macro assumes that the first and last data fields have values for every record. Instructions in B:B5 and B:B6 would not include every record if some of the fields were blank.

Modifying the Macro You can modify the macro to change the field the Data Sort command uses for a key by changing the cell address in B:B7 and B:B8. Enter the specific range address for the database, although this approach means modifying the macro as the database range expands.

Command Language Macros

Command language macros are more powerful than the keyboard alternative macros described in the last chapter. Command language macros allow you to perform repetitive tasks with ease, and automate applications so that even novice users can handle complex worksheet tasks. They also allow you to use features that are not part of the 1-2-3/G menu structure.

The macro command set in 1-2-3/G provides a number of new options. However, command language macros are built with 1-2-3/G's command language, which is essentially a programming language. As with any programming language, you are likely to have moments of frustration as you strive to make 1-2-3/G understand your needs. To create command language macros successfully, you must be willing to define your needs with precision, and to persist with the task until the macro works correctly.

This chapter provides strategies for creating command language macros as easily as possible. The first part of the chapter includes general strategies for creating macros, and discusses specific techniques used by programmers working in other programming languages. Since the 1-2-3/G macro command language is also a programming language, some of these techniques should prove helpful when you write your macros. The second section of this chapter discusses each macro command separately, providing both a description and a working example.

TWENTY THREE

Differences Between Command Language Macros and Keyboard Macros

You enter command language macros just as you enter keyboard macros. Like keyboard macros, command language macros are label entries stored in a column of worksheet cells, named with a backslash and a single letter key. Naturally, you must follow rules when entering instructions from 1-2-3/G's macro command language. The command keyword and any arguments it requires must always be enclosed in curly braces—for example, {BRANCH A9}. Arguments must always be entered in the prescribed order.

How do you know when to use command language macros and when to use keyboard macros? When a keyboard macro will work, use it. However, to accomplish tasks that menu commands cannot handle, you should use command language macros.

Your first command language macros may use only a few statements. For example, consider the following macro, which enters a payment formula in five cells:

```
\d      {LET z1,0}
top     {IF z1=5}{BRANCH end}
        @PMT(
        {?}
        '
        {?}
        '
        {?}
        )~
        {DOWN}
        {LET z1,z1+1}
        {BRANCH top}
end     {QUIT}
```

After you master simpler command language macros, you can begin to think of more sophisticated tasks to delegate to 1-2-3/G. Many of these tasks will require the use of command language instructions, but they are also likely to employ the familiar 1-2-3/G functions, formulas, and menu options.

Constructing and Using Command Language Macros

A command language macro normally consists of a number of detailed steps that must be executed in a logical order. When you communicate instructions to another person, you can often be less than fully specific and still get the desired results. That is because people can interpret directions and make assumptions about how a task should be performed.

When you tell a computer to do something, however, there are no interpretations and no assumptions. You get exactly what you ask for, whether or not it is what you want. If you leave out a step or provide the steps in the wrong sequence, you get results that differ from what you expect.

For this reason, you need to create a road map showing what you want the computer to do for you. If you create this road map on paper, it is easy to separate logic and syntax. *Logic* refers to the steps in the task you wish the computer to perform, and *syntax* refers to the detailed instructions in the 1-2-3/G macro command language, and the specific order of arguments that they need to execute successfully. If you haven't worked out the logic of your macro, you won't be able to solve the problem by entering specific instructions. You need to know where you are going and the general route you plan to follow before you start.

Entering Command Language Macros

Having mapped out a plan for your macro, you are ready to begin entering the actual code. You enter command language macros the same way you enter keyboard alternative macros. You can enter them in a macro library or as part of a file that contains worksheet or data management entries. If you enter command language macros within an existing file, consider using a separate sheet. It is a good idea to place command language macros language in an out-of-the-way location that has room for a blank column on both sides of the macro instructions column. This allows you to use the column to the left of the macro for the macro name and any range names you might assign to different sections of the macro. If you place a macro on a worksheet that contains text and data, consider using a worksheet location where other data is not stored in the same columns or rows. This way, if you insert rows or columns in the other portion of the sheet, the macro is not affected.

You can use either upper- or lowercase for macro commands, argument names, cell address references, keyboard commands, and macro names. You must follow the command syntax exactly, using the curly braces around each command entry, and the exact spelling for each command keyword.

You can have 1-2-3/G do some of the work: Type the curly brace {, and press F3 (Name). 1-2-3/G lists all the macro key names and commands. Typing a letter moves the highlight to the next macro instruction or key name that starts with that letter. You can double-click the one you want, or highlight the one you want and press ENTER to have 1-2-3/G add it to your cell entry. You must separate each of the command's arguments are entered with semi-colons or commas. You must then supply the proper type of data for each type of argument. Although you can use the specific type of entry within the macro, you can also use range names, cell addresses, or an appropriate formula to supply the necessary argument information. A closing brace follows the last argument entry.

Arguments that are literal strings usually require quotation marks around them. Quotation marks are necessary when the string contains separator characters (a comma, a semicolon, a colon, or a period).

Each cell in the column where you make your macro entries can contain up to 512 characters, since each macro instruction is entered as a label. However, you shouldn't use entries that even approach this upper limit. Forty or fifty characters is a reasonable upper limit if you want your macros to be readable. Try to complete each macro instruction in the cell in which you begin entering it.

Naming Command Language Macros

You name command language macros just as you name keyboard macros. The name of any command language macro that you wish to execute directly from the keyboard should consist of a single letter preceded by a backslash (\). This naming convention allows you to execute the macro quickly from the keyboard. You can also use any valid range name if a quick entry alternative is not required. Upper-and lowercase letters are treated as equivalent, so you can construct 26 unique macros that can be executed from the keyboard. Remember that you can also have one special automatic macro in each file—such macros start executing as soon as you retrieve the worksheet containing it. This assumes that the check boxes under Worksheet Global Default Autoexec command are selected. You must give this macro the name of \0.

Since command language macros have branching instructions as well as subroutine calls to execute other macros, you can name macros with regular range names. These macros are executed when invoked by another macro. You can also execute them by pressing ALT-F3 (Run) and selecting the macro name.

In all cases, you only need to name the top cell in a macro. Macros are considered to continue until a blank cell, a cell containing a value, or a {QUIT} instruction is encountered.

Tip: If you like, you can code all of your macro instructions at once. It often works better, however, to code just the major instructions first. This method speeds up your testing process significantly, since you can test the program's basic logic by invoking each subroutine and checking the special message it displays. Once you check the execution flow, you can add the detailed code.

Creating Interactive Macros

Interactive macros are macros that change as they are executed. They can change logic flow in response to entries by the operator. They can even change entries in instructions, such as filenames.

Macros that Respond to Operator Input

Several of the various macro commands in this chapter accept operator input. These include {?}, {GETLABEL}, {GETNUMBER}, {GET}, and {LOOK}. You can use the information obtained from these entries to control {BRANCH} instructions and subroutine calls, as well as other processing within the macro.

Dynamically Altered Macros

Dynamically altered macros store information that is input or calculated during execution as part of the macro itself. For example, in a file retrieve instruction, you might want to change the file retrieved depending on the application that you are working on. To do this, use a menu selection to determine the application, and have this instruction alter the following macro instruction sequence:

```
{MENU}fr

blank

~
```

In this example, the macro cell that contains the word "blank" would actually be an empty cell. You want to have the macro make an appropriate entry in this cell, using either a {PUT} or {LET} instruction. In this way, the macro alters itself to perform the exact action you want. Here is an example of this type of dynamically altering macro:

	A	B	C
1	save_name	{GETLABEL Enter your name,B3}	Ask for name
2		{MENU}fs{ESC 2}	Select File Save
3		Campbell	Use name provided
4		~	Finalize command

This macro uses the {GETLABEL} command to enter in B3 the filename that the macro uses to save the file. When you execute this macro, 1-2-3/G updates the entry in B3 to your entry from the {GETLABEL} prompt.

The macro instruction can also be a string formula. As an example, suppose that you want to save the file using the same filename, but you want to save it to drive A. In a file called MY_FILE.WG1, the macro instructions might look like this:

```
{MENU}fs{ESC 2}A:\
MY_FILE.WG1
~
```

In this example, the second macro instruction looks like a label, but the cell actually contains this formula:

```
@RIGHT(@CELLPOINTER("filename"),@LENGTH(@CELLPOINTER("filename"))-15)
```

This formula uses the @CELLPOINTER filename to return the path and filename. The @LENGTH function calculates the length of the path and filename. The @RIGHT function returns only the filename from the results of @CELLPOINTER by subtracting 14, which is the number of characters in C:\123G\WORK\, the default work file directory. This formula constantly updates the value of the second macro instruction to be the current filename.

Documenting Command Language Macros

You can add comments to the worksheet to document your macro. The main purpose of documentation is to make each macro step clear. This is especially useful to someone who didn't create the macro. However, documentation can also be helpful when you look back at a macro you wrote, say, three months ago.

You should give meaningful names to variables in a macro. This minimizes the need for supplemental documentation and makes formulas in the macro easier to read.

You can document the name of your macro by placing it in the column to the left of the top macro instruction. When naming subroutines, place the name to the left of the top cell in each subroutine. You should document macro instructions by writing a description to the right of each instruction. Be as brief as possible, but make sure that you describe all formulas or other entries that might not be clear later.

Testing Command Language Macros

Don't assume that a macro will work correctly unless you have tested it. A multiple-step testing process is the most efficient, and should ensure that your macro works under all conditions. Here are some macro testing guidelines:

1. Your first test should be an easy one. If the macro performs calculations, use even numbers so that you can check its answers mentally. If you choose a complicated number, you might make arithmetic mistakes yourself while testing it.

2. If your macro is an iterative one (one that is executed numerous times), test only two or three iterations of its cycle. This saves time and makes it easier to check results.

3. Next, check what the macro does with exceptions or unusual conditions that occur only sporadically.

4. Now check for error conditions. If the macro prompts you for the number of times you wish to execute a certain routine, enter **−25**. If it asks for a number of vacation days, enter **560**. If it asks for a salary increase, respond with **1500%**. See whether it responds to the error conditions as you would expect.

5. If your macro fails at any step, correct the error condition and go back to the first step for a quick recheck. Never assume that a change to one part of a macro does not affect another part.

6. If others will use your macro, involve them in the testing process. No one knows better the type of data that will be entered into the macro than the person who will use the program every day. This approach also helps you discover whether you have misinterpreted the user's needs. For instance, you may have allowed for the entry of an invoice amount, whereas the user expected the macro to compute a total invoice amount based on entry of detail figures.

7. If you are designing a macro to work in multiple files, make sure to test its operation in more than one file.

Tip: When Undo is enabled, you can check the steps a macro performs by pressing ALT-BACKSPACE (Undo). Each time you press ALT-BACKSPACE, you remove the effects of the macro instructions one step at a time, which may help you find an error.

Executing Command Language Macros

It's easy to execute a completed command language macro. As with a keyboard macro, simply hold down the CTRL key and press the letter key of the macro's name. You can also press ALT-F3 (Run) and select the name of the macro to be executed. If the macro is in another file, you should select the file from the list and then select the macro name when 1-2-3/G lists the range names in the selected worksheet file. With macros stored in a macro library, you don't need to select the filename. You can simply type the name of the macro from the prompt.

Using Undo While Running Macros

As mentioned, if you run a macro with Undo enabled, you can press ALT-BACKSPACE to cancel the last macro. Undo eliminates the effect of menu selections and macro commands within the normal scope of its capabilities (that is, Undo cannot eliminate File Saves and print operations that are completed). If 1-2-3/G does not have sufficient memory to run the macro with Undo enabled, it prompts you before turning Undo off. If you turn off Undo, you can start the macro again from the beginning.

Updating the Worksheet

Some of the macro commands update worksheet cells. They don't always recalculate immediately, and sometimes you must recalculate the worksheet after one of these commands. For some commands, you can just press the ENTER to cause the updating. You should follow these commands with a tilde (~) if immediate update is critical to the successful execution of the macro. Other commands require that the worksheet be recalculated.

The following commands will update the worksheet if you follow them with a tilde (~) or {CALC}:

{CONTENTS}
{DEFINE}
{FILESIZE}
{FOR}
{GET}
{GETLABEL}
{GETNUMBER}
{GETPOS}
{LOOK}
{ONERROR}
{PUT}
{READ}
{READLN}

Stopping a Macro

Unless you have disabled the BREAK key by including {BREAKOFF} in your macro, you can interrupt a macro simply by pressing CTRL-BREAK. This displays a message on the screen. If you select OK, you can leave the macro and return to Ready mode. {BREAKOFF} is described in the "Interactive Macro Commands" section later in this chapter.

Macro Commands

1-2-3/G provides macro commands for creating advanced macros. The macro commands are grouped into categories: commands that affect the screen, interactive macro commands, macro commands that affect the flow of execution, macro commands that manipulate data, macro commands that handle files, and macro commands that manipulate windows.

Syntax of Macro Commands

There are two types of macro commands: commands without arguments and commands with arguments. Both types include a keyword in braces. For a subroutine, the subroutine name is the keyword. See Table 23-1 for a list of macro commands and their functions.

A command without arguments is nothing more than a keyword enclosed in braces. Examples are {RETURN}, {RESTART}, and {QUIT}.

The format of a command with arguments consists of the keyword followed by a blank space and a list of arguments separated by commas. As with @function arguments, no spaces are allowed between or within arguments. The entire entry is enclosed in braces. Here are two examples:

```
{GETLABEL "Enter your name:",A2}

{FOR Counter,1,20,1,Loop}
```

Conventions for Macros in this Chapter

Whenever possible, the same conventions are used for all of the example macros. The macro name is shown in column A to the left of the top cell in the macro. Subroutine names are also shown in column A. The macro instructions are written in column B as labels, except for menu macros, which extend to the right into additional columns. The columns on the sheets where the macros are entered are widened to allow for the complete entry of each element.

Whenever possible, documentation is placed in column C. Each description extends to the right and sometimes displays in the columns to the right of column C or in a widened column C. When you create macros of your own, you should make sure to document them.

Lowercase characters are used for menu selections and responses to menu prompts. Filenames, command keywords, and special key indicators—such as {HOME}, {ESC}, {IF}, and {MENUBRANCH}—are shown in uppercase. Range names, which also serve as subroutine

Macro Command	Function	Type of Macro
{?}	Accepts keyboard input	Interactive
{ALERT}	Displays dialog box with message and command buttons	Interactive
{APPENDBELOW}	Appends one or more rows of data below an existing database	Data
{APPENDRIGHT}	Appends one or more columns of data to the right of an existing database	Data
{BEEP}	Sounds bell	Screen
{BLANK}	Erases cell or range	Data
{BRANCH}	Changes execution flow to a new routine	Flow
{BREAKOFF}	Disables BREAK key	Interactive
{BREAKON}	Restores BREAK key function	Interactive
{CLEARENTRY} or {CE}	Removes existing contents of text box or control line	Data
{CLOSE}	Closes an open file	File
{CONTENTS}	Stores the numeric contents of a cell as a label in another cell	Data
{DEFINE}	Specifies location and type of arguments for a subroutine call	Flow
{DISPATCH}	Branches to a new location indirectly	Flow
{FILESIZE}	Determines number of bytes in a file	File
{FOR}	Loops through a macro subroutine multiple times	Flow
{FORBREAK}	Cancels current {FOR} instruction	Flow
{FORM}	Allows you to use a form for input. Can monitor keystrokes and execute subroutines	Interactive
{FRAMEOFF}	Turns off the worksheet frame	Screen
{FRAMEON}	Restores the worksheet frame	Screen
{GET}	Halts macro to allow single-keystroke entry	Interactive
{GETLABEL}	Halts macro to allow label entry	Interactive
{GETNUMBER}	Halts macro to allow number entry	Interactive
{GETPOS}	Returns to pointer position in a file	File
{GRAPHOFF}	Restores graph settings to before {GRAPHON}	Screen
{GRAPHON}	Displays a graph or activates a set of graph settings	Screen
{IF}	Causes conditional execution of command that follows	Flow
{INDICATE}	Changes mode indicator	Screen
{LET}	Stores a number or label in a cell	Data

Table 23-1. The Macro Language Commands (*continued on next page*)

Macro Command	Function	Type of Macro
{LOOK}	Checks to see if keyboard entry is made	Interactive
{MENUBRANCH}	Allows the construction of a custom menu	Keyboard
{MENUCALL}	Executes a custom menu as a subroutine	Interactive
{ONERROR}	Branches to an error processing routine	Flow
{OPEN}	Opens a file for read or write access	File
{PANELOFF}	Eliminates Control Panel program updating	Screen
{PANELON}	Restores Control Panel program updating	Screen
{PUT}	Stores a number or label in one cell of a range	Data
{QUIT}	Ends the macro and returns to Ready mode	Flow
{READ}	Reads characters from file into cell	File
{READLN}	Reads a line of characters from a file	File
{RECALC}	Recalculates formulas in a range, row by row	Data
{RECALCCOL}	Recalculates formulas in a range, column by column	Data
{RESTART}	Clears subroutine pointers	Flow
{RETURN}	Returns to the instruction after the last subroutine call or {MENUCALL}	Flow
{*routine*}	Calls the subroutine specified by *routine*	Flow
{SETPOS}	Moves the file pointer to a new location in the file	File
{SYSTEM}	Executes an OS/2 command	Flow
{TONE}	Sounds a tone of set pitch and duration	Screen
{WACTIVATE}	Selects open window to make active	Window
{WAIT}	Waits until a specified time	Keyboard
{WAITDIALOG}	Waits until macro operator selects OK or Cancel command button in a dialog box	Keyboard
{WINDOWSOFF}	Suppresses window updating	Screen
{WINDOWSON}	Restores window updating	Screen
{WMOVE}	Moves window on desktop	Window
{WRITE}	Places data in a file	File
{WRITELN}	Places data in a file and adds a carriage return/line feed at the end	File
{WSIZE}	Changes size of window	Window

Table 23-1. The Macro Language Commands

names, are shown in lowercase. Arguments in the text are shown in italics.

The macro commands in the following sections are grouped according to these categories: commands that affect the screen, commands that interact with the keyboard operator, commands that control the flow of execution within a macro, commands that affect data entry, and commands that access file data. (These are the categories used in the 1-2-3/G manual.) For each command, there's a description, format rules, descriptions of arguments (if any), suggestions for use, and an example. Special setup procedures are also described, if any are required.

Macro Commands that Affect the Screen

Macro commands that affect your screen can handle such tasks as updating the Window option and menu bar. If the macro commands display as they execute you have an indication of where the macro is at any particular moment. As a macro progresses quickly a flicker may appear as the screen is updated. You can eliminate this flicker with the screen macro commands. These macros also enable you to create your own mode indicator, and to sound your computer's bell to get the operator's attention.

{BEEP}

The {BEEP} command sounds your computer's bell.

Format The format for the {BEEP} command is

{BEEP *number*}

where *number* is an optional argument to set the tone of the bell. The *number* argument can have any value from 1 to 4, with 1 as the default when no number is specified.

Use You can use the beep to alert the operator to an error, indicate that you expect input, show periodically that a long-running macro is still functioning, or signify the conclusion of a step.

Example In this example, the beep indicates that an input instruction follows:

```
{BEEP 3}
{GETNUMBER "Enter your account number",F2}
```

This {BEEP} instruction rings the computer's bell with tone 3 right before the input message is displayed.

Tip: If you disable the computer's beep with the Control Panel program, the {BEEP} command has no effect.

Note that when you use a tone argument other than 1 through 4, 1-2-3/G divides the number by 4 and uses the remainder for the tone value.

{FRAMEOFF}

The {FRAMEOFF} command allows you to further customize the screen by turning off the display of the worksheet frame. This is identical to unselecting the Grid lines, Column frames, and Row frames check boxes in the Worksheet Global Screen Attributes dialog box.

Format The format for the {FRAMEOFF} command is

{FRAMEOFF}

This command has no arguments.

Use The {FRAMEOFF} command allows you to create a help display or data entry form that doesn't contain column letters, row numbers, and grid lines. The frame is not restored to the display until a {FRAMEON} instruction is encountered or the macro ends.

Example The screen in Figure 23-1 is created with text entries and format commands. The {FORM} command displays the form and controls input within the defined input area. If the {FRAMEOFF} command

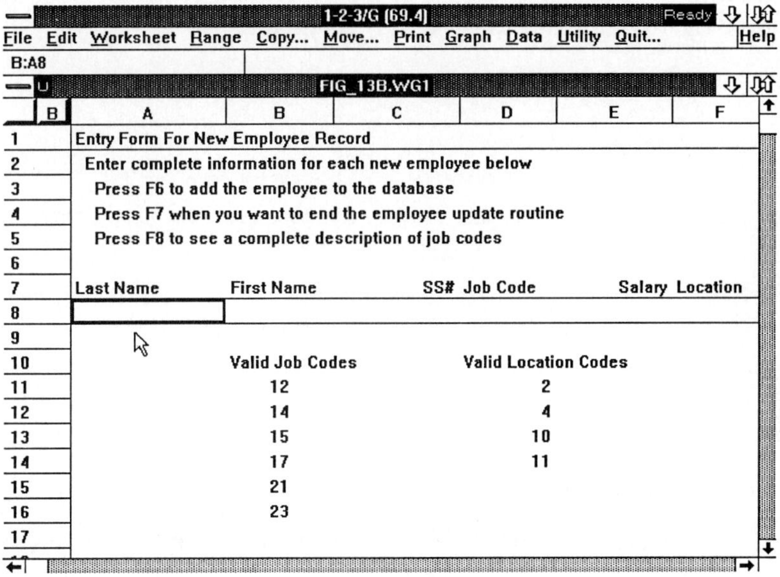

```
1-2-3/G (69.4)                                              Ready
File Edit Worksheet Range Copy... Move... Print Graph Data Utility Quit...   Help
B:A8
FIG_13B.WG1
B     A            B            C            D            E            F
1   Entry Form For New Employee Record
2     Enter complete information for each new employee below
3       Press F6 to add the employee to the database
4       Press F7 when you want to end the employee update routine
5       Press F8 to see a complete description of job codes
6
7   Last Name       First Name            SS#  Job Code          Salary  Location
8
9
10                  Valid Job Codes            Valid Location Codes
11                       12                           2
12                       14                           4
13                       15                          10
14                       17                          11
15                       21
16                       23
17
```

Figure 23-1. Data entry form with a frame

is added to the macro code before executing the {FORM} command, the row and column headings are eliminated.

{FRAMEON}

The {FRAMEON} command allows you to restore the display of the worksheet row and column frame after it has been disabled with {FRAMEOFF}.

Format The format of the command is

{FRAMEON}

This command has no arguments.

Use You can use the {FRAMEON} command to restore the display of the frame when a task requiring cell pointer positioning is required.

Example The following code illustrates the restoration of the frame after the execution of the {FORM} command:

	A	B	C
1	addrec	{FRAMEOFF}	Eliminate frame and grid lines
2		{FORM custadd}	Use custom form for add
3		{FRAMEON}	Restore frame and grid lines

Setup You must create the range name CUSTADD before invoking this macro. The range should be unprotected with the Range Unprotect command, since this is the area where entries are made on the form.

{GRAPHOFF}

The {GRAPHOFF} command moves the active graph window from the top to the bottom of the desktop.

Format The format of the command is

{GRAPHOFF}

The command has no arguments.

Use You can use {GRAPHOFF} after you have made a graph window the current window on the 1-2-3/G desktop. You may display a graph with {GRAPHON} for a fixed amount of time or allow the user to make an entry that removes it. Either way, when you want to move the graph window to the bottom of the desktop, use {GRAPHOFF}.

Example The following macro code displays and removes a graph:

	A	B	C
1	dispgrph	{GRAPHON pie1}	Display pie graph
2		{WAIT @NOW+@TIME(0,0,20)}	Wait 20 seconds
3		{GRAPHOFF}	

The graph displays on the top of the desktop for the 20 seconds generated by the {WAIT} instruction. Next, the graph is moved to the bottom of the 1-2-3/G desktop with the {GRAPHOFF} command.

{GRAPHON}

The {GRAPHON} command displays a named graph or the current graph in the graph window with the same name as the active worksheet window. While this command displays the graph window on top of the 1-2-3/G desktop, it doesn't activate the graph window, so subsequent macro instructions are performed in the window that is still active.

Format The format of this command depends on the specific action desired. {GRAPHON} with no arguments displays the current graph in the graph window. If the desktop does not have a graph window with the same name as the current worksheet file, this command opens it or creates it. To make a specific named graph current and display it in the graph window, use the format

{GRAPHON *named-graph*}

where *named-graph* is a set of graph definitions saved with the current worksheet file. Another format of this command is

{GRAPHON *named-graph,no-display*}

Although the named graph is still made current, it is not displayed on the screen. The graph window remains displayed until the macro ends or 1-2-3/G performs a {GRAPHOFF}, {INDICATE}, {GETLABEL}, {GETNUMBER}, {MENUCALL}, {?}, or {MENUBRANCH} macro command.

Use You can use the {GRAPHON} command to display a graph on the screen. Since the macro continues to process commands, you can use {GETLABEL} instructions to make enhancements to the graph without the user needing to know the commands required to make enhancements to the graph.

You can also use this command to make a set of graph specifications current, yet not display them immediately.

Example You can use {GRAPHON} to create a slide show of graphs. Since the macro continues to execute, you can use commands that display prompts and accept user input that affects the graph. The following macro displays a bar graph and prompts the user about the addition of grid lines to the graph:

	A	B	C
1	dispbar	{GRAPHON bar1}	Display graph bar 1
2		{WAIT @NOW+@TIME(0,0,10)}	Wait 10 seconds
3		{GETLABEL "Do you want see the graph again?",answer}	
4		{IF answer="N"}{QUIT}	Add grid lines if Y
5		{GRAPHON}	Display the graph
6		{WAIT @NOW+@TIME(0,0,10)}	Wait 10 seconds

The graph BAR1 is displayed by the first instruction. The {GETLABEL} instruction removes the graph from the screen, and then determines if the user wants to see the graph again. If the user types an N, 1-2-3/G terminates the macro by executing the {QUIT} command. (You would need to add instructions to this example to add the grid lines if the answer weren't N.) The {GRAPHON} instruction redisplays the graph for ten seconds. The graph is then removed when the macro ends.

{INDICATE}

The {INDICATE} command enables you to customize the mode indicator in the upper-right corner of the desktop title bar.

Format The format of the {INDICATE} command is

{INDICATE *string*}

where *string* is any character string. The string supplied is displayed in place of 1-2-3/G's regular indicator. Using an empty string—that is, {INDICATE ""}—removes the mode indicator from the desktop title bar. Using no string—that is, {INDICATE}—returns the indicator to 1-2-3/G's default. If the indicator is lengthy, it moves the desktop name to the left.

Use The indicator you select with this command remains in effect until you use the command again to establish a new setting.

The {INDICATE} command is useful when you are designing automated applications. When a macro is performing varied tasks, you can use the {INDICATE} command to indicate the macro's progress.

Example The macro shown here changes the mode indicator several times:

	A	B	C
1	\I	{INDICATE "SETUP"}	Change indicator to Setup
2		{MENU}wcs10.5~	Change column width to 10.5
3		{MENU}rfc0~{DOWN 5}~	Format as currency with 0 decimals
4		{INDICATE "SPLIT"}	Change indicator to Split
5		{DOWN 5}	Move down 5 cells
6		{MENU}wwh	Create horizontal window
7		{INDICATE}	Return indicator to default

You may want to watch this macro execute in Step mode, since 1-2-3/G performs the commands between the two {INDICATE} commands very quickly.

The first step in the macro changes the indicator to Setup. The macro then performs worksheet commands to set up the worksheet with a new column width adjustment and Currency format.

The instruction in B4 changes the indicator to Split. A horizontal second window is then created. Finally, the {INDICATE} command is used without an argument to return to the default setting of Ready mode when the macro ends. Without this last instruction, the mode indicator would still read Split after the macro executed. This indicator instruction is most useful in a long macro when you stay for the most part in a set mode.

{PANELOFF}

The {PANELOFF} command prevents 1-2-3/G from updating the desktop title bar, menu bar, and control line.

Format The format for the {PANELOFF} command is

{PANELOFF}

or

{PANELOFF clear}

When you use the second form, the menu bar and control line are cleared before being frozen.

Use The {PANELOFF} command reduces the flicker that occurs when macro instructions are executed. It is also useful if you don't want the user to know the exact instructions being executed.

Example The following macro lets you determine whether to update the first three lines of the 1-2-3/G desktop as you execute the macro:

	A	B	C
1	\p	{GETLABEL "Update Control Panel?",update}	
2		{IF update="Y"},{BRANCH yes}	If Y, update
3		{PANELOFF}	Disables updating
4		{BRANCH finish}	Skip next command
5	yes	{PANELON}	Display updating
6	finish	{GOTO}a:d1~	Go to A:D1
7		{MENU}rfc2~~	Format currency
8		{MENU}wcs12~	Set column width
9		{GOTO}a:f3~	Go to A:F3
10		{MENU}rfp3~{DOWN 3}~	Format percents

This macro lets you choose whether or not to update the top of the desktop. The first instruction expects a Y, if you want to update the top of the desktop and an N if you don't. Your entry is stored in a range (cell) called update, which is checked by the {IF} statement in B2. If the entry in Update is a Y, control passes to B5. If it is any other value, control passes to B3, where {PANELOFF} disables updating of the desktop title bar, menu bar, and control line. B4 branches to the subroutine called FINISH to bypass the instruction that restores updating. The remainder of the macro moves the cell pointer to D1, then invokes a Range Format and a Worksheet Column Set width command. The cell pointer is moved to F3, and another format instruction is issued before the macro ends.

Setup Besides entering the macro instructions and naming the macro \p, you must select a cell to contain the response to the {GETLABEL} instruction. This cell is assigned the range name UPDATE. Range names must also be assigned to two sections of the macro. B5 is assigned the range name YES, and B6 is assigned the range name FINISH. You may wish to assign the names with Range Name Labels Right.

{PANELON}

The {PANELON} command causes 1-2-3/G to update the top of the desktop with each instruction executed. This is the default.

Format The format for the {PANELON} command is

{PANELON}

This command has no arguments.

Use {PANELON} is useful when you want to reactivate updating of the desktop title bar, menu bar, and control line in the middle of a macro.

Example See the example for the {PANELOFF} instruction.

{TONE}

The {TONE} command creates a sound of a specific pitch and duration. Like the {BEEP} command, {TONE} has no effect if the sound is disabled with the Control Panel program.

Format The format for the {TONE} command is

{TONE *frequency,duration*}

where *frequency* is an argument to set the tone of the bell. This is the value of hertz, with the lower numbers such as 110 representing low pitched sounds and higher numbers such as 7040 representing higher sounds. The *duration* is the number of milliseconds (1/1000th of a second) for which the pitch is held.

Use You can use {TONE} to create different sounds that are not available with {BEEP}.

Example The following macro uses the {TONE} instruction to tell the user that a significant response is being requested:

	A	B	C
1	\e	{TONE 220,1000}	Sound first pitch
2		{TONE 440,1000}	Sound second pitch
3		{TONE 220,1000}	Sound third pitch
4		{ALERT "Do you want to erase the worksheet?",,2}{QUIT}	
5		{MENU}weyn	Erase worksheet file

This macro erases the worksheet file if the operator selects the OK command button when prompted for a confirmation. When this macro is executed, it sounds three pitches to indicate that input is needed. The {ALERT} command requests a confirmation for erasing the worksheet. If the user selects the OK command button, the active worksheet file is erased. If the operator selects the Cancel command button, the macro quits. You can include a macro like this can be included in the macro library, since you can use it in any worksheet file.

{WINDOWSOFF}

The {WINDOWSOFF} command freezes the windows, with the exception of the desktop title bar, menu bar, and control line.

Format The format for the {WINDOWSOFF} command is

{WINDOWSOFF}

This command has no arguments.

Use Using {WINDOWSOFF} reduces the flicker that occurs on the windows when each new macro instruction is executed. Without this command, the screen flickers as ranges are selected, the cell pointer is moved, and entries are generated for worksheet cells. Eliminating window updating also reduces execution time for long macros, since it means that 1-2-3/G does not have to redraw the desktop every time you move the cell pointer or manipulate data.

Example The following macro allows you to monitor the effects of updating the window or freezing it during the execution of the macro:

	A	B	C
1	\w	{GETLABEL "Update Windows?",update}	
2		{IF update="Y"},{BRANCH yes}	If Y, update
3		{WINDOWSOFF}	Disables updating
4		{BRANCH finish}	Skip next command
5	yes	{WINDOWSON}	Display updating
6	finish	{GOTO}a:d1~	Go to A:D1
7		{MENU}rfc2~~	Format currency
8		{MENU}wcs12~	Set column width
9		{GOTO}a:f3~	Go to A:F3
10		{MENU}rfp3~{DOWN 3}~	Format percents

With just one response to a prompt, you can change the window updating option, which lets you see the difference between updating and freezing.

The first instruction expects a Y if you want to update the windows while the macro executes, and an N if you don't. The entry you make is stored in the cell named UPDATE, which is checked by the {IF} statement in B2. If the entry is a Y, control passes to B5, where {WINDOWSON} is executed. If the entry is any other value, control continues to B3, where {WINDOWSOFF} disables updating of the window portion of the desktop. B4 branches to the subroutine called FINISH to bypass the instruction that turns on window updating. The remainder of the macro moves the cell pointer to D1, then invokes a Range Format and a Worksheet Column Set Width command. The cell pointer is moved to F3, and another format instruction is issued before the macro ends.

Setup Besides entering the macro instructions and naming the macro \w, you must select a cell to contain the response to the {GETLABEL} instruction. You should assign this cell the range name UPDATE. You must also assign range names to two sections of the macro. Assign B5 the range name YES, and assign B6 the range name FINISH. You may want to enter these labels in column A as documentation and assign the names with Range Name Labels Right.

{WINDOWSON}

The {WINDOWSON} instruction causes 1-2-3/G to update the windows with each instruction. This is the default setting.

Format The format of the {WINDOWSON} command is

{WINDOWSON}

This command has no arguments.

Use You use {WINDOWSON} to reactivate window updating. For instance, you may want to update the window with the current results.

Example See the example under {WINDOWSOFF}.

Interactive Macro Commands

Interactive macro commands enhance the ability of a user to interact with a macro. Interactive macro commands provide features that display a message on the screen while waiting for operator input. Interactive macro commands also offer advanced features such as the ability to create custom menus and entry forms.

{?}

The {?} command is actually an advanced macro instruction, although it is introduced in Chapter 22. As you know, {?} allows the user to enter information from the keyboard.

Format The format for the {?} command is

{?}

This command has no arguments.

Use The {?} command is useful when you need to obtain a few pieces of information from the operator.

Example A macro from the last chapter allowed you to enter a date in a cell. With some formulas like @PMT, you may want to try different combinations of principal, interest and loan term. You can add a loop for a fixed number of iterations to enhance the basic macro shown in Chapter 22 under {?}. The modified macro might appear as follows:

	A	B	C
1	\d	{LET a14,0}	Initialize A14 to 0
2	top	{IF a14=10}{QUIT}	Check for maximum value in counter
3		{LET a14,a14+1}	Increment counter
4		@PMT(	Enter first part of function
5		{?}	Pause for entry of principal
6		,	Add a comma separator

(Continued)

	A	B	C
7		{?}	Pause for entry of interest rate
8		,	Add a comma separator
9		{?}	Pause for entry of # of years
10		)~	Closing parenthesis and finalize
11		{DOWN}	Move cell pointer down one cell
12		{BRANCH top}	Begin loop again

In this version of the macro, the {?} is enhanced to produce multiple versions of the same formula rather than a single entry.

Setup Besides entering the macro instructions and a macro name assignment of \d, you must assign the range name TOP to B2 of the macro. You can assign both the \d and top at the same time with the Range Name Labels Right command.

{ALERT}

The {ALERT} command displays a message in a dialog box. You can select the types of command buttons that appear at the bottom and the icon that appears to the left of the dialog box's message.

Format The format for the {ALERT} command is

{ALERT *message,type,icon*}

Where *message* is a string that must be enclosed in double quotation marks if it contains any punctuation or a cell reference, range name, or formula that produces a string. The message can be up to 30 or 34 characters, depending on whether an icon is chosen for display.

The *type* and *icon* arguments select the command buttons that appear in the dialog box and the icon that appears before the message. The *type* is 1, 2 or 3. If you don't provide a type number, 1-2-3/G uses 1. 1 displays an OK command button, 2 displays OK and Cancel command buttons, and 3 displays Yes and No command buttons. With types 2 and 3, if the user selects Cancel or No, 1-2-3/G performs any macro instructions on the same line after the {ALERT} command before performing the macro instruction in the cell below. With any type, when the user selects OK or Yes, 1-2-3/G performs the macro instructions recorded in the cell below the {ALERT} command. The user can select the command buttons with either the keyboard or the mouse.

The *icon* argument determines the icon that appears to the left of the message. If you omit an icon argument, no icon appears in the dialog box. *Icon* can be 1, 2, 3, or 4. 1 displays a hand (OS/2 version 1.1) or stop sign (OS/2 version 1.2), 2 displays an exclamation point, 3 displays a question mark, and 4 displays an asterisk (OS/2 version 1.1) or I icon (OS/2 version 1.2)

Use The {ALERT} command can display messages to the user and ask for a choice between two alternatives.

Example The {ALERT} command provides interaction between the macro and the macro operator. For example, this macro backs up the current file if drive A contains a disk:

	A	B
1	\s	{ALERT "Does drive A have a disk?",3,1}{QUIT}
2		{MENU}fs{CE}A:\BACKUP~
3		{ALERT "File saved successfully",,1}

The first macro instruction displays the dialog box like this:

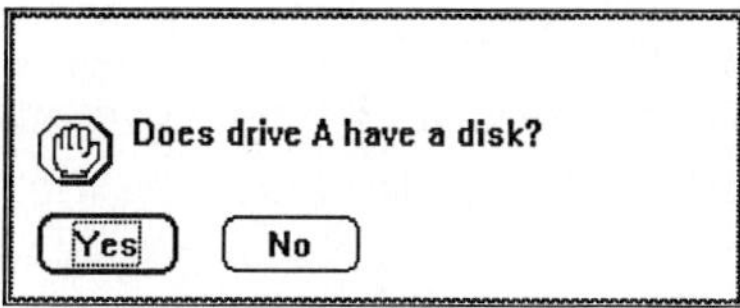

(In OS/2 version 1.2, the dialog box displays a stop sign in place of the hand). This dialog box prompts you to select Yes if drive A contains a disk or No if it does not. If you select No, the {QUIT} command recorded on the same line stops the macro execution. If you select Yes, the macro saves the file to drive A using the filename BACKUP.WG1, and displays a message that the file has been saved successfully.

Setup Before you can execute this macro, you must name B1 \s.

{BREAKOFF}

The {BREAKOFF} command disables the BREAK key function, thereby preventing the interruption of a macro.

Format The format of the {BREAKOFF} command is

```
{BREAKOFF}
```

This command has no arguments.

Use You can disable the Break feature by placing {BREAKOFF} in your macro. Be sure to test your macro before doing this, since you can only stop a macro with an infinite loop and {BREAKOFF} by closing the 1-2-3/G desktop. To close the desktop, highlight 1-2-3/G in the Task Manager or Task List window, and then select Close from the Task pull-down menu in OS/2 version 1.1 or click the End Task command button.

Example Since the {BREAKOFF} command keeps CTRL-BREAK from stopping runaway macros, it can be dangerous, leaving you no way to interrupt the macro.

However, this may be exactly what you want if you have enabled the Protection feature and wish to ensure that entries are restricted to the cells you choose.

The macro that controls input with the features described above follows:

```
    A          B                                C
23  \0         {}                               Insert {BREAKOFF} here
24             {GETLABEL ask_name,r1}           Ask to update names
25             {IF r1<>"Y"}{BRANCH address}
26             {MENU}ria2..b20~                 Update names
27  address    {GETLABEL ask_add,r2}            Ask to update addresses
28             {IF r2<>"Y"}{BRANCH phone}
29             {MENU}ric2..f20~                 Update addresses
30  phone      {GETLABEL ask_phone,r3}          Ask to update phone #
31             {IF r3<>"Y"}{BRANCH salary}
32             {MENU}rig2..g20~                 Update phone #
33  salary     {GETLABEL ask_pass,r4}           Ask to update salaries
34             {IF r4<>a:z1}{BRANCH salary}
35  end        {BREAKON}{QUIT}                  Finish macro
36
37  ask_name   Do you wish to update employee names?
38  ask_add    Do you wish to update employee addresses?
39  ask_phone  Do you wish to update employee phone numbers?
40  ask_pass   Enter password to update salaries
41  update     {MENU}rih2..h20~                 Update salaries
42             {BREAKON}{QUIT}                  Finish macro
```

The first instruction, in B23, will eventually contain {BREAKOFF}, but it is best not to add this instruciton until you test the macro. B23 currently contains {}, so 1-2-3/G skips this macro instruction. From here, the macro controls the updating of various sections of an employee database. Certain fields cannot be changed, others can be changed as desired, and you can update salaries only if you know the correct password.

The {GETLABEL} instruction in B24 checks whether you want to update the section of the database that includes employee names. This command displays the label stored in the cell named ask_name as the prompt for the {GETLABEL} command. If you respond with Y, the macro proceeds to the Range Input instruction in B26. The names in the database for this example are located in worksheet columns A and B, and this instruction allows you to change any of them.

If you don't want to alter any names and respond with N, the ADDRESS section of the macro is executed next. Again, you respond to the {GETLABEL} prompt, and if updates are needed, a new Range Input instruction is executed.

The next section is PHONE, which allows you to update phone numbers in the same manner. When you are is finished with this section, SALARY is next. In this section, the {GETLABEL} instruction expects a password. This password must match the one stored in cell Z1. Since BREAK is disabled, you must know the password, since you cannot interrupt the macro to look at the contents of Z1. If your entry matches Z1, the macro branches to UPDATE and allows updates to the salaries section of the worksheet. In the example, this is H2..H20.

{BREAKOFF} is then canceled with {BREAKON} before the macro ends (this is not mandatory, since ending a macro automatically disables {BREAKOFF}). This macro leaves the worksheet vulnerable to unauthorized changes after the update is completed. To prevent this, you can replace the two {BREAKON}{QUIT} instruction sequences can be replaced with

{MENU}fs{TAB}cr{TOOLMENU}c

to save the worksheet and close the window. If you do this, you have forever locked both the operator and yourself out of this worksheet unless Undo is enabled. You can also prompt for another password just before the file is saved and the window is closed. If the password is provided, the macro would stop with the worksheet file still on 1-2-3/G's desktop.

Setup You need to complete a number of steps in addition to entering and naming the macro:

- The cells H2..H20 must be unprotected with Range Unprotect so you can alter their contents with the Range Input command.

- Range names of \0, ADDRESS, PHONE, SALARY, END, ASK_NAME, ASK_ADD, ASK_PHONE, ASK_PASS, and UPDATE must be assigned to B23, B27, B30, B33, B35, B37, B38, B39, B40, and B41, respectively. You can do this all at once with the Range Name Labels Right command.

- The password to allow salary updates must be stored in Z1. Unlike 1-2-3/G's file passwords, such passwords are not case sensitive. Although you can assign any password you wish, "LOCK" is used for this macro.

- You may wish to freeze titles on the screen. Test the macro once and then decide. If you wish to make this change, use the command Worksheet Titles. You may decide to incorporate this command into the macro to change frozen titles for each section.

{BREAKON}

The {BREAKON} command restores the BREAK key function so that you can press CTRL-BREAK to interrupt a macro.

Format The format of the {BREAKON} command is

{BREAKON}

This command has no arguments.

Use You can disable the Break function during part of a macro and then restore its operation for a later section, for printing or data entry. Break is always restored at the end of a macro.

Example See the example under {BREAKOFF}.

{FORM}

The {FORM} command suspends macro execution, allowing you to enter data in an unprotected range. Although the concept is similar to Range

Input, {FORM} allows to define either included or excluded keystrokes. You can also define keys that invoke subroutines during the execution of the {FORM} instruction.

Format The basic format of the {FORM} command is

{FORM *input-location*}

where *input-location* is a range of unprotected cells in which you want to make entries. Normally, *input-location* is an area on a form that you design for data entry. Since {FORM} is frequently used with {APPENDBELOW} for adding records to a database, *input-location* is likely to be a row.

The {FORM} command has three optional arguments, as shown here:

{FORM *input-location,call-table,include-list,exclude-list*}

Input-location is a range of cells where you want to make entries. You can supply a range name or address for these arguments.

Call-table allows you to associate keystrokes like function keys or other entries with subroutines. It is supplied as a range address or range name. The entries in this range are expected to be placed in two adjacent columns; the first listing the keystroke, and the column to its immediate right containing the subroutine commands that are executed in response to the keystroke. The keystroke entries are case sensitive. These assignments are only effective while the form is active.

You can use *include-list* to limit the keys that can be used while the form is active. When you use *include-list,* 1-2-3/G will ignore *exclude-list.* Any key not listed is disabled. You can include typewriter keys, pointer movement keys, and function keys in the list. *Include-list* is specified as a range address or range name in which these keystrokes are stored. The *exclude-list* allows you to list the keys that you wish to inactivate. Any keys not in this list are enabled. The *exclude-list* argument is provided as a range address or range name in which these keys are stored. *Include-list* and *exclude-list* are both case sensitive.

Use You can use the {FORM} command to improve the data-entry process. Rather than entering information directly into a database, you can make your entry on a form and then transfer it to the database with {APPENDBELOW}.

Example Figure 23-2 shows a form developed for entering new employee information. The range A8..F8 is unprotected with Range Unprotect—unprotected cells are the only cells you can alter during a {FORM} command. The input location is named RECS and the cells containing the new employee record is named NEWREC.

Next, the macro code in Figure 23-3 is entered. The first instruction hides the grid lines and the row and column frames. Then the macro activates the form and allows for input in the unprotected cells in the range RECS. You can define subroutines to be invoked with an optional argument *call-table.* For this instruction, the call table is a two-column range named SUBRTNS located in K4..L6. The keys are recorded using standard macro representation, such as {WINDOW} for the F6 key. Actions assigned to each of these keys are noted on the form and are placed in the table. The optional argument for *include-list* is not supplied, so an extra comma separates *exclude-list* from *call-table.* The exclude list is named EXCLKEYS and is located in K8. The keys in this list are not operational when {FORM} is active.

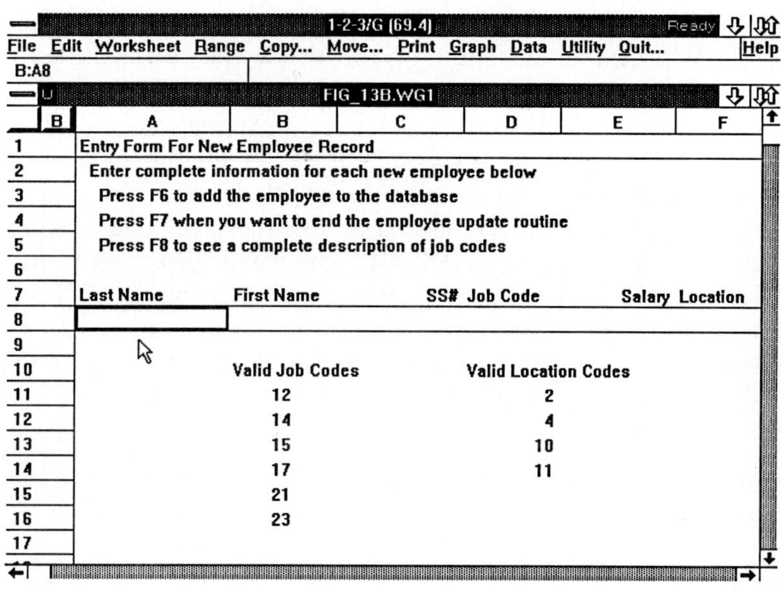

Figure 23-2. Data entry form used by {FORM}

1-2-3/G (69.4) Ready

File Edit Worksheet Range Copy... Move... Print Graph Data Utility Quit... Help

A:K1 '{FRAMEOFF}

FIG_13B.WG1

	A	J	K	L	M	N	O
1		\e	{FRAMEOFF}		Remove grid lines, column and row frames		
2			{FORM recs,subrtns,,exclkeys}		Prompt for form entry		
3							
4		subrtns	{WINDOW}	{APPENDBELOW employdb,newrec}{BLANK newrec}			
5			{QUERY}	~{MENU}fs{TAB}cr{QUIT}			
6			{TABLE}	~{GOTO}help10~{CALC}{WAIT @NOW+@TIME(0,0,10)}~			
7							
8		exclkeys	{EDIT}{LEFT}{NAME}				

Figure 23-3. Macro code using {FORM} with a call table and excluded keys

Tip: Be careful not to make your *exclude-list* an *include-list.* Remember the extra comma separators to replace unused optional arguments. If you forget this comma, 1-2-3/G misinterprets your {FORM} command entries.

If the user presses F6 (Window), F7 (Query), or F8 (Table), special actions occur. F6 appends the input information to the area below the database named employdb and then blanks the range named newrec. Once the subroutine is finished, 1-2-3/G automatically branches to the top of the macro for the entry of another form. This loop continues until the user presses F7 or F8. F7 saves the file and quits the macro. F8 displays a special help screen that you create for ten seconds and returns to the form entry. The ~ in the second and third subroutines suspends the restricted input of the {FORM} command. You could also use {GETLABEL} to let the user determine the length of the display. Alternatively, you could use a horizontal window split, with the help information always in the bottom window while the operator works on the form in the top window.

Setup Besides naming the macro before invoking it, you must establish range names RECS, NEWREC, SUBRTNS, and EXCLKEYS.

{GET}

The {GET} command is designed to accept the entry of a single character from the keyboard.

Format The format of the {GET} command is

{GET *location*}

where *location* is the storage location for the single character you enter from the keyboard. Your entry can be an alphabetic character, a numeric digit, or any other key, including one of the special function keys such as F9 (Calc) or F2 (Edit).

Use The {GET} command can restrict the keyboard response to a single character. {GET} is ideal when you wish to build your own full-screen menu and expect a one-letter code for each selection.

Example Figure 23-4 presents a full-screen menu that offers selections in Smith Company's accounting application. Letter selections represent a budget update, aging of receivables, and other accounting functions.

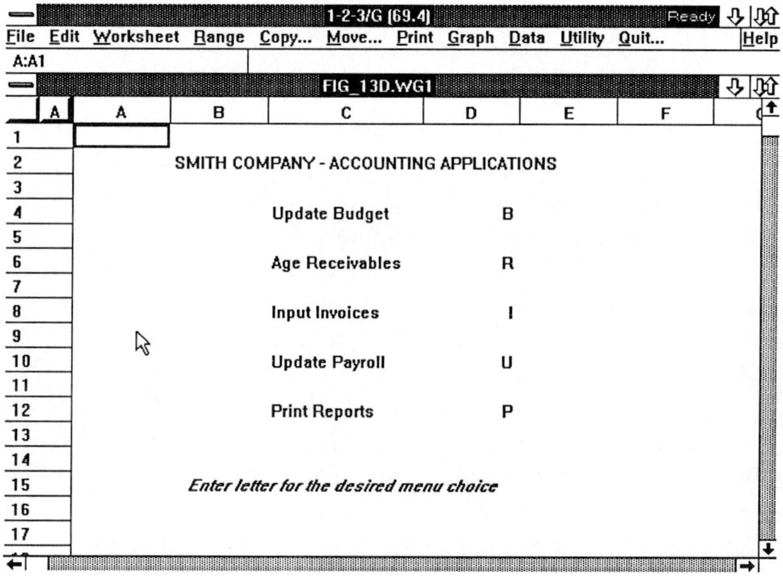

1-2-3/G [69.4] Ready
File Edit Worksheet Range Copy... Move... Print Graph Data Utility Quit... Help
A:A1
FIG_13D.WG1
SMITH COMPANY - ACCOUNTING APPLICATIONS
Update Budget B
Age Receivables R
Input Invoices I
Update Payroll U
Print Reports P
Enter letter for the desired menu choice

Figure 23-4. Menu for {GET} example

The following macro works with this menu:

```
     J         K
1    \g        {BLANK a17}
2              {INDICATE}
3              {GOTO}a1~
4              {GET choice}
5              {IF choice="B"}{BRANCH budget}
6              {IF choice="R"}{BRANCH rec}
7              {IF choice="I"}{BRANCH inv}
8              {IF choice="U"}{BRANCH payroll}
9              {IF choice="P"}{BRANCH report}
10             {INDICATE "Error"}
11             {LET a17,"Incorrect entry reexecute macro"}~
12
13   budget    {ALERT "Budget routine"}
14
15   rec       {ALERT "Receivables Routine"}
```

The macro begins with a {BLANK} instruction to make sure that A17 is erased. (This cell presents an error message to the operator when incorrect entries are made. You must start each new selection process with no entry in this cell.) The {INDICATE} instruction in K2 assures that the mode indicator is in its default state.

Next, the cell pointer is moved to A1 to allow the display of the entire screen. The {GET} instruction accepts a single-character response and stores it in a cell that previously is assigned the range name CHOICE.

The next five instructions check the value of CHOICE and then branch to appropriate subroutines. Only two of these subroutines are shown in the listing, but they all follow the same pattern. They are established as shell routines that simply display a message indicating which routine has been reached. These shells can be expanded later to include a full set of instructions for the appropriate processing.

If none of the branches is taken, the operator entered an unacceptable character. When this happens, the mode indicator is set to Error in line 10, and an error message is placed in A17 with the {LET} instruction, which assigns a string value to A17.

{GETLABEL}

The {GETLABEL} command permits the entry of a character string from the keyboard in response to a prompt message.

Format The format for the {GETLABEL} command is

{GETLABEL *prompt message,location*}

where *prompt message* is a string that must be enclosed in double quotation marks if it contains a character that can be used as an argument separator (a comma, colon, semicolon, or period), or a cell reference, range name, or formula that produces a string. When 1-2-3/G executes the {GETLABEL} command, it displays a dialog box in the middle of the desktop. The prompt message displays up to 88 characters. If you supply a longer string, the extra characters do not appear.

The *location* argument is a reference to a cell, range, or range name in which the information entered from the keyboard is stored. Up to 512 characters are accepted as input. If you supply a range for the argument, the character string entered is stored in the upper-left cell of the range.

Use The {GETLABEL} command stores your entry as a label in the location specified using the global label alignment. This command is this appropriate for numeric entries that you want placed at the left edge of the cell so they can be read as macro keystrokes.

You might use this command to obtain the name of a vendor with the following instruction:

```
{GETLABEL "Enter Vendor Name...",a2}~
```

Here, the name you enter is stored as a left-justified label in A2.

Example Figure 23-5 shows a screen that might capture data-entry information. Although you cannot use {APPENDBELOW} with this type of form, it may seem more familiar to your users than entering record

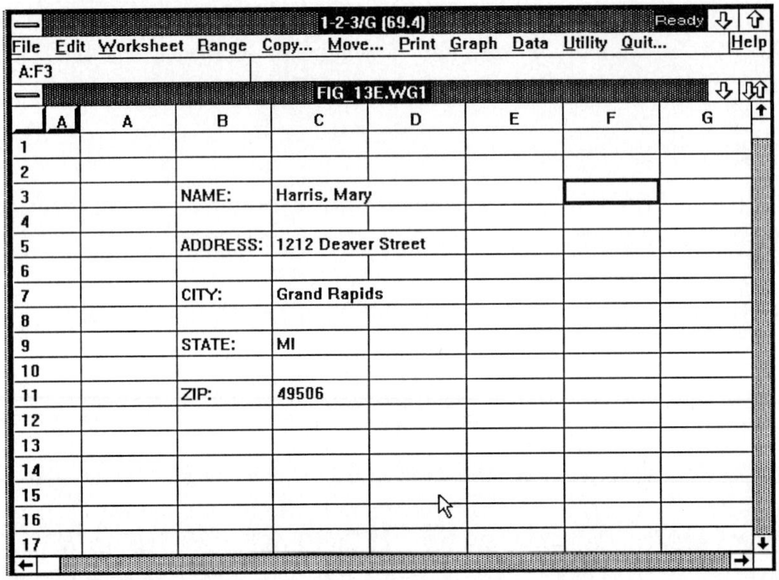

1-2-3/G (69.4) Ready

File Edit Worksheet Range Copy... Move... Print Graph Data Utility Quit... Help

A:F3

FIG_13E.WG1

A	A	B	C	D	E	F	G
1							
2							
3		NAME:	Harris, Mary				
4							
5		ADDRESS:	1212 Deaver Street				
6							
7		CITY:	Grand Rapids				
8							
9		STATE:	MI				
10							
11		ZIP:	49506				
12							
13							
14							
15							
16							
17							

Figure 23-5. Data-entry screen for {GETLABEL} example

information across a row. The following instructions are an extract from a macro that might be used with this data-entry screen:

```
     J      K                        L

1    \e     {HOME}                   Move to A1

2           {GOTO}c3~                Move to C3

3           {GETLABEL prompt,c3}     Ask for name
```

The macro moves the cell pointer to A1 and then C3. Next, the {GETLABEL} instruction uses the label in the cell named PROMPT to prompt the operator for the name. The macro stores the response in C3. Other instructions would provide a prompt for each new piece of required information and store it in the current cell.

Setup The first macro example expects that the entries in column B are already made. Before you can execute this macro, you must name K1 \e, and K13 prompt, respectively.

{GETNUMBER}

The {GETNUMBER} command permits the entry of numeric information from the keyboard in response to a prompt.

Format The format for the {GETNUMBER} command is

{GETNUMBER *prompt message,location*}

where *prompt message* is a string that must be enclosed in double quotation marks if it contains a character that can be used as an argument separator, or a cell reference, range name, or formula that produces a string. The string displays up to the first 88 characters of the prompt message in a dialog box in the middle of the desktop.

The *location* argument is a reference to a cell, range, or range name in which the information entered from the keyboard is stored. You can enter a numeric value, formula, or range name referencing a numeric value. If you supply a range for the argument, the numeric value entered is stored in the upper-left cell of the range. The location contains ERR if you enter something other than a value.

Use You can use {GETNUMBER} any time you want to prompt the operator for a numeric only:

Example The following code could be used to determine how many times the user wanted to enter a built-in @function like @PMT:

	A	B	C
1	\d	{LET a15,0}	Initialize A15 to 0
2		{GETNUMBER ask,a15}	Ask for number of formulas
3	top	{IF a15=10}{QUIT}	Check for maximum value in counter

```
(Continued)

     A      B                    C
 .
 .
 .
14   ask   How many @PMT formulas would you like to enter?
```

The first instruction initializes a counter. Next, the number of iterations is determined by requesting input from the operator.

{LOOK}

The {LOOK} command checks the keyboard buffer for characters and places the first character in this buffer as an entry in the range identified by the *location* argument. {LOOK} is similar to {GET}, but {LOOK} allows the operator to type ahead.

Format The format of the {LOOK} command is

{LOOK *location*}

where *location* is a cell address or range name that stores the character from the type-ahead buffer. If finds the buffer is blank, {LOOK} erases the contents of the *location* cell.

Use Unlike {GET}, {LOOK} does not suspend macro execution while waiting for an entry. Normally, you use {LOOK} within a loop, allowing a certain amount of time for an entry before canceling the instruction. You may or may not wish to update the file before canceling.

Example The following macro uses {LOOK} to process a menu request from the application designed earlier for {GET}:

```
        I          J
1       \l         {INDICATE}{HOME}
2                  {LET time,@NOW}
3       looking    {LOOK selection}
4                  {IF selection<>""}{BRANCH process}
```

(Continued)

	I	J
5		{IF @NOW<(time+@TIME(0,10,0))}{BRANCH looking}
6		{INDICATE "ERROR"}
7		{LET a17, "No selection made - Reexecute macro"}
8		{QUIT}
9		
10	process	Macro instructions to process menu selection

Unlike {GET}, {LOOK} uses a loop to control the amount of time it waits if the selection is not in the type-ahead buffer.

The macro first sets the indicator to its default and moves the cell pointer to A1. Then it places the current date and time in a cell named TIME.

The next instruction begins the loop for checking the type-ahead buffer. {LOOK} is executed and stores the first character from the type-ahead buffer, if present, in SELECTION. The next instruction, in line 4, checks whether anything is placed in SELECTION. If anything is stored there, the macro branches to PROCESS. If the cell is empty, the macro continues to the {IF} instruction in line 5. This {IF} instruction compares the current time against the time stored at the beginning (in TIME) plus an acceptable wait interval. For this example, the wait time is set at ten minutes. If the current time is less than ten minutes after the beginning time, the macro continues to look for an entry by branching to the LOOKING subroutine. If the chosen time interval elapses, the macro sets the indicator to Error and displays an error message in A17. An alternative strategy would be to save the file, clear memory, and quit 1-2-3/G. The PROCESS section of this macro is not shown, but would contain instructions similar to those in the {GET} example.

Setup The example macro requires that cells for the storage of variables be named TIME and SELECTION. The range names LOOKING and PROCESS must be assigned to locations in the macro, as shown.

{MENUBRANCH}

The {MENUBRANCH} command allows you to branch to a location containing information required to build a customized dialog box. Once this branch occurs, the macro executes instructions based on selections in the dialog box. If you select the Cancel command button in the dialog box, 1-2-3/G performs the macro instructions located after the {MENUBRANCH} command.

Format The format of the {MENUBRANCH} command is

{MENUBRANCH *location*}

where *location* is a cell address or range name that represents the upper-left cell in the area used for menu storage. This area must be a minimum of three rows deep and two columns wide. You may have up to eight columns of menu information.

Use You must organize information for the customized menu according to specific rules:

- The top row of the menu area contains the menu selection words to be used. Each of these words should begin with a different character, as in 1-2-3/G's menus. This allows the operator to enter the first letter of an option, or to point to the option. Like other 1-2-3/G menus, 1-2-3/G underlines the unique letter. Menu selection words are entered one to a cell, and may be up to 70 characters. 1-2-3/G accepts up to 128 characters, but the resulting dialog box may not display more than 70. You can use up to eight cells across, providing eight dialog box options.

- The second row of the menu area contains the expanded description for each menu choice. This description displays in the dialog box title bar when you highlight the dialog box item.

- Place the remainder of the macro instructions for each choice in the column with the menu item and expanded description. Begin these instructions in the cell immediately under the expanded description, and extend as far down the column as you need. You may include a branch to a subroutine.

Example Figure 23-6 shows a dialog box that was created by the macro shown in Figure 23-7. The macro begins with the {MENUBRANCH} instruction and has all the menu options stored at a

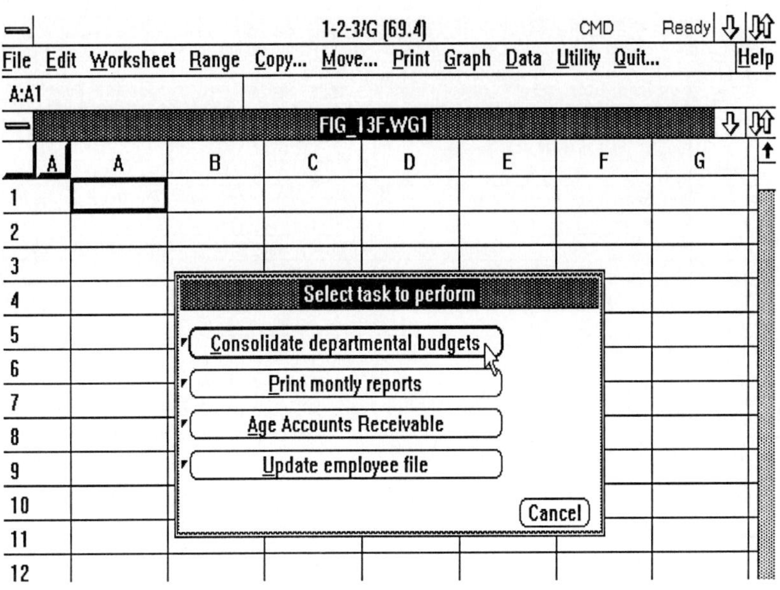

Figure 23-6. Custom dialog box

location named SELECT. The range name, SELECT, is located at J3, and descriptions extend down from there and to the right.

The menu selections are shown in J3..M3. As required, each word begins with a different letter, which is underlined in the dialog box. The expanded descriptions appear in cells J4..N4. In this example, they indicate the action that the user should take. As you select a command button in the dialog box, the dialog box title bar displays the text in the cell below the command button text. While the command button names and descriptions overlap in the worksheet, they appears in full at the top of the dialog box.

The last step in creating a menu macro is to fill in the cells underneath the descriptions with all the instructions for each choice. In the example, these instructions occupy only row five. However, menu instructions could potentially extend down in the columns to row 50 or more.

In this macro, each option has a branch to a different subroutine. At this point, the routines are simply shells to allow you to check the logic. Selecting each new choice just changes the indicator to the entry specified.

1-2-3/G [69.4] Ready

File Edit Worksheet Range Copy... Move... Print Graph Data Utility Quit... Help

A:J4 'Select task to perform

FIG_13F.WG1

A	I	J	K	L	M
1	\m	{MENUBRANCH select}			
2					
3	select	Consolidate	Print montly reports	Age Accounts Receivable	Update employee file
4		Select task	Select task to perfo	Select task to perform	Select task to perform
5		{BRANCH C	{BRANCH Prt}	{BRANCH Rec}	{BRANCH Employ}
6					
7	con	{ALERT "In Con subroutine"}			
8					
9	prt	{ALERT "In Prt subroutine"}			
10					
11	rec	{ALERT "In Rec subroutine"}			
12					
13	employ	{ALERT "In Employ subroutine"}			
14					
15					
16					
17					

Figure 23-7. Macro for creation of custom menu

Setup You must enter the entire menu section before you can test a macro like this. This is the only type of macro that can extend across as many as eight columns, (actually, it is eight individual macros in adjacent columns).

All the names listed in column I must be assigned to the respective cells in column J. Range Name Labels Right is the easiest way to handle this task.

{MENUCALL}

Like {MENUBRANCH}, {MENUCALL} displays a custom dialog box, but it executes the menu as a subroutine rather than as a branch. This affects the execution flow at the end of the menu processing. With {MENUBRANCH}, the macro ends when the code for the selected option completes. With {MENUCALL}, control returns to the statement below {MENUCALL} in the main code for the macro, and execution begins again.

Format The format of the {MENUCALL} command is

{MENUCALL *location*}

where *location* is a cell address or range name that represents the upper-left cell in the area used for menu storage. This menu area must be a minimum of three rows deep and two columns wide. You may have up to eight columns of menu information.

Use Information for the menu must be organized according to specific rules, which are listed under the {MENUBRANCH} command.

Example An example of {MENUCALL} would be just like the one for {MENUBRANCH}, but you would expect to see statements after {MENUCALL} in the main code. These would be executed after the {MENUCALL} subroutine processing had completed.

{WAIT}

The {WAIT} command halts the execution of a macro until a specified time.

Format The format of the {WAIT} command is

{WAIT *time_number*}

where *time_number* is a decimal value that represents the serial time number for the time of day that you want execution to continue.

Use The {WAIT} instruction is useful when you want to limit the display of information to a fixed amount of time.

Example You can compute a time value for WAIT by adding a time value to the value computed with @NOW to create a fixed delay. For example, you could display information on the screen for 30 seconds like this:

```
{WAIT @NOW+@TIME(0,0,30)}
```

This adds 30 seconds to the current time and waits until that time is reached before continuing execution.

Suppose you want an operator to read the instruction screen. There are several ways to proceed after the information is displayed. You can have the user enter a character to proceed, which you can use the {GET} instruction to process. In this situation, the operator may move past the screen without reading it. An alternative is to include a {WAIT} instruction in the macro. This allows you to freeze the displayed screen for a period of time, increasing the chance that the information is read. If you use this approach, these instructions might appear in your macro:

```
 ...                          Preceding macro instructions
{HOME}                        Position cell pointer in the window
{WAIT @NOW+@TIME(0,0,25)      Wait 25 seconds before proceeding
 ...                          Subsequent macro instructions
```

{WAITDIALOG}

The {WAITDIALOG} command halts the execution of a macro while the user completes a dialog box, at which point the macro continues. Unlike {?}, {WAITDIALOG} takes commands from both the keyboard and the mouse.

Format The format of the {WAIT} command is

{WAITDIALOG}

This command has no arguments.

Use The {WAITDIALOG} command lets the user make any entries in a dialog box. The macro selects and displays a dialog box to alter, and lets the user finish the entries.

Example If you want an operator to select the default font that the current worksheet uses, you can use the {WAITDIALOG} command to halt the macro temporarily. A macro that uses this command is

	A	B	C
1	\p	{MENU}wgaf	Display dialog box
2		{ALERT "Select the font to use"}	Display message
3		{WAITDIALOG}	Wait until OK
4		{MENU}fppra1..f20~gq	Print worksheet

This macro displays the Worksheet Global Attributes Font dialog box and then prompts the user to select the font to be used. The macro does not regain control of 1-2-3/G until the user selects the OK or Cancel command button in the same dialog box that displays when {WAITDIALOG} is performed.

Macro Commands that Affect Flow of Execution

Macro execution normally proceeds from the first instruction to the last. If you use macro commands that affect the execution flow you can alter the execution flow. The instructions in this group support branching to different locations, subroutine calls, and iterative processing of instructions.

{BRANCH}

The {BRANCH} command allows you to move the flow of execution in your macro to a new location.

Format The format of the {BRANCH} command is

{BRANCH *location*}

where *location* is a cell address or a range name that tells 1-2-3/G the location of the next macro instruction to execute. If you specify a range name that refers to a range of cells, 1-2-3/G begins execution with the keystrokes in the upper-left cell of the range.

Use {BRANCH} is frequently used with a condition test to change the flow of execution.

Example Here is an excerpt from a macro that combines the data in four files:

```
      A      B
1     \c     {GETLABEL "Begin combine?",h21}
2            {IF h21<>"Y"}{BRANCH stop}
```

The excerpt begins by asking the operator whether to proceed with the consolidation. The logical {IF} in the next line checks for any value other than Y and uses the {BRANCH} instruction to alter the execution flow to STOP if such a value is found. STOP recalculates the worksheet and ends the macro.

Note that {BRANCH} is frequently confused with {GOTO}. However, {GOTO} repositions the cell pointer without affecting the execution of the macro, whereas {BRANCH} alters the macro's execution flow but does not move the cell pointer.

{DEFINE}

The {DEFINE} command stores arguments passed to subroutines and establishes the type of information that they contain. It is the first macro instruction in a subroutine that uses arguments.

Format The format of the {DEFINE} command is

{DEFINE *location1:type1,location2:type2,. . .location:typen*}

where *location* is a cell in which the value passed to the subroutine is stored. You specify this cell with a cell address or a range name. A range name is preferable, since it is updated automatically when the worksheet is restructured. If you specify a range name that references a group of cells, the upper-left cell in the range is used for storage.

The argument *type* tells 1-2-3/G whether value or string data is to be passed to the subroutine. You may enter *type* as either value or string, like this:

```
{DEFINE Price:value,supplier:string}
```

where PRICE and SUPPLIER are range names that are used for passing the arguments to the subroutine. PRICE ontains value data, and SUPPLIER ontains strings. String is the type default. Value and string can be abbreviated as v and s.

Use The {DEFINE} command is an essential entry in every subroutine that you call with arguments in the subroutine call.

Example If you want to call a subroutine and pass it three numeric arguments to it, the subroutine requires a {DEFINE} statement to specify storage locations for the three arguments. Since you want these arguments to be treated as values, you must specify the type, because string is the default. Your {DEFINE} statement for the example might look like this:

```
{DEFINE z1:value,z2:value,z3:value}
```

If any of the arguments passed to these locations are arithmetic formulas, they are evaluated before storage, since the value type is specified.

For an additional example, see {*routine*} later in this section.

{DISPATCH}

The {DISPATCH} command allows you to use the contents of a cell to determine the branch location where the macro will continue processing.

Format The format of the {DISPATCH} command is

{DISPATCH *location*}

where *location* is a cell address or a range name that refers to a single cell. This cell, in turn, must contain a cell address or a range name of another cell. {DISPATCH} reads this information from the cell and branches to the location represented by its contents.

Use {DISPATCH} is useful when you need to set up a variable branching situation based on the contents of data fields or other worksheet results. In contrast to {BRANCH}, which immediately executes the instructions in the cells beginning at location, {DISPATCH} first reads the location cell to determine the final branch location at which it executes instructions.

Example Here is an example of {DISPATCH}:

	A	B
1	\d	{IF due_date>@NOW}{LET routine,"not_due"}
2		{IF due_date<=@NOW}{LET routine,"over_due"}
3		{DISPATCH routine}
4		
5	not_due	{ALERT "Account not yet due"}
6		
7	over_due	{ALERT "*** Account Overdue ***"}

The macro is designed to take two different paths, depending on whether the date in DUE_DATE is greater than today's date. The first instruction checks DUE_DATE against @NOW. If DUE_DATE is greater, it places the string NOT_DUE in the cell named ROUTINE. If the opposite condition is true, the string OVER_DUE is placed in ROUTINE.

The worksheet is calculated to place these values in ROUTINE, so you can see them display if you use the Step mode. {DISPATCH}, the next instruction, reads the entry in ROUTINE and then branches to the appropriate location. Again, the two subroutines are set up as shells in the example, but they can be expanded easily to handle whatever tasks you require.

{FOR}

The {FOR} command permits you to execute the code at a given location numerous times through a loop that the macro establishes.

Format The format of the {FOR} command is

{FOR *counter,start,stop,increment,routine*}

where *counter* is a location within the worksheet that the {FOR} instruction can use to count the number of iterations performed. {FOR} initializes this location with the value you specify for *start.*

The argument *start* is the initial value for counter. The argument *stop* is the end value for *counter—counter* never exceeds this value. The argument *increment* is the amount that should be added to *counter* for each iteration of the loop. The argument *routine* is a cell address or range name that specifies the location of the routine to be executed repeatedly.

None of these values should be altered from within the subroutine. *Start, stop,* and *increment* are maintained internally by 1-2-3/G.

Use Using {FOR} can simplify looping tasks, since it automatically handles initialization of the counter, increments it with each iteration, and checks for the last execution of the loop. When you create an iterative process outside of {FOR}, you must manage these tasks yourself.

The rules {FOR} uses to process a loop are as follows:

- Before each pass through the loop, {FOR} compares *counter* and *stop.* If *counter* is less than or equal to *stop,* the loop is processed. If *counter* is greater than *stop,* control passes to the instruction following {FOR}.

- At the end of the *start* routine or at a {RETURN}, control passes to the top of the loop. *Counter* is now increased by *increment.*
- If *stop* is less than *start,* the loop is not executed. A loop with an *increment* of 0 is an infinite loop; you can stop it only by pressing CTRL-BREAK.
- If you use {QUIT} or {FORBREAK} is used at the end of the loop rather than {RETURN}, the loop ends after the first pass.

Example The following macro allows the user to enter a column of numbers from the numeric keypad, and then sums the numbers. An arbitrary limit of 20 numbers is established, but if you want to stop sooner, enter z.

The macro instructions are as follows:

	A	B	C
1	\f	{FOR counter,1,20,1,numbers}	
2		{DEL}	Delete current cell
3		{UP}{MENU}rafau~~{DOWN}	Underline last value
4		@SUM(	Start @SUM formula
5		{UP}{END}{UP}.{END}{DOWN}	Select cells
6		)~	Finish formula
7			
8	numbers	{?}~	Get next number
9		{IF @CELLPOINTER("contents")="z"}{FORBREAK}	
10		{DOWN}	Move cell pointer

The first instruction sets up the loop with an initial value of 1, an *increment* of 1, and a *stop* value of 20. A cell named COUNTER store the number of iterations performed, and NUMBERS is the location of the code that begins the loop.

NUMBERS is executed next. In every iteration, it expects you to enter a value. You can use the numeric keypad if you disable the movement keys with NUM LOCK.

The next instruction checks whether the current cell contains a z. If it does, the {FOR} loop ends (via {FORBREAK}), regardless of the number of iterations completed, and control returns to line 2. If a z is not entered, the cell pointer moves down one cell. The *counter* is incremented by 1, and the loop begins again.

When control returns to B2, the current cell is erased. It is either blank or contains a z, depending on how the loop ended. B3 underlines the last value. The @SUM instruction is added to the cell below the last value. All the numbers you entered are then added and the @SUM function finalized.

Setup The range name \f and NUMBERS must be assigned to B1 and B7, respectively. You must also assign a range name to *counter.* Before executing the macro, position your cell pointer in the desired location for the column of numbers to be entered, and turn on NUM LOCK, since you cannot do this from the macro.

{FORBREAK}

The {FORBREAK} command cancels processing of a {FOR} loop before the stop value is reached.

Format The format of the {FORBREAK} command is

{FORBREAK}

This command has no arguments.

Use Normally, {FORBREAK} is used in conjunction with an {IF} statement that checks the value of a variable and, on a certain condition, exits the loop. As an example, suppose you want to process a loop 20 times, or until the account balance is zero. {FORBREAK} can be executed based on a test of the account balance.

Example See the example {FOR}.

{IF}

The {IF} command conditionally executes the command on the same line as {IF}.

Format The format of the {IF} command is

{IF *condition*}

where *condition* is any expression with either a numeric or a string value.

Use The statement on the same line as the {IF} statement is treated as a THEN clause: "IF the expression is true, THEN the subsequent instruction is executed." Any numeric expression is considered true as long as it is not the numeric value zero. A false condition, blank cells, ERR, NA, and string values all evaluate as zero.

The instructions on the line after {IF} are regarded as the ELSE clause. Normally, the THEN clause contains a {BRANCH}; otherwise, the macro executes the instructions in the ELSE clause after completing the THEN instructions.

Example This macro provides an example of the {IF} command:

	A	B	C
1	\h	{GOTO}i1~	Display directions in window
2		{GET k1}	Get type
3		{IF k1="C"}{LET c15,i20}	Check Budget Year/Set heading
4		{IF k1="P"}{LET c15,i19}	Set heading for previous year

This macro establishes a heading for a budget report and uses the {IF} command to determine which budget year to print at the top of the report.

At the beginning of the macro, the cell pointer moves to I1, where directions are displayed. Then {GET} waits for a single-character entry of **C** for current or **P** for previous.

The {IF} statements in lines 3 and 4 check the character entered to determine the proper heading to use—this character is then placed in C15. The statement following each {IF} on the same line is executed only if the condition shown for that {IF} is true.

Setup The macro expects to find headings for the previous and current budget years in I19 and I20, respectively.

{ONERROR}

The {ONERROR} command allows you to intercept errors, or process them yourself, during macro execution. This command does not intercept all errors including command syntax errors.

Format The format of the {ONERROR} command is

{ONERROR *location,message_location*}

where *location* is the location to which 1-2-3/G branches for error processing when an error is encountered.

The argument *message_location* is a cell containing the message that 1-2-3/G displays when an error occurs. This argument is optional, but you may not be able to determine what type of error occurred if you do not supply it.

Use Since the {ONERROR} command is not effective until 1-2-3/G executes it within the flow of the macro, you should place it near the beginning of your macro. It remains in effect until another {ONERROR} command is executed, an error is encountered, CTRL-BREAK is pressed, or the macro ends. Since CTRL-BREAK registers as an error, you can use {ONERROR} to intercept BREAK requests without using {BREAKOFF}. Once {ONERROR} intercepts an error, it is not normally available again in the same macro. If you want to reinstate {ONERROR} after using it, the routine at *location* should contain another {ONERROR} command.

Example The following macro shows the macro and message 1-2-3/G uses when an error occurs. This macro automatically executes when the file is retrieved. The {ONERROR} command directs 1-2-3/G to execute the macro starting at the cell called restart if an error occurs while 1-2-3/G executes the update_pay macro. If an error occurs, 1-2-3/G displays the message in the cell labeled Message before retrieving the file again so you can start over. You could use this type of error condition when you want to prevent batch transaction processing if an error has occurred. If the macro cannot perform *all* of the changes and save the modified file, it does not save *any* changes. In a payroll example, you wouldn't want to perform, payroll computations for only half of your employees—you want to make the computations for all employees or none.

	A	B	C
1	\0	{ONERROR restart,message}	If error, restarts
2		{update_pay}	Updates payroll
3		{MENU}fs{TAB}cr	Saves results
4			
5	restart	{ALERT message}	Display message
6		{MENU}frPAYROLL~n	Retrieve file again
7			
8	message	Unable to complete process, starting over	

{QUIT}

The {QUIT} command terminates a macro.

Format The format of the {QUIT} command is

{QUIT}

This command has no arguments.

Use The {QUIT} command can be the macro instruction at the end of a condition test—for example, {IF a1 > 10}{QUIT}. When the condition evaluates as true, the macro, and all of its subroutines end.

{RESTART}

The {RESTART} command cancels the execution of the current subroutine and eliminates all pointers to routines that called the current subroutine so that 1-2-3/G does not return to the subroutine.

Format The format of the {RESTART} command is

{RESTART}

This command has no arguments.

Use When you include {RETURN} anywhere within a called subroutine, it immediately cancels the call, completes the routine, and continues executing from that point downward. All upward pointers to higher level routines are canceled.

Tip: Use the {RESTART} command when you are using the {FORM} command with a call list if you want one of the macros in the call list to stop using the form that the macro uses.

{RETURN}

The {RETURN} command returns from a subroutine to the calling routine. It is used in conjunction with {MENUCALL} and {*routine*}. When a blank cell or one containing a numeric value is encountered in a subroutine, it has the same effect as {RETURN}.

Format The format for the {RETURN} command is

{RETURN}

This command has no arguments.

Use Placing {RETURN} anywhere in a called subroutine sends the flow of control back to the instruction following the one that called the subroutine. Unlike {RESTART}, {RETURN} does not cancel upward pointers. Check the example under {*routine*} for more on {RETURN}.

Note: Don't confuse {RETURN} with {QUIT}. {RETURN} continues processing after returning to the calling routine. {QUIT} ends the macro. With {QUIT}, no further instructions are processed.

{subroutine}

The {*subroutine*} command calls the specified subroutine. Unlike the other macro commands, it contains no keyword, but only the argument *subroutine* and any optional value arguments you choose.

Format The format of the {*subroutine*} command is

{*subroutine argument1,argument2,argumentn*}

where *subroutine* is a range name assigned to a single cell. This name must not be the same as any of the function-key or cell pointer movement key names, such as {UP}, {EDIT}, or {CALC}.

The *arguments* are optional values or strings passed to the subroutine. They must have corresponding entries in a {DEFINE} statement.

Use The use of a subroutine allows you to use the code from different areas of the macro and allows you to remove repetition in the main macro code.

Example The following macro provides an example of the use of a subroutine call.

	A	B	C
1	\r	{GETNUMBER "How many items?",k1}	
2		{LET counter,0}	Initialize counter
3		{LET K5,0}{LET K6,0}	Initialize K5,K6
4		{purchase K1}	Execute Purchase
5		{INDICATE "Done"}	Change indicator
6		{GOTO}q1~The total purchased is :~	
7		{RIGHT 2}+K6~	Supply text & number
8		{MENU}rfc2~~	Format number
9			
10	purchase	{DEFINE K2:value}	Define argument
11	loop	{IF Counter=K2}{BRANCH end}	Check if finished
12		{GETNUMBER "Enter Purchase Amount",K5}	
13		{LET K6,K6+K5}	Increase total cost
14		{LET counter,counter+1}	Increment counter

(Continued)

	A	B	C
15		{BRANCH loop}	Start loop again
16	end	{RETURN}	Finished calculation

This macro lets you enter any number of purchase amounts, and totals them for you.

The first instruction prompts you for the number of items purchased. This number is stored in cell K1. The next two instructions do some housekeeping by zeroing counters that the macro uses.

The subroutine call is in line 4. Notice that the optional argument passes the value in K1 to the subroutine.

The subroutine that begins in line 10 first uses a {DEFINE} statement to set aside K2 for the information passed to it, and declares this information to be a numeric variable. It uses COUNTER to loop within the subroutine until COUNTER is equal to the number of purchases specified. Until that time, it increments cell K6 by the purchase amount each time, increments COUNTER by 1, and then branches back to the loop.

When all purchases are processed, the subroutine branches to END, here a {RETURN} statement is located. This statement returns control to line 5 in the \r macro. The mode indicator then changes to Done and the total amount purchased is displayed.

{SYSTEM}

The {SYSTEM} command allows you to suspend your work with 1-2-3/G temporarily and execute an OS/2 operating system command. 1-2-3/G opens a OS/2 window, performs the OS/2 command, and closes the OS/2 window.

Format The format of the {SYSTEM} command is

{SYSTEM *command*}

where *command* is the OS/2 command that is performed. It is a string in quotes or a cell address or name for a cell containing the OS/2 command. *Command* can be a batch file, a program name, or an operating system command of up to 128 characters.

Use You can use {SYSTEM} any time you want to perform an OS/2 command during a macro.

Example A macro might use {SYSTEM} to format a floppy disk before backing up a large file. The macro would need to contain these instructions:

```
{SYSTEM "format a:"}

{MENU}fs{CE}A:BACKUP~
```

The first macro instruction formats the disk in drive A, and the second saves the current worksheet file to drive A using the name BACKUP.WG1. Before OS/2 formats the disk, the message in the OS/2 window tells you to insert a diskette into the drive and press ENTER.

Macro Commands that Manipulate Data

The macro commands in this section allow you to manipulate values and strings stored in worksheet cells. You can use these commands to blank out a section of the worksheet or store a value or string in a cell. You can also use commands from this section to recalculate the worksheet in row or column order.

{APPENDBELOW}

The {APPENDBELOW} instruction lets you append information to an existing database. This command extends the defined range of the database to include the extra row that it adds.

Format The format of {APPENDBELOW} is

{APPENDBELOW *target-location,source-location*}

where *target-location* is a range or range name that references an existing database. The argument *source-location* is the range of entries across a row or rows, for one or more records, to add to the existing database. The number of rows in the source location cannot exceed the number of rows available below the target location in the worksheet. 1-2-3/G does not write over existing entries when executing this command.

Use You can use {APPENDBELOW} to enter new records in a database. Generally, it is used in conjunction with Range Input or {FORM} to add the information as a new record in the database. This command can also join the contents of two database tables with an identical format.

Example You can use a custom input form and have 1-2-3/G append new records to a database automatically; Figure 23-8 shows the Entry Form that is designed for this purpose. The macro used with this data was shown in Figure 23-3. The form in the example is invoked with

```
{FORM recs,subrtns,,exclkeys}
```

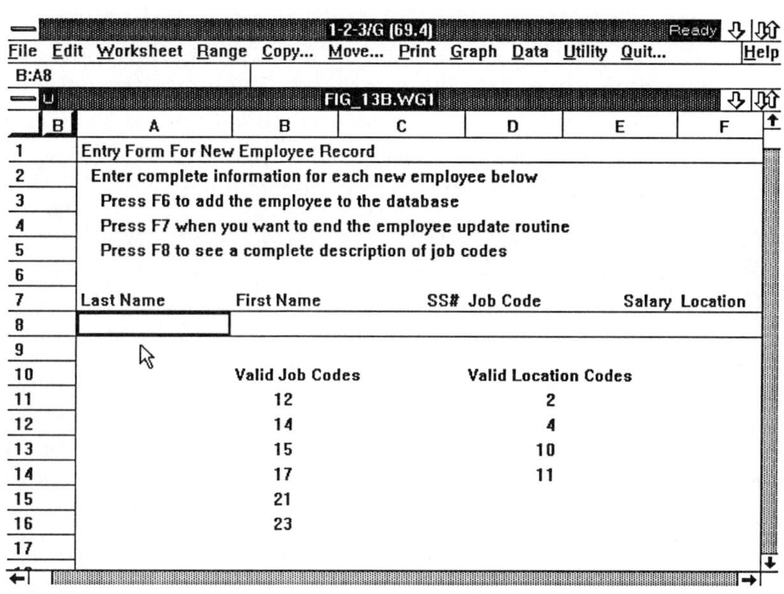

Figure 23-8. Entry form for new employee record

and accepts entries in much the same way as Range Input. When the user presses F6 (Window), the {FORM} instruction executes

```
{APPENDBELOW employdb,newrec}{BLANK newrec}
```

which adds the new record to the database. The Unprotect attribute makes the new entry appear green or highlighted, depending on your monitor. You can continue to append records to the database.

{APPENDRIGHT}

The {APPENDRIGHT} command adds fields of data to an existing database. It extends the range of the database to include the new columns of information.

Format The format of the {APPENDRIGHT} command is

{APPENDRIGHT *target-location,source-location*}

where *target-location* is a range name that references an existing database. *Source-location* is a range name referring to one or more columns that you want to append to the right edge of the existing database. The number of columns in the source location should not exceed the number of columns to the right of the target location. 1-2-3/G does not write over existing entries when executing this command.

Use If you have two databases that are in the same table sequence and contain information about identical objects, you can use {APPENDRIGHT} to add several columns of one database to another.

Example The left half of Figure 23-9 shows records from an employee salary database. Other information on the same employees is recorded in the personnel database on another sheet in the same file, as shown in the right half of the figure. Notice that the employee information is listed in the same order. You can use {APPENDRIGHT} to join to the employee database the last two columns of information in the personnel database.

1-2-3/G (69.4) Ready

File Edit Worksheet Range Copy... Move... Print Graph Data Utility Quit... Help

D:A1 "SS#

FIG_13B.WG1

C	A	B	C
1	SS#	Last Name	Salary
2	313-78-9090	Hatwick, E	$31,450
3	670-90-1121	Preverson, G	$27,600
4	560-90-8645	Smythe, G	$65,000
5	431-78-9963	Justof, J	$41,200
6	817-66-1212	McCartin, J	$54,600
7	569-89-7654	Campbell, K	$32,000
8	198-98-6750	Deaver, K	$24,600
9	459-34-0921	Caldor, L	$32,500
10	214-89-6756	Miller, L	$18,700
11	212-11-9090	Patterson, L	$21,500
12	215-67-8973	Hawkins, M	$19,500
13	543-98-9876	Larson, M	$12,000
14	219-89-7080	Samuelson, P	$28,900
15	560-55-4311	Lightnot, P	$23,500
16	312-45-9862	Kaylor, S	$32,900
17	219-78-8954	Stephens, T	$17,800

D	A	B	C	D
1	SS#	Health	Life	
2	313-78-9090	1	0	
3	670-90-1121	0	0	
4	560-90-8645	0	1	
5	431-78-9963	0	0	
6	817-66-1212	1	0	
7	569-89-7654	1	0	
8	198-98-6750	1	0	
9	459-34-0921	1	0	
10	214-89-6756	1	1	
11	212-11-9090	1	1	
12	215-67-8973	1	0	
13	543-98-9876	1	0	
14	219-89-7080	1	0	
15	560-55-4311	1	0	
16	312-45-9862	0	0	
17	219-78-8954	0	1	

Figure 23-9. Salary and personnel information

As a precaution, you should initially append all three personnel database columns, as shown in Figure 23-10. This figure shows the worksheet after you've set the column widths of D, E, and F and entered the formula

@IF(A2=D2,"","SS#'s DO NOT MATCH")

in column G to verify that the social security numbers are identical. Assuming that no errors display, delete columns D and G to remove the extra copy of the social security numbers and the unneeded formula. The defined database size automatically readjusts.

The result of joining the two database tables with {APPENDRIGHT} is shown in Figure 23-10 after setting the column widths and adding the formula to column G. If the employee database is named EMPLOYDB and the personnel database is named PERSONNEL, the append instruction

1-2-3/G [69.4] Ready

File Edit Worksheet Range Copy... Move... Print Graph Data Utility Quit... Help

C:G2 @IF(A2=D2,"",SS#'S DO NOT MATCH")

FIG_13B.WG1

C	A	B	C	D	E	F	G	H
1	SS#	Last Name	Salary	SS#	Health	Life		
2	313-78-9090	Hatwick, E	$31,450	313-78-9090	1	0		
3	670-90-1121	Preverson, G	$27,600	670-90-1121	0	0		
4	560-90-8645	Smythe, G	$65,000	560-90-8645	0	1		
5	431-78-9963	Justof, J	$41,200	431-78-9963	0	0		
6	817-66-1212	McCartin, J	$54,600	817-66-1212	1	0		
7	569-89-7654	Campbell, K	$32,000	569-89-7654	1	0		
8	198-98-6750	Deaver, K	$24,600	198-98-6750	1	0		
9	459-34-0921	Caldor, L	$32,500	459-34-0921	1	0		
10	214-89-6756	Miller, L	$18,700	214-89-6756	1	1		
11	212-11-9090	Patterson, L	$21,500	212-11-9090	1	1		
12	215-67-8973	Hawkins, M	$19,500	215-67-8973	1	0		
13	543-98-9876	Larson, M	$12,000	543-98-9876	1	0		
14	219-89-7080	Samuelson, P	$28,900	219-89-7080	1	0		
15	560-55-4311	Lightnot, P	$23,500	560-55-4311	1	0		
16	312-45-9862	Kaylor, S	$32,900	312-45-9862	0	0		
17	219-78-8954	Stephens, T	$17,800	219-78-8954	0	1		

Figure 23-10. Result of joining two tables with {APPENDRIGHT}

```
{APPENDRIGHT employdb,personnel}
```

handles the task.

{BLANK}

The {BLANK} command is functionally equivalent to Range Erase: It erases a range of cells on the worksheet. However, you can use {BLANK} in the middle of other 1-2-3/G commands, which you can't do with Range Erase.

Format The format of the {BLANK} command is

{BLANK *location*}

where *location* is a range of cell addresses or a range name associated with one or more worksheet cells.

Use The {BLANK} command can clear a data entry area from the worksheet.

Example Figure 23-11 presents a data entry screen to be used with a macro. The screen contains the data from the previous entry, which may confuse an operator ready to enter a new record. To clear the entries, add {BLANK a:c} or {BLANK c3..c11} (depending on if you have other entries in the column) to an existing macro, placing them so they are executed following the processing of the current record. If you use {BLANK a:c}, you must include the sheet letter and colon so that 1-2-3/G knows you want to use a column rather than a range name.

{CLEARENTRY} or {CE}

The {CLEARENTRY} command removes the contents of the control line, or dialog text box. This command ensures that the current entry you make replaces any previous setting.

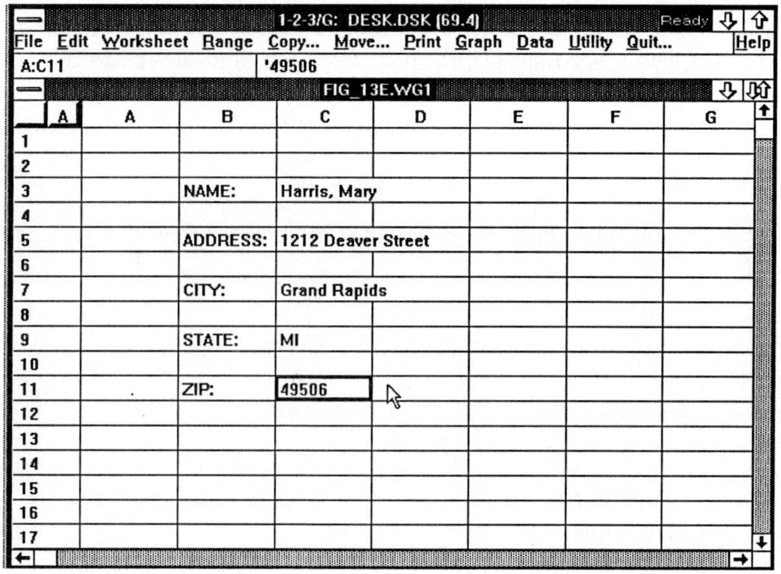

Figure 23-11. Data-entry screen containing old data

Format The format of the {CLEARENTRY} command is

{CLEARENTRY}

or

{CE}

This command has no arguments.

Use {CLEARENTRY} can clear data from cell entries and dialog boxes.

Example When you save a file using a new filename, you may want to remove the existing filename before you supply a new one. A macro that performs this task looks like this

```
{MENU}fs{CE}A:BACKUP~
```

This macro uses {CE} to remove the existing filename from the Filename text box in the File Save dialog box. Once the old file name is removed, the macro supplies a new filename and saves the file.

{CONTENTS}

The {CONTENTS} command stores a numeric value in a cell as a label with a specified format.

Format The format for {CONTENTS} is

{CONTENTS *destination,source,width,format*}

where *destination* is the location in which you want to store the label. It is a cell address or a range name.

Source is the location of the value entry you want stored in *destination* as a string (label). You may specify this location as a cell address or a range name.

Width is an optional argument, unless you specify *format,* in which case *width* is required. *Width* determines the width of the string entry. If you don't specify a width, it is obtained from the *source* location.

Format is an optional argument that allows you to determine the exact manner in which the *source* value is formatted in the destination string. Table 23-2 shows a list of the values you can select for this argument.

Use The {CONTENTS} command can be used to store a numeric value within a macro since it stores the value as a label with the format you specify. You can also use it to display information for a macro user.

Code	Associated Format
0 to 15	Fixed format with 0 to 15 decimal places, depending on the number. 0 means zero decimal places and 15 means 15
16 to 32	Scientific format with 0 to 15 decimal places
33 to 47	Currency ($) format with 0 to 15 decimal places
48 to 63	Percent (%) format with 0 to 15 decimal places
64 to 79	Comma (,) format with 0 to 15 decimal places
112	+/− format
113	General format
114	Date format 1 (DD-MMM-YY)
115	Date format 2 (DD-MMM)
116	Date format 3 (MMM-YY)
117	Text display
118	Hidden
119	Date format 6 (HH:MM:SS AM/PM)
120	Date format 7 (HH:MM AM/PM)
121	Date format 4 (Long International date)
122	Date format 5 (Short International date)
123	Date format 8 (Long International time)
124	Date format 9 (Short International time)
127	Worksheet global numeric display format

Table 23-2. Codes and Associated Formats for the Contents Command

Example The {CONTENTS} command allows you to display the formula behind a cell at a given location. Suppose that the *source* location is D1, and it contains the formula +Z1*Z3, although a 30 displays in the cell. You can display the formula behind D1 in D5 with the following macro statement:

```
{CONTENTS D5,D1,9,117}~
```

In this statement, D5 represents the *destination* location and D1 represents the *source.* A *width* of 9 is established, and the *format* represented by 117 is selected. The number 117 specifies Text display, so the formula behind D1 displays in D5. Remember that this is a string rather than a formula once it is stored in *destination.*

{LET}

The {LET} command permits you to assign a number or string to a location on the worksheet.

Format The formats for the {LET} command are

{LET *location,entry*}

where *location* is the address or range name of the cell in which you wish to store the value or label. If you specify *location* as a range, only the upper-left cell in the range is used.

The argument *entry* is a string, numeric value, formula, or cell address or name to a label or value that is stored in *location.*

Use {LET} is useful whenever you wish to control the value in a worksheet cell. You can use it with a loop to increment a counter.

Example The {LET} command can initialize and increment a counter when you want to set up your own loops. The following shell shows the format of a loop that uses {LET} in this way:

```
\s        {LET counter,1}          Initialize value of counter
top_loop  {IF counter>stop}{BRANCH end_loop}
```

```
         ...                       Additional macro instructions
         {LET counter,counter+1}   Increment value of counter
         {BRANCH top_loop}         Perform top_loop again
end_loop ...                       More macro instructions
```

Tip: If you use the {LET} command with multiple worksheet files, remember to include the filename in double angle brackets to store a value or label in a worksheet other than the current one.

{PUT}

The {PUT} command enables you to put a value in a location within a range. Unlike {LET}, which accepts only a cell address, {PUT} lets you select a row and column offset within a range.

Format The format for the {PUT} command is

{PUT *location,column offset,row offset,entry*}

where *location* is a range of cells identified by cell addresses or a range name. *Column offset* is the column number within the *location* range. The first column in the range is column 0. *Row offset* is the row number within the *location* range. The first row in the range is row 0. *Entry* is the value or string you wish to store at the specified *location.*

Use {PUT} is similar to {LET}, but it lets you store values within a range.

Example The {PUT} command can supply the values for a database table. You might have entries such as this in your macro:

- {PUT table,0,0,100}
- {PUT table,0,1,d5/2}

where TABLE is the named range of your database table.

Note: The row and column offsets must be within the range you establish with the *location* argument. If not, an error occurs. This error cannot be processed with {ONERROR}.

{RECALC}

The {RECALC} command recalculates the formulas row by row within the range you specify. This command makes macros perform faster by limiting recalculation to a specific area of one worksheet file.

Format The format for the {RECALC} command is

{RECALC *location,condition,iteration*}

where *location* is the range of the worksheet you wish to recalculate.

The optional *condition* argument specifies a condition that must be true before the selected *location* range is no longer recalculated. As long as the condition is false, 1-2-3/G continues to recalculate the worksheet. *Condition* is used in conjunction with *iteration,* which specifies a maximum number of iterations.

The optional argument *iteration* specifies the number of times that formulas within the location range are recalculated as long as condition is false. When *condition* is true, recalculation stops automatically. Each iteration reduces the count by 1. When the count is zero, no further recalculations occur.

Use Use {RECALC} when the area you are recalculating is below and to the left of the cells referenced by the formulas in this area. Use {RECALCCOL} when the area you are recalculating is above and to the right of the cells referenced by the formulas in this area. If the formula is *both* above and to the left of cells with new values, you must use {CALC} and recalculate the entire worksheet.

Example If you have a macro that changes the value of cell AB10 and you want to know the value of cell Z12, which is affected by AB10, you can use this {RECALC} instruction in your macro:

```
{RECALC z1..ab12}
```

1-2-3/G recalculates row by row to obtain the correct result for of AB10 and thus for Z12.

{RECALCCOL}

The {RECALCCOL} command recalculates the formulas within the range you specify, proceeding column by column within this range.

Format The format for the {RECALCCOL} command is

{RECALCCOL *location,condition,iteration*}

where *location* is the range of the worksheet you wish to recalculate.

The optional argument *condition* specifies a condition that must be true before the *location* range selected is no longer recalculated. As long as the condition is false, 1-2-3/G continues to recalculate the worksheet. This argument is used in conjunction with *iteration*, which specifies a maximum number of iterations.

The optional argument *iteration* specifies the number of times that formulas within the location range is recalculated as long as condition is false. When *condition* is true, recalculation stops, even though you may not have used all the iterations. With each iteration the count is reduced by 1. When it is zero, no further recalculations occurs.

Remember, when you use {CALC}, the entire worksheet is recalculated. You can use {RECALCCOL} instead when the area you are recalculating is above and to the right of the cells referenced by the formulas in this area.

Example {RECALCCOL} follows the same syntax rules as {RECALC}. Refer to the example under {RECALC} for additional information.

Macro Commands that Handle Files

The file macro commands provide sequential file-handling capabilities equivalent to the ones in programming language. You can use these commands in macros to read and write records to text files. If you haven't worked with files, you should review a section from a data processing text that overviews records, file size concepts, file input and output procedures, and other basic file use terminology before you try to use these macros.

The commands in this section are interdependent. For example, you cannot use {READLN}, {READ}, {WRITE}, or {WRITELN} unless you first open the file with {OPEN}. There are short examples with each command. The examples under {WRITE}, {WRITELN}, {READ}, {READLN}, and {FILESIZE} show commands used in context with other requred commands.

{CLOSE}

The {CLOSE} command closes the file you opened with the {OPEN} command. You must close one file before opening a second one.

Format The format for the {CLOSE} command is

{CLOSE}

This command has no arguments.

Use 1-2-3/G ignores this command if you use it when there are no open files. For an example, see {FILESIZE}.

{FILESIZE}

The {FILESIZE} command allows you to determine the number of bytes or characters in your file.

Format The format for the {FILESIZE} command is

{FILESIZE *location*}

where *location* is the cell address or range name of the cell in which you want 1-2-3/G to store the number representing the length of your file.

Use The file must be open before you use [FILESIZE}. Remember, the character for the end-of-file condition is included in the count for {FILESIZE}. If you know the length of the records, you can use {FILESIZE} to determine how many records the file contains.

Example The following macro uses the {FILESIZE} command:

```
     A    B
1    \f   {OPEN "B:TEST.PRN",r}
2         {FILESIZE a5}{CALC}
3         {CLOSE}
```

First, the macro opens the file, since a file must be opened before you can use {FILESIZE}. The entry in line 2 determines the number of bytes in the file and places this number in cell A5. {CALC} updates the worksheet cell immediately, and then the file is closed.

{GETPOS}

The {GETPOS} command determines your current position in a file.

Format The format for the {GETPOS} command is

{GETPOS *location*}

where *location* is the address or range name of the cell in which you wish the current position number stored. Remember that the first character in a file is considered to be position 0.

Use You can use {GETPOS} to monitor your progress through a file, comparing the current position to the file size so that you don't attempt to read beyond the end of the file.

Example After reading a record, you might include a {GETPOS} instruction, like this:

```
{READLN a10}

{GETPOS current}
```

You could then compare CURRENT and the result from the {FILESIZE} command to determine the number of records left to be read.

{OPEN}

The {OPEN} command allows you to open a file and specify whether you plan to read the file, write to it, or both.

Format The format for the {OPEN} command is

{OPEN *file,access*}

where *file* is a string or range name referring to a single cell containing a string or string formula that references the name of the text file you want to open. The cell string can include the entire path name and subdirectory, as well as the filename extension.

The argument *access* is a single character that controls the type of access you have to the file. The possible code characters are as follows:

- R means read-only. You cannot write to the file if your access mode is R.
- W means write-only. This argument opens a new file or recreates an existing file. You cannot read from the file if your access mode is W.
- M allows modifications to the file, permitting both read and write access.
- A means append. This argument opens the existing file; any data written is appended to the file. You can both read and write data.

Use If you want to use an error routine in case {OPEN} fails, you can place this routine on the same line as {OPEN} as a subroutine call. For example,

```
{OPEN SALES.PRN,R}{fix_err}.
```

{READ}

The {READ} command reads the specified number of characters into the location you define, starting at the file pointer's present location.

Format The format for the {READ} command is

{READ *byte-count,location*}

where *byte-count* is the number of characters you want to read from the file, beginning at the current position. If the number of bytes is larger than the number of characters remaining in the file, {READ} takes the amount of data remaining. *Byte-count* must be a numeric value or formula that evaluates to one. The number should be between 0 and 512.

The argument *location* is the address or range name for the cell in which you want to store the string of characters. The data is stored in this location as a label.

Use The {READ} command is useful when you need to work with selected information in a text file. Rather than read an entire line of a text file as with the {READLN} command, {READ} allows you to specify the number of characters that you want to read.

Example The following macro illustrates the use of the {READ} instruction:

	A	B	C
1	\r	{OPEN "b:TEST.PRN",r}	Open B:TEST.PRN for reading
2		{SETPOS 6}	Set the file pointer
3		{READ 9,g22}	Read nine characters
4		{CALC}	Recalculate any formulas
5		{CLOSE}	Close B:TEST.PRN

The first instruction opens the file for reading. The file pointer is then set at 6, which would be the seventh character in the file. Nine bytes (characters) are read from the file and stored in cell G22. The worksheet is recalculated immediately to show this entry, and is then closed.

{READLN}

The {READLN} command copies a line of characters (a record) from a file and places it at the specified location.

Format The format for the {READLN} command is

{READLN *location*}

where *location* is the cell address or range name that specifies the cell in which you want to store the line of data.

Use The {READ} command works based on the number of bytes specified as incoming text. {READLN}, by contrast, looks for a carriage return/line feed to define how many characters to read. Like {READ}, it uses the current file pointer position as the starting point and can be used with {SETPOS}.

Example The following macro reads one line from a text file.

	A	B	C
1	\z	{OPEN "b:TEST.PRN",r}	Open B:TEST.PRN for reading
2		{READLN place}~	Read first line from file
3		{RIGHT}	Move cell pointer right
5		{CLOSE}	Close B:TEST.PRN

First the file is opened. Then {READLN} reads the first line from the file and places these characters in PLACE. A tilde rather than {CALC} updates the worksheet, since the tilde represents ENTER and causes an update while requiring only one keystroke. The cell pointer is moved to the right, and then the file is closed.

{SETPOS}

The {SETPOS} command positions the file pointer at the location you specify.

Format The format for the {SETPOS} command is

{SETPOS *number*}

where *number* is a numeric value or an expression that results in a numeric value that tells 1-2-3/G which character in the file the pointer should be positioned on. Remember that the first character in the file is considered to be position 0.

Use 1-2-3/G doesn't prevent you from positioning the pointer at a location beyond the end of the file. You should always use {FILESIZE} to ensure that this doesn't happen.

Example Suppose you have the following information stored in a file:

```
ABC Company, LaCrosse, MI
```

Setting the pointer to 4 would place it on the "C" in the word "Company."

{WRITE}

The {WRITE} command places a set of characters in a file that you have opened.

Format The format for the {WRITE} command is

{WRITE *string*}

where *string* is a character string, an expression evaluating to a character string, or a range name assigned to a single cell that contains a string.

Use When you use {WRITE}, 1-2-3/G writes a string to the file at the current location of the file pointer. Then it moves the pointer to the end of this entry so it's ready to write the next set of characters.

Example If you have a column of worksheet cells that contains the days of the week, as in G1..G7 of Figure 23-12, use {WRITE} to write this list of names to a file. The names will be all in one line (record) of the file.

Assuming that you position your cell pointer at G1 where the first day name is located, pressing CTRL-Z to execute the macro writes all seven names for you. The first instruction opens the file for write access. A counter is initialized in line 2. The {FOR} loop repeats the top subroutine seven times. After the seventh iteration, the macro ends by closing the file.

When 1-2-3/G executes the top subroutine, the contents of the current cell are written to the file using the built-in @function @CELLPOINTER. The pointer is moved down, and the {FOR} command checks whether the subroutine should be performed again. The macro continues in this cycle until it writes all seven entries to the file. Each entry starts at the endpoint of the previous statement unless you reset the cell pointer using {SETPOS}.

1-2-3/G (69.4) Ready

File Edit Worksheet Range Copy... Move... Print Graph Data Utility Quit... Help

A:A1 '\z

FIG_13M.WG1

A	A	B	C	D	E	F	G
1	\z	{OPEN "together.prn",w}		Open new file for writing			Monday
2		{FOR ctr,1,7,1,top}		Start FOR loop for each day			Tuesday
3		{CLOSE}		Close file			Wednesday
4							Thursday
5	top	{WRITE @CELLPOINTER("contents")}					Friday
6		{DOWN}		Write day and move cell pointer			Saturday
7							Sunday
8	ctr	8					
9							
10	\y	{OPEN "together.prn",w}		Open new file for writing			
11		{FOR ctr,1,7,1,days}		Start FOR loop for each day			
12		{CLOSE}		Close file			
13							
14	days	{WRITELN @CELLPOINTER("contents")}					
15		{DOWN}		Write day and move cell pointer			
16							
17							

Figure 23-12. Macros to write days of the week to a file

Since entries are written sequentially on the same line, the result of this macro is

```
MondayTuesdayWednesdayThursdayFridaySaturdaySunday
```

assuming that the first cell contained Monday and the days proceeded in order throughout the week as you moved down the column.

Setup The macro requires that you assign the range names TOP and CTR to appropriate cells. Also, the days of the week must already be in the worksheet, and your cell pointer must be positioned on the first day before you execute the macro.

{WRITELN}

The {WRITELN} command places characters in an open file. Unlike {WRITE}, it adds a carriage return/line feed to the end of each character string, so it creates a new line or record in the file each time it is used.

Format The format for the {WRITELN} command is

{WRITELN *string*}

where *string* is a character string, an expression evaluating to a character string, or a range name assigned to a single cell that contains a string.

Use When you use [WRITELN}, 1-2-3/G writes a string to the file at the current file pointer location. It then moves the pointer to the beginning of the next line so it's in ready to write the next set of characters.

Using {WRITELN ""} generates a carriage return/line feed at the current position in the file. You might want to build a record with a series of {WRITE} commands, and then use {WRITELN} to add a line feed before beginning the next record.

Example You can use {WRITELN} to create a file with each day of the week on a separate line. This macro uses a loop construction just like the \z macro for the {WRITE} command in Figure 23-12. It writes to the file the days of the week, which are stored in worksheet cells G1. . .G7. It's like the {WRITE} example, but each day of the week appears in a separate line (record) of the file.

If you import the text file created with this macro into the worksheet with your cell pointer in J1, J1..J7 contains one day name per cell.

Since each day is written to a separate line when the file is created, each day is on a different line when the file is imported.

Macro Commands that Manipulate Windows

The new category of macro commands determines the window that is active, and its size and position. These commands allow you to affect screen appearance during macro execution.

{WACTIVATE}

The {WACTIVATE} command selects which open window is active, thus determining the window affected by subsequent macro instructions.

Format The format for the {WACTIVATE} command is

{WACTIVATE *windowname*}

where *windowname* is the name of the window that you want to activate. It is either enclosed in quotes, or can be a cell address or range name to a cell containing the name of the window. The window name must match the window name that appears in the list when you select Window from the Desktop Control menu.

Use {WACTIVATE} is used when a macro employs multiple windows and you want to change the window that is active.

Example For example, this macro opens two windows and prints from both of them:

	A	B	C
1	\p	{MENU}foGRAPH1.WG1~	Open worksheet window
2		{MENU}fo{BACKTAB 3}g	Select a graph tool to open
3		{TAB 3}GRAPH1.GPH~	Select graph file for window
4		{MENU}fppsp	Print graph to screen preview
5		{WACTIVATE "GRAPH1.WG1"}	Switch to worksheet window
6		{MENU}fpprprint1~sgq	Print worksheet
7		{WACTIVATE "Preview"}	Switch to preview window
8		{MENU}pp	Send window contents to print

This macro opens a worksheet window that contains GRAPH1.WG1 and a graph window that contains GRAPH1.GPH. With the graph window active, the macro prints the half-sized graph. The {WACTIVATE} command in B5 activates the worksheet window containing GRAPH1.WG1. After printing some worksheet data, the {WACTIVATE} command in B7 makes the Preview window active and prints its contents.

Setup This macro requires that the graph dimension is previously set and the range to print is named PRINT1. Also, you must give B1 the name \p.

{WMOVE}

The {WMOVE} command repositions the window on 1-2-3/G's desktop.

Format The format for the {WMOVE} command is

{WMOVE *x*,*y*,*windowname*}

x is the horizontal distance between the left edge of the desktop and the left side of the window's new location. *y* is the vertical distance between the bottom of the desktop and the bottom of the window's new location. These distances are in inches or millimeters, depending on the setting selected in Utility User Settings International Measurement. *Window-name* is the name of the window that you want to move. If you don't supply this optional argument, 1-2-3/G moves the current window. You can provide a window name, or you can use a cell address or range name to a cell containing the name of the window. If the window name contains special characters, enclose it within quotes if you enter it directly in the macro instruction.

Use Use {WMOVE} to reposition a window on 1-2-3/G's desktop.

Example For example, this macro opens and positions two windows:

	A	B	C
1	\m	{MENU}foGRAPH1.WG1~	Open worksheet window
2		{MENU}fo{BACKTAB 3}g	Select a graph tool
3		{TAB 3}GRAPH1.GPH~	Select graph file
4		{WSIZE 10,3}	Resize graph window
5		{WSIZE 10,3,"GRAPH1.WG1"}	Resize worksheet window
6		{WMOVE 0,0}	Move graph window
7		{WMOVE 0,3,"GRAPH1.WG1"}	Resize worksheet window

This macro opens a worksheet window that contains GRAPH1.WG1 and a graph window that contains GRAPH1.GPH. With the graph window active, {WSIZE} changes the window size to 3 inches high and 10 inches wide. The {WSIZE} command in B5 changes the size of the worksheet window containing GRAPH1.WG1. Once the windows are sized, the {WMOVE} command in B6 moves the graph window to the bottom of the desktop. The {WMOVE} command in B7 moves the window containing GRAPH1.WG1 to the top of the desktop, just below the control line. The {WSIZE} in B4 and the {WMOVE} in B6 use the window argument to move a window that is not the active window. You must simply give B1 the name \m.

{WSIZE}

The {WSIZE} command alters the size of a graph or worksheet window.

Format The format for the {WSIZE} command is

{WSIZE *x,y,windowname*}

x is the horizontal distance between the left edge and the right edge of the window that the command affects. *y* is the vertical distance between the top and the bottom of the resized window. These distances are in inches or millimeters, depending on the setting of Utility User Settings International Measurement. *Windowname* is the name of the window that you want to size. If you don't supply this optional argument, 1-2-3/G alters the size of the current window. Either enclose the window name within quotes, or select a cell address or range name to a cell containing the name of the window.

Use {WSIZE} is used to change the size of any desktop window that you can also size with the Window Control menu.

Example See the example for the {WMOVE} instruction.

Translating Macros from Other 1-2-3 Releases

Developing a macro to handle complex tasks often takes a great deal of time. If you are upgrading to 1-2-3/G an application from a previous release of 1-2-3, you will want to use your macros in the new release.

You can use File Retrieve or File Open to access worksheets created with prior releases of 1-2-3. However, the macros in these sheets may not work. Some of the commands from previous releases, especially print features, are reduced and replaced with other commands or OS/2 features. Other commands execute differently. In addition, you make selections differently because you use dialog boxes. 1-2-3/G handles the required changes to your macros with a translate utility, which can translate macros from Release 2.01, 2.2, and 3.0 into a 1-2-3/G macro.

You can access this translate utility from within the Utility menu, or directly from the DOS or OS/2 prompt. Entering the request from the DOS or OS/2 command prompt provides some options not available from the menu.

Translating Macros from Within 1-2-3/G

You can translate macros from earlier releases of 1-2-3 by selecting Utility Macros Translate. A dialog box allows you to select the macros to translate, the file that contains the old macros, the file to contain the new macros, and the file in which to report any macro instructions that the couldn't be translated. If a Release 2.01, 2.2, or 3.0 file is in the active window, 1-2-3/G suggests this file for translating. You can accept these suggestions or alter the filenames in the text boxes. If the file names are not displayed, type the name of the Release 2.01, 2.2, or 3.0 file to be translated in the Translate file text box, type the file to contain the new macros in the Into file text box, and type the filename to contain any problems in the Create report text box. The check boxes under Translate allow you to determine the scope of the translate action within the chosen worksheet file. Selecting All macros translates all macros in the file, selecting Backslash macros translates macros named \a through \z and \0, and selecting Selected ranges translates the macros that start in the selected range. If you choose the last option, you must also supply the range address containing the macros to translate. When you select OK, 1-2-3/G translates the macros. Figure 23-13 shows a macro before and after translation. Once the macro is translated, you may want to review it and remove unnecessary macro instructions such as the WGD{esc 3} and /wgd{esc 4}.

If you plan to use the macros in 1-2-3/G immediately, you should specify a .WG1 file extension for the Into worksheet file. You will need to retrieve and save this file after the translation to establish a file with a .WG1 format, since the translate utility writes the file in its original

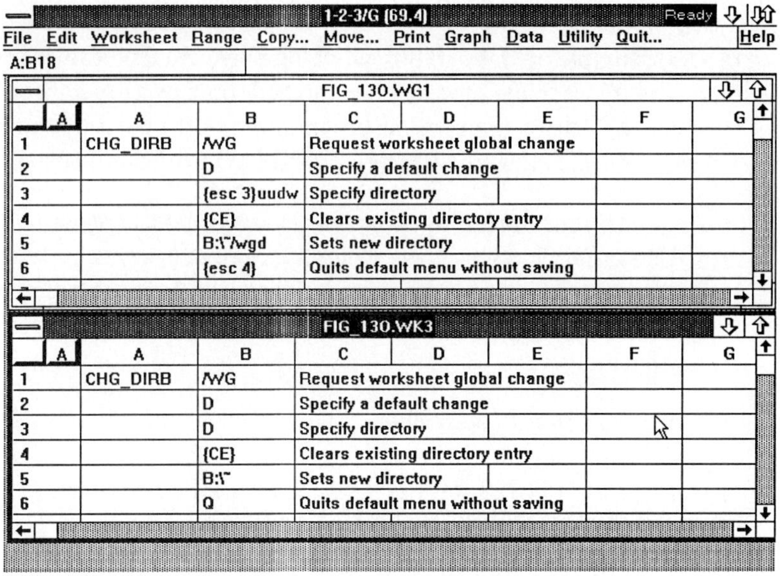

1-2-3/G (69.4) Ready

File Edit Worksheet Range Copy... Move... Print Graph Data Utility Quit... Help

A:B18

FIG_130.WG1

A	A	B	C	D	E	F	G
1	CHG_DIRB	/WG	Request worksheet global change				
2		D	Specify a default change				
3		{esc 3}uudw	Specify directory				
4		{CE}	Clears existing directory entry				
5		B:\~/wgd	Sets new directory				
6		{esc 4}	Quits default menu without saving				

FIG_130.WK3

A	A	B	C	D	E	F	G
1	CHG_DIRB	/WG	Request worksheet global change				
2		D	Specify a default change				
3		D	Specify directory				
4		{CE}	Clears existing directory entry				
5		B:\~	Sets new directory				
6		Q	Quits default menu without saving				

Figure 23-13. Macro before and after translation

format such as .WK3. This is like the temporary file format of files created with the File Xtract command.

Translating from a Command Prompt

Translating from the command prompt offers many new options. You can view errors and translated code on your screen and you can create a detailed report on the translation. If you have many worksheet files containing macros to translate, you should translate them from a DOS or OS/2 command prompt. From a DOS or OS/2 command prompt window, you can enter 123GXMAC followed by as many as six arguments. Here is the format of the request with the required and optional arguments is:

> 123GXMAC [*display-option*] [*international-option*] *worksheet-types macro-files* [*report-options*] [*translation-options*]

The optional arguments are bracketed.

- *Display-option* determines what displays during the translation. Use -de to display errors encountered during translation, -do to display the entire translation process, or -ds to turn of the display. If you omit this argument, the 123GXMAC program uses -de.

- *International-option* determines the argument separator for macros. Use -a followed by a semicolon, period, or comma to tell 1-2-3/G the argument separator used in functions and macro commands. If you omit this argument, the 123GXMAC program uses a comma for the separator.

- *Worksheet-types* describes the release of 1-2-3 that the 123GXMAC program is translating. Use -m followed by 123R201 for Release 2.01, 123R22 for Release 2.2, or 123R30 for Release 3.0.

- *Macro-files* lists the worksheet files that 123GXMAC uses. Use -i followed by the worksheet files to be translated, a space, and -o followed by the worksheet files that contain the translated macros. The filenames must include the path if they are different than the current directory. The filenames must also include the extensions.

- *Report-options* select the reports that the 123GXMAC program creates. Use -l followed by en for a report of errors, b to list the original and translated cell contents, s to display the original cell contents, and x to display the translated cell contents. The last three options should be followed by either v to show only the cells 1-2-3/G used in the translation, or a to show all strings and labels.

- *Translation-options* controls the scope of the translation performed on the worksheet file. Use -r followed by a list of range names separated by commas to translate specific macros. You can also supply a range address to translate all macros in a range. Use -k to translate all backslash macros like \a, and \0. If you use either -r or -k the 123GXMAC program translates the selected macros and any macros in the worksheet file that are used by the named or backslash macros. If you omit this argument, the translate utility translates all macros on the worksheet.

Table 23-3 provides some example entries and shows the specific instructions that they provide to the translate utility.

Translation Problems

Although the translation utility can translate most of your macro instructions, the translated macro occasionally does not perform the same task. As a general rule, you should check each macro you translate to ensure that it performs the same task before you use it. The macro may not translate correctly when it contains one of these features:

- Self-modifying macros that must be altered, especially if the cells to be modified are blank.
- Macros that don't start in Ready mode. The translate program does not understand your menu selection if the macro starts in Menu mode.
- Macros that print and create graphs. Since OS/2 now handles many of the features that earlier 1-2-3 releases handled, several of the Print menu commands have disappeared. In addition, the graph tool menu handles many graph features that the Graph menu used to handle, so many of the graph menu commands have disappeared.

Entered at Command Prompt	Results
123GXMAC -m123R301 -iMACRO.WK3 -oMACRO.WG1 -lenMACRO.LOG	Translates all macros in the MACRO.WK3 worksheet file and lists any errors in a file called MACRO.LOG
123GXMAC -m123R201 -iMACRO.WK1 -oMACRO.WG1 -rA1..B20	Translates macros in the range A1..B20 from the MACRO.WK1 worksheet
123GXMAC -a; -m123R301 -iMACRO.WK3 -oMACRO.WG1 -lxvMACRO.RPT -k	Translates all backslash macros from the MACRO.WK3 worksheet file. These macros use a semicolon as the argument separator. The translation program reports the cells used during translation to the MACRO.RPT file.

Table 23-3. Sample Entries for 123GXMAC Program

- Macros that extract files to worksheets other than .WG1 worksheets. If you want to extract to a Release 2.01, 2.2, or 3.0 worksheet, modify the macro to extract the file to a .WG1, and then save the resulting file to a .WK1 or .WK3 file.

- Macros with names that match macro command keywords. For example, the 123GXMAC program is confused by a macro named {GOTO}.

- Macro commands in Release 3.0. macros that navigate between files. Alter the macro afterward to change the macro commands such as {LASTFILE} and {NEXTFILE} to the macro command {WACTIVATE}.

- Macros that aren't separated by a blank cell. To translate these macros correctly, you must specifically name the macros with -r and the range names for the translation-options argument or by selecting the Selected ranges check box.

- Macros that contain commands that no longer exist. These commands include the printing and graph commands mentioned earlier, as well as File Erase, File List, Worksheet Global Default (when used with All, Status, and Update), and Worksheet Window Graph. These untranslated command are described in the translate report that is created whether you translate from within 1-2-3/G or from a command prompt.

The quickest way to check that your macro has translated correctly is to check the .LOG file that you select in the Macro Translate dialog box or the reports that the 123GXMAC program creates with the report options. If you translated the macros in 1-2-3/G, you can use File Import Text to import the report file.

PART SEVEN

Appendixes

System Requirements and Installation
OS/2 Essentials
Release Differences
Command Map
Lotus Character Set

System Requirements and Installation

Installing 1-2-3/G takes about 20 minutes. During this time, you need to do little other than be available to supply another disk or make a few entries. 1-2-3/G even sounds its bell when it is time to supply another disk, allowing you to focus on another task until you are needed.

Hardware Requirements

To ensure that the installation proceeds smoothly, you should check that your system includes the following:

- An IBM PS/2 Model 50 or higher, or an AT. A machine that is 100 percent compatible with one of the IBM models is also acceptable. Although a 286-based machine is acceptable, a 386 machine is recommended.
- An EGA, VGA, or IBM 8514 monitor.
- An Epson, Hewlet-Packard LaserJet, or PostScript printer. Another printer with an OS/2 driver might also work.
- OS/2 1.1 or 1.2 with Presentation Manager installed.
- A minimum of 4 megabytes of RAM—5 is recommended.
- A minimum of 6.5 megabytes of disk space for 1-2-3/G and for OS/2's SWAPPER.DAT file.

The 1-2-3/G Installation Process

If your machine includes all the necessary hardware and software, you are ready to begin the installation process. Follow these steps to complete the installation:

1. Place the 1-2-3/G Install disk in drive A. Then type **A:** and press ENTER to make drive A the active drive.

2. Type **INSTALL** and press ENTER. If you have a monochrome screen, type **INSTALL MONO** instead.

3. Press ENTER again to begin the program. If you need to interrupt the installation program and return to the operating system, you can press F3 at any time. If you need help at any time during the install procedure, you can press F1.

4. Type your name and press ENTER. The name should not exceed 30 characters.

5. Type your company name and press ENTER. Again, the name should not exceed 30 characters.

6. Check the spelling of your last two entries. If you need to make changes type **N** and then make the necessary corrections. Once you have accepted the changes by typing **Y** and pressing ENTER, you can not alter these entries.

7. Press ENTER to accept the default of the C drive or type a new drive letter before pressing ENTER.

8. Press ENTER to accept the default directory name of 123G or type a new directory name before pressing ENTER. If the directory name you specify does not exist, 1-2-3/G will create it.

9. Follow the screen instructions for entering each of the installation disks. A beep sounds when it is time to enter each new disk. When the files are copied from the last disk, you'll see the message "All files copied successfully."

10. You must accept the default directory names or supply a different new name for each. To accept the defaults, press ENTER at each new directory display. To use different names, type a new

name before pressing ENTER. The default directories are 123G\WORK for worksheet and graph files, 123G\TEMPLATE for template files, 123G\BACKUP for backup files, and 123G\TEMP for temporary files needed by commands such as UNDO.

11. Select a country driver from the list by highlighting the name of the desired country and pressing ENTER.

12. If your keyboard speed is not set to fast, the Install program prompts you to accept the default speed of fast to achieve optimal worksheet performance. The keyboard speed is set in the file STARTUP.CMD. If you don't change the option, the keyboard speed remains at its current setting.

13. The OS/2 configuration files needs certain changes that 1-2-3/G's Install program can add automatically: LIBPATH needs 123/G added, IOPL must be set to YES, and THREADS must be set to 64 or greater.

Install will make the needed modifications automatically if you OK them.

14. 1-2-3/G's Install program will add 1-2-3/G to the Start Programs window in OS/2 1.1 or the Group-Main window in OS/2 1.2 if you confirm that this addition is acceptable.

15. Install will automatically install the Helvetica, Times, and Courier fonts if they are not available on your system.

16. You can use existing installed OS/2 printer drivers with 1-2-3/G. If 1-2-3/G is the first OS/2 application you are installing on your system, you should select a printer from the list if you have an Epson, HP LaserJet, or PostScript printer.

17. Accept the default name for the selected printer by pressing ENTER or type a new name and then press ENTER.

18. Select an unassigned port for the printer. If the port you want to use is already assigned, use the OS/2 Control Panel program to unselect the current connection and make it available for use with this driver.

Install will copy the printer files to the OS2/DLL directory. If you want to define forms or make other custom changes, you need to use the OS/2 Control Panel program after leaving the 1-2-3/G Install program.

19. After reading the final installation screen, reboot your system with CTRL-ALT-DEL to enact the new selections.

Installing Fonts

OS/2 1.2 automatically installs the Helvetica, Courier, and Times fonts during the OS/2 installation process. If you acquire other fonts, you will want to install them. The installation procedure is slightly different in OS/2 1.1 and OS/2 1.2. In both versions, you need to restart your system to make the fonts available.

Follow these steps to add fonts with OS/2 1.1:

1. Activate the Start Programs window by pressing CTRL-ESCAPE and selecting Start Programs.

2. Press F10 to activate the menu; select Group and 2. Utility Programs. You can also use the mouse to make the same selections.

3. Select Control Panel from the list below the menu bar.

4. Press F10 to activate the menu in the Control Panel. Then select Installation or use the mouse to click Installation.

5. Select Add Font.

6. Place the font disk in drive A and press ENTER.

7. Select the font from the list and press ENTER again.

8. Select Add and then select Yes.

9. Press ALT-F4 to return to the Start Programs window.

Follow these steps to add fonts with OS/2 1.2:

1. Activate the Desktop Manager window by pressing CTRL-ESCAPE and selecting Desktop Manager.

2. Press F10 to activate the menu then select Utilities or use the mouse to make the same selection.

3. Press F10 to activate the menu in the Control Panel. Then select Installation or use the mouse to make the same selection.
4. Select Add Font.
5. Place the font disk in drive A and press ENTER.
6. Select the font from the list and press ENTER again.
7. Select Add and then select Yes.
8. Press ALT-F4 to return to Start Programs.

Installing Printers

The 1-2-3/G installation program installs the printer drivers for the printers you will use. If you change your printer, you need to change the printer information that OS/2 uses. Installing a printer involves several steps. The installation procedure is slightly different between OS/2 1.1 and OS/2 1.2.

Adding a Printer in OS/2 1.1

You use the Control Panel program to make most of the selections for installing a printer with OS/2 1.1. Follow these steps to install a printer with OS/2 1.1:

1. Activate the Start Programs window by pressing CTRL-ESCAPE and selecting Start Programs.
2. Press F10 to activate the menu, and then select Group and 2. Utility Programs. You can also use the mouse to make the same selections.
3. Select Control Panel from the list below the menu bar.
4. Press F10 to activate the menu in the Control Panel. Then select Installation or use the mouse to click Installation.
5. Select Add printer driver.

6. Place the disk containing the printer driver files in drive A and press ENTER.

7. Select the printer from the list.

8. Select Add and then select Yes. The Control Panel program displays the drive and directory in which OS/2 will copy the driver file.

9. Select Yes.

10. Select Setup and Printer connections from the menu bar.

11. Click the Names command button in the Printer box or press the TAB key twice to select the Names command button and then press ENTER.

12. Type a name for the printer in the Printer name text box.

13. Press TAB and type any network information in the Network Options text box.

14. Click the Add command button or press TAB and the RIGHT ARROW four times to move to the Add button and then press ENTER.

15. Click the Enter command button or press TAB twice and press ENTER. This adds the new printer name to the list of available printer names.

16. Double-click the new printer name in the Printer Name list box, or press SHIFT-TAB twice and use UP ARROW and DOWN ARROW to highlight the printer name you have just added.

17. Click the connection between your computer and the printer in the list under the Port Names list box. Alternately, press TAB and use UP ARROW and DOWN ARROW to highlight the communications port the printer uses. If another printer is assigned to the communication port you want, press SHIFT-TAB, highlight the other printer, press TAB, and select a different communications port using None if the other choices are not suitable. Then repeat steps 16 and 17.

18. Click the Drivers command button or press TAB, the RIGHT ARROW, and ENTER.

19. Select the printer that the printer name represents. You can select a printer by clicking the printer from the list or by using the UP ARROW and DOWN ARROW to highlight the printer and then pressing SPACEBAR. You may need to unselect a printer by clicking it or by using UP ARROW or DOWN ARROW to highlight the printer to unselect and pressing SPACEBAR. The goal is to display the printer you want assigned to the printer name in the Default device driver text box.

20. Click the Enter command button or press ENTER.

21. Click the Setup command button or press RIGHT ARROW and ENTER.

22. Select the printer that you are using in the Selected device driver list. Click the Change command button or press TAB and ENTER. OS/2 displays a window similar to the dialog box that appears when you select File Destination Setup from a 1-2-3/G tool window.

23. Make any desired changes to the printer settings. The actual selections available depend on the printer that you are using.

24. Select the Enter or OK command button at the bottom of the window.

25. Press ESCAPE to return to the Printer Connections window.

26. If the printer is connected to a serial port, click the Comms command button or press TAB and ENTER. Make the selections for the communications port, the baud rate, the word length, parity, stop bits, and handshake protocol. Click the Enter command button or press TAB to select the Enter command button and press ENTER.

27. Click the Enter command button or press TAB to select the Enter command button and press ENTER. This returns you to the window that appears when you select Printer Connections from the Setup pull-down menu.

28. If you want the printer that you have just added to be the default printer (unless you select a different printer in the application), select Printer defaults from the Setup pull-down menu. Select the printer name from the Default printer list box that you want most OS/2 applications to use. From this window, you can also provide the timeout information (the time OS/2 waits before telling you that the printer is not working). Device not selected indicates the number of seconds that OS/2 waits before telling you that the

printer is not accepting information either because it is not turned on, the cable between the computer and the printer is not connected, or the printer is not online. For Transmission retry, you are providing the number of seconds that OS/2 waits to determine that a packet of information that was sent to the printer has not been received and should be send again. When you have finished making selections, click the Enter command button or press TAB to select Enter and press the ENTER key.

29. Press ALT-F4 to close the Control Panel program and return to the Start Programs window.

At this point, you are ready to use the new printer in your OS/2 applications. If the printer you added is the default printer, 1-2-3/G will use it unless you select a different printer with the File Destination command. If the printer you added is not the default printer, you can use it by selecting File Destination Printer and selecting the printer name from the list box.

Adding a Printer in OS/2 1.2

You use the Control Panel program and the Print Manager to install a printer with OS/2 1.2. Follow these steps to install a printer with OS/2 1.2:

1. Activate the Task List window by pressing CTRL-ESCAPE.

2. Either select Group-Utilities from the Task List window or select Desktop Manager from the Task List window and Utilities from the Desktop Manager window.

3. Select Control Panel from the list.

4. Press F10 to activate the menu in the menu bar. Then select Installation or use the mouse to click Installation.

5. Select Add printer driver.

6. Place the disk containing the printer driver files in drive A and press ENTER.

7. Select the printer from the list by clicking it or by using the UP ARROW and DOWN ARROW keys to highlight the printer and pressing SPACEBAR. You can also change the drive and directory to which the printer driver file will be copied by pressing TAB or clicking the Copy Printer files to drive/directory text box.

8. Select the Add command button or press ENTER.

9. If the printer will be connected to a serial port, select Options and Communications port. Make the selections for the communications port, the baud rate, the word length, parity, stop bits, and handshake protocol. Click the Enter command button or press TAB to select the Enter command button and press ENTER.

10. Press F3 to close the Control Panel window.

11. Press CTRL-ESCAPE to display the Task List window. Either select Group-Main from the Task List window or select Desktop Manager from the Task List window and Utilities from the Desktop Manager window.

12. Select Print Manager from the Group-Main window.

13. Select Setup and Printers.

14. Click the Add command button or press TAB to select the Add command button and type **A**.

15. Type the name for the printer in the Printer name text box.

16. Press TAB or click the Description text box and type the description of the printer in the Description text box.

17. Accept the device name assigned to the printer or press UP ARROW and DOWN ARROW to display other possible selections. Since OS/2 will not let you assign the two printers to the same port, you may need to change the device assignment of another printer before you can assign the new printer name to the printer device you want.

18. To use different timeout information, press TAB or click the Device not selected text box and type the number of seconds OS/2 waits before indicating that the printer is not accepting information either because it is not turned on, the cable between the computer and the printer is not connected, or the printer is not online. Then press TAB to click the Transmission retry text box and type the

number of seconds that OS/2 waits to determine that a packet of information that was sent to the printer has not been received and should be send again. Unless you know that this information needs to be changed, you can accept the defaults.

19. In the list box, select the printer that the printer name represents. You can click the printer from the list, you can use or the UP ARROW and DOWN ARROW keys to highlight the printer and then press the SPACEBAR. You can unselect a printer by clicking it or by using UP ARROW and DOWN ARROW to highlight the appropriate printer and pressing SPACEBAR. The goal is to display the printer you want assigned to the printer name in the Default device driver text box.

20. Click the Printer Properties command button or press TAB twice and type **P**. OS/2 displays a window that contains many of the printer selections available when you select File Destination Setup from a 1-2-3/G tool window.

21. Make any changes to the printer settings. The actual selections available depend on the printer you are using.

22. Select the Enter or OK command button at the bottom of the dialog box.

23. Click the Add command button or type **A**. If another printer uses the same printer device that you selected in step 17, OS/2 displays a message that the two printers cannot use the same device and changes the device for the added printer to None. You can use the Change command button later to change the device that the printer uses.

24. Click the OK command button or press LEFT ARROW to move to the OK command button and press ENTER. Now the printer driver is available to be added to the printer queue.

25. Select Setup and Queues.

26. If you want to add network options, press TAB twice and type any network options in the Network options text box.

27. Under the Names and Descriptions list box, select the printer name you have added.

28. Click the Job Properties command button or press TAB until the Change command button is selected and type **J**. From the window OS/2 presents, you can make additional selections about print jobs. You will see some of the options available when you select File Destination Setup from a 1-2-3/G tool window.

29. Select the OK command button or press TAB until OK is selected and press ENTER.

30. Click the Change command button or type **C**. This finalizes your changes and returns control to the Queues window.

31. Select the OK command button or press LEFT ARROW twice so OK is selected. Then press ENTER.

32. If you want the new printer to be the default printer (unless you select a different printer in the application), select Application defaults from the Setup pull-down menu. Click the printer name that you want most OS/2 applications to use and click the Set command button. You can also press TAB and use UP ARROW or DOWN ARROW to highlight the printer to use as the default and press ENTER.

33. Minimize the Print Manager window by clicking the minimize icon or pressing ALT-F9.

At this point, you are ready to use the new printer in your OS/2 applications. If the printer you added is the default printer, 1-2-3/G will use it unless you select a different printer with the File Destination command. If the printer you added is not the default printer, you can use it by selecting File Destination Printer and selecting the printer name from the list box.

OS/2 Essentials

Advantages of Using OS/2 Rather than DOS
Versions of OS/2
Installing OS/2
Running Programs with OS/2
Types of OS/2 Programs
Starting and Stopping Applications
Spooling Output

APPENDIX B

OS/2 is the latest microcomputer operating system offered by IBM. It offers a number advantages over its predecessor, DOS. If 1-2-3/G is your first OS/2 application, you should learn about some of OS/2 advantages and major features. Although you don't need to be an OS/2 expert to use 1-2-3/G productively, you should understand how it differs from DOS.

Advantages of Using OS/2 Rather than DOS

Unlike DOS, OS/2 can operate multiple software programs or system tasks in system memory at the same time. This makes OS/2 a multitasking operating system, in contrast to the single task orientation of DOS. Multitasking means that your computer system needn't devote all its resources to the first program you load; you can also run other programs concurrently. For example, you can print from an OS/2 word processing program while making entries in an OS/2 spreadsheet program. OS/2 ensures that your computer's resources are allocated among the concurrent application programs and that commands issued from one program do not affect commands or other applications in the memory of your system.

In addition, OS/2 has a much larger memory address capacity than the 640K limit imposed by DOS. OS/2 can address up to 16 megabytes of memory. Besides using RAM, OS/2 uses some of your disk space for virtual memory when it needs to hold and swap information in and out of memory. You will need at least 6.5 megabytes of free disk space for the OS/2 SWAPPER.DAT file used to swap information out of memory when other information requires the space. This disk space will be shared by all active applications in addition to 1-2-3/G.

The third advantage of OS/2 is its graphical user interface. Graphic screen elements represent application tools and software programs. You can double-click a graphic element called an icon to activate a particular program. You can also manipulate the screen display by using a mouse or the Presentation Manager function keys to resize windows and desktop items, rather than typing a series of commands to revise display formats.

OS/2 also offers the advantage of compatibility with IBM's Systems Application Architecture (SAA). This means that the user interfaces in all OS/2 programs are similar. In addition, programs offered on the larger mainframe IBM 370 have a compatible interface with their PC counterparts. Common help options, function keys, and menus all speed up the learning process as you begin to work with multiple OS/2 applications.

Versions of OS/2

OS/2 has already gone through five different versions, beginning with OS/2 version 1.0. Version 1.0 was followed by OS/2 version 1.1 standard edition. Next, an extended edition of 1.1 offered capabilities new to a PC operating system, such as communications and data management. The latest versions are OS/2 version 1.2 standard and extended editions. Although you can run 1-2-3/G with either version 1.1 or 1.2, the standard or extended edition of OS/2 version 1.2 is recommended.

Installing OS/2

You must have OS/2 up and running on your machine to install 1-2-3/G. Fortunately, the standard installation procedure for OS/2 is quite simple and is enough to get you started with 1-2-3/G. You can accept the defaults provided by the OS/2 Install program and make changes later if performance problems occur.

Since 1-2-3/G uses the services of the OS/2 Presentation Manager rather than operating all of the system services directly, OS/2 requires more setup than DOS. For one, you need to install print devices. Consult Appendix A to learn the basic procedure for installing OS/2's print features. These instructions should provide a valuable reference, since 1-2-3/G may be your first OS/2 application. Appendix A also explains how to install the fonts provided on your OS/2 disks.

Running Programs with OS/2

OS/2 provides an operating mode for both OS/2 programs and DOS programs. The OS/2 operating mode is called *protect mode*. You can run several different types of OS/2 programs in a protect mode system. The single application environment under which DOS programs run is simply called *DOS mode*.

OS/2 or Protect Mode

Protect mode offers the multitasking environment that allows you to run several OS/2 programs at the same time. Each active program in OS/2 is placed in a window on the screen. (Each window is also referred to as a session.) If you start 1-2-3/G, OS/2 places it in a window on the screen.

Each session is either a foreground or a background session. As an analogy, if you are washing your car, that activity is your foreground task—it is your main activity. You might also be performing background tasks at the same time. You might have the car radio playing, and be trying to think of a birthday present for your daughter, or you might occasionally water some nearby flowers, or playfully squirt the dog.

Foreground Sessions

You can think of the foreground application as the current application that is using more of your computer's resources than background applications. You can interact with a foreground program from the keyboard or your mouse, since it is at the front of the potential stack of active applications. You should run an application in the foreground when you want maximum speed and performance, because OS/2 assigns a higher priority to the needs of a foreground application.

Background Sessions

You can also run one or more background programs. A background program is a program running out of your view that is not currently interactive. You can alter the status of active programs by altering the status of the window or session in which they are running.

When you start a new program, it is placed in the foreground session. Other active programs are automatically made into background sessions since you can only have one foreground application at a time.

A background session that requires user input will be suspended until it becomes the foreground application. You can then supply the needed information and the application will continue.

DOS Mode or Real Mode

In OS/2, you can run programs in DOS mode. When you run a program in DOS mode, it must be the foreground application, although you can continue your OS/2 applications from the background mode. The DOS application will use your entire screen and does not support windows.

Some DOS programs will not work when run under OS/2's DOS mode. These include network programs and other applications that are timing dependent or programs that require more than the 512K that is allocated to DOS with the OS/2 install program.

Types of OS/2 Programs

You can run three different types of OS/2 programs within OS/2 sessions. These include text-windowed applications, full-screen applications, and Presentation Manager applications.

Text-windowed applications run in a window on your screen. They display text information and allow you to enter text. However, they lack the graphical elements found in Presentation Manager applications. You can run OS/2 commands in a text-windowed application.

Full-screen applications offer no windowing capability and occupy your entire screen. Like text-windowed applications, they are limited to text display. Although a full-screen application doesn't let you see the windows for other background sessions, these will still run while you work in the full-screen display. You can run OS/2 commands from a full-screen display.

Presentation Manager applications offer the biggest advance over DOS since they allow windowing within applications. They also use graphical elements in addition to screen text to present information and allow direct manipulation of the display items. Being able to have multiple windows on the screen makes it easier to switch between active foreground applications. 1-2-3/G is a Presentation Manager application.

Starting and Stopping Applications

The way you start applications is almost identical in OS/2 1.1 and 1.2, but the terminology differs a little. In OS/2 version 1.2, two groups of applications are provided in the desktop manager: Main and Utilities. When you install 1-2-3/G, you can add it to one of the groups. If you add it to the Main group, you can start it from the Group-Main window by double-clicking it with the mouse or highlighting 1-2-3/G and pressing ENTER.

In OS/2 1.1, the various options are organized by the Task Manager. From this window, you can select Start Programs where your application options are organized. When you use OS/2 1.1, 1-2-3/G is added to the Start Programs window and is selected in the same way.

Switching Between Applications

To switch to a different program in OS/2, you can use CTRL-ESCAPE regardless of the release you are using. In OS/2 version 1.2, this will activate the Task List window. You can select Group-Main to start a new program, or pick the name of the background task you want to run in the foreground with either the mouse or the keyboard. If you are running OS/2 version 1.1, pressing CTRL-ESCAPE activates the Task Manager, allowing you to make the same selection.

Ending Applications

Since you can have many application programs running concurrently, make sure that you consider the impact for all applications when you turn off your system. You might complete a DOS application and end normally yet have two or three OS/2 applications still active. Turning off the power would end these applications abruptly, and could result in a loss of data.

If you need to check the status of each application individually, you can use CTRL-ESCAPE to check each one. You can shut down all applications at once if you are certain that you will not lose any data. The OS/2 Shutdown option will ensure that files are closed and applications are ended in an orderly fashion, although it does not force each application to save its data.

To shut down all programs with OS/2 1.2, follow these steps:

1. Activate the Desktop Manager.
2. Select Desktop.
3. Select Shutdown.

To shut down all programs from OS/2 version 1.1, follow these steps:

1. Activate the Task Manager.
2. Select Shutdown.
3. Select Shutdown Now.

Spooling Output

With DOS, all of your output was sent directly to the output device. OS/2 uses a spooler to store your output in temporary files and send it to the output device based on the other print jobs managed by the spooler. This process is similar to spoolers used on networks, which manage print requests sent from many different workstations. The use of spooler allows you to schedule print output better, since the output can be written to a temporary disk file quickly and transmitted to the printer at any time.

OS/2 automatically provides a spooler. 1-2-3/G prefers to run without sharing the output devices, and would rather that you not use the spooler, although it does support the spooler. If you disable the spooler, you can follow these steps within OS/2 version 1.2:

1. Activate the Print Manager by double-clicking.
2. Select Setup from the Print Manager menu.
3. Click on Spooler and then click the button to turn it off.
4. Click on Set.
5. Reboot your machine by simultaneously pressing CTRL-ALT-DEL.

If you are using OS/2 version 1.1, here are the steps for disabling the spooler:

1. Activate the Control Panel program.
2. Select Setup from the Control Panel menu bar, then select Spooler options.
3. Press SHIFT-TAB and SPACEBAR, or click the Spooler enabled check box.
4. Press ENTER or click the OK command button.
5. Exit the Control Panel program by pressing ALT-F4.
6. Reboot your machine by simultaneously pressing CTRL-ALT-DELETE.

For both releases, when your system reboots, the spooler will not be available.

Some printer drivers are not available for OS/2 version 1.1, and most printers that you can use with 1.1 cannot be used with the printer spooler. You are therefore advised to disconnect the printer spooler if using 1.1.

Release Differences

1-2-3/G has many new features not available in any other 1-2-3 release. Other features are new if you use 1-2-3 Release 2.01 or 2.2, although they should not be new to a 1-2-3 Release 3 user.

Solver and Backsolver Technology

A Solver utility locates and identifies problem solutions that meet multiple analysis goals or constraints. A Solver reporting capability creates a variety of reports that let you explore solutions or attempts in detail.

A Backsolver utility solves backward from a solution to a variable value needed to reach the desired result.

Three Dimensions

Each worksheet file automatically contains 256 sheets. Although 1-2-3 Release 3 also supports up to 256 sheets, you don't need to insert sheets in a 1-2-3/G worksheet to make them available, as you would with a Release 3 file.

A Worksheet Window Perspective command allows you to view as many as five sheets at once within a window. The Worksheet Window Clear command lets you switch back to a single sheet view of a worksheet file.

You can use CTRL-PGUP and CTRL-PGDN to move between sheets quickly.

Network Support

1-2-3/G supports reservations to ensure single user update access to a file. 1-2-3/G will automatically supply the reservation for a file if you open it when no one else is accessing the file. You can change the setting for this default with File Admin Reservation.

You can seal a file and prevent changes to the reservation setting with File Admin Seal. File Admin Seal requires a password and prevents format changes to the file.

Template Files

There are template files for both worksheets and graphs. You can change DEFAULT.WG1 and DEFAULT.GPH to save settings and data that you want to use with each new worksheet or graph. You can also create other template files to allow consistency and quick customization for a variety of applications.

Graphical User Interface

1-2-3/G runs under OS/2 Presentation Manager. This allows 1-2-3/G to employ all of the new graphical capabilities of the operating system. You can accomplish many tasks with direct manipulation of screen objects. Fonts, colors, type styles, and being able to turn off the grid and frame give you new possibilities in worksheet design.

You can change row and column sizes by pressing a mouse button and moving the mouse on the work surface to make adjustments.

Multiple Windows

You can open as many as 16 windows on the screen at once. These open windows can contain the Worksheet or Graph tools or utilities like Solver, help, notes, or a print preview. Windows can be stacked one on top of the other or tiled next to one another. You can also use custom sizing and placement for windows.

File Links

You can use File link formulas or Presentation Manager's Dynamic Data Exchange to link files with 1-2-3/G. External link formulas are easy to enter since the only addition is an external file reference. Files referenced in an external link can be open or on disk. Links are refreshed when you retrieve the worksheet containing them or when you use File Admin Link Refresh. You access the DDE link capability through the Edit Link commands. Although the file to which you are linking must be open, it can be in any application that supports DDE. This allows you to transfer data from Microsoft Excel or another application package.

Desktop Files

1-2-3/G uses your screen as a desktop with as many as 16 different windows open at once. These files can contain worksheets, graphs, notes, or other utility data such as help or Solver information. A desktop file contains information about the files in any open windows, although it does not contain the data for any of the files. The desktop file contains information on the name and location of each file on that desktop, links between files, and the information needed to return each file window to its current size and position.

Improved Screen and Print Appearance

Fonts and type style assignments allow you to customize both the screen display and printed output. Since font assignments are separate for print and display, you can use different setups for the different modes. This means that you can use as many fonts as your printer supports, even if you can only display Courier on your screen.

You can use as many as 16 colors when displaying or printing information. You can use color for the data, cell background, worksheet frames, grid lines, and borders. You can use different colors to distinguish different types of data, and positive and negative numbers.

You can establish borders around cells and ranges.

Improved User Interface

In addition to the standard 1-2-3 menu, you can access options through a desktop control menu and a window control menu. Desktop control menu options allow you to save the desktop, change the active window, and size and position the desktop on your screen. The window control menu allows you to size and position the current window.

Options beneath the main menu are presented in cascade menus that allow you to see the path of previous selections or dialog boxes. Dialog boxes have many new graphical elements, such as boxes and buttons, that simplify your selections. You can make all menu and dialog box selections with the mouse to save time.

User Settings

To supplement Worksheet Global options, 1-2-3/G provides a User Settings menu that you can access via the Utility menu or the desktop control menu. New customization options allow you to select whether you wish to see the Worksheet or Graph tool when you start 1-2-3/G. You can also set ENTER and ESCAPE to be compatible with prior releases of 1-2-3 or with Presentation Manager. You can display markers to indicate which underlined letters you can type to make selections. In addition, you can display the function keys at the bottom of the screen to allow for mouse selection.

Graph Capabilities

You can access graph commands through the worksheet tool menu and through the new graph tool menu. Graph View and Setup options allow you to create instant graphs without making a whole series of menu selections.

New graph types include a high-low-open-close graph, which is excellent for displaying financial market data. Overlapped bars, 3-D bar, and combination graphs offer additional presentation options.

You can manipulate graph objects directly with the mouse. A gallery of graph types and text, arrows, lines, colors, and fonts offer many new customization features that are easy to apply.

Status Information

Additional status information is provided through both mode indicators in the desktop title bar and status indicators in the window title bar.

Cell indicators display in the window title bar on the left and provide display information for the current cell.

New Function Keys

1-2-3/G provides additional features that you can access through function keys. The new function key assignments include ALT-F4 (Close desktop) to close the 1-2-3/G desktop; CTRL-F4 (Close tool) to close the active window; SHIFT-F4 (Bound) to limit cell pointer movement to selected cells; SHIFT-F8 (Detach) to detach the cell pointer from the current selection; SHIFT-F7 (Group) to activate or deactivate Group mode; SHIFT-F6 (Hide) to hide or display hidden worksheets, columns, and rows; CTRL-F6 (Next window) which activates the next open window; and SHIFT-F3 (Options) which displays the Options box for certain commands. In addition, with the Utility User Settings Preferences command you can display a function key map which lists the function each key performs, at the bottom of the 1-2-3/G desktop.

Collections and Other New Range Options

Collections are discontinuous ranges that can be defined like ranges and used for most 1-2-3/G commands that accept ranges. You can use one command to apply changes to an entire collection or to print areas of the worksheet that are not adjacent. 1-2-3/G allows you to detach the cell pointer from the current selection in order to begin the selection of another range for the collection.

Ranges can now span worksheets. These 3-D ranges include the same cells on whatever span of sheets you select.

Group Mode

Group mode allows you to work with a selection of worksheets as if they were one. Selections made in one sheet are made in the entire group. Changes made to a sheet in the group affect all sheets in the group. 1-2-3/G's Group mode implementation differs from 1-2-3 Release 3's by allowing you to control whether existing settings on the current sheet are copied to all sheets in the group when you first establish the group.

Improved Print

1-2-3/G offers the following new print options since it has access to all of OS/2's new print features:

- You can print to an encoded file to retain all of the printer specific information for deferred printing.
- There is a Print Preview utility for viewing output before printing.
- You can print text and graphs on the same page.
- You can print multiple ranges on the same page.
- You can create and name multiple print settings.
- You can access OS/2's printer setup options from within 1-2-3/G.
- There are print options available from the File command included in the Graph tool and 1-2-3/G utilities.
- You can convert color display output to black-and-white mapped patterns.

Help

There is now a Help utility that allows you to continue working in another window while help is displayed on the screen. The help information provided is context sensitive. It is also much more extensive than the help provided with earlier versions of 1-2-3.

Note Utility

You can use the Note utility to add as many as four notes to each cell or range. Each note can be as long as 512 characters.

Clipboard

The Clipboard provides the interface between 1-2-3/G and other Presentation Manger applications. Although you access it through the Edit command options in 1-2-3/G's main menu, the Clipboard allows you to transfer data between 1-2-3/G and any other Presentation Manger application that supports the Dynamic Data Exchange.

New Undo Capabilities

1-2-3/G allows you to undo the effect of as many as 20 previous commands. You can use ALT-BACKSPACE or Edit Undo to access this feature.

New Copy Options

A special Options button available after selecting Copy allows you to restrict the type of information copied.

Search and Replace Options

You can use the new Range Search command to locate specific data on the worksheet.You can search through labels or formulas and can specify a replacement for the entry.

User-Defined Formats

In addition to the many standard formats, you can now create your own formats. The Format Description Language allows you to create formats for values, including special date and time serial number formats.

Memory

1-2-3/G uses virtual (disk) memory in addition to RAM. This prevents your computer's hardware from limiting the OS/2 and 1-2-3/G features you can use.

Recalculation

Recalculation is much more efficient since it is performed in the background while you work on other tasks. It is also minimal, since 1-2-3/G recognizes the cells that require recalculation and limits its worksheet update to these cells.

Data Management

Data management supports external database access through the Data External command. This allows you to access information in another type of file, such as a dBASE file, directly from your 1-2-3/G worksheet.

A Data Query Output range can contain computed columns. You can use aggregate @functions like @SUM and @AVG to head these computed columns as well as other formulas.

1-2-3/G supports multiple database tables. This allows you to use Data Query Extract after joining data in the two tables with a join formula, which connects the data in one table with the data in another.

1-2-3/G supports as many as 255 sort keys for Data Sort. You can also enter criteria for as many as 255 fields.

A new Data Table command allows you to create a three-way table to vary as many as three variables systematically. A Data Table Labeled command allows you to use an unlimited number of variables while calculating multiple formulas. Labeled tables also allow more variation in the appearance of the output.

Data Query Modify allows you to extract data records from a database table, modify them, and replace them in the original table.

New @Functions

There are 14 new @functions in 1-2-3/G compared to the offerings in 1-2-3 Release 2.01. The new functions are

@COORD	@ISRANGE
@DGET	@SHEETS
@DQUERY	@SOLVER
@DSTDS	@STDS
@DVARS	@SUMPRODUCT
@D360	@VARS
@ISEMPTY	@VDB

In addition, you can use the F3 (Name) key to select and insert @function names into your formulas.

New Macro Features

There are 17 new macro commands in 1-2-3/G, beyond those offered by 1-2-3 Release 2.01. The new macro commands are

{ALERT}	{MENUBRANCH}
{APPENDBELOW}	{MENUCALL}
{APPENDRIGHT}	{SYSTEM}
{CLEARENTRY}	{TONE}
{FORM}	{WACTIVATE}
{FRAMEOFF}	{WAITDIALOG}
{FRAMEON}	{WMOVE}
{GRAPHOFF}	{WSIZE}
{GRAPHON}	

There are also many new macro key names.

A Keystroke Editor allows you to work with the keystroke history that 1-2-3/G captures as you make command selections. You can cut, copy, and paste captured keystrokes to create macros.

A macro translator provides an easy upgrade for macros created in 1-2-3 2.01, 2.2, and 3.0.

Command Map

APPENDIX D

Worksheet Menu

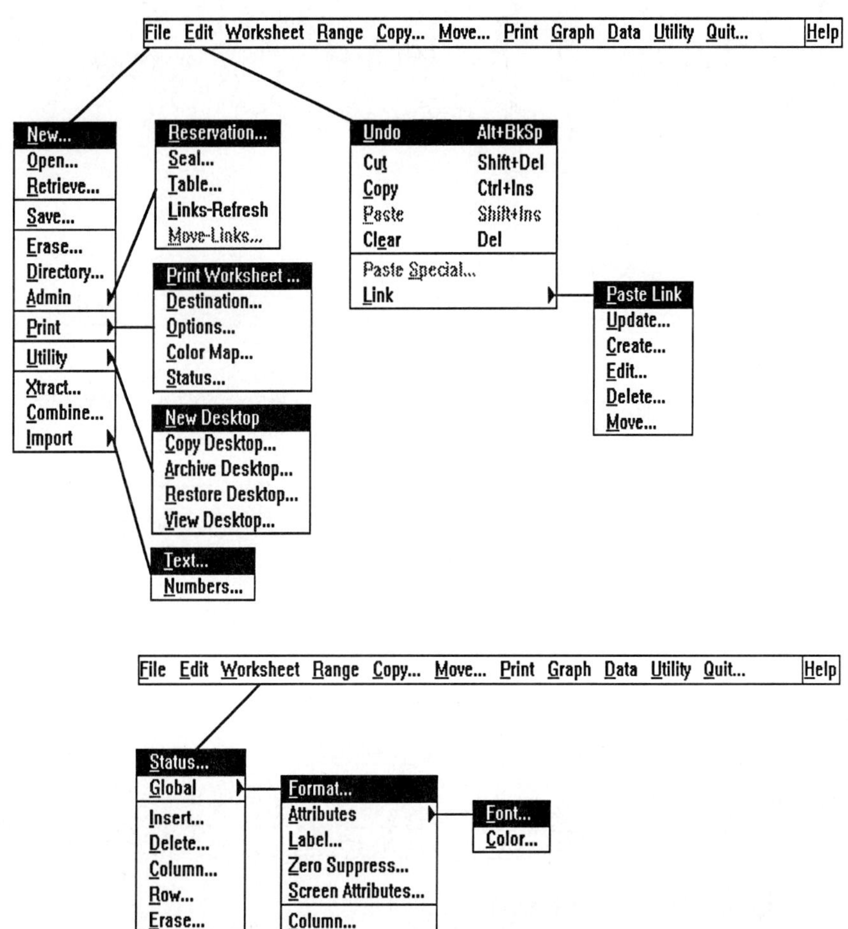

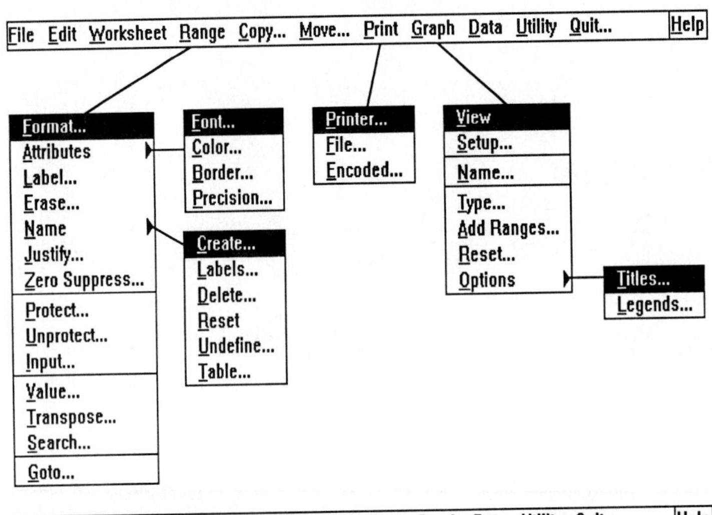
File Edit Worksheet Range Copy... Move... Print Graph Data Utility Quit... Help
Format...
Attributes
Label...
Erase...
Name
Justify...
Zero Suppress...
Protect...
Unprotect...
Input...
Value...
Transpose...
Search...
Goto...
Font...
Color...
Border...
Precision...
Create...
Labels...
Delete...
Reset
Undefine...
Table...
Printer...
File...
Encoded...
View
Setup...
Name...
Type...
Add Ranges...
Reset...
Options
Titles...
Legends...

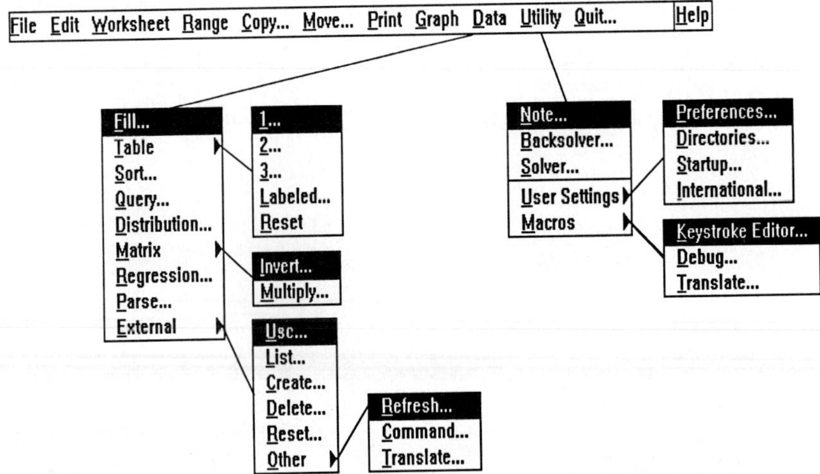
File Edit Worksheet Range Copy... Move... Print Graph Data Utility Quit... Help
Fill...
Table
Sort...
Query...
Distribution...
Matrix
Regression...
Parse...
External
1...
2...
3...
Labeled...
Reset
Invert...
Multiply...
Use...
List...
Create...
Delete...
Reset...
Other
Refresh...
Command...
Translate...
Note...
Backsolver...
Solver...
User Settings
Macros
Preferences...
Directories...
Startup...
International...
Keystroke Editor...
Debug...
Translate...

Graph Menu

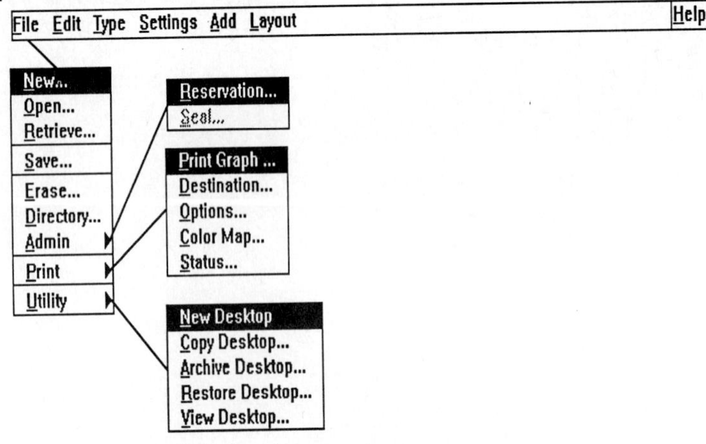
File Edit Type Settings Add Layout Help
New...
Open...
Retrieve...
Save...
Erase...
Directory...
Admin
Print
Utility
Reservation...
Seal...
Print Graph ...
Destination...
Options...
Color Map...
Status...
New Desktop
Copy Desktop...
Archive Desktop...
Restore Desktop...
View Desktop...

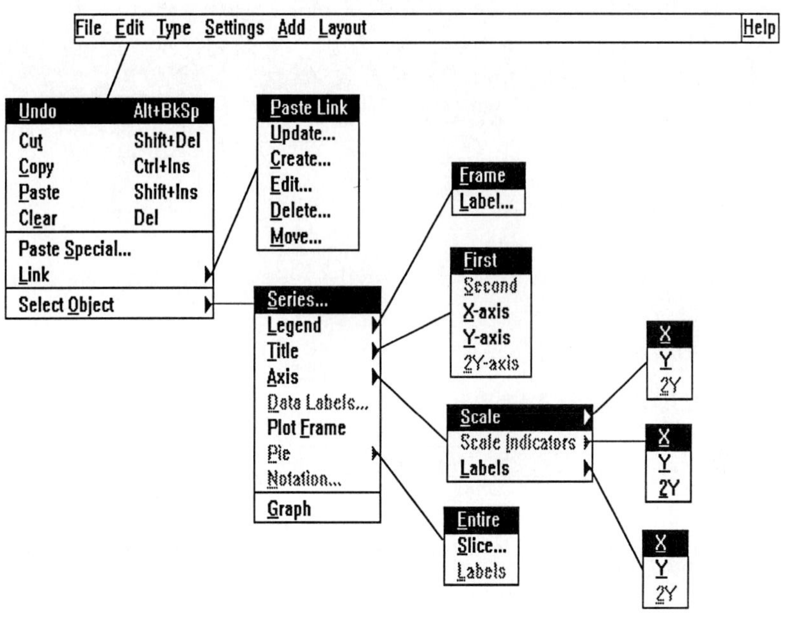
File Edit Type Settings Add Layout
Help
Undo Alt+BkSp
Cut Shift+Del
Copy Ctrl+Ins
Paste Shift+Ins
Clear Del
Paste Special...
Link
Select Object
Paste Link
Update...
Create...
Edit...
Delete...
Move...
Series...
Legend
Title
Axis
Data Labels...
Plot Frame
Pie
Notation...
Graph
Frame
Label...
First
Second
X-axis
Y-axis
2Y-axis
Scale
Scale Indicators
Labels
Entire
Slice...
Labels
X
Y
2Y

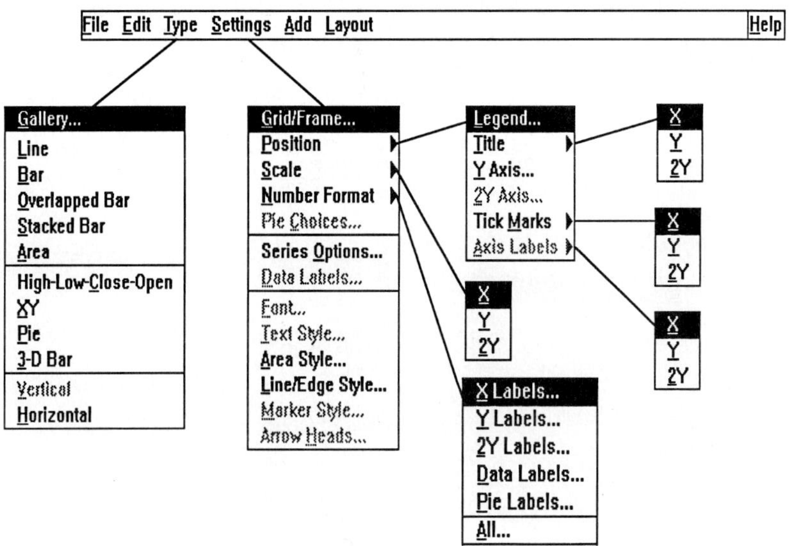
File Edit Type Settings Add Layout
Help
Gallery...
Line
Bar
Overlapped Bar
Stacked Bar
Area
High-Low-Close-Open
XY
Pie
3-D Bar
Vertical
Horizontal
Grid/Frame...
Position
Scale
Number Format
Pie Choices...
Series Options...
Data Labels...
Font...
Text Style...
Area Style...
Line/Edge Style...
Marker Style...
Arrow Heads...
Legend...
Title
Y Axis...
2Y Axis...
Tick Marks
Axis Labels
X Labels...
Y Labels...
2Y Labels...
Data Labels...
Pie Labels...
All...
X
Y
2Y

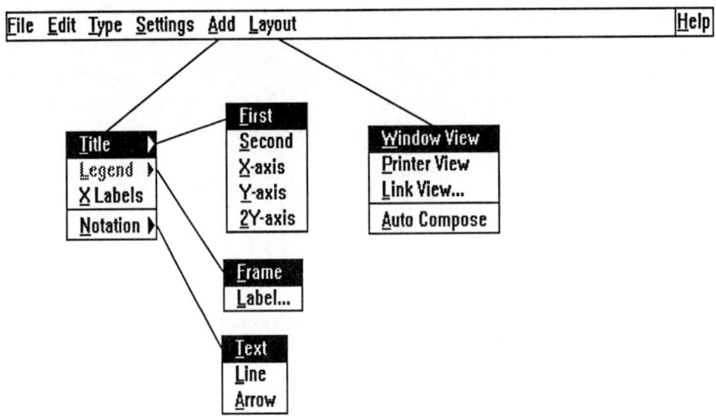
File Edit Type Settings Add Layout
Help
Title
Legend
X Labels
Notation
First
Second
X-axis
Y-axis
2Y-axis
Window View
Printer View
Link View...
Auto Compose
Frame
Label...
Text
Line
Arrow

Solver Menu

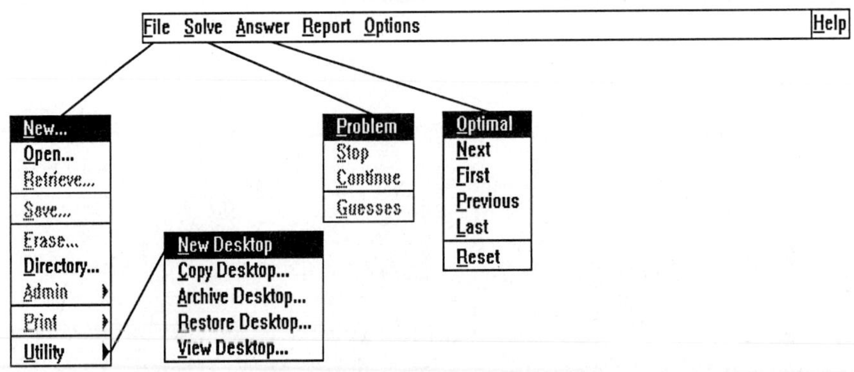
File Solve Answer Report Options
Help
New...
Open...
Retrieve...
Save...
Erase...
Directory...
Admin
Print
Utility
New Desktop
Copy Desktop...
Archive Desktop...
Restore Desktop...
View Desktop...
Problem
Stop
Continue
Guesses
Optimal
Next
First
Previous
Last
Reset

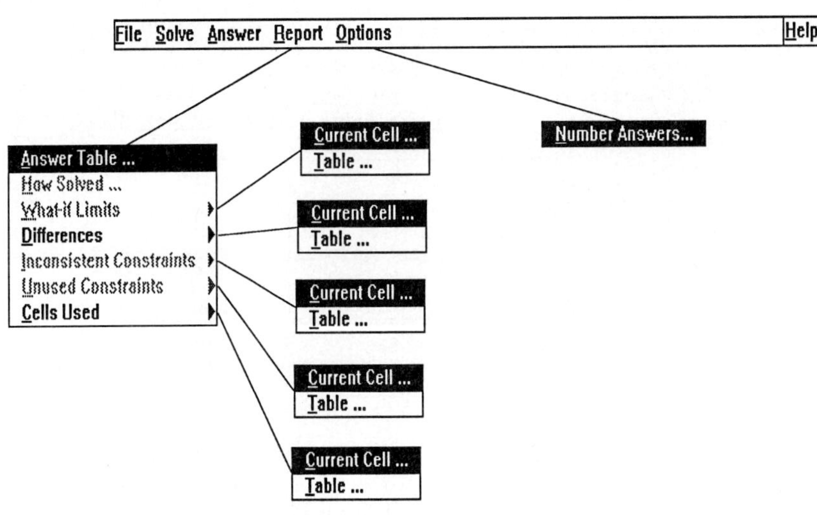
File Solve Answer Report Options
Help
Answer Table ...
How Solved ...
What-if Limits
Differences
Inconsistent Constraints
Unused Constraints
Cells Used
Current Cell ...
Table ...
Current Cell ...
Table ...
Current Cell ...
Table ...
Current Cell ...
Table ...
Current Cell ...
Table ...
Number Answers...

Note Menu

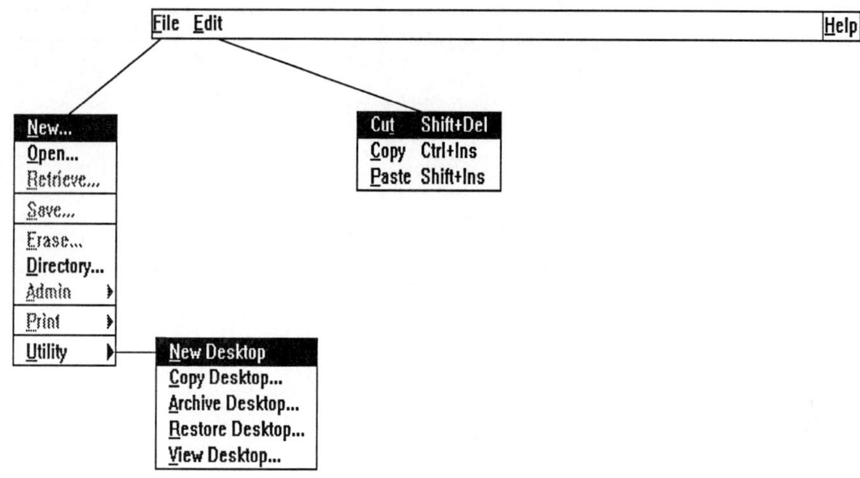

Preview Menu

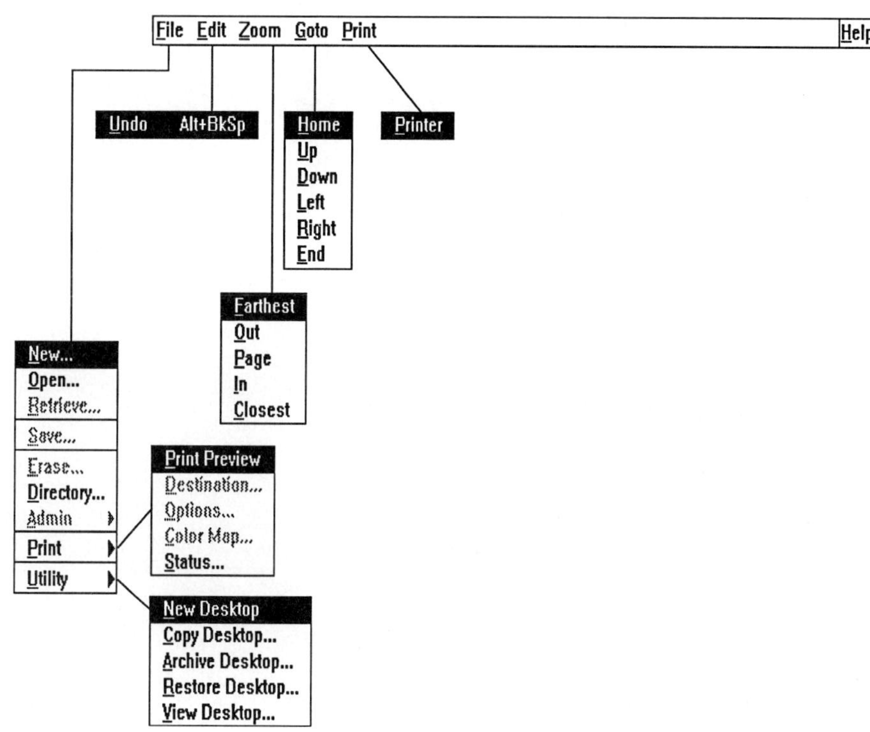

Keystroke Editor Menu

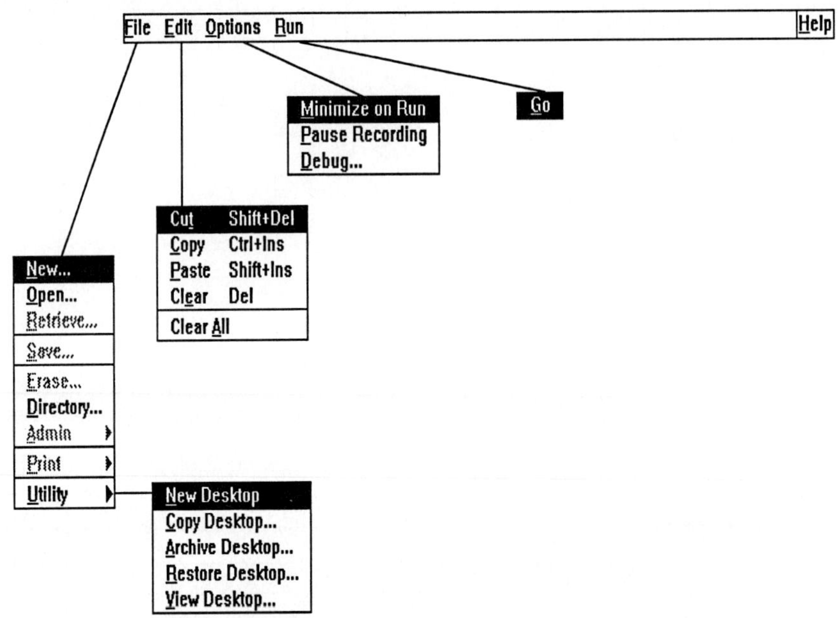

Lotus Character Set

APPENDIX E

Code Page Value	Character	Description	Compose Sequence
1	☺	Smiling face	
2	☻	Smiling face, reversed	
3	♥	Heart suit symbol	
4	♦	Diamond suit symbol	
5	♣	Club suit symbol	
6	♠	Spade suit symbol	
7	•	Bullet	
8	◘	Bullet, reversed	
9	○	Open circle	
10	◙	Open circle, reversed	
11	♂	Male symbol	
12	♀	Female symbol	
13	♪	Musical note	
14	♫	Double musical note	
15	☼	Sun symbol	
16	►	Forward arrow indicator	
17	◄	Back arrow indicator	
18	↕	Up-down arrow	
19	‼	Double exclamation points	
20	¶	Paragraph symbol	! p
21	§	Section symbol	S O

Code Page Value	Character	Description	Compose Sequence
22	▬	Solid horizontal rectangle	
23	↨	Up-down arrow, perpendicular	
24	↑	Up arrow	
25	↓	Down arrow	
26	→	Right arrow	
27	←	Left arrow	m g
28	∟	Right angle symbol	
29	↔	Left-right symbol	
30	▲	Solid triangle	b a
31	▼	Solid triangle, inverted	e a
32		Blank space	
33	!	Exclamation point	
34	"	Double quotes	
35	#	Number sign	+ +
36	$	Dollar sign	
37	%	Percent sign	
38	&	Ampersand	
39	'	Close single quote	
40	(	Left parentheses	
41	)	Right parentheses	
42	*	Asterisk	
43	+	Plus sign	
44	,	Comma	
45	−	Minus sign	
46	.	Period	
47	/	Forward slash	

Code Page Value	Character	Description	Compose Sequence
48	0	Zero	
49	1	One	
50	2	Two	
51	3	Three	
52	4	Four	
53	5	Five	
54	6	Six	
55	7	Seven	
56	8	Eight	
57	9	Nine	
58	:	Colon	
59	;	Semicolon	
60	<	Less than	
61	=	Equal sign	
62	>	Greater than	
63	?	Question mark	
64	@	At sign	a a
65	A	Uppercase A	
66	B	Uppercase B	
67	C	Uppercase C	
68	D	Uppercase D	
69	E	Uppercase E	
70	F	Uppercase F	
71	G	Uppercase G	
72	H	Uppercase H	
73	I	Uppercase I	
74	J	Uppercase J	
75	K	Uppercase K	

Code Page Value	Character	Description	Compose Sequence
76	L	Uppercase L	
77	M	Uppercase M	
78	N	Uppercase N	
79	O	Uppercase O	
80	P	Uppercase P	
81	Q	Uppercase Q	
82	R	Uppercase R	
83	S	Uppercase S	
84	T	Uppercase T	
85	U	Uppercase U	
86	V	Uppercase V	
87	W	Uppercase W	
88	X	Uppercase X	
89	Y	Uppercase Y	
90	Z	Uppercase Z	
91	[	Open square bracket	((
92	\	Backslash	/ /
93	]	Close square bracket	))
94	^	Circumflex	v v
95	_	Underscore	
96	`	Open single quote	
97	a	Lowercase a	
98	b	Lowercase b	
99	c	Lowercase c	
100	d	Lowercase d	
101	e	Lowercase e	
102	f	Lowercase f	
103	g	Lowercase g	

Code Page Value	Character	Description	Compose Sequence
104	h	Lowercase h	
105	i	Lowercase i	
106	j	Lowercase j	
107	k	Lowercase k	
108	l	Lowercase l	
109	m	Lowercase m	
110	n	Lowercase n	
111	o	Lowercase o	
112	p	Lowercase p	
113	q	Lowercase q	
114	r	Lowercase r	
115	s	Lowercase s	
116	t	Lowercase t	
117	u	Lowercase u	
118	v	Lowercase v	
119	w	Lowercase w	
120	x	Lowercase x	
121	y	Lowercase y	
122	z	Lowercase z	
123	{	Open curly brace	(-
124	|	Vertical bar	^ /
125	}	Close curly brace	) -
126	~	Tilde	– –
127	⌂	Delete	
128	Ç	Uppercase C cedilla	C ,
129	ü	Lowercase u umlaut	u "
130	é	Lowercase e acute	e '

Code Page Value	Character	Description	Compose Sequence
131	â	Lowercase a circumflex	a ^
132	ä	Lowercase a umlaut	a "
133	à	Lowercase a grave	a `
134	å	Lowercase a ring	a *
135	ç	Lowercase c cedilla	c ,
136	ê	Lowercase e circumflex	e ^
137	ë	Lowercase e umlaut	e "
138	è	Lowercase e grave	e `
139	ï	Lowercase i umlaut	i "
140	î	Lowercase i circumflex	i ^
141	ì	Lowercase i grave	i `
142	Ä	Uppercase A umlaut	A "
143	Å	Uppercase A ring	A *
144	É	Uppercase E acute	E '
145	æ	Lowercase ae diphthong	a e
146	Æ	Uppercase AE diphthong	A E
147	ô	Lowercase o circumflex	o ^
148	ö	Lowercase o umlaut	o "
149	ò	Lowercase o grave	o `
150	û	Lowercase u circumflex	u ^
151	ù	Lowercase u grave	u `
152	ÿ	Lowercase y umlaut	y "
153	Ö	Uppercase O umlaut	O "

Code Page Value	Character	Description	Compose Sequence
154	Ü	Uppercase U umlaut	U "
155	ø	Lowercase o slash	o /
156	£	British pound symbol	L =
157	Ø	Uppercase O slash	O /
158	×	Multiplication symbol	x x
159	ƒ	Florin symbol	f f
160	á	Lowercase a acute	a '
161	í	Lowercase i acute	i '
162	ó	Lowercase o acute	o '
163	ú	Lowercase u acute	u '
164	ñ	Lowercase n tilde	N ~
165	Ñ	Uppercase N tilde	N ~
166	ª	Masculine ordinal indicator	a _
167	º	Feminine ordinal indicator	o _
168	¿	Inverted ?	? ?
169	®	Trademark	R O
170	¬	End-of-line symbol (logical not)	-]
171	½	One half	12
172	¼	One quarter	14
173	¡	Inverted !	! !
174	«	Left angle quotes	«
175	»	Right angle quotes	»
176	░	Light solid fill	
177	▒	Medium solid fill	
178	▓	Heavy solid fill	
179	│	Center vertical bar	

Code Page Value	Character	Description	Compose Sequence
180	┤	Right box side	
181	Á	Uppercase A acute	A '
182	Â	Uppercase A circumflex	A ^
183	À	Uppercase A grave	A `
184	©	Copyright	C O
185	╣	Double right box side	
186	║	Double center vertical bar	
187	╗	Double upper right corner	
188	╝	Double lower right corner	
189	¢	Cent sign	c |
190	¥	Yen sign	Y =
191	┐	Upper right corner	
192	└	Lower left corner	
193	┴	Lower box side	
194	┬	Upper box side	
195	├	Left box side	
196	─	Center horizontal bar	
197	┼	Center intersection	
198	ã	Lowercase a tilde	a ~
199	Ã	Uppercase A tilde	A ~
200	╚	Double lower left corner	
201	╔	Double upper left corner	
202	╩	Double lower side	

Code Page Value	Character	Description	Compose Sequence
203	╦	Double upper side	
204	╠	Double left box side	
205	═	Double center horizontal bar	
206	╬	Double center intersection	
207	¤	International currency sign	X O x o X 0 or x 0
208	ð	Lowercase Icelandic eth	d –
209	Đ	Uppercase Icelandic Eth	D –
210	Ê	Upppercase E circumflex	E ^
211	Ë	Uppercase E umlaut	E "
212	È	Uppercase E grave	E `
213	ı	Lowercase dotless i	i <space>
214	Í	Uppercase I acute	I '
215	Î	Uppercase I circumflex	I ^
216	Ï	Uppercase I umlaut	I "
217	┘	Lower right corner	
218	┌	Top left corner	
219	█	Solid fill character	
220	▄	Lower half of solid fill character	
221	¦	Broken vertical line	/ <space>
222	Ì	Uppercase I grave	I `
223	▀	Uppercase half of solid fill character	
224	Ó	Uppercase O acute	O '

Code Page Value	Character	Description	Compose Sequence
225	β	German sharp	s s
226	Ô	Uppercase O circumflex	O ^
227	Ò	Uppercase O grave	O `
228	õ	Lowercase o tilde	o ~
229	Õ	Uppercase O tilde	O ~
230	µ	Lower mu	/ u
231	þ	Lowercase Icelandic thorn	p –
232	Þ	Uppercase Icelandic thorn	P –
233	Ú	Uppercase U acute	U ′
234	Û	Uppercase U circumflex	U ^
235	Ù	Uppercase U grave	U `
236	ý	Lowercase y acute	y ′
237	Ỳ	Uppercase Y grave	Y `
238	–	Overline character	^ –
239	′	Acute accent	
240	-	Hyphenation symbol	– =
241	±	Plus/minus sign	+ –
242	‗	Double underscore	_ _
243	¾	Three quarters sign	3 4
244	¶	Paragraph symbol	
245	§	Section symbol	
246	÷	Division sign	÷ –
247	¸	Cedilla accent	′ ′
248	°	Degree symbol	^ 0

Code Page Value	Character	Description	Compose Sequence
249	¨	Umlaut accent	
250	•	Center dot	^ .
251	¹	One superscript	^ 1
252	³	Three superscript	^ 3
253	²	Two superscript	^ 2
254	▪	Square bullet	
255		Null	

INDEX

This index is separated into five sections: Subject Entries, Keys, Commands, Functions, and Macros.

Subject Entries

A

E

G

L

M

N

O

P

Commands

Functions